PSALMS

Also by James Montgomery Boice

Witness and Revelation in the Gospel of John
Philippians: An Expositional Commentary
The Minor Prophets: An Expositional Commentary (2 volumes)
How to Live the Christian Life (originally, *How to Really Live It Up*)
Ordinary Men Called by God (originally, *How God Can Use Nobodies*)
The Last and Future World
The Gospel of John: An Expositional Commentary (5 volumes)
The Epistles of John: An Expositional Commentary
"Galatians," in the *Expositor's Bible Commentary*
Can You Run Away from God?
Our Sovereign God, editor
Our Savior God: Studies on Man, Christ and the Atonement, editor
Does Inerrancy Matter?
The Foundation of Biblical Authority, editor
Making God's Word Plain, editor
The Sermon on the Mount
Genesis: An Expositional Commentary (3 volumes)
The Parables of Jesus
The Christ of Christmas
The Gospel of Matthew: An Expositional Commentary (2 volumes)
Standing on the Rock
The Christ of the Empty Tomb
Foundations of the Christian Faith (4 volumes in one)
Christ's Call to Discipleship
Transforming Our World: A Call to Action, editor
Ephesians: An Expositional Commentary
Daniel: An Expositional Commentary
Joshua: An Expositional Commentary
Nehemiah: An Expositional Commentary
The King Has Come
Romans: An Expositional Commentary (4 volumes)
Mind Renewal in a Mindless Age
The Glory of God's Grace (originally, *Amazing Grace*)
Psalms: An Expositional Commentary (3 volumes)
Sure I Believe, So What?
Hearing God When You Hurt
Foundations of God's City (originally, *Two Cities, Two Loves: Christian Responsibility in a Crumbling Culture*)
Here We Stand!: A Call from Confessing Evangelicals, editor
   with Benjamin E. Sasse
Living by the Book: The Joy of Loving and Trusting God's Word
Acts: An Expositional Commentary
The Heart of the Cross, with Philip G. Ryken
What Makes a Church Evangelical?
The Doctrines of Grace, with Philip G. Ryken

Psalms

Volume 2
Psalms 42–106

JAMES
MONTGOMERY
BOICE

BakerBooks
Grand Rapids, Michigan

© 1996 by James Montgomery Boice

Published by Baker Books
a division of Baker Publishing Group
P.O. Box 6287, Grand Rapids, MI 49516-6287
www.bakerbooks.com

Paperback edition published 2005
ISBN 0-8010-6585-2

Printed in the United States of America

The Library of Congress has cataloged the hardcover edition as follows:
  Boice, James Montgomery, 1938–
    Psalms : an expositional commentary / James Montgomery Boice.
        p. cm.
      Includes bibliographical references and indexes.
      Contents: v. 1. Psalms 1–41. v. 2. Psalms 42–106.
      ISBN 0-8010-1077-2 (v. 1)
      ISBN 0-8010-1118-3 (v. 2)
      1. Bible. O.T. Psalms—Commentaries. 2. Bible. O.T. Psalms—Homiletical use. I. Title.
    BS1430.3.B64 1994
    223′.2077—dc20   93-36246

To
Jesus Christ,
Our Great Refuge and Strength,
an Ever-Present Help in Trouble

Contents

Preface

In the preface to the first volume of this three-volume series on the psalms, I pointed out how I first approached the task of teaching these chapters with considerable fear and trepidation. I have always thought of the psalms as the deepest and most spiritual portion of the Word of God, and I knew that I was nowhere near mature enough to expound them. I only began the task because I wanted to study the psalms for my own benefit as well as the benefit of others—and because there are many psalms and I was not getting any younger.

I found the study to be a great blessing for myself. But what I was not prepared for was the extent to which others found these sermons to be a blessing too. I have probably received more favorable comments per sermon on these chapters from members of Tenth Presbyterian Church, where they were first preached, and from listeners to the Bible Study Hour, where they were aired later, than from any other comparable teaching. The reason, of course, is that the psalms touch deeply on the hurts, joys, and spiritual aspirations of God's people. So any honest attempt to explain and apply them inevitably reaches and blesses most Christian people where they live.

Several things have struck me especially in the more than four years I have already spent on these studies.

First, I have been amazed at the utter honesty of the men who wrote these verses. That was true for me from the beginning, but it has been especially true as I have moved from book one of the Psalter into books two, three, and four. The only thing that can be said for these writers is that they "tell it like it is," to use Howard Cosell's popular radio and television phrase. They do this even when what they are describing seems to be opposed to all good biblical theology or a challenge to the "good name" of God. Even more remarkable perhaps is that they tell the truth about themselves. These are no plaster saints, no media-conscious, popularity-seeking religious personalities. They are people who doubt, hurt, worry, cry out, and even expose their own deep spiritual faults and failing faith.

Second—and this is most important—they never lose their grasp on God or their faith in him as the great, sovereign, wise, and loving God he is. We might ask how they can hold to this and express their doubts too. But it is precisely because they have such a faith that they can doubt. By contrast, we frequently pretend to a higher level of faith and to a greater trust in God than we actually possess, not because we are stronger than the psalmists but because we are weaker. It takes a spiritually strong person to express a strong doubt strongly.

Third, I have been impressed with the care that has gone into the construction of these verses as literature. When we first begin to read the psalms it is easy to think of them as powerful but more or less random outbursts of religious passion. The passion is part of it, of course. It is one reason why they are such great literature. But they are also carefully constructed, which means that their expressions are anything but random. And this is especially true when at first glance a particular phrase or stanza does not seem to fit in. When they see such a thing the liberal scholars of our time will frequently call foul, speaking of bad editorial work on the part of the compiler or just bad writing. But it is usually, if not always, the case that such a judgment only reveals the failure of the interpreter to understand or appreciate what the psalmists are doing. It is arrogant to suppose that we can improve on such time-tested poetry. Even worse, it is unbelief to suppose that we can improve or correct the verbally inspired and thus perfect Word of God.

Here, as in my other books, I need to thank the Session of Tenth Presbyterian Church for allowing me to spend so much of my time studying the Bible and writing sermons. I also want to thank the staff, particularly the ministerial staff, for attending to the many thousands of demands of a thriving inner-city church that I no longer have time for personally. I owe special thanks to Miss Joan Borgard, my executive assistant, who handles my schedule and carries forward much of my work.

It is my prayer that these studies may be a source of spiritual nurture, grace, instruction, and comfort for you as you read them. May God, who gave them to us for exactly those ends, bless you in your personal study. "Praise be to the LORD, the God of Israel, from everlasting to everlasting. Let all the people say, 'Amen!' Praise the LORD" (Ps. 106:48).

Book Two of the Psalter

Psalms 42–43

An Upward Look by a Downcast Soul

As the deer pants for streams of water,
so my soul pants for you, O God.
My soul thirsts for God, for the living God.
When can I go and meet with God?
My tears have been my food
day and night,
while men say to me all day long,
"Where is your God?" . . .

Why are you downcast, O my soul?
Why so disturbed within me?
Put your hope in God,
for I will yet praise him,
my Savior and my God.
42:1–3; 43:5

It is hard for me to imagine that a book about depression would be very popular, but in 1965 D. Martyn Lloyd-Jones, the pastor of Westminster Chapel in London, published a book entitled *Spiritual Depression: Its Causes and Cure*, which became one of the most highly valued and widely circulated books he ever wrote.[1] The only conceivable reason it has been so popular is not that the subject itself is attractive, but that so many people, including Christians, are depressed and looking for solutions.[2]

We are all depressed at times. We get down in the dumps. We sing the blues. We feel that God has forgotten us and that we will never be able to get on track with God again. It is a condition the old mystics accurately labeled "the dark night of the soul."

It is a puzzling condition too. We wonder why it is happening, especially if we are Christians. We identify with Erma Bombeck, who asks in the title of one of her best-selling books, *If Life Is a Bowl of Cherries, Why Am I Living in the Pits?*

Psalms 42 and 43, which open book two of Psalms, are about depression, and I suppose the facts that have made D. Martyn Lloyd-Jones's book so popular are the same facts that have made these among the best loved and most frequently consulted of the psalms. Since most of us are downcast at some time or another, we turn naturally to a psalm that asks honestly and forthrightly, "Why are you downcast, O my soul?" (42:5). And we are encouraged when it answers hopefully, "Put your hope in God, for I will yet praise him, my Savior and my God" (42:11; 43:5).

"I will yet praise him!" The words mean that my present downcast mood is not the final act of my life's drama.

The Sons of Korah

There are a number of interesting changes at this point in Psalms, and the first is that the compositions shift from being almost exclusively psalms of David to being those of a variety of authors. In the first section (Psalms 1–41), thirty-seven psalms are ascribed to David. The first two are introductory, and two others have no opening ascription. David is the only author identified in the first book. In the second section (Psalms 42–72), eighteen are ascribed to David. But in addition, one is assigned to Asaph, another to Solomon, and seven (eight if Psalm 43 is assumed to have the same author as Psalm 42) to the Sons of Korah. Three have no names with them. There are more psalms of Asaph, David, and the Sons of Korah, as well as one more by Solomon and a few by other authors later on.

Psalm 42 (as well as Psalm 43, which needs to be taken with it as the second part of a longer original composition) is by the Sons of Korah.[3] There are two collections under this name: Psalms 42–49 (to which we have now come) and Psalms 84–88, with the exception of Psalm 86.

The Korahites were Levites, descended through Kohath, Korah's father (1 Chron. 6:22–48; 9:17–32; 2 Chron. 20:19). They were employed in the performance of the temple music. But the interesting thing is this: When the Israelites were wandering in the desert, Korah led a rebellion of 250 community leaders against Moses and perished by God's judgment along with the other leaders and their families (Numbers 16; cf. Jude 11). For some reason the Sons of Korah were spared, and it seems from their later employment that, in gratitude to God and his mercy, they must have dedicated themselves to producing and performing the music used to praise God at the wilderness tabernacle and later in the temple in Jerusalem (cf. Num. 26:11). This interesting fact is a reminder that there can be devout children of reprobate fathers as well as devout fathers with reprobate children, and that no child needs to be kept from serving God because of his or her parents' sins.

Another interesting change as we pass from book one to book two of Psalms is that the frequency of the two most important names for God also changes noticeably. According to Franz Delitzsch, in book one the name Jehovah occurs 272 times and Elohim only 15. But in book two, Elohim occurs 164 times and Jehovah only 30 times.[4]

Causes of Spiritual Depression

Psalms 42 and 43 need to be taken together for several reasons: (1) in a number of the Hebrew manuscripts the psalms are joined together as one unit; (2) Psalm 43 has no introductory title, although every other psalm in book two, except for Psalm 71, does; and (3) the thrice-repeated refrain links the compositions (42:5, 11; 43:5).[5] The chief reason for taking the psalms together, however, is that both deal with spiritual depression. They give at least six reasons for it, and they indicate the cure.

What are the causes of spiritual depression? There are undoubtedly more than these psalms list, but the place to begin is with the causes they identify.

1. *Forced absence from the temple of God, where God was worshiped* (42:1–2). We do not know from the title of this psalm who the particular person was who composed it. He is presumably just one of the Sons of Korah. But whoever he was, we know the chief thing that was bothering him. He was far from Jerusalem and its temple worship on Mount Zion, and he therefore felt himself to be cut off from God. The psalm begins with his panting after God "as the deer pants for streams of water" when he cannot find it.

We do not know exactly where this unknown author was, either, or why he was there, but we can come close to answering the first question at least. He says he is writing "from the land of the Jordan, the heights of Hermon—from Mount Mizar" (42:6). Mizar means "little hill" (or "little mountain"). We know of no hill by that name, but "the land of the Jordan" is the region beyond the Jordan to the north and east, where Mount Hermon is. So Mizar was probably a lesser mountain in the Hermon range. This area is pretty far from Jerusalem, and some writers have suggested that if a traveler (or captive, which the author could be) were headed east in the direction of Babylon, this is the last point from which he might glimpse the familiar mountains of his homeland to the south.

So the psalmist is far from home and feels that he is therefore also far from God. It is not that he does not believe that God is everywhere, or that

God is not with him. He is praying to God in these psalms, after all. But his being away from home has gotten him down, and his depressed state has caused him to feel that God is absent.

There is another dimension to this sense of alienation. We need to remember that the employment of the Sons of Korah was at the temple in the performance of the temple music. So the author's forced absence from Jerusalem was also an absence from his work and therefore from his sense of being useful. It reflected on his whole purpose for living. Perhaps you have felt the force of that in one way or another. I am sure you have if you have ever lost a job or perhaps are stuck in a dead-end job. An early forced retirement will lead to depression like this for some people. So will old age, when a person feels that his or her useful days are done.

2. *The taunts of unbelievers* (42:3, 10). In this distant land the psalmist was also surrounded by unbelievers who taunted him with the biting challenge, "Where is your God?" This must have hurt him a lot, because he repeats the line twice in just this one composition. In ancient times almost no one was a true atheist. The first real atheism came with Greek philosophy. So the taunt did not mean that God did not exist but that God had abandoned the psalmist. It meant, "Where is your God when you need him? Where is your God now?"

That is a cause for deep depression. Where is God indeed? Where is God when I am in a far country, separated from my usual work, taunted by enemies? Why doesn't God seem to hear my cries? Why doesn't he intervene to change my circumstances?

3. *Memories of better days* (42:4). The psalmist was also troubled by memories of better days. There is a proper use of memory in times when we are depressed, remembering God's past acts as an encouragement to believe that he will act for us again. But that is not the first use of memory we find in these psalms. What we find here is the writer's wistful remembrance of the good days when he

> . . . used to go with the multitude,
>   leading the procession to the house of God,
> with shouts of joy and thanksgiving
>   among the festive throng (42:4).

It is hard for us to feel the extent of this longing for the exuberant joy of Jewish worship by an ancient Israelite, but C. S. Lewis captures a bit of it in a chapter called "The Fair Beauty of the Lord" in *Reflections on the Psalms*. He calls it an "appetite for God" and argues that it had "all the cheerful spontaneity of a natural, even a physical, desire. It is gay and jocund. They are glad and rejoice (9, 2). . . . Let's have a song, bring the tambourine, bring the 'merry harp with the lute,' we're going to sing merrily and make a cheerful noise (81, 1, 2). Noise, you might well say. Mere music is not enough. Let everyone, even the benighted gentiles, clap their hands. . . . Let us have clashing cymbals, not only well tuned, but *loud,* and dances too (150, 5). Let even the remote islands (all islands were remote, for the Jews were no sailors) share the exultation (97, 1)."[6]

Our services do not have the same exuberance as the temple religion, and there are some good reasons for that. Nevertheless, for many Christians some of their very best memories are of worshiping with other believers in church, perhaps at a special holiday season—Christmas or Easter, for example. The absence of these times as well as their remembrance can contribute to depression.

4. *The overwhelming trials of life* (42:7). A bit further on in this psalm the writer speaks of the overwhelming trials of his life, referring to them as "waves and breakers" that have swept over him. We do not know what these trials were, though we can imagine that they were the adverse circumstances that had borne him away from Jerusalem. Perhaps he is seated by a mountain stream, watching the tumbling cataracts and currents. Under other circumstances this might be a delightful experience, one likely to draw out thanks to God for creating such beauty. As it is, he sees the waves as cataracts of evil fortune that have broken on his head.

5. *Failure of God to act quickly on our behalf* (42:9). Verse 9 is a painful cry to God for having forgotten him. It reminds us of nothing so forcefully as Jesus' cry from the cross, "My God, my God, why have you forsaken me?" (Matt. 27:46), though the words of Jesus were actually borrowed from Psalm 22:1. It is not unusual for a depressed person to feel forsaken by God.

6. *Attacks from ungodly, deceitful, and wicked persons* (43:1). The second of these two psalms brings in another cause of depression. It is attacks by unscrupulous and deceitful enemies. These are probably the same people who taunted the psalmist earlier, asking, "Where is your God?" But in this section we learn that they had also been attacking him unjustly, since he prays for vindication and a pleading of his cause by God. Most of us can relate to this too, since it is not unusual for those who try to live for God to be unjustly accused, attacked, and slandered. Jesus said, "You do not belong to the world, but I have chosen you out of the world. That is why the world hates you. . . . If they persecuted me, they will persecute you also" (John 15:19–20). It is an unusual person who will not be occasionally depressed by malicious and hurtful treatment.

And what about those many additional causes of depression that the poet does not even mention? We could add the ones listed in *Spiritual Depression* by D. Martyn Lloyd-Jones: *temperament* (some people are just more inclined to depression than others), *physical conditions* (we can be affected by adverse physical health), *a down reaction after a great blessing* (an example is Elijah after his great victory over the prophets of Baal on Mount Carmel), *the attacks of Satan* (one of his strategies is to get us to take our eyes off God), and *simple unbelief* (probably the most significant cause of all).

Maybe you have some things of your own to add: a great disappointment in life, some personal failure, the burden of getting old. The list is probably endless.

The Cure for Spiritual Depression

But we have looked at the causes of depression enough. What is the cure for spiritual depression?

The world turns to many false cures. Some people try to escape the depressing realities of their lives through divorce, excessive entertainment, or frequent vacations. Some pop pills. Some are on habit-forming drugs. There must be millions who echo the thoughts of the young character Mallory of the television program *Family Ties,* who said, "When I get depressed I go shopping." They buy a new dress or a Miata. These "cures" are ineffective. At best they merely lift our spirits for a time.

It is different when we study what the author is teaching us in this important two-part psalm. The psalm tells us how the godly person can win out over depression.

1. *He takes himself in hand.* The most important thing to be said about the approach to depression taken by the author of this psalm is that he does not give in to depression or self-pity but rather takes himself in hand and wrestles through it. He reminds himself of what he really knows and finds that "no reasons for being cast down are so strong as those for elation and calm hope."[7]

Lloyd-Jones makes a great deal of this point, stressing that talking to ourselves rather than allowing circumstances to talk to us is the very essence of wisdom in this matter. It is a case of the mind speaking to the emotions rather than the emotions dictating to the mind: "You have to take yourself in hand, you have to address yourself, preach to yourself, question yourself. You must say to your soul: 'Why art thou cast down'—what business have you to be disquieted? You must turn on yourself, upbraid yourself, condemn yourself, exhort yourself, and say to yourself: 'Hope thou in God'—instead of muttering in this depressed, unhappy way."[8]

In a similar vein, J. J. Stewart Perowne speaks of "the struggle between the spirit of faith and the spirit of dejection, between the higher nature and the lower, between the spirit and the flesh."[9]

2. *He challenges himself to do what should be done.* The second step in the battle against depression follows from the act of addressing oneself in this manner. Indeed, it is a part of it. It is to challenge oneself to do what the spiritual self knows should be done: "Put your hope in God." There can be no lasting hope in anything else in this sinful, failing world. There never has been. There never will be. Besides, the believer has put his or her trust in God in past days. He can do so again. It is a mark of simple sanity to do what the psalmist urges should be done.

3. *He reminds himself of a great certainty.* To "hope in God" leads to the final step in the crusade against depression, the reminder, based on the character of the God we trust, that "I will yet praise him." This is a great certainty. God has not changed. Therefore, his purposes for me have not changed. He has led me to uplifting victories in times past. He will do so again. Therefore, instead of looking at the past glumly as something I have lost, I will look to it as a foretaste of the many good things yet to come. We can find multiple examples of this in the lives of the Bible's characters, people like Joseph, Moses, Joshua, and David.

Good Medicine

Does medicine such as the psalmist prescribes really help? Does it effect a cure? The progress achieved by it is evident throughout the psalm.

Look how the thought flows and the mood rises throughout this two-part composition. In the first stanza the psalmist remembers the former days at the temple and is oppressed by the memory; in stanza two he draws on memory again, but this time it is to remember God and his goodness. In the first stanza he is troubled by the taunts of enemies who say to him, "Where is your God?"; in the second stanza he answers that God is with him (v. 8). In verse 1, God is absent. In verse 9, God is his "Rock." By the time we come to Psalm 43:2, God is his "stronghold," and he is praying confidently that God will guide him back to the place of worship and the joys of former days. The first two stanzas were laments; the third has become a strong, believing prayer.

The same movement carries into the flow of thought in the last stanza, for the motion he anticipates from God is marked out in four anticipatory stages. First, it is backward to Mount Zion, the "holy mountain" of verse 3 from which he has been removed. Second, it is to the temple upon Mount Zion, "the place" where God dwells. Third, it is to the "altar of God" before the temple (mentioned in v. 4). Finally, it is "to God" himself.

> Then will I go to the altar of God,
>   to God, my joy and my delight (43:4).

Is there a cure for depression? Yes. But it is not in us. It is in God. The cure is to seek God's face, so ours will not be downcast, which is what the psalmist does.

Psalm 44

Sheep That Conquer

If we had forgotten the name of our God
or spread out our hands to a foreign god,
would not God have discovered it,
since he knows the secrets of the heart?
Yet for your sake we face death all day long;
we are considered as sheep to be slaughtered.

Awake, O Lord! Why do you sleep?
Rouse yourself! Do not reject us forever.
Why do you hide your face
and forget our misery and oppression? . . .

Rise up and help us;
redeem us because of your unfailing love.
verses 20–26

God never sleeps," wrote the Scottish commentator Murdoch Campbell in his opening observation on this psalm.[1] Maybe not, but he seems to, at least at times. He seems to be sleeping when his people cry out to him in their troubles.

I begin this way because one of the verses of Psalm 44 is an appeal to God to wake up—"Awake, O Lord! Why do you sleep? Rouse yourself! Do not reject us forever" (v. 23)—and it is obviously an intense cry that we must take seriously if we are to understand the psalm. Besides, it is hard to read it without thinking of a time in the earthly ministry of Jesus Christ when he and his disciples were crossing the lake of Galilee in a small boat after a hard day's work. A furious squall came up, and Jesus was in the stern, sleeping on a cushion. The disciples were experienced fishermen, but this was a bad storm and they were afraid they would drown. So they called to Jesus to wake up: "Teacher, don't you care if we drown?" Of course, Jesus did care and did wake up. He quieted the storm, leaving them wondering, "Who is this? Even the wind and the waves obey him!" (Mark 4:35–41). But still, Jesus was sleeping for a time.

It was out of just such a frightening experience that Psalm 44 was written.

Like the psalms before it, this psalm was written by one of the Sons of Korah, which means that we do not know who the author was precisely. Nor do we know the exact circumstances or time of composition. The nation of Israel had experienced a great military defeat, but we do not know when this was. Guesses range from as early as the time of David to the Persian or even to the later Maccabean period. Whenever it was, the author is asking God to hear him and save the people as he did in the past. He cannot understand why God has not yet done so.

This psalm is a lament. Some other categories of psalms are hymns, thanksgiving psalms, psalms of confidence, psalms of remembrance, wisdom psalms, and kingship psalms, some of which are messianic.

Psalm 44 is most easily considered in three parts: (1) the past (vv. 1–8), (2) the present (vv. 9–22), and (3) the future (vv. 23–26). The past concerns God's former acts of deliverance. The present concerns the painful, puzzling contrast between those past acts and what is happening now. The future section consists of a prayer for help yet to come.

God's Past Acts of Deliverance

A person would never expect this psalm to be a lament from reading the beginning stanzas, a remembrance of God's past acts of deliverance (vv. 1–8). These by their very nature are both positive and grounds for thanksgiving. At this point we would expect the psalm to be a thanksgiving psalm, a praise psalm, or a psalm of confidence. These remembrances are mature remembrances, too. The author and his contemporaries know that Israel's past military victories had not been achieved by their own exceptional might or skill, but by the power of God.

J. J. Stewart Perowne recognizes this in his study:

> The psalm opens with a glance at the past history of the nation and the acknowledgment that, from the first, every victory which they had won had been won not by their own strength, but by the immediate hand of God. This was, it might be said, the perpetual lesson of their history. They did not

rise upon their Egyptian masters, but God bowed the heart of the monarch and the people by his signs and wonders, till they thrust them out in haste. At the Red Sea they did not turn to fight with the chariots and the horsemen of Pharaoh; they were but to *stand still* and see the victory of Jehovah. When they came to Canaan, their first exploit was not a feat of arms, for Jericho fell by a miracle. The Roman army by the lake Regillus attributed its victory to the two mysterious horsemen who, on their white horses, led the charge. The Jewish host with a better faith believed that in every battle an invisible Captain led them and knew that, whenever they conquered their enemies, it was because an invisible arm gave them the victory.[2]

A quick look at this opening section (vv. 1–8) will show that it has two parts, separated into two stanzas in the New International Version.

1. *The distant past.* The first part recalls victories of the distant past, which the writer's generation had heard about and rightly understood to have been accomplished by God and as the sole result of his favor. He refers to these as things "our fathers have told us, what you did in their days, in days long ago" (v. 1). What follows makes clear that this refers to the conquest of Canaan by the tribes that came out of Egypt. In those days God drove out the nations that were in the land before them and crushed their enemies. The section concludes:

> It was not by their sword that they won the land,
>   nor did their arm bring them victory;
> it was your right hand, your arm,
>   and the light of your face, for you loved them (v. 3).

Our equivalent of this memory would be reflections on our own spiritual heritage, on events like the Protestant Reformation, the Wesleyan Revivals, or the Great Awakenings. Those distant past events are part of what we are, and we acknowledge rightly that they were accomplished by the will and power of God. Our "fathers" told us of those things, and we are thankful for them.

2. *The immediate past.* The second part of this opening section recalls victories in the immediate past, acknowledging, as in the preceding part, that they were achieved not by any strength or virtue of the people, but by God. In this stanza the subject of the sentences becomes singular ("my" and "I"), rather than plural ("we," "us," and "our") as in stanza one. This does not mean that suddenly there is another speaker at this point, as if this were a liturgical exchange between a priest and the people, as some scholars think. Rather, it is a way of intensifying the poet's testimony to God's past acts of deliverance. "It is not only that you did those things long ago for other people," he says. "You have also done them for us, for me. I can testify to such victories."

> I do not trust in my bow,
>   my sword does not bring me victory;

> but you give us victory over our enemies,
>> you put our adversaries to shame.
> In God we make our boast all day long,
>> and we praise your name forever (vv. 6–8).

Putting this in terms of our own experience, it is as if we were to say, "We have also experienced what those who came before us did. Not to the same degree perhaps, but you have nevertheless worked in our days as you worked in theirs. We give you glory."

If Psalm 44 had ended with verse 8, it would have been a victory hymn. It is positive, expectant, trusting. But the psalm does not end here. It goes on to the lament of verses 9 and following, which means that these opening verses, in spite of the positive statements, must have been uttered in a puzzled tone of voice. As we will see in part 2, God had not been helping the people currently, which raised the question, "How come? Why is he not helping us when he has helped us so effectively in the past?"

The Puzzling Present

This second section of the psalm opens with the contrasting words "but now." We find this phrase again and again in the Bible, usually comparing our sad condition apart from God's grace with what we have because of it. A classic example is in Romans 3:21, where Paul passes from his description of the hopeless condition of the human race in its sin to what God has done in providing a way of salvation through Jesus Christ. The text says, "*But now* a righteousness from God, apart from law, has been made known."

The contrast is exactly the opposite in this psalm. Instead of moving from a sad past to a glorious present, the words move us from a glorious past to a tragic present. Look at the contrast.

Verse 7:

> You give us victory over our enemies.

Verses 9–10:

> *But now* you have rejected and humbled us;
>> you no longer go out with our armies.
> You made us retreat before the enemy,
>> and our adversaries have plundered us.

Is that what the people of God are to expect from the One who has been their champion in past days?

This situation is so painful and puzzling in view of the people's past experience of God that this second section seems to be searching desperately for an explanation. A few possibilities lie in the background.

1. *Perhaps God was temporarily looking the other way, and the people's enemies used that moment to gain the upper hand.* That explanation might work for pagans, who know nothing of the true God. But it can never work for the followers of Jehovah. Jehovah is not indifferent. He is not sleeping, even though that may seem to be the case. If he is not sleeping or is not indifferent or is not impotent, then he must be behind what is happening.

Note the repetition of the word *you*. "*You* have rejected and humbled us; *you* no longer go out with our armies. *You* made us retreat before the enemy, . . . *You* gave us up to be devoured like sheep. . . . *You* sold your people for a pittance. . . . *You* have made us a reproach to our neighbors. . . . *You* have made us a byword among the nations. . . . *you* crushed us" (vv. 9–14, 19). The people's defeats are no accident. God is behind them, since God is responsible for all things.

This is what makes the problem so puzzling. A mere accident is not puzzling. A disaster is only puzzling if God is in control, is favorable to us, but lets it happen anyway. Nevertheless, although it makes the situation puzzling, the realization that God is in control is still both the proper way to approach such problems and the only possible way to find a solution to them. The secularist has nowhere to turn. Not only does he not have an answer, he does not even have a way of finding one.

As for the believer, he may not understand God's ways, but he knows that the only way to proceed is by recognizing that God is as active in defeats as he is in victories and waiting for his explanation.

2. *Perhaps the defeat is not as bad as it appears, and the people are exaggerating.* This is the second approach the psalmist is rejecting. The Pollyanna approach will not do here, because there is no escaping the magnitude of the disaster. The soldiers have been slaughtered like sheep and scattered (v. 11). Even worse, the people have been made a reproach to their neighbors; they have been disgraced and covered with shame (vv. 13–16).

3. *Perhaps the people themselves are at fault, and God has sent defeat as a judgment for their sins.* This is the best explanation so far since it takes both the sovereignty of God and the magnitude of the defeat at full value. What is more, the people often had sinned and had been judged for it. Their past history was as much a testimony to that fact as it was to the intervention of God on their behalf. The problem is that at this point of their history the people were keeping God's covenant and following God's way faithfully. At least that is what the psalmist says.

> All this happened to us,
> > though we had not forgotten you
> > or been false to your covenant.
> Our hearts had not turned back;
> > our feet had not strayed from your path (vv. 17–18).

He is arguing that they were obeying God and yet were defeated.

Can this really be? We are conscious of sin in ourselves. Very few Christians would want to claim utter faithfulness in following after God, as the psalmist does. Perhaps the writer is mistaken. Perhaps the explanation of this tragic defeat is to be found in precisely this self-righteousness. That explanation does not work here for two reasons.

First, because of verses 20–21:

> If we had forsaken the name of our God
>   or spread out our hands to a foreign god,
> would not God have discovered it,
>   since he knows the secrets of the heart?

This does not mean merely, "If we had sinned, God would know about it since God knows everything." That would lead to the conclusion, "Therefore, we must have sinned, since God is punishing us," and that is not what the psalm is saying. There would be nothing puzzling about the present situation under those circumstances. The words "would not God have discovered it" mean "would not God have discovered it *to us.*" That is, "Wouldn't God have told us what we have done wrong, if we had done wrong? Therefore, since he has not revealed any particularly outstanding sin to us, our sin cannot be the explanation of why we are suffering these military setbacks." An example of a sin that was revealed to the people as the cause of their defeat in war would be the defeat at Ai following the conquest at Jericho, where the cause was revealed to be Achan's disobedience in taking articles of clothing and precious metals from an enemy tent (cf. Josh. 7).

The second reason why we cannot handle the text this way—which also brings it directly into our own experience—is that Paul quotes verse 22 in Romans 8 as a confirming statement that the people of God suffer innocently. But he says this in the midst of a powerful affirmation concerning the keeping love of God:

Who shall separate us from the love of Christ? Shall trouble or hardship or persecution or famine or nakedness or danger or sword? As it is written:

> "For your sake we face death all day long;
>   we are considered as sheep to be slaughtered."

No, in all these things we are more than conquerors through him who loved us (Rom. 8:35–37).

Paul and other Christians had served God faithfully, yet they were made to face death all day long.

So, as easy as it would be to say that the people of God suffer defeat because they are being punished for their sins, this is not a fully adequate explanation, at least not in all instances, including Psalm 44 and Romans 8.

Prayer for Deliverance in the Future

So what is the explanation? None is given in this psalm. There is a suggestion of one, but the answer the psalmist finds is not an explanation, however much he might have appreciated one, but rather a practical clinging to God and beseeching God for help in spite of God's apparent sleep or silence.

Does God seem to be asleep? "Forget whether he really sleeps or not or what he may or may not be sleeping for," the psalmist seems to be saying. "Pray to him. Get practical and rouse him, if you must, with your prayers."

> Awake, O Lord! Why do you sleep?
>   Rouse yourself! Do not reject us forever.
> Why do you hide your face
>   and forget our misery and oppression? . . .
>
> Rise up and help us;
>   redeem us because of your unfailing love (vv. 23–24, 26).

One of the early commentators expressed the psalm's thought like this: "You helped us in the past. You must help us now. But you are not helping us, even though we have done nothing to prohibit your helping us. So help us."[3] The psalm is as simple as that.

But let us return to the suggestion of an explanation for trouble we find in the psalm. There are actually two clues that are "starters" for further thinking.

First, there is the phrase "for your sake" in verse 22, the verse Paul quotes in Romans. Psalm 44 has no elaboration of this idea, but we cannot miss remembering that it was developed at length by Jesus, who spoke of those who would be "persecuted because of righteousness" and "because of me" (Matt. 5:10–11), and who told his disciples, "'No servant is greater than his master.' If they persecuted me, they will persecute you also" (John 15:20). Paul was using the same idea when he quoted Psalm 44:22 in Romans, because it is for God's sake that the people of God often suffer.

Second, there is the last phrase of the psalm: "your unfailing love" (v. 26). That is a very important ending. Although nothing like it has appeared in the psalm thus far, it means, if it is to be taken at full value, that the love of God is of such quality that even the terrible defeats of the present moment are not without a purpose and will not, even in the worst extremity, sever the believing one from God. This is exactly how Paul handles the problem of suffering in Romans 8, too. Early in the chapter he explains that sharing in Christ's sufferings now means that we will share in his glory later, concluding, "I consider that our present sufferings are not worth comparing with the glory that will be revealed in us" (Rom. 8:18). Then, at the end of the chapter, after having quoted from Psalm 44, he concludes, "For I am convinced that neither death nor life, neither angels nor demons, neither the present nor the future, nor any powers, neither height nor depth, nor anything else in all creation, will be able to separate us from the love of God that is in Christ Jesus our Lord" (vv. 38–39).

With a faith like that, those who are accounted only as "sheep to be slaughtered" always will conquer, whatever defeats they may suffer in this life. They will conquer because God is in control of all history, his love is unfailing, and he guarantees the ultimate outcome of everything that happens to us . . . and the victory.

Psalm 45

A Messianic Wedding Song

You are the most excellent of men
    and your lips have been anointed with grace,
    since God has blessed you forever.
Gird your sword upon your side, O mighty one;
    clothe yourself with splendor and majesty.
In your majesty ride forth victoriously
    in behalf of truth, humility and righteousness;
    let your right hand display awesome deeds.
Let your sharp arrows pierce the hearts of the king's enemies . . .

Listen, O daughter, consider and give ear:
    Forget your people and your father's house.
The king is enthralled by your beauty;
    honor him, for he is your lord.

                                    verses 2–5, 10–11

Psalm 45 is unique, unlike any other psalm. It is a beautiful poem prepared on the occasion of a royal wedding, evoking all the sights, sounds, movement, splendor, and emotion of such an important occasion. It is at the same time a messianic psalm, as the words "O God" in verse 6 and the use of verses 6–7 in the first chapter of Hebrews in reference to Jesus Christ clearly show.

We do not know which earthly king and bride it was originally composed about, though it might fit the marriage of Solomon to the princess of Egypt, as many of the early commentators supposed. Other guesses have been Solomon and a princess of Tyre, Joram and Athaliah, a Persian king and his bride, even—ludicrously in my opinion—Ahab and Jezebel.[1] Yet, even as a hymn depicting the wedding glories of Solomon, the most likely choice, the psalm still seems to require much more for its interpretation, because the language is so exalted. As Alexander Maclaren wisely wrote, "Either we have here a piece of poetical exaggeration far beyond the limits of poetic license, or 'a greater than Solomon is here.'"[2] We are to assume, then, that the poet is writing of a specific Jewish king, whose identity is unknown, but that he is also looking ahead and upward to that ideal promised King whose perfect and eternal reign was foreshadowed by the Jewish monarchy.

A number of the psalms have messianic elements, though they are not in themselves wholly messianic. Examples are Psalms 8 and 40, parts of which are applied to Jesus in Hebrews (Psalm 8:4–6 in Hebrews 2:6–8, and Psalm 40:6–8 in Hebrews 10:5–7), though the psalms as a whole have other meanings. The specifically messianic psalms, in which all or most of the material refers to Jesus Christ, include Psalms 2, 16, 22, and 110. Psalm 45 is in this later category.

This psalm has a short introduction (v. 1) and a short conclusion (vv. 16–17) in which the poet speaks in the first person. These bracket the main body of the psalm (vv. 2–15), which is divided between an address to the groom (vv. 2–9) and an address to the bride (vv. 10–15).

Ancient Wedding Customs

Walter J. Chantry, author and pastor of Grace Baptist Church, Carlisle, Pennsylvania, has an excellent study of three messianic psalms (Psalms 2, 45, and 110) in which he argues that in order to understand Psalm 45 we need to know something about ancient betrothal and wedding customs.[3] He uses this background to trace the psalm's description of a procession from the home of the bridegroom to the home of the bride and back again, along the lines of traditional wedding day processions.

In ancient times the first step leading to a wedding was the betrothal. This was a very formal act, usually arranged by the parents of the future bride and groom, though quite often taking the wishes of their children into account. Betrothal meant more than engagement does to us. It was a legal procedure enacted before witnesses and confirmed by oaths taken by the couple. It was so weighty a matter that the couple could be called husband and wife, even though there had been no physical union. That was the case with Joseph and Mary at the time Jesus was conceived. It required something like a divorce to break this covenanted union.

One normal feature of the betrothal was a commitment on the part of the husband's family to provide a dowry. This feature, as well as propriety and the possibly young age of the couple, meant that there was often a long delay between the betrothal and the time of the wedding itself.

When the day of the wedding finally came, the friends and attendants of the bride gathered at the bride's home, where she prepared herself in her finest clothing and jewelry. At the same time, the attendants of the groom would gather at his house. Then there would be a grand procession through the streets of the city as the groom and his attendants went to fetch the bride, followed by a second procession of the entire party, both the bride and the groom's entourage, from the bride's home back to the groom's. At the groom's home there would be a joyful wedding feast, which could last as long as one or two weeks, depending on the status and wealth of the groom's family. Jesus' parable about the five wise and the five foolish virgins has as its setting such a returning procession and feast.

We have to keep these movements in mind as we study Psalm 45. In verses 2–9 we see the king coming for his bride. In verses 10–12 we find advice being given to the bride as she waits eagerly for her bridegroom. In verses 13–15 the bride is led out to the king, the procession makes its way to his home, and the wedding party enters the palace. The final verses are the poet's personal blessing upon the marriage and its union.

God's Poet Laureate

In a psalm unique among the psalms of the Psalter, we also find a unique introduction (v. 1). In it the poet tells how the theme assigned to him as court poet has stirred his emotions. His is "a noble theme," and he has been moved to pour all his considerable skill into the effort.

And well he might! This would be a moving challenge if the wedding were only that of an earthly monarch and bride. But as we have seen, it is at the same time a picture of that heavenly wedding in which the divine groom, Jesus Christ, takes the church, his bride, to himself. So this is not only a noble theme; it is the theme of themes. It is the ultimate meaning of all history, the story of the ages. No wonder the poet is stirred as he considers what he is to say in praise of this great King and the advice he is to give to this highly favored bride.

The language in this verse is so unusual that some commentators believe the poet is claiming special inspiration. Herman Gunkel even translates the verse, *Mein Herz wallt ueber von begeisterten Worte* ("My heart overflows with inspired words").[4]

In Praise of King Jesus

The main body of the psalm begins with praise of the divine King and bridegroom, who is Jesus (vv. 2–9). If these words were written of a mere earthly king, they would need to be understood as conventional court flattery. But as a description of him who is "the fairest of ten thousand" they are only the smallest part of what needs to be said.

There is something of a natural sequence in these themes.

1. *The King's character.* The divine King of this beautiful wedding ode is called "the most excellent of men" (v. 2), which leads some scholars to observe that in the ancient world the chief praiseworthy characteristics of a monarch were physical attractiveness and gracious speech or words. So what is new? These are exactly the characteristics that get politicians elected to high office today. It would be a mistake to limit this phrase to mere physical attractiveness, however. In fact, in a list of praiseworthy attributes mere physical attractiveness would come fairly low in God's scale, far behind such traits of character as "truth, humility and righteousness," which are mentioned in verse 4. Jesus excels in all these desirable characteristics. There is no good quality, no grace that is not found to the highest possible degree in him.

2. *The King's words.* When Jesus was on earth he spoke with authority and charm, so much so that when his enemies sent soldiers to arrest him, the soldiers returned, saying, "No one ever spoke the way this man does" (John 7:46). On another occasion, when the masses of the people were deserting Jesus and he challenged the twelve, asking if they wanted to leave too, Peter replied for all of them, "Lord, to whom shall we go? You have the words of eternal life" (John 6:68). When he was on earth, the words of Jesus had power to still the storm, send demons from those who were possessed, restrain enemies, and draw men and women who were trapped by sin to faith. They still do today.

3. *The King's military victories.* Though expressed in graphic battle language, we must remember that the victories of Jesus during his lifetime and in this present age are not military conquests but victories won on behalf of "truth, humility and righteousness" (v. 4) and by these qualities. This was the way Jesus triumphed during his earthly ministry. From a purely physical point of view Jesus' enemies were victorious, since they succeeded in having him condemned and executed. But in terms of truth, humility, and righteousness, Jesus won, since he upheld these characteristics in his person and conduct, even when he was being unjustly treated. This is the truth captured in the hymn "Ride On, Ride On in Majesty," based on verse 4.

Christians must remember that their victories are to come in the same way, not by force or coercion. Whenever the church has succumbed to the use of force as a way of asserting Christian truth or values, as it did in the Middle Ages, it has lost the spiritual battle and has become like the world, adopting the very evils it opposes.

In other words, the only sword we are to use is the sword of Jesus, which is the truth of the "word of God," the Bible (Eph. 6:17).

4. *The King's wedding.* The final verses of this section (vv. 8–9) turn from the personal qualities and military victories of King Jesus to the wedding,

which is the occasion for the psalm. Jesus is dressed in robes "fragrant with myrrh and aloes and cassia" and has come from "palaces adorned with ivory" (v. 8). This verse inspired the hymn "Out of the Ivory Palaces," which describes Jesus entering this "world of woe" out of love for his espoused bride. The marriage, this long-anticipated event, is amplified in the New Testament as the marriage supper of the Lamb.

Verse 6 calls for special comment. It is extraordinary because it addresses the bridegroom of this wedding ode as God: "Your throne, O God, will last for ever and ever." Then, in a manner some find puzzling, the next verse speaks of the groom as a man once again, saying, "Therefore, God, your God, has set you above your companions."

Naturally, there have been many attempts to sidestep what is being said. For example, some take the word *God* as meaning "divine" and translate the phrase as "your divine throne." Others say things like "Your throne is like God's throne, eternal" and "Your throne is God's forever and ever." Thus, the Revised Standard Version has "your divine throne," the New English Bible has "your throne is like God's throne," and other versions likewise try to avoid the clear meaning of the text. It needs to be noted, however, that the ancient versions all support the Hebrew and that the New Testament takes this meaning as well when it applies verses 6–7 to Jesus in Hebrews 1:8–9. The words of these two verses together are incomprehensible unless they are understood to refer to the incarnation of Jesus Christ. Only he can be called God and at the same time have the Father as his God.

Did the writer of this psalm understand what he was saying? It is hard to know how much the Old Testament writers understood the truths the Holy Spirit led them to put down. But J. J. Stewart Perowne is probably right when he concludes "that in the use of such language the psalmist was carried beyond himself, and that he was led to employ it by a twofold conviction in his mind, the conviction that God was the King of Israel, combined with the conviction that the Messiah, the true King, who was to be in reality what others were but in figure, was the son of David."[5]

That the Septuagint translates these verses as the New International Version has them indicates that even the ancient Jewish translators regarded these words as referring to the Messiah.

Comfort for the King's Bride

While the groom has been on his way to the bride's home with his attendants, the bride has been waiting in joyful expectancy, but also with just a touch of anxiety since the arrival of the groom will mean leaving her family and ancestral home forever. Therefore, in what is surely one of this psalm's most engaging touches, the writer turns to the bride in a fatherly manner to reassure her that the future is bright. There are three parts to his counsel (vv. 10–12).

1. *Forget the past.* The writer's first words of counsel to the bride remind us immediately of God's call to Abraham to "Leave your country, your people and your father's household and go to the land I will show you" (Gen. 12:1). They say, "Forget your people and your father's house" (v. 10). Strong words! Yet this is the same thing Christians are called upon to do. The Lord Jesus Christ said, "If anyone would come after me, he must deny himself and take up his cross daily and follow me" (Luke 9:23), and "If anyone comes to me and does not hate his father and mother, his wife and children, his brothers and sisters—yes, even his own life—he cannot be my disciple" (Luke 14:26). Even allowing for a certain amount of Semitic hyperbole in the last statement (hatred for close relations, even life itself), the point is clear that no human relationships must be allowed to restrain us from a wholehearted following after Jesus, if we would be his.

Speaking of marriage, the Bible says, "For this reason a man will leave his father and mother and be united to his wife" (Gen. 2:24). If we would be Christ's bride, we must leave all other loyalties behind.

Do you hear this counsel yourself? Can you follow it? Here is the way Walter Chantry makes the application:

> It is painful to leave behind mother and father, son and daughter. We are attached to the beauties and friendships of this world. "Forget" them all! The King will more than make up for all. Some day you will look back upon the parting with temporal things and think your hesitation silly and ill-founded. When you sit in the ivory palace, arrayed in the gold of Ophir, at the right hand of the eternal King, you will wonder what you saw in those former things. You will never regret it! . . . Carry through with your discerning choice. . . . The King must be your one and only love henceforth.[6]

2. *Honor (obey) your lord.* The second word of counsel from the writer to the bride of this psalm is to "honor . . . your lord." The word *honor* here literally means to "bow down." This is a far cry from the popular and generally immoral love stories that so frequently fill people's heads today. This is a holy relationship in which the sublime love of the bridegroom for the bride and the humble reverence of the bride for the groom are both beautifully maintained (cf. Eph. 5:22–33).

Chantry writes:

> If a marriage union is to endure, the husband must express his love to his wife by tenderly cherishing her as part of his own body, by considerateness, by sharing all the goodness of God in his life with her. She in turn must express love by holding her husband in high esteem and by submitting to him in all things. Thus the church must bow down to Christ both because he is her Lord and Sovereign and because he is her Lord and Husband. Since the bride loves her Lord, it is a pleasant thing to serve his interests. She desires to bring Christ honor, to fulfil his will, to worship his name.[7]

3. *Look ahead.* The last word of advice this wise counselor has for the bride of the psalm is to look to what the future holds for her as the bride of this great king, knowing that her choice of him was the right choice to have been made. The writer sees three things in her future: first, the love of her king (v. 11); second, the honor that will be given her because of her relationship to him (v. 12); and third, the "joy and gladness" that will be hers with him forever.

Then, having advised her to look ahead, the poet himself looks ahead by returning to his description of the wedding procession. In these verses (vv. 13–15) he describes the bride being led out to the king and then accompanying him, together with their many attendants, back to the king's palace, where they enter with rejoicing. This climax is handled modestly by the poet, as he himself seems to stop at the door, since "no eye has seen, no ear has heard, no mind has conceived what God has prepared for those who love him" (1 Cor. 2:9).

"Yes, I Am Coming Soon"

In verse 16 the pronouns *you* and *your* are masculine, which means that at this point the writer turns his attention back to the king once again, offering a kind of benediction or blessing on the marriage: "Your sons will take the place of your fathers" and "you will make them princes throughout the land." If we think of this in terms of the Messiah, it must refer to the "many sons" who will be brought into glory as a result of his fruitful union (Heb. 2:10, 13). As for the poet himself, "I will perpetuate your memory through all generations; therefore the nations will praise you for ever and ever," he says (v. 17).

This leads us to wonder: Are we doing as the psalmist did? Do we praise him who has purchased us to himself to be his bride? Are we working to see that the nations come to honor him as well?

Even more, are we waiting for his coming, as the bride of this psalm was? Jesus came a first time to join us to himself in a spiritual betrothal. He will come a second time to take us to himself forever. Are you ready for that coming? Are you looking forward to it? The Bible describes Christians as having "turned to God from idols to serve the living and true God, and to wait for his Son from heaven, whom he raised from the dead—Jesus, who rescues us from the coming wrath" (1 Thess. 1:9–10). If you are waiting for him, you will purify yourself in preparation for his coming (1 John 3:3). Jesus said, "In my Father's house are many rooms; if it were not so, I would have told you. I am going there to prepare a place for you. And if I go and prepare a place for you, I will come back and take you to be with me that you also may be where I am" (John 14:2–3). Are you looking for that return?

Revelation 1:7 says, "Look, he is coming with the clouds, and every eye will see him." Then, at the very end of the same book, we read, "He who testifies to these things says, 'Yes, I am coming soon.'" The church rightly replies, "Amen. Come, Lord Jesus" (Rev. 22:20). So let it be! Amen.

Psalm 46

Martin Luther's Psalm

God is our refuge and strength,
an ever-present help in trouble.
Therefore we will not fear, though the earth give way
and the mountains fall into the heart of the sea,
though its waters roar and foam
and the mountains quake with their surging. Selah

There is a river whose streams make glad the city of God,
the holy place where the Most High dwells.
God is within her, she will not fall;
God will help her at break of day.
Nations are in uproar, kingdoms fall;
he lifts his voice, the earth melts.

The LORD Almighty is with us; ‹
the God of Jacob is our fortress.   Selah

Come and see the works of the LORD,
the desolations he has brought on the earth.
He makes wars cease to the ends of the earth;
he breaks the bow and shatters the spear,
he burns the shields with fire.
"Be still, and know that I am God;
I will be exalted among the nations,
I will be exalted in the earth."

The LORD Almighty is with us;
the God of Jacob is our fortress.   Selah
verses 1–11

Almost everyone associates Martin Luther with the Book of Romans, particularly Romans 1:17, "The just shall live by faith" (KJV). We tend to forget that Luther was converted not only

387

by his study of Romans, but also by his study of the psalms. Luther taught the psalms for years and loved them very much, even late in life. His favorite was Psalm 46. It is said of Luther that there were times during the dark and dangerous periods of the Reformation when he was terribly discouraged and depressed. But at such times he would turn to his friend and coworker Philipp Melanchthon and say, "Come, Philipp, let's sing the forty-sixth Psalm." Then they would sing it in Luther's own strong version:

> A sure stronghold our God is He,
> A timely shield and weapon;
> Our help he'll be and set us free
> From every ill can happen.

We know it as "A Mighty Fortress Is Our God."

Luther said, "We sing this psalm to the praise of God, because God is with us and powerfully and miraculously preserves and defends his church and his word against all fanatical spirits, against the gates of hell, against the implacable hatred of the devil, and against all the assaults of the world, the flesh and sin."[1]

A great Lutheran scholar, H. C. Leupold, wrote, "Few psalms breathe the spirit of sturdy confidence in the Lord in the midst of very real dangers as strongly as does this one."[2]

"A Mighty Fortress Is Our God"

No part of Luther's hymn is as close to Psalm 46 as the first stanza, which calls God "a mighty fortress" and "a bulwark" in trouble. In the Hebrew text, as in Luther's hymn, the emphasis is on God himself, the point being that God alone is our refuge, he and no other. Nothing in the universe can be a comparable refuge.

Some people think they will be secure if only they have enough money. So they lay it up in bank accounts, stocks, and other tangible assets. Like the rich man of Jesus' parable they say, "You have plenty of good things laid up for many years. Take life easy; eat, drink and be merry" (Luke 12:19). Jesus called a person who does that a fool, since in the end death comes and he or she must stand before God at his final judgment. Money cannot protect us from judgment. It cannot even shield us against heartbreak, failure, sin, disease, or disaster in this world.

Other people think they will be secure because of their specialized training, skills, or personal talents. But even the best-educated and highly skilled people suffer sudden reversals of fortune.

Still others expect security from their families, friends, or business connections. But these are all only human supports. They are uncertain at best, and at times they are suddenly swept away. The Reformers knew how unstable and uncertain these things could be. They knew that God is unshakable and trustworthy.

> Let goods and kindred go,
> This mortal life also;
> The body they may kill:
> God's truth abideth still;
> His kingdom is forever.

Verse 1 looks to God for two kinds of help, indicating that he is: (1) a stronghold into which we can flee and (2) a source of inner strength by which we can face calamities. Sometimes God shields us from what is going on around us and it can be said of us, quoting the later psalmist, "A thousand may fall at your side, ten thousand at your right hand, but it will not come near you. You will only observe with your eyes and see the punishment of the wicked" (Ps. 91:7–8). In such times God is our fortress.

At other times we are afflicted and do suffer. Then we find that God is our help. We are able to say, "God is my strength, my ever-present help in trouble."

God is our help even if the worst imaginable calamities should come upon us. This is what verses 2–3 are about, as the psalmist imagines the return of chaos, in which the "earth gives way and the mountains fall into the heart of the sea," thus reversing the work of God on the third day of creation. Sometimes life is like that. The foundations of our established worlds are shaken, and chaos seems to have come again.

I seldom read these verses without thinking of Elisabeth Elliot. She suffered the loss of two husbands. The first, Jim Elliot, was killed by Auca Indians in Ecuador while trying to reach them with the gospel. The second, Addison Leitch, was slowly consumed by cancer. In relating what these experiences were like, she referred to this psalm, saying that in the first shock of death "everything that has seemed most dependable has given way. Mountains are falling, earth is reeling. In such a time it is a profound comfort to know that although all things seem to be shaken, one thing is not: God is not shaken."[3] She added that the thing that is most needful is to do what the psalmist does later, to "be still" and know that God is God. God is God whether we recognize it or not. But it comforts us and infuses strength into our faltering spirits to rest on that truth.

"His Kingdom Is Forever"

Psalm 46 is divided into three stanzas, each ending with the word *selah*, which probably indicates a pause in the music or a pause for contemplation. In addition, the second and third stanzas end with the refrain, "The LORD Almighty is with us; the God of Jacob is our fortress." Stanza one (vv. 1–3) is a general statement stressing that God alone is our refuge, even in the worst calamities. In the next stanza (vv. 4–6) the poet emphasizes the defense of God's city.

This has two points of reference. The first is the earthly city of Jerusalem. The immediate occasion of the psalm was probably some great intervention of God to destroy enemy armies that were marching against Jerusalem. In this time of danger those who resided in Jerusalem were secure, because God was in their midst. He was with them. In this setting the "river" of verse 4 is the stream of Siloam, the only natural supply of fresh water in Jerusalem. The "holy place" is the temple mount. Thus, with great poetic beauty, right against the picture of chaos in verses 2–3, comes the picture of the perfect peace and safety of Jerusalem in verse 4. This probably explains why the refrain following verses 7 and 11 is left out here, where it would otherwise belong.

Quite a few psalms concern the city of Jerusalem, among them Psalms 48, 76, 84, 87, and 122. They are called "songs (or psalms) of Zion."

Yet no one can read this psalm perceptively without sensing that this earthly reference fails to exhaust its meaning. This is because the "city of God," the theme of verses 4–6, is also a major theme of the whole of Scripture and concerns not only the security of earthly Jerusalem but also the nature and safety of the people of God throughout history. It has its culmination in the new spiritual Jerusalem, a symbol of heaven, which has been prepared by God as the final dwelling place of the saints. In this frame of reference the "river" of verse 4 is the river that flows from God's throne (see Ezek. 47:1–12; Zech. 14:8; Rev. 22:1–2) and the "holy place" is the dwelling place of God in heaven. This is the city for which Abraham looked, not a mere earthly Jerusalem but "the city with foundations, whose architect and builder is God" (Heb. 11:10).

What earthly circumstances lie behind this account of God's defense of Jerusalem? There are two main theories.

1. *The destruction of the armies of Ammon, Moab, and Mount Seir during the reign of Jehoshaphat* (2 Chron. 20:1–30). When Jehoshaphat was told that armies from the east were coming against him, he appealed to God for help and God answered, saying that he would deliver the inhabitants of Jerusalem. The people were not to fight the invading armies but were to station themselves at a high vantage point to see what would happen. When they did, they saw the soldiers of Ammon and Moab turn against the soldiers from Mount Seir. That is, the armies fought each other and destroyed themselves. The text says, "When the men of Judah came to the place that overlooks the desert and looked toward the vast army, they saw only dead bodies on the ground; no one had escaped" (v. 24).

The great German scholar Franz Delitzsch believed that this is what lies behind Psalm 46.[4] The best argument for it is the mention of the Sons of Korah in the account and their celebration of God's promise of deliverance. Since Psalm 46 is ascribed to the Sons of Korah, it is easy to see it as their own personal praise of God for his deliverance on this occasion.

2. *The destruction of the army of the Assyrian King Sennacherib during the reign of Hezekiah* (2 Kings 18–19). This is the better known of the two incidents. On this occasion Sennacherib's field commander stood before the walls of Jerusalem and called on the people to surrender, boasting that none of the gods of the nations had been able to stand against the Assyrian armies. He then sent a letter to Hezekiah, boasting of the same thing. When Hezekiah received it he went into the temple and spread it before the Lord, and God answered him through the great prophet Isaiah, who said that God would defend the city and that Sennacherib would return to Nineveh and perish there. That night God sent an angel through the camp of the Assyrians, killing 185,000 soldiers. The account says, "When the people got up the next morning—there were all the dead bodies! So Sennacherib king of Assyria broke camp and withdrew. He returned to Nineveh and stayed there" (2 Kings 19:35–36).

The nineteenth century romantic poet Lord Byron wrote a poem about this event called "The Destruction of Sennacherib," beginning with these well-known lines:

> The Assyrian came down like the wolf on the fold,
> And his cohorts were gleaming in purple and gold.

With the exception of Delitzsch, most of the major commentators believe this is the deliverance lying behind Psalm 46. The best evidence is the appearance of Isaiah in the story and the similarity between his prophecies and the chief ideas of the psalm, such as the quiet river that makes glad the city of God (Isa. 8:6; 66:12), the shaking of the mountains (Isa. 54:10), and Immanuel who is "God with us" (Isa. 7:14; 8:8).

In my judgment there is insufficient evidence to decide between the two theories. But it does not matter, since the point of the psalm does not depend on the identification. Whatever the original circumstances, it is true that God alone is our defense and that our ultimate security does not rest in any earthly city, but in the heavenly city prepared for us by God.

"Above All Earthly Powers"

G. Campbell Morgan has a nice outline of the psalm's sections: (1) the challenge of confidence, (2) the secret of confidence, and (3) the vindication of confidence.[5] We come to the third of those sections now (in vv. 8–10). Although the language grows out of the earlier material—that is, the historical deliverance of the people from either the armies of Ammon, Moab, and Mount Seir or Sennacherib—the stanza is not really looking to the past but ahead to the future when God shall defeat all armies and establish his eternal reign. In other words, the stanza is written along the same lines as Psalm 2 in which God mocks those who take arms against him and his anointed. He tells the Son, "I will make the nations your inheritance, the ends of the earth your possession. You will rule them with an iron scepter; you will dash them to pieces like pottery" (Ps. 2:8–9).

When verse 9 says, "He makes wars cease to the ends of the earth," it is not presenting God as a peace negotiator but as a conqueror. In other words, this peace is not to be compared to the SALT treaties, negotiated disarmament pacts between mutually powerful nations. It is more like the Allies' bombardment of Iraq, which established "peace" by imposing it on the conquered party.

There is an interesting illustration of this contrast from the days of the Roman empire. A Roman medal was struck by Vespasian after completing his wars in Italy and other places, showing the goddess of peace holding an olive branch in one hand and a torch setting fire to heaps of armor in the other. The olive branch represents a negotiated peace. The torch and destroyed armor represent an imposed peace. Both are peace, but it is the second that is being presented in Psalm 46:8–10.

Therefore, in this setting, "be still, and know that I am God" is not advice to us to lead a contemplative life, however important that may be. Elisabeth Elliot was not wrong to say that this should be our goal in times of emotional turmoil. It means rather, "Lay down your arms. Surrender, and acknowledge that I am the one and only victorious God." Of course, the time to do this is now, while a desirable peace can be yours through the work of Jesus on the cross. If you will not surrender now, you will do so one day in spite of yourself, though it will be for judgment rather than blessing. This is because God is God, and in the end it will be his power and holiness that are exalted. No one can hope to resist him.

"Lord Sabaoth His Name"

The conclusion and proper application of this psalm is the response that has already appeared following stanza two (v. 7) and now appears a second and final time in verse 11: "The LORD Almighty is with us; the God of Jacob is our refuge." Who is he, this God who is his people's refuge? The answer is given in the two names of God in this refrain.

First, he is "the LORD Almighty." The words are literally "the LORD of Hosts (Jehovah Sabaoth)." "Hosts" refers to the armies of Israel, on the one hand, and to the angelic armies of God, on the other. This makes the name especially apt in this psalm, since the psalm is based on a historical deliverance of the people from earthly armies, whatever their origin, and also looks forward to a final deliverance when God will subdue the hostile forces of rebellious man forever. It is a particularly striking name in this psalm because the name Jehovah does not occur much in this second book of the psalms; the name is usually Elohim.

We have a wonderful insight into the power of God's hosts in the story of Elisha at Dothan. The city of Dothan had been surrounded by the armies of Ben-Hadad of Syria in an attempt to capture Elisha, and they were discovered early in the morning by Elisha's young servant. When he saw the soldiers and chariots positioned around the city he rushed back inside and cried out to Elisha, saying, "Oh, my lord, what shall we do?" (2 Kings 6:15). Elisha prayed that God would open the eyes of his servant to see the heavenly hosts protecting him, and when God did, the servant saw that the hills were filled with horses and chariots of fire around Elisha. Elisha reminded his servant that "Those who are with us are greater than those who are with them" (2 Kings 6:16).

> Did we in our own strength confide,
> Our striving would be losing;
> Were not the right man on our side,
> The man of God's own choosing.
> Dost ask who that may be?
> Christ Jesus, it is he,
> Lord Sabaoth his name,
> From age to age the same,
> And he shall win the battle.

Second, God is the God of Jacob. Jacob was the third of the three Jewish patriarchs and the least outstanding of the three. He was a schemer, as his name implies. It took him a lifetime to learn to trust God. Yet the God of Abraham was his God no less than he was the God of Abraham. The great Bible expositor Alexander Maclaren has a wonderful study of these two names in which he concludes, "The God of Jacob is the Lord of hosts. More wondrous still, the Lord of hosts is the God of Jacob."[6]

This is your God, too, if you have come to him through faith in Jesus Christ. And if he is your God, then he is with you at all times, which is what this important couplet says.

On the day he died John Wesley had already nearly lost his voice and could be understood only with difficulty. But at the last with all the strength he could summon, Wesley suddenly called out, "The best of all is, God is with us." Then, raising his hand slightly and waving it in triumph, he exclaimed again with thrilling effect, "The best of all is, God is with us." Is the Lord Almighty with you? Is the God of Jacob your refuge, as he was for Martin Luther and John Wesley? Make sure that he is. The storms of life will come, and the greatest storm of all will be the final judgment. Make Christ your refuge now, while there is still time.

Psalm 47

King of All the Earth

Clap your hands, all you nations;
shout to God with cries of joy.
How awesome is the LORD Most High,
the great King over all the earth!
He subdues nations under us,
peoples under our feet.
He chose our inheritance for us,
the pride of Jacob, whom he loved.   Selah

God has ascended amid shouts of joy,
the LORD amid the sounding of trumpets.
Sing praises to God, sing praises;
sing praises to our King, sing praises.

For God is the King of all the earth;
sing to him a psalm of praise.
God reigns over the nations;
God is seated on his holy throne.
The nobles of the nations assemble
as the people of the God of Abraham,
for the kings of the earth belong to God;
he is greatly exalted.

verses 1–9

There are quite a few places in the Old Testament in which God is addressed as the God of Israel almost exclusively—that is, as if he is the Jews' God as opposed to being one of the gods of the nations round about. In fact, the Jews are repeatedly warned against serving these other gods. The first of the Ten Commandments is one example: "I am the LORD your God, who brought you out of the land of Egypt, out of the land of slavery. You shall have no other gods before me" (Exod. 20:2–3). I count forty-eight similar warnings in the Book of Deuteronomy alone. If we are to read these or other texts uncritically, without the whole biblical revelation in mind, we might get the idea that the world is ruled by what scholars call "tribal deities" and that the Jewish God, Jehovah, is merely the greatest of the lot.

That would be a terrible misconception, however. For there is only one God. His name is Jehovah, and all the other "gods" are, in fact, mere idols. Isaiah especially makes fun of such gods, explaining in irony how a worshiper finds a piece of wood, uses half of it to make a fire to cook his meal, and then carves the other half into an idol. Such idols "know nothing, they understand nothing," he says (Isa. 44:18; cf. vv. 9–20). In the same chapter he quotes God as declaring, "I am the first and I am the last; apart from me there is no God" (v. 6).

What follows from this is important: If the gods of the nations are mere idols and there is no true God but One, then that One is God of all the earth and King of all the nations—whether the people who compose those nations acknowledge it or not.

We have a soaring expression of this idea in Psalm 47. In this psalm, in sharp contrast to many other passages, God is praised clearly as King of all the earth and people of all nations are invited to praise him.

But there is even more to the psalm than this. "More than poetry," writes Derek Kidner, "this is prophecy, whose climax is exceptionally far-reaching."[1] The psalm envisions a day in which the nations will, in fact, praise God and come to him freely "as the people of the God of Abraham" (v. 9). In other words, in this psalm we have an anticipation of that climactic moment in Revelation in which the nations will have been subdued before God and, we are told, "The kingdom of this world has become the kingdom of our Lord and of his Christ" (Rev. 11:15).

A Few Observations

It will help to make a few observations about Psalm 47 and its place in the Psalter. First, Psalm 47 follows quite naturally after Psalm 46. Psalm 46 is focused on the security of God's people, noting how God had delivered them from one of their great enemies.[2] It challenged the nations to observe that deliverance and stand in awe before God.

> Be still, and know that I am God;
> I will be exalted among the nations,
> I will be exalted in the earth (v. 10).

God himself is speaking. Now, in Psalm 47, the writer addresses the same people, saying, "Clap your hands, all you nations; shout to God with cries of joy. How awesome is the LORD Most High, the great King over all the earth!"

(vv. 1–2). In other words, he is following up on what God had himself said earlier. Some commentators also see another connection between these psalms. They think that Psalm 47:5 may be referring to the same deliverance of Jerusalem from foreign armies that lies behind the writing of Psalm 46.

A second useful observation is that Psalms 46, 47, and 48 are what are often called Songs of Zion, because they focus on the city of Jerusalem and God's protection of it. Psalms 46 and 48 speak of Jerusalem explicitly, calling it "the city of God" (Ps. 46:4), "the city of our God" (Ps. 48:1, 8), and "the city of the Great King" (Ps. 48:2). Psalm 47 refers to the city indirectly by speaking of God's "ascending amid shouts of joy," perhaps to Jerusalem, and of his being seated there "on his holy throne" (vv. 5, 8).

There is no general agreement regarding the overall outline of this psalm. Since the word *selah* comes at the end of verse 4 and seems to indicate a break there, some writers see two stanzas of four verses each, followed by a final prophetic note in verse 9. The New International Version obviously sees three stanzas (vv. 1–4, 5 and 6, and 7–9). In my opinion, attempts to work out a specific outline are not very helpful in this case. It is more useful to follow the flow of the thought, which is from the universal reign of God over all the nations to the more particular reign of God over Israel (and his acts on her behalf) and then back again to thoughts of a universal (future) reign, where the first two ideas are combined.

Our God Reigns

The psalm begins, then, with praise of God as "the great King over all the earth," and it invites people of the nations to join the psalmist in this praise (v. 2). Of course, at the present time the world's peoples may not all acknowledge God's rule, but he is their ruler nonetheless. He sets up kings and he dethrones them. This is one thing that is meant whenever the Bible talks about God's kingdom.

In 1934 the great British historian Arnold Toynbee began a study of world history that occupied him until 1961 and eventually filled twelve large volumes.[3] In this massive work Toynbee isolated thirty-four distinct civilizations, including thirteen "independent" civilizations, fifteen "satellite" civilizations, and six "abortive" civilizations. Each of these came upon the pages of history for a time and then passed away. Egypt was once a great world power, but it is weak today. Babylon was mighty, but its territory has been divided, and even the discovery of great stores of oil in that area of the world has not restored it or the surrounding nations to a dominant position on the world stage. Greece and Rome, once wonders of mankind, have fallen. The Soviet Union fell apart. Even the United States of America, though now at the very pinnacle of world power, is in decline and will not escape the inexorable law of history, namely, that "Righteousness exalts a nation, but sin is a disgrace to any people" (Prov. 14:34).

When they are strong and victorious, nations fondly suppose that they control their own destinies. Yet it is not they but God who is "King over all the earth." Moreover, the God who is King requires righteousness. So when the nations depart from his ways and arrogantly exalt themselves, God brings them down.

The Bible book that makes this point most emphatically is Daniel. The story of King Nebuchadnezzar teaches it forcefully, as God humbled Nebuchadnezzar by judging him with insanity. But I pass over Nebuchadnezzar's story to that of his son Belshazzar, which is built on it. Belshazzar had given a party in which he had defiled the vessels that had been taken from the temple of God in Jerusalem when Nebuchadnezzar sacked the city. In the midst of this party, the fingers of a human hand appeared, writing on the palace wall. Belshazzar and his guests became frightened.

The writing said, "MENE, MENE, TEKEL, PARSIN"[4] (Dan. 5:25). It meant "numbered, numbered, weighed, divided." That is, God had numbered the days of Belshazzar's reign and brought it to an end; Belshazzar had been weighed and found wanting, and now his kingdom was to be divided and given to the Medes and Persians.

When Daniel was summoned to the banquet and asked to explain what this meant, he told Belshazzar,

> The Most High God gave your father Nebuchadnezzar sovereignty and greatness and glory and splendor. . . . But when his heart became arrogant and hardened with pride, he was deposed from his royal throne and stripped of his glory. He was driven away from people and given the mind of an animal; he lived with the wild donkeys and ate grass like cattle; and his body was drenched with the dew of heaven, until he acknowledged that the Most High God is sovereign over the kingdoms of men and sets over them anyone he wishes. But you his son, O Belshazzar, have not humbled yourself, though you knew all this (Dan. 5:18, 20–22).

That night the city was overthrown, Belshazzar was killed, and Darius the Mede reigned in his place.

Daniel spoke to Belshazzar in the name of the "Most High God." It is significant, therefore, that this is the name the author of Psalm 47 uses in verse 2 when he exclaims, "How awesome is the LORD Most High, the great King over all the earth!" Awesome indeed! The kingdoms of this world rise and fall, but over them all, determining their course and end, stands the "Most High God," the God of all history.

"King of the Jews"

After this "awesome" beginning, the psalmist seems to drop down a note and reflect on the powerful acts of God on the part of Israel, as if to say that in addition to his being "King over all the earth" Jehovah is Israel's God specifically. He mentions three things.

First, *the subjection of the land of Canaan under Joshua* (v. 3). This is what verse 3 is about. The details of the conquest are in Joshua 6–12.

Second, *the gift of the land of Canaan to Jews as their inheritance* (v. 4). At first glance, the order between these two items seems backward, since we tend to think first of God giving the land to the Jewish people and then of the people conquering it. But the psalmist is probably thinking of the division of the land subsequent to the conquest, which is the order found in Joshua. The partitioning of the land, according to the instructions given earlier by Moses, is described in detail in Joshua 13–21. The phrase "pride of Jacob" refers to this land, calling it "our inheritance."

Third, *a more recent deliverance, which is the occasion for Psalm 46 and probably for Psalm 47, too* (v. 5). There are two ways God's ascending "amid shouts of joy" and the "sounding of trumpets" may be taken. Most scholars see this as the carrying of the ark of the covenant, symbolizing the presence of God, back into Jerusalem following a battle in which the Jewish armies were victorious. They refer us to 2 Samuel 6, in which David brings the ark back to the city after the years it has been in the house of Obed-Edom. They are particularly impressed with the words of verse 15: "The entire house of Israel brought up the ark of the LORD with shouts and the sound of trumpets." Here is a great tumult, as in Psalm 47. Besides, scholars like the idea of an ascending and enthroned ark because it fits with current speculations about a supposed annual enthronement festival in Israel.

That may be the meaning of the reference, of course. But the problem I see is that 2 Samuel 6 does not describe a battle. In fact, normally the ark did not accompany the people into battle, and the one time they tried to use it in this way, when they were fighting the Philistines, the ark was captured and the battle was lost (cf. 1 Sam. 4:1–7:1).

The other way of taking the reference in verse 5 to God's ascending amid shouts of joy is to the lifting up of the cloud of God's glory, the Shekinah, from over the ark of the covenant, which was in the middle of the Israelite camp during their years of wandering. There are more than fifty verses in the Old Testament that speak of this phenomenon. In them the rising of the Shekinah indicated that God was leading his people forward. When he moved they were to break camp and follow him. Later, when the Shekinah settled down over the ark and tabernacle, they were to settle down also. This is described clearly at the end of Exodus (Exod. 40:36–38). In Numbers 10 we are told that when the cloud raised up and the ark was lifted up by the priests to follow it, Moses said,

> Rise up, O LORD!
> May your enemies be scattered;
> may your foes flee before you (v. 35).

And when the cloud returned, he said,

> Return, O LORD,
>   to the countless thousands of Israel (v. 36).

This cloud was no longer with the people, leading them, when Psalm 47 was written, of course. Therefore, the reference to the cloud in verse 5 cannot be literal. I believe it refers to God going out to meet Israel's foes and defeating them, either in the reign of Jehoshaphat or in the reign of Hezekiah. The point is that God showed his presence with his people in that recent victory just as he had shown his presence at the time of the conquest.

Verse 6 of the second stanza is an invitation to praise God for his continual presence and deliverance.

Your Kingdom Come

In verse 7 we come to the part of the psalm that caused Derek Kidner to call it a prophecy. It starts mildly enough, seeming only to reiterate what has been stated forcefully earlier: "God is King of all the earth" (v. 7) and "God reigns over the nations" (v. 8). But it ends with the nations actually assembling before God as his people:

> The nobles of the nations assemble
>   as the people of the God of Abraham,
> for the kings of the earth belong to God;
>   he is greatly exalted (v. 9).

This has not happened yet. That is why we call it prophecy. But it will happen, and we look forward to it. It is why we are so active in evangelism, bringing the gospel to the nations, and why we so often pray in the words taught us by Jesus, saying, "Your kingdom come" (Matt. 6:10; Luke 11:2).

This is a good place to remember the very different picture of the nations drawn for us in Psalm 2. In that psalm the kings of the earth are opposing the Lord and his Christ. They are saying, "Let us break their chains . . . and throw off their fetters" (v. 3). In that psalm God is laughing at such impotent folly. He scoffs at it and rebukes the people, saying, "I have installed my King on Zion, my holy hill" (v. 6). He admonishes, "Be wise; be warned, you rulers of the earth. . . . Kiss the Son, lest he be angry and you be destroyed in your way" (vv. 10, 12). Psalm 2 reminds us that there are two kinds of compliance with the just reign of God and Jesus Christ. There is a willing, joyful compliance on the one hand, but there is also an unwilling, forced compliance on the other.

Our task is to bring the gospel to the nations now so that, by God's grace and by the power of the Holy Spirit, many might willingly bow before Jesus Christ and thus come under the banner of his blessed rule.

That is where history is going. It is what life is all about.

I take you back to the early chapters of Genesis, in which God calls Abraham to be his follower, promising,

I will bless those who bless you,
    and whoever curses you I will curse;
and all peoples on earth
    will be blessed through you (Gen. 12:3).

From the very beginning God had said that he purposed to bless all nations and all peoples through Abraham and his descendants, particularly through his one great descendant, the Messiah, Jesus Christ. And that is what he has done and is doing. He is building Christ's spiritual kingdom with people from all nations and races.

There were times when the Jewish people thought in exclusively ethnic or nationalistic terms, as nations generally do. They thought that the blessings of God's kingdom were for them alone. But the psalmist knew differently, and so did that great Jewish theologian, Paul, who wrote that Abraham "is the father of all who believe but have not been circumcised [that is, Gentiles], in order that righteousness might be credited to them" (Rom. 4:11). And again, "The promise comes by faith, so that it may be by grace and may be guaranteed to all Abraham's offspring—not only to those who are of the law but also to those who are of the faith of Abraham. He is the father of us all. As it is written: 'I have made you a father of many nations'" (Rom. 4:16–17).

A number of years ago someone asked me whether the kingdom of God is past, present, or future. The questioner had in mind the debate that once raged in scholarly circles among such people as C. H. Dodd, Rudolf Bultmann, and Albert Schweitzer. I replied that the answer is far bigger than the question.

It is impossible to describe the kingdom of God as being merely past, merely present, or merely future. It is all of those and more, for it is also internal and external. It involves willing compliance as well as forced compliance. This is because the kingdom of God is God's rule, and God rules everywhere and all things. The only meaningful question is, Are you a member of that kingdom? Are you a part of it? Am I?

There is only one way to become a willing part of God's kingdom, and that is by personal surrender to the claims of Jesus Christ, the divine Son of God and Savior of his people. It is to bow before him, for he is the only true "King of kings and Lord of lords" (Rev. 19:16).

In this age God is building his kingdom by calling out a people to himself. They are from every imaginable people, nation, condition in life, and race—Americans and Africans and African Americans; tribal people, street people, and sophisticated urban dwellers; working men and men without work; judges and those who have been judged; all types of people. And he is turning them into men and women in whom the kingdom of Jesus Christ is present and in whom his loving, winsome, and upright character can be seen. There is nothing in life more important or more wonderful than belonging to that kingdom.

Psalm 48

City of Our God

Great is the LORD, and most worthy of praise,
in the city of our God, his holy mountain.
It is beautiful in its loftiness,
the joy of the whole earth.
Like the utmost heights of Zaphon is Mount Zion,
the city of the Great King.
God is in her citadels;
he has shown himself to be her fortress. . . .

Walk about Zion, go around her,
count her towers,
consider well her ramparts,
view her citadels,
that you may tell of them to the next generation.
For this God is our God for ever and ever;
he will be our guide even to the end.
verses 1–3, 12–14

W̄e are used to symbolism in poetry, and it would be hard to find a psalm that did not employ much of it. But Psalm 48 exceeds most others in the sense that its very theme is symbolic.

It is called a Song of Zion because of its references to Jerusalem as the "city of God." Those words occurred once in Psalm 46 (v. 4). Psalm 46 is the first of the Songs of Zion. The others are Psalms 76, 84, 87, and 122. Psalm 84 begins, "How lovely is your dwelling place, O LORD Almighty!" Psalm 122 begins, "I rejoiced with those who said to me, 'Let us go to the house of the LORD.'" All these psalms praise Jerusalem as the dwelling place of God. But if ever a psalm was truly a Song of Zion, it is the one we come to now. In it the words "city of our God" or their equivalent occur three times (in vv. 1, 2, 8), and the people are actually invited to walk around the city, count its towers, and meditate on the strength of its great ramparts: "Walk about Zion, go around her, count her towers, consider well her ramparts, view her citadels" (vv. 12–13).

All this carries us beyond the mere city of Jerusalem, if read with understanding. For one thing, the city is not the Jews' delight alone; it is "the joy of the whole earth" (v. 2). And God is not only to be praised by his own people; he is to be praised everywhere (v. 10).

Even more, as Derek Kidner suggests, in this psalm Zion itself seems to become more than a mere earthly capital, and the struggle described becomes more than local. It concerns the whole earth and the whole span of time. Thinking ahead to the final chapters of Revelation, which describe heavenly Jerusalem, Kidner says, "The outlines of 'the Jerusalem above,' with its great walls and foundations which are 'for ever,' are already coming into view."[1]

There is yet another way the psalm exceeds our expectations. Ostensibly in praise of Jerusalem, Psalm 48 is in reality a psalm in praise of God, for this is what Jerusalem stands for. We see this as early as verse 1.

In Praise of God

In fact, we see it not only in the opening couplet (v. 1) but also at the very end (v. 14). These two verses, in which God is praised, are a poetical device scholars call *inclusio,* a single idea that both opens and closes a poem or section of a poem. It binds its parts together and sometimes, as here, indicates how the material that is enclosed should be taken.[2] Psalm 8 is a good example of *inclusio.* It begins and ends with the words, "O LORD, our Lord, how majestic is your name in all the earth!" (vv. 1, 9), showing that the created order comes from and should praise God.

This device is less obvious in Psalm 48, but what it accomplishes is nevertheless clear. It tells us that its praise of Zion, which the body of the poem consists of, is actually praise of God. It begins:

> Great is the LORD, and most worthy of praise,
>> in the city of our God, his holy mountain (v. 1).

It ends:

> For this God is our God for ever and ever;
>> he will be our guide even to the end (v. 14).

These observations support Peter C. Craigie's view, who says, "The substance of the Songs of Zion may appear superficially to be the praise of

Mount Zion in the holy city; [but] at a deeper level, it is the praise of God, whose presence and protection is symbolized by the holy mountain and its sanctuary."[3] In a similar vein, H. C. Leupold writes, "The conclusion that this psalm draws is that the God who dwells at Zion is immeasurably great and will be a sure defense of all who put their trust in him, as Psalm 46 had already pointed out with emphasis."[4]

In Praise of Zion

After the opening couplet in praise of God, which sets the tone for the psalm, the psalmist praises God's city itself. The first part of this praise is in verses 2–8. It has three sections.

1. *Praise of Jerusalem.* Jerusalem is not the highest point of the hill country of Israel, though it is twenty-five hundred feet above sea level. If you approach from the south, from Hebron, you actually go down a bit to reach it. But the city's setting is such that one seems always to be impressed with its "loftiness," the word the psalmist uses. From the north, west, and east, and even from the immediate south, the way to Zion is uphill, which is why the psalms always speak of going "up" to Jerusalem. There on the lofty hills of Zion the towering ramparts of the city rose, and the breathtaking beauty of the city beckoned.

Yet the beauty of Jerusalem was not in her physical appearance alone, any more than true beauty is to be found in mere appearances today. The real beauty was the beauty of the Lord, who had chosen to reside in Zion. "God is in her citadels; he has shown himself to be her fortress," he says (v. 3).

2. *Remembrance of a great deliverance.* That last line leads naturally to what the poet wants to say next, for the statement "he has shown himself to be her fortress" leads to the question, How has he shown himself to be her fortress? The answer is, "by the recent deliverance of the city from our enemies." This deliverance seems to link Psalms 46, 47, and 48 together, though it is impossible to say with certainty what specific deliverance they refer to. The two possibilities are: (1) the deliverance of the people from the armies of Ammon, Moab, and Mount Seir in the days of Jehoshaphat, as described in 2 Chronicles 20, and (2) the deliverance of the people from the armies of Sennacherib in the days of Hezekiah, as described in 2 Kings 18–19. The reference in Psalm 48:4 to "the kings" (plural) joining forces to advance against the city seems to fit the combined armies of Ammon, Moab, and Mount Seir better than the single army of Sennacherib. But these armies were turned back before they actually "saw" Jerusalem. So the specific references in this psalm, as well as those in the others, are inconclusive.

The most striking feature of the account of this deliverance is the use of four terse verbs in verse 5. In fact, the verse consists almost entirely of these verbs. The effect is not as vivid in the English translations as it is in Hebrew, particularly since the New International Version gives us only two sentences. But in Hebrew the words are similar to the well-known report of Julius

Caesar about his victories in Gaul: *Veni, vidi, vici* ("I came, I saw, I conquered"). Only here the kings did not conquer; they fled from the city in terror. The verbs literally say, "They saw [Jerusalem is implied]; they were dumbfounded; they were overwhelmed; they fled in panic." The fast pace of the language captures the confusion and fearful flight that must have overtaken the enemy armies when God moved against them.

Two effective images round out this description: (1) a woman in labor and (2) the scattering of the mightiest ships before a powerful Mediterranean east wind (vv. 6–7). The first image portrays the fierce enemy warriors as helpless to avoid or delay their hour of destruction. The second image suggests the overwhelming scope of the rout. The ships of Tarshish were the mightiest ships of the day. This is why Ezekiel, echoing the words of Psalm 48, also describes their destruction as an amazing judgment by God: "Your oarsmen take you out to the high seas. But the east wind will break you to pieces in the heart of the sea" (Ezek. 27:26). Interestingly, the idea is then picked up by the apostle John in Revelation in connection with the fall of Mystery Babylon, which represents the godless world system (cf. Rev. 18:17–20; Ezek. 27:29–36).

History provides us with a later, literal illustration of such massive naval destruction. In 1588 the "invincible" Spanish Armada set sail from Lisbon under orders from the Spanish King Philip II to invade and subdue England. It consisted of 130 great galleons and supply ships, 7,000 sailors, and more than 17,000 soldiers. The British fleet under command of Sir Francis Drake met it in the English Channel and engaged it in a series of battles extending over about a week in late July. The Spanish ships were massive and well armed. The English ships were light and more maneuverable. The battle went to the English, who successfully destroyed and captured many ships. But the real victory came when the weather changed and the wind blew the Spanish ships up the Channel toward Scotland, which they attempted to round and thus return to Spain by passing across the North Sea and down the westward coast of Ireland. Scores of these ships were wrecked on the Irish coast, and their crews were massacred. Others sank at sea. Less than half managed to return to Spain and Portugal, and the defeat was so complete that prior Spanish domination of the "ocean sea" was ended.

Most modern authors attribute the English success to their superior navy. But it is significant that the English themselves attributed the victory to God. They struck a medal to celebrate the defeat of the Armada on which were these words: "God blew upon them and they were scattered." That is the way the psalmist viewed the destruction of the enemy kings.

3. *A corporate testimony.* The third item in this section of the psalm is the people's corporate testimony to the deliverance, expressed in the words "As we have heard, so have we seen . . ." (v. 8). It means, "We have heard about the powerful

acts of God in past days. Our fathers and mothers have told us about them. Now we have seen the power of God for ourselves. He has acted in our time also."

This should be the testimony of every mature child of God. It is important to know about God's past acts. Indeed, it would be impossible to be a Christian without knowing about them, for we become Christians through faith, and faith consists in knowing, believing, and acting upon what God has done, especially what he has done for us in the death and resurrection of Jesus Christ. But our experience shouldn't stop there. We have also heard what God has done in the lives of other people, how he provided for them in hard times, protected them in moments of danger, and comforted them in loss. Perhaps you were told of such special acts of God by your parents. As you learn to trust him, you should begin to experience such personal blessings yourself, and you should be able to say, "As I have heard, so have I seen."

This section ends with the testimony that it is God who made the city of Jerusalem secure. Remember that it is God who makes you secure too. Think about that. The psalm invites you to consider it since the section ends with the word *selah,* which indicates a pause.

Rejoicing in God

Thus far in Psalm 48 we have seen an opening ascription of praise to God, followed by a longer section of praise of Jerusalem which, of course, is itself praising God. In verse 9 and following, this pattern repeats itself again, though in a more personal and direct way. In verses 9–11, the people offer a prayer of praise and thanksgiving. In verses 12–13, they are invited to circle the city and see for themselves how thoroughly God had delivered them.

The point of this is that the name of God will be exalted in increasing ways. One is spacial. That is, the praise of God will extend outward from Jerusalem to the "villages" round about (v. 11) and to "the ends of the earth" (v. 10). We are engaged in this same work when we send missionaries to distant places to tell others about Jesus Christ. The other way these verses view the increasing praise of God is temporal—that is, from generation to generation (v. 13). We do this work when we pass on our faith to our children.

Rejoicing in Zion

One of the nicest parts of this psalm is the concluding section, in which the people are invited to walk around the city, count the towers, and consider the ramparts and citadels, that the perfect nature of God's recent deliverance might be impressed on their minds so they might be able to remember it vividly and so be able to pass it on to their children and their children's children (vv. 12–13).

The great Puritan theologian John Owen used the King James Version when he studied this psalm, and the King James Version has the word *bulwarks* for "ramparts" in verse 13. It says, "Mark ye well her bulwarks." Owen thought that this is a very good thing for us to do. Only he was thinking of heavenly Zion, the church, and of our security in Jesus Christ. He said that heavenly Zion has five great bulwarks.[5]

1. *"The designation and constitution of Jesus Christ to be King of the church, King of Zion."* The world has seen many different kinds of rulers throughout its history. Some have been cruel and cunning, like King Richard II of England. Some have been magnanimous, like Cyrus of Persia. Some have been weak. Claudius of Rome hid behind a curtain when the emperor's guard chose him to replace his predecessor. Others have been strong. But there has never been a king like King Jesus. He is utterly sovereign, wonderfully compassionate, all-wise, and extraordinarily patient—all at the same time. Moreover, he is the King of kings and Lord of lords. And his is an eternal kingdom. The Bible says,

> The kingdom of this world has become the kingdom
> of our Lord and of his Christ,
> and he will reign for ever and ever (Rev. 11:15).

If we belong to the Lord and are members of his kingdom, then nothing will ever diminish our security, and we can know that we will reign with him forever. That bulwark is the first great rampart of the church.

2. *"The promises of God, which are innumerable."* A Bible teacher once promised a class of children that he would give ten dollars to anyone who could think of a promise that God had not given to his people. He said later that he might as well have offered a million dollars, for God has promised to meet all our needs and to give us all good things, whatever those needs may be. If we are wise, we will pay attention to those promises. We will mark those blessings. We will impress them on our minds in order to live by them and pass them to the next generation.

3. *"The watchful providence of God over the church."* If you and I care for something very much, we keep a watchful eye on it. But we do not always successfully protect the thing we love. We may look away at just the wrong moment, allowing a child to run out into the street and be hit by a car, for instance. Or, even if we are watching, we are not always able to prevent the disaster.

God is not subject to our limitations. His watchful eye is everywhere, seeing all things. We speak of this when we say that he is omnipresent and omniscient. He is also all-powerful, so he is able to care for, protect, defend, and preserve us perfectly. We get a sense of how carefully God cares for his church from Jesus' prayer for it just before his crucifixion. He prayed, "Holy Father, protect them by the power of your name—the name you gave me—so that they may be one as we are one" (John 17:11).

4. *"God's special presence in his church."* The ancient devout Jew was conscious of the presence of God in Jerusalem, symbolized by the ark of the covenant that rested within the Most Holy Place of the temple. It is why he

could say, "God is in her citadels" (v. 3). We cannot say that God is in our cities in the same way, or even in our churches. But we have something better: God in us, in the person of his Holy Spirit. When Jesus was about to leave this world he said to his disciples, "I will ask the Father, and he will give you another Counselor to be with you forever—the Spirit of truth. The world cannot accept him, because it neither sees him nor knows him. But you know him, for he lives with you and will be in you" (John 14:16–17). To have the Holy Spirit within us is a very great bulwark against the world, the flesh, and the devil, against all sin and temptation.

5. *"The last bulwark unto which all others may be reduced . . . the covenant of God."* Owen is right when he suggests that the greatest bulwark is the covenant that God has established with us, since it embraces all else and is confirmed by the precious blood of his own Son.

In fact, with this important note we are led to a section of Hebrews in which the new Jerusalem is declared to be superior to the old, and the new covenant, sealed with the blood of Jesus Christ, is declared to be superior to the old covenants that preceded it. The author begins by telling us that today Christians have not come to Mount Sinai, where the first covenant was proclaimed. That was a frightening place before which even Moses trembled. Rather, "You have come to Mount Zion, to the heavenly Jerusalem, the city of the living God. You have come to thousands upon thousands of angels in joyful assembly, to the church of the firstborn, whose names are written in heaven. You have come to God, the judge of all men, to the spirits of righteous men made perfect, to Jesus the mediator of a new covenant, and to the sprinkled blood that speaks a better word than the blood of Abel." He concludes, most aptly in view of Psalm 48, "Therefore, since we are receiving a kingdom that cannot be shaken, let us be thankful, and so worship God acceptably with reverence and awe" (Heb. 12:22–24, 28).

A Closing Couplet

The last couplet of the psalm says, "For this is our God for ever and ever; he will be our guide even to the end" (literally, "even unto death"). There are commentators who have considered this personal note inappropriate as an ending to a psalm about Zion. But they surely miss the point, since a personal note is exactly what we need. It is wonderful to know that God has established Zion forever, even more wonderful to know that he has established his church. But what about me? And what about death, the great separator? The last verse assures us that the God of Zion is our personal God too and that he will keep us even as he keeps his church and city. Can you say this with the psalmist,

> For this God is our God for ever and ever;
> he will be our guide even to the end.

Psalm 49

You Can't Take It with You

*No man can redeem the life of another
    or give to God a ransom for him . . .*

*Do not be overawed when a man grows rich,
    when the splendor of his house increases;
for he will take nothing with him when he dies,
    his splendor will not descend with him.
Though while he lived he counted himself blessed—
    and men praise you when you prosper—
he will join the generation of his fathers,
    who will never see the light of life.*

*A man who has riches without understanding
    is like the beasts that perish.*

verses 7, 16–20

Because the Bible is a book of progressive revelation, it is often the case that a New Testament passage can be read as a commentary on part of the Old Testament. But sometimes it works the other way around. Sometimes an Old Testament passage is a commentary on something in the New Testament.

Psalm 49 is like that. It is a commentary on Jesus' story about the rich fool, recorded in Luke 12:13–21. The story concerns a rich landowner whose ground produced such an abundant crop that he said to himself, "I will tear down my barns and build bigger ones, and there I will store all my grain and my goods. And I'll say to myself, 'You have plenty of good things laid up for many years. Take life easy; eat, drink and be merry'" (vv. 18–19). But God said to him, "You fool! This very night your life will be demanded from you. Then who will get what you have prepared for yourself?" (v. 20).

Jesus said, "This is how it will be with anyone who stores up things for himself but is not rich toward God" (v. 21).

The Path of Wisdom

Psalm 49 is a wisdom psalm about the emptiness of riches. We have not read anything quite like it up to this point in our studies. In fact, the opening verses (vv. 1–4) sound more like Proverbs or another "wisdom" section of the Old Testament than a psalm.

It begins, like the Book of Proverbs, with a call to wise men everywhere. It is for "all who live in this world, both low and high, rich and poor alike." All are included, ourselves as well as others. Christians in our day sometimes think they are above such appeals. But this is never the case—we all need to attend to the Bible's wisdom—and it is certainly not the case in this area. Most of us in the West, even when we are very active in Christian work, are materialistic. That is, we think in terms of the things we see rather than spiritual realities we cannot see, and we are inclined to trust wealth or what we can accomplish with it. Not many years ago, the well-known Christian psychiatrist and writer John White wrote a book titled *The Golden Cow,* in which he faithfully exposed the blatant materialism of the twentieth-century Western church.[1]

Trust in riches is a persistent and universal problem.

What the psalmist proposes is wisdom given to him by God. In the Hebrew text, the words *wisdom* and *understanding* are both plural ("wisdoms" and "understandings"), which has the effect of heightening the importance and value of what he is to say. Lest we miss the point, verse 4 says, "I will turn my ear to a proverb." That is, the psalmist will listen to what God has to say on the subject. More than one commentator has pointed out that the one who would teach others must first be taught himself. The preacher who would speak in God's name must begin by listening.

The psalmist calls what he is about to expound a "riddle." It is what we might call "the *mystery* of life, death, and prosperity" or the lack of it. This is the theme. But it is a sophisticated treatment in that it enlarges on this basic theme to include the oppression that wealth frequently makes possible and encourages, and deals with the fear the poor often have of those who have money. It tells the listener not only to be aware that death is the great leveler but also not to fear wealthy persons.

J. J. Stewart Perowne handles the psalm's theme well:

It is no mere commonplace on the shortness of life and the uncertainty of riches. It is no philosophical dissertation, which bids us bear up bravely in our perils and sufferings, telling us that virtue is its own reward. It goes at once to the root of the matter. It shows us not only the vanity of riches, but the end of those who "boast in their riches." It comforts the righteous in their oppression and affliction, not merely by the assurance that they shall finally triumph over the wicked, but by the more glorious hope of life ever-lasting with God. . . . It is this doctrine specially enunciated, which gives the Psalm its distinctive character, and which leads the Psalmist himself to claim for it so attentive a hearing.[2]

Nearly all commentators divide Psalm 49 into the same five parts, although they sometimes combine them under comprehensive headings. They are: (1) the introduction, (2) the foolishness of trusting riches (vv. 5–9), (3) the inescapability of death (vv. 10–12), (4) the contrast between those who trust riches and those who trust God (vv. 13–15), and (5) an appeal to all persons to be wise (vv. 16–20).

The Foolishness of Trusting Riches

The foolishness of trusting wealth comes from the obvious truth that it cannot save a person from death (vv. 5–9). It is wisdom to remember that and the height of folly to forget it. Since we are eternal creatures, we ought to focus on how we might prepare for eternity rather than on how we might accumulate increasing wealth here and perish with it.

The French atheist and scourge of Christianity, Voltaire, was a very rich man. He was the most famous person of the European enlightenment in the sophisticated eighteenth century, and his writings, particularly his satirical attack on Christianity, *Candide,* were read everywhere. Yet when Voltaire came to die, it is reported that he cried to his doctor in pained desperation, "I will give you half of all I possess if you will give me six months more of life." But, of course, it was beyond the doctor's ability to do that, and all Voltaire's great wealth could not slow death's advance. He died despairing.

Verse 7 uses this truth to say that "no man can redeem the life of another or give to God a ransom for him." That is, no one can save another from death by money.

Writers have pointed out that it would seem more natural if verse 7 should speak of a man redeeming his own life, rather than "the life of another." Hence, many have tried to emend the text to make it say this.[3] But, as is usually the case, such scholarly changes miss the point. The reason the psalmist speaks at this point of redeeming the life of another, which is impossible for man, is because later he is going to speak of God redeeming us. The point of the parallel is that God alone can redeem. We can't.

The Inescapability of Death

But maybe the foolishness of those who trust their wealth is not that they think that somehow money can redeem their lives from death, but rather that they somehow think that they themselves are invincible, that they will not die (vv. 10–12). If this is the case, it is an even greater example of folly than the first absurdity. "For," as the psalmist says,

> all can see that wise men die;
>> the foolish and the senseless alike perish
>> and leave their wealth to others (v. 10).

The point is that death is inevitable and that, when it comes, we must leave everything behind.

Two men met in a streetcar one day and began to talk about a millionaire whose death had been announced in that morning's paper. "How much did he leave?" one asked the other.

"Everything he had!" replied his companion.

Years ago, when burial customs were a bit different from what they are now, people used to make the same point when they said, "Shrouds have no pockets."

This is so obvious a truth that all people can see it: "All can see that wise men die" (v. 10). Yet although they *can* see it, they also *fail* to see it because they *refuse* to see it. Although they know they will die, they behave as if they will live forever.

One of the early commentators, cited by Spurgeon in his remarkable work on the psalms, tells about a wealthy landowner in Massachusetts. He had spent most of his life acquiring property. It was his passion. But his extensive lands were marred by a poorer neighbor who held a small plot in the middle of his expanding domain. The poorer farmer got into financial trouble, was sued, and judgments were rendered against him, all of which meant that he would probably lose his land. The wealthy man was delighted and waited on the sidelines to buy up the land as soon as the smaller parcel should become available. But somehow the poor man met his payments, and the debt was paid off without the land being sold. When he heard of it the wealthy, greedy landowner exclaimed, "Well, my neighbor is an old man; he cannot live long, and when he is dead I will buy the lot."

"But," wrote this ancient writer, "the neighbor was fifty-eight, and the wealthy man was sixty!"[4]

After these wise observations, the psalmist ends the first half of the poem with a couplet that will be repeated with some slight but significant variations at the end.

> But man, despite his riches, does not endure;
>> he is like the beasts that perish (v. 12).

It is a recurring theme in much ancient literature, not only in the Bible, that to live without understanding is to live like an animal, since it is the ability to think and reason that sets human beings apart from the remainder of creation. Yet how animal-like we are when we fail to consider the shortness of our days and prepare for how we will spend eternity! The Hebrew text is more powerful than the translations at this point, for the phrase "does not endure" literally means "does not pass the night." It suggests that in view of death a person's position in life is not as secure even as a traveler who turns into an inn for the evening. In our case, life is so short that we do not even make it to the morning.

Yet there will be a bright "morning" for some whom the psalmist calls "upright" (v. 14).

The Great Contrast

This brings us to the second half of the psalm, to a section that introduces a contrast between those who trust riches and those who trust God (vv. 13–15). It is a contrast we have been expecting. For although thus far the psalmist's words have been entirely about foolish persons who trust riches and refuse to think about death, the writer is nevertheless speaking to those who should be wise enough to listen to him and learn from him.

1. *Those who trust riches.* The first part of this contrast involves those he has been discussing all along, the rich who trust riches. But verse 13 adds a new and very important element, "their followers." It is a way of saying that not all who are foolish are rich; there are also foolish people who follow them, aspire to be like them, and approve their sayings or philosophy of life. You do not have to have wealth to perish because of wealth. You can perish equally well merely by making money your goal and forgetting spiritual things.

For that is part of the contrast—not merely the goals of those who are materialistic and those who are upright, but also their ends. The person who is preoccupied with money has security, health, long life, and a lasting reputation as his goals. But the true end of such a person is death—and not only physical death, but spiritual death too.

Verse 14 compares the foolish to sheep destined for slaughter, itself an apt image. But then it also adds literally, "Death shall shepherd them." Alexander Maclaren wrote a sermon on this verse in which he compares the shepherding of death with the good shepherding of Jesus, suggesting that the psalmist may have been thinking of the well-known words of Psalm 23, "The LORD is my shepherd," when he wrote, "Death is *their* shepherd" in this psalm.[5]

2. *Those who trust God.* The most remarkable thing about this section, indeed of the psalm as a whole, is the statement of verse 15, which expresses faith in life for the righteous after death. Its first words, "But God," are one of the great "but God" contrasts of the Bible. They teach that those who trust riches will die, be buried and soon be forgotten, but those who trust

God will be redeemed *by him* and be taken *to him* to enjoy personal life and fellowship *with him* forever.

Strangely, Peter C. Craigie, in other respects an excellent student of the psalms, takes verse 15 as a mistaken self-confident boast of the wicked, meaning, "Surely God will redeem my soul. . . ." This leads him to conclude somewhat later that "the psalm, in keeping with the Psalter as a whole, has no explicit theology and hope of life after death."[6] But one can argue the other way. H. C. Leupold asks why the psalmist does not elaborate on this important matter if it is really so striking an insight of faith. He answers: "It must be that the hope of life with God was more real in Old Testament days than many commentators would allow for."[7] In other words, it was not a novelty to say that the upright would be preserved by God in order to have fellowship with him in the afterlife. It was a commonplace. Most if not all the Old Testament writers understood and believed this.

I would argue that the next line also suggests it, since the verb "take me" in the phrase "take me to himself" is used of Enoch in Genesis 5:24. That verse says, "Enoch walked with God; then he was no more, because God took him away." It would have been known to all devout Jews. If Enoch "was taken from this life, so that he did not experience death" (Heb. 11:5), then there must be a life for the righteous beyond death, and it is this life to which the psalmist refers. His was not a well-informed faith, since Jesus had not yet come and no one could fully anticipate the significance of his triumphant resurrection. Yet it was a true faith found, once we know to look for it, in many Old Testament writers.[8]

Moreover, we need to give the fullest possible meaning to "the morning" in verse 14. This could refer only to a later day, as if the psalmist were saying that given enough time the materialist will die and the righteous will inherit his possessions. But that is not always the case. In this life the rich frequently outlive the upright. So I believe the early commentators were right when they suggested that the verse is actually an anticipation of the morning of the resurrection, when the saints shall be raised to glory and receive their spiritual rewards.

Here is an important question: *What makes the difference in the fate of the upright?* Why are they assured of seeing God, while those who trust only in their riches perish?

The answer surely is not in what they do or can do, since that is the error of those who "trust in themselves" (v. 13). The difference is "God," whom the upright trust. God "redeems" the soul of the righteous in contrast to men, who cannot redeem another (v. 7) or themselves (vv. 8–9). In this stage in the history of biblical revelation it would be too much to suggest that the psalmist anticipated the redemption of sinners by the death of Jesus Christ, as the New Testament presents it—for example, in Romans 3:22–24 ("There is no difference, for all have sinned and fall short of the glory of God, and are justified freely by his grace through the redemption that came by Christ Jesus") or in 1 Peter 1:18–19 ("For you know that it was not with perishable things such as silver or gold that you were redeemed from the empty way of life handed down to you from your forefathers, but with the precious blood of Christ, a lamb without blemish or defect"). Nevertheless, "redeem" is exactly the right word to use in this context.

We must remember that *redeem* is a commercial term, meaning "to buy," "buy out," or "buy [a slave so that he or she need never again return to the marketplace]." Spiritually, it refers to God's work in buying us out of sin's marketplace and setting us free. Who can do that? No one but God. The psalmist has already pointed out that no mere human being can redeem another person from death:

> No man can redeem the life of another
> or give to God a ransom for him— (v. 7).

But this is precisely what God does. He redeems the lives of those who trust him rather than riches (v. 15). In this verse "he" and "me" strike a personal note, causing one commentator to write wisely, "We leave the world either with God or with nothing."[9]

An Appeal to Be Wise

This leads naturally to the appeal to be wise that ends the psalm (vv. 16–20), telling us not to be overawed by those who have riches or to trust our soul's eternal destiny to wealth. Why? We say, You can't take it with you. The psalmist says, "He will take nothing with him when he dies" (v. 17).

Do you trust Jesus as your Redeemer, or are you trusting your wealth? Now is the time to get your priorities straight, for you will be in no frame of mind to do it when you're dying. A preacher was called to speak to a dying old miser who wanted him to pray for his soul but was unwilling to take his hand as he did so. They talked about the afterlife, and when the preacher asked him pointedly what he was actually trusting at that moment, the miser confessed that (even as he seemed to be breathing his last) under the bedclothes his hands were clutching the keys to his storage cabinet of treasures. He feared that his money would be taken from him when he died. It was why he would not take the preacher's hand.[10]

Don't be so foolish. Relax your grip on perishing treasures, and place your hand in the hand of Jesus, who died to save you from your sin.

Psalm 50

The Mighty God, the Lord

The Mighty One, God, the Lord,
   speaks and summons the earth
   from the rising of the sun to the place where it sets.
From Zion, perfect in beauty,
   God shines forth.
Our God comes and will not be silent;
   a fire devours before him,
   and around him a tempest rages.
He summons the heavens above,
   and the earth, that he may judge his people:
"Gather to me my consecrated ones,
   who made a covenant with me by sacrifice."
And the heavens proclaim his righteousness,
   for God himself is judge.

verses 1–6

$$I$$n the introduction to Psalm 49 I pointed out that, because the Bible is a progressive revelation, it is often the case that a New Testament passage is a commentary on an Old Testament text. In the case of Psalm 49 it was the other way around; the psalm can be viewed as an exposition of Jesus' well-known parable of the rich fool. Psalm 50 is an example of the normal pattern. Its theme is devel-

415

oped in 1 Peter 4:17, where Peter writes, "For it is time for judgment to begin with the family of God; and if it begins with us, what will the outcome be for those who do not obey the gospel of God?"

A theme like this calls for sober reflection by God's people.[1]

Summons to Judgment

Psalm 50 is a judgment psalm, and the opening verses are a call to judgment in words that evoke memories of the solemn setting of the giving of the law on Mount Sinai in the days of Moses. In Exodus 19, the chapter that immediately precedes the Ten Commandments, we are told:

> On the morning of the third day there was thunder and lightning, with a thick cloud over the mountain, and a very loud trumpet blast. Everyone in the camp trembled. Then Moses led the people out of the camp to meet with God, and they stood at the foot of the mountain. Mount Sinai was covered with smoke, because the LORD descended on it in fire. The smoke billowed up from it like smoke from a furnace, the whole mountain trembled violently, and the sound of the trumpet grew louder and louder (Exod. 19:16–19).

We have exactly this setting in the first six verses of Psalm 50, which are a summons to judgment in which God presents himself on Mount Zion as he did on Mount Sinai, accompanied by fire and a tempest. This theophany is not so extensively described as the one in Exodus. This is a psalm after all, not history. Nevertheless, there is no mistaking the author's intention. And lest we miss it, later on there are other echoes of the language of Mount Sinai. The summons of the people in verse 7 ends with the words "I am God, your God," which echoes the first words of the Ten Commandments, "I am the LORD your God" (Exod. 20:1), and in verses 18–19 there are explicit references to the eighth, seventh, and ninth commandments.

It is hard to imagine anything more solemn than this opening summons to God's court. Note three important elements.

1. *The names of God.* The first line contains three names of God: *El, Elohim,* and *Yahweh* (Jehovah). J. J. Stewart Perowne argues that the first two are not names but are rather to be understood as "the God of gods," thus identifying Jehovah as that One ("The God of gods, Jehovah . . .").[2] But most commentators understand these to be three distinct names, each with its own specific overtones. The New International Version captures some of this by its translation: "the Mighty One, God, the LORD." Thus, "The psalm opens with a majestic heaping together of the divine names, as if a herald were proclaiming the style and titles of a mighty king at the opening of a solemn assize. . . . El speaks of God as mighty; Elohim, as the object of religious fear; Jehovah, as the self-existent and covenant God," says Alexander Maclaren.[3]

2. *The universal scope of the impending judgment.* The next important element in this opening summons to judgment is the scope of the call itself. It extends to the whole "earth from the rising of the sun to the place where it sets" (v. 1). Indeed, it is even greater than that. For having traversed the earth from east to west in verse 1, the psalmist then looks up and down as he refers to God summoning "the heavens above, and the earth" in verse 4. All are included. None are left out. We seem to be on the very edge of God's final judgment of the ungodly, as indeed we are, though it is not in the sense we might have been expecting.

3. *The sudden focus on God's own people.* Suddenly there is a surprise. We were expecting God's final judgment on the heathen, but now we discover that the summons is to God's own people.

> He summons the heavens above,
>> and the earth, that he may judge *his people:*
> "Gather to me *my consecrated ones,*
>> *who made a covenant with me by sacrifice*" (vv. 4–5).

This is why I began this study by Peter's words concerning judgment for God's people: "It is time for judgment to begin with the family of God." For it is not the heathen, but the people of God who are in view.

Appropriately, this opening summons ends with the word *selah* (v. 6). *Selah* seems usually to indicate a break in what is being said, calling for quiet and reflection. If that is accurate, it could not be more significant than here. That one word says well what the prophet Habakkuk said elsewhere in a similar reference to God's judgment, when he wrote,

> The LORD is in his holy temple;
>> let all the earth be silent before him (Hab. 2:20).

The First Indictment: Formalism

There are two categories of God's alleged people summoned to judgment: (1) those writer Derek Kidner calls the "nominally orthodox" or "mechanically pious"[4] (vv. 7–15) and (2) "hypocrites" (vv. 16–21). The first are people who, when God reproves them for a lack of genuine love for him and a thankful spirit, retreat into ritual.

Ritual is not bad in itself, of course, which is why God says, "I do not rebuke you for your sacrifices or your burnt offerings" (v. 8). In this case, the burnt offerings and sacrifices did two good things. First, they remind the worshiper that all we have comes from God; even in our worship we only give back a portion of what God has already given us. Second, they teach that the only way of approaching God is by atonement for sins. They remind us that we are sinners and need salvation. But what this boils down to is that rituals, whether the Old Testament system of sacrifices and feasts or the New Testament sacraments of baptism and the Lord's Supper, are for our benefit, not God's. Therefore, they function rightly only when they inculcate a spirit of thankfulness in the worshiper. As soon as we begin to think that we are doing God a favor by our worship we dishonor God and slide into a false religion of works righteousness.

This is why what is emphasized in the psalm as the right approach to God is thankfulness and honor (vv. 14–15, 22), and not faith. Thankfulness embraces other items, but it is stressed here because it emphasizes what God has done and not what we imagine ourselves as being able to do.

The real problem with ritual is that, if forms are all there is to our religion, they give us feelings of being right with God when actually we may be guilty of the most terrible sins. This happened to the Pharisees in the days of Jesus. They hated him and were trying to get rid of him. Eventually they murdered him. But they did so religiously, breaking the law when they had to but at the same time keeping up every possible outward appearance of piety. Since it was the time of the Passover Feast, they would not defile themselves by going into Pilate's courts. They insisted that Pilate come out to them. Yet they had already arrested Jesus by night, which was illegal. They had forged various and unrelated charges against him, which was illegal. They condemned him unanimously without allowing anyone to speak on his behalf, which was illegal. Students of Jewish law say that scores of safeguards, all of which were meant to protect an innocent person, were recklessly abandoned in Jesus' trial. Yet in spite of this most horrible of sins, the Pharisees nevertheless kept themselves ritually clean and certainly observed the Passover with clear (though hardened) consciences the next day.

Formalism leads easily to such hardening, which is why the psalm speaks so strongly about it.

The psalmist seems to say that the cure is to realize afresh that God does not need anything from us. That is, the cure is a good dose of spiritual reality. It is what verses 9–13, the longest treatment of any single theme in this psalm, say:

> I have no need of a bull from your stall
>   or of goats from your pens,
> for every animal of the forest is mine,
>   and the cattle on a thousand hills.
> I know every bird in the mountains,
>   and the creatures of the field are mine.
> If I were hungry I would not tell you,
>   for the world is mine, and all that is in it.
> Do I eat the flesh of bulls
>   or drink the blood of goats?

To suppose that our worship contributes anything to God or meets a need in God is the height of absurdity. We need to see that. But we also need to see the positive side, namely, that what God requires of us is a thankful heart attitude.

Toward the end of the Old Testament, the prophets speak out against the system of sacrifices on the grounds that the only thing that actually matters in worship is a right attitude. Formalism without a right heart makes the sacrifices, which are otherwise good in themselves, detestable (cf. Isa. 1:11–14; Jer. 7:21–23; Micah 6:6–8).

The Second Indictment: Hypocrisy

With verse 16 there is an unmistakable movement to a second class of people, since the verse begins, "But to the wicked, God says . . ." Yet it is important to see that even here we are not in the presence of the heathen but rather still with the alleged people of God. Derek Kidner calls these "the nominally orthodox," "hypocrites," and "hardened characters."[5]

Their problem is that they are only the *alleged* people of God. They are unconverted, which they prove by supposing that they can worship God and disobey him at the same time. In verse 16 we find that they are reciting God's laws and taking his covenant on their lips. That is, they are mouthing everything they are supposed to. But verse 17 tells us that they actually hate God's instruction and ignore the Bible's precepts. The theological term for this perilous state is *antinomianism,* meaning "against the law." It is the religion of those who think they can belong to God and nevertheless sin freely.

The church is full of people like that, and many are even highly visible. They are fodder for the scandal sheets. They bring discredit to Christianity and dishonor the Lord.

What is even worse, there is a type of evangelical theology that refuses to face the fact that such persons are not Christians and indeed even encourages them in the delusion that they can belong to God and at the same time continue willfully to disobey him. In our day the way this is expressed is to say that it is possible to have Jesus as Savior without having him as Lord. In other words, it is possible to be saved by him without having to follow him in obedient discipleship. Or, as I would also say, it is the mistaken notion that it is possible to be justified without being regenerated or born again. Let me say it clearly: It is possible for Christians to sin; they do sin. But it is not possible for them to be hypocrites. If they are not intending to do the right thing and wanting to do the right thing, as defined by the moral law of God, they are not Christians, any more than the "wicked" people of this psalm were truly God's people.

This is why the psalm speaks so extensively of the law of God at this point, just as it had spoken against the notion that God needed sacrifices or something to eat in part one. The ritualists of part one needed to be reminded that God is spirit and must be worshiped in spirit and truth (cf. John 4:23). The hypocrites need to know that God is moral.

As is often the case in such passages, the psalm refers to several of the Ten Commandments (in this case three) as representative of all.

1. *"You shall not steal"* (v. 18). The first commandment mentioned is the eighth, recorded in Exodus 20:15 and Deuteronomy 5:19. It concerns the property of another. We break this commandment not only in big ways, by robbing a bank or stealing from the petty cash box, for example, but in such small things as wasting our employer's time or failing to give him our best efforts, which is what we are paid to do. Or we steal spiritually by withholding the worship due to God, using the Lord's day for our own pleasures rather than for spiritual service and refreshment, or even by refusing to support the Lord's work. If unbelievers fail to do these things, it is not surprising. They are not Christians. The scandal is when those who profess the name of Christ refuse to do them. Yet all it really does is show that they are hypocrites.

2. *"You shall not commit adultery"* (v. 18). The second reference is to the seventh commandment, found in Exodus 20:14 and Deuteronomy 5:18. It concerns sexual relations with another person's wife or husband. But it is also broader than that, since it embraces all kinds of sexual sins, including the outward sin of fornication and the inner sins of impure thoughts or lust. Jesus said that "anyone who looks at a woman lustfully has already committed adultery with her in his heart" (Matt. 5:28).

At this point there is a strong temptation for us to dismiss the force of the commandment. We live in an exceedingly lustful age, and we tend to excuse this sin on the grounds that if even thinking about adultery is adultery, then all are guilty and therefore it cannot be so bad. But notice that this is not what the psalm does. In the previous example, the psalmist condemned these hardened hypocrites not necessarily because they stole things from others, though they probably did, but because they joined the company of thieves. So also in this case. These alleged people of God are condemned not necessarily because they have been guilty of adultery themselves, though they may have been, but because they threw in their lot with adulterers. That is, they liked to hang around them. They liked their approach to life and their stories. My point is that the Bible does the very opposite of what we do. It does not lessen the force of the commandment; it heightens it. It condemns us for pretending to worship and enjoy God when what we actually enjoy is sin.

3. *"You shall not bear false witness"* (vv. 19–20). The third and last representative commandment is the ninth, from Exodus 20:16 and Deuteronomy 5:20. It deals with truth. We tend to treat words lightly, excusing slander by the claim, "I didn't mean it," or a lie by the excuse, "I was mistaken." Or, even worse, we hear, "I said it; so what?" God does not take these false representations or lies lightly. He is a God of truth. In fact, to judge by the space given to each of these commandments in the psalm, it would seem that he regards lying as even worse than stealing and adultery. The first two are

combined in one verse of two lines, while discussion of this single sin fills two verses and four lines.

> You use your mouth for evil
>   and harness your tongue to deceit.
> You speak continually against your brother
>   and slander your own mother's son (vv. 19–20).

The last verse seems to highlight a sad characteristic of lying, namely, that it becomes a habit. Once we fall into it, it is something we do "continually." It becomes a pattern of speech that we cannot break. Moreover, we become indiscriminate in our lying; we speak not only against our brothers (or sisters) in the broadest sense of those terms, but also against our "own mother's son"—that is, to the one with whom above all we should be truthful, our own blood brother or sister.

What is the problem with such people? They have forgotten that God is a moral God. God says, "You thought I was altogether like you" (v. 21). We excuse sin and take moral requirements lightly. God does not. We assume that because God is silent for long periods of time, he is as indifferent to righteousness as we are. But God is not indifferent. Peter referred to those who mock God's judgment because it is delayed, saying, "Where is this 'coming' he promised?" But Peter replied, "The Lord is not slow in keeping his promise, as some understand slowness. . . . But the day of the Lord will come like a thief. The heavens will disappear with a roar; the elements will be destroyed by fire, and the earth and everything in it will be laid bare." He then asks, "Since everything will be destroyed in this way, what kind of people ought you to be?" (2 Peter 3:9–11).

What kind, indeed?

The Judge's Final Charge

This is where Psalm 50 ends. It ends with a final charge to God's real and alleged people, reminding them of the judgment that is coming and challenging them to remember God by a repentance leading to thanksgiving.

There have been two kinds of people in this psalm, though outwardly they may seem to be the same: formalists and hypocrites. Both "forget God" (v. 22), but they do so in different ways. The first are genuine believers, but they fall into formal patterns of worship by forgetting that God is spirit and must be worshiped spiritually, with the heart and mind. The second are wolves in sheep's clothing. They are not believers. They forget that God is a moral God and that he will not be mocked. They forget that their sin will surely be judged one day.

It is hard to think of a psalm that is as relevant to our day as this one. Alexander Maclaren once wrote, "The psalm has as keen an edge for modern as for ancient sins. Superstitious reliance on externals of worship survives, though sacrifices have ceased; and hypocrites, with their mouths full of the Gospel, still cast God's words behind them."[6] Who can deny the truth of that? It is as descriptive of our time as any, perhaps our time particularly. What we need to do is learn from it by humbling ourselves before God, repenting of our many sins, and honoring God by offering our lives to him.

Psalm 51

Cleansed by the Blood: Part 1

Confession and Cleansing

Have mercy on me, O God,
  according to your unfailing love;
according to your great compassion
  blot out my transgressions.
Wash away all my iniquity
  and cleanse me from my sin.

For I know my transgressions,
  and my sin is always before me.
Against you, you only, have I sinned
  and done what is evil in your sight,
so that you are proved right when you speak
  and justified when you judge.
Surely I was sinful at birth,
  sinful from the time my mother conceived me.
Surely you desire truth in the inner parts;
  you teach me wisdom in the inmost place.

Cleanse me with hyssop, and I will be clean;
  wash me, and I will be whiter than snow.
Let me hear joy and gladness;
  let the bones you have crushed rejoice.
Hide your face from my sins
  and blot out all my iniquity.

verses 1–9

A person who does not have much experience studying the Bible is likely to think that a well-known passage must be easy to elaborate. "It must be easy to teach John 3:16, the twenty-third Psalm, or the Christmas story," he might say. Actually, the opposite is the case. The well-known passages are the hardest, and some seem almost impossible to expound.

This is true of Psalm 51. "This is the fourth, and surely the greatest, of the 'penitential' psalms," says Derek Kidner.[1] Yet who can properly expound it? Charles Haddon Spurgeon was the prince of expositors. He could get more out of a passage than anyone I have ever heard or read. But in the preface to the second part of his first large volume on the psalms, Spurgeon tells how he postponed working on Psalm 51 week after week and often sat down to it and got up again without having written a line. He concluded,

> It is a bush burning with fire yet not consumed, and out of it a voice seemed to cry to me, "Draw not nigh hither, put off thy shoes from off thy feet." The psalm is very human, its cries and sobs are of one born of woman; but it is freighted with an inspiration all divine, as if the Great Father were putting words into his child's mouth. Such a psalm may be wept over, absorbed into the soul, and exhaled again in devotion; but, commented on—ah! where is he who having attempted it can do other than blush at his defeat?[2]

But to start, a few simple things should be noted.

1. Psalm 51 is the first of a series of psalms that, in this second book of the Psalter, are ascribed to David. In fact, from this point on in book two all but four of the psalms are ascribed to him (Psalms 51–65 and 68–70). Psalms 66, 67, and 71 are unnamed. Psalm 72 is attributed to Solomon.

2. Psalm 51 has been a favorite of many well-known historical figures, particularly when they were dying. It was recited in full by Sir Thomas More and Lady Jane Grey when they were on the scaffold in the bloody days of Henry VIII and Queen Mary. Henry V had it read to him as he lay on his deathbed. William Carey, the great pioneer missionary to India, asked that it might be the text of his funeral sermon.[3]

3. There are six easily noted parts to the psalm: (1) the psalmist's approach to God, which is a cry for forgiveness (vv. 1–2); (2) the confession of his sin (vv. 3–6); (3) an appeal for cleansing (vv. 7–9); (4) a desire for inward renewal or the creating of a pure heart (vv. 10–12); (5) a promise to teach others the lessons about forgiveness he has learned (vv. 13–17); and (6) a concluding prayer for the prosperity of Zion (vv. 18–19).

We will look at the first three parts in this study and the last three parts in the next.

David's sin, in which he committed adultery with Bathsheba and later, after discovering that she was pregnant, arranged to have her husband, Uriah, killed in battle, is the dark background for the psalm (see 2 Sam. 11–12). But this very blackness led David to the light. Murdoch Campbell writes:

> David had committed two sins for which the Mosaic law provided no forgiveness. For deliberate murder and adultery death was the inevitable penalty. He knew that before God there was no forgiveness through any sacrifices which he might offer or any gifts which he might present. With Micah he could have asked the solemn question: "Will the Lord be pleased with thousands of rams or with ten thousands of rivers of oil? Shall I give my first-born for my transgression, the fruit of my body for the sin of my soul?" No! By such offerings God cannot be appeased. David might have said: "If I build him an house, a magnificent temple; if I plead my hitherto circumspect life and all my good deeds in his service, will these not compensate for my lapse, and restore me to his favor?" No! "We are all as an unclean thing, and all our righteousnesses are as filthy rags."
>
> There is but one way back to God. And David knew it. It is through the merits of the Lamb of God.[4]

This, though cast in Old Testament language, is the psalm's wonderful message and the secret of its great appeal.

The Psalmist's Cry for Help

David begins by approaching God, whom he is asking to help him in his sinful state (vv. 1–2). But this is no simple approach. It is perceptive, moving, genuine, and profound.

Two things come together in these verses. The first is a fierce, almost desperate clinging to God's mercy. This is profound because, as many commentators have pointed out, mercy is the sole basis of any approach to God by sinners.[5] We cannot come to God on the basis of his justice; justice strikes us with fear and causes us to hide from him. We are not drawn to God by his wisdom; wisdom does not embolden us, though we stand in awe of it. No more does omniscience, omnipotence, or omnipresence. The only reason we dare come to God and dare hope for a solution to our sin problem is his mercy.

Where do we learn that God is merciful? God himself has revealed it to us.

After Israel's national disaster in worshiping the golden calf, Moses asked God to teach him his ways so that Moses might know him. "Show me your glory," he said. God answered Moses that he could not show him his face, because "no one may see me and live." However, he would place him in a cleft of the rock, cover him with his hand, and then pass by. God said, in words that would certainly have been known by David, "I will cause all my goodness to pass in front of you, and I will proclaim my name, the LORD, in your presence. I will have mercy on whom I will have mercy, and I will have compassion on whom I will have compassion" (Exod. 33:12–23). According to this revelation, the very essence of God and the most important thing that sinners can ever know about him is that he is merciful.

David begins this way. And lest we miss the force of this important beginning, he elaborates his opening by two other words that also highlight this important aspect of God's character: "unfailing love" and "compassion." *Mercy* denotes God's loving assistance to the pitiful. *Unfailing love* points to the continuing operation of this mercy. *Compassion* teaches that God feels for our infirmities.

The second striking thing in these opening verses, which comes together with the first, is David's profound awareness of his sin and its true nature. In verse 1 he used three words to describe God's compassion. In verses 1 and 2 he uses three corresponding words to describe his sin.

The first word is *transgressions* (Hebrew, *pesha*). It refers to crossing a forbidden boundary with the thought that this is a serious rebellion. You will recall from the annals of Julius Caesar that as long as the general remained to the north of the river Rubicon he was on peaceful terms with the Roman Senate. But once he crossed the Rubicon, which the Senate had forbidden him to do, he was at war with that legislative body. Caesar did cross, crying, *Iacta alea est* ("the die is cast"), and civil war resulted. That is what we have done with God. We have crossed the boundary of his moral law and are at war with him in consequence. "It is not merely, then, that we go against some abstract propriety, or break some impersonal law of nature when we do wrong, but that we rebel against a rightful Sovereign," says Maclaren.[6]

The second word is *iniquity* (Hebrew, *ʿawon*). It means "perversion" and refers to what we usually call "original sin" or the "depravity" of our natures. Significantly, it is the word used in the first part of verse 5, in the phrase "sinful from birth."

The third word is *sin* itself (Hebrew, *chattath*). It means "falling short" or "missing the mark." We miss God's high mark of perfection, falling short of it in the same way an arrow might fall short of a target. But it is also true that sin misses its own mark, since we never hit what we are aiming at by sinning.

These three words occur again later in the psalm (in vv. 3, 4, 5, 9, and 13). All refer to personal failure, which David emphasizes by speaking of "*my* transgressions, *my* iniquity, and *my* sin" (vv. 1–2).

We should note, too, that this opening of the psalm is similar to that of Psalm 32, which also begins with the same three words for sin. In fact, the relationship of the psalms is close. Both seem to have grown out of the same moral failure on David's part, though Psalm 51 is more intense and personal and seems to have been written close to the event, while Psalm 32 is more reflective and was probably written later. It may be that Psalm 32, which is identified as a *maskil* (possibly meaning "instruction"), is a fulfillment of the promise David makes to "teach transgressors your ways" in Psalm 51:13.

Confession of Sin

Psalm 51 seems to be constructed on the basis of parallel statements in sets of threes. Part one contains three words that describe God as being merciful: *mercy, love,* and *compassion.* There are also three words for sin: *transgressions, iniquity,* and *sin.* In this second section of the psalm, in which David confesses his sin (vv. 3–6), we find three strong statements:

1. *I am aware of my sin* (v. 3). This may seem self-evident and almost trite. "If David is confessing his sin, he must have been aware of it; if he were not, he would not be confessing," we might think. But most of our problems with sin begin at just this point. We do not confess our sins because we do not believe ourselves to be sinners, and this is because we do not recognize that what we do is sin.

Moreover, David was *very much aware* of his sin. Psalm 32:3–4 seems to be a comment on his state of mind at this time, for he speaks there of his bones wasting away and of his "groaning all day long." He says that before he confessed his sin his "strength was sapped as in the heat of summer."

2. *I know that it is sin* (v. 4). In my judgment, this is the meaning of the much-discussed sentence "Against you, you only, have I sinned." Many people have objected that this is not entirely right since David had not only sinned against God but had sinned also against Bathsheba, her husband, Uriah, and even against the nation that eventually also suffered for his wrongdoing. Commentators usually answer that the offense against God was so great in David's mind that it more or less forced from his mind these other lesser matters.

Yet that hardly seems right. I think J. J. Stewart Perowne is on the right track in his excellent treatment of this statement. He approaches it in two ways. First, sin by its very definition is against God, since it is only by God's law that sin is defined as sin. A wrong done to our neighbor is an offense against humanity. In the eyes of the state, which measures wrongs by its own laws, that wrong may be a crime. Only before God is it a sin.

Second, it is only because God is in the picture that even a wrong done to our neighbor is a wrong. It is because our neighbor is made in God's image and is endowed with rights by God that it is wrong to harm him or her. Perowne writes, "All wrong done to our neighbor is wrong done to one created in the image of God; all tempting of our neighbor to evil is taking the part of Satan against God, and, so far as in us lies, defeating God's good purpose of grace toward him. All wounding of another, whether in person or property, in body or soul, is a sin against the goodness of God."[7] Only when a person sees that is he or she ready to acknowledge that God is utterly right in his words and justified in his judgments, which is what David says in the latter half of verse 4, a verse the apostle Paul quotes in Romans 3:4. David did exactly that when Nathan came to him and exposed his sin, confessing, "I have sinned against the LORD" (2 Sam. 12:13).

3. *I confess that sin springs from my thoroughly evil nature* (v. 5). This is the most perceptive statement of all, for it is the equivalent of what we today

call the doctrine of original sin. When David says, "Surely I was sinful at birth, sinful from the time my mother conceived me," he is not blaming his mother for his sin, of course. The whole tone of the psalm is against any such idea. David is confessing his sin and taking full responsibility for it. He is confessing that there was never a moment in his existence when he was not a sinner. As one of the early commentators says, "He lays on himself the blame of a tainted nature instead of that of a single fault."[8]

Verse 6 provides the positive side of this same truth. It teaches that God desires inward purity. This goes along with verse 5, for David's sin was that of an inward nature disposed to sin as well as the act itself, and what God requires is a pure nature as well as upright conduct. The second half of the psalm develops this thought further. In other words, the sinner has two needs: pardon for sin and purity of heart. The first half of the psalm talks about the first need. Verses 10–12 describe the second.

Cleanse Me with Hyssop

The pattern of triple parallel statements continues in verses 7–9, with a list of three things David wanted God to do: "cleanse me with hyssop" (v. 7), "wash me" (v. 7), and "blot out all my iniquity" (v. 9). The verbs are repeated from verses 1–2.

Cleanse means "purge." It is based on the word for sin *(chattath)* and literally means "de-sin" me. David wanted to have his sin completely purged away. He did not want to retain even a stain of it. *Wash* refers to the lustrations of the law. Centuries later Isaiah would write,

> Though your sins are like scarlet,
>   they shall be as white as snow;
> though they are red as crimson,
>   they shall be like wool (Isa. 1:18).

David wanted to be washed until he was as clean as that. *Blot out* refers to removing writing from a book, perhaps removing an indictment. It is the exact opposite of Pilate's words at the time of Jesus' trial and crucifixion: "What I have written, I have written" (John 19:22).

Here is an illustration. There are certain ancient Bible manuscripts called palimpsests. They are pieces of papyrus (or some other ancient book material) that at one time contained a different text. But because this text was no longer needed and the material on which it was written was expensive, someone rubbed out the old writing, turned the sheet sideways, and wrote new words. This is what David wanted and what we all desperately need. The books of our lives have been written upon with many sins, and these stand as a terrible indictment against us. Unless something is done, they are going to be read out against us at the last day. But God can and will do something, if we ask him. God will rub out the ancient writing, turn the pages sideways, and write over the newly prepared surface the message of his everlasting compassion through the work of Jesus Christ.

This is not possible without great cost, of course. This is taught in the four words that begin verse 7, words that I think are the most important in the entire psalm though they are probably also the least understood: "Cleanse me with hyssop."

Hyssop was a small plant frequently found growing in the crevices of stone walls, as Solomon observed (1 Kings 4:33). Because of its shape and structure, it was used as a small brush. In the ceremonies of the temple it was used to sprinkle blood. The first time it is mentioned in the Bible is at the Passover when the Jews were leaving Egypt: "Take a bunch of hyssop, dip it into the blood in the basin and put some of the blood on the top and on both sides of the doorframe" (Exod. 12:22). When the angel of death saw the blood he passed over the Jewish households, and the firstborn in those homes did not die. After that we are told how hyssop was used to sprinkle blood on one who had been healed of some infectious skin disease in an act of ceremonial cleansing (Lev. 14:4, 6) and how it was used in a similar ceremony to cleanse one who had defiled himself by touching a dead body (Num. 19:18).

The author of Hebrews is informative. He indicates that hyssop was used in the enacting of the covenant in Moses' day:

> When Moses had proclaimed every commandment of the law to all the people, he took the blood of calves, together with water, scarlet wool and branches of hyssop, and sprinkled the scroll and all the people. He said, "This is the blood of the covenant, which God has commanded you to keep." In the same way, he sprinkled with blood both the tabernacle and everything used in its ceremonies. In fact, the law requires that nearly everything be cleansed with blood, and without the shedding of blood there is no forgiveness (Heb. 9:19–22).

David understood this, and when he asked that God cleanse him with hyssop he meant "cleanse me by the blood. Forgive me and regard me as cleansed on the basis of the innocent victim that has died."

That is how we must come to God too. We need forgiveness badly. But "without the shedding of blood there is no forgiveness." It is only on the basis of the shed blood of Jesus Christ, the Son of God, that we may find God's mercy. Have you found mercy? Your sin may be as great as David's, even greater. But however great it is, you will find God to be wonderfully merciful if you will come to him as David did.

Psalm 51

Cleansed by the Blood: Part 2

Renewal and Testimony

Create in me a pure heart, O God,
and renew a steadfast spirit within me.
Do not cast me from your presence
or take your Holy Spirit from me.
Restore to me the joy of your salvation
and grant me a willing spirit, to sustain me.

Then I will teach transgressors your ways,
and sinners will turn back to you.
Save me from bloodguilt, O God,
the God who saves me,
and my tongue will sing of your righteousness.
O Lord, open my lips,
and my mouth will declare your praise.
You do not delight in sacrifice, or I would bring it;
you do not take pleasure in burnt offerings.
The sacrifices of God are a broken spirit;
a broken and contrite heart,
O God, you will not despise.

In your good pleasure make Zion prosper;
build up the walls of Jerusalem.
Then there will be righteous sacrifices,
whole burnt offerings to delight you;
then bulls will be offered on your altar.

verses 10–19

Because the psalms are poetry, as a whole they do not have the kind of outlines we expect from didactic literature. The verses do not build on one another with statements, reasons for those statements, and conclusions. We do not find many connective words like *therefore, so, thus,* and *but.* This does not mean that the psalms do not have orderly progressions, however. Psalm 51 obviously does. It has six parts, as we saw in the last study, and these flow naturally from God, with whom the psalm begins, to the psalmist, who is praying for forgiveness and renewal, to the people whom his experience of forgiveness and renewal will affect. The outline goes like this:

1. The approach to God, a cry for forgiveness (vv. 1–2)
2. Confession of sin (vv. 3–6)
3. An appeal for cleansing (vv. 7–9)
4. Desire for inward renewal, creating of a pure heart (vv. 10–12)
5. A promise to teach others the lessons he has learned (vv. 13–17)
6. A concluding prayer for the prosperity of Zion (vv. 18–19)

These six sections also fall into two easily definable psalm parts, corresponding to the psalmist's two great needs. The first need is of forgiveness. David, who is writing the psalm, had sinned against God by his adultery with Bathsheba and the murder of her husband, Uriah, and he knew that he needed to have his sin forgiven and cleansed by God, who alone could cleanse it. He knew that this comes only through the blood of a sacrifice, meaning that an innocent victim has died in the sinner's place. The sacrifices pointed forward to the atonement for sin made by Jesus Christ. He writes of those sacrifices,

> Cleanse me with hyssop, and I will be clean;
> wash me, and I will be whiter than snow (v. 7).

Verses 1–9 deal with this necessity, showing the only path to forgiveness, which is confession of sin and an appeal to God's mercy and compassion.

Yet forgiveness is not the only need David has. He is aware that his sins of adultery and murder came from a sinful heart. He sinned because he is a sinner. Because he is a sinner he is certain to sin again and again, unless God helps him. Therefore, he also needs an inward renewal, which he describes as the creation of a pure heart and the renewal of a steadfast spirit. The second half of the psalm, verses 10–19, deals with this necessity.

Pardon and purity! Those are the two great needs of every human being, since we are all sinners by deed and by nature, just as David was. We need first, cleansing, then the creation of a new spirit or heart.

A New Creation

In some ways the most important and perceptive part of the psalm is the fourth section (vv. 10–12), in which David prays for inward renewal. It indicates that his confession of sin in part one was genuine, because it shows that he could not be content merely with forgiveness. His sin and its effects were so terrible to him that David did not want to fall into sin again. In addition, this fourth section shows David's awareness of his true problem, that his sinful acts sprang from a sinful heart that would certainly cause him to sin repeatedly unless God dealt with it.

Following the pattern of triple parallel statements noted in the last study, we find David asking God to do three things for him in this section.

1. *Create a pure heart.* This is a startling request, and we must not miss its force. The word that begins this section is the Hebrew verb *bara,* which is used in Genesis 1 for the creation of the heavens and the earth by God. Strictly used, this word describes what only God can do; to create *ex nihilo,* out of nothing. It is true that you and I, being made in God's image, can create things too, but not in the same way. We create out of existing material, using preexisting mental forms or ideas. God creates out of nothing, as only God can. In Genesis 1 *bara* is used at three pivotal points of the narrative to describe: (1) the creation of matter, the heavens and the earth (v. 1); (2) the creation of self-conscious life, the animals (v. 21); and (3) the creation of God-conscious life, human beings (v. 27). At all other points less powerful verbs are employed.

Bara is the word David uses in verse 10 of the psalm, where he asks God to "create" a pure heart in him. In other words, as Derek Kidner writes, "With the word *create* he asks for nothing less than a miracle."[1] He desires what only God can provide.

Moreover, he is acknowledging that this must be a creation out of nothing. This is very important, because it means that David knew, as the apostle Paul would later write in Romans, "that nothing good lives in me, that is, in my sinful nature" (Rom. 7:18). If the work was to be any good, it could not use anything that was already in David. It would have to be a creation from nothing, since if any of it came from David himself, that little bit would contaminate everything, like deadly germs in drinking water. It is a way of saying that if we are ever going to have victory over sin, God is going to have to start over with us from the beginning.

And he does! He has promised to. Ezekiel quoted God as saying,

> I will sprinkle clean water on you, and you will be clean; I will cleanse you from all your impurities and from all your idols. I will give you a new heart and put a new spirit in you; I will remove from you your heart of stone and give you a heart of flesh. And I will put my Spirit in you and move you to follow my decrees and be careful to keep my laws (Ezek. 36:25–27).

It is a wonderful truth and promise. It is a promise to which we cling.

2. *Do not cast me away.* Even if God should re-create him, David is still worried that he might again fall into sin. Hence there is much in these verses about God sustaining him in his renewed state. He prays for "a steadfast spirit" (v. 10). He uses the word *sustain* itself in verse 12. The positive is also expressed by the negative in verse 11: "Do not cast me from your presence or take your Holy Spirit from me."

This verse has been a problem to commentators. The idea of God removing the Holy Spirit from someone comes from the account of God's withdrawal of his blessing from King Saul, David's immediate predecessor as king of Israel (see 1 Sam. 16). But what did David mean by such a prayer? Did he mean that it is possible to be born again, which is the work of the Holy Spirit, and then to be unborn? Did he mean that it is possible to be saved and then lose your salvation because of sin? Or is he referring only to God's continued favor and blessing? We can understand how we might lose the full blessing of God on our lives because of sin, but if that is all David means, why does he refer to God casting him away or taking away his Holy Spirit?

John Calvin believed in eternal security, of course. So when he came to this verse he argued that David's prayer that God not take away the Holy Spirit showed that he still possessed the Holy Spirit. Hence, even his great sins of adultery and murder had not threatened David's perseverance in grace. The bottom line of Calvin's answer to the apparent problem of this verse would seem to be that David did not need to pray as he did, since the removal of God's Spirit from a born-again son or daughter of God is an impossibility. Calvin wrote, "It is natural that the saints, when they have fallen into sin, and have thus done what they could to expel the grace of God, should feel an anxiety upon this point; but it is their duty to hold fast the truth, that grace is the incorruptible seed of God, which can never perish in any heart where it has been deposited."[2]

Fundamentalists of a few years ago, most of whom were greatly influenced by dispensational ideas, distinguished between the working of the Holy Spirit in Old Testament times and the activity of the Holy Spirit since Pentecost. Sometimes they would say that before Pentecost the Holy Spirit would come "on" a person chosen for a special task but that after Pentecost he dwells "within" all believers. They would say that only since Christ's coming are people truly "born again." The bottom line of this second answer to the problem is that David's prayer was appropriate to one living in the Old Testament dispensation, but that it is inappropriate for God's people today. Arno C. Gaebelein, one of the editors of the famous Scofield Reference Bible, wrote, "The prayer of the eleventh verse needs not to be prayed by the saint in the New Testament, for he is accepted in the Beloved One. He is saved and safe in him; he may grieve the Holy Spirit, but he is the abiding Holy Spirit, by whom we are sealed unto the day of redemption."[3] In other words, the Old Testament saints could lose their salvation; we cannot.

Today most commentators recognize that David is not talking about eternal security or the fear of losing his salvation at all. He is only acknowledging that he is unable to live a holy life without God. Therefore, he needs the help and power of the Holy Spirit every single moment if he is to be able to overcome temptation and follow after godliness. J. J. Stewart Perowne writes along these lines, explaining, "It is the cry of one who knows, as he never knew before, the weakness of his own nature, and the strength of temptation, and the need of divine help."[4] Alexander Maclaren has the same idea in mind when he says, "The psalmist is recoiling from what he knows only too well to be the consequence of an unclean heart—separation from God."[5]

3. *Restore the joy of your salvation.* The third of David's requests in this section is that God would restore the joy of his salvation. It is important to note that David is not praying that God would restore his salvation, as if he had lost it and needed to get it back again. It is not the salvation he had lost, but the joy of it. As long as he was living in sin he had no joy. His fellowship with God was broken. Now that he has repented of his sin, found cleansing, and is seeking a renewed spirit, he wants to have that joy again.

How relevant to many people's thinking today. Many think that the way to joy or a good time is by sinning. They think that godliness is dull. Actually the opposite is the case. Sin brings sorrow. Righteousness brings rejoicing. Allowed to continue, sin will remove every good thing from our lives—joy, health, wealth, and at last even life itself. Only righteousness will restore them. One commentator notes wisely, "The fact that the psalmist prays for so many things [in vv. 7–12] indicates how many things he knew he had lost when he plunged into sin."[6]

Sinners Then Shall Learn from Me

Religion is a personal thing, and the confession of sin is particularly personal. We must confess our own sin, not someone else's. This does not mean that true religion can ever be individualistic or entirely private, however. We see this in the last two sections of the psalm. For having been forgiven, cleansed, and renewed by God, David now recognizes that he has a duty to those around him. In section five he vows to teach what he has learned about sin and forgiveness to other sinners, so they may confess their sin and turn back to God too. In the final section he prays for Zion, which was also affected by his transgression. As I pointed out in the first study of this psalm, Psalm 32 is probably the fulfillment of the vow in verses 13–15.

There are two things that David says he is going to teach others: (1) the "ways" of God (v. 13), and (2) "your righteousness" (v. 14). The "ways" of God is a broad designation that usually means the path of righteousness set out in the law. "Righteousness" itself usually means that upright character of God that we associate with his holiness. Probably neither of these terms means exactly that here.

In the context, the "ways" of God probably means his ways with sinners—that is, the way in which he afflicts them in their sin and accounts them righteous on the basis of the sacrifices, which point forward to the atoning work of Christ, when they confess it. Psalm 51 would require this interpretation all by itself, since that is what it is about. But if Psalm 32 is the fulfillment of the vow David makes to teach God's ways to others, the point is even clearer. For that psalm contains a painful description of the psalmist's state when he was continuing in his sin, as well as the very verses Paul quotes in Romans to show that David understood the doctrine of justification by the grace of God through faith and trusted in it.

> Blessed is he
>> whose transgressions are forgiven,
>> whose sins are covered.
> Blessed is the man
>> whose sin the LORD does not count against him
>> and in whose spirit there is no deceit
>> (Ps. 32:1–2; cf. Rom. 4:7–8).

This is what needs to be taught to sinners. It is what gospel preaching is all about, in our day as well as in the past.

Similarly, the word *righteousness* in verse 14 is not so much the righteousness of God as he is in himself, but rather his righteousness in the justification of sinners. Perowne therefore says rightly, "The righteousness of God is that attribute according to which he gives to every one his own, to those who with repentance and faith turn to him, the forgiveness which they ask, and which he has promised to bestow."[7] It is exactly the way the word is used in 1 John 1:9, where we are told, "If we confess our sins, he is faithful and just and will forgive us our sins and purify us from all unrighteousness." In that verse the word *just (dikaios)* has the same root as the word *righteousness (dikaiosune)* and means that God acts justly and in faithfulness to his promise when he forgives sin. He is just because he does it on the basis of Christ's atonement, and he is faithful because he has promised to forgive all who will confess their sin and come to him through faith in Jesus.

Teaching is not the only thing David wants to do, however. He also wants to praise God rightly. He wants to praise God out of a broken spirit and a contrite heart.

This is the way in which we are to understand his words about sacrifices and burnt offerings in verse 16. Earlier I pointed out that the prayer "cleanse me with hyssop" in verse 7 is a reference to ceremonial purification by sprinkling with the blood of an animal sacrificed for sin. It is a recognition that "without the shedding of blood there is no forgiveness" (Heb. 9:22). Does verse 16 mean that David is contradicting himself now, that he was wrong earlier and that God does not actually want sacrifices? Or that sacrifices have no value? Not at all! Forgiveness is on the basis of the sacrifice made by Jesus Christ. There is no forgiveness without faith in him. However, having been justified by faith in Christ, we are not to think that a right relationship with God is now somehow to be retained or advanced ceremonially, as if sacrifices without an upright heart can please God. They cannot. What God requires in regenerate people is a yielded spirit, which will express itself in willing obedience.

To put it in New Testament terms, it is what Paul writes in Romans when he asks those who have been justified, "What shall we say, then? Shall we go on sinning so that grace may increase?" and answers, "By no means! We died to sin; how can we live in it any longer?" (Rom. 6:1–2). The proof of the forgiveness described in Psalm 32:7–9 is found in the altered heart attitudes depicted in verses 13–17.

Blessing for Zion

This changed attitude is evident in verses 18–19, too. These two verses, the last of the six sections of this psalm, are a prayer for God's blessing on Zion, that God would prosper the city, build up its walls, and make it a place where godly people could continue to present their sacrifices.

These last verses have been used by some writers, even conservative ones, as an argument against David's authorship of the psalm or at least his authorship of the final verses. Alexander Maclaren argues that these verses are a liturgical addition since the walls were not down and did not need to be rebuilt.[8] Derek Kidner and Stewart Perowne believe that the words were added during the Jewish captivity or following the exile.[9] This is possible, of course. But it is also possible that the verses are not added or misplaced, but that David, having confessed his sin, now contemplates the bad effect it may have had upon the nation and prays about it.

As for the walls being built up, two views are possible. David may be speaking metaphorically, suggesting that the strength of Jerusalem is in the righteousness of its people and that this had been weakened because of his sin and now needed to be restored. Or he may be speaking literally, since the walls, buildings, and temple were not completed until the days of Solomon (see 1 Kings 3:1). In this case, David would be praying that this important work might not be hindered by his sin and might continue.

Let us remember that everything we do affects other people, whether for good or evil. It is not true that we can sin "as long as it does not hurt anyone," because sin always hurts someone. But it is also true that those who confess their sin find forgiveness and renewal, teach others the ways of God, and become a blessing.

Psalm 52

Righteous Judgment for a Wicked Man

Why do you boast of evil, you mighty man?
  Why do you boast all day long,
  you who are a disgrace in the eyes of God?
Your tongue plots destruction;
  it is like a sharpened razor,
  you who practice deceit.
You who love evil rather than good,
  falsehood rather than speaking the truth.   Selah
You love every harmful word,
  O you deceitful tongue!

Surely God will bring you down to everlasting ruin:
  He will snatch you up and tear you from your tent;
  he will uproot you from the land of the living.   Selah
The righteous will see and fear;
  they will laugh at him, saying,
"Here now is the man
  who did not make God his stronghold
but trusted in his great wealth
  and grew strong by destroying others!"

But I am like an olive tree
  flourishing in the house of God;
I trust in God's unfailing love
  for ever and ever.
I will praise you forever for what you have done;
  in your name I will hope, for your name is good.
  I will praise you in the presence of your saints.

verses 1–9

437

In the vast collection of Hebrew verse that we call the Psalter only a few psalms are given a specific historical setting. Psalm 51 is one of these. It is introduced as "A psalm of David. When the prophet Nathan came to him after David had committed adultery with Bathsheba." Other examples are Psalms 3, 18, 34, 54, 56, 57, 59, 60, 63, and 142. All these concern incidents from the life of David, and the part of the Psalter we are in now contains the largest number of such historically situated psalms (eight from Psalms 51 to 63).

The heading for Psalm 52 gives the context as one of the most bitter experiences in the life of David: "When Doeg the Edomite had gone to Saul and told him: 'David has gone to the house of Ahimelech.'"

As a result of this report and at Saul's command, eighty-five of the priests of Nob together with their wives, children, and other citizens of the town were killed by Doeg. David had two responses to this tragic massacre that have been recorded for us. The first is in 1 Samuel 22:22–23, where the story is recorded. The second is our psalm. In the first of these responses David recognized and confessed his own unwitting responsibility for the massacre. In the second he documented the primary and deliberate wickedness of Doeg, who is the "evil, . . . mighty man" of the psalm (v. 1).

David and Ahimelech

But first the story. David had been forced to flee Jerusalem after his sad parting with Jonathan in the field outside the city, and he had come to Nob, one of the cities of the priests. Ahimelech was the chief priest, and David presented himself to Ahimelech, asking for help. Ahimelech must have suspected that something was wrong because David had come unarmed and alone, without his customary band of soldiers. We are told that Ahimelech trembled when he saw David. But David lied to him, saying that Saul had sent him on a secret errand and that he had arranged to meet his soldiers later. Then he asked for food and was given the consecrated bread that had been on the Table of Shewbread, presented to the Lord. Because David had no weapon Ahimelech also gave him the sword of Goliath, which had been kept in the sanctuary at Nob and was the only weapon available.

In the midst of this story we find this solemn notation: "Now one of Saul's servants was there that day, detained before the LORD; he was Doeg the Edomite, Saul's head shepherd" (1 Sam. 21:7).

In the next chapter the scene shifts to a hillside at Gibeah where Saul was assembled with his officials and personal military guard. The king was feeling sorry for himself and isolated, because he had heard that David was gathering supporters in Judah; he knew that Jonathan was David's friend and had made a covenant of friendship with him, and no one was sharing any of this with him or telling him what else was going on.

Sadly, Doeg was present, and seeing this as an opportunity to insinuate himself into even greater favor with the king, Doeg volunteered, "I saw the son of Jesse come to Ahimelech son of Ahitub at Nob. Ahimelech inquired of the LORD for him; he also gave him provisions and the sword of Goliath the Philistine" (1 Sam. 22:9–10). This infuriated Saul. So Saul called for Ahimelech and accused him of conspiracy. Ahimelech replied correctly that no one in the kingdom was more loyal to Saul than David. Besides, how was he to know there was a problem between David and the king? When David came to Nob, he assisted David just as he had done many times previously and would expect to do always.

Saul was irrational. "You will surely die, Ahimelech, you and your father's whole family," he said (v. 16). But when Saul ordered his guards to kill the priests they refused to do so, considering it sacrilege to lift a hand against the anointed servants of the Lord.

Saul then ordered Doeg to kill the priests, and he did: "So Doeg the Edomite turned and struck them down. That day he killed eighty-five men who wore the linen ephod. He also put to the sword Nob, the town of the priests, with its men and women, its children and infants, and its cattle, donkeys and sheep" (vv. 18–19). One man, Abiathar, a son of Ahimelech, escaped by fleeing to David, who took him in and protected him. It was to Abiathar that David confessed his own unwitting part in this terrible tragedy: "That day, when Doeg the Edomite was there, I knew he would be sure to tell Saul. I am responsible for the death of your father's whole family" (v. 22).

This story is never mentioned again anywhere else in the Bible, except in the introduction to Psalm 52. This psalm is David's personal evaluation of Doeg and the tragic events he precipitated. It has three parts: (1) a description of Doeg's wickedness (vv. 1–4), (2) the prophesied end of this exceedingly evil man (vv. 5–7), and (3) a final contrasting portrait of David himself, showing what he was and what he hoped always to do and continue being (vv. 8–9).

Portrait of a Very Wicked Man

As we read the first stanza of this historical psalm, we find Doeg's evil character described in three aspects.

First, he was *proud*. The word used in the psalm is *boast,* and it occurs twice, both times in verse 1: "Why do you boast of evil, you mighty man? Why do you boast all day long?" The thought conveyed in this Hebrew word is not necessarily that of a person strutting around making extravagant claims to others about his or her abilities. Rather it is that of a smug self-sufficiency that does not parade itself openly simply because it is so convinced of its superiority. Sometimes outward boasting is a cover-up for a person's inner insecurities, but that was not what Doeg was like. As the British scholar Derek Kidner writes, "The real point is the man's self-satisfaction. He thinks himself clever, he is absorbed in his intrigues."[1]

There is some evidence for this evil element of Doeg's character in the story itself. For if we read it carefully, we notice that there was a considerable time gap between the day Doeg was in Nob and saw David and when he reported this fact to King Saul. The end of 1 Samuel 21 tells of David's escape to Achish, one of the rulers of the Philistines, and the start of the next chapter tells of David gathering his mighty men about him while in the stronghold at Adullam. Both of these events intervene between the time Doeg saw David with Ahimelech in Nob and when he reported this to Saul. So it was not a case of the Edomite's merely blurting out what he knew at the first opportunity. On the contrary, he knew he had a piece of valuable information and kept it to himself until it would best serve his interests to divulge it. He saw his opportunity when Saul complained that none of his retainers was concerned about him or told him anything.

Second, Doeg *loved evil*. Verse 3 says, "You love evil rather than good, falsehood rather than speaking the truth." The fact that Doeg told Saul what he knew would not be proof of his love of evil necessarily. He might simply have been trying to advance himself with Saul. But his ruthless murder of the priests of Nob and their families showed that he actually hated all who stood for righteousness—Ahimelech stood for righteousness and had spoken truthfully when he was interrogated by Saul—and Doeg wanted to eliminate such people and thus advance and align himself with the most evil aspects of Saul's deteriorating moral character.

Third, Doeg *used words as his weapon*. At first glance this does not seem so bad to us. In fact, it seems out of place. We know that boasting is bad, and loving evil is bad by definition. But words? Words seem relatively harmless. Yet when we look carefully at the stanza we see that this is the vice most emphasized.

> Your tongue plots destruction;
> it is like a sharpened razor,
> you who practice deceit.
> You love evil rather than good,
> falsehood rather than speaking the truth.
> You love every harmful word,
> O you deceitful tongue (vv. 2–4).

This tells us something about the nature of falsehood, deceit, and lies as well as the potentially murderous effects of words. It teaches that words are not morally neutral. They are a powerful force either for evil or good. Yet the statements of the psalm do something else too. They also bring this denunciation of Doeg's character closer to us and warn us of the evil of which we are capable.

Believers in Jesus Christ should not be able to see themselves as people who love evil. In fact, if they do love evil rather than good, they are not Christians. Neither should they be able to be described as those who are self-satisfied, clever, or absorbed in their intrigues. But words? Failing to tell the truth? Deceit? These are things that come much closer to where we live and are a rebuke to any loose talk or less than honest or upright conversation.

If this were not a danger for us, why would James have written about the harm the tongue can do in that extensive treatment found in chapter 3?

> The tongue is a small part of the body, but it makes great boasts. Consider what a great forest is set on fire by a small spark. The tongue also is a fire, a world of evil among the parts of the body. It corrupts the whole person, sets the whole course of his life on fire, and is itself set on fire by hell.
>
> All kinds of animals, birds, reptiles and creatures of the sea are being tamed and have been tamed by man, but no man can tame the tongue. It is a restless evil, full of deadly poison.
>
> With the tongue we praise our Lord and Father, and with it we curse men, who have been made in God's likeness. Out of the same mouth come praise and cursing. My brothers, this should not be (James 3:5–10).

The whole passage is sobering, but especially those last words: "Brothers, this should not be." "Brothers" means Christians. So this is a statement that believers in Christ are sometimes guilty of the same vice seen in wicked Doeg and that they do corresponding harm.

In England during World War II a war poster designed to warn against the unwitting disclosure of troop movements or other military secrets was displayed all over the country. It contained the words "Loose talk costs lives." That is true spiritually as well. So instead of being people whose talk is undisciplined or loose, we should be people whose conversation is constructive and above all truthful.

When I say grace before meals one of the prayers I frequently make is that God will "guide our conversation." It is a prayer we might all make at all times and on all occasions.

A Prophesied Judgment

Having described Doeg's evil character, David next prophesies his end. It is an important principle in the psalms, often stated by David but also by others, that in a moral universe ultimately evil does not prosper but is instead brought down. And by contrast, the righteous excel.

This is not to be taken as a truth with no exceptions, of course, for clearly the righteous sometimes do suffer, even death. After all, Ahimelech and the other priests as well as their families were killed by Doeg. That is the very occasion of the psalm. And the wicked do sometimes flourish. That is one of the things that bothers the psalm writers. They can't understand why evil people frequently do prosper or why the judgment of God on such persons is often long delayed. The psalm writers were not naive. In fact, they were far more sensitive to these anomalies than we customarily are. But underlying these observations and more basic was their steadfast conviction that in the end the wicked are brought down and the righteous are preserved and blessed by God.

This stanza contains two main ideas: first, what God will do to Doeg eventually, and second, what the righteous will do when at last they witness God's judgment.

The statement of God's judgment on Doeg contains four vigorous verbs meant to stress the utter totality of his ruin. The first is *bring down*. It has the idea of tearing something down in order to break it into pieces, as when an altar is torn down and demolished so that it might never be raised up again. The second verb is *snatch up,* which has the additional thought of twisting something up or out, as trees are sometimes torn out of the ground by twisting them. The third verb is *tear* (or *sweep*) *away.* The New International Version reads "tear you from your tent," but other scholars believe the idea is actually "so you may no longer be a tent"—that is, a family in Israel. As Doeg had destroyed the families of the priests, so he and his family would be expunged from Israel. The final verb, *uproot* (or *eradicate*), reinforces this idea.

At this point we might expect something about punishment in the life to come, judgment of the soul as well as of the body. But instead we find two verses describing what the righteous will do when they witness God's judgment on the evil man. They will "see" it and "fear" (v. 6). That is, they will stand in awe of God's mighty judging acts. And they will "laugh," drawing the appropriate conclusion on Doeg's folly in pursuing evil rather than good and falsehood rather than truth.

> They will laugh at him, saying,
> "Here now is the man
>   who did not make God his stronghold
> but trusted in his great wealth
>   and grew strong by destroying others!" (vv. 6–7).

It is the lesson drawn from God's judgment that keeps the laughter of the righteous from being what we would call mere selfish delight at the fall of some mighty enemy. This is not mockery at another person's misfortune. It is satisfaction at the rightness of things when God intervenes to judge those who have done great harm to others.

A Contrasting Portrait of the Righteous

We have to be careful at this point, of course, because we are sinners too, and it is fatally easy for us to forget our own evil when we see how others are brought down and find improper satisfaction in it. This is why we have the third, final stanza. In it David suggests what the proper attitude of the righteous should be, using himself as an example:

> But I am like an olive tree
>> flourishing in the house of God;
> I trust in God's unfailing love
>> for ever and ever.
> I will praise you forever for what you have done;
>> in your name I will hope, for your name is good.
> I will praise you in the presence of your saints (vv. 8–9).

We know from the story of David's later life that he did not always live up to a righteous standard. But at the time he wrote this he could honestly say that he was "like an olive tree flourishing in the house of God." The olive is one of the most lasting of all trees. With its dark, waxen leaves it survives even the worst summer droughts. It is valuable in its ability to produce a yearly crop of olives.

At this point it is difficult not to think back to Psalm 1, of which Psalm 52 is a specific illustration. Psalm 1 contrasted the way of the righteous with the way of the wicked, showing the righteous person to be "like a tree planted by streams of water, which yields its fruit in season and whose leaf does not wither" (v. 3), while the wicked are described as "chaff that the wind blows away" (v. 4). "Therefore," says the psalmist,

> the wicked will not stand in the judgment,
>> nor sinners in the assembly of the righteous.
>
> For the LORD watches over the way of the righteous,
>> but the way of the wicked will perish (vv. 5–6).

Assuming the prophecy of Doeg's eventual end to have been fulfilled, the ways of David and Doeg illustrate that teaching.

Do you and I believe that? Do we believe that God really is in control of this world and that evil will be judged and righteousness will be rewarded in the end, even if not openly in every case right now? If we do, then the last verse of Psalm 52 describes what we will do and be like. In it David does three things. First, *he praises God* ("I will praise you forever for what you have done," v. 8). Second, *he trusts God for the future* ("I trust in God's unfailing love for ever and ever" and "in your name I will hope, for your name is good," vv. 8–9). Third, *he bears witness of these truths before others* ("I will praise you in the presence of your saints," v. 9).

Charles Haddon Spurgeon wrote, "Before or among the saints David intended to wait, feeling it to be good both for him and them to look to the Lord alone, and wait for the manifestation of his character in due season. Men must not too much fluster us; our strength is to sit still. Let the mighty ones boast, we will wait on the Lord; and if their haste brings them present honor, our patience will have its turn by-and-by, and bring us the honor which excelleth."[2] That is true. It will surely happen. The honor of God stands behind such an outcome. But when it does happen, make sure you are faithful in telling others about it, as David did.

Psalm 53

A Psalm That Is Repeated

The fool says in his heart,
"There is no God."
They are corrupt, their ways are vile;
there is no one who does good.

God looks down from heaven
on the sons of men
to see if there are any who understand,
any who seek God.
Everyone has turned away,
they have together become corrupt;
there is no one who does good,
not even one.

Will the evildoers never learn—
those who devour my people as men eat bread
and who do not call on God?
There they were, overwhelmed with dread,
where there was nothing to dread.
God scattered the bones of those who attacked you;
you put them to shame, for God despised them.

Oh, that salvation for Israel would come out of Zion!
When God restores the fortunes of his people,
let Jacob rejoice and Israel be glad!

verses 1–6

W e now come to a psalm that is a
near repetition of one we have already examined, Psalm 14, except for a few
minor changes and the last three lines of verse 5. This suggests two questions:
Why is it repeated? and What can I say about the psalm the second time?

Since God has seen fit to repeat Psalm 14 with only minor changes, I am
tempted to follow God's lead and repeat the earlier study. When we studied
Psalm 14 I pointed out that, in addition to Psalms 14 and 53 being almost
identical, the most important part of these psalms is also repeated in
Romans 3 as verses 10–12. I said, "Anything God says once demands attention. Anything he says twice demands our most intent attention. How then
if he says something three times, as he does in this case? This demands our
keenest concentration, contemplation, assimilation, and even memoriza-
tion. These are words which, to use the often-quoted phrase of the collect
from the Book of Common Prayer, we are to 'read, mark, learn and
inwardly digest.'" That is why I say it might be appropriate if I followed
God's lead and simply repeated the earlier study.

Yet somehow I think that would be missing the point. Probably the psalm
is repeated because God thinks we have much to learn from it. We have not
learned all we could learn in our first study. Therefore, if we turn to the
psalm a second time, we will find that it has new lessons for our growth and
blessing.

Spurgeon thought that we profit from it more as we grow older. He
wrote, "All repetitions are not vain repetitions. We are slow to learn, and
need line upon line." Assuming that Psalm 53 was written by David late in
life and that he had written Psalm 14 earlier, Spurgeon said, "David after a
long life, found men no better than they were in his youth. Holy Writ never
repeats itself needlessly, [therefore] there is good cause for the second copy
of this Psalm." Making a point by the numbering of the psalms, he noted,
"If our age has advanced from fourteen to fifty-three, we shall find the doctrine of this psalm more evident than in our youth."[1]

Slightly Different

There are a few differences between the psalms, however, so we may start
by noting them. Most are slight. In verse 1, "deeds" in Psalm 14 is changed
to "ways" in Psalm 53. In verse 3, "All have turned aside" is changed to
"everyone has turned away." In verse 4, "*the* evildoers" replaces "evildoers."
The only apparent effect of these minor changes is to intensify or heighten
the sentiments slightly.

A change that is a bit more significant is the replacing of the name
Jehovah ("LORD") with *Elohim* ("God") throughout Psalm 53. Each psalm
refers to God seven times. In Psalm 14, however, *Elohim* appears three times
and *Jehovah* four times, while in Psalm 53 the word is *Elohim* in every

instance. If Psalm 14 is the original psalm, as most of the commentators think, it is hard to explain the change of *Jehovah* to *Elohim* in Psalm 53, except to say that *Jehovah* is the word for God that predominates in book one of the Psalter while *Elohim* predominates in book two.

The only significant variation in Psalm 53 is verse 5, which replaces verses 5–6 of Psalm 14. The earlier psalm seems to be addressing fools in Israel, saying,

> There they are, overwhelmed with dread,
>   for God is present in the company of the righteous.
> You evildoers frustrate the plans of the poor,
>   but the LORD is their refuge (Ps. 14:5–6).

The later psalm is addressing evildoers who have attacked Israel, presumably Gentiles, whom it refers to, saying,

> There they were, overwhelmed with dread,
>   where there was nothing to dread.
> God scattered the bones of those who attacked you;
>   you put them to shame, for God despised them (Ps. 53:5).

We can only guess what specific incident this refers to, but something like the scattering of the armies of Sennacherib in the days of Hezekiah and Isaiah would explain it well (cf. 2 Kings 18–19). If verse 5 does refer to the defeat of alien armies in the time of one of these kings, then a later poet probably altered David's original psalm to apply it more specifically to the new situation.

Fools and Their Folly

That is not our situation, of course. So if the psalm is to speak to us, it needs to speak in a different way. When we studied Psalm 14, I looked at Paul's use of verses 1–3 in Romans and followed his analysis of the way the human race has rejected God. In that analysis the fool is one who knows that God exists because of God's revelation of himself in nature but who suppresses that knowledge because he does not want to acknowledge God. That is sin, of course. So recognizing that it is sin, we could define a fool by saying, "A fool is anyone who sins, acting as if there is no God." If we do this, we can look at the psalm for what it has to teach about sin, considering its nature, fruit, and consequences.

Matthew Henry does that. He finds eight points in the psalm, seven of which have to do with sin and the eighth, by contrast, with the faith of the saints. All begin with the letter *f*. I am adopting his outline for what follows.[2]

1. *The fact of sin.* Henry begins with the reality of sin, arguing his point from the truth that "God looks down from heaven" and sees it (v. 2). You

and I do not always see sin, and the chief reason for our blindness is that we choose to close our eyes to transgressions. We often do that with others, turning a blind eye to their actions. We nearly always do it with ourselves. If we are confronted with the reality of our sin, we defend ourselves by such excuses as, "I didn't mean to do it," "You don't understand what happened," "It wasn't really like that," "It wasn't my fault," or "You should see what the other person did to me first." In other words, we pretend either that the act was not sin or that it was justified.

In the Garden of Eden, on the occasion of the first sin, Adam tried to deny his fault by blaming Eve: "The woman you put here with me—she gave me some fruit from the tree, and I ate it" (Gen. 3:12).

Eve blamed Satan: "The serpent deceived me, and I ate" (v. 13).

The problem with denial is that we are not the court of last appeal. In fact, we are not even judges. We are the accused, and the one who knows the facts of the case, prepares the indictment, handles the prosecution, and renders the ultimate judgment is God. The omniscient God sees perfectly and knows all things. Before him all hearts are open, all desires known, and it is he who says,

> All have turned aside,
>   they have together become corrupt;
> there is no one who does good,
>   not even one (Ps. 14:3).

It will do us no good to pretend that sin is not sin or that we are not sinners, as long as God is on his throne.

2. *The fault of sin.* Another way we deal with sin so we can live with it and not feel too guilty is to minimize sin, thinking of sin as a weakness or imperfection perhaps but certainly not as a serious transgression that inevitably harms us and wounds others. It is evidence of our folly that we do this, but God is no fool, and he "tells it like it is."

God says that sinners are "corrupt" and that "their ways are vile" (v. 1). He describes them as having "turned away" from the correct path (v. 3). He says that they are "evildoers" who "devour" other people (v. 4). These terms describe sin accurately in terms of three basic relationships: to God, ourselves, and others. So far as God is concerned, we have turned from him. Indeed, the verb is even stronger than this; it means that we have turned around entirely and are now pursuing a completely "anti-God" path. So far as we are concerned, we have become corrupt and vile. This means that we are destroying ourselves and that our sin is offensive both to God and others. So far as others are concerned, we are harming them by our actions. Sin is no small thing. It is a very great fault and very harmful.

3. *The fountain of sin.* "How comes it that men are so bad?" asks Henry. "Surely it is because there is no fear of God before their eyes."[3] It is because they say in their hearts, "There is no God" (v. 1).

I pointed out in our study of Psalm 14 that this does not necessarily describe what we would call theoretical atheism, the atheism of one who literally denies the existence of a Supreme Being. There are quite a few theoretical atheists in our day, but an atheist like this was rare in the ancient world. What is in view here is rather what we might call practical atheism—that is, the outlook of one who would concede that there is a God but who would maintain that God has nothing to do with the world as it now is and therefore that God has no practical bearing on how we are to live or what we do. This is clearer in the Hebrew text than in the English translation, because in Hebrew the phrase *There is* in the sentence "There is no God" is missing, and what the text actually says is, "No God." That is, "No God for me." Whether or not God exists, the fool does not act as if there is one.

This is the source of our troubles, of course. I pointed out in our study of Psalm 8 that God has placed man in a mediating position in the universe, midway between God and the angelic beings, who are above him, and the animals or beasts, who are below. It is man's privilege and duty to look up and so become increasingly like the one to whom he looks. But if man will not look up, if he determines to act as if "there is no God," then the only way he can look is down, in the direction of the animals, and as a result he will begin to behave like animals. In fact, he will behave even worse than animals. He will multiply sin and invent new ways of doing evil (Rom. 1:28–32). His path will be downhill, and there will be no depths to which he will not go.

I have noticed by reading the newspapers and newsmagazines that as soon as people get disturbed by this obviously downward inclination and begin to search for standards—"community standards" beyond which we will not go—this is precisely where the culture does go. Sinners embrace the vice as soon as it is mentioned, so great is our self-destroying, beastlike, lemminglike run into the sea.

4. *The folly of sin.* This is utter folly, of course, the fourth of Henry's points. It is folly because God exists, whether we acknowledge him or not, and because it is certain that one day we will have to stand before him to give an accounting of every word we have spoken and every deed we have done. If you are a person who has been living as if there is no God, what do you suppose you will say to God on that day? What excuse will you make?

"I didn't know you existed"?

How do you think that will sound to God, who has gone to such lengths to reveal himself to you? He has revealed himself in creation, in Jesus Christ, and in the Bible. Have you taken time to study creation for its revelation of God? To investigate the claims of Jesus Christ? To read the Bible?

"I didn't think you were important"?

How insulting to God! You thought television was important, the latest football or baseball scores were important, your bank account was important. Didn't you think God was important? Can you imagine how stupid that will sound to the exalted, almighty, all-wise God?

"I didn't have time for you"?

You had time for everything else, everything you believed was important. If you have not exerted yourself to know God and to love and serve him with all your heart, mind, soul, and strength, you will be revealed as the greatest of all fools on the day you must give an accounting. And you will know that you were a fool, whether you will acknowledge it openly or not.

5. *The filthiness of sin.* One of the deceptive features of sin is that it masquerades as something beautiful and desirable while actually it is hideous and destructive. The words the psalm uses are *corrupt* and *vile* (v. 1).

When Magic Johnson, the handsome professional basketball personality, revealed that he had AIDS (acquired immune deficiency syndrome) the first, immediate reaction of the sportswriters and pundits was jubilation that at last we had an attractive way to look at the killer disease. One newspaper I read actually spoke of the "smiling face of AIDS," because Magic Johnson is so often seen smiling. Another paper said that we now know that AIDS is not a danger only for some groups of people but that anyone can get it. That is not true, of course. AIDS is not acquired by those who obey the moral law of God, except in a few tragic cases involving the transfusion of contaminated blood. So far as the "smiling face of AIDS" is concerned, anyone can smile at the beginning. It is the end that is horrible, and there are few deaths that are as horrible as those of AIDS sufferers.

The Bible says, "There is a way that seems right to a man, but in the end it leads to death" (Prov. 14:12). The apostle Paul wrote, "The wages of sin is death, but the gift of God is eternal life in Christ Jesus our Lord" (Rom. 6:23).

6. *The fruit of sin.* Sin destroys the one who pursues it, of course. But verse 4 also shows how it impacts others. The verse uses a simple image, describing evildoers as "those who devour my people as men eat bread." In the Middle East, as in the Western world, bread is the most common of food staples. It is eaten regularly and with scarcely a thought. This seems to be how the psalmist regards evildoers as acting when they further their own interests. They devour the weak and poor in order that they might grow strong and rich themselves. What an apt description of our own dog-eat-dog world! We know people who function exactly like that. They don't care what happens to anyone else. Underneath the glamour, that is sin's true nature.

The righteous do care what happens to others. Therefore, they will do the right thing even at great personal cost, and they are generous with what is theirs in order to help others.

7. *The fear and shame that attends sin.* Verse 5 is the new addition and variant in this repeated psalm, and it seems to refer to a historical incident, though we cannot be sure which one. I have already mentioned the scattering of the armies of Sennacherib in the days of Hezekiah as a possibility (2 Kings 18–19), but there are numerous examples of God sending unrea-

soning terror into the hearts of Israel's foes. Joshua 10:10 tells of the confusion of the armies of southern Canaan when the Jewish troops fell on them at Gibeon. Judges 7 recounts the battle of Gideon and his small army of three hundred men against the Midianites, when all they did was surround the Midianite camp by night, expose their lanterns, and blow their trumpets. The Midianites were terrified and turned against one another, killing their own countrymen in the night. In 1 Samuel 14, after Jonathan and his armor-bearer had killed some twenty of the Philistines, "panic struck the whole army" and Saul and his larger army routed them (v. 15).

In these cases panic overtook Israel's enemies when there was no adequate human cause for it. But if that has been so when there was no cause, how much greater the fear will be when sinners are confronted by the enormity of their transgression before the presence of the thrice holy God. Jesus said of sinners that in the day of God's judgment, "They will say to the mountains, 'Fall on us!' and to the hills, 'Cover us!'" so great will be their dread (Luke 23:30). But the hills will answer to God who created them, not those who have been opposed to him, and the wicked will be forced to give an accounting of all they have done.

The Faith of the Saints

The last of Matthew Henry's points maintains the alliteration of words beginning with the letter *f* (the fact, fault, fountain, folly, filthiness, fruit, and fear of sin). But the last point turns from sin to the contrasting portrait of the true people of God found in verse 6. Henry calls this verse "The faith of the saints."

These people live in a world in which fools do indeed act and speak as if "there is no God." It is a world in which sin abounds and in which the perpetrators of evil habitually destroy the righteous as if they were merely eating bread. Yet in the midst of this present evil world, made cruel by sin, the saints look upward and wait for the "salvation" that comes from Zion. In the days of the psalmist that salvation was still future, for properly assessed it was not an earthly deliverance from such threats as the Canaanite, Midianite, Philistine, or Assyrian armies. These were temporary, physical deliverances. The "salvation" to which the righteous looked was God himself, particularly the Savior-God whose coming had been prophesied so many times over in the Old Testament.

That Savior was Jesus. So now, we who live on the after side of his coming look back to him as the one who alone delivers us from sin. We put our faith in him and his work, rather than in our own works, as the basis of our salvation. And we look forward to his second coming too, knowing that in that day sin will be punished, good will be rewarded, and the folly of those who have lived as if there is no God will be revealed.

If you have been living as if there is no God, I urge you to repent of your folly and become wise instead. The person who is wise knows that he or she needs a Savior. When that Savior is revealed, the wise person believes on him and follows him forever.

Psalm 54

Betrayed

Save me, O God, by your name;
vindicate me by your might.
Hear my prayer, O God;
listen to the words of my mouth.

Strangers are attacking me;
ruthless men seek my life—
men without regard for God.   Selah

Surely God is my help;
the Lord is the one who sustains me.

Let evil recoil on those who slander me;
in your faithfulness destroy them.

I will sacrifice a freewill offering to you;
I will praise your name, O LORD,
for it is good.
For he has delivered me from all my troubles,
and my eyes have looked in triumph on my foes.
        verses 1–7

P salm 54 follows nicely upon Psalm 53. The earlier psalm was about people who act as if "there is no God," the moral and spiritual "fools" of this world. In Psalm 54 the psalmist is surrounded by just such people. He speaks of them as "ruthless men . . . men without regard for God" (v. 3). The earlier psalm ends with "the faith of the saints," that is, the faith of believers living in just such a world. Psalm 54 is by one of those saints, David.

451

Psalm 54 is about betrayal, and that links it not only to Psalm 52, which describes David's betrayal by Doeg the Edomite, but also to Psalm 55, which speaks of David's betrayal by a close friend.

Psalms 52 and 54

Psalm 52 and Psalm 54 are also intertwined historically since, according to their titles, they come from the same period in David's life, when David was fleeing from King Saul.

You will recall from study of the earlier psalm that David had fled suddenly on advice from his close friend Jonathan, Saul's son. He had gone to the priestly city of Nob and had been given food and the sword of Goliath, which had been stored there since the day he had killed the great Philistine champion. An evil man named Doeg was present when David arrived, and some time later, when Saul was feeling sorry for himself because it seemed to him that no one would tell him what was going on in regard to David, Doeg revealed that David had gone to Nob and had been helped by the chief priest of Nob, whose name was Ahimelech. Saul turned on Ahimelech, demanding his death, and when the soldiers refused to lift their hands against God's priest, Doeg obliged the king by killing not only Ahimelech but his entire family and all the other priests and families of Nob. In all eighty-five priests were killed, and the inhabitants of Nob were massacred. Only one man, Abiathar, a son of Ahimelech, escaped to tell David what happened.

David confessed to Abiathar, "That day, when Doeg the Edomite was there, I knew he would be sure to tell Saul. I am responsible for the death of your father's whole family" (1 Sam. 22:22). It was one of the darkest moments of David's life.

The immediate background for Psalm 54 picks up at this point. According to 1 Samuel 23, the Philistines were attacking a Jewish border town called Keilah. David asked God if he should attack the Philistines and rescue the citizens of Keilah, and when God gave him leave to do so, he drove the Philistines off and rescued the endangered city. Keilah was a walled city. So when news came to Saul, who was still pursuing David, that David was in Keilah, Saul marched his armies south to capture David in the city since, he said, "David has imprisoned himself by entering a town with gates and bars" (v. 7).

Fortunately, Abiathar, the son of Ahimelech who had escaped to David after the massacre of the priests of Nob, had brought with him the sacred ephod, used to discern the will of God in specific situations. David used it to ask whether the citizens of Keilah, whom he had just rescued, would deliver him over to Saul if Saul surrounded the city and was told that they would indeed surrender him to Saul. So David slipped out of the city before Saul arrived and went further south into the hills of the inhospitable desert area of Ziph.

Even in this remote area David was not safe. When he was in Horesh, one of the towns of this region, the Ziphites went to Saul at Gibeah to tell him where David was hiding. They said, "Is not David hiding among us in the strongholds at Horesh, on the hill of Hakilah, south of Jeshimon? [It was a very specific set of directions.] Now, O king, come down whenever it pleases you to do so, and we will be responsible for handing him over to the king" (1 Sam. 23:19–20). It pleased Saul to do so right away. So he moved against David, pursuing him out of Horesh into the southern wilderness before he was forced to break off to defend the country against the Philistines who were invading further north.

Later, when David and his men were hiding in Hakilah in the same southern region the Ziphites went to Saul again and reported, "Is not David hiding on the hill of Hakilah, which faces Jeshimon?" (1 Sam. 26:1). The title of Psalm 54 refers to these betrayals by the people of Ziph when it says, "A *maskil* of David. When the Ziphites had gone to Saul and said, 'Is not David hiding among us?'"

So this was a bad period for David. It was a time when seemingly he had nowhere to turn. He was unsafe even in the wilderness, and there was hardly anyone he could trust. He had saved one of the cities of his tribesmen in the south, but even these people were against him. Derek Kidner says, "To be betrayed by Doeg the Edomite had been hardly a surprise (1 Sam. 22:22), but now David finds himself rejected by men of his own tribe."[1] He was rejected, pursued, betrayed. But it was out of this dark, dangerous, and disillusioning situation that he called upon God in the words of Psalm 54 and found God to be his sure and steadfast help.

This is a psalm for anyone who feels abandoned, rejected, or betrayed. Have you been abandoned by a husband or wife, or by your children? Have you been publicly denounced by someone you thought was your close ally and friend? Do you feel that no one is on your side, that no one cares for you? You need to do what David did and turn to God. In this psalm we see what that means and how David did it.

The Fugitive's God

One lesson we learn from David is that whenever he had a problem he brought it to God, which is what he does in the opening part of this psalm (vv. 1–3). In other words, he prayed. If Joseph Scriven's popular hymn of 1855 had been known in his day, David would have understood it and identified with it completely:

> Have we trials and temptations?
> Is there trouble anywhere?
> We should never be discouraged:
> Take it to the Lord in prayer!
> Can we find a friend so faithful,

Who will all our sorrows share?
Jesus knows our every weakness:
Take it to the Lord in prayer!

Do thy friends despise, forsake thee?
Take it to the Lord in prayer!
In his arms he'll take and shield thee,
Thou wilt find a solace there.

So David prayed. But equally important is the fact that he prayed to God; that is, he prayed to the true God whom he had come to know by studying Scripture and by personal experience. He reminds us how important this is by saying in the first line of the psalm, "Save me, O God, by your name" (v. 1).

What does David mean when he asks God to save him "by your name"? That idea does not have a great deal of importance for us, because we do not often think of the "name" itself being particularly significant. We think of God but not the name of God. For the Old Testament saints it was different. For them names were important generally. They were understood to sum up the character and personality of the person named. That is why there are so many descriptive or symbolic names in the Old Testament and why we find such significant episodes as God naming one of the Old Testament characters or one of these characters inquiring after the name of God. We remember how Jacob inquired after the name of God when he wrestled with him at the brook Jabbok (Gen. 32:29) and was given a new name himself instead, or how Moses asked God for his name when God called him at the burning bush.

Moses asked, "Suppose I go to the Israelites and say to them, 'The God of your fathers has sent me to you,' and they ask me, 'What is his name?' Then what shall I tell them?" (Exod. 3:13).

God answered, "I AM WHO I AM. This is what you are to say to the Israelites: 'I AM has sent me to you'" (v. 14).

This example is particularly important for understanding Psalm 54. For the name God gave Moses, "I AM" (*Yahweh* or *Jehovah*, usually translated "LORD" in our Bibles), is the name David is appealing to in this psalm.

Notice how he does it, heightening the importance of the name by delaying pronouncing it until verse 6. The psalm begins, "Save me, O God, by your name." But the word for God in the opening verse is not *Jehovah*. It is *Elohim*, the name most often used for God in the second book of the Psalter. Moreover, this is the name that prevails up to and including verse 4. It is in verse 2, "Hear my prayer, O *God*." We have it again in verse 3, ". . . men without regard for *God*." And again in verse 4, "Surely *God* is my help." Verse 4 goes a step further by introducing the title *Adonai* (translated "Lord" in our Bibles). But it is not until verse 6 that the name appealed to in the opening sentence is actually introduced. Verse 6 reads literally: "I will sacrifice a freewill offering to you; I will praise your name, O *Jehovah (Yahweh)*, for it is good."

Scholars are divided on the exact meaning of the name *Jehovah,* but that is only because it is so great and so encompassing that nothing we can say ever seems to do it justice. The name is the root of the Hebrew verb *to be,* which is why it is translated "I AM" in Exodus 3:14. It is in the present tense, of course. So it reveals God as the eternal present, as the one who has always existed and who will always exist, the unchangeable God. Eternal existence also implies self-existence and self-sufficiency. Self-existence means that God has no origins and is therefore answerable to no one. Self-sufficiency means that God depends on no one and therefore has no needs. God helps those who call on him, but he needs no help himself. We often find ourselves in situations that have no conceivable human solution. But our "impossible" circumstances are not impossible to God. Jesus said, "With God all things are possible" (Matt. 19:26).

The Fugitive's Prayer

After the opening cry of verse 1, which sets the theme for the psalm, David begins the prayer in which he asks Jehovah to rescue him in his forsaken situation. His prayer has the following five parts.

1. *He asks God to hear his lament* (v. 2). When Jesus prayed, he said on one occasion, "Father, I [know] that you always hear me" (John 11:42). It is also true that God always hears us in the sense that he knows all things and therefore obviously also hears all things. Nevertheless, it is good to ask God to hear us. For the very act of asking reminds us of who God is and that there are things that, if they do not hinder him from hearing us, at least hinder him from responding when we ask. Sin is one such hindrance. That is why God said through Isaiah,

> Surely the arm of the LORD is not too short to save,
>> nor his ear too dull to hear.
> But your iniquities have separated
>> you from your God;
> your sins have hidden his face from you,
>> so that he will not hear (Isa. 59:1–2).

When we ask God to hear us, as David's example encourages us to do, we are taking time to see if there is any reason why God should not hear us. If there is a reason, we must confess the sin or correct the situation.

2. *He describes the situation he faces* (v. 3). Some people are reluctant to say if something is bothering them or admit they have a problem, probably because they want to save face or keep up appearances. Christians are often among their number, even when they are talking to God. David was not like this, and one of the most refreshing aspects of the psalms written by David is that he is not the least hesitant to say what he thinks and describe a situation as he sees it. In this verse he says that he is being attacked by ruthless

men. These men have no regard for God, and they want to kill David. That was literally true, of course. Saul was seeking his life. Those who were loyal to Saul were part of Saul's evil design, and David never knew when someone who seemed to be his friend might betray his whereabouts in hopes of securing the present king's favor.

If you are facing some hard problem, I encourage you to tell God about it in detail. God knows it already, of course. But it will do you good to spell it out, and mentioning details will remind you that God also knows and cares about them. You will also be remembering that he cares for you.

3. *He encourages himself by remembering who God is* (v. 4). David does not merely wallow in his problems. There is a danger of doing that when we lay our troubles before God, but David does not fall into that trap. As soon as he has described his situation (v. 3), he breaks off completely and spends time reminding himself of who God truly is. "Surely God is my help," he says. "The Lord is the one who sustains me."

In 1 Peter 5:7, the apostle who had learned to trust Jesus rather than himself in all situations says, "Cast all your anxiety on him because he cares for you." (The very next psalm is the place Peter got that text, cf. Ps. 55:22.) In Psalm 54, David has "cast his anxiety on God." That is what verses 1–3 have been about. Now, having done it, he is ready to encourage himself by remembering that God is indeed his help and that he has been sustaining him and will continue to sustain him in his difficulties. It is what Isaac Watts captures in his poetic rendering of Psalm 90:

> Our God, our Help in ages past,
> Our Hope for years to come;
> Be thou our Guard while troubles last,
> And our eternal Home.

4. *He makes his request* (v. 5). Finally, David makes the specific request that God might destroy those who are attacking him. In the case of Doeg, pictured in Psalm 52, he has already prophesied what his end would be. It was to be pulled down, snatched up, twisted out, and torn from Israel, even from the land of the living (v. 5). David is not so graphic in Psalm 54, but he does pray that evil might "recoil on those who slander" him and that God might be faithful to him by destroying them.

This prayer has bothered a number of commentators, who say that this is somehow unworthy of a man of God and that we have been taught better in the New Testament. For example, A. Weiser complains about "human self-will and man's low instincts of vindictiveness and gloating," suggesting that the proper response is to pray for one's enemies.[2] It is true, of course, that we have been taught to pray for our enemies. But that does not mean that we are to cease to care for righteousness or pray that justice should be done by God. It is worth noting that judgment did eventually come to David's enemies. David was right to pray for it.

But, it is equally important to remember that when David had the opportunity he did not take justice against Saul into his own hands. The text that provides the background for Psalms 52 and 54 tells how David received what seemed to be "God-given" opportunities to kill Saul but records how he spared Saul's life on at least two occasions (cf. 1 Sam. 24, 26).

5. *He promises God a freewill offering* (vv. 6–7). This is not a case of offering a bribe to God—"I will bring you an offering if you deliver me from my enemies." This is a thank offering, promised to God in advance of his deliverance on the grounds of his firm confidence that God would indeed deliver him. How does he know God will do it? It is because of who God is ("God is my help"), and because God has delivered him in the past. David may not have begun this psalm with confidence. But having brought his anxieties to God and having reminded himself of who God is, he finds, as he did in so many other psalms, that he is restored to a quiet trust and confidence in God by the end of it.

Charles Haddon Spurgeon wrote, "Let us trust that if we are as friendless as this man of God, we may resort to prayer as he did, exercise the like faith, and find ourselves ere long singing the same joyous hymn of praise."[3]

Man of Sorrows

Here is one last thought. I have said several times in these studies that we must be careful not to turn all the psalms into prophecies of the coming of Jesus Christ or of events of his or the very last days. Augustine sees almost everything in them as a prophecy of Christ, and Arno Gaebelein sees nearly everything as a prophecy of the experience of Israel just before the Lord's second coming. These narrow perspectives greatly limit the value of their commentaries. Most of the psalms are not prophecy at all. But a few are. They are the messianic psalms. And there are other psalms that, although they are not about Jesus Christ specifically, nevertheless aptly describe what we know were his experiences from the account we have of them in the New Testament.

Psalm 54 may be in this latter category. This is because if you study it with the passion of Christ in mind, you will find that it is an excellent expression of the hope of him who called on God in the midst of his suffering on the cross and was heard by him. For example,

> Save me, O God, by your name; . . .
> Strangers are attacking me; . . .
> Surely God is my help; . . .
> He has delivered me from all my troubles.

The Father did hear, did help, and did save Jesus, even as he heard, helped, and saved David. You can be sure that Jesus will also hear, help, and save you.

Psalm 55

Betrayed by a Close Friend

If an enemy were insulting me,
 I could endure it;
if a foe were raising himself against me,
 I could hide from him.
But it is you, a man like myself,
 my companion, my close friend,
with whom I once enjoyed sweet fellowship
 as we walked with the throng at the house of God. . . .

Cast your cares on the LORD
 and he will sustain you;
 he will never let the righteous fall.
But you, O God, will bring down the wicked
 into the pit of corruption;
bloodthirsty and deceitful men
 will not live out half their days.

But as for me, I trust in you.

verses 12–14, 22–23

P salms sometimes have meaningful relationships with one another, and that is the case with Psalms 52, 54, and 55. According to their titles, each is by David and each involves David's betrayal by some person or group. In Psalm 52 David's presence in Nob had been disclosed to Saul by Doeg the Edomite. It concerns David's betrayal by a foreigner. In Psalm 54 David has been betrayed by the people of Ziph—that is, by his own countrymen. This short series of betrayal

458

psalms reaches a climax in Psalm 55 with its description of David's betrayal by an intimate friend.

Who was this friend? The best guess is Ahithophel, David's most trusted counselor, who sided with Absalom at the time of Absalom's rebellion. But this is a "best guess" only because we have no other story from David's life to link it to. Ahithophel's story is told in 2 Samuel 15–17. It tells us that he was close to David and that he betrayed him in order to side with Absalom, later hanging himself when Absalom rejected his advice in favor of another counselor. But there are problems with this view. The writer of Psalm 55 is presumably in Jerusalem. But in the account of Absalom's rebellion given in 2 Samuel, David learned of Ahithophel's defection only after he had left the city. Again, although David valued the advice of Ahithophel and trusted him, it would be hard to say that he was as close to David as Psalm 55 describes the betrayer having been: "my companion, my close friend, with whom I once enjoyed sweet fellowship" (vv. 13–14).

These difficulties have caused some commentators to ascribe the psalm to another writer entirely, to Jeremiah or to someone writing in a later, declining period of the monarchy. But the title says the psalm is by David, and we should probably assume that it is merely about an incident that is not recounted in the historical books. At best those books give a summary of what was obviously a long and very complex career.

Many commentators offer a three-part outline for this psalm, the most striking form being by G. Campbell Morgan: (1) fear (vv. 1–8), (2) fury (vv. 9–15), and (3) faith (vv. 16–23).[1]

Marvin E. Tate, one of the more modern commentators, finds ten parts.[2]

In my judgment, the best way of getting into the psalm is to focus on its alternating pattern of six or seven parts. We have seen something like this before, in Psalms 5, 18, and 42–43, for example. In the case of Psalm 55, the stanzas alternate between disclosures of the psalmist's own state of mind and his descriptions of the wicked who are causing him problems. As is usual with such psalms, the descriptions of the psalmist's state show improvement as David moves from anguish of mind and pain to quiet confidence in God. I outline the psalm like this: (1) the first disclosure of the psalmist's anguish (vv. 1–8); (2) the first description of the wicked (vv. 9–11); (3) the second disclosure of the psalmist's anguish (vv. 12–14); (4) the second description of the wicked (v. 15); (5) the psalmist's faith in God (vv. 16–19); (6) the third description of the wicked (vv. 20–21); and (7) the psalmist's final conclusion and advice (vv. 22–23).[3] The psalm is a combination of the lament, prayer, and wisdom genres.

The Psalmist's Personal Anguish

There is a significant difference between the setting of the two earlier psalms of betrayal and this one. In Psalms 52 and 54 David is in the wilderness fleeing from his enemy, Saul, a low point in his career, while in Psalm 55 he is apparently established in Jerusalem, his capital city. This must mean that Saul is dead and that David is now king. We would expect this situation to be good. David's troubles should be over. But we find that this is not the case and that David is as much troubled in his ascendancy as he was when a fugitive.

In fact, the pain of these verses (vv. 1–8) may even be greater, for this is strong language. David begins by saying that he is "distraught" (v. 2) and in "anguish" (v. 4), and the words increase in intensity after this. The "terrors of death" assail him (v. 4). "Fear and trembling" beset him. "Horror" overwhelms him (v. 5).

In verses 6–8 we find something new. The writer is so distraught by what he finds around him that he is thinking of how wonderful it would be to escape from his troubles. We have not seen anything like this before in David's psalms. He has been fearful before. But always he has seemed ready to confront the evil boldly. Nowhere before has he expressed a wish to escape his trouble, to fly away and be at rest. Yet here he does.

> I said, "Oh, that I had the wings of a dove!
>   I would fly away and be at rest—
> I would flee far away
>   and stay in the desert;
> I would hurry to my place of shelter,
>   far from the tempest and storm."

What is happening? Why do we find this new element? We have here the weariness that comes to a valiant warrior or worker late in life or at least after the passing of youthful battles and triumphs. When we are young we do not expect life to be easy, and if we are energetic we tackle problems with optimism and with our full strength. We achieve certain victories too. But as life goes on we find that the problems we thought we had overcome earlier are still around. The company we work for is still in trouble. Our taxes are still high. The murder and felony rates have not declined. Our children continue to cause trouble. In addition, we are getting older and therefore have less energy to cope with problems. We find ourselves thinking how nice it would be merely to fly away and escape them.

Many do, of course, at least if they have sufficient money to retire and even travel in retirement. It is desires like theirs that enable the tourist industry to flourish. But it is not always possible to escape our problems—David did not have "the wings of a dove"—and God does not always give us leave to leave either, especially if the problems we face involve continuing responsibilities on our part.

At this point the psalm becomes a lesson to us in steady perseverance, particularly perseverance in middle or late age. Perseverance is one of the virtues God looks for in his children.

Bad Times in the City

Having unburdened himself of his troubled inner feelings, the psalmist now turns to the wicked who are wreaking havoc in the city. His description of this evil is in words people who live in cities in our day can readily understand (vv. 9–11).

We might have thought from David's reference to "the enemy" in verse 2 that he was concerned about the hostile nations that surrounded the Jewish kingdom. But now we discover that the enemy is not without but within. The psalmist is saying, as Pogo said in one of the best-known Pogo cartoons, "We have met the enemy, and he is us." These verses personify six vices in three pairs of two each. Violence and Strife prowl about on its walls. Malice and Abuse are within the city. Threats and Lies never leave the streets. It is a grim picture, because we know that these are not just forces in themselves. They are present because wicked people are present, and these wicked people are within the gates. They are ourselves.

That is what is wrong with the cities of America, of course. We want to blame our problems on the environment or government programs or the lack of government programs. But the problem is not "out there." It is within. The problem is that we are sinners, and this means that there will never be a substantial improvement in the moral state of our cities (or the country as a whole for that matter) until there is a deep moral improvement in America's people. And that happens in only one way—by revival, by a people rediscovering God. There is nothing America needs so much right now as a Holy Spirit produced revival and reformation.

But until that comes we can at least pray that evil will be frustrated and the doers of evil confused. This is what David prays for in verse 9, asking God to "confuse the wicked" and "confound their speech," using words deliberately reminiscent of the confusion God brought upon the builders of the tower of Babel (cf. Gen. 11:1–9). God does it too. Thank God, he does. We would be many times worse off if evil people could actually get their acts together and work in harmony against the righteous instead of fighting among themselves, as they habitually do.

The Psalmist's Pain

It is possible to see verses 12–14 as an extension of the psalmist's description of the evil in Jerusalem. But it is better to see it as a return to the revelation of his own anguish and pain. In fact, like a trained psychologist probing deeply for the root of his pain, David explores his own heart and reveals that what is bothering him most is that his own close friend has betrayed him. The friend's betrayal is part of the general evil, of course. If these verses refer to Absalom's rebellion, the rebellion might even have greatly contributed to the pain David feels. But more than this, the betrayal is the root of David's personal pain and his understandable desire to run away from what is hurting him and be at rest.

How well he knows himself and how perceptively he describes this painful situation.

> If an enemy were insulting me,
> I could endure it;
> if a foe were raising himself against me,
> I could hide from him (v. 12).

David had endured insults from enemies. When he was fleeing Jerusalem and Shimei (a noted enemy) cursed him from the hillside, crying, "Get out, get out, you man of blood, you scoundrel! The LORD has repaid you for all the blood you shed in the household of Saul, in whose place you have reigned," the king did not allow his men to retaliate by killing Shimei. He said, "My son, who is of my own flesh, is trying to take my life. How much more then, this Benjamite! . . . It may be that the LORD will see my distress and repay me with good for the cursing I am receiving today" (2 Sam. 16:5–14).

David bore Shimei's cursing well. But this was not Shimei, an enemy. This was his companion, his close friend, one with whom he had enjoyed sweet fellowship, a person in whose presence he had worshiped at the house of God. It does not require a special revelation to observe that it is those who are closest to us who hurt us most. Spurgeon said, "None are such real enemies as false friends."[4]

Destruction for the Wicked

Verse 15 seems to stand alone. It is the low point of the psalm and is a prayer or wish in which David longs for the destruction of his foes. The language is important because, just as verse 9 uses words that deliberately recall the confusion of speech at the building of the tower of Babel, so here the throwback is to the destruction of Korah and his followers in the days of Moses. On that occasion "the ground under them split apart and the earth opened its mouth and swallowed them, with their households and all Korah's men and all their possessions. They went down alive into the grave, with everything they owned; the earth closed over them, and they perished and were gone from the community" (Num. 16:31–33). David is referring to this unprecedented destruction in the language of verse 15.

But why such vehemence? J. J. Stewart Perowne explains it by his friend's betrayal: "To have trusted, and to find his trust betrayed; to have been one with a man in public and in private, bound to him by personal ties, and by the ties of religion, and then to find honor, faith, affection, all cast to the winds—this it was that seemed so terrible, this it was that called for the withering curse."[5]

That may be, of course. But it seems significant that David does not specifically mention his former friend in this malediction. In fact, he seems to have distinguished between his enemies, who are cursed here, and his former friend in the previous section, who is not cursed.

A Turning Point in the Psalm

What is important is that a turning point comes with verse 16. Earlier the writer had called on God. The psalm began, "Listen to my prayer, O God, do not ignore my plea; hear me and answer me" (vv. 1–2). But that was uttered out of the writer's anguish. Here the tone is different. In these words the psalmist explains that when he calls on God, as he has just done, the Lord actually hears him and saves him. He explains his experiences of God's grace in three moving phrases: "the LORD saves me" (v. 16), "he hears my voice" (v. 17), and "he ransoms me unharmed" (v. 18). Because of this past experience of God's grace, which he has remembered, the psalmist knows that God will destroy the enemies that still confront him and will deliver him from them (v. 19).

This is faith, of course. It is the point we come to when problems are honestly faced and brought to God—and brought to him again and again. For that is the point of the alternating structure of the psalm. There are psalms that are a short, fierce statement of concern, thrown up to God in quick desperation. But this is not one of them. This is a prayer in which the psalmist unburdens himself of his anguish, describes the terrors he is facing, reflects on the evil of his foes, asks God for help, and then persists in laying the same things before God again and again, stanza after stanza. This psalm is a lesson in perseverance.

It is also an illustration of how such persevering prayer first changes us, strengthening our faith, before God intervenes in response to change our desperate situation.

A Final Glance at the Wicked

The alternating structure of the psalm continues in verses 20–21, where David casts a final glance at the friend who has betrayed him. But the tone has changed now. Earlier David was deeply pained by the betrayal. Here, having laid the matter before God and having assured himself that God is his Savior and that he will surely deliver him from such evil, David steps away from his own feelings and reflects on the wrongdoing itself. The real problem is that the man is a covenant breaker, and the reason he breaks covenant is that he is a hypocrite. He pretends one thing but plots another. He speaks peace, but actually he is devising war. It is advancing a step to see the evil for what it is dispassionately.

Conclusion and Practical Advice

But enough about evil. There will always be traitors and hypocrites and covenant breakers in this fallen world. Righteousness we may hope for and sometimes discover; sin we can count on. Sin is everywhere and in all people. The question is, What are the righteous to do in such deplorable times and conditions? Significantly, the psalm ends by answering this question. It tells us:

> Cast your cares on the LORD
>   and he will sustain you;
>   he will never let the righteous fall (v. 22).

This statement is the verse picked up by the apostle Peter and commended to us in the fifth chapter of his first epistle: "Cast all your anxiety on him because he cares for you" (1 Peter 5:7). Early in his life Peter had been a very anxious person. In the final days of Jesus' earthly life Peter had been greatly worried about what might happen to Jesus, and then, when Jesus was arrested, he was even more worried about what might happen to himself. Peter was a great worrier, and not without cause. But as he grew older he learned not to worry but rather to do what he then also commended to others, to cast his cares on God.

Why should we do that? Isn't this just another form of escapism, the kind of thing David was wanting to do early in Psalm 55? No. In fact, it is the exact opposite. It is learning to cast our cares on God that enables us not to run away but to stand tall and carry on with the task God has assigned us. Casting our cares on God enables us to be steadfast. The last verses give three reasons why we should cast our cares on God.

First, "he will sustain you." When we are down it is natural to think that we will never be able to bear up under the troubles that are pressing in from every side. We are sure we will be beaten down. But that is not the case. The Bible says, "No temptation has seized you except what is common to man. And God is faithful; he will not let you be tempted beyond what you can bear. But when you are tempted, he will also provide a way out so that you can stand up under it" (1 Cor. 10:13).

Second, "he will never let the righteous fall." Peter was sure he was going to fall when he was trying to walk toward Jesus over the water of the Sea of Galilee. He looked at the waves and began to sink. "Lord, save me!" he cried (Matt. 14:30). This is exactly what David has been praying in this psalm. He wants to be saved. And the Lord did it. He saved David, just as he saved Peter and all who cast their cares upon him. David is not exaggerating when he says, "the LORD . . . will never let the righteous fall."

Third, "God . . . will bring down the wicked." Evil persons may succeed for a time, but it is the promise of God as well as the judgment of history that they soon perish and are destroyed, just as they had sought so hard to destroy other people.

The bottom line is the psalm's last sentence: "But as for me, I trust in you"—that is, in God. That is David's final testimony. Is it yours? If you are focusing on the evil around you, you may not be able to say, "But as for me, I trust in you." But you will be able to say it, if you have really cast your cares on God.

Psalm 56

"What Can Man Do to Me?"

Be merciful to me, O God, for men hotly pursue me;
all day long they press their attack.
My slanderers pursue me all day long;
many are attacking me in their pride. . . .

In God, whose word I praise,
in the LORD, whose word I praise—
in God I trust; I will not be afraid.
What can man do to me?

I am under vows to you, O God;
I will present my thank offerings to you.
For you have delivered my soul from death
and my feet from stumbling,
that I may walk before God
in the light of life.

verses 1–2, 10–13

What can man do to me?

We know the answer to that, and we do not have to think about it very much: A lot! And to prove it, all we have to do is read the morning's newspaper. The week I wrote this sermon, on just one day, I read these stories: (1) an account of an attack on Serbian, Bulgarian, Romanian, and Vietnamese refugees in Germany by neo-Nazis, while German police looked on. To their credit the refugees fought back and injured ten of their attackers. (2) A United Nations vote to look into reports of war crimes by the Serbian government against Moslems in Bosnia. The Serbs were murdering thousands of Moslems in an offensive they call "ethnic cleansing." (3) The trial of a man who sold an unsuspecting family a home with a defective gas heater, knowing it was dangerous. It emitted carbon monoxide, and the night it was first turned on three in the family, including an infant, were killed. (4) The murder of a manager of a fast food restaurant and the wounding of a coworker by two young punks who wanted to rob them. (5) The sentencing of two men for insurance fraud. (6) An abduction. (7) Several cases of sexual abuse.

Sometimes I count the number of murders on a weekend in Philadelphia. Often there are up to half a dozen. But these are only the tip of the iceberg of evil in one city, a small, partial proof of what the nineteenth-century poet William Wordsworth aptly called "man's inhumanity to man."

What can man do to me?

Man can oppress, slander, hurt, hate, maim, and murder me, for starters. But, of course, that is not the answer David is giving us in Psalm 56. His answer is: Nothing! Not if God is for me and stands against the opposition.

Into Death's Jaws

I suppose the immediate reaction to a statement like that is along these lines: "Well, that was easy for David to say. He was a king. He commanded an army. He lived in a fortified city. None of us are so lucky." I want to stress that this was not the situation David was in when he wrote this psalm. The title sets us straight on that. It tells us that the psalm was written about the time "when the Philistines had seized him in Gath."

Here is the story. When we were studying Psalm 52 we saw that early in his life David had been forced to escape from King Saul because he was trying to kill him. David went to Nob, one of the towns of the priests, where Ahimelech, the head priest, assisted him by giving him food and a weapon. Unfortunately, Doeg the Edomite was present when David arrived in Nob, and Doeg later reported this to Saul, which led to the king's demand that Ahimelech be killed. Doeg obliged Saul by killing Ahimelech. In fact, Doeg killed all the priests of Nob, eighty-five in all, together with their entire families.

In our study of Psalm 52, I pointed out that there was a lapse of time between David's visit to Nob and the report of his visit to Saul by Doeg. In fact, 1 Samuel 21–22 tells of two incidents that filled this interval. The first is David's flight to the fortified Philistine city of Gath, where he thought he would be safe from Saul. The second story tells that when he found he was not safe in Gath, David escaped into the wilderness, to the cave at Adullam, where his brothers and other discontented people began to gather around him. At the end of this period David had collected about four hundred valiant men who eventually became the core of his army.

Psalm 56 was written about David's time in Gath—that is, between the time of his passing through Nob and his arrival at Adullam. Three things are worth noting.

1. *David was alone.* He had fled from Saul without any soldiers, in fact, even without food or weapons. We think of him having at least four hundred valiant men with him when he was in the wilderness. We think of him

having hearty companionship and at least some protection. But according to 1 Samuel 22, the gathering of his army occurred after the time in Gath. So David was entirely alone at this time. There was no one with him.

2. *David was desperate.* Gath had been the home of the giant Goliath, whom David had killed just a few years before. Goliath was a Philistine hero, and he had certainly been the pride of Gath. What except desperation would cause anyone to walk alone into the hometown of the hero he had killed?

And there is this, too. When David was at Nob only days before he had asked Ahimelech if he had any weapons, and Ahimelech had given him the only weapon he had, the sword of Goliath. The sword is not described in the account of David's fight with Goliath in 1 Samuel 17, but the account does say that Goliath was over nine feet tall and that his body armor and bronze javelin were unusually large and heavy. His sword must have been large too, and it was certainly remembered by the people of Gath and was easily recognized by them. There are only two ways any sane man would walk into Gath under those conditions: either in arrogant pride or in desperation. Since we know from the psalm that David was afraid rather than arrogant, he must have gone to Gath in near despair.

Derek Kidner begins his study by noting this: "To have fled from Saul to Gath of all places, the home town of Goliath, took the courage of despair; it measured David's estimate of his standing with his people." David's attempt to find safety in Gath was not successful, of course. So Kidner adds, "This has failed, and [David] is [now] doubly encircled."[1]

3. *David was afraid.* We are told this explicitly in 1 Samuel. When David arrived in Gath his presence was reported to the king of Gath, a man called Achish. The people told Achish,

Isn't this David, the king of the land? Isn't he the one they sing about in their dances:

"Saul has slain his thousands,
    and David his tens of thousands"? (1 Sam. 21:11).

Those "tens of thousands" were Philistines, and some of the former people of Gath as well as their hero Goliath were among them. Therefore, the next sentence is not a surprise: "David took these words to heart and was very much afraid of Achish king of Gath" (v. 12). Since David had no one to defend him he resorted to cunning, pretending to be out of his mind so Achish would despise him rather than kill him, and so he eventually escaped.

With this in mind we now read the central verses of the psalm.

When I am afraid,
    I will trust in you.
In God, whose word I praise,
    in God I trust; I will not be afraid.
    What can mortal man do to me? (vv. 3–4)

Do you ever feel afraid? Desperate? Alone? If so, you will find this psalm to be encouraging, for it is not merely about loneliness and fear. It is about faith that gives victory over those very real states and terrible emotions. I notice with approval that J. J. Stewart Perowne described the psalm as being about "the victory rather than the struggle of faith."[2]

But first, one more word about the title. It contains the notation: "To the tune of 'A Dove on Distant Oaks.'" We know nothing about these tunes, but the reference to a dove makes us think back to Psalm 55, in which David cried, "Oh, that I had the wings of a dove! I would fly away and be at rest" (v. 6). When we studied Psalm 55 we saw that David did not have the wings of a dove. But here we learn that he had something better. He had God who made the dove, and he found the peace he was seeking by trusting him.

Psalm 56 seems to have been popular with the other biblical writers, since it is quoted elsewhere. Verses 4 and 11 are picked up in Psalm 118:6 and quoted by the author of Hebrews in 13:6. Verse 9 is referred to by Paul in Romans 8:31. The first part of verse 13 is quoted in Psalm 116:6 with only slight alteration, and the last phrase, "the light of life," reappears in the third of Jesus' "I am" sayings in John's Gospel: "I am the light of the world. Whoever follows me will never walk in darkness, but will have the light of life" (John 8:12).

The Outline

At this point in the Psalter we come upon a number of psalms that have a repeating chorus. For example, the chorus of Psalm 57 is "Be exalted, O God, above the heavens; let your glory be over all the earth" (vv. 5, 11). Psalm 59 has the chorus "O my Strength, I watch for you; you, O God, are my fortress, my loving God" (vv. 9, 17).

The same thing occurs in Psalm 56 and is the key to outlining it. In Psalm 56 the refrain is what I earlier called the central verses of the psalm. It is found first in verse 4 and then a second time, slightly expanded, in verses 10–11. The psalm follows this pattern. First, there is a brief description of the trouble in which David finds himself (vv. 1–2). Second, there is a strong statement of faith, including the words of the chorus (vv. 3–4). Third, there is a further elaboration of the problem (vv. 5–9), followed, fourth, by a slightly expanded version of the chorus (vv. 10–11). Fifth and last, David promises to present a thanksgiving offering to God when he is saved by him (vv. 12–13).

The Voice of Fear

I mentioned Perowne's opinion that Psalm 56 is about "the victory rather than the struggle of faith." That does not mean that fear is missing from the psalm. On the contrary, the fear described in 1 Samuel 21:12 is evident in the opening verses (vv. 1–2) and also in David's second, longer elaboration of the danger (vv. 5–9). There are two emphases.

1. *The fury of the attack.* Sometimes language can be used to capture the feeling of a moment, and that is the case in verses 1–2, where David conveys the relentless fury of his enemies' pursuit by striking word repetitions. There are three of them. "Pursue," "attack," and "all day long" are each repeated in verse 2 after being introduced first in verse 1. We have: "men hotly *pursue* me" and "my slanderers *pursue* me," *"all day long"* and *"all day long,"* and finally "they press their *attack*" and "many are *attacking* me." It is a striking way of saying, "I am overwhelmed, simply overwhelmed; because no matter what direction I turn they are always after me, after me, pursuing me, always pursuing me."

2. *The nature of the attack.* The second, later description of the problem (vv. 5–9) is not so furious. Rather, it is a calmer description of the nature of the attacks being made. We might think from the setting that all David would be concerned about was his immediate physical danger. But even in verse 2 he spoke not merely of military attacks but of "slanderers," and now he explains that it is the slander that bothers him even more than the danger. They want to kill him, of course. But to justify their doing it (or perhaps to win the necessary numbers to their side) his enemies twist his words to make it seem that he is speaking against King Saul.

> All day long they twist my words;
>   they are always plotting to harm me.
> They conspire, they lurk,
>   they watch my steps,
>   eager to take my life (vv. 5–6).

This section ends with a prayer that God will judge these enemies (v. 7) and with a request that God will remember his sorrows, making a list of them (v. 8). David knows that God knows what he is going through and that he will remember it. In fact, he presents the tender concerns of God for himself and his people in an image that has been of immense comfort to generations of sorrowing believers. We know it best in the words of the King James Bible: "Put thou my tears in thy bottle." But the idea is much the same in the New International Version: "list my tears on your scroll" or "put my tears in your wineskin" (footnote). The meaning is that God will never forget nor ever be indifferent to the cares of any one of his much-beloved people.

The Voice of Faith

I have already pointed out that the chorus, which occurs in verses 4, 10, and 11, is the very heart of the psalm. We have been invited to observe David's fear, but now in even clearer tones we hear the voice of faith.

> In God, whose word I praise,
>> in God I trust; I will not be afraid.
>> What can mortal man do to me? (v. 4).

And again, slightly expanded,

> In God, whose word I praise,
>> in the LORD, whose word I praise—
> in God I trust; I will not be afraid.
>> What can man do to me? (vv. 10–11).

1. *Confidence in God.* In these verses there are two parts to David's confidence, and the first is that he is confident in God. He trusts God, whom he calls *Elohim* four times (two times in verse 4, once each in verses 10–11) and Jehovah once (in verse 10). Not man! Not circumstances! Not his own cunning, as useful as that seemed to have been at Gath! He trusts God: "In God I trust." It is because of this that he could ask, "What can man do to me?" and expect the answer, "Nothing."

So let me ask, Do you trust God? If you are a Christian, you have trusted him in the matter of your salvation. That is the greatest thing. God has saved you from sin, hell, and the devil. If you are a Christian, you believe he has done that. But if he has done that, can you not also trust him in lesser things like loneliness or even those sometimes dangerous circumstances that cause fear and desperation? The Bible teaches that God will take care of you if you belong to him and are following after Jesus Christ. David wrote in an earlier psalm, "I was young and now I am old, yet I have never seen the righteous forsaken or their children begging bread" (Ps. 37:25). The psalm immediately before this one urged, "Cast your cares on the LORD and he will sustain you" (Ps. 55:22). The apostle Paul wrote to the Philippians, "My God will meet all your needs according to his glorious riches in Christ Jesus" (Phil. 4:19).

2. *Confidence in the Word of God.* There is another aspect to David's confidence in God—it is also based upon the Word of God. In this repeated chorus the phrase "whose word I praise" occurs three times. This is very important, because apart from the Word of God we do not know what God is like, and we certainly do not know what he has promised to do for us. What is this "word of God" to which David refers? Clearly it is the entire self-revelation of God in Scripture given up to that time—the Pentateuch (the first five books) and possibly Joshua and Judges. That is only a portion of our Bible, but it was enough to make God's character and desires for his people known. In the chorus of Psalm 56 David therefore praises God for his Word, recognizing it as one of the greatest of all God's good gifts to men and women.

It may also be the case, however, that David is thinking specifically of the words of God that were brought to him by the prophet Samuel, assuring him that he would be king over Israel (cf. 1 Sam. 16:1–13). That must have seemed a long way off when David was in Gath or hiding in the cave of Adullam. But no matter! It was the word of God, and though the fulfillment of that word might be long delayed, it was nevertheless absolutely certain. Therefore, it was not only in God but also in the specific words of God that David trusted.

You and I do not have individualized revelations from God delivered to us today by God's prophets. We have the Bible. But the Bible we have is more extensive than David's. It contains all we need to know about spiritual things. Equally important, we have the Holy Spirit to give us understanding of what has been written as well as the ability to apply it to specific areas of our lives.

New Life in Christ

The last two verses of Psalm 56 are like the ending of Psalm 54, in which David vows to present a thanksgiving offering to God when he is delivered, so certain is he that God will deliver him in time.

> I am under vows to you, O God;
> I will present my thank offerings to you.
> For you have delivered me from death
> and my feet from stumbling,
> that I may walk before God
> in the light of life (vv. 12–13).

This is a great vow of confidence, like the confidence of Psalm 34, which is also based on the incident at Gath. David got this confidence by praying, and so can we. Confidence comes to the person who prays and trusts God.

But I want you to see one thing more before I end this study. The fact that Jesus seems to have used the last words of verse 13 in John 8:12 makes us think of verse 13 in light of the deliverance Jesus brings to those who trust him and the "life" as his gift of salvation by the Holy Spirit. That is the ultimate fulfillment of the psalm, of course. As Alexander Maclaren says, "The really living are they who live in Jesus, and the real light of the living is the sunshine that streams on those who thus live, because they live in him."[3] So I end this way. If you really want to move out of your fear, despair, and loneliness and bask in God's sunshine, live looking upward always into the face of Jesus Christ. Then will you find yourself saying firmly, "In God I trust; I will not be afraid. What can man do to me?"

Psalm 57

Hiding in Thee

Have mercy on me, O God, have mercy on me,
for in you my soul takes refuge.
I will take refuge in the shadow of your wings
until the disaster has passed.

I cry out to God Most High,
to God, who fulfills his purpose for me.
He sends from heaven and saves me,
rebuking those who hotly pursue me;
God sends his love and his faithfulness.

I am in the midst of lions;
I lie among ravenous beasts—
men whose teeth are spears and arrows,
whose tongues are sharp swords.

Be exalted, O God, above the heavens;
let your glory be over all the earth.

They spread a net for my feet—
I was bowed down in distress.
They dug a pit in my path—
but they have fallen into it themselves.

My heart is steadfast, O God,
my heart is steadfast;
I will sing and make music.
Awake, my soul!

Awake, harp and lyre!
I will awaken the dawn.

I will praise you, O Lord, among the nations;
I will sing of you among the peoples.
For great is your love, reaching to the heavens;
your faithfulness reaches to the skies.

Be exalted, O God, above the heavens;
let your glory be over all the earth.
verses 1–11

For several chapters we have been look-
ing at psalms that are linked to that early desperate period of David's life
when he was forced to flee into the wilderness from King Saul who wanted
to kill him. Psalm 52 began this set of psalms. It refers to Doeg the
Edomite, who told Saul that David had gone to Nob and had been helped
by Ahimelech the priest. Because of Doeg's self-serving betrayal, Ahimelech and eighty-four of the priestly families were killed. Psalm 54 is
another such psalm. It tells of David's betrayal by the Ziphites, who were
his countrymen and who should have protected him. Worst of all, Psalm
56 describes David's desperate plight in the Philistine town of Gath, which
he went to alone, desperate, and afraid.

After David left Gath he faded into the wilderness and hid in a large cave
known as Adullam, to which the title of Psalm 57 probably refers.[1] David
was also alone there, at least at the beginning. But this place was a turning
point in his fortunes. First Samuel 22 tells us that it was while he was at
Adullam that his brothers and his father's household and all who were in
distress or debt or discontented began to gather around him. In all, about
four hundred men came to him, and he became their leader. Although
there is nothing in Psalm 57 to indicate that this had begun to happen by
the time the psalm was written, there is nevertheless a very noticeable
change in the tone of the composition. The earlier psalms were mostly
uncertain, fearful, even desperate. Psalm 57 is settled, and its prevailing
note is praise.

What makes the difference? In the earlier psalms David was hiding *from
his enemies,* in Gath or in the wilderness of the Ziphites. Here he is hiding *in
God,* which is what the cave comes to symbolize. David sings a great song in
Psalm 57. But if he had not composed Psalm 57 and if he had only our
hymn "Hiding in Thee" instead, he might have sung,

O safe to the rock that is higher than I,
My soul in its conflicts and sorrows would fly;

> So sinful, so weary, thine, thine would I be;
> Thou blest Rock of Ages, I'm hiding in thee.

"Hiding in thee" is what Psalm 57 is about.

The Psalm and Its Outline

How should the psalm be outlined? The psalm's eleven verses could be divided into three parts: (1) a call to God for mercy (vv. 1–3); (2) a description of the problem that caused David to ask for mercy (vv. 4–6); and (3) concluding praise of God (vv. 7–11). But in view of the refrain that is repeated in verses 5 and 11, it is best to take the psalm in two main parts, each ending with the refrain. This is the outline suggested by J. J. Stewart Perowne and H. C. Leupold, who says rightly, "The first section, vv. 1–5, is a confident cry for deliverance from cruel enemies; the second section, vv. 6–11, is a resolve to praise God for deliverance."[2]

Verses 7–11 appear again as the opening verses of Psalm 108 (the second half of Psalm 108 is likewise borrowed from Psalm 60:5–12), and a number of phrases echo words, verses, and images found in other places.[3]

Part One: Safe in God's Shadow

The first of the psalm's two parts begins with David asking for mercy even as he takes refuge in God. Since the title of the psalm speaks of the cave in which David was hiding, it is natural to think that the cave suggested the idea of a "refuge." But we should notice that David does not call the cave his refuge, though it was a refuge in a certain physical sense. Rather it is God whom he calls his refuge. Indeed, to use the image of the second half of verse 1, although David may have been hidden physically in the dark shadows of the vast cave of Adullam, he knows that it is actually under the shadow of the wings of God that he has found safety.

Here is the point to notice how prominent God is in this psalm and thus also in the mind of the young fugitive. In this psalm God is referred to twenty-one times either by name or pronoun, and there are other words and phrases like "refuge" and "shadow of your wings" that are used to refer to him as well.

"Shadow of your wings" is a particularly rich image, and Bible students have looked at it generally either in one of two ways.

1. *The wings of the cherubim.* The most frequent Old Testament use of the word *wings* is to refer to the wings of the golden cherubim that were upon the lid of the ark of the covenant in the Most Holy Place of the temple or tabernacle. They are mentioned first in Exodus 25:17–20: "Make an atonement cover of pure gold—two and a half cubits long and a cubit and a half wide. And make two cherubim out of hammered gold at the ends of the cover. Make one cherub on one end and the second cherub on the other; make the cherubim of one piece with the cover, at the two ends. The cheru-

bim are to have their wings spread upward, overshadowing the cover with them. The cherubim are to face each other, looking toward the cover." This description occurs again in Exodus 37:9 and 1 Kings 6:27, and there are additional references to the cherubim's "wings" in 1 Kings 8:6–7, 1 Chronicles 28:18, 2 Chronicles 3:13 and 5:7–8. Apparently, Ezekiel in his visions of heaven saw the heavenly beings, of which the golden cherubim were but representations, and in that book the word *wings* occurs more than twenty times. There is a similar vision and reference in Revelation 4:8.

The tabernacle and its divinely appointed articles of furniture were so prominent in the religious outlook of the Jewish people that it is easy to suppose that David might have been thinking of the wings of the cherubim here, especially since the wings of the temple cherubim encompassed the space where God was supposed to dwell symbolically. If this is what is intended, David would be saying that he is as secure as if he were himself within the Most Holy Place, next to or virtually one with God.

The difficulty, of course, is that Psalm 57:1 does not speak of the wings of the cherubim, however significant they may have been, but of "your wings," which means the wings of God. It is much more natural therefore to think along the lines of Jesus' use of the image in Matthew 23:37, where he said, "O Jerusalem, Jerusalem, you who kill the prophets and stone those sent to you, how often I have longed to gather your children together, as a hen gathers her chicks under her wings, but you were not willing" (cf. Luke 13:34).

2. *The wings of God.* The problem with the first image has led other commentators to explain David's reference as to the wings of God himself. To the objection that God does not have wings or that the image is unworthy of the Almighty we answer that God speaks along these lines himself in several places. Indeed, the earliest biblical use of the word *wings* is an example. In Exodus 19:4, God declares, "You yourselves have seen what I did to Egypt, and how I carried you on eagles' wings and brought you to myself." This initial use of the image later lends itself to several variations. Thus, in the Song of Moses God is compared to

> an eagle that stirs up its nest
>   and hovers over its young,
> that spreads its wings to catch them
>   and carries them on its pinions (Deut. 32:11).

The phrase "*shadow* of your wings," occurring in Psalm 57:1, is also in Psalms 17:8, 36:7, 61:4, and 63:7. In Psalm 91:1 the phrase becomes "shadow of the Almighty," and verse 4 of the same psalm says, in words that are very close to Psalm 57,

> He will cover you with his feathers,
>   and under his wings you will find refuge;
>   his faithfulness will be your shield and rampart.

In the second stanza of part one (vv. 2–3) David refers to God as "God Most High." This name occurs first in the Bible in the story of Abraham and Melchizedek, where Abraham presents offerings to this otherwise unknown king of Salem. Melchizedek said, "Blessed be Abram by God Most High, Creator of heaven and earth . . . who delivered your enemies into your hand" (Gen. 14:19–20). Derek Kidner thinks this name is intended to draw attention to Abraham as "another homeless man."[4] But in David's situation it is more likely that it is chosen for the sake of the accompanying phrase "who delivered your enemies into your hand." This is what David needed (as well as being delivered from his enemies), and it is what God did. First God delivered David. Then he delivered Saul, David's chief enemy, into David's hand. He did it more than once (cf. 1 Sam. 24 and 26).

In these desperate early days, wherever David went he seemed to be "in the midst of lions" (v. 4). But when he lay down in the cave of Adullam "in the shadow of [God's] wings," he was as safe as Daniel in the lions' den. If Daniel had lived before David and if David had known Daniel's words, David might well have used them to tell Saul, "My God sent his angel, and he shut the mouths of the lions. They have not hurt me, because I was found innocent in his sight. Nor have I done any wrong before you, O king" (Dan. 6:22).

Part Two: A Heightened Testimony

I want to deal now with part two of this psalm, holding consideration of the chorus or refrain for last. Generally speaking, part two has the same themes as part one. But seeing how they are introduced and what happens to them the second time around will help you to understand something about Hebrew poetry.

First, look at the general subject matter of the three stanzas the New International Version rightly identifies as stanzas in part one. Verse 1 is the first. It is an appeal to God for mercy, coupled with a resolute determination to take refuge in him. Verses 2 and 3 are the second stanza. They are a testimony to God's faithfulness to David. Verse 4 is the third stanza, the last of part one, apart from the chorus. It is a description of David's enemies and of the danger he is in because of them.

Now look at part two. These same general themes occur here, but in inverse order. The first stanza is verse 6. It deals with David's enemies, which is what the third stanza did in part one. The second stanza, verses 7–8, also deals with faithfulness or steadfastness, only here the steadfastness is David's. Because God is faithful, David will also be faithful and will sing praises to him. The third stanza, verses 9–10, is like the first in part one in that it is another cry to God. So the structure of the psalm is:

A, B, C / chorus
followed by C, B, A / chorus

But notice this. The second time around each of the three themes is raised a notch or two higher, and the tone of the psalm becomes gloriously strong and confident, all because the psalmist is focusing on God primarily—he is hiding in God, after all—and not on his problems.

The stanzas that I have identified as "C" deal with David's enemies, but the description of danger that is found in the first part gives way to the confidence that the pit they have dug for David will trap them. They will fall into it themselves.

The stanzas that I have identified as "B" deal with David's relationship to God. But the earlier expression of confidence, which is already on a very high note, rises even higher as David moves from confidence in God to actual singing, so wonderful does God seem to him.

> . . . my heart is steadfast;
> I will sing and make music.
> . . . Awake, harp and lyre!
> I will awaken the dawn (vv. 7–8).

The stanzas that I have identified as "A" are direct addresses to God. But the appeal for mercy in part one rises to pure praise in part two.

> I will praise you, O Lord, among the nations;
>   I will sing of you among the peoples.
> For great is your love, reaching to the heavens;
>   your faithfulness reaches to the skies (vv. 9–10).

This is not the first occurrence of the words *love* and *faithfulness* in this psalm. They are found first in verse 3, at the beginning, and now also here in verse 10, at the end. In between we have David's believing declaration "My heart is steadfast," repeated twice for emphasis (a Hebrew poetic device). Because God is faithful, David will be faithful. This makes verse 7 the emotional focal point of the psalm.

So I apply the psalm here, asking: Are you faithful in this sense? Is your heart steadfast?

Alexander Maclaren preached a sermon on this verse titled "The Fixed Heart" in which he provided wise words and asked some searching questions:

> For a fixed heart I must have a fixed determination and not a mere fluctuating and soon broken intention. I must have a steadfast affection, and not merely a fluttering love that, like some butterfly, lights now on this, now on that sweet flower, but which has a flight straight as a carrier pigeon to its cot, which shall bear me direct to God. And I must have a continuous realization of my dependence upon God and of God's sweet sufficiency going with me all through the dusty day. . . .
>
>   Ah, brethren! How unlike the broken, interrupted, divergent lines that we draw! . . . Is our average Christianity fairly represented by such words as

these of my text? Do they not rather make us burn with shame when we think that a man who lived in the twilight of God's revelation, and was weighed upon by distresses such as wrung this psalm out of him, should have poured out this resolve, which we who live in the sunlight and are flooded with blessings find it hard to echo with sincerity and truth?

Fixed hearts are rare amongst the Christians of this day.[5]

Maclaren died more than fifty years ago, about the time I was born. But who would argue that the situation has improved even a trifle in the last half century?

To God Be the Glory

After what we have seen so far in the psalm we are not surprised to find the chorus calling for God to be exalted: "Be exalted, O God, above the heavens; let your glory be over all the earth" (vv. 5, 11). God is exalted above the heavens. His glory does fill the earth. The goal of history is that God might be known as God and be honored for it. Nothing will frustrate this worthy purpose of the Almighty.

But this repeated chorus is not a statement that God has or will be exalted. It is a prayer that he might be exalted. And that raises questions: How so? In what manner? And by whom? The answer is that David wants God to be exalted in his own personal circumstances and by the way he trusts and praises him even in difficulties. This makes me think of the third chapter of Ephesians. Paul is writing of the glory of what God is accomplishing in the church in which Jews and Gentiles are being brought together into one body and in which even their sufferings demonstrate the sufficiency of God in all circumstances. He has been speaking of this for several chapters, but here he intensifies his tone, arguing that even the angels marvel at this manifestation of God's wisdom:

> His intent was that now, through the church, the manifold wisdom of God should be made known to the rulers and authorities in the heavenly realms, according to his eternal purpose which he accomplished in Christ Jesus our Lord. In him and through faith in him we may approach God with freedom and confidence. I ask you, therefore, not to be discouraged because of my sufferings for you, which are your glory (Eph. 3:10–13).

This is exactly what David is saying in Psalm 57. The world thrills when human beings are exalted. It fawns on kings, rulers, and statesmen, the rich and the famous. But those who know God rejoice when God is exalted, and they rejoice that they have the great privilege of exalting him themselves, especially in circumstances that are disappointing or difficult.

Psalm 58

Low Deeds in High Places

> Do you rulers indeed speak justly?
>> Do you judge uprightly among men?
> No, in your heart you devise injustice,
>> and your hands mete out violence on the earth.
> Even from birth the wicked go astray;
>> from the womb they are wayward and speak lies.
> Their venom is like the venom of a snake,
>> like that of a cobra that has stopped its ears,
> that will not heed the tune of the charmer,
>> however skillful the enchanter may be.
>
> Break the teeth in their mouths, O God;
>> tear out, O LORD, the fangs of the lions!
> Let them vanish like water that flows away;
>> when they draw the bow, let their arrows be blunted.
> Like a slug melting away as it moves along,
>> like a stillborn child, may they not see the sun.
>
> Before your pots can feel the heat of the thorns—
>> whether they be green or dry—the wicked will be swept away.
> The righteous will be glad when they are avenged,
>> when they bathe their feet in the blood of the wicked.
> Then men will say,
>> "Surely the righteous still are rewarded;
>> surely there is a God who judges the earth."
>
> *verses 1–11*

There was a time in American political history when anyone reading Psalm 58 would have thought it somehow unreal, at least where the United States is concerned. Psalm 58 is about

480

unjust rulers, and in those earlier halcyon days America was favored for the most part with leaders whose characters were upright and whose actions were above reproach. No longer. Today corruption is widespread even at the highest levels of political leadership, and Psalm 58 seems to be an apt prophetic description of our times.

Even secular observers see it. Speaking of our national life, the *Washington Post* said recently that "common decency can no longer be described as common." The *New Republic* magazine declared, "There is a destructive sense that nothing is true and everything is permitted."[1]

On April 4, 1991, Charles W. Colson gave an address on ethics at the Harvard Business School. Not long before this the business school had established a Chair on Ethics, recognizing that the moral decline of American leadership is a significant social problem, and Colson had objected that "Harvard's philosophical relativism precludes the teaching of ethics." Now he was invited to address this intelligent and highly critical body. He expected the worst. Only a few years earlier the Nobel prize-winning neurobiologist Sir John Eccles had been booed when he had suggested that although we can account for brain cells through evolution, the consciousness of the mind is something that has to have come from God. Nevertheless, when Colson reviewed the recent moral scandals involving America's leadership, he received a respectful hearing.

He spoke of the Keating Five, five United States senators tried, in effect, by their own tribunal for complicity in the savings and loan scandal; Senator Dave Durenberger, who was censured by the Senate; Marion Barry, the mayor of the District of Columbia, arrested for drug use; congressmen, who have been turned out of office by the scores; and perhaps most reprehensible of all, the HUD scandal in which people were embezzling large sums of money from funds intended to help the poor.

Colson referred to a recent press release in which the Department of Justice boasted that in 1990 they had prosecuted *and convicted* fifteen hundred public officials, the highest number in the history of the country. Boasting about it![2] It was a sad commentary on the corruption that has become epidemic in contemporary American life, corruption the business school students seemed to recognize even though they did not know what to do about it.

A Vigorous Protest

The audience that heard Colson's address was mostly passive, however, as many Americans seem to be today. Americans tend to dismiss corruption, saying simply, "Well, that's just the way people are." And they are, of course! That is what original sin is all about. G. K. Chesterton said that the doctrine of original sin is the only philosophy that has been empirically validated by thirty-five hundred years of human history. But the fact that "all have sinned" and that low deeds in high places are so frequent does not mean that we are to accept sin or corruption passively. Especially not in our leaders! And not in ourselves!

David did not accept such sin, either here or elsewhere. On the contrary, Psalm 58 is a particularly vigorous protest against the evil he saw in ancient Israel at least a thousand years before the birth of Jesus Christ.

One of the great early commentators, J. J. Stewart Perowne, wrote,

> This psalm is a bold protest against unrighteous judges. It opens with an indignant expostulation on their deliberate perversion of justice, whilst they pretend to uphold it. It lays bare their character and that of those whom they favor, as men thoroughly, habitually, by their very nature, corrupt. And finally, because they are thus beyond all hope of correction or amendment, it calls upon God to rob them of their power and to bring all their counsels to nought.[3]

Psalm 58 is an imprecatory psalm, calling for God to judge the ungodly, in this case the unjust judges. Many people are disturbed by these psalms, but I have answered some of their objections elsewhere, showing that they do not express hatred of others or a desire for revenge on the part of the writer but only that God will intervene in history to judge the worst sins and permit righteousness to flourish. It is a matter of the writer siding with God and his righteousness and not with evil.

But the imprecatory psalms have another function too; they remind us to make sure we are not like those being faulted for their evil. The people described in this psalm are habitual offenders, people who are impervious to correction. As we study the psalm we should make sure that we are not like them, that our sin is covered by the blood of Jesus Christ, and that God has given us ears to hear what the Holy Spirit of correction says to us about our own evil ways.

A Description of the Wicked

The stanzas of the New International Version are a reasonable way to outline this psalm. The first stanza is itself in two parts, since verses 1–2 address the wicked directly while verses 3–5 describe what they are like. But there is a sense in which the entire stanza is a portrait of these people. Stanza two, verses 6–8, is a prayer that they might be overcome or destroyed, a malediction. The final stanza, verses 9–11, is a prediction of the end of the wicked and the vindication of the righteous. It concludes with a striking summary in verse 11.

The opening verses, then, are a rebuke of the corrupt rulers of David's day. They are addressed directly, and they are accused of failing to do the one thing they are appointed to do, which is to speak and judge justly.

But there are problems with the text, which you can easily see by comparing the English translations. What I have just said is clear in any translation.

But there is a problem with the Hebrew word the New International Version translates as "rulers" (v. 1). The word is *elem,* which means "muteness" or "silence." It is hard to fit this word and its form into the text, but the older versions do the best they can and come up with something like the new King James Version, which says, "Do you indeed speak righteousness, you silent ones?" However, because the word is close in form in Hebrew to the word *elohim,* which means "gods," and because *elohim* is used in the sense of "mighty ones" or "rulers" in the psalms, some of the more recent versions take *elem* as referring to the judges themselves. So we have translations like this: "Do you rulers indeed speak justly?" (NIV).

I am not sure it is possible to reach certainty about how the text should be taken. But I tend to stick with how the text actually reads and avoid emendations, however reasonable, and if that is right, then the problem is that these judges did not speak up for the right course of action when evil was being planned. Perowne says, "They are *dumb* when they ought to speak, as afterwards they are said to be *deaf* when they ought to hear."[4] The next sentences show that these evil persons also plotted evil and put it into practice. If "silence" is the right translation in verse 1, then the opening stanza accuses them of silence and reminds us that to remain silent when evil is planned is also an evil and deserves God's condemnation.

Are you careful to stand up for righteousness when evil is proposed and good is challenged? Remember that a courageous, good word can be extremely effective. It was because of the protest of one righteous man, Ebed-Melech, a Cushite, that the prophet Jeremiah was saved when his enemies had thrown him into a cistern to die (cf. Jer. 38:1–13).

Verses 3–5 add two damaging accusations to the charge against the unjust judges or rulers.

1. *They are evil from birth* (v. 3). David is thinking of this special class of evildoers, as opposed to occasional wrongdoers or the righteous. But we should remember that this is also an accurate description of all men and women in their natural state. No one is born righteous. We are born sinners. In fact, it is because we are born sinners that we sin. Even David said, "Surely I was sinful at birth, sinful from the time my mother conceived me" (Ps. 51:5). He meant that there was never a moment of his life, even from his conception, when he did not possess a sinful nature. It is because we are sinners that we both sin and need a Savior.

2. *They will not listen to appeals to act differently* (vv. 4–5). Psalm 58 is noteworthy for its striking images, and one of these is its description of evildoers as snakes. This is not an uncommon image for us, since we also might call some particularly devious person a snake. But here David calls attention to the snake's venom or poison. The snake's bite kills. Then he adds an additional striking thought, describing these persons as snakes that cannot hear and therefore cannot even be controlled by the tunes of the snake charmer. I am told that snakes do not actually hear very much, if anything. They are

controlled more by the motion of the flute than by the tune. But that is irrelevant to the writer's image. His point is that people intent on evil will not listen to those trying to dissuade them, either to man or God. Therefore, they are equally deaf both to reason and to revelation.

God told Ezekiel, "Son of man, you are living among a rebellious people. They have eyes to see but do not see and ears to hear but do not hear, for they are a rebellious people" (Ezek. 12:2). Isaiah said, "You have seen many things, but have paid no attention; your ears are open, but you hear nothing" (Isa. 42:20). That is true of all of us in our natural state.

A Prayer against the Wicked

The second stanza of Psalm 58 moves from a description of the wicked to a prayer that they and their evil might be overthrown by God. It contains five images for what David is asking God to do. These images move from what is powerful to what is increasingly weak, from what is awe inspiring to what is merely tragic or sad.

1. *The teeth of a lion.* The most awe-inspiring image is that of a lion, which is fierce and able to kill and do great damage. David had used the image in Psalm 57, where he described himself as being "in the midst of lions . . . among ravenous beasts" (v. 4). Here he is asking God to defang his fierce enemies, to break the teeth of those who would consume him. God did this when he caused the armies of Saul to be defeated by the Philistines in the battle that preceded the call of David to be king.

2. *Water that flows away.* Water can also be destructive when it comes in large quantities as in a flood. It can wash away houses, even whole villages, and claim lives. But it is also a characteristic of water that it flows downhill and therefore quickly moves away and vanishes. David uses this image to ask that God will cause the workers of evil to pass by quickly and vanish into the earth like water into parched soil.

3. *Blunted arrows.* Arrows are less destructive than masses of water, but in the hands of a skilled archer they can wound and kill. David has used this image in the previous psalm too, describing his enemies as "men whose teeth are spears and arrows" (Ps. 57:4). He knew the piercing, wounding, killing power of evil words. Yet God can blunt words' effects. David knew that too. So he prays in these verses, "When they draw the bow, let their arrows be blunted" (v. 7). At the time of Absalom's rebellion, David prayed that the wise counsel of Ahithophel might fall on deaf ears and so be disregarded. It was. Absalom listened to Hushai instead of Ahithophel and eventually lost the war (cf. 2 Samuel 16–17).

4. *A melting slug.* A slug does not actually melt away as it moves along the ground leaving its slimy trail behind. But it seems to, and it is this low image that David creates to describe the self-destructing pathway of the wicked. As Alexander Maclaren says, "Opposition to God's will destroys itself by its own activity."[5] David expressed the same thought with another image in Psalm

57 when he said, "They dug a pit in my path—but they have fallen into it themselves" (v. 6).

5. *A stillborn child.* That last image is of a child born dead, what we call a stillbirth. So it is David's prayer that the lives of these evil ones might be nipped at the beginning. This image corresponds closely to his statement in verse 3 that the wicked have gone astray "from birth." His thinking is that if they have been evil from birth, they should be cut off at birth.

It's God's World After All

The last stanza of Psalm 58 is a prophecy, a confident statement that the wicked will be judged by God and the righteous rewarded. It is the climax of the psalm. The moral is that although judgment may tarry long, it will come, and when it comes the way of the righteous will be seen to have been right.

But there is a problem with verse 9. I wrote earlier that translators cannot agree on the meaning of verse 1 because of the word *silent.* Those problems are increased manyfold in this verse, because there are several words for which the meaning is unclear. The word translated "pots" (NIV) can mean either "a pot used for cooking" or "a thorn." The word rendered "green," as in wood that has not yet dried out, can mean either that or "raw" as in raw or uncooked meat. The words "the heat of" have been added, meaning that the text actually says only "feel the thorns." There are a few other more minor problems too. If you compare Bible translations, you can see at once how these cause the translations to differ.[6]

On the other hand, in spite of these problems of translation the general meaning is clear. As Alexander Maclaren says, "It is a homely and therefore vigorous picture of half-accomplished plans suddenly reduced to utter failure, and leaving their concocters hungry for the satisfaction which seemed so near."[7]

The climax of the psalm comes in the moral of verse 11, that, although judgment may tarry long, it will come, and when it comes the way of the righteous will be seen to have been right.

> Then men will say,
>   "Surely the righteous still are rewarded;
>   surely there is a God who judges the earth."

That is something worth remembering. We tend to forget that it is true, especially when we see evil winning out for a time, as evil often does. But those who fix their eyes on God and believe God and his word will remember it. They will have a long-range perspective and will live accordingly. They will do right and stand for righteousness, knowing that evil will be judged and good rewarded in the end.

Look back at the title of this psalm for a moment, to the word *miktam*. No one is entirely sure what this means, which is why it appears as *miktam* rather than being translated. But the word seems to have its root in a verb meaning "to engrave," and this seems to have been the understanding of the translators of the Septuagint version, since they rendered it by *stelographia,* which means an inscription on a stele or column. Noting this, John Jebb, writing in 1846, had this suggestion:

> It appears by the titles of four out of these six psalms, that they were composed by David while flying and hiding from the persecutions of Saul. What, then, should hinder us from imagining that they were inscribed on the rocks and on the sides of the caves which so often formed his place of refuge? This view would accord with the strict etymological meaning of the word, and explain the rendering of the Septuagint.[8]

Whether or not these words were actually inscribed on the rock walls of the cave of Adullam, let them be inscribed on your heart. Let this climactic saying be a *miktam* to you. Assure yourself on the basis of God's revelation in the Bible that "the righteous still are rewarded" and that "there is a God who judges the earth."

And equally important, make sure that you live for him and stand for righteousness. You cannot do it by yourself. But you can by the power of Christ who lives in you, if you are a Christian.

I began this study by citing some things Charles Colson said to students in the Harvard Business School in 1991. I return to what he said now, because he ended his speech on this note:

> Even the most rational approach to ethics is defenseless if there isn't the will to do what is right. On my own—and I can only speak for myself—I do not have that will. That which I want to do, I do not; that which I do, I do not want to do.
>
> It is only when I can turn to the One whom we celebrate at Easter—the One who was raised from the dead—that I can find the will to do what is right. It's only when that value and that sense of righteousness pervade a society that there can be a moral consensus. I would hope I might leave you, as future business leaders, the thought that a society of which we are a part—and for which you should have a great sense of responsibility and stewardship—desperately needs those kind of values. And, if I might say so, each one of us does as well.[9]

Psalm 59

God Is My Fortress

Deliver me from my enemies, O God;
   protect me from those who rise up against me.
Deliver me from evildoers
   and save me from bloodthirsty men.

See how they lie in wait for me!
   Fierce men conspire against me
   for no offense or sin of mine, O LORD.
I have done no wrong, yet they are ready to attack me.
   Arise to help me; look on my plight!
O LORD God Almighty, the God of Israel,
   rouse yourself to punish all the nations;
   show no mercy to wicked traitors.   Selah

They return at evening,
   snarling like dogs,
   and prowl about the city.
See what they spew from their mouths—
   they spew out swords from their lips,
   and they say, "Who can hear us?"
But you, O LORD, laugh at them;
   you scoff at all those nations.

O my Strength, I watch for you;
   you, O God, are my fortress, my loving God. . . .

O my Strength, I sing praise to you;
   you, O God, are my fortress, my loving God.
                              verses 1–9, 17

Psalm 59 is another psalm with a his-
torical setting from the life of David, the great poet of the first two books
of psalms. These historically based psalms have appeared in more or less
alternating order since Psalm 51. That is, when we look at the titles to
these psalms, we find historical references for Psalms 51, 52, 54, 56, 57,
and now 59 and 60. Most of these are linked to the days when David was
hiding from King Saul, first at Nob, then at Gath, next in the wilderness of
Ziph, and finally in the wilderness cave of Adullam. As the collection
comes to an end, we find Psalm 60 looking ahead to something that happened later in David's life when he had been king for some time, and
Psalm 59 looking back to David's first troubles with the king.

Psalm 59 is about the time "when Saul had sent men to watch David's
house in order to kill him." The story is in 1 Samuel 19:11–18.

David's Escape

David was still with Saul in those days. But it was the time following
David's victory over Goliath, and the women of Israel had been singing,
"Saul has slain his thousands, and David his tens of thousands" (1 Sam.
18:7). Saul was jealous. Twice he became so distraught that he threw his
spear at David (1 Sam. 18:10–11; 19:9–10), but each time David escaped.
After the second attempt on his life David thought it would be wise to leave
Saul and his court and go to his own home, but that night the king sent soldiers to surround David's house, watch it, and kill him in the morning.
David was married to Saul's daughter Michal at this time. She loved David
and warned him, "If you don't run for your life tonight, tomorrow you'll be
killed" (1 Sam. 19:11). Michal seems to have known her father well, just as
her brother Jonathan, David's friend, also did. So that night Michal let
David down through a window of the house, presumably outside the city's
walls or into a back alley, and he escaped.

Michal also bought David time. She put an idol in his bed, covered it
with a blanket, and set some goat's hair at its head. When the soldiers came
in the next morning, it looked as if David was asleep. "He is ill," Michal said.
The soldiers reported this to Saul. Saul told them to bring David to him on
the bed so he could kill him anyway. But when the soldiers went back to
David's house and discovered the ruse, David was long gone.

The psalm is quite understandable against this background, but a few
phrases suggest that it may have been expanded at a later time to apply more
broadly the lessons David learned in these early days.[1] Thus, there are two
references to the surrounding nations ("all the nations," v. 5, and "all those
nations," v. 8) and one reference to "the ends of the earth" (v. 13).[2] The
point seems to be that just as God protected and delivered David when he

was surrounded by the hostile forces of King Saul, so also will God protect and deliver his elect people from whatever enemies may surround them.

Marvin E. Tate observes rightly that "the psalm reminds us that we have not escaped the problem of enemies and their evil work in human society. The 'dogs' prowl about in our communities and towns as they did in the ancient world—'dogs' which embody the devouring, malignant persons and forces in human affairs. . . . Law no longer mediated justice." He reminds us that today, "Like ancient Israelite communities, we too are dependent on Yahweh for deliverance."[3]

This is another psalm that is divided into two parts by a refrain, but here the two parts are also much like one another. In fact, there are repetitions within the two halves. The simplest outline goes like this: (1) David's appeal to God (vv. 1–5); (2) a description of David's fierce foes (vv. 6–8); (3) a refrain (v. 9); (4) David's second appeal to God (vv. 10–13); (5) a second description of his foes (vv. 14–16); and (6) the refrain repeated (v. 17).

David's First Appeal to God

From where we sit, in safety and comfort and frequently surrounded by luxuries, the psalms sometimes seem to be little more than quaint poetry containing noble thoughts. We lose a feel for their urgency. Yet the psalms are often very urgent and their prayers almost desperate. We catch something of the urgent quality of this psalm in the imperatives that begin each of the four swift sentence prayers of verses 1 and 2: *deliver, protect, deliver,* and *save.* These are not casual utterances. In them we can sense David's awareness of danger and of his desperate aloneness except for God.

There is a lesson here, however. The urgency that leads us to utter swift sentence prayers does not preclude our praying thoughtfully and thus presenting a reasoned case to God. I say this because of the second stanza. It contains three reasons why God should hear David's prayer.

1. *The danger facing David* (v. 3). God is omniscient. He sees and knows all things. But this does not stop David from calling God's attention to the danger he is facing. "See how they lie in wait for me!" he tells God. "Fierce men conspire against me." Are you in danger? Tell God about it. Are you discouraged? It is not wrong to call it to God's attention. If you lack wisdom, ask him for wisdom; he has promised to supply it. David's reminding God of his dangerous situation reminds us of the aged saint who, when people were threatening him, told God, "God, your property is in danger." He knew that he belonged to God and that God saw his problem, loved him, and was able to take care of him.

2. *David's innocence* (vv. 3–4). In the last phrase of verse 3 and in verse 4 David protests his innocence: "for no offense or sin of mine, O LORD" and "I have done no wrong." David is not claiming to be sinless, of course. This is not a matter of his innocence before God but rather of his innocence before Saul, his enemy. It is an important point. If you are innocent of

wrongdoing before other people, then you can appeal to God bravely and with confidence. If you are guilty of wrongdoing, then you cannot pray boldly and you will appear before God convicted of sin rather than vindicated and assured. Are you innocent before other people? Can you truly say, "I have done no wrong" (v. 4)?

3. *The character of God* (v. 5). One of the most striking features of this psalm is its names for God, and here they appear in profusion: "O LORD God Almighty, the God of Israel." In Hebrew this is quite a mouthful of names: *Yahweh,* the great personal name of God revealed to Moses on Sinai, means, "I am who I am." *Elohim Sabaoth,* "the God of hosts," refers to both the armies of Israel and to the heavenly hosts who stand behind them and give victory. *Elohi Israel,* "the God of Israel," refers to the God who has entered into a lasting covenant relationship with his people. Leupold says, "The writer recalls God's unique power by employing the various most familiar names by which he was known in Israel."[4] He is right. When we can pray, "Lord God, Lord of hosts, God of Israel, my God," we have said a great deal and have a powerful argument.

David's Doglike Foes

Most people who live in the West today have little appreciation for the role of the numerous wild dogs of an ancient Eastern city. For us, dogs are pets for the most part—or at least guard dogs that patrol an area but are not allowed to roam wild. It was not like that in the East. Occasionally people may have had small dogs as pets. Jesus' words to the Canaanite woman seem to imply this: "It is not right to take the children's bread and toss it to their dogs" (Matt. 15:26). But generally the dogs of an Eastern city were wild scavengers that roamed in packs, particularly at night, when they searched the streets and alleys for garbage or other food that may have been discarded by the citizens.

One nineteenth-century English writer describes what it was like during a visit he made to Constantinople:

> The whole city rang with one vast riot. . . . The yelping, howling, barking, growling, and snarling were all merged into one uniform and continuous even sound, as the noise of frogs becomes when heard at a distance. For hours there was no lull. I went to sleep and woke again, and still, with my windows open, I heard the same tumult going on; nor was it until daybreak that anything like tranquility was restored.[5]

I suppose, as I read that description, that having lived in a major Western city for nearly thirty years I would probably not have found the noise of the city's dogs that overwhelming. The Englishman was probably raised in an English village or on the downs. Still, it gives us an idea of what such packs of dogs were like and of how aptly David applies the image to the soldiers who were prowling about his village seeking to kill him.

Should he be afraid of these "dogs"? Hardly, since the Lord his God was laughing at them. These vile creatures are no threat to God; and if they are no threat to God, they are no threat to the one protected by him. The idea of God laughing at his foes takes us back to Psalm 2:4 ("The One enthroned in heaven laughs; the Lord scoffs at them") and Psalm 37:13 ("The Lord laughs at the wicked, for he knows their day is coming").

The Refrain

I will consider this refrain more fully the second time around, when it reappears in verse 17. But note the one difference in the two versions of it. Verses 9 and 17 are the same except for the phrase "I watch for you" in the earlier verse, which becomes "I sing praise to you" in the latter. Verse 9 says, "O my Strength, I watch for you; you, O God, are my fortress, my loving God."

"I will watch" reminds us of the minor prophet Habakkuk's similar words when he was in danger and overcome by fear. He declared,

> I will stand at my watch
>   and station myself on the ramparts;
> I will look to see what he will say to me,
>   and what answer I am to give to this complaint (Hab. 2:1).

Habakkuk did not understand why the things that were happening in Israel in his day were happening, any more than David understood what the Lord was doing when he allowed him to be hunted by Saul's soldiers. But Habakkuk did the same thing David did. Habakkuk committed himself to God and waited faithfully and expectantly for God's deliverance.

There are many situations in which you and I can do no more. We cannot alter them, but we can commit them to God and wait for his solution.

David's Second Appeal to God

In the psalmist's first appeal (vv. 1–5), the emphasis seemed to be on David's danger and therefore on the bloodthirsty men who had been set against him. In this second parallel appeal (vv. 10–13), David's description of the danger shifts to what he is asking God to do to these enemies.

He is asking God to destroy them, of course: "bring them down" (v. 11), "let them be caught in their pride" (v. 12), "consume them in wrath, consume them till they are no more" (v. 13). But what is unique in this second appeal is his asking that these enemies not be destroyed at once but rather gradually so that people will see it, learn from it, and not forget God's justice. David says,

> But do not kill them, O Lord our shield,
> or my people will forget (v. 11).

This says something important about evil and God's willingness to let evildoers survive for a time. For some this is an offense, even a reason for disbelieving in God: "If there is a God, why would he permit such things to happen?" Here is the answer. God allows evil to flourish for a time so that we might learn from it. We can see that evil is short-lived. We can learn that sin carries the seeds of its own destruction in itself. We can know that judgment does come upon the wicked in the end. If God did not permit evil, we would never learn any of this and would not grow by it.

Verse 13 sums this up. When evil emerges, is tolerated for a time, is allowed to stagnate and fall because of its own inner corruption, and then is eventually judged decisively by God, "Then it will be known to the ends of the earth that God rules over Jacob" (v. 13). This understanding of evil must have been in David's mind for a long time, for these are almost the same words he used when he went out to fight Goliath. He told the Philistine champion, "This day the LORD will hand you over to me, and I'll strike you down and cut off your head. . . . and the whole world will know that there is a God in Israel" (1 Sam. 17:46).

David's Foes and God Almighty

This fifth section of the psalm is like the second, even to the point of exact verbal repetitions. But there is this difference. In section two David was describing the conduct of his enemies, portraying them as wild Near Eastern dogs. Here he is noting their punishment, particularly their howls of frustration when they are "not satisfied."

Remember that. Not only does evil carry within it the seeds of its own destruction, it is not capable of being satisfied either. In fact, it is the very nature of evil to be dissatisfied: wanting, but never having enough; eating, but never getting full; grasping, but always seeing the object of the desire slipping from one's hands. There is a picture of this in God's judgment on the serpent in the Garden of Eden, described in Genesis 3. God told the serpent, "You will crawl on your belly and you will eat dust all the days of your life" (v. 14). A snake does not eat dirt, of course. This is a way of saying that for those who pursue evil everything they taste will turn to ashes in their mouths.

As for the godly, they know that God will "prepare a table" for them even "in the presence of [their] enemies" and that "goodness and love will follow [them]" all the days of their lives (Ps. 23:5–6).

The Refrain

Now we come to the refrain the second time around. It is a great testimony ("O my Strength, I sing praise to you; you, O God, are my fortress, my loving God" [v. 17]), particularly when we remember that outwardly the psalmist's circumstances had not changed a bit. The same situation that caused David to cry out to God in verses 1–2 is still there. But here at the end he is not only testifying that God is his "Strength" and "fortress." He is actually singing praises to God in the very midst of the danger. In fact, the singing begins even before this, in verse 16.

What has brought him to a point of vigorous jubilation? The answer is in the slight variation I noted earlier between verses 9 and 17. In verse 9 he is waiting on God, watching for his eventual deliverance. It is because he has been waiting and because God has provided encouragement, though not yet the expected deliverance, that David can sing. In the Hebrew the words *watch* and *sing* are identical except for one letter, which is a way of saying, I suppose, that keeping one's eyes on God is only a stroke away from singing his praises and otherwise rejoicing in him.

Do you lack joy? Is it hard for you to sing God's praises? If so, it is probably because you are not watching for God, are not looking to him. Remember Habakkuk, who was waiting on his watchtower to see what God would say to him. Nothing changed outwardly for him, either. He was as much in danger and as much perplexed at the end of his prophecy as at the beginning. But Habakkuk was changed as a result of waiting upon God, and for that reason his short book ends with what we can only regard as singing.

> Though the fig tree does not bud
>   and there are no grapes on the vines,
> though the olive crop fails
>   and the fields produce no food,
> though there are no sheep in the pen
>   and no cattle in the stalls,
> yet I will rejoice in the LORD,
>   I will be joyful in God my Savior.
> The Sovereign LORD is my strength;
>   he makes my feet like the feet of a deer,
>   he enables me to go on the heights (Hab. 3:17–19).

Those are the words of one who has learned to wait on God and to trust him completely. They are words any Christian should be able to say.

Alexander Maclaren says, "Trust [God] as what he is, and trust him because of what he is, and see to it that your faith lays hold on the living God himself and on nothing besides."[6] If you do that, regardless of the circumstances that surround you, even if you are surrounded by "dogs" who seek your life, you will end up singing.

Psalm 60

If God Does Not Go with Us

You have rejected us, O God, and burst forth upon us;
*   you have been angry—now restore us!*
You have shaken the land and torn it open;
*   mend its fractures, for it is quaking.*
You have shown your people desperate times;
*   you have given us wine that makes us stagger.*

But for those who fear you, you have raised a banner
*   to be unfurled against the bow.*   Selah

Save us and help us with your right hand,
*   that those you love may be delivered.*
God has spoken from his sanctuary:
*   "In triumph I will parcel out Shechem*
*   and measure off the Valley of Succoth.*
Gilead is mine, and Manasseh is mine;
*   Ephraim is my helmet,*
*   Judah my scepter.*
Moab is my washbasin,
*   upon Edom I toss my sandal;*
*   over Philistia I shout in triumph."*

Who will bring me to the fortified city?
*   Who will lead me to Edom?*
Is it not you, O God, who have rejected us
*   and no longer go out with our armies?*
Give us aid against the enemy,

for the help of man is worthless.
With God we will gain the victory,
and he will trample down our enemies.
                                                              verses 1–12

Psalm 60 is the last of the psalms with a historical setting from the life of David. The title is the longest such introductory title in the Psalter, occupying three and a half lines in our text and about the same amount of space in the standard Hebrew Bible. In the Hebrew text the titles are numbered as verses, and the title is actually the first two verses of the psalm.

It tells us that these words are about the time David "fought Aram Naharaim and Aram Zobah [that is, the Arameans of the Mesopotamian River valley[1]], and when Joab returned and struck down twelve thousand Edomites in the Valley of Salt." The only possible time for these battles is after David had become king and had reigned for a considerable number of years. But if this is so, then Psalm 60 is an important historical document, for, as Derek Kidner says, "[Except] for this psalm and its title we should have no inkling of the resilience of David's hostile neighbors at the peak of his power."[2] The only other accounts we have of this period speak of it as a time of uninterrupted military victories.

That highlights two strange things about Psalm 60. First, the title is about a victory, Joab's victory over the Edomites in the Valley of Salt, but the psalm is about a defeat ("You have rejected us, O God, and burst forth upon us," v. 1). Second, the title sets the psalm in a soaring account of David's many and geographically widespread victories.

The Historical Background

But maybe there is a lesson even in that. Let me explain.

The background is in 2 Samuel 8:1–14.[3] In the part of the book immediately before this, several things are recorded. First, David becomes king over all Israel (2 Sam. 5:1–5). Second, he conquers Jerusalem and makes it his capital (5:6–16). Third, he achieves decisive victories over the Philistines (5:17–25). Fourth, he brings the ark to Jerusalem as a focus for the people's worship (ch. 6). Fifth, God sends Nathan to him with the greatest message David received in his entire lifetime, that God was going to establish his throne forever (ch. 7). It was a prophecy of the Messiah, which David immediately recognized. Immediately after these events, the chapter about David's many military victories, the setting for Psalm 60, occurs:

> In the course of time, David defeated the Philistines and subdued them, and
> he took Metheg Ammah from the control of the Philistines.

David also defeated the Moabites. . . .

Moreover, David fought Hadadezer son of Rehob, king of Zobah, when he went to restore his control along the Euphrates River. [These are the areas mentioned in the title of Psalm 60.] David captured a thousand of his chariots, seven thousand charioteers and twenty thousand foot soldiers. He hamstrung all but a hundred of the chariot horses.

When the Arameans of Damascus came to help Hadadezer king of Zobah, David struck down twenty-two thousand of them. He put garrisons in the Aramean kingdom of Damascus, and the Arameans became subject to him and brought tribute. The LORD gave David victory everywhere he went. . . .

And David became famous after he returned from striking down eighteen thousand Edomites in the Valley of Salt.

He put garrisons throughout Edom, and all the Edomites became subject to David. The LORD gave David victory everywhere he went (2 Sam. 8:1–6, 13–14).

What seems to have happened, if we put the title of Psalm 60 together with this account, is that the Edomites took advantage of David's being away from Jerusalem, fighting along the Euphrates River, and staged an uprising. They must have succeeded in this to the extent described in Psalm 60, as a result of which David dispatched Joab, one of his chief commanders, to subdue the Edomites. Joab did, achieving the victory described in the title of Psalm 60, after which David returned and completed the conquest, even of the Edomite strongholds. That sequence of events might explain why Joab is credited with killing twelve thousand Edomites in Psalm 60, while David is credited with striking down eighteen thousand Edomites in 2 Samuel 8:13.[4]

This tells us that even in times of unprecedented blessing there are nevertheless defeats. Some Jewish cities were still being overrun by enemies. Some people were still being killed. Should we expect things to be different? It is a fallen world. Even in times of blessing we can expect some things to go wrong. In fact, even when we are closest to the Lord ourselves, we can be sure that there are still areas of our lives that will cause us trouble and need correcting.

The psalm seems to fall into three parts of four verses each: (1) a lament on the occasion of a great defeat (vv. 1–4); (2) an appeal to God and God's answer, an oracle (vv. 5–8); and (3) two important lessons to be drawn (vv. 9–12).

Defeat in the Midst of Victory

We do not know specifics of the defeat that came to Israel at this time, but the opening verses of Psalm 60 portray it as a great disaster. It was so great that two powerful images are used to describe what it was like.

First, *an earthquake* (v. 2). We are aware how damaging and terrifying earthquakes can be because we have heard about many of them: the many earthquakes in California; the earthquake that killed many people in Cairo; earthquakes in Central America, Turkey, and the former Soviet Union. In these earthquakes tremendous damage was done and many lost their lives. It is easy to see how such a strong image might apply to a military defeat in which city walls have been broken down and some of the defenders killed. David says, "You have shaken the land and torn it open; mend its fractures, for it is quaking" (v. 2).

The second image describes the effect of the battle and defeat on the people. It is the image of *drunkenness:* "You have shown your people desperate times; you have given us wine that makes us stagger" (v. 3). This is a frequent Old Testament image for God's outpoured wrath. The image occurs in Psalm 75:8:

> In the hand of the LORD is a cup
>> full of foaming wine mixed with spices;
> he pours it out, and all the wicked of the earth
>> drink it down to its very dregs.

This image is also in Isaiah 51:17, 22; Jeremiah 13:13; 25:15–16; 49:12; and other prophetic passages. Isaiah 51:17, a typical passage, says,

> Awake, awake!
>> Rise up, O Jerusalem,
> you who have drunk from the hand of the LORD
>> the cup of his wrath,
> you who have drained to its dregs
>> the goblet that makes men stagger.

We might say that the attack by the Edomites left the people reeling from the blow.

Yet the worst thing about this defeat, as David describes it, is that it was because the Lord was angry with the people and had rejected them (v. 1). This does not seem to refer to everyone. For example, there is no reason to think that God was angry with David, at least at this period of his life. Nor was he even angry with all the people in the defeated territories. In fact, the fourth verse makes a distinction, saying, "But for those who fear you, you have raised a banner to be unfurled against the bow." These people were obedient and godly. Still, there were some who had displeased God, and David takes their acts and God's consequent displeasure seriously. Because of their sin many were defeated, just as the army of Israel was defeated at Ai because of Achan's disobedience at Jericho (cf. Josh. 7).

Charles Spurgeon has an interesting comment at this point. He says, "To be cast off by God is the worst calamity that can befall a man or a people; but the worst form of it is when the person is not aware of it and is indiffer-

ent to it."[5] David was aware of it, however. He wrote the psalm to show that
he was not indifferent.

Let's apply this to the church. Isn't it true that the church fails to achieve
great victories because of the sin of some? Churches are sometimes torn
open because of a few factious members. Denominations fail to achieve
their potential because some bring disgrace on the gospel or others deny or
even attack it. What shall we do when we see that happening? We need to
make sure we are not the cause of the trouble, first of all. But then we need
to do something else too. We need to rally around the banner God has
given us. That banner is the gospel. Those who fear the Lord will do that
(v. 4). Their actions will show that they fear him, and he will provide for
them and defend them.

It is significant that a *selah* occurs at this point in the psalm. It probably
means "stop and consider, pay attention to that."

An Appeal to God and God's Answer

The second section of the psalm contains an appeal to God to help those
who have been attacked by the Edomites (v. 5), followed by God's answer in
the form of an oracle (vv. 6–8). The oracle follows so closely upon the
appeal that we know that faith has already won a victory.

There are two ways verses 6–8 may be understood. They are introduced
as a word that "God has spoken from his sanctuary." The sanctuary is the
tabernacle precinct in Jerusalem, so it is possible that this was a special revelation from God that could have been brought to David by Nathan or one
of the other priests or prophets. In that case, it is a statement that God has
given the land of Israel to the Jewish people and a promise that he would
give them victory over the enemies that were trying to take it from them. If
this is that kind of oracle, it may have been preserved in writing separately
from the psalm, which might explain why verses 5–12 also appear as the latter half of Psalm 108, verses 6–13.[6]

The other way of looking at these verses is suggested by the fact that the
place names are not what we might expect at this point in David's
career—we would expect the names of the tribal territories perhaps—and
by the fact that they seem to come from and trace the early history of the
occupation of the land from the time of the patriarch Jacob onward.
Shechem was the place Jacob settled after his return to Canaan from
Paddan Aram, where he had lived for twenty years with his uncle and later
father-in-law, Laban (Gen. 33:18). Succoth was the last place he had been
prior to that (Gen. 33:17). These two places represent the eastern and western sides of the Jordan River. Gilead and Manasseh represent larger areas of
the eastern side of the Jordan River occupied by Israel at the time of the
conquest under Joshua. Ephraim and Judah represent the most prominent
tribes to the west.[7] If these names are meant to remind us of this early his-

tory and of the fact that God had given the land to the people from the time of the patriarchs, then verses 6–9 are not necessarily an oracle from David's own time but rather a new phrasing of these older promises.

But notice this: In either case, as H. C. Leupold writes, "The word of God (vv. 6–8) is made the basis of [the faith expressed in verse 5]. Thus faith should always seek the foundation of the Word of God."[8]

Biblical faith is not optimism, as some think. Nor is it a positive mental attitude worked up to help us through tough times. According to the Bible, faith is believing the Word of God and acting on it, which is what David expresses in this psalm and what he apparently did in actuality. Because God had promised him victory over Edom as well as over Moab and Philistia, David sent Joab to fight the armies of Edom in the Valley of Salt. Wouldn't we be more active in gospel work if we believed God's promise to bless it? Some have believed God and have made an impact on cities and even continents.

Two Lessons to Be Drawn

When was Psalm 60 written precisely? We know from 2 Samuel 8 that David eventually joined Joab and conquered Edom, placing garrisons throughout the country. In the last stanza of the psalm he is thinking about that final triumph, asking, "Who will bring me to the fortified city? Who will lead me to Edom?" (v. 9). It would seem, therefore, that David wrote the psalm while on his campaign near the Euphrates River after Joab was dispatched but before the final victories.

What is in David's mind at this time? What lessons is he learning as he reflects, first on the people's defeat by Edom and second on the promises of God to give an eventual victory? It seems to me that there are two of them.

1. *Only God can give victory.* There were a number of well-fortified cities in Edom, the source of the country's strength and great pride. But when David speaks of "*the* fortified city" he can only mean Petra, the most inaccessible and apparently impregnable mountain stronghold of Edom. I have had the privilege of visiting Petra twice. It is approached through a narrow cut in the limestone cliffs that winds inward for about two miles and is called a *siq*. The cliffs rise upward for thousands of feet on both sides, and in places the passage is so narrow that no more than two horses can pass abreast. A handful of brave men could defend this *siq* against an army. But even if the passage could be breached, the defenders could retreat into the mountains surrounding the hidden inner valley and defend themselves from there. Only God could give victory over a fortress like that, and David knew it. So he cries to God, acknowledging that "the help of man is worthless" (v. 11).

2. *We must ask for it.* David was also learning that although only God can give victory, we must nevertheless ask for it. And so he did. That is what he is doing in the final stanza of the psalm. Moreover, because he is asking for help he anticipates God's positive answer, saying,

> With God we will gain the victory,
>   and he will trample down our enemies (v. 12).

Thus, as Leupold says, "The psalm closes on a strong note of confidence which was engendered by the promises of God, which were grasped in faith."[9]

You and I are not kings, as David was. We do not have military battles to fight, and we have never seen an Edomite. But I want to suggest that the lessons of this psalm are directly applicable to us in terms of the spiritual battles we are called to fight. We are members of the kingdom of the Lord Jesus Christ, and our task is to advance his kingdom in this spiritually hostile world. The apostle Paul said, "For our struggle is not against flesh and blood, but against the rulers, against the authorities, against the powers of this dark world and against the spiritual forces of evil in the heavenly realms" (Eph. 6:12). Compared to the conquest of these hostile spiritual forces, the victory over Edom and the overthrow of its mountain stronghold Petra was a piece of cake. How can we gain this greater victory? Not by ourselves, or even with the help of other Christians. In this battle "the help of man is [truly] worthless." We need God to fight with us and on our behalf.

The second lesson applies to us too: We must ask for God's help. The Book of James says, "You do not have, because you do not ask God" (James 4:2). Jesus expressed the other side of James's words when he said, "Ask and it will be given to you; seek and you will find; knock and the door will be opened to you" (Matt. 7:7). We can ask for many things wrongly and so fail to receive them. James speaks of that too (James 4:3). But the one thing we can be sure of receiving is victory on behalf of the gospel. Do you remember Nebuchadnezzar's vision, the one that he could not remember but that troubled him so much? It was a vision of a great statue representing in sequence all the many great kingdoms of this world. At the end of the vision a rock "not cut by human hands" struck the statue and destroyed it, and then grew up to become "a huge mountain" that "filled the whole earth" (Dan. 2:34–35). That rock is the Lord Jesus Christ, and that mountain is his kingdom, which is destined to triumph.

If you believe that, then this is the banner around which you must rally and on behalf of which you can confidently fight.

Psalm 61

The Rock That Is Higher Than I

Hear my cry, O God;
*   listen to my prayer.*
From the ends of the earth I call to you,
*   I call as my heart grows faint;*
*   lead me to the rock that is higher than I.*

For you have been my refuge,
*   a strong tower against the foe.*
I long to dwell in your tent forever
*   and take refuge in the shelter of your wings.*   Selah

For you have heard my vows, O God;
*   you have given me the heritage of those who fear your name.*

Increase the days of the king's life,
*   his years for many generations.*
May he be enthroned in God's presence forever;
*   appoint your love and faithfulness to protect him.*

Then will I ever sing praise to your name
*   and fulfill my vows day after day.*
*   verses 1–8*

In the *Trinity Hymnal,* the hymnbook we use in our church, William O. Cushing's hymn "O Safe to the Rock That Is Higher Than I" is linked to Psalm 94 because of verse 22, which speaks of God as a rock of refuge. But it is hard to read Psalm 61 without supposing that Cushing had it in mind rather than Psalm 94 when he composed the hymn. Psalm 61 says, "Lead me to the rock that is higher than I," and Cushing wrote:

> O safe to the rock that is higher than I
> My soul in its conflicts and sorrows would fly;
> So sinful, so weary, thine, thine would I be;
> Thou blest Rock of Ages, I'm hiding in thee.
> Hiding in thee, hiding in thee—
> Thou blest Rock of Ages, I'm hiding in thee.

People who have lived with the Lord for any length of time know the force of that hymn and the image it is based upon. Life is filled with sorrows, and there are times when there is no one to whom we can turn for understanding, comfort, or help. Some people spend most of their lives alone. Others are surrounded by an unsympathizing family, perhaps because these others are not Christians and resent the believer's convictions and lifestyle. Some have an unbelieving husband or wife, or they may be resented by people at work. Others have simply grown old, and all their friends and relatives have died. Whatever the cause, many know what it is like to have no one human to whom they can turn for understanding.

Yet if they are Christians and have any experience of the Lord at all, they know that God is a rock to which they can turn, a rock higher and wiser and stronger than they are themselves.

The title to Psalm 61 identifies it as a psalm of David, but it could be from nearly any period in his career, since we know that David often felt alone, even after he had become king.

There are various ways of outlining this psalm. Some divide it into two parts of four verses each, separated at the *selah* following verse 4.[1] Leupold divides the psalm into three petitions, the first two ending with a reason for the petition, the third with a vow.[2] Alexander Maclaren has the most interesting arrangement. He argues that there is an introductory verse, followed by three matched pairs of verses, ending with an additional single verse to match verse 1.[3] In my opinion, any of these outlines is equally valid, but none is more helpful than the others. This is a very simple psalm, and the most helpful way of studying it is merely to look in order at the various points that are made. There are five to notice.

Trust When Far from Home

The setting for a psalm provides a background for interpreting it, and in this case the setting is found in the fact that the psalmist is far from home. He feels he is very far away indeed, because he is calling to God from what he regards as the very "ends of the earth" (v. 2).

For any Jew the center of the universe was (and is) Jerusalem, where the ark of God was located. So the phrase "ends of the earth" must mean that David was far from or felt himself to be far from Jerusalem. Is this to be taken literally, as a geographical reference? If so, it could refer to any time David was absent from the capital—when he was fleeing from Saul or Absalom or when he was absent on a military campaign. Verses 6–7 make clear that at the time of writing David was already king. So at the very least, the days when he was fleeing from Saul are eliminated. David could be writing during the days of Absalom's rebellion. Again, the placing of Psalm 61 immediately after Psalm 60 might suggest that the psalm was written at the time of the campaign along the Euphrates River, which is the earlier psalm's setting. Certainly the words "ends of the earth" would be more appropriate to that location than the Judean wilderness where David fled from Absalom.

But there is another possibility, and that is that the words "ends of the earth" are metaphorical. This idea appeals to Marvin E. Tate, who concludes his study with a section suggesting that the chief value of the psalm is its metaphorical richness. He believes that "the dominant metaphor in the psalm is that of distance from God. . . . a sense of far-awayness from the divine presence, an at-the-end-of the earth experience" and that the psalm was written to overcome this faraway feeling. He adds, "Breaking down a perceived distance and the creation of a sense of nearness and presence is a major function of prayer."[4]

This may very well be right, and in any case it is how you and I should apply the words to ourselves, at least in most instances. From time to time, perhaps often, you and I feel far from God. When we do, we should do as David did and pray along the lines of this psalm.

A Rock Higher Than Ourselves

The second point to notice is the image David uses for God in verse 2, calling him "the rock that is higher than I." The idea of God being a rock is common in the psalms, appearing twenty times.[5] In fact, it occurs three times in the next psalm, Psalm 62, alone. We have already looked at it at some length in our study of Psalm 18, where it is used four times in an interesting progressive sequence:

> The LORD is my rock (v. 2).
> My God is my rock (v. 2).
> Who is the Rock except our God? (v. 31).
> Praise be to my Rock (v. 46).

The thought of God being a rock is prominent in the Davidic psalms because David had used the rocks of the Judean wilderness as places of refuge and protection during the years he was forced to hide from King Saul and later Absalom. David knew every cranny, track, and hiding place in the vast, rocky wilderness. So when he fled to the rocks he knew that he was safe in their protection.

Each of the psalms has its own way of writing about God as a rock, however, and this is no less true of Psalm 61. There are two unique features to David's use of the rock image here.

1. *This rock is "higher" than David.* It is natural to think of God being higher or greater than ourselves when we are suffering some severe reversal of fortune, when we are somehow down and out. We know we need God then. But when we are on top, as David seems to have been at this time—he was the king of all Israel, after all—we forget about God and consider ourselves able to deal with any need that can arise. David never made this mistake. He never forgot that God was infinitely above him and that it was always God he needed. The people of Israel may have looked to David as their rock, but David looked to a rock that was higher than he.

2. *We must be led to this rock.* The other unique feature of David's speaking of God as his rock in Psalm 61 is that he asks to be "led" to it, that is, led to God. It is hard to know exactly what David was thinking of when he wrote this, but Charles Haddon Spurgeon said that, for our part, not only do we need a rock, we also need the Holy Spirit to lead us to him. Our rock is Christ, but none of us come to Christ by ourselves. We need the Holy Spirit to quicken our dead souls, awaken us to our spiritual need, renew our wills, and bring us to the point of personal commitment to the Savior.

In Spurgeon's day ships often ran upon the rocks off the coast of England, and mariners were cast into the water and drowned. At times the mariners would find themselves struggling at the base of high cliffs, knowing they would be safe if they could only get up the steep, slippery face of the rocks. But they could not. At one place, according to Spurgeon, a man who lived at the top of one of these cliffs carved stone steps into the rock face so wrecked mariners could climb up. And when the steps became badly worn and impassable over time, someone else added stanchions and a chain railing to help the struggling survivors.

Observed Spurgeon,

> How infinitely higher than we are is the salvation of God. We are low and grovelling, but it towers like some tall cliff far above us. This is its glory, and it is our delight when we have once climbed [onto] the rock and claimed an interest in it; but while we are as yet trembling seekers, the glory and sublimity of salvation appall us, and we feel that we are too unworthy even to be partakers of it; hence we are led to cry for grace upon grace, and to see how dependent we are for everything, not only for the Savior, but for the power to believe on him.[6]

Spurgeon thought of the steps and chain in his illustration as God coming to assist us in our weakness. Salvation is of God and is entirely of grace.

Is God your rock? Have you been led to him? If you have not trusted in Jesus Christ yet, there is nothing wrong with asking God to lead you to him. It is a case of saying, "I do believe; help me overcome my unbelief" (Mark 9:24). That is a prayer God loves to hear and answer.

What God Is to His Trusting People

The next thing to notice about Psalm 61 is that its second stanza adds to the image of God as David's rock by four metaphors that elaborate what God is to his trusting people. God is so great that any number of images might be provided at this point. What is significant about these images is that they are arranged to become increasingly warm and intimate.

1. *A refuge.* This image is closest to that of God being a rock and, in fact, is frequently linked to it: "my rock, in whom I take refuge" (Ps. 18:2), "my rock of refuge" (Pss. 31:2; 71:3), "my mighty rock, my refuge" (Ps. 62:7), and "the rock in whom I take refuge" (Ps. 94:22). It calls to mind a retreat such as David used when fleeing from King Saul.

2. *A strong tower.* A tower is a refuge for people in times of attack from enemies, but it differs from a wilderness refuge in that it is part of a walled city. So here the idea is not of a person fleeing from home but of a person defending himself in his home city when threatened by hostile forces. Presumably he is not alone in this condition. Others would be taking refuge in the tower with him and would be helping him defend it.

3. *A tent.* The word *tent* conjures up a domestic scene in which a host might welcome strangers, as Abraham welcomed the three heavenly visitors outside his tent near the great trees of Mamre. A visitor in such a situation would be entitled to his host's most solicitous care and protection. Yet there may be more in the image than this, since the word *tent* is also translated as "tabernacle" and in the Old Testament frequently refers to the wilderness tabernacle where the ark of God was kept. If David is using the word in this sense, as he probably is, he is asking to dwell where God himself dwells, an idea he also expresses elsewhere:

> One thing I ask of the LORD,
>   this is what I seek:
> that I may dwell in the house of the LORD
>   all the days of my life,
> to gaze upon the beauty of the LORD
>   and to seek him in his temple (Ps. 27:4).[7]

This means that the images used thus far move us from the wilderness to the fortified city, presumably Jerusalem, and to the tabernacle, which means closer and closer to God.

4. *A sheltering mother bird.* Thus we are prepared for the last and most intimate image of all, that of dwelling under the shadow of God's wings. When

we studied Psalm 57 we saw that commentators often interpret this image as having to do with the wings of the cherubim on the lid of the ark of God within the tabernacle, which would make a natural sequence in this stanza, especially if the tent image refers to the tabernacle where the ark was kept. But I argued in the earlier study that strictly speaking the wings are not called the wings of the cherubim but the wings of God and that this is an even more powerful and intimate image. Some might think it indelicate, but David would not consider it wrong to want to be sheltered beneath the wings and against the very breast of God.

Nor should we. Never fear to be intimate with God. God desires to be intimate with you and is only hurt when you remain at a distance or draw back from his embrace.

A Prayer Fulfilled in the Messiah

In verses 6–7 the psalmist apparently ceases to pray for himself and prays instead that God will "increase the days of the king's life, his years for many generations," that he will be "enthroned in God's presence forever," and that God will appoint his "love and faithfulness to protect him." At first glance, it seems that another hand has added these words, perhaps at a later date, and that is the way many commentators have understood them. Yet it can also be argued that David is writing about himself as king, merely switching to the third from the first person for stylistic effect. The last verse seems to imply this since it returns to the first person, promising that the speaker will praise God if the earlier petition is answered. David could do that if God promised to prolong his reign for generations.

Yet this must also be said: Whether this prayer was by David or is for David, ultimately it is about and is fulfilled in the Messiah. "Increase the days of the king's life"? That can easily be understood of an earthly king. "His years for many generations"? That too perhaps, by stretching things a little. But not, "May he be enthroned in God's presence *forever*," at least not if that is literally understood.

And it probably should be. I say that because this is the way David responded when God sent Nathan to him to promise that a descendant of his would sit upon his throne forever: "When your days are over and you rest with your fathers, I will raise up your offspring to succeed you, who will come from your own body, and I will establish his kingdom. He is the one who will build a house for my Name, and I will establish the throne of his kingdom forever" (2 Sam. 7:12–13). Some of that might be understood to have been fulfilled in Solomon, David's immediate successor. But not the forever part, which David seems to have recognized at once since he responded, "Is this your usual way of dealing with man, O Sovereign Lord?" (v. 19). Nothing merely of man lasts forever. So if God was promising a forever kingdom, it must be a kingdom to be established and maintained by a divine Messiah, who would be God become man. The promise made to

David was about the eternal kingdom of the Lord Jesus Christ, and if this is what David was thinking about in Psalm 61, this is another messianic psalm.

Enduring Praise for God

As we look back over Psalm 61 we are reminded that David began it feeling at "the ends of the earth," far from God. But as he thought about God and prayed to him, he drew closer to God and grew in confidence until he ends actually expecting to be established in Jerusalem, his capital, for many days and many generations. That is something to praise God for. And that, quite naturally, is how the psalm ends.

> Then will I ever sing praise to your name
> and fulfill my vows day after day (v. 8).

Shouldn't that be true for you as well? It is not only David who had such a great God, or those who lived with him in this Old Testament period. His God is our God, and it is our privilege to know him even more intimately than David did, for we know him in the Lord Jesus Christ. Jesus is the rock that is higher than we are, infinitely higher. He is very God of very God, as the creeds say. He is the Rock of Ages. But he is also the rock that has been cleft for us, crucified, that we might be saved from sin.

> Rock of Ages, cleft for me,
> Let me hide myself in thee.

Jesus is our refuge, but not only a refuge from human enemies and foes. He is a refuge from the wrath of God to be poured out at the final judgment. He is our tower that we can run into and be safe. He is our tabernacle. The apostle John used this very word when he wrote, "The Word became flesh and made his dwelling among us" (John 1:14). In the Greek the words "made his dwelling" are literally "tabernacled." Jesus is the one who said of the city of Jerusalem, "O Jerusalem, Jerusalem, you who kill the prophets and stone those sent to you, how often I have longed to gather your children together, as a hen gathers her chicks under her wings, but you were not willing" (Matt. 23:37). But he has gathered *us* to himself.

Sometimes we need to feel we are at "the ends of the earth" before we can discover how wonderful Jesus is. That is what the great Augustine was thinking of when he wrote, "They that are godly are oppressed and vexed in the church or congregation for this purpose: that when they are pressed, they should cry; and when they cry, that they should be heard; and when they are heard, that they should laud and praise God."[8] We will be happy Christians if we learn to do just that.

Psalm 62

Rest in God Alone

My soul finds rest in God alone;
  my salvation comes from him.
He alone is my rock and my salvation;
  he is my fortress, I will never be shaken.

How long will you assault a man?
  Would all of you throw him down—
    this leaning wall, this tottering fence?
They fully intend to topple him
  from his lofty place;
    they take delight in lies.
With their mouths they bless,
  but in their hearts they curse. . . .

One thing God has spoken,
  two things have I heard:
that you, O God, are strong,
  and that you, O Lord, are loving.
Surely you will reward each person
  according to what he has done.
                    verses 1–4, 11–12

Do you ever feel like an endangered species? If we are to believe what we read in the papers, there are a lot of endangered species these days, and many powerful organizations have been brought into existence to try to save them. There are endangered whales, endangered seals, endangered plants and animals, even the

508

endangered snail darter that held up a major hydroelectric project in the South for many years. When we are discouraged, depressed, or threatened we sometimes feel that we too are one of these endangered species and that we are soon going to be destroyed, wiped out, or forgotten.

David did. That is what Psalm 62 is about. David was surrounded by enemies who were treating him as if he were a leaning, tottering wall, and they were doing everything they could to push him over. Yet in spite of their hostility, in this psalm David is not worrying about them but rather is trusting God.

That is probably the most important thing to be said about the psalm. David is in danger, but in spite of the danger his trust in God is so strong that the psalm is wonderfully serene and confident. H. C. Leupold wrote, "There is scarcely another psalm that reveals such an absolute and undisturbed peace, in which confidence in God is so completely unshaken, and in which assurance is so strong that not even one single petition is voiced throughout the psalm."[1] J. J. Stewart Perowne observed, "Scarcely anywhere do we find faith in God more nobly asserted, more victoriously triumphant; the vanity of man, of human strength and riches, more clearly confessed; courage in the midst of peril more calm and more unshaken, than in this psalm."[2]

Clearly this is a psalm for you if you feel threatened or in danger.

The psalm falls naturally into three stanzas of four verses each, the three parts separated by the *selahs* that follow verses 4 and 8. The last four verses are longer than the earlier ones, however, which encouraged the translators of the New International Version to divide the psalm into four parts. In what follows, I am holding to the NIV arrangement.

God and the Psalmist's Enemies

The first stanza (vv. 1–4) introduces us to the three interacting agents in the psalm: God, the psalmist, and the psalmist's enemies. His enemies are trying to throw him down, but David is trusting God, who is his "rock," his "salvation," and his "fortress" (v. 2). The critical point is that David is trusting in God only, in God alone.

It is hard to see this in the English text, because the Hebrew is almost untranslatable, but in the Hebrew text the word *only* or *alone* occurs five times in the first eight verses (in vv. 1, 2, 4, 5, 6), and once in verse 9. The Hebrew word is *ʾak,* and the reason its use in the psalm is almost untranslatable is that no one English word seems to be an adequate translation in all the six occurrences. Moreover, in the Hebrew text the word occurs at the beginning of each of the six verses for emphasis, and that too does not lend itself to any easy translation into English. *Alone* is probably the best word for us to use, which is what the New International Version does in four of the six occurrences: "My soul finds rest in God *alone*" (v. 1), "He *alone* is my rock" (v. 2), "Find rest, O my soul, in God *alone*" (v. 5), and "He *alone* is my rock" (v. 6). But in verse 4, the translators thought they needed to use the word *fully* ("They *fully* intend to topple him"), and in verse 9, they use the pale word *but* ("Lowborn men are *but* a breath").

Marvin Tate makes a stab at a more reflective rendering by using the word *yes*. His lines go:

> Yes, my soul waits calmly for God . . .
> Yes, he is my rock where I am secure . . .
> Yes, despite being a person of high status . . .
> Yes, calmly wait for God, O my soul . . .
> Yes, he is my rock where I am secure . . .
> Yes, ordinary people are only a breath . . .[3]

Tate's effort captures something of the poem's style, but it misses the psalmist's emphasis upon God being his *only* object of faith and trust, which is the most important thing after all.

So I repeat what I have been saying: The most important thing about Psalm 62 is that the psalmist is making God his *only* object of trust. He is not trusting something other than God, nor is he trusting God and something else, or God and someone else. His trust is in God only, and that is why he is so confident.

Alexander Maclaren, one of the best of all commentators and preachers on the psalms, captures this when he says, "That one word *[only]* is the record of conflict and the trophy of [the psalmist's] victory."[4]

I think this is something Christians in our day especially need to learn. As I see it, our problem is not that we do not trust God, at least in some sense. We have to do that to be Christians. To become a Christian you have to trust God in the matter of salvation at least. It is rather that we do not trust God *only,* meaning that we always want to add in something else to trust as well.

I think this is what was disturbing John MacArthur when he wrote the book *Our Sufficiency in Christ*.[5] Quite a few people did not like that book, because it criticized the way many of today's Christians depend on mystical experiences, pragmatic solutions to problems, and psychology rather than fully trusting Christ for guidance, help, and wholeness. The critics wanted to argue for a proper use of these experiences, methodologies, and tools. They had their point, of course, because there is a legitimate place for experience, pragmatism, and professional counseling help, just as there is a legitimate place for doctors even though God is the ultimate source of bodily healing. Nevertheless, when I read the book I felt myself siding more with John MacArthur than his critics. For I am a pastor, as he is, and I too find that Christians in our day are far more inclined to trust the world's tools and mechanisms than to trust Jesus Christ wholly. For many of today's believers Jesus really is not sufficient for all things, regardless of what they may profess publicly.

Not long ago I was interviewed by a staff writer from *Christianity Today* about the impact of culture on the ministry, and I explained that television has turned our age into an entertainment-oriented culture and that preachers therefore increasingly try to be entertainers. I explained how many churches have almost eliminated prayer from their services, substituted brainless music for the great theological hymns, and reduced the content of most sermons to a series of need-defining comments, trivial "teaching" lines, and funny anecdotes. The person interviewing me did not necessarily disagree, but he wondered what I would say to the argument that you have to begin where people are and that if people want entertainment, you have to provide it in order to have them listen.

I answered in two ways. I said that the simplest response, a simplistic answer but one that nevertheless has some truth in it, is that of course that is true. You do have to begin where people are. Moreover, I said, anyone who is any good at communicating does that, even those who are determined to teach the Word of God. People have to be trained to listen. And like any other subject, you have to master the ABCs of biblical content and theology before you can go on to higher and more complicated matters.

But, I said, there is also another answer, and in my opinion it is here that the real problem lies. The real problem is a crisis of faith, lack of belief in God and the power of the Word of God, which he has given. The real reason preachers do not teach the Bible and resort to other devices such as "lite" theology and funny stories is that they do not trust God. They do not believe that God actually works through his Word to convert unbelievers and strengthen and form character in Christians. I think John MacArthur is aware of this and is dismayed by the current drift of evangelical Christianity too, which is why he wrote *Our Sufficiency in Christ.*

But doesn't it work? someone will ask. Doesn't "felt-need" preaching and entertainment fill churches? Well, yes, when it is well done it often does fill churches. If you give people what they want, they will come for it. But this is not the same thing as serving Jesus faithfully as an undershepherd or doing kingdom work.

Moreover, it is a betrayal of God. For, as one of the early Bible teachers said, "They trust not God *at all* who trust not him *alone.*"[6]

To pretend to trust God but not to trust him only is like having one foot on a solid foundation and another on an object that is unstable and is moving away from the foundation. When I was a teenager my family had a cottage on a lake in New York state, and my grandmother, who was a very heavy woman, came to visit us in the summer. On one of these visits my father took her out in our motorboat, and after the ride he returned to the dock and began to help my grandmother up out of the boat. Unfortunately, he had not tied the boat to the dock. So as soon as she had one foot on the dock her weight began to push the boat away from it. The boat began to drift, and there was nothing to be done but to watch her slowly sink down between the dock and boat and splash into the water.

That is what will happen to you if you try to trust God *and something else.* You will find that you are actually not trusting God at all and that you will fall down doing it. David did not make that mistake. He had learned that if he was to trust God at all, he had to trust him only, and when he did, he found that God was indeed his "rock," his "salvation," and his "fortress." Fixed on that rock, David knew that he would "never be shaken," as he says in verse 2.

Still Will We Trust

Yes, but still he had to keep trusting, and he knew how variable and weak the faith of a man in God can be. This is what is emphasized in the second stanza. David had trusted God. But now he also: (1) encourages himself to continue to trust God (vv. 5–7), and (2) urges the people to trust God too (v. 8).

There is a great deal of similarity between the first and second stanzas of this psalm, because the first two verses are repeated again as verses 5–6, which begin stanza two. They are not a refrain (like the refrains in Psalms 57 and 59), but rather a thematic statement that repeats the necessity for trusting God alone. They are repeated because this is what the psalm is emphasizing.

There is a slight change the second time around, however. In the first occurrence David declared that he did trust God and had found rest in him. In the second stanza David urges himself to find rest in God or to continue in it. How does he do this? Well, in the first case, after he had expressed trust in God alone, he looked aside to reflect on the evil of those surrounding him, the people who were trying to knock him over like they might destroy a tottering wall. In this second instance, where he is encouraging himself to continue to trust God, he does not think about his enemies but rather focuses on God instead.

He focuses on God by repeating in verse 7 the images and epithets he has used to describe God in verses 2 and 6, bringing them before his mind once again. He says in verse 7,

> My salvation and my honor depend on God;
> he is my mighty rock, my refuge.

"Salvation," "rock," and "refuge" ("fortress") were mentioned in verse 6, just one verse before.

Here is a point where we can all obviously learn from David. Alexander Maclaren had a sermon in which he compared verses 1 and 5, pointing out that although the settled confidence that David shows in verse 1 may be beyond us, his desire to "find rest" in God is nevertheless something we can copy. "This man's profession of utter resignation is perhaps too high for us; but we can make his *self-exhortation* our own" is his summary.[7] That is precisely what David urges on the people in verse 8: "Trust in him at all times, O people; pour out your hearts to him, for God is our refuge."

A New Look at Weak Man

If we are to divide the psalm into three stanzas, marked by the *selahs* at the end of verses 4 and 8, then the last stanza (vv. 9–12) echoes the first in that each is about both God and man. The first is about God and David's enemies, in that order. The third is about mankind in general and God; the matter is the same but the order is reversed. Yet there is an even bigger difference the second time around. True, David is thinking about his enemies in this stanza too. But in the meantime he has settled himself on God, and as a result his focus has changed significantly.

I noted that there were three interacting agents in stanza one: God, the psalmist, and the psalmist's enemies. Those agents are also here (the presence of the psalmist is implied). But in the earlier stanza David was looking at his enemies in relationship to himself, and he was primarily aware of the danger he was in. They were about to push him over like a tottering wall. Here he is looking at his enemies in relationship to God, whom he has continued to trust (particularly in stanza two), and by that comparison he sees that these supposedly dangerous men are "only a breath." They are not worth fearing. In fact, "If weighed on [this] balance, they are nothing" (v. 9).

Derek Kidner suggests that there are two important points here: (1) We have nothing to fear from man, and (2) we have nothing to hope from man, either.[8] These are both true, and both flow out of the lessons the psalm as a whole has been teaching.

Most of us are willing to agree, at least verbally, that we do not have to fear man, assuming we are Christians. We believe that Jesus is strong and that God is able to care for us. We find the words "Surely I am with you always, to the very end of the age" (Matt. 28:20) to be a great comfort. It is the second part we have trouble with. We trust God, but we want to trust man too, or at least look to other people for something we doubt God is able or willing to supply. But other people will always let us down. They are sinners, as we are. They cannot be trusted. But even if they could be, they are still "but a breath" and are quickly taken away and are gone. If God has given you faithful and good friends or a loving life companion, thank him for it. It is a great gift. But do not place your deepest hope in man. Instead trust him who is eternal and unchanging, and you will never be shaken when people disappoint you.

Two Lessons Learned about God

The last two verses of Psalm 62 are intended as a summary of what David has been learning, but they also go a step beyond it. David says that he has learned two lessons: that God is strong and that God is loving.

The opening lines ("one thing God has spoken, two things have I heard") can be taken in three ways. First, they can mean that God has spoken one thing twice. That is, God has repeated his lesson for emphasis.

Second, they can mean that God has taught David two lessons, "one" and "two" being only a Semitic literary device. Third, they can mean that God spoke once but that David learned two things from it. David probably means that he has learned two great things about God as a result of God's continuing self-revelation of himself.

First, God is strong; that is, he is sovereign in all the events of history, including the dangers that have threatened David. Second, God is loving or merciful, even in these apparently contradictory things. The word David uses is *hesed,* which refers to God's faithful covenants with his people. It means that he is a covenant-keeping God.

If you know anything about God and the salvation he has provided for you in Jesus Christ, you should be rejoicing in these two great attributes of God also, as David did. Why? Because there would be no salvation for you or anyone else if God lacked either. If God had power but lacked mercy, he would be able to save mankind but would have no inclination to do so. If God was merciful but lacked power, he might desire to save us, but he would not be able to do it. Fortunately, God is both all-powerful and compassionate. Therefore, he has reached out to save us and has been successful in doing so through Jesus Christ.

J. J. Stewart Perowne reflects on these attributes in a slightly broader way, saying, "This is the only truly worthy representation of God. Power without love is brutality, and love without power is weakness. Power is the strong foundation of love, and love is the beauty and the crown of power."[9] This is why we can also "rest in God alone." We can come to God for help, because he loves us and invites us to come to him. Once there, we can rest in perfect contentment, because we know that God is also able to protect us. Indeed, he is more than able. He is an impregnable fortress.

Psalm 63

A Love Better Than Life

O God, you are my God,
earnestly I seek you;
my soul thirsts for you,
my body longs for you,
in a dry and weary land
where there is no water.

I have seen you in the sanctuary
and beheld your power and glory.
Because your love is better than life,
my lips will glorify you.
I will praise you as long as I live,
and in your name I will lift up my hands.
My soul will be satisfied with the richest of foods;
with singing lips my mouth will praise you.

On my bed I remember you;
I think of you through the watches of the night.
Because you are my help,
I sing in the shadow of your wings.
I stay close to you;
your right hand upholds me.
They who seek my life will be destroyed;
they will go down to the depths of the earth.
They will be given over to the sword
and become food for jackals.

But the king will rejoice in God;
all who swear by God's name will praise him,
while the mouths of liars will be silenced.
verses 1–11

There are three types of people in any Christian gathering. There are those who are Christians in name only. They seem to be following after God and Jesus Christ and say they are, but theirs is a false following, like that of the five foolish virgins who did not truly know the Lord and were rejected by him. The second class are those who are following Jesus but are following "at a distance," like Peter at the time of Jesus' arrest. The third type are those who, as Murdoch Campbell suggests, "in storm and sunshine, cleave to him and enjoy daily communion with him."[1] These people want God, and they want him intensely, because they know that he and he alone will satisfy the deep longing of their souls. David was a person who desired God above everything else, and Psalm 63 is a classic expression of this longing.

The Setting of the Psalm

The title of Psalm 63 identifies it as "a psalm of David" and indicates that it was written "when he was in the desert of Judah." There were only two periods in David's life this can apply to, either (1) when he was in the wilderness early in his life fleeing from King Saul or (2) later when he was in the wilderness fleeing from his son Absalom. The second must be the case here, because in verse 11 David refers to himself as "the king," and he was not yet king when he was fleeing from Saul.

The story of Absalom's rebellion is told in 2 Samuel 15–19. Absalom was estranged from his father because he felt that David had mistreated him. He spent four years doing his utmost to win over the hearts of the people of Israel, and when he thought he was ready he set up a rival kingship in the nearby city of Hebron. Caught off guard, David feared an attack on Jerusalem and fled the city with those who remained loyal to him. From a military standpoint Absalom should have attacked David at once, while he was still off balance and unable to resist an assault. But God caused Absalom to listen to counselors who advised delay, and by the time the battle finally came, David was ready, and Absalom's army was soundly defeated by David's battle-seasoned soldiers led by his faithful general, Joab. Twenty thousand men perished in that battle, and Absalom was one of them. He was caught in a tree while fleeing on a mule and was slain by Joab personally.

This historical setting throws light on some of the psalm's expressions: "better than life," "as long as I live," and "those who seek my life," for instance (vv. 3, 4, 9). They remind us that David was in danger of death at

Absalom's hand. The setting also gives added weight to David's description of himself as "the king," reminding everyone that he was the true king as opposed to the pretender.

This background helps us appreciate the emotional passion of the psalm. Separated from God's sanctuary, which was in Jerusalem and which David loved, David is longing for a sense of the presence of God as a friend longs for one from whom he is separated, or as a lover longs for his beloved. This makes the psalm almost a love song for God, especially when David says, "My soul thirsts for you, my body longs for you" (v. 1). Commentator Derek Kidner says, "There may be other songs that equal this outpouring of devotion; [but there are] few if any that surpass it."[2] J. J. Stewart Perowne says, "This is unquestionably one of the most beautiful and touching psalms in the whole Psalter."[3]

The longing for God expressed here is similar to that in some of the psalms of the Sons of Korah, especially Psalms 42, 43, and 84. Psalm 63 is similar in tone to Psalms 61, 62, and 64, which means that the historical setting of those psalms might also be the period in which David fled from Absalom.

Longing for God

There are several ways of outlining the eleven verses of this psalm, and they can be found in various commentaries. The New International Version is probably on track, however, when it sets verse 1 off as a stanza to itself. This is because the verse expresses the longing of David's soul for God and because the next section (vv. 2–8) describes how that longing has been answered in the past and is being honored in the present.

Verse 1 is a wonderful expression of the very heart of religion. David is in the desert of Judah, one of the most barren regions on earth, and he uses that as a poetic background for his condition apart from God. He has been driven from Jerusalem, where God was present in his sanctuary and where he regularly worshiped and beheld God's glory. He sees himself now as thirsting for God as a man might thirst in the desert, "where there is no water," and as longing physically for God as a traveler through such hostile country might long for rest at the end of his debilitating journey.

This intense physical longing for God, almost an appetite for God, is something that impressed C. S. Lewis when he was preparing his *Reflections on the Psalms*. He wrote,

> These poets knew far less reason than we for loving God. They did not know that he offered them eternal joy; still less that he would die to win it for them. Yet they express a longing for him, for his mere presence, which comes only to the best Christians or to Christians in their best moments. They long to live all their days in the temple so that they may constantly see "the fair beauty of the Lord" (Ps. 27:1). Their longing to go up to Jerusalem

and "appear before the presence of God" is like a physical thirst (Ps. 42). From Jerusalem his presence flashes out "in perfect beauty" (Ps. 50:2). Lacking that encounter with him, their souls are parched like a waterless countryside (Ps. 63:2).[4]

How little this is found today! Most people do not even know that it is God their souls truly desire. They are seeking satisfaction in other things. Others know God but do not cultivate his presence; they do not long after him. Is it not this above everything that explains the weakness of the contemporary church? Is it not this that makes us so hollow spiritually?

One other thing is worth noting about verse 1. The verb *seek* is an unusual verb that is related to the Hebrew noun for *dawn,* and it can be translated two ways, either as "to seek early" or "to seek earnestly." The New International Version has chosen the second option ("earnestly I seek you"), probably rightly, but many of the older versions, including the King James Version, had "early." This caused Christians to think of Psalm 63 as a morning psalm, and in many places it was sung at the beginning of each day. For example, it was used this way by the early Greek churches and remains such in the liturgy of the Armenian church.

Liturgy is not the point, however. The point is the desirability of a regular, early, daily longing after God. Do you have that desire for God? Probably not. But do you want to? Are you willing to develop it? There is no better way to start each day than by earnestly seeking God's face through personal Bible study, meditation, and devout prayer.

Satisfaction in God

About a thousand years after these words were written, David's greater descendant, Jesus Christ, said, "Ask and it will be given to you; seek and you will find; knock and the door will be opened to you" (Matt. 7:7). David did not know these specific words, of course. But he did know the reality of them, since he elaborates this idea in the next section (vv. 2–8).

There are various ways these verses can be studied. For example, they might be outlined as God's past, present, and future satisfying of David. *The past:* "I have seen you in the sanctuary and beheld your power and your glory" (v. 2). It is the memory of those joyous moments that makes David's present circumstances painful. *The present:* "Your love is better than life" (v. 3), "On my bed I remember you; I think of you through the watches of the night" (v. 6), "You are my help" (v. 7), "Your right hand upholds me" (v. 8). Even though he is cut off from the sanctuary in Jerusalem, God has not cut himself off from David. As Spurgeon said, "There was no desert in his heart, though there was a desert around him."[5] *The future:* "My soul will be satisfied as with the richest of foods; with singing lips my mouth will praise you" (v. 5). Because God is the same and does not change, the one who has found God able to satisfy his longings in the past can know that he will continue to satisfy him completely in the present and in the future too.

If we outline the verses in this way, they become a means of exploring God's character and stressing his inexhaustible capacity for satisfying our deepest spiritual desires. They are a development of Saint Augustine's well-known words: "Our hearts are restless till they find rest in thee."[6]

Again, this section can be studied for how David praises God. Thomas Le Blane, one of the early commentators, saw David doing this in seven ways. Using the King James translation, he wrote,

> First, he extols the loving-kindness of God with *his lips* (v. 3): "My lips shall praise thee." Secondly, with *his tongue* (v. 4): "Thus will I bless thee while I live." Thirdly, with *his hands:* "I will lift up my hands in thy name." Fourthly, with *his will* (v. 5): "My soul shall be satisfied as with marrow and fatness." Fifthly, with *his mouth:* "And my mouth shall praise thee with joyful lips." Sixthly, with *his memory* (v. 6): "When I remember thee upon my bed." Seventhly and lastly, with *his intellect:* "And meditate on thee in the night watches."[7]

If we handle the verses in this way, they become a means of exploring what it means to be a human being and how each part of a person's physical and emotional makeup can be used to praise God. This would be a worthwhile study in itself. Most people only use about a tenth of their brain, and it would be highly worthwhile to find out how to use just a few percentage points more of our mental capacities. In the same way, it would be worthwhile to find out how to use just a bit more of our potential capacity for praising God.

Let me suggest another way of looking at this section of the psalm. We can see it as statements first of David's satisfaction in God and then of two results flowing from it.

1. *David is satisfied with, in, and by God.* This is the main point of what he is saying certainly, and it flows from his opening expression of deep longing. David longs for God, and therefore David is satisfied with God. God does not hold himself back from those who seek him. Rather he gives himself to them fully and in increasingly fuller ways. That is why David can speak of past, present, and future satisfaction.

It is also why he speaks of God's love being "better than life" (v. 3). This verse contains two things, each of which is acknowledged as good, and it compares them, concluding that the loving-kindness of God is best. Everyone acknowledges that life is good. Therefore most of us try to hang on to life at whatever cost. We will give up our money rather than be shot by a thief who wants our wallet. We will submit to painful surgical procedures or even to amputations of a limb if those things will restore us to even partial health and prolong our days. Satan used this truth to slander righteous Job: "Skin for skin! A man will give all he has for his own life" (Job 2:4). For nearly everyone, life is the most precious of all possessions.

However, says David, there is something even better than life, and that is the love of God. The word he uses is *hesed*, which is often translated "loving-kindness" or "covenant-love." It stresses the faithful continuance of God's love. God's love is steady and unchangeable, which is why it is better than even the best thing in life, which is life itself. Life itself can be lost, even though we value it and try to protect it at all costs. However, the covenant-love of God can never be lost. The apostle Paul wrote, "For I am convinced that neither death nor life, neither angels nor demons, neither the present nor the future, nor any powers, neither height nor depth, nor anything else in all creation, will be able to separate us from the love of God that is in Christ Jesus our Lord" (Rom. 8:38–39).

In view of such great love, isn't it strange that we spend so much time trying to find satisfaction elsewhere, even in earthly loves, and so little time seeking and enjoying the lasting love of God?

When I remember that David wrote earlier in the psalm about seeking God as a thirsty man seeks water, I think of a fountain on Sedgley Hill in Philadelphia, where I live. If a person makes his way out along the eastern side of the Schuylkill River, he will come to the statue of a pilgrim where a small spring empties into the river. Then, if he follows the course of that stream upward onto the hill, he will come to a spring, which is its source, and he will see an inscription erected there years ago by the government of the city. It reads: "Whosoever drinketh of this water shall thirst again," a quotation from Jesus' conversation with the woman of Samaria (John 4:13).

That quotation tells us that all earthly satisfactions ultimately are unsatisfying, just because they are earthly. That is, they are not eternal and we are beings made for eternity. Jesus went on to say, "But whoever drinks the water I give him will never thirst. Indeed, the water I give him will become in him a spring of water welling up to eternal life" (John 4:14). David had drunk of the spring of the covenant-love of God, and he was forever satisfied.

2. *As a first result of being satisfied by the eternal loving-kindness of God, David praises God.* David was so abundantly satisfied with the love of God that he wanted everyone else to know about God's love too.

In the days of Elisha the armies of Ben-Hadad, the king of Aram, were besieging Samaria, and God scattered them by causing them to hear the sound of chariots, horses, and a great army so that they panicked and fled, leaving their tents and provisions behind and their arms and other valuables strewn over the route they fled by. There were about forty lepers at the entrance of Samaria's city gate. They decided to go to the camp of the enemy soldiers to get some food from them, because the lepers, like the shut-up citizens of Samaria, were starving. When they arrived in the camp they discovered that it was deserted. So they had a great time. They ate and drank and took the silver and gold and costly clothing and carried it off and hid it. Then they came back and took more.

At last they came to their senses and said, "We're not doing right. This is a day of good news and we are keeping it to ourselves. If we wait until daylight [that is, until tomorrow], punishment will overtake us. Let's go at once and report this to the royal palace" (2 Kings 7:9). They did, and by nightfall sacks of flour and barley, which had been nearly nonexistent just a day before, were being sold for pennies in the market.

The point is that it is both natural and right to share good news. King David knew this, and his song of unmixed praise of the God who satisfies our deepest longings is the result. Verse 3 says, "*Because* your love is better than life, my lips will glorify you," and verse 7 makes the same connection: "*Because* you are my help, I sing in the shadow of your wings." John Donne wrote of verse 7 that "as the spirit and soul of the whole book of Psalms is contracted into this psalm, so is the spirit and soul of the whole psalm contracted into this verse."[8] He meant that the Psalter shows how the person who has found satisfaction in God sings about it.

3. *As a second result of being satisfied by the great loving-kindness of God, David wants to stay close to God.* This too is a natural consequence of being deeply satisfied. Verse 8 says, "My soul clings to you." *Cling* is a word used of the attachment between a husband and wife or of other tight relationships, such as Ruth's attachment to her mother-in-law, Naomi (Ruth 1:14). If you have been satisfied by God, isn't it true that you will want to cling to him too? If you are not clinging to him, perhaps it is because you have never sought him enough to be truly and deeply satisfied.

Vindication by God

The last three verses of the psalm look to the future and express David's confidence that in time his enemies will be destroyed, the mouths of those who have slandered him will be silenced, and he will again be openly praising God with others who also love and seek him. Pedantic commentators feel that these last verses are an unworthy blemish upon what was otherwise a particularly beautiful psalm, and some have suggested that they were tacked on later by a somewhat insensitive editor. But this is not the case at all. They simply bring us back to where we started, in the desert with David, and they remind us that this is a real world after all and that, if we are to be genuinely satisfied with God's love, it must not be in some never-never land but right here in the midst of this world's disappointments, frustrations, and dangers. In other words, it is at the very time when his son had betrayed him and was seeking to kill him that David found the Lord's love to be richly satisfying.

Given these circumstances, the psalm is an amazing triumph of faith. But, as G. Campbell Morgan writes, "Two things are necessary for such triumph as this. These are indicated in the opening words of the psalm. First, there must be the consciousness of personal relationship, 'O God, Thou art my God'; and secondly, there must be earnest seeking after God, 'Early will I seek Thee.'"[9] Because that is true, a wise person will desire both.

Psalm 64

Sudden Destruction for the Wicked

Hear me, O God, as I voice my complaint;
protect my life from the threat of the enemy.
Hide me from the conspiracy of the wicked,
from that noisy crowd of evildoers.

They sharpen their tongues like swords
and aim their words like deadly arrows.
They shoot from ambush at the innocent man;
they shoot at him suddenly, without fear.

They encourage each other in evil plans,
they talk about hiding their snares;
they say, "Who will see them?"
They plot injustice and say,
"We have devised a perfect plan!"
Surely the mind and heart of man are cunning.

But God will shoot them with arrows;
suddenly they will be struck down.
He will turn their own tongues against them
and bring them to ruin;
all who see them will shake their heads in scorn.
All mankind will fear;
they will proclaim the works of God
and ponder what he has done.
Let the righteous rejoice in the LORD
and take refuge in him;
let all the upright in heart praise him!

verses 1–10

I t is not very often that David finishes a psalm without mentioning his enemies. Psalm 23 pictures God as David's loving and wise shepherd. But verse 5 says, "You prepare a table before me in the presence of *my enemies*." The fact that David mentions his enemies so often gives some idea of how many enemies he had and what his life as the king of Israel was like.

This particular block of Davidic psalms began with Psalm 51, and with the sole exception of that psalm, which is a psalm of repentance for David's sin with Bathsheba, every single psalm up to this point has mentioned David's enemies, usually using that very word. That is going to change. But for now we have been given a sizable collection of material describing the king's enemies, through whom we may learn about our own, and many useful examples of David's turning to God as his ever-present help in trouble. In fact, those are the two main themes of this collection: God and David's enemies. In the last psalm the focus was on God, and the threat from David's enemies was suppressed. They were mentioned in verses 9–10 only. In Psalm 64 the situation is reversed: the emphasis is on the enemies, and there is less written about God. Nevertheless, the ending of both psalms is virtually the same. Psalm 63 ends with the words,

> But the king will rejoice in God;
>> all who swear by God's name will praise him,
>> while the mouths of liars will be silenced (v. 11).

Psalm 64 concludes,

> Let the righteous rejoice in the LORD
>> and take refuge in him;
>> let all the upright in heart praise him! (v. 10).

Surrounded by enemies, the psalmist has no human help. But he does have God; he calls to him, and he finds that the help he desires is not lacking. The great Scottish preacher, Alexander Maclaren, applied this lesson, saying, "However high and closely engirdling may be the walls that men or sorrows build around us, there is always an opening in the dungeon roof through which heaven is visible and prayers can mount."[1]

The key word in Psalm 64 is *suddenly*, meaning "unexpectedly" or "without warning." It is used in the two main sections of the psalm: first, of the unexpected attacks of the wicked on the righteous ("they shoot at him suddenly, without fear," v. 4) and, second, of the unexpected judgment of the wicked ("But God will shoot them with arrows; suddenly they will be struck down," v. 7). The parallel image, shooting with arrows, helps to enhance the contrast. Together the two shootings strike a note of poetic justice, which carries throughout the psalm. The wicked are done in by their own weapons.

The Psalmist's Complaint

The psalm begins by David asking God to hear his complaint. To us the word *complaint* is negative. We associate it with complaining, and we don't like people who complain. But that is not the sense in which *complaint* occurs here. Here the word refers to a formal allegation, in this case against the wicked by one who is being unjustly treated by them. Our clearest parallel example would be a complainant in a legal proceeding—that is, one who initiates an action calling for reparation or redress. David brings his case to God. Do you, when you are unjustly accused or attacked in some underhanded way? Most of us don't. We retaliate in kind. We try to be our own defenders. That is wrong, of course. God says, "It is mine to avenge; I will repay" (Deut. 32:35; cf. Rom. 12:19). For our part, we are told to love our enemies and overcome evil with good (cf. Rom. 12:21). Retaliation is not only wrong, but it is also particularly ineffective where secret slander rather than outright opposition is involved, which is the case here. In this psalm David's enemies are not attacking him openly and directly, but rather behind his back and by malicious words. There is no adequate defense against that. So David does the only wise and effective thing, and that is to bring his complaint to God.

We would be wise to bring everything to God, whatever our particular burden may be. Peter learned to do that and later wrote to others, telling them, "Cast all your anxiety on him because he cares for you" (1 Peter 5:7).

The Threat from the Wicked

As noted in the introduction, this psalm spends most of its time on the wicked who are attacking David, rather than on God. The result is that we are provided with a helpful study of this particular kind of evil. Looking carefully at verses 2–6, we find them analyzing: (1) the nature of this evil, (2) the weapons of these evil people, (3) their methods, (4) their plans, and (5) their fierce but complacent pride.

1. *Their nature* (v. 2). Wickedness takes many forms, but in this case it involves its practitioners in a "conspiracy" to do harm. Conspiracy describes any familiar conversation, so technically it can describe a good, upright, or profitable discussion among friends. The negative sense usually predominates, however, and that is the case here. What David faced was the secret plotting of his enemies to bring him down. They were not foreigners, warlords, or generals plotting in some foreign capital how they might attack and overthrow the kingdom of Israel. These were people from within David's own court in Jerusalem, even, as we learn from the accounts of his reign in the historical books of the Old Testament, from within David's own family, even from Absalom, his son.

Nothing hurts more than when a person close to us turns against us and tries to harm us. It is like a snake striking from a bush, unseen. The poison from such a wound rankles and can poison a life of otherwise useful service. David has not allowed the conspirators to do this to him. He has brought his burdens to God.

2. *Their weapons* (v. 3). Verse 3 describes the weapons his enemies are using, and we find in this case that the weapons are words. These people "sharpen their tongues like swords and aim their words like deadly arrows." This theme has been developed in other psalms in this same section of the Psalter (see Psalms 52, 57–59); in Psalms 57 and 58 David even compared the words of his enemies to arrows shot at him secretly from hiding, as he does here. So we know that this was something David was very much afraid of and unable adequately to counter. That is also true for every one of us, isn't it? Forthright assaults we can sometimes handle. But when a person is talking about us behind our backs, creating suspicions, slandering us, and telling lies, it is almost impossible to deal with what is happening, and the results can be terribly destructive. In politics careers are sometimes ruined by so-called unconfirmed reports or information supplied by "someone close to the source who declines to be identified."

The apostle James had strong words to say about this evil:

Consider what a great forest is set on fire by a small spark. The tongue also is a fire, a world of evil among the parts of the body. It corrupts the whole person, sets the whole course of his life on fire, and is itself set on fire by hell.

All kinds of animals, birds, reptiles and creatures of the sea are being tamed and have been tamed by man, but no man can tame the tongue. It is a restless evil, full of deadly poison (James 3:5–8).

When we think of the evil that can be done by words, it is helpful to remember that although the most effective weapon of the wicked may be words, words are also the chief weapon of the Holy Spirit. The words of the righteous are effective, especially when they are uttered in a Spirit-blessed prayer (James 5:16). The words of God are even more effective.

> As the rain and the snow
>   come down from heaven,
> and do not return to it
>   without watering the earth
> and making it bud and flourish,
>   so that it yields seed for the sower and bread for the eater,
> so is my word that goes out from my mouth:
>   It will not return to me empty,
> but will accomplish what I desire
>   and achieve the purpose for which I sent it
>   (Isa. 55:10–11).

Remember that we are called upon to fight the Lord's battles with the Lord's weapons, not the weapons of the world. The world's weapons are money, power, and influence. Our weapons are the Word of God and prayer. It is said of the warfare of the saints against Satan in Revelation, "They overcame him by the blood of the Lamb and by the word of their testimony" (Rev. 12:11).

3. *Their methods* (v. 4). Verse 4 outlines the methodology of the ones who were conspiring against David. It was secret, sudden warfare: "They shoot from ambush at the innocent man; they shoot at him suddenly, without fear." This is particularly effective against the innocent, just because the innocent person *is* innocent. A guilty person is probably on his guard. The innocent person is not on guard. A sudden surprise attack can overthrow him.

This is the first place in the psalm where the key word *suddenly* occurs. "Strike suddenly when your enemy is least expecting it" is the idea. This has worked well in military campaigns. The Romans were masters of it; Julius Caesar used it effectively in Gaul. These evil persons have discovered that it also works well against innocent people, such as David. Who can protect us from the arrow that is launched by night or from some hidden covert? Only God, who is the psalmist's trust.

4. *Their plans* (v. 5). In verse 5 the word *encourage* is actually a bit stronger than the English word suggests. For this is not a matter of bucking one another up but rather of "strengthening" others with the goal, in this case, of "hardening" those people in their evil purposes. On this verse Charles Haddon Spurgeon wrote wisely, "Good men are frequently discouraged and not unfrequently discourage one another, but the children of darkness are wise in their generation and keep their spirits up, and each one has a cheering word to say to his fellow villain."[2] If the wicked can do that, what is wrong with us? Shouldn't Christians encourage and strengthen one another, rather than attacking one another, as we often do?

The question asked in the last phrase of verse 5, "Who will see them?" is indirect, so that it actually means, "Who will see *us?*" It is referring to the wicked themselves, not to their plots. These people are working secretly and in the dark. They do not think anyone can see them or that their plots can be uncovered. But they have forgotten God, who sees everything. Before him all hearts are open, all desires known.

5. *Their pride* (v. 6). The last thing said about the wicked, in verse 6, is that they think they have "devised a perfect plan." They are proud, even smug in their devisings. They think that nobody is as clever as they are. They look down on the innocent as naive, foolish, even stupid people. But, as we will see, it is actually the wicked who are foolish, because they have forgotten God. Anyone who leaves God out of his or her life or life calculations is a fool, according to the Bible (see Pss. 14:1; 53:1; Rom. 1:21–23).

The last phrase of this section, the last sentence of verse 6, contains the psalmist's comment on the nature of man and the terrible evil that is within him. The Hebrew literally speaks of men's hearts as being "deep," the idea being that they are almost bottomless in their supply of evil deeds and cunning. This is a shrewd comment on human nature—not that people are nice or dependable or generous or any other good quality, though people are capable of kind acts from time to time, but rather that we are all bottomless in our ability to work harm. Surely, as Jeremiah wrote, "The heart is deceitful above all things and beyond cure" (Jer. 17:9). Or as Paul said in Romans,

> "All have turned away,
>   they have together become worthless;
> there is no one who does good,
>   not even one."
> "Their throats are open graves;
>   their tongues practice deceit."
> "The poison of asps is on their lips."
>   "Their mouths are full of cursing and bitterness."
> "Their feet are swift to shed blood;
>   ruin and misery mark their ways,
> and the way of peace they do not know."
>   "There is no fear of God before their eyes" (Rom. 3:12–18).[3]

Derek Kidner captures the thrust of David's summary when he says, "The pointed comment of 6b on human nature . . . is a remark which warns the reader that the deception (and self-deception) which he has just observed may have their counterparts much nearer home."[4]

God's Sudden Intervention

In the last chapter of Paul's letter to the Thessalonians, the apostle writes of the wicked, saying, "While people are saying, 'Peace and safety,' destruction will come on them suddenly, as labor pains on a pregnant woman, and they will not escape" (1 Thess. 5:3). That is what happens in Psalm 64. For five verses the wicked have been hatching their nefarious plots against King David. They have done it secretly, cunningly, and with mutual encouragement. They have reached the point of congratulating themselves on their efforts, saying, "We have devised a perfect plan" and "Who will see us?" But *suddenly,* just when they think they have succeeded brilliantly, God, who has been watching it all from heaven, launches his bolt against them and quickly brings them down. Indeed, they have been in his sights all along, and it does not require a quiver full of arrows to destroy them. One arrow does the job.

If you read this carefully, you may notice that the psalm's structure reflects what the words are saying. There are a lot of verses telling about the laborious, drawn-out plotting of the wicked. They build to a climax. But then destruction comes quickly, in just a verse and a half.

It is hard to read about the sudden destruction of the wicked without thinking of the story of Haman and Mordecai in the Book of Esther. Mordecai was a Jew who worked in the court of Xerxes, the king of Persia. Haman was a high official. Most people deferred to Haman, bowing to him almost as if he were the king. Mordecai would not do this. Therefore, Haman hated him for the perceived affront and plotted to get him killed. Haman did this by a particularly nasty bit of anti-Semitism, telling the king that there was a race of people in the kingdom who did not obey the king's laws and were subversive. He got the king to approve a secret, sudden uprising against the Jews, while he himself prepared a gallows on which he planned to hang his great enemy, Mordecai.

Mordecai had a niece whose name was Esther. Her Jewish ancestry was not known, and she had been taken into the palace where she had won Xerxes' favor and became his queen. Esther was present at this strategic moment, and God used her to alert Xerxes to what was really going on and to expose Haman. Xerxes, Esther, and Haman were at dinner when she did this. She told the king of a person who was plotting to destroy both herself and her family. The king couldn't believe someone would try to kill his queen. "Who is he?" he demanded. "Where is the man who has dared to do such a thing?"

Esther pointed to the man sitting next to her, saying, "The adversary and enemy is this vile Haman" (Esther 7:5–6).

Haman must have been struck with terror like a man turned to stone. He was exposed—suddenly, and there was no escape. The king was furious, and that very day Haman was hanged on the gallows he had prepared for Mordecai. Poetic justice? Yes. But even more important than that: sudden and certain justice, just like that which will come on all who despise God and reject his Son and our Savior, Jesus Christ.

Three Lessons to Be Drawn

The last two and a half verses of the psalm sketch three lessons to be drawn. First, the wicked will be exposed, so that those who are watching from the sidelines will "shake their heads in scorn" (v. 8). Second, people will be directed to "fear" God and "ponder what he has done" (v. 9). This tends to happen when some particularly wicked person or nation is brought down. Third, the righteous will "rejoice in the LORD and take refuge in him" (v. 10). In Psalm 64 the judgment of these evil people is still in the future, but God's people are told to rejoice even now, because the eventual, sudden judgment of the wicked is so certain.

It takes faith to trust God and look ahead to the future destruction of the wicked. But true faith wins that victory.

Psalm 65

All Good Gifts from Our Good God

Praise awaits you, O God, in Zion;
to you our vows will be fulfilled. . . .

You care for the land and water it;
you enrich it abundantly.
The streams of God are filled with water
to provide the people with grain,
for so you have ordained it.
You drench its furrows
and level its ridges;
you soften it with showers
and bless its crops.
You crown the year with your bounty,
and your carts overflow with abundance.
The grasslands of the desert overflow;
the hills are clothed with gladness.
The meadows are covered with flocks
and the valleys are mantled with grain;
they shout for joy and sing.

verses 1, 9–13

Psalm 65 is an extraordinary, exquisite poem about nature. But it is also predominantly about the God of nature, who is gracious to man, powerful in his acts, and the source of all nature's bounty—which is what we would expect of a song written by David, the great poet of Israel.

In his brilliant little study of the Psalms, the English professor and Christian apologist C. S. Lewis has a section on the Jews' appreciation of nature, pointing out that, not having many large cities, hardly any of the ancients, Jew or Gentile, loved or thought of "the country" as we do—that is, as a peaceful place to get away to, in contrast to the hectic life of the town. Pastoral lyrics are written by city people, not farmers. Yet, being close to nature as they were, the Jews, who were largely farmers, knew nature and delighted in it a great deal more than we do. Citing Psalm 65 specifically, he writes, "The psalmists, who are writing neither lyrics nor romances, naturally give us little landscape. What they do give us, far more sensuously and delightedly than anything I have seen in Greek, is the very feel of weather—weather seen with a real countryman's eyes, enjoyed almost as a vegetable might be supposed to enjoy it."[1] Lewis quotes selected verses from Psalm 65:9–14 to illustrate this point.

Another way of speaking about Psalm 65 is as a harvest hymn, a song to be sung when crops were gathered in. We have our harvest hymns too, of course, such as "Come, Ye Thankful People, Come" and "We Plough the Fields and Scatter." These were more popular when people in the West lived closer to the soil. But none of our harvest hymns has the freshness and abounding delight in God's bounty in nature that this ancient composition has.

Derek Kidner says,

> The climax of this psalm, a stanza as fresh and irrepressible as the fertility it describes, puts every harvest hymn to shame as plodding and contrived. Here we almost feel the splash of showers, and sense the springing growth about us. Yet the whole song has this directness, whether it is speaking of God in his temple courts (1–4) or in his vast dominion (5–8) or among the hills and valleys which his very passing wakens into life (9–13).[2]

H. C. Leupold says, "We venture the claim that this is the most eloquent and beautiful description of the blessings that God bestows on field and meadow to be found anywhere in such brief compass."[3]

The Occasion and Outline of the Psalm

This psalm could have been sung in Israel at any time, of course, and probably was. But since it deals with the bounty of a good harvest, it is likely that it was composed for the Jews' annual harvest festival, the Feast of Tabernacles. This was the longest and most joyful feast of the Jews. It began on the fifteenth day of the seventh month, which was observed as a Sabbath, and it continued until the twenty-second day of the month, which was also observed as a Sabbath, for a total of eight days in all. This was after the crops were brought in and the people were celebrating the abundance of the harvest. Part of the celebration consisted in offering the first fruits to God (see Lev. 23:33–43; Num. 29:12–39).

There is another feature of the psalm that would also place it at this time of year. Psalm 65 is one of only three psalms in the Psalter that use the word *atone* or *atonement* (in v. 3, inexplicably rendered "you forgave our transgressions" in recent NIV editions). That it does may be significant in light of the fact that the Day of Atonement occurred almost immediately before the Feast of Tabernacles in the Jewish calendar, on the tenth day of the seventh month. Therefore, the first stanza of the psalm, where the reference to atonement occurs, might be thought of as looking back to that immediately preceding day.

There is little question about how the psalm should be outlined, since virtually all commentators do it the same way. There are three stanzas, just as in the New International Version text: verses 1–4, verses 5–8, and verses 9–13. Derek Kidner titles these three sections: (1) God of Grace, (2) God of Might, and (3) God of Plenty. The emphasis is on the last of these three sections, which is also the longest. The first two stanzas prepare for this final stanza and build to it.

The God of Saving Grace

A psalm as focused on a national Jewish festival as this one might easily have become narrowly nationalistic—that is, a psalm in praise of One who is thought to be the God of Israel only. But however special the relationship between Jehovah and his specially chosen people may be, the God of Israel is nevertheless the God of all other peoples too, and this important balance is maintained in the opening verses. Verse 1 declares that praise awaits God "in Zion"—that is, in Jerusalem, where the great Jewish Feast of Tabernacles was held. But the next verse, verse 2, recognizes that God is a prayer-hearing God "to whom *all* men will come."

This is a right and proper kind of universalism, not a universalism that presupposes the equal truth and validity of all religions but that welcomes all of whatever race who will come to the true God. This is exactly the position Jesus took with the Samaritan woman whose story is told in John 4. When she asked him to compare the religion of the Samaritans with that of the Jews, he replied by saying that the Jewish God was the true God and that he was to be worshiped in Jerusalem, as he had commanded: "You Samaritans worship what you do not know; we worship what we do know, for salvation is from the Jews" (v. 22). That is a "narrow" statement. But at the same time, Jesus welcomed the woman, as well as pointing to a day when people would worship neither in Jerusalem or Samaria but in spirit and truth because of the changes he himself would bring about. "God is spirit, and his worshipers must worship in spirit and in truth," he said (v. 24).

This right kind of universalism is also found in stanza two of Psalm 65 in the words "the hope of all the ends of the earth" (v. 5) and "those living far away fear your wonders" (v. 8). It is worth noting that it is in the three following psalms also (Pss. 66:1, 4, 7, 8; 67:2–5; and 68:32).

How can sinful men and women, Jews as well as Gentiles, come before a God who is holy? How can sinners hope to have their prayers heard or their desires satisfied? The only possible answer is the atonement, God providing a sacrifice by which an innocent victim bears the punishment of those who are actually guilty. Isaiah 59:1–2 explains the problem:

> Surely the arm of the Lord is not too short to save,
>   nor his ear too dull to hear.
> But your iniquities have separated
>   you from your God;
> your sins have hidden his face from you,
>   so that he will not hear.

Sin causes God to cover or hide his face from us. But the sacrifice covers, or atones, for the sin, so that God can deal with us graciously again. The word *atonement (kopher)* actually means "a covering" and refers to the way the blood of the sacrifice was sprinkled on the cover of the ark of the covenant by the Jewish high priest. Since the ark held the two stone tablets of the law, containing the Ten Commandments, which we have broken, the blood covered over those transgressions, shielding our sins from the gaze of the thrice holy God and pointing to the coming, only sufficient sacrifice of the Lord Jesus Christ upon the cross. His sacrifice not only covers our sins but also removes them from us forever.

The word *atonement* is common in Leviticus but, as noted earlier, it is found only three times in the Psalter (Pss. 65:3; 78:38; 79:9).

Perhaps the most striking thing about this psalm's uncommon reference to atonement is that it is described as something God himself does. For it is not the people who make atonement, or even the high priest; it is God. "*You* forgave [actually, atoned for] our transgressions" (v. 3). This is because God is exceedingly gracious, which is what the rest of the psalm will show. Indeed, even the next verse shows it, for it speaks of the one who has been brought near to God by virtue of the atonement now being blessed with every good thing.

> We are filled with the good things of your house,
>   of your holy temple (v. 4).

This verse sets up the rest of the psalm, in which some of these good gifts of God for his people are laid out.

J. J. Stewart Perowne provides an especially well-stated summary of this stanza:

> In Zion God is known, there he is praised and worshiped. He is the hearer of prayer; that is his very character, and therefore all flesh comes to him. All who feel their weakness, all who need help and grace, seek it at his hand. It

is true that they who thus come, come with the burden of sin upon them: their iniquities rise up in all their strength and might, and would thrust them away from the presence of the Holy One. But he himself, in the plenitude of his mercy, covers those iniquities, will not look upon them, and so suffers sinners to approach him. And how blessed are they who, reconciled and pardoned, are thus suffered to draw nigh. Of that blessedness may we ourselves be partakers, may we be filled and satisfied therewith.[4]

Do you know that blessedness? You will never know the God of the abundant blessing of nature (or any other blessing) until you first know him as the one who has made atonement for your sin.

The Mighty God, the Lord

It is one thing to be gracious, as God is. It is quite another and also important thing to be able to help out. In January 1994, a strong earthquake struck southern California. Roadways were destroyed, buildings collapsed, fires erupted. I read of one apartment building where scores of people were trapped and of a man who worked strenuously for hours to free them. He saved the lives of dozens of people, but there was one man he was unable to save, and in the stress of the day this strong, helpful man wept uncontrollably. He wanted to save all the people, but he could not do it.

It is not this way with God. God is gracious, but he is mighty too, as the second stanza of the psalm points out. God's strength is more than equal to any gracious design he may have. In this stanza the psalm mentions three specific displays of God's power: (1) in raising the mountains, (2) in calming the seas, and (3) in quieting the nations.

The high mountains and the turbulent, unpredictable seas are some of the most awesome displays of nature known to man. Before the space age they were probably the most awesome of all. The Alps or Himalayas tower above us in their hard, cold, remote, and frightening grandeur, and the seas change in a moment from a peaceful rolling motion to a mass of unruly, foaming, and potentially deadly billows. Then they quiet down again. Who controls these elements? "God!" cries the Bible. For the Bible traces all effects to God. As H. C. Leupold says of the mountains, "They did not set themselves into place or become firm and immovable, *God* established them, giving proof thereby that he is girded with power." And of the seas, "They never composed themselves; God calmed them."[5]

This is true of planting and harvest too, which is what the psalm is coming to. The hymn by Matthias Claudius (written in 1782 and translated by Jane M. Campbell in 1861) states it well:

> We plough the fields and scatter
> The good seed on the land.
> *But it is fed and watered*

By God's almighty hand;
He sends the snow in winter,
The warmth to swell the grain,
The breezes and the sunshine
And soft refreshing rain. (italics added)

In the Bible the seas are often an image for the turbulent nations of the world, and it is probably mention of the seas that causes David to add, after saying that God "stilled the roaring of the seas" and "their waves," that he also stilled "the turmoil of the nations." This is a way of saying that God is the only real source of world peace—not the cunning of this world's statesmen, not peace treaties, but God. Hence, it is right to pray for peace and to try to live righteously as a people so God will grant it.

Verse 8 says that the report of God's work spreads throughout the earth to all peoples, which calls for songs of joy. Such songs are sung sometimes. But more often human tongues are silent while only speechless nature cries out (see v. 13).

God of a Plenteous Harvest

We come then to the stanza for which the two preceding sections have prepared us. It is about the people's harvest, and it tells us that the God who is gracious to his people and all-powerful in effecting his purposes has shown both his grace and his power in blessing the harvest and the land.

The first thing we read about is God's caring for the land by watering it. Indeed, this is the dominant thought in verses 9–10. Those of us who live in lands that are well watered, sometimes overwatered, can hardly appreciate the value of water in an otherwise barren land, as Canaan is. For people in that place and day, the coming of abundant rains to water the crops was literally the blessing of life rather than death. It is hard for most of us today to fully appreciate that.

Here is a point at which a writer on the psalms should be a farmer or at least have spent some significant time in the country at some period in his or her life. I have not had that privilege. But I remember sitting in a fresh Alpine meadow high in the Swiss Alps in the spring shortly after the passes opened after being closed by the winter snows. Millions of wild mountain flowers were beginning to open their multicolored petals to the sun. What struck me most was the abundance of water. There was water everywhere. Not in rivers or lakes, but in hundreds of tiny, twisting mountain rivulets that literally laced the meadows. It was hard to walk without stepping into water. And being high in the mountains, as I was, and therefore close to the very face of God (as it seemed) it was hard to miss understanding that all this great bounty was from God.

I did not know what Psalm 65 was about at the time. But in those high Alpine meadows I could have well and wisely declared:

> You care for the land and water it;
>> you enrich it abundantly.
> The streams of God are filled with water
>> to provide the people with grain,
>> for so you have ordained it.
> You drench its furrows
>> and level its ridges;
> you soften it with showers
>> and bless its crops (vv. 9–10).

Then there are the crops, which verse 10 also mentions. In the same way, unless you have been a farmer it is hard to appreciate the immense joy and wonder of looking out on fertile fields and watching the rising rows of soybeans, corn, or other grain stretching out beautifully in the sun. Any farmer works. He works hard and long. But it is not the farmer who makes the crops grow. It is God! And for the believing farmer the abundance of God's work in making the fields prosper is a matter for praise.

I remember an experience I had when I was just a boy. I was visiting some friends of my family who had a small farm. It was August, and there was a field of corn that was just ready to be harvested. In fact, we had corn that afternoon, freshly picked from the fields. What I remember most was walking with one of my friends through the many rows of corn. It was another world, a mysterious, wonderful, virile world entirely separate from the predictable, normal world from which we came. It was like diving under the ocean to be with fish or climbing high into the mountains. It sharpened my perception, and I remember being aware of the wonder of what God does in bringing crops to such abundant fruition and giving such great gifts to men.

Shouting for Joy

The last line of the psalm is striking and unexpected. For after having described how God has watered the earth and caused it to bring forth and bud, David suddenly says that the meadows, valleys, flocks, and grain all "shout for joy and sing" (v. 13). It is a poetic fallacy, of course. Meadows and valleys, flocks and grain, do not shout or sing or do anything else that only self-conscious, articulate personalities do. But in their harvest splendor they seem to, as if they had awakened singing after a long, dead winter or a dry summer. Besides, if they could literally cry out, they would do it. After all, Jesus said at the time of his triumphal entry into Jerusalem, when the Pharisees wanted him to rebuke his disciples for their praise, "If they keep quiet, the stones will cry out" (Luke 19:40).

The point is that since inanimate objects cannot literally praise God, we who are made in God's image and can praise God, should!

Psalm 66

A Praise Psalm of Thanksgiving

Shout with joy to God, all the earth!
Sing to the glory of his name;
make his praise glorious!
Say to God, "How awesome are your deeds!
So great is your power
that your enemies cringe before you.
All the earth bows down to you;
they sing praise to you,
they sing praise to your name." Selah
verses 1–4

There is a link between the last verse of Psalm 65 and the first two verses of Psalm 66, which is probably why Psalm 66 is placed where it is in the Psalter. The last verse of Psalm 65 was about the meadows and valleys of the land, and it is said of them that "they shout for joy and sing." The first verses of Psalm 66 call for this same response from the entire earth.

Shout with joy to God, all the earth!
Sing to the glory of his name.

But there is a difference. It is said of the world of nature that it does praise God. It does not need to be urged to do so. Unfortunately, praise from human beings is usually lacking, with the result that you and I need to be told repeatedly to praise God. This psalm tells us to praise and thank God, and it is itself the product of one who is doing just that.

Two Overlapping Movements

There are two overlapping movements in this psalm, and it is useful to note them before looking at it in greater detail. The first movement is from the praise of God on a large scale ("Shout with joy to God, all the earth," v. 1), to the praise of God by the specific nation of Israel ("Praise our God, O peoples," v. 8), to the praise of God by a single individual ("I will come to your temple with burnt offerings and fulfill my vows to you," v. 13). Verses 1–7 complete the first section, verses 8–12 are the second, and verses 13–20 are the third. Derek Kidner notes this and titles the psalm "God of All—of Many—of One."

There is a sense then in which the psalm begins broadly and ends narrowly. What happens can be illustrated by one of the more interesting symphonies of Franz Joseph Haydn: Symphony No. 45 in F sharp minor, known as the "Farewell Symphony." The reason this piece is called the Farewell Symphony is that it begins with the entire orchestra on the platform, but then, as the piece develops, the various sections of the orchestra and its members get up one by one and leave the platform until at the very end only two violinists are left. When the piece was first performed in Vienna in 1772, as each instrumentalist finished his part he blew out a lantern that was at his place to illuminate the music. So, as the musicians left, the lights went out too.

In Psalm 66 the number of participants likewise narrows down—from the whole earth, to the Jewish nation, to the psalmist. But unlike the symphony, which just fades away, the psalm grows in intensity and power as the passion and sincerity of the psalmist break through. In this respect it is a very remarkable composition.

The other overlapping movement is an alternating pattern between praise either given or called for and an invitation to others to "come and see what God has done." First, praise is offered to God from the whole earth (vv. 1–4). Second, an invitation is given to everyone to come see what God has done (vv. 5–7). Third, praise is offered to God by God's elect people (vv. 8–12). Fourth, the psalmist himself comes to offer sacrifices and praise to God (vv. 13–15). Finally, the whole earth is again invited, this time to hear what God has done for the psalmist (vv. 16–20). Thus the last stanza comes back to the theme of the first stanza and the psalm is thereby made complete.

Everybody Praise God

Most Bible students know that later in its history, after the Babylonian captivity, the nation of Israel became religiously exclusive. The masses of Jews looked down on Gentiles, who were thought of as being excluded from any relationship to the true God, and deservedly so. It is somewhat surprising therefore to find many times a considerably broader and inclusive view in the psalms. We are in a little block of such psalms now. Psalms 65–68 each call on all the nations of the world, not just Israel, to praise and worship God.[1]

The call to the earth to praise God in verses 1–7 is a proper kind of universalism, meaning that God is God of the whole earth and that all the peoples of the earth should acknowledge him as God and be thankful. But the fact that the peoples of the earth must be invited to "come and see what God has done" betrays the reality of the situation; although people ought to praise God and be thankful, they actually do not do it (cf. Rom. 1:21). True, they are sometimes awed by the power of God in or over nature, as those who witnessed his deliverance of the Jews from Egypt by turning "the sea into dry land," thus enabling them to pass over "on foot" (v. 6). The people who learned of the overthrow of Jericho and other Jewish victories as part of the conquest of Canaan must have been likewise impressed. They might have said of God, "How awesome are your deeds!" (v. 3). But this does not mean that they bowed down to God or worshiped him.

What happens is illustrated by comments on the earthquake that occurred in southern California early in 1994. By later estimates the California earthquake was the most destructive and costly natural disaster ever to occur in the United States of America. Some thought that might be significant. Noting the closeness of the Los Angeles riots, the destructive brush fires of the previous fall, and the earthquake of the winter, one person observed in an interview on network television, "Maybe God is trying to tell us something." Another person said, "Maybe God doesn't like what is going on in California." These people (and others) were impressed with the power of God displayed in nature and were led to draw God into their thinking and conversation, as they probably had not done before the earthquake. But it does not mean that they repented of personal sin and sought God through faith in Jesus Christ.

It would be difficult to document any significant turning to God in our country as the result of this or any other natural disaster.

Singing, Praise, and Thanksgiving

It is also worth reflecting on what the opening verses of this psalm say about singing, praise, and thanksgiving.

The fact that the peoples of the earth are encouraged to "sing to the glory of his [that is, God's] name" makes us think about the role of music in worship and of the fact that it is natural for Christians to sing. Have you ever thought about that? The world sometimes sings too, of course, but not in the same way or for the same reasons or even very often. Usually the world just listens to singing, which means it is mere entertainment, some of it highbrow like opera, some of it lowbrow like most popular music. A generation or two ago, when people were less "sophisticated" but perhaps had a better time, people sang some of the popular tunes. That was true during the war years, for example, when the songs were mostly morale boosters or patriotic numbers. But today people don't even sing songs like that. In fact, the majority of popular songs are unsingable, except by rock groups (and I am not even sure that they are really singing them). We live in a noisy world, including the noise of contemporary music. But there is little real singing, probably because there is not very much to sing about.

Singing requires a certain amount of emotion. It can flow from sadness or from joy. But when there is joy, singing follows naturally, and that is why Christians have always been a singing people. They can't help but sing praises to God; for he is a great God, he has redeemed them from their sin, and they are looking forward to being with him and seeing him when they die. Moreover, it is natural for them to encourage the world to sing too.

But there is also this. From a Christian perspective singing in worship is not merely to express emotion, as if the focus were on us. On the contrary, the focus is on God, and though there may and should be true emotion, this is because of who God is and because praise is a proper and natural response to him. In other words, the content of our worship, even by music, should not be our experiences, however intense or powerful, but rather God and God's glory. That is why the psalmist says,

> Shout with joy to God, all the earth!
>> Sing to the glory of his name;
>> make his praise glorious!
> Say to God, "How awesome are your deeds!
>> So great is your power
>> that your enemies cringe before you" (vv. 1–3).

And

> Come and see what God has done,
>> how awesome his works in man's behalf! (v. 5).

There is one more matter that is also part of this picture, and that is the interesting balance between the praise of God and thanksgiving. It is true that the psalmist praises God and wants the entire creation to do so too. But so far as he is concerned, a major reason for this is what God has done for him personally. He is thankful for it.

Marvin E. Tate has some thoughts about this combination that can help in guiding us when we worship God:

> The structure of the psalm reminds us that thanksgiving should be set in a theological context larger than that of purely personal concerns. . . . "Thanks" can become a self-centered and even commercialized expression with little of the spontaneity of real praise. Praise requires concentration on the thing, person, or deity being praised. Thanks tend to be focused on what the *speaker has received,* and thus may become rather narrow and perfunctory. In the expression of thanksgiving the self may become the primary subject, but this is much less likely to happen in praise. . . . On the other hand, praise without thanksgiving moves toward a sterile religious experience in which the praise becomes purely ritualistic. Why should anyone sing the praise of God when there is nothing for which to be thankful?[2]

Let the People of God Praise God

This brings us to the second major section of the psalm in which the specific nation of Israel is invited to praise God (vv. 8–12). The world should "shout with joy to God" and "sing to the glory of his name." But it usually does not, simply because it is not aware of the many blessings for which it should be thankful. Even an official Thanksgiving holiday does not make it thankful. It is different for the people of God, since they have come to know God and are aware of the way he has kept them and blessed them even in the most difficult times.

When the author was calling to the Gentile nations, he invited them to see how God had intervened in nature to deliver and preserve his people. But they were invited only to look on from the outside. Israel is on the inside; therefore, the people are invited to praise God for what he has done for them personally. Here the first person plural pronouns are used.

> Praise *our* God, O peoples,
>   let the sound of his praise be heard;
> he has preserved *our* lives
>   and kept *our* feet from slipping.
> For you, O God, tested *us:*
>   you refined *us* like silver.
> You brought *us* into prison
>   and laid burdens on *our* backs.
> You let men ride over *our* heads;
>   *we* went through fire and water,
>   but you brought *us* to a place of abundance (vv. 8–12).

The nations of the world can praise God in a general way for his mighty acts in nature and can be awed by his power in delivering his people. But the people of God can praise him as other people cannot.

For what do they praise him? In the second stanza, where the nations are invited to praise God, the references seem to be to the specific acts of God in delivering the Jews from Egypt and bringing them into the Promised Land. Obviously, these were dynamic interventions the pagan nations could see. In stanza three, where the Jewish people are told to praise God, the references are not specific but are rather poetic expressions that embrace a variety of salvation experiences.[3]

> He has preserved our lives
>   and *kept our feet from slipping.*
> For you, O God, tested us;
>   you *refined us like silver.*
> You *brought us into prison*
>   and *laid burdens on our backs.*
> You *let men ride over our heads;*
>   we went *through fire and water,*
>   but you brought us to a place of abundance
>   (vv. 9–12, italics added).

The reason for this choice of words seems to be that the deliverances of the people of God are too many and too personal to be adequately listed in a single psalm, though later psalms will in fact review the nation's many deliverances in detail. This stanza simply means: You have preserved us at all times and in every situation. The final image, "through fire and water," embraces every extreme, like saying, "come hell or high water" or "from the mountains to the valleys to the oceans white with foam." That is, whatever the time or circumstances, the people of God can say, "[God] has preserved our lives and kept our feet from slipping" (v. 9).

Listen While I Praise God

In the final two stanzas of the psalm (vv. 13–15, 16–20), the joyful tumultuous praise of the nations, including the praise of Israel, fades away and the individual psalmist himself remains standing on the stage. In the quiet of this moment he speaks twice, first to God, then to anyone who might be listening.

1. *The psalmist's words to God* (vv. 13–15). I mentioned earlier that although the participants in the psalm shrink from the many peoples of the world to the single nation of Israel to the individual psalmist, the passion and intensity of the psalm actually grows. That is particularly clear in this stanza, where the psalmist says he is going to bring a variety of sacrifices to God's temple.

He says that these will be "burnt offerings" (v. 13). Burnt offerings were distinguished from fellowship offerings in that they were to be entirely consumed by fire on the altar while only parts of fellowship offerings were consumed. The other parts were eaten by the worshiper and his friends. Fellowship offerings were something like a religious party or even a barbecue held for religious reasons. By its very nature a burnt offering was more serious, signifying something like the complete dedication or consecration of himself to God by the worshiper. The psalmist is saying that what he intends to do is as serious as anything could possibly be.

He also lists the variety of animals he intends to offer, and they are rams, bulls, and goats (v. 15). That is a lot of animals—two of each at least—and they would have been costly. So this is no casual rite that the writer is pursuing. As he says, he was in great trouble, and he cried to God in his trouble, promising such offerings if he should be delivered. He was delivered, and now he intends to pay his vow. Moreover, all this is directed to God himself. Unlike most of us, who make promises easily and then just as easily forget them, the psalmist intends to carry his religious resolutions and devotions through to the end.

2. *The psalmist's testimony* (vv. 16–20). Having spoken to God of what he intends to do, the writer now turns to those who may be looking on and invites them to hear what God has done for him. In other words, he gives a testimony. He tells what God has done, how he heard his prayer and delivered him from trouble. Therefore, he concludes,

> Praise be to God,
>   who has not rejected my prayer
>   or withheld his love from me! (v. 20).

John Bunyan did exactly what the psalmist is doing when he invited people to read his great spiritual biography, *Grace Abounding to the Chief of Sinners*. That classic testimony to God's grace has as its motto or theme sentence verse 16 of this psalm: "Come and hear, all ye that fear God, and I will declare what he hath done for my soul" (KJV).

The psalm ends with a striking, redirected syllogism. Syllogisms have three parts: proposition *a*, proposition *b*, and a conclusion drawn from putting the two initial statements together. Here is an example: (1) All men are mortal; (2) Socrates was a man; (3) therefore, Socrates was mortal. Now notice the psalmist's syllogism. First proposition: "If I had cherished sin in my heart, the Lord would not have listened" (v. 18). That is a sound statement; it is exactly what is also affirmed in Isaiah 59:1–2 ("Surely the arm of the LORD is not too short to save, nor his ear too dull to hear. But your iniquities have separated you from your God; your sins have hidden his face from you, so that he will not hear"). Second proposition: "But God has surely listened and heard my voice in prayer" (v. 19). That is also a sound statement, the proof of which is the psalmist's previous testimony. The very fact that he is present to testify and not dead is the evidence.

But now, what is the expected conclusion? (1) If I had sinned God would not have heard my prayers, but (2) he has heard my prayers. Therefore, what? Obviously: "I have not cherished sin in my heart." Ah, but this is not the psalmist's line of logic. Instead of reverting to himself with what would be a self-serving conclusion to his syllogism, he concludes instead, "Praise be to God, who has not rejected my prayer or withheld his love from me!" In other words, he ends with God and God's grace. Thomas Fuller, one of the earlier commentators on the psalms, noted this twist, saying, "David hath deceived, but not wronged me. I looked that he should have clapped the crown on his own, but he puts it on God's head. I will learn this excellent logic; for I like David's better than Aristotle's syllogisms, and whatever the premises be, I make God's glory the conclusion."[4]

So should we all! For whatever our triumphs may be, they are always by the grace of God and we must always say, "To God alone be glory."

Psalm 67

The Shining Face of God

May God be gracious to us and bless us
  and make his face shine upon us;   Selah
may your ways be known on earth,
  your salvation among all nations.

May the peoples praise you, O God;
  may all the peoples praise you.
May the nations be glad and sing for joy,
  for you rule the peoples justly
  and guide the nations of the earth.   Selah
May the peoples praise you, O God;
  may all the peoples praise you.

Then the land will yield its harvest,
  and God, our God, will bless us.
God will bless us,
  and all the ends of the earth will fear him.
                                        verses 1–7

Some of the Bible's psalms are popu-
lar, so popular that whenever psalms are mentioned they come immediately to mind, like Psalm 23: "The LORD is my shepherd, I shall not be in
want" (v. 1), or Psalm 14: "The fool says in his heart, 'There is no God'"
(v. 1). Psalm 67 is not one of these well-known psalms. Most of the com-

mentators seem to share this opinion since they deal with it in brief compass, a page or two perhaps, usually not more. Martin Luther skips the psalm entirely, even though we have five large volumes of his studies of these important compositions.

There is an exception to this neglectful evaluation, however, and that is the treatment Psalm 67 has received from John R. W. Stott, the well-known author and speaker, and former rector of All Souls Church in London. Stott has selected it along with only thirty-seven other psalms for inclusion in his book of *Favorite Psalms*. Why favorite? I'm sure it is because Psalm 67 is what one commentator calls "a missionary psalm," and John Stott is very concerned with world missions.

Alexander Maclaren, another commentator, wrote, "This psalm is a truly missionary psalm, in its clear anticipation of the universal spread of the knowledge of God, in its firm grasp of the thought that the Church has its blessings in order to the evangelization of the world, and in its intensity of longing that from all the ends of the earth a shout of praise may go up to the God who has sent some rays of his light into them all, and committed to his people the task of carrying a brighter illumination to every land."[1] Charles Haddon Spurgeon struck a similar note when he said of Psalm 67, "The great theme of the psalm is the participation of the Gentiles in the worship of Jehovah."[2]

The structure of the psalm supports this. It has three stanzas (vv. 1–2, 3–5, and 6–7) of which the second (vv. 3–5) is both the longest and the core around which the rest of the psalm is built. It is the "missionary" part.

God's Blessing on Israel

When a section of a psalm begins and ends with a similar verse, phrase, or emphasis, scholars call it *inclusio*. This is a literary device that sets the included subject matter apart and gives it emphasis. We have two such "inclusions" in this psalm, one within another. The second, middle stanza is set apart in this way, and is the clearest example because it begins and ends with the same verse: "May the peoples praise you, O God; may all the peoples praise you" (vv. 3, 5). The less apparent example is the psalm itself, which begins and ends with the prayer that God might bless Israel and that the God of Israel might be known and feared among the Gentiles (vv. 1, 7).

1. *The Aaronic blessing.* The language of verse 1 is drawn from the great Aaronic blessing of Numbers 6. Numbers is an important part of the law God gave Moses to give to the Jewish people during the years of their desert wandering after they left Egypt, and part of it is this blessing. The text says that God told Moses to have Aaron bless the people, saying,

> "The LORD bless you
>   and keep you;
> the LORD make his face shine upon you

and be gracious to you;
the LORD turn his face toward you
and give you peace" (vv. 24–26).

A shining face is the opposite of an angry or scowling face, and a face turned toward someone is the opposite of a face turned away in indifference or disgust. A shining face implies favor, the favor of the one whose face is shining, and it implies the friendliness of warm personal relationships too. So what is meant by this blessing is something more than what we normally think of when we ask God to "bless us." Usually all we mean is that we want God to help us to succeed at something or enable us to make money or give us the job, house, or car we desire. But although such forms of material blessing are not excluded by the Aaronic benediction, they are only part of it—and a lesser part at that. More desirable is that God would himself enter into a gracious personal relationship with his people.

This is what real blessing is, of course. We usually think that God has blessed us if we get to be rich. But Jesus overthrew that narrow, selfish idea of blessing when he asked the crowds pointedly, "What good is it for a man to gain the whole world, yet forfeit his soul?" (Mark 8:36). If spiritual blessing, which is to know God, does not lie at the base of all our blessings, including the possession of material things and of a happy life, then these other blessings are hollow and may even be a dangerous deception and snare. On the other hand, to know God and be favored by God is the greatest blessing anyone can experience either in this life or afterward.

This, then, is the blessing alluded to in the opening sentence of Psalm 67. But it is not the only psalm that does this. The Aaronic benediction found in Numbers 6:22–27 is echoed in several other places, such as Psalms 4:6; 29:11; 31:16; and 80:3, 7, 19. The only significant variation from the original benediction is that in Psalm 67 the speaker identifies himself with those who are to receive the blessing: "Bless us" rather than "Bless you."

2. *Gentile salvation.* The point I have been making, that the shining face of God is to be thought of as God's entering into a personal, gracious relationship with his people, is made abundantly clear in verse 2. For the purpose of the blessing on Israel is that "your ways [may] be known on earth, your salvation among all nations"—that is, that the Gentiles may come to possess the same blessing possessed by Israel, which is to know God. Or to put it in other words, it is that the nations of the world might come to hear and believe the gospel and so be saved.

God's Blessing on the Nations

Yet how are the nations of the world to get to know God? How is this great blessing to be known throughout the earth? This question is raised inescapably by stanza two (vv. 3–5), which is a prayer for God's blessing on the nations parallel to the prayer for his blessing on Israel in stanza one.

This is the longest stanza, as noted earlier; hence it is the one that should receive the most emphasis. It is also set apart in that it opens and closes with an identical verse, the second *inclusio*.

These verses ask that the Gentiles might come to know and praise God, that they might understand his just dealings among the earth's peoples, that they might be informed of his ways. But again I ask, How is this to happen? How are the nations to get to know God?

1. *The power of God in his people.* One way is by their observing God's blessing of his people, which would be the ultimate end of the prayer to God to "bless us," if this is what "blessing us" means. John Stott sees it like this:

> If only Aaron's blessing would come true! If only God's mercy were granted to them! If only God were specially to bless them, and the light of his smile were to be upon them and with them always! Surely then the nations would see for themselves? Then the nations would have visual proof of the existence, activity and grace of God? Then the nations would come to know his way and his salvation, and experience themselves that God rules righteously and leads his people like a shepherd (v. 4).

> The same principle operates today. Non-Christian people are watching us. We claim to know, to love and to follow Jesus Christ. We say that he is our Savior, our Lord, and our Friend. "What difference does he make to these Christians?" the world asks searchingly. "Where is their God?" It may be said without fear of contradiction that the greatest hindrance to evangelism in the world today is the failure of the church to supply evidence in her own life and work of the saving power of God. Rightly may we pray for ourselves that we may have God's blessing and mercy and the light of his countenance—not that we may then monopolize his grace and bask in the sunshine of his favor, but that others may see in us his blessing and his beauty, and be drawn to him through us.[3]

Does your life show forth the presence of God within? Does anyone ever look at you and think, "God certainly makes a difference for that Christian." As one person has pointedly asked, "If being a Christian were a crime, would there be enough evidence to convict you?"

2. *The power of God's Word through his people.* But there is also another answer to the questions I asked earlier (How are the nations of the world to get to know God? How is this great blessing to be known throughout the earth?), and it is clearly that we must tell them. Stott says that a great hindrance to evangelism is the church's failure to give evidence of the power of God in each individual and in her corporate life, and that is surely true. But an equally great problem is our failure simply to do evangelism itself, our failure to tell others about God.

Here I want to go back to the idea of the "priestly" blessing and ask how the blessing of the priest, Aaron or any other, was actually to come to the people. Magically? Mechanically by the laying on of hands, or something of that sort? No. Blessing comes to God's people by someone bringing his Word to them. The Word of God comes to them today by our speaking it to them—that is, instructing them from the Bible. The Old Testament priest dramatized the word of the gospel by performing the sacrifices, but he spoke the Word too.

Here are three important texts.

First, Romans 15:15–16. Paul is writing to the largely Gentile Christians at Rome and is describing his ministry to them, which he calls a "priestly duty." He says, "I have written you quite boldly on some points, as if to remind you of them again, because of the grace God gave me to be a minister of Christ Jesus to the Gentiles with the *priestly duty* of proclaiming the gospel of God, so that the Gentiles might become an offering acceptable to God, sanctified by the Holy Spirit." This is a priestly ministry described in priestly language ("that the Gentiles might become an offering acceptable to God, sanctified by the Holy Spirit"). But it is a ministry accomplished by "proclaiming the gospel of God." In other words, Paul saw himself as a priest. But the way he exercised his priesthood was by evangelism, by teaching others about God.

The second text is Exodus 19:5–6: "Now if you obey me fully and keep my covenant, then out of all nations you will be my treasured possession. Although the whole earth is mine, you will be for me a kingdom of priests and a holy nation." These verses say that in the fullest and most important sense of the word, all God's people are and should be priests. How? Clearly by living for God as God's people and by telling others about him.

The third text is 1 Peter 2:9–10, which is written to the Gentiles but which draws on the verses in Exodus that I have just quoted. Peter tells them, "But you are a chosen people, a royal priesthood, a holy nation, a people belonging to God, that you may declare the praises of him who called you out of darkness into his wonderful light. Once you were not a people, but now you are the people of God; once you had not received mercy, but now you have received mercy." Here Peter is calling not only all believing Jews but also all believing Gentiles God's priests, and he is saying that their function and inescapable duty as priests is to "declare the praises of him who called [them] out of darkness into his wonderful light." That is our calling. As Jesus said in Acts, "You will receive power when the Holy Spirit comes on you; and you will be my witnesses in Jerusalem, and in all Judea and Samaria, and to the ends of the earth" (Acts 1:8).

One of the early commentators whom Charles Haddon Spurgeon quotes in his *Treasury of David* is William Binnie, who speaks of the balance in this psalm between the desire that others might be saved and our responsibility to tell them how. Binnie wrote:

How admirably balanced are the parts of this missionary song! The people of God long to see all the nations participating in their privileges, "visited with God's salvation, and gladdened with the gladness of his nation" (Ps. 106:5). They long to hear all the nationalities giving thanks to the Lord and hallowing his name; to see the face of the whole earth, which sin has darkened so long, smiling with the brightness of a second Eden. This is not a vapid sentiment. The desire is so expressed as to connect with it the thought of duty and responsibility. For how do they expect that the happy times are to be reached? They trust, in the first instance, to the general diffusion of the knowledge of God's way, the spreading abroad of the truth regarding the way of salvation. With a view to that, they cry for a time of quickening from the presence of the Lord, and take encouragement in this prayer from the terms of the divinely-appointed benediction. As if they had said, "Hast thou not commanded the sons of Aaron to put thy name upon us, and to say: The Lord bless thee and keep thee; the Lord cause his face to shine on thee and be gracious to thee? Remember that sure word of thine. God be gracious unto us and bless us, and cause his face to shine upon us. Let us thus be blessed, and we shall in our turn become a blessing. All the families of the earth shall, through us, become acquainted with thy salvation."

Such is the church's expectation. And who shall say it is unreasonable? If the little company of a hundred and twenty disciples who met in the upper chamber at Jerusalem, all of them persons of humble station, and inconspicuous talents, were endued with such power by the baptism of the Holy Ghost, that within three hundred years the paganism of the empire was overthrown, one need not fear to affirm that, in order to the evangelization of the world, nothing more is required than that the churches of Christendom be baptized with a fresh effusion of the same Spirit of power.[4]

Blessings Now and Later

The third and final stanza of this psalm is a bit surprising in one respect, its mention of God causing the land to yield a good harvest (v. 6). Nothing has been said about harvests or any other specific material blessing thus far in the psalm, and we wonder why this seems to be thrown in. The answer is probably that if material blessings are to be thought of at all, the most evident place they can be seen is in an abundant harvest. The desire of the people is that God will bless them there so that the surrounding nations may see how God provides for a people who love him and seek to walk in his ways.

There is a question about how the tense of the verb in verse 5 should be taken. In fact, there are questions about most of the tenses in this psalm. In the main part of the psalm, following verse 1, the verbs are in the Hebrew imperfect tense, which is usually rendered in English as the present tense. However, the imperfect is also used wishfully (called an optative), and most translators understand that and therefore translate these verses as the New International Version does: "*May* your ways be known . . . ," "*May* the peoples praise you . . . ," and "*May* the nations be glad . . ." (vv. 2–5).

So far so good. The problem is that in verse 6 "yield" suddenly appears in the past tense, which is why some Bibles say, "The earth has yielded its produce" (see the New American Standard Bible, for example). Should it be translated as something that has already happened—the Lord has blessed us, therefore, he will bless us (vv. 6–7)? That is possible, but most students of the psalm feel this breaks the pattern of the other verses in which the imperfects are used to express a wish for what the people want to see happen in the future. Therefore, because the past can also sometimes be used of the future (in this case "will have yielded"), more commentators today take verse 6 to be future. This is what the New International Version does: "Then the land will yield its harvest, and God, our God, will bless us."

It is no small matter to look forward to such abundant blessing from our good God. Indeed, the thought of blessings on the land is exactly what is set out in Deuteronomy as the result of faithful obedience by God's people:

> If you fully obey the LORD your God and carefully follow all his commands I give you today, the LORD your God will set you high above all the nations on earth. All these blessings will come upon you and accompany you if you obey the LORD your God:
>
> You will be blessed in the city and blessed in the country.
> The fruit of your womb will be blessed, and the crops of your land and the young of your livestock—the calves of your herds and the lambs of your flocks.
> Your basket and your kneading trough will be blessed.
> You will be blessed when you come in and blessed when you go out (Deut. 28:1–6).

The opposite of such blessing is the list of curses found in the remainder of the chapter. The future blessing of God on our lives and labors for him is a very great thing.

But still, the greatest blessing will be to see God, which takes us back to the beginning of the psalm and its prayer that God might "be gracious to us and bless us and make his face shine upon us." Do you remember the prayer of Moses found in Exodus 33? Moses made three requests in that prayer: first, that God would teach him his way so that he might know him and continue to find favor with him; second, that God would remain with the people and never take his presence from them; and third, that he might look on God's face and see his glory (vv. 12–18). God granted the first two of those requests. He even said, "I will cause all my goodness to pass in front of you, and I will proclaim my name, the LORD, in your presence. I will have mercy on whom I will have mercy, and I will have compassion on whom I will have compassion. But . . . you cannot see my face, for no one may see me and live" (vv. 19–20).

That is profoundly true, of course. No sinner, however devout or pious, as Moses was, can possibly look upon the face of God and survive that holy, piercing sight. But one day we shall! We shall look upon God in the day when all his redeemed people, drawn from every tribe and tongue and nation and purged of even the slightest taint of sin, stand before his throne to sing praises to the almighty God and to the Lamb. In that day God's face will shine upon us in the fullest measure—we will see him "face to face"—and the ultimate beatific vision anticipated by Psalm 67 will be ours. In that day our joy will be even greater because great multitudes from all the nations of the earth will be praising God with us.

Psalm 68

God Who Saves: Part 1

Looking Back

May God arise, may his enemies be scattered;
may his foes flee before him.
As smoke is blown away by the wind,
may you blow them away;
as wax melts before the fire,
may the wicked perish before God.
But may the righteous be glad
and rejoice before God;
may they be happy and joyful.

verses 1–3

Psalm 68 is a song of military triumph. It was the battle song of the French Huguenots. Henry of Navarre was the Protestant champion. On one occasion he and his armies were confined in the fortified town of Dieppe, threatened with destruction by the armies of the Catholic League under the Duc of Mayenne. Fog had rolled in, which kept Henry's artillery from taking aim on the enemy. Reinforcements had failed. The soldiers' courage had been crushed by the overwhelming strength of the enemy. "Come," said the king, "lift the psalm. It is full time."

Thus, above the din of the clashing armies there rose the austere melody of Psalm 68, set to the words of Theodore de Beza (1519–1605).

> Que Dieu se montre seulement,
> Et on verra soudainement
> Abandonner la place
> Le camp des ennemis espars,
> Et ses haineux, de toutes pars,
> Fuir devant sa face.

Pressing onward to the psalm's sound, the men of Dieppe forced through the royalist lines, splitting their forces. The fog cleared, and Henry's cannon fired on the opposing ranks of soldiers, the cannon actually marking the cadence of the psalm. The League was scattered. The year was 1589.

Sixteen years earlier, in 1573, the Protestant stronghold of Rochelle was under royalist attack. Four times the battle lines advanced, and four times they were driven back while the defenders raised their song of triumph from the ramparts: "May God arise, may his enemies be scattered; may his foes flee before him." The siege was raised, and Rochelle was spared.

One night, at the siege of Montauban in August 1621, a Protestant who was serving in the king's army marched under the town's battlements playing the tune of Psalm 68. It was a signal that the siege was soon to be lifted. It happened the next day.

Charlemagne and Oliver Cromwell loved the sixty-eighth psalm.

In 1812, after the French general Napoleon's disastrous retreat from Moscow, a service was held to celebrate the city's deliverance and the Metropolitan of the city preached from Psalm 68:1, "Let God arise, and let his enemies be scattered."

Outline and Historical Setting

In the introduction to the last study I said that very little has been written about Psalm 67. That is not true of Psalm 68. A great deal has been written about this psalm, and there are many theories about it, in part because it contains a large number of verses that are hard to understand.

Psalm 68 has ten stanzas. We will study five in this chapter and five in the next. The psalm has a prologue (vv. 1–6) and an epilogue (vv. 32–35). In between is a central section divided into two parts (vv. 7–18 and 19–31). The song is about God's mighty acts on his people's behalf. Derek Kidner says, "Flanked by the ebullient prologue and epilogue, the two main parts of the psalm celebrate, first, God's victorious march from Egypt, with its culmination at Jerusalem (vv. 7–18), and secondly the power and majesty of his regime seen in the ascendancy of his people and the flow of worshippers and vassals to his footstool (vv. 19–31)."[1]

One feature of the psalm is that it abounds in names for God. Six are explicit: *Yahweh, Yah, Elohim, El, Adonai,* and *Shaddai.* Others are in the form of descriptive words or phrases: him who rides on the clouds (v. 4), a father to the fatherless, a defender of widows (v. 5), the One of Sinai (v. 8), God our Savior (v. 19), the Sovereign LORD (v. 20), my God and King (v. 24), and he who rides the ancient skies above, who thunders with mighty voice (v. 33). Each stanza relates something different about God, progressing from God's mighty acts in the past to the present and eventually even to an anticipation of the future. The psalm's survey of the majestic sweep of God's doings is superb. It is hard to find another psalm to equal it.

If there is a specific event for which the psalm was written and to which it refers, it is probably the occasion of the entrance of the ark into Jerusalem in the time of David, recorded in 2 Samuel 6. The *Commentary on the Psalms* by J. J. Stewart Perowne contains a survey of many other theories about the psalm's origin, but Perowne also gives several cogent reasons for its having been written in David's time.[2] If we take seriously the fact that David is identified as the author, as we should, noting at the same time that the references in the psalm lead up to his historical period but not beyond it, except as prophetic anticipations of the messianic age, then a setting in David's reign when the ark of God was brought to Jerusalem seems reasonable.

The Prologue: "Arise, O Lord"

Just as the opening stanzas of this psalm have a long history extending onward to the time of the wars of religion in France and beyond, so also do they have a history moving backward in time. For the opening line at least has its origin in the ancient cry of the setting out of God's people, found in Numbers 10:25–36.

The setting is the end of the encampment of the Jews at Mount Sinai, where they had received the law and constructed the wilderness tabernacle and its furnishings. The most important item of these furnishings was the ark of the covenant, which was kept out of sight within the Most Holy Place of the tabernacle. It was thought of as the earthly abode of God, and God favored this understanding by descending upon the tabernacle and its ark visibly in the form of the massive Shekinah glory, or cloud, when the structure was first set up. The cloud rose up and moved out ahead of the people when they were being instructed to march forward. It settled down over the tabernacle when they were to stop and camp. Therefore, as Numbers relates,

> Whenever the ark set out, Moses said,

> "Rise up, O LORD!
>   May your enemies be scattered;
>   may your foes flee before you."

Whenever it came to rest, he said,

"Return, O LORD,
to the countless thousands of Israel" (vv. 35–36).

That is a dramatic historical memory, and it is to this that the opening of Psalm 68 refers. Only in Psalm 68 the prayer ("Arise, O Lord") is turned into a historical remembrance or declaration (literally, "God arises"). Yet this is a declaration of faith that is looking to the future because of the past; the New International Version is on the right track when it translates, "May God arise, may his enemies be scattered."

Two things are said of God in this prologue. First, he scatters his enemies, who are the wicked (vv. 1–2). Second, he cares for the weak and the abandoned (vv. 5–6). Specifically, he is "a father to the fatherless, a defender of widows," one who "sets the lonely in families," and who "leads forth the prisoners with singing." This is a revelation of God's character, which is always to uplift the downtrodden and comfort the lonely.

The Virgin Mary understood this about God and may even have deliberately echoed Psalm 68 in her Magnificat (Luke 1). She said of God,

"He has performed mighty deeds with his arm;
he has scattered those who are proud in their inmost thoughts.
He has brought down rulers from their thrones
but has lifted up the humble.
He has filled the hungry with good things" (vv. 51–53).

The kings and other rulers of this world do not act like this. They surround themselves with the noblest and richest of their lands, those who can enhance their glory and strengthen their power. The highest glory of God is that he cares for the miserable and surrounds himself with them. Therefore, the righteous must be glad and praise him. They do at the end of stanza one (v. 3) and at the start of stanza two (v. 4).

The March: Setting Out from Sinai

The words that begin the third stanza (vv. 7–10), the first of the main body of the psalm, pick up directly from the prologue, for the cry "Arise, O God" was raised when the people finally set out from Sinai on the march to Canaan, which is what these verses describe. There is a jumble of images here, poetically compacted: the shaking of the earth, which was associated with the theophany at Sinai (Exod. 19:18–19; see Heb. 12:26); rain, perhaps that which defeated Sisera (see the Song of Deborah, Judges 5:4); and showers of blessing, which were part of God's provision for the poor (vv. 9–10). This image reminds us of Psalm 65:9–13 and ties stanza three to stanza two.

The March: Victory over the Kings

The fourth stanza (vv. 11–14) relates to the conquest of Canaan. Once again we have a fast-moving mixture of images: kings and armies fleeing (vv. 12, 14); Jewish armies dividing the plunder (v. 12); and the ease of the conquest, like snow falling gently on the land (v. 14).

Verse 13 is the first of several verses that are extremely puzzling. Whatever does "the wings of [God's] dove . . . sheathed with silver" mean? And what is the context of "while you sleep among the campfires"? Derek Kidner lists a number of possibilities: Israel basking in prosperity, the enemy in flight, the glory of the Lord revealed in battle, a particular trophy seized from the enemy, even, "the women of 12b preening themselves in their new finery."[3] It is probably best to confess simply that we do not know what this means. Someday we may, but in the meantime, we can be sure that its meaning was known to those for whom the psalm was first written.

Verse 11 has taken on importance in the church far beyond its original context in the psalm. In the original setting the verse probably referred to God's promise to Israel of victory on some specific occasion, followed by the spreading of reports of that victory by the Jewish women. Perowne says, "The deliverance of Israel from Pharaoh's host, the overthrow of Sisera, and David's victory over Goliath were all thus celebrated."[4] However, the verse has been picked up by the church as the announcement of the Christian gospel and referred to the commission Jesus gave his disciples to spread the gospel to every corner of the globe.

Charles Haddon Spurgeon has some helpful notes on this verse. For example, he quotes William Bridge, who observes that in the Hebrew text the word that our versions translate "company" is actually "army" ("host"); so it reads, "great was the army of preachers." This leads him to say, "An army of preachers is a great matter; nay, it is a great matter to have seven or eight good preachers in a great army; but to have a whole army of preachers, that is glorious."[5] Spurgeon also quotes William Strong, who said, "The Lord did give his word at his ascension, and there were a multitude of them that published it, and by this means kings of armies were put to flight: they conquered by the word."[6] Spurgeon himself wrote, "O for the like zeal in the church today that, when the gospel is published, both men and women might eagerly spread the glad tidings of great joy."[7]

The problem today is that zeal like this does not seem to exist, except in a very few people, and those are not always well equipped to teach the gospel. And where is the army of preachers? There are many pulpiteers, but those who proclaim the Word of the Lord are few indeed. May God raise them up and thus begin a new work of reforming grace in our time!

The March: Arriving at Mount Zion

The picture of snow falling gently on Mount Zalmon in verse 14, whatever it may mean literally, leads naturally to a description of the high, rugged mountains of Bashan at the start of stanza five. The peaks of Mount Hermon on the northern fringe of the Bashan range are nine thousand feet above sea level and can be thought of as a worthy counterpart to Zalmon, which is also high. But what about Mount Zion, which David chose as the site of his capital and where the ark of God was to rest? Compared with the majestic, rugged mountains of Bashan, Zion is unimpressive, rising only a few hundred feet above the surrounding valley floors. Judging by appearances, Zion should stand in awe of Bashan. But inverting the picture, the psalmist imagines the higher mountains envying small Zion, since Zion is "the mountain where God chooses to reign, where the LORD himself will dwell forever" (v. 16).

This fifth stanza is the longest in the psalm, which is a way of showing that these verses are the high point of the composition and the climax of the poem's first half. Several points are particularly worth noting.

1. *God's choice of small things.* There is an important biblical principle here, which is that God is not impressed by greatness, as we think of it, but rather chooses the weak and lowly things of this world as vehicles for his great acts in order that the glory for what is accomplished might go to himself. We have already had a taste of this principle in the prologue, where God was introduced as the champion of the weak. We noted it in Mary's Magnificat, which speaks of God lifting up the humble and filling the hungry with good things. It is not alien to the spirit of these verses to remember also that David, the author, was of a lowly family and was additionally the youngest and therefore least prominent of Jesse's eight sons. Yet God chose him to be king of Israel. Indeed, he became the greatest of all Israel's kings.

Here is how Paul puts it in 1 Corinthians:

> Brothers, think of what you were when you were called. Not many of you were wise by human standards; not many were influential; not many were of noble birth. But God chose the foolish things of the world to shame the wise; God chose the weak things of the world to shame the strong. He chose the lowly things of this world and the despised things—and the things that are not—to nullify the things that are, so that no one may boast before him. It is because of him that you are in Christ Jesus, who has become for us wisdom from God—that is, our righteousness, holiness and redemption. Therefore, as it is written: "Let him who boasts boast in the Lord" (1 Cor. 1:26–31).

If you think of yourself as being poor, weak, or unimportant, do not consider that as a handicap or disadvantage but instead as an opportunity for God to show his power in you. God has said, "I am the LORD; that is my name! I will not give my glory to another" (Isa. 42:8). If you try to take

God's glory to yourself, you will become merely a resounding gong or a clanging cymbal. But if you are content to be nothing, which you truly are, then God will show himself to be everything in you.

2. *The entrance of God into his sanctuary.* If stanza five is the high point of the psalm and the climax of the psalm's first half, then verse 17 is certainly the climax of the climax. It describes the entrance of God into his sanctuary.

> The chariots of God are tens of thousands
> and thousands of thousands;
> the Lord has come from Sinai into his sanctuary.

This is pretty exalted language, suggesting more than a merely human event or procession. The "thousands of thousands" of God's chariots sound more like legions of angels than merely human armies (see 2 Kings 6:17). But if this is a psalm written on the occasion of the bringing of the ark of the covenant up to Jerusalem in the time of David, then it is right to think of it as the culmination of the journey that began at Sinai hundreds of years before. It is because this was so important, so eternally significant, that it is lifted to such cosmic standards. David had been told that God would not abandon either him or his descendants and that he would indeed dwell in Zion forever (v. 16). If this was to be accomplished, it would have to be by superhuman power, by the force of the heavenly hosts, which were the true defenders of the precarious Jewish kingdom.

3. *Paul's use of verse 18.* One of the most fascinating things about Psalm 68 is the way the apostle Paul used verse 18 in his letter to the Ephesians. He referred it to Jesus Christ, saying in the well-known fourth chapter of that letter,

> But to each one of us grace has been given as Christ apportioned it. This is why it says:
>
> > "When he ascended on high,
> > he led captives in his train
> > and gave gifts to men" (vv. 7–8).

It is not so strange that Paul would take a verse that in the Old Testament refers to the arrival of the ark of the covenant at Mount Zion and refer it to Jesus who, in a similar way, ascended to the heavenly tabernacle after his resurrection to reign over the church. What is puzzling is that in the psalm God is described as *receiving* gifts from men, even from people who have been rebellious, while in Ephesians Paul describes Jesus *dispensing* gifts to men. It seems to be a wrong or at least an unjustified twisting of the Old Testament quotation.

Some commentators have suggested that Paul just boldly altered the text for his own purposes, but it is hard to be satisfied with that since there was no compelling reason for him to quote the psalm at all. The point in

Ephesians does not depend on it. The solution may be in the image itself; a victorious king would both receive gifts and dispense them, particularly dispensing the spoils of his conquest. The solution may also be in the meaning of the Hebrew word translated "received," since it can also be rendered "brought." This is supported by the fact that two ancient versions of Psalm 68, the Aramaic and Syriac, translate the Hebrew word as "gave." So whatever Paul was intending in Ephesians, his view was not a novel but an established interpretation.

The point, of course, is that what is so beautifully described in the psalm has its ultimate fulfillment in the work of Jesus Christ, for which all the Old Testament pictures are but prophecies. It is he who has delivered us from slavery to sin and brought us from Sinai to Mount Zion, where we are to dwell forever. May Jesus Christ be praised!

Psalm 68

God Who Saves: Part 2

Looking Forward

Summon your power, O God;
show us your strength, O God, as you have done before.
Because of your temple at Jerusalem
kings will bring you gifts.
Rebuke the beast among the reeds,
the herd of bulls among the calves of the nations.
Humbled, may it bring bars of silver.
Scatter the nations who delight in war.
Envoys will come from Egypt;
Cush will submit herself to God.

verses 28–31

Is Psalm 68 messianic? Early writers, such as Saint Augustine and even Martin Luther, call all the psalms messianic. Augustine did it to such an excessive degree that I find his work almost useless for my own studies. But even more modern writers do the

same thing. The great Bible scholar and teacher Arno C. Gaebelein considered most of the psalms to refer to Christ or to a future day of messianic blessing for the people of Israel. Bible teacher William L. Pettingill
was more particular. He spoke of only fourteen psalms as messianic. But
he included Psalm 68 as one of them in a little book titled *Christ in the
Psalms*,[1] judging it to be about Jesus on the basis of Paul's use of verse 18
as referring to Jesus in Ephesians 4:8.

If the criterion for a messianic psalm is that a verse or portion of it
should be explicitly used of Jesus Christ in the New Testament, then there
are indeed fourteen messianic psalms.[2] But, of course, other psalms also
contain less obvious messianic or prophetic themes.

So what about Psalm 68? We have already seen that the theme of the
psalm is God's victorious march from Egypt to Jerusalem, with its culmination in the entrance of the ark of the covenant into the holy city (vv. 7–18),
and then the power and majesty of the divine regime seen in the ascendancy of his people and the flow of worshipers and vassals to his footstool
(vv. 19–31). This means that at least the first half is not explicitly messianic.
But to our surprise, it is in the first half that the most explicit reference to
Jesus Christ occurs, in verse 18, which Paul cites in Ephesians.

Perhaps that is the answer. Perhaps there is a turning point here. It is
true that much of what follows can be explained well by the reign of God in
Zion in David's time. But the psalm also looks beyond David's time to a day
of future blessing, and that certainly has to do with the kingdom of the
Lord Jesus Christ.

It is not inappropriate that Psalm 68 is assigned to Whitsunday in the
Anglican Prayer Book, thereby associating it with the dispensing of the Holy
Spirit, by whom Christ's gifts are given to individual members of the church.

Salvation Now and to Come

A major shift in Psalm 68 occurs at verse 19, marked by the word *daily*.
Up to this point the psalm has looked back to what God has done for Israel
in the past, in history. At this point it begins to praise God for being the
same in the present as he has been in the past, and that basic shift causes
the writer to look ahead in time to what God will yet do.

Following up on the first half of the psalm, the people of God are now
established in Zion, David is king, and the ark is in God's sanctuary. What
are they to do now? The answer is twofold.

1. *They are to praise God.* They were told to do this earlier, in the prologue
(vv. 3–4), but nothing was said about praising God during the historical
recap of God's progress from Sinai to Jerusalem (vv. 7–18). That follows naturally only after their victories are past and the kingdom is settled on a firm
foundation. From this point on we find praise of God more often. It is in
the procession section in verses 24–27. It comes to a peak in verses 32–35. It
is the note on which the psalm ends: "Praise be to God!" (v. 35). This is the

way our relationship to God goes. God acts, his acts result in his people's salvation, and they praise him for it.

Have God's saving acts in Christ resulted in your salvation? Then it is the most natural thing in the world for you to praise him for that, as the psalmist does. He sets the pattern.

2. *They are to continue to trust God.* The second thing the people are to do is trust God. Because he has shown himself to be "God [their] Savior," they are to trust him to bear their daily burdens. Because he is "a God who saves," they are to trust him even as they come face to face with death. The last reference could mean only that God will deliver his people from death in battle, especially since the next stanza begins to speak about battles. But it is probably wrong to limit it to that if only because the psalm is moving from the past through the present to the future. God may indeed save his people in the day of battle, but death comes anyway in time. What are they to expect of God then? Will death be the end? Will God abandon them? Not at all! "God is a God who saves" is in a continuous present tense. God has saved in the past. He saves today. Therefore, he can be expected to save in the future (and forever) also.

"Salvation comes from the LORD" (Jonah 2:9). That is the theme of the Bible. But we must remember that it is not a philosophical statement but a confident hope of present and future blessing founded on the character of God, who has acted for us savingly in the past. It is because God has saved that we believe he does and will. It is because of Jesus that we have a steadfast hope of eternal life.

Salvation to Come: Future Victories

The seventh stanza (vv. 21–23) deals with the people's future victories. It is the place where the verbs of the psalm turn from past or present tenses to the future. But the victories described are set down in such bloodthirsty language that more than one commentator has been troubled by it. How shall we reply? If "plung[ing] your feet in the blood of your foes, while the tongues of your dogs have their share" is to be referred only to a routine historical victory by Israel over one of her surrounding hostile foes, we may reply that in that case the words do indeed seem bloodthirsty, and the claim that theirs was a more violent, less sophisticated age than ours does not help much. On the other hand, if this is a messianic reference, if we are to think not of Israel's enemies primarily but of God's enemies, then it is appropriate to think of such a complete destruction and rejoice in it.

A proper comparison reference might be the rejoicing of the righteous at the fall of Babylon, described in Revelation 18–19. Babylon represents the whole of the secular world system with all its evil, sin, extortions, excess, greed, debauchery, and godlessness. When it falls the kings of the earth and the world's merchants, who profited from Babylon, cry, "Woe!" That is the theme of chapter 18. But in chapter 19 in heaven the righteous, who seek God's glory above all and deplore the world's evil, rejoice, shouting,

> Hallelujah!
> Salvation and glory and power belong to our God;
>> for true and just are his judgments.
> He has condemned the great prostitute
>> who corrupted the earth by her adulteries.
> He has avenged on her the blood of his servants (vv. 1–2).

And again, in one of my favorite Bible statements:

> Hallelujah!
> The smoke from her goes up for ever and ever (v. 3).

It would be wrong for us to rejoice over the fall of anyone like that in this life, because we are sinful ourselves and this is still the day of God's grace. But it will not be inappropriate in heaven. In heaven we will glory in righteousness and rejoice at the punishment of evil.

The reference to God's people being brought from Bashan and from the depths of the sea in verse 22 is probably to be explained by a passage like Amos 9:1–3, which describes God fetching people to judgment from the most remote and even inaccessible places. It may be that the psalm verses should be read as the older versions have them, referring to sinners being brought to judgment and not to the righteous wallowing in their enemies' blood. Amos wrote,

> Not one will get away,
>> none will escape.
> Though they dig down to the depths of the grave,
>> from there my hand will take them.
> Though they climb up to the heavens,
>> from there I will bring them down.
> Though they hide themselves on the top of Carmel,
>> there I will hunt them down and seize them.
> Though they hide from me at the bottom of the sea,
>> there I will command the serpent to bite them.

Certainly there will be no avoiding God by anyone on the day of his certain and most just judgment.

Salvation to Come: Procession of the Tribes

The eighth stanza of Psalm 68 (vv. 24–27) describes a procession that is making its way up the steep rising pathways to Jerusalem and its sanctuary. If the psalm was written on the occasion of David's bringing the ark of the covenant to Jerusalem, then it is a fuller description of what is recorded less poetically in 2 Samuel 6:5 and 1 Chronicles 13:8 and 15:16–28. The first passage says, "David and the whole house of Israel were celebrating with all their might before the LORD, with songs and with harps, lyres, tambourines, sistrums and cymbals." The second text is like it but has "trumpets" instead of "sistrums" (whatever that is; the meaning is unclear). The third text mentions the instruments the others do, but in addition it tells of the appointment of singers from among the Levites. It records their names.

No one is sure why the four tribes mentioned in verse 27 are singled out: Benjamin, Judah, Zebulun, and Naphtali. But they are probably chosen representatively, two from the south (Benjamin and Judah) and two from the north (Zebulun and Naphtali). Benjamin is called the "ruler" (the one "leading them," NIV) because Saul, the first king, was a Benjamite.

Salvation to Come: The Messianic Age

The final stanza of this middle portion of the psalm, stanza nine (vv. 28–31, before the epilogue, which is stanza ten), is another climax, much as stanza five was a climax to part one. It describes the gathering of the people and nations of the world to God's city. There are two things to note about these verses.

1. *All the nations will come.* The psalmist was unable to list all the nations of the world by name, of course, not even the limited number of nations that would have been known to him. But he mentions a few by name and suggests others by poetic language. The specific nations mentioned are Egypt, Israel's great neighbor to the southwest, and Cush (or Ethiopia), which was probably the most remote nation known to Israel. It lay to the far south at the uppermost reaches of the Nile. The "beast among the reeds" must be either a crocodile or a hippopotamus, and in that case it is probably a way of referring to Egypt, especially since Egypt is mentioned specifically in verse 31. The "herd of bulls among the calves of the nations" (v. 30) would then probably refer to lesser nations. But this is another verse whose meaning has divided commentators.

This is the point at which Psalm 68 develops what I have called a right kind of biblical universalism, thus falling in line with what we have seen in Psalms 65–67, immediately before this. There is no discrimination among the nations. All may come to Zion. In fact, all or representatives of all will come, according to this prophecy. It is nevertheless to the God of Israel, the true God, and not to some other god (their own gods, for example) that they must and will come.

The gathering of the pagan nations to worship God in Jerusalem is an important theme in the prophets, particularly the later prophets. Derek Kidner notes rightly that this theme is developed with great beauty, power, and fullness in Isaiah 60, saying, "Its initial fulfillment is by now a matter of history, as a spiritual rather than political conquest, in the Gentile influx into the Kingdom."[3] Isaiah describes nations coming to Israel's light and kings to the brightness of her dawn, obvious references to the day when the glory of God will shine out fully from Zion. He mentions many far-flung nations by name. According to some interpretations of prophecy—I think this way myself—Isaiah's chapter as well as stanza nine of Psalm 68 probably refer to a time still in the future when Jesus will actually reign on earth, the millennium, though there is certainly a kind of fulfillment now through Christians' obedience to the Great Commission and the resulting advance of worldwide Christianity.

2. *It is the power of God that will draw them.* However we take this reference—either to the gathering of the nations through the proclamation of the Christian message today or to a future day when Jesus will reign on the earth—it is the power of God alone that will draw the people: "Summon your power, O God; show us your strength, O God, as you have done before" (v. 28).

This is sound Bible theology. "No one can come to me unless the Father who sent me draws him," said Jesus (John 6:44). And "You did not choose me, but I chose you" (John 15:16). Do you believe that? Do you believe that salvation is by the power and grace of God alone? If we really did believe it, we would pray for God's power to be seen in our evangelism much more than we do. In fact, we would pray exactly as the psalmist does here, saying something like, "Summon your power, O God; show us your strength, O God, as you have done before." God has worked powerfully before—in the very early church, at the time of the Reformation, and in some phases of the modern missionary movement. Why not again? Why not now?

Epilogue: "Praise Be to God!"

We come, then, to the final stanza, the epilogue, in which the kingdoms of the earth are called upon to praise God (vv. 32–35).

> Sing to God, O kingdoms of the earth,
>   sing praise to the Lord,   *Selah*
> to him who rides the ancient skies above,
>   who thunders with mighty voice.
> Proclaim the power of God,
>   whose majesty is over Israel,
>   whose power is in the skies.
> You are awesome, O God, in your sanctuary;
>   the God of Israel gives power and strength to his people.

Here it is worth thinking back to the prologue where the psalm began. The prologue was uniquely Israel's, harking back to the days at Sinai and to God's going before the advancing hosts of Israel in the glory of the Shekinah cloud. No other nation has ever had an experience of God and his glory that was like that. But now, in the epilogue, the praise of God that was once Israel's alone has become universal ("Sing to God, O kingdoms of the earth"), reflecting the movement of the psalm from Sinai to Jerusalem and on to the messianic age. Nevertheless, God is still "the God of Israel." Jehovah remains the one, only, and true God. He alone is to be worshiped.

Keep Pressing On

At the beginning of the previous study, I wrote that Psalm 68 is a song of military triumph, and I illustrated this by the way the Huguenots used it and by how it was popular with Charlemagne, Oliver Cromwell, and other strong military figures who were Christians. It is easy to understand how Psalm 68 appealed to them. They were responsible for fighting people they considered to be God's enemies, and the idea of God rising up to scatter his enemies and defeat his foes was the very thing they desired and for which they prayed. If we had been in their shoes, we would probably have used the psalm as they did.

But I cannot help observing, having studied the psalm, that in the final analysis none of those military efforts was an unqualified success, at least in the long haul. It is true that Henry of Navarre won several major campaigns and that the Huguenots were able to defend themselves for many years. But eventually the Edict of Nantes was revoked, thousands of French Protestant Christians were murdered, and the rest were driven into exile to the benefit of other nations such as England, Holland, and the United States, to the impoverishment of France.

Charlemagne had some success reviving the so-called Roman Empire. But his empire was in no way an equivalent of the ancient Roman Empire. And although he had famous victories over the Moors, who were regarded as the ruthless enemies of Christianity, in a short while these very Moors swept across North Africa, over the Near East, and into Europe. Even the Crusades, for all their great effort and piety, were unable to defeat them utterly or completely drive them out.

And Cromwell? He was an unusual leader, and some would regard the era of Puritan ascendancy as a great thing. But even if it was a good thing, it was only a short while after Cromwell's death that England turned from its immediate Puritan past, brought Charles II back from exile, and reinstated the monarchy.

None of this is meant to lessen any appreciation of any of the victories or accomplishments of any of these leaders. But it does remind us that the goal of the church of God in this age is not military triumphs, however noble or highly motivated they may be, any more than its methodology is to be the world's methodology. Our commission is to preach the gospel of salvation by the grace of God through faith in Jesus Christ throughout the whole world and leave the conquest of the world to Jesus. This is because he alone is King. Indeed he is the King of kings and Lord of lords (Rev. 19:16).

He is in complete control of all things. He will reign in power. All nations will come to him, and before him every knee will bow,

> in heaven and on earth and under the earth,
> and every tongue confess that Jesus Christ is Lord,
> to the glory of God the Father (Phil. 2:10–11).

What should be our response to that? Obedience, of course. Jesus is our king too, and kings require obedience. But how about praise? Psalm 68 is a praise psalm among other things, and this is even how it ends: "Praise be to God!" So let us praise him, even if others do not do so yet. Let us remember that even though we may suffer discouragements now and sometimes be defeated, we can still press on in steady faith, knowing that Jesus is on the throne and that everyone will eventually bow before him. And let us be encouraged by remembering that we will reign with him in that day.

Psalm 69

Man of Sorrows: Part 1

A Plea for Help in Suffering

Save me, O God,
  for the waters have come up to my neck.
I sink in the miry depths,
  where there is no foothold.
I have come into the deep waters;
  the floods engulf me.
I am worn out calling for help;
  my throat is parched.
My eyes fail,
  looking for my God.
Those who hate me without reason
  outnumber the hairs of my head;
many are my enemies without cause,
  those who seek to destroy me.
I am forced to restore
  what I did not steal.

verses 1–4

Toward the end of our study of Psalm 68, I said that it is not easy to discern whether the psalm is messianic. In some ways it is messianic; in some ways it is not. There is no difficulty answering that question about Psalm 69, because it is clearly about Jesus. In fact, it is one of the most obviously messianic psalms in the psalter. This is why, for instance, next to Psalms 22 and 110, it is the psalm most frequently cited in the New Testament. Seven of its thirty-six verses are directly quoted, and others furnish themes relating to Christ's work that are expanded in the Gospels.

Arno C. Gaebelein captures something of this flavor when he says of Psalm 69, "What a precious psalm it is! It begins with the cry of the one who bore our sins in his body, who suffered for our sake. It ends with the glorious results of his atoning work."[1]

The Original Setting

The setting of Psalm 69 is the condition of a hurting man who is asking God for help against his many troubles and foes. We must note this, because some of the psalm's expressions fit this original situation and do not relate to Jesus, even though the psalm is messianic. Verse 5 is an example.

> You know my folly, O God;
>   my guilt is not hidden from you.

Obviously, that cannot have been said or thought by Jesus Christ.

Psalm 69 is identified as a psalm of David. Can it be, especially in light of verse 35, which speaks of rebuilding the cities of Judah? That sounds like something written after the destruction of the cities of Judah by Nebuchadnezzar and his armies. Recognizing this problem, a number of commentators assign the psalm to Jeremiah, but this is only a calculated guess based on the time at which Jeremiah wrote and perhaps because he had been put into a cistern, since the author of the psalm begins by saying that "the waters have come up to [his] neck" and that he is sinking "in the miry depths where there is no foothold" (vv. 2–3).

If the psalm is by David, the ending was probably added to relate it to a later historical situation. But there is nothing strange about that. It only shows that the psalm touches on common human experiences and relates to any people and any time.

The way to study the psalm is to keep three important and overlapping reference points in mind: (1) David's situation (or that of another ancient Jewish writer), (2) the person and work of Jesus Christ, and (3) our own experiences and problems. When we think of David we will remind ourselves of how difficult life must have been for him, even though he was the powerful and esteemed king of Israel. When we think of Jesus we will try to enter into his genuine humanity and realize more fully what he endured from sinful human beings for our sakes. When we think of ourselves and our experiences we will be encouraged to endure and carry on faithfully for God, looking to Jesus as our great enabling example.

We will remember how the author of Hebrews said,

Let us fix our eyes on Jesus, the author and perfecter of our faith, who for the joy set before him endured the cross, scorning its shame, and sat down at the right hand of the throne of God. Consider him who endured such opposition from sinful men, so that you will not grow weary and lose heart.

In your struggle against sin, you have not yet resisted to the point of shedding your blood (Heb. 12:2–4).

A Lament and a Plea for Help

The tone of the psalm is set in the first four verses, which are at the same time both a lament about the psalmist's sad plight and a plea to God to help him. The psalm is a classic lament.

I am sure you have felt like the psalmist—overwhelmed. We often feel overwhelmed with problems we cannot seem to solve, pressures we don't see how we can sustain, and demands on us and our time we know we cannot meet. Then, in addition, we feel that we are at the end of our ability even to pray, to petition, to plead, to place our hurts and needs before God. The psalmist relates to us at this point, because he uses powerful images that vividly describe how he was feeling. I have already mentioned how he talks about being in waters up to his neck and stuck in the mire where he cannot gain a foothold. In a similar way, we too speak of drowning in deep troubles or being stuck somewhere and being unable to get out.

Two things seem to make this pain particularly intense for the psalmist. First, he has not given his enemies cause to bring these evils on him. They hate him "without reason" and oppose him "without cause" (v. 4). Second, he has been pleading with God for help and God has not answered (v. 3). Have you ever gone through times like that? If so, remember this: Although the psalmist was worn out with calling on God, he did not stop calling. He continued to pray. This psalm is proof of it.

Let's recall here that we need to study this psalm on three levels: (1) what it meant to David in his situation, (2) what it tells us about Jesus and his suffering, and (3) what it ought to mean to us. We have begun to explore points one and three. What about point two? What does the psalm tell us about Jesus and his suffering?

The first question we might ask along these lines is whether Jesus could have prayed like this. The answer is, Of course. Not only could he have prayed like this, he did. He prayed like this in the Garden of Gethsemane at least, and perhaps on other occasions. In John 15:25 Jesus quotes verse 4 of himself, saying, "This is to fulfill what is written in their Law: 'They hated me without reason.'"

The best commentary on verses 1–4 in terms of Jesus' earthly experience is Hebrews 5:7–10:

During the days of Jesus' life on earth, he offered up prayers and petitions with loud cries and tears to the one who could save him from death, and he was heard because of his reverent submission. Although he was a son, he learned obedience from what he suffered and, once made perfect, he became the source of eternal salvation for all who obey him and was designated by God to be high priest in the order of Melchizedek.

These verses tell us that in his humanity Jesus was not exempt from those feelings of being almost overwhelmed that sometimes overtake us. But Jesus prayed, was heard by the Father, and grew in the knowledge of God's ways and in obedience as a result of his suffering. Obviously that is to be our pattern. When we feel overwhelmed we must pray and trust God to keep and teach us too.

A Brief Confession of Sin

The next verse is one that could not have been spoken by Jesus.[2] It is the psalmist's brief confession of folly, guilt, or transgression (v. 5). In itself this is not surprising. We should all constantly confess our sins to God. What is surprising is that this is not what we would expect at this point of the psalm. We would expect to find a protest of innocence on the psalmist's part, because he has just said,

> Those who hate me without reason
>   outnumber the hairs of my head;
> many are my enemies without cause,
>   those who seek to destroy me.
> I am forced to restore
>   what I did not steal (v. 4).

We would expect him to say, "And you know, God, that I really did not steal it, regardless of what they say." Or "Really, I didn't give them any reason to hate me." Instead we find David acknowledging his foolishness and guilt (transgressions). This is a real inversion, but it is the kind of thing we learn to expect from the godly. As much as they can, they live without blame before other men and women. But they nevertheless know their lack of wisdom and acknowledge their deep guilt before God. In fact, it is their profound awareness of their guilt before God that keeps them close to God and causes them to lead morally upright lives.

A First Renewal of the Lament

Each of the psalms has its own unique outline, and the unique pattern of this psalm is to repeat, first the lament introduced in verses 1–4 and then the appeal for help introduced in the same verses. Thus, we have a first renewal of the lament in verses 6–12, a first renewal of the plea for help in verses 13–18, a second renewal of the lament in verses 19–21, and a second renewal of the plea in verses 22–28. This is followed at the end by a one-verse interjection similar to that in verse 5, in verse 29, and a two-part conclusion in verses 30–36.

Verses 6–12 contain the first renewal of the lament. Yet they go beyond what was said in the first stanza, as each of the repetitions also goes beyond what has come before. In the opening stanza the writer complained that he was being unjustly attacked. Here he explains why; it is "for your sake" (v. 7) and because "zeal for your house consumes me" (v. 9). This is very much like Jeremiah 15:15, where the prophet said that he suffered reproach for God's sake. Even more to the point, it reminds us of Jesus' teaching about suffering for righteousness' sake in the Sermon on the Mount.

> Blessed are those who are persecuted because of righteousness,
>   for theirs is the kingdom of heaven.
> Blessed are you when people insult you, persecute you and falsely say all
>   kinds of evil against you because of me (Matt. 5:10–11).

Clearly the key phrases here are "because of righteousness" and "because of me." This is not a promise of blessing for people who are persecuted because they are obnoxious or fanatics. It is for those who suffer because of righteousness and for their identification with Jesus Christ.

Two lines in this section are explicitly identified with Jesus in the New Testament. The first is the first half of verse 9 ("zeal for your house consumes me"). John tells us that the disciples remembered that verse and applied it to Jesus on the occasion of his cleansing the temple (John 2:17). The second is the second half of the same verse ("the insults of those who insult you fall on me"), which Paul applied to Jesus in Romans 15:3.

Paul's point is that Jesus' behavior is an example for us in the sense that we should not seek to please ourselves but rather work for others' well-being. Moreover, this should be true even in situations where we are being slandered by our enemies, rejected by our family, ridiculed by mockers, and criticized by people who are in authority over us. If we read through the first part of the psalm with situations like that in mind, we will find many examples of the kind of insults (or other abuses) Jesus endured for us that we should be willing to endure for God and others.

1. *Enemies.* The first example goes back to stanza one, where the psalmist complains that his enemies "outnumber the hairs of [his] head" (v. 4). Since Jesus quoted this verse of himself, there can be no doubt of its application. Donald Grey Barnhouse wrote about how these verses apply to Jesus Christ:

> There were those among the scribes and Pharisees, the priests and the Levites, who simply hated him. The reason is not far to find. Until he came and stood beside them, they looked like good men. Linen bleaching on the grass seems white until the snow falls; it then appears gray. Thus it was for the so-called "spiritual" leaders of the people. They hated him freely; they hated him without a cause in himself. The only cause was in their evil hearts. When we turn to the New Testament we shall see what channel their hatred took.[3]

2. *His brothers*. Verse 8 says, "I am a stranger to my brothers." Barnhouse also applied this to Jesus' experience:

After Jesus was born, the Virgin Mary was fully and completely married to Joseph, and the Bible tells us that she bore him at least six children. We read there were at least two daughters, and the names of four sons are recorded in Mark 6:3. . . . The presence of Jesus in that household certainly caused diffi-culties. It is hard to live with near-perfection; how much harder to live with absolute perfection! After Christ came to manhood, his half-brothers wanted him to declare himself and use his power. They knew that he had turned water into wine, and that he had healed the sick and fed the multitudes. They could not be unaware of the potential of such power as advantage to them, and they wanted him to live according to the dictates of the advertising agen-cies. In John's Gospel we read, "Now the Jews' feast of the tabernacles was at hand. So his brothers said to him, 'Leave here and go to Judea, that your dis-ciples may see the works you are doing. For no man works in secret if he seeks to be known openly. If you do things, show yourself to the world.' For even his brothers did not believe on him" (John 7:2–5). Truly he had become a stranger to his brothers, an alien to his mother's children.[4]

3. *A proverb*. Barnhouse writes,

Still further in this psalm we see that he became a proverb to the people—a byword (v. 11). We know how a Christian student may be sneered at on a col-lege campus—called a "Christer" or a "Holy Joe." [Today we speak of "reli-gious nuts," the "radical right" or the "God squad."] We do not know what the slang phrase was by which Christ was thus deprecated, but our text leaves no doubt of the fact. He was a byword to the people.[5]

4. *The rulers*. Barnhouse says,

In the next clause we read: "They that sit in the gate speak against me" (v. 12). To sit in the gate meant to be a ruler of the people. Of the diligent woman described in the last paragraph of Proverbs it is said, "Her husband is known in the gates, when he sits among the elders of the land" (Prov. 31:23). Thus, those who sat in the gate were the rulers of the people, the honorable ones, and they were against him.[6]

5. *The drunkards*. Barnhouse concludes,

Finally, we read, "And I was the song of the drunkards" (v. 12). Solomon reminds us that "Fools make a mock of sin" (Prov. 14:9), but here we find men who mock at the Savior who died for them.[7]

A Lifetime of Insults

Jesus bore a lifetime of insults for God and our sake. When he spoke the truth about sin, the leaders were incensed. Jesus showed them that they were children of their fathers, who had stoned the prophets and killed those who were sent to them. "You are doing the things your own father does," he told them (John 8:41). They turned on him with wrath and reproached him with illegitimacy. They knew, undoubtedly, that Jesus had been born shortly after the marriage of Joseph and Mary, and not knowing that he was conceived by the Holy Spirit, they flung in his teeth that he was rumored to be illegitimate: "*We* are not illegitimate children." Jesus knew that he had been begotten by the Holy Spirit and took this reproach gently, but he let them know their true background: "You belong to your father, the devil" (v. 44).

The first time that Jesus ever spoke in public, his message on salvation by the simple, electing grace of God aroused fury in the Pharisees. He had not spoken twenty lines before they rose up and led him to the brow of the hill on which the city was built, intending to push him over the precipice (Luke 4:29). When he cast out demons, his enemies reproached him for working by the power of the devil: "It is only by Beelzebub, the prince of demons, that this fellow drives out demons" (Matt. 12:24). When he was on the cross, they mocked him with the claims he had made: "You who are going to destroy the temple and build it in three days, save yourself! Come down from the cross, if you are the Son of God!" (Matt. 27:40). They flouted his claim to deity and more than implied that he was himself a great deceiver.[8]

If there was ever an example of one who was willing to bear even the worst of abuses in order to please God the Father, it was Jesus Christ. If there was ever one whose personal experiences in life reflected the words of this psalm, it was the Savior.

A First Renewal of the Plea for Help

We just saw that verses 6–12 contained the first renewal of the psalmist's lament. In a similar way, verses 13–18 are a first renewal of the psalmist's plea for help. This stanza renews the imagery of the first verses, referring once again to "the mire" and the danger of sinking in it (v. 14), "deep waters" (v. 14), and the "flood" (v. 15). One new image is a "pit," which was likely to "close its mouth over" the psalmist (v. 15). The word *pit* refers to a cistern, which would normally have water at the bottom and be closed at the top with a stone. The idea of a cistern closing its mouth over the psalmist means something like being buried alive.

The new idea in this stanza is David's description of himself as God's "servant" in verse 17. This makes us think at once of the great "servant songs" found in Isaiah 42, 49, 50, and 53, which point to Jesus as God's unique servant. He said, "The Son of Man did not come to be served, but to serve, and to give his life as a ransom for many" (Matt. 20:28).

Christ's Life through Christ's Power

The point of this is that Jesus is to be an example for us, that we might behave as he did. We have been told by Jesus that if we seek to please God, we will be hated by the world, because we are not of the world: "If you belonged to the world, it would love you as its own. As it is, you do not belong to the world, but I have chosen you out of the world. That is why the world hates you. . . . If they persecuted me, they will persecute you also" (John 15:19–20). Nevertheless, although we may bear abuse for his sake—and we certainly will if we are living close to him and are bearing a genuine witness for him and for righteousness—we are to bear persecutions patiently without trying to retaliate, that we might please God.

This is an enormous privilege and a daunting challenge. If it were not for the power of Jesus Christ within, we would not respond to either, because we would put ourselves first, as the world does, and avoid the insults. To live as Christ, we must grow in his power by close fellowship with him.

Psalm 69

Man of Sorrows: Part 2

Judgment and Redemption

> May the table set before them become a snare;
>   may it become retribution and a trap.
> May their eyes be darkened so they cannot see,
>   and their backs be bent forever.
> Pour out your wrath on them;
>   let your fierce anger overtake them.
> May their place be deserted;
>   let there be no one to dwell in their tents.
> For they persecute those you wound
>   and talk about the pain of those you hurt.
> Charge them with crime upon crime;
>   do not let them share in your salvation.
> May they be blotted out of the book of life
>   and not be listed with the righteous.
>   *verses 22–28*

I pointed out in the introduction to the last study that if there was ever a messianic psalm, it is Psalm 69. Seven of its thirty-six verses are quoted in the New Testament, and there are themes that are developed in a general way in reference to Jesus Christ in the Gospels. In exploring the application of this psalm to Jesus, we looked at points that are illustrated by Jesus' earthly experience, saw how he endured them for the sake of the Father and for us, and observed how we should also willingly endure such trials for Jesus. We saw that we will be able to do this only through the power and grace he supplies.

I also noted the outline of the psalm. It begins with a stanza in which the psalmist both laments his sad situation and also calls on God to help him (vv. 1–4). This is followed by a one-verse acknowledgment of the psalmist's folly and guilt (v. 5).

At this point the psalm begins to repeat itself: first the lament and then the plea for help, doing both twice. Verses 6–12 contain the first renewal of the lament. Verses 13–18 contain the first renewal of the plea for help. Those are the sections we looked at in the last study. In the section of the psalm we are to look at now, verses 19–21 contain the second renewal of the lament and verses 22–28 contain the second renewal of the plea. That constitutes the main body of the psalm. It then closes with a short, one-verse interjection similar to verse 5, in verse 29, and a formal conclusion in which the reader is invited to praise God along with the psalmist, in verses 30–36.

A Second Renewal of the Lament

Verses 19–21 contain a second renewal of the psalmist's lament, but like the other renewals these verses also introduce new elements. The first new element is the writer's claim that God knows how he is being scorned (v. 19). This is the second time he has claimed that God knows something. Earlier it was his folly and guilt (v. 5). Here it is his mistreatment.

It is helpful for us to know that God knows what we are going through, and there is comfort in knowing that he knows. I think this is why the hymn by Joseph Scriven (c. 1855), "What a Friend We Have in Jesus," is so popular. It is not great poetry, and the tune is rather bland. But it has drawn forth an echoing note in countless devout hearts, people who have taken their sad troubles to Jesus and been comforted simply by knowing that he knows about them and has gone through them himself.

> What a Friend we have in Jesus,
> All our sins and griefs to bear!
> What a privilege to carry
> Everything to God in prayer!
> O what peace we often forfeit,
> O what needless pain we bear,
> All because we do not carry
> Everything to God in prayer.
>
> Have we trials and temptations?
> Is there trouble anywhere?
> We should never be discouraged:

> Take it to the Lord in prayer!
> Can we find a friend so faithful,
> Who will all our sorrows share?
> Jesus knows our every weakness—
> Take it to the Lord in prayer!

When we are hurting, either from physical ills or mistreatment, the most natural thing in the world is to look around for someone who might at least be able to show us some sympathy or offer comfort. But David says that in his trouble there was no one, no one who offered sympathy. No one provided even a little comfort.

That may be your experience too. Many people are alone in their grief and suffering, and people do not naturally identify with the unfortunate or console them. If that is your case, remember that there is One who knows what you are going through, because he has gone through it himself. When he was in his greatest agony on the cross no one showed any sympathy for him; they mocked him instead.

> He was despised and rejected by men,
>   a man of sorrows, and familiar with suffering.
> Like one from whom men hide their faces
>   he was despised, and we esteemed him not (Isa. 53:3).

That is what makes Jesus such an empathizing help to us. The author of Hebrews wrote,

> Therefore, since we have a great high priest who has gone through the heavens, Jesus the Son of God, let us hold firmly to the faith we profess. For we do not have a high priest who is unable to sympathize with our weaknesses, but we have one who has been tempted in every way, just as we are—yet was without sin. Let us then approach the throne of grace with confidence, so that we may receive mercy and find grace to help us in our time of need (Heb. 4:14–16).

Verse 21 deserves some special consideration. Not many verses in the Old Testament are quoted in the New Testament. Even fewer are quoted more than once. This verse is cited or alluded to in each of the four Gospels in the accounts of Christ's crucifixion (Matt. 27:34, 48; Mark 15:23, 36; Luke 23:36; John 19:29). The reference in John is most explicit, because John says that Jesus was offered wine vinegar to drink "so that the Scripture would be fulfilled," an unmistakable reference to this psalm.

A Second Renewal of the Plea for Help

The second renewal of the plea for help, in verses 22–28, also goes a step beyond the earlier prayers in that it now is no longer merely a plea for personal deliverance from trouble but is also a request for God's swift and utter judgment on the psalmist's enemies. It is an imprecatory prayer that is equal in its fierce power to any of the explicitly imprecatory psalms and should be handled as they must be.

> May the table set before them become a snare;
>   may it become retribution and a trap.
> May their eyes be darkened so they cannot see,
>   and their backs be bent forever.
> Pour out your wrath on them;
>   let your fierce anger overtake them.
> May their place be deserted;
>   let there be no one to dwell in their tents.
> For they persecute those you wound
>   and talk about the pain of those you hurt.
> Charge them with crime upon crime;
>   do not let them share in your salvation.
> May they be blotted out of the book of life
>   and not be listed with the righteous.

These imprecations build in intensity, ending in the most terrible words of all: "May they be blotted out of the book of life and not be listed with the righteous" (v. 28). We pull back from words wishing that someone else might go to hell. But if those others are persistently and ultimately unrepentant, that is the only place they could possibly go and be. If they were taken into heaven, they would ruin heaven.

How do we handle something as explicitly vengeful as these verses? I could repeat some of the things I have said before in reference to similarly imprecatory verses. First, although David is calling for God's swift vengeance on his enemies, it is significant that he is asking God to render judgment and not proposing or even wanting to take vengeance himself. Second, it is David, the anointed one of God, who is speaking. Therefore, his enemies are God's enemies. David's calls for vindication are therefore never merely an individual matter.

But there is more. We should remember that Jesus told us to forgive our enemies: "You have heard that it was said, 'Love your neighbor and hate your enemy.' But I tell you: Love your enemies and pray for those who persecute you, that you may be sons of your Father in heaven" (Matt. 5:43–45). Jesus, when he was being crucified, even being given vinegar mixed with gall to drink (v. 21), did not curse his enemies but prayed for them instead. He prayed, "Father, forgive them, for they do not know what they are doing" (Luke 23:34). We are likewise told to forgive and not to take vengeance.

Alexander Maclaren handles the seeming incompatibility of Psalm 69 with these texts by saying, "It is impossible to bring such utterances into harmony with the teachings of Jesus, and the attempt to vindicate them ignores plain facts and does violence to plain words. Better far to let them stand as a monument of the earlier stage of God's progressive revelation, and discern clearly the advance which Christian ethics has made on them."[1]

Blessings That Become Curses

Yet this is not the whole story. It is true that we are not to take vengeance. Paul says this in Romans, writing, "Do not take revenge, my friends, but leave room for God's wrath, for it is written: 'It is mine to avenge; I will repay,' says the Lord" (Rom. 12:19). But just because we are not to take judgment into our own hands does not mean that we should not want justice to be done or that God will not punish sin eventually. It is significant in this respect that Paul, the same author who says, "Do not take revenge . . . but leave room for God's wrath," also quotes verses 22–23 of Psalm 69 (in Rom. 11:9–10) as a prophecy of a judicial blinding of the majority of the people of Israel because of their rejection of Jesus Christ.

What is unique about Paul's use of these verses in Romans is his teaching that in their unbelief even those things that should have been a great blessing to the Jewish people—presumably the things he lists at the start of chapter 9 ("the adoption as sons; . . . the divine glory, the covenants, the receiving of the law, the temple worship and the promises . . . the patriarchs," vv. 4–5)—have become a "snare," "trap," "stumbling block," and "retribution" for them in their unregenerate state.

This is a critical point. It means that if the blessings of God are misused—and they always are misused unless we allow them to lead us to faith in Jesus as our Savior—they will inevitably harden our hearts, propel us into further sins, and eventually lead to even greater judgment.

There is a powerful statement of this principle at the very end of the Old Testament, in Malachi. Malachi's days were bad days. The people, led by their priests, were far from God. They were so far from God that when he sent Malachi to rebuke them, their response was one of hostile surprise and confrontation: "How have you loved us? . . . How have we shown contempt for your name? . . . How have we defiled you? . . . How have we wearied him? . . . How are we to return? . . . How do we rob you? . . . What have we said against you?" (Mal. 1:2, 6, 7; 2:17; 3:7, 8, 13).

The priests were chiefly to blame for this attitude. So the strongest judgments are pronounced against them: "If you do not listen, and if you do not set your heart to honor my name, . . . I will send a curse upon you, and I will curse your blessings. Yes, I have already cursed them, because you have not set your heart to honor me" (Mal. 2:2).

Here is where Psalm 69:22–23 and Paul's use of these verses in Romans come home forcefully to us. If individual Jews, who were a chosen nation, missed salvation because of their rejection of Christ and if, as a result, the blessings of God that had been given to them became a curse for these people, then it is entirely possible (indeed probable) that many sitting in the evangelical churches of America today are also missing salvation because of their failure to trust Jesus in a personal way and that their blessings have become curses too.

This means that if you will not allow the good things we enjoy as allegedly Christian people to lead you to Christ, which is what God has given them to us for, then they will be worse than worthless to you. They will actually be harmful and propel you inevitably into an even greater spiritual stupor, hardness of heart, and sin.

Here are four examples.

1. *Baptism.* Baptism is an outward sign of an inward, spiritual union with Jesus Christ. It is meant to strengthen our faith by making the inward reality more palpable to us. But countless allegedly Christian people have trusted the outward sign without the inward commitment. They have judged themselves to be saved persons without any true following after Jesus Christ. Therefore, the very thing that should have been an instruction and blessing to them has become a false ground of hope.

2. *The Lord's Supper.* Entire branches of the church teach that grace is somehow imparted in the physical partaking of the elements, so that the physical act by itself conveys salvation. But the reality is not physical. The Lord's Supper is meant to show us the broken body and atoning blood of Jesus Christ and lead us to trust him and place our faith in him, not the ceremony. Thus, if we do not trust Christ, the sacrament, which is intended to do us good, actually becomes a curse for us and we become superstitious and even pagan in our practice.

3. *Material possessions.* Money and other material goods are from God. But they can be dangerous, particularly when we possess them in abundance. They should lead us to God in gratitude. More often they lead us from him.

4. *The Lord's Day.* My fourth example is our misuse of the Lord's Day. On December 7, 1941, the air force of imperial Japan bombed the American navy at Pearl Harbor, bringing the United States into World War II and altering the course of history. It was a terrible disaster for this country, since it crippled the Pacific fleet and claimed 2,403 young lives. The bombing took place on Sunday morning. What is not well known is that after the defeat of Japan in 1945, General Douglas MacArthur took control of the archives of the Japanese war department and set translators to work on the enemy's papers. They discovered that in the years prior to the war the Japanese had sent professors to the United States to study America's national character to determine at what point and in what manner we would be most vulnerable to attack, when it should come. Their reports stated that we would be most vulnerable on a Sunday morning following a Friday on which both the army and the navy had a payday.

And that is precisely what December 7, 1941, was. In earlier years Sundays were sacred days of rest and worship for the majority of Americans, and even those who were not Christians respected them. But that had changed by the winter of 1941. Our day of national blessing had become a national hangover, and God turned this former blessing into a curse. That weekend at Pearl Harbor was a debauch of vast proportions, and we were unprepared and unable to meet the Japanese attack when it came.[2]

God is not mocked. We must remember that the judgment of God will in time surely be meted out to sinners, even though that is not a task assigned to us. That includes our own use or abuse of God's gifts. We forget a truth like this at our great cost and peril.

A Brief Interjection

Verse 29 is a brief interjection, corresponding to verse 5 in the first part of the psalm. But it is different. The first one-verse section was a confession of sin, occasioned by the psalmist's profession of innocence toward his enemies. Though innocent before them, he acknowledged that he was not innocent before God. He was both foolish and guilty. In verse 29 David seems merely to reiterate his profound pain and once again calls on God to protect him. In other words, it is a one-verse summary of the opening lament and plea for help.

What it seems to do is draw the main body of the psalm to a close and prepare for the quite different material and tone of the closing stanzas in which the psalmist praises God and calls on others to praise God too.

Conclusion: Let God Be Praised

There is a great deal of sorrow and tragedy in this life. A person would have to be blind not to see it. But for the Christian tragedy is never the final word. The final word is always victory and praise. So this is the note on which the psalm ends, just as Psalm 22, which was also a psalm of pain and suffering, ended on a note of victory.[3] In this case the psalmist first voices his praise to God, then calls on "heaven and earth . . . the seas and all that move in them" to praise God also.

Assuming that David was the original author of this psalm, as the title of the psalm says, and that the reference to rebuilding the cities of Judah in verse 35 came from a later age than David's, the last stanza was probably added by a later hand for the benefit of a later congregation's worship. If that is so, then the original psalm would have ended with verse 33, which would have been a perfect conclusion. Even so, verse 33 is the key to the psalm and the most important verse.

> The LORD hears the needy
>   and does not despise his captive people.

I wish I could plant that truth in your mind so that nothing would ever blot it out and that it could ring there with a constant glad clarity. In this world there is always much pain and evil. It is what life is like. What is more,

God does not always remove the pain or troubling times. Jesus prayed in great agony in Gethsemane, asking that the cup he was about to drink might be taken from him, and God did not remove the cup. Jesus had to drink it. God nevertheless heard his prayer and did not despise his agony. Moreover, he sent angels to minister to him and strengthen him so that he might go through his trial gloriously for God.

Be assured that this will be the case with you also. Whatever cross you are given, tell God about it and know that he will hear your prayers and come to strengthen you. You will certainly praise him for it one day.

Psalm 70

"Let God Be Exalted"

Hasten, O God, to save me;
*O L*ORD*, come quickly to help me.*
May those who seek my life
be put to shame and confusion;
may all who desire my ruin
be turned back in disgrace.
May those who say to me, "Aha! Aha!"
turn back because of their shame.
But may all who seek you
rejoice and be glad in you;
may those who love your salvation always say,
"Let God be exalted!"

Yet I am poor and needy;
come quickly to me, O God.
You are my help and my deliverer;
*O L*ORD*, do not delay.*

verses 1–5

For the second time in our study of the psalms we come to a psalm that is a virtual repetition of words found earlier. The first time this happened was more obvious, because it involved the almost exact duplication of Psalm 14 as Psalm 53. This psalm repeats only a portion of an earlier psalm. It is a repetition of verses 13–17 from Psalm 40. Nevertheless, it is a repetition, which makes us ask about the relationship between the two psalms as well as question whether there is any reason for the several slight differences that exist.

Psalm 40 and Psalm 70

In the study of Psalm 40 in volume one of this series, I pointed out that some Old Testament scholars, particularly those of the critical school, think that Psalm 40 was originally two psalms, verses 1–12 being the first and verses 13–17 being the second, and that they were put together somewhat awkwardly by an unknown editor. They consider the combination to be awkward because the first part of Psalm 40 speaks of deliverance from a desperate situation and the second part is still seeking a deliverance. This kind of combination is not strange to the psalms, however, and it is equally possible that Psalm 70 was detached from the longer psalm in order to salvage it for general use in a later period.

The placing of the two psalms in the Psalter, the first in an early section among the many psalms of David and the second in a later, somewhat more eclectic section, may point in this direction.

If Psalm 70 was detached from Psalm 40 with the goal of making it into a distinct composition for later use, the intent seems to have been to stress the urgency of the psalmist's plight and highlight the need for God to hurry to his defense.

This is because of the small differences between Psalm 70 and the nearly identical material in Psalm 40. For example, Psalm 40:13 begins with the words *be pleased,* but they are omitted here. In fact, Psalm 70 does not even have the word *hasten* at the start, as the NIV suggests, but begins literally, "God, to deliver me; LORD, to my help, hurry." That sounds just about as urgent in English as it does in Hebrew. Again, the Hebrew text of Psalm 40:14 has the word *together* after the word *confounded* and *to destroy it* after *seek my life.* These words do not occur in Psalm 70. (They do not occur in the NIV of Psalm 40 either, though they are in the Hebrew. It is hard to imagine why the NIV translators have excised them, unless it is merely to make the two psalms concur with each other.)

The Psalmist's Plight

What is immediately apparent about Psalm 70 is that the writer is in serious trouble and that he is calling on God to help him quickly before it is too late. We do not know what his trouble was, though it clearly had to do with enemies, who were not only mocking him, saying, "Aha! Aha!" (v. 3), but were also seeking to take his life (v. 2). With the exception of the years in which David was hiding from King Saul and the time, much later, when he was forced to flee Jerusalem because of the rebellion of his son Absalom, we do not know what these specific dangers might have been. But we discern from this as well as from other psalms that David faced such dangers much of the time.

That is an important thing to notice. I remind you that David was the beloved king of Israel, who reigned powerfully and well for forty years. He was installed, blessed, and approved by God, who called him "a man after his own heart" (1 Sam. 13:14). David was nearly always in close fellowship with God. Yet he had constant troubles and was in nearly constant danger for his life. In Psalm 40 he described himself as having been stuck in a pit from which he was unable to escape and in which he might die.

If that was true for David, should we be surprised that it is often our experience too? Should we be astonished that troubles and dangers, enemies, and even muddy pits are our frequent lots in life?

We should not even be surprised if our situation seems desperate, as is David's case here. Look how often he uses the word *hasten* or its synonyms. The idea occurs twice in verse 1: "*Hasten*, O God, to save me; O Lord, come *quickly* to help me." Then it occurs twice more at the end of the psalm, in verse 5: "Come *quickly* to me, O God. . . . O Lord, *do not delay.*" Four times in just five verses! Have you ever felt like that? I am sure you have. It may be a situation at work or in your family. It may involve a serious illness. You may be telling God, "I need help now. If you don't step in and help me right away, it will be too late." You may even be saying, "If I don't get some relief from this immediately, I think I am going to crack up."

The Psalmist's Prayer

What do you do in such times? The answer for those who know God is to pray, turning to God. For however desperate the situation seems to us, we can know that it is never desperate for God but rather is under his control. This is why Paul told the Philippians, "Do not be anxious about anything, but in everything, by prayer and petition, with thanksgiving, present your requests to God. And the peace of God, which transcends all understanding, will guard your hearts and your minds in Christ Jesus" (Phil. 4:6–7).

So here is another important thing to notice. Psalm 70 is a prayer throughout. In it David prays for three things.

1. *For himself: for quick deliverance.* Some years ago someone taught me a little acrostic for prayer. It is the word ACTS, where *A* stands for adoration, *C* for confession, *T* for thanksgiving, and *S* for supplication, or prayers for others. I have always found this helpful, since it begins with who God is and confesses sin and expresses thanks to God before asking for anything. I always appreciate it when a pastoral prayer follows those main lines.

But this is not what David does here, is it? There are psalms in which he spends a great deal of time praising God for who he is, confessing sin, and thanking God for his many blessings. But not here! Here David gets right to his point and calls on God to help him, praying first not even for others but for himself: "Hasten, O God, to save me; O LORD, come quickly to help me" (v. 1). Why doesn't David follow a more acceptable or selfless pattern in this prayer? The answer is obvious. It is because he needs help now. Tomorrow will be too late. It may even be too late if he is overly lengthy in his prayer. So there is no beating around the bush, no nice formalities. "Help me quickly" is where his prayer both begins and ends.

We are not always in situations like this, of course. So our prayers should usually be less hurried and cover far more ground, especially for the needs of other people. When we are in desperate need, however, there is nothing wrong with getting to the point and praying urgently for exactly what we need, as David does.

I suppose it was its directness that made this psalm appeal to Martin Luther. Because the psalm is short and because it is a virtual repetition of verses 13–17 of Psalm 40, most commentators tend to skip it or pass over it with brief comments. Not Luther. In the massive collection of the Reformer's works ten pages are given to Psalm 70's exposition. Luther says at one point, "This prayer is the shield, spear, thunderbolt and defense against every attack of fear, presumption [and] lukewarmness . . . which are especially dominant today."[1] I am sure this was because of the dangers Luther himself faced. He identified with David's urgent petition.

2. *For his enemies: for their shame and confusion.* The second subject of David's prayer is his enemies (vv. 2–3). It is not the way Jesus taught us to pray for our enemies, is it? We are to pray charitably and for their help or salvation: "You have heard that it was said, 'Love your neighbor and hate your enemy.' But I tell you: Love your enemies and pray for those who persecute you, that you may be sons of your Father in heaven" (Matt. 5:43–44). In this psalm David prays that: (1) those who seek his life "may . . . be put to shame and confusion"; (2) those who desire his ruin "may . . . be turned back in disgrace"; and (3) those who mock him, saying "Aha! Aha!" "may . . . turn back because of their shame."

I want to suggest that there is no conflict between these two types of prayers for enemies and that both are proper in their place.

It is true that we may have trouble with the kind of imprecatory prayer we saw in the last psalm, in which David asks that his enemies might "be blotted out of the book of life and not be listed with the righteous" (Ps. 69:28)—in other words that they might be sent to hell. But that is not the case here. Here David is merely asking that his enemies' evil plans against him might be frustrated and that they might be turned back in shame and confusion. That is what we should all pray in regard to those who do evil, that the evil might be turned back and that they might be ashamed. We certainly wouldn't want to pray that their evil plans would prosper.

Moreover, our desire for our enemies' well-being demands the same thing. For success in evil encourages even more evil and establishes the evildoer in his or her ways. The kindest thing we can pray for people who do wrong is that their plans will fail, for it may be that in their frustration they will see the folly and true end of evil and be reached for God.

Before we leave this record of how David prayed for his enemies, we need to remind ourselves that what David describes these people as doing is what the enemies of Jesus did at the time of his crucifixion. They were seeking his life, of course. They were also desiring his ruin. But what I am most interested in here is the way they mocked him, saying "Aha! Aha!" Matthew describes it in the fullest manner, writing,

> Those who passed by hurled insults at him, shaking their heads and saying, "You who are going to destroy the temple and build it in three days, save yourself! Come down from the cross, if you are the Son of God."
> In the same way the chief priests, the teachers of the law and the elders mocked him. "He saved others," they said, "but he can't save himself! He's the king of Israel! Let him come down now from the cross, and we will believe in him. He trusts in God. Let God rescue him now if he wants him, for he said, 'I am the Son of God'" (Matt. 27:39–43).

Jesus bore these taunts in order to achieve our salvation by obeying God the Father. We should be willing to bear similar insults too, if we are as serious about following in our Lord's steps as we profess to be.

3. *For the righteous: for their delight in God.* The third subject of the psalmist's prayer is the number of the righteous or, as he puts it, those who "seek" God and "love [his] salvation" (v. 4).

Why does he pray for them, especially when his own situation is so urgent? Well, for one thing it is good to be reminded that there are other righteous people, those who are trying to follow after God and do the right thing, just as we are. We often forget this. We struggle against our particular enemies, grow tired and discouraged, and find ourselves slumped under a juniper tree like Elijah, crying out, "I have been very zealous for the LORD God Almighty. The Israelites have rejected your covenant, broken down your altars, and put your prophets to death with the sword. I am the only one left, and now they are trying to kill me too" (1 Kings 19:10). When that happens we need to remind ourselves (or be reminded by God) that there are yet "seven thousand in Israel—all whose knees have not bowed down to Baal and all whose mouths have not kissed him" (1 Kings 19:18). It is important to remember that there are other people who are trying to do exactly what we are trying to do.

Again, it is important to pray for them, because if other believers are going through what we are going through and if we need prayer ourselves, then so do they. And we, above all others, should be the ones to pray for them. If you are sick, you should be able to pray for those who are sick, even better than those who are well. If you are being abused by your coworkers or family, you should be able to pray for Christians who are likewise being abused and insulted. If you are in a dead-end job or see no future to what you are doing, you should be able to pray for other believers in the same situation. Let your trials teach you how to pray for other Christians.

But I notice this also. Since David is praying for his own deliverance he might want to pray that others who are righteous would also be delivered. But what he actually prays for here is that they might "rejoice and be glad" in God and be able to say always, "Let God be exalted!"

For that is the real victory! Not that we should escape our troubles, though we can pray for deliverance and are often delivered by God when we do, but rather that we should be able to praise God for whatever he chooses to do with us. We think of Job, who praised God even when he was going through the worst of his terrible tribulations. God allowed Satan to take away all his possessions, even the lives of his ten children. But we read at the end of that terrifying account,

> At this, Job got up and tore his robe and shaved his head [two well-known symbols of mourning]. Then he fell to the ground in worship and said:
>
> > "Naked I came from my mother's womb,
> > and naked I will depart.
> > The LORD gave and the LORD has taken away;
> > may the name of the LORD be praised."
>
> In all this, Job did not sin by charging God with wrongdoing (Job 1:20–21).

It is a great thing when the people of God can say in any circumstance, "Let God be exalted!" For he will be! It is fitting when we can acknowledge this and praise God openly.

The Psalmist's Persuasion

The last verse of Psalm 70 is what I call the psalmist's most basic belief or persuasion. It has two parts: (1) that he is "poor and needy," and (2) that God is his "help and . . . deliverer."

In his short but helpful observations on this psalm, the great preacher G. Campbell Morgan says that the faith that is displayed in this last stanza "is not the highest type of faith" because, though it believes in God's ability to help, it doubts whether help will arrive in time.[2] In my opinion this is not right. Help might not arrive in time. Since none of us knows the mind of God or has any special insight into his ordering or timing of events, none of us can say with certainty that God will intervene to save us from whatever danger we are praying about. Therefore, the height of faith is not to presume on what God will or will not do but to be convinced precisely of what

David is convinced: that we are needy, that we cannot help ourselves, and that God is the only one who can help us.

Many people get off base on the very first of these two points because they assume, as virtually all unbelievers do, that human beings are perfectly able to help themselves. In other words, they are not "poor"—they have great natural resources—and they are not "needy," certainly not in spiritual areas! If they are going to get to heaven, it will be by their own efforts. They are the masters of their souls. They are the captains of their fates. According to a recent public opinion poll, over 60 percent even of so-called evangelical Christians believe that the saying "God helps those who help themselves" is in the Bible!

Those who know their Bibles don't want anything to do with that false teaching. They know that they can't help themselves. So they say with David, who by all outward appearances was a rich and very powerful man, "Yet I am poor and needy; come quickly to me, O God." Above all they confess their utter need of God in salvation. They know that there is no salvation to be found anywhere except in Jesus Christ.

The second part of David's confession is important too, for it is only this that makes the prayer hopeful. David knew his weakness and need, but he also knew God's grace and greatness. Therefore, even though he is weak he turns to God strongly. And though needy, he comes to the one who is able to satisfy his need. Do you know that? Do you know God as the one who offers deliverance from the penalty and power of your sin through the work of Jesus Christ? The very name *Jesus* means "Jehovah saves." It is Jesus' work as Redeemer to set his enslaved people free.

This is not weak faith, but great faith, crying out to God urgently because the need is great.

"Even So, Come, Lord Jesus"

The very last line of this psalm returns us to the note struck at the beginning: "O LORD, do not delay." The prayer that the Lord might make haste, come quickly, or not delay is the psalm's watchword and theme. It is a cry often on the tongues of God's people.

We ought to remind ourselves that this was often the prayer of the early church as it waited for the return of Jesus Christ. The Christians of that day did not have the freedoms we do or enjoy protection from an enlightened democratic state. They were under constant danger from hostile authorities, and they were frequently plunged into times of terrible persecution. In their trials they cried out to God, and their prayer was that Jesus might quickly come again. Like the saints in the Book of Revelation, they cried to God, saying, "How long, Sovereign Lord, holy and true, until you judge the inhabitants of the earth and avenge our blood?" (Rev. 6:10). Life is one long trouble, since ours is a sinful, evil world. Jesus said, "In this world you will have trouble." The saints wanted God to come quickly, to hasten.

And so at times do we. But then we turn in our trouble to the very last verses not of Psalm 70, but of the Bible. And there we find the Lord Jesus himself speaking, and what he says is this: "I am coming soon" (Rev. 22:20).

To us the coming of Jesus may seem long delayed, but it is not long in the great sweep of history. What we must do, despite our weariness and frequent lack of faith, is to endure, looking to him who is our present help and ultimate deliverance:

Therefore, since we are surrounded by such a great cloud of witnesses, let us throw off everything that hinders and the sin that so easily entangles, and let us run with perseverance the race marked out for us. Let us fix our eyes on Jesus, the author and perfecter of our faith, who for the joy set before him endured the cross, scorning its shame, and sat down at the right hand of the throne of God (Heb. 12:1–2).

Psalm 71

A Psalm for Old Age

Do not cast me away when I am old;
  do not forsake me when my strength is gone.
For my enemies speak against me;
  those who wait to kill me conspire together.
They say, "God has forsaken him;
  pursue him and seize him,
  for no one will rescue him."
Be not far from me, O God;
  come quickly, O my God, to help me.
May my accusers perish in shame;
  may those who want to harm me
  be covered with scorn and disgrace.

But as for me, I will always have hope;
  I will praise you more and more.
My mouth will tell of your righteousness,
  of your salvation all day long,
  though I know not its measure.
I will come and proclaim your mighty acts, O Sovereign LORD;
  I will proclaim your righteousness, yours alone.
Since my youth, O God, you have taught me,
  and to this day I declare your marvelous deeds.
Even when I am old and gray,
  do not forsake me, O God,
till I declare your power to the next generation,
  your might to all who are to come.

verses 9–18

Almost all the psalms in the second book of the Psalter have title lines. In fact, with the exception of this psalm, the only other psalm that does not is Psalm 43, which seems to belong with Psalm 42. Since Psalm 71 likewise has no title line, some commentators think it might once have belonged with Psalm 70, both therefore being ascribed to King David.

Certainly there are elements in Psalm 71 that pick up on Psalm 70,[1] and there are even more expressions drawn from other psalms that are ascribed to David: "rock of refuge" and "my rock and my fortress" (v. 3), "my enemies" (v. 10), "Be not far from me, O God" (v. 12), "come quickly, O my God, to help me" (v. 12), and others. The first three verses are taken directly from the opening verses of Psalm 31, which is by David. Moreover, since we are near the ending of book two of the Psalter and since it ends with the words "This concludes the prayers of David son of Jesse," it is appropriate that a psalm of David's written in and about his old age should appear at this point. It is consistent with this view that the author seems to have been a public person (he says that he has become a "portent," a well-known example or warning to many, v. 7) and a person of greatness or honor (v. 21). The Septuagint ascribes the psalm to David.

In this study I will be assuming David's authorship. But on the other hand, the fact that it is or might be by David contributes little. For the psalm is a song of old age and is therefore for all who are old or will be, which is going to be true for most of us sooner or later. Charles Haddon Spurgeon says, "We have here the prayer of the aged believer who in holy confidence of faith, strengthened by a long and remarkable experience, pleads against his enemies and asks further blessings for himself."[2]

As far as the psalm's outline goes, there may be six stanzas, as in the New International Version. But the important points overlap, and according to H. C. Leupold, "No two commentators divide the psalm in the same way."[3] Leupold splits it into two parts (vv. 1–12 and 13–24). Marvin E. Tate divides it into five parts (vv. 1–4, 5–12, 13–18, 19–20, 21–24). Derek Kidner has six sections, like the New International Version, but he does not follow the stanzas of the NIV (vv. 1–3, 4–6, 7–11, 12–16, 17–21, 22–24).

It is probably best to think of this psalm in terms of what it says, rather than its outline. It handles four subjects: (1) old age and its problems, (2) how the past looks from the perspective of old age, (3) the future in terms of what is yet to be done, and (4) praise from one who has lived long enough to have observed God's faithful ways.

Old Age and Its Problems

It is not fun to be old, especially in America. At other times and in other cultures old age had advantages to offset its disadvantages. Elderly persons were honored and respected. Their wisdom was valued. That is no longer true in America or in the West generally. Here we value youth, and the culture is so oriented to youthful interests that many old people even try to dress and act like teenagers. David didn't have those problems, of course. But the problems he had as a result of his old age were serious and even universal. In fact, they are the most basic problems of all.

1. *Weakness, the loss of former strength or abilities.* One problem with getting old is that you lose the strength and many of the abilities you had when you were younger. John Wesley, the great Methodist evangelist, lived to be eighty-eight years old (1703–91). He kept a diary throughout most of his life, and for June 28, 1789, there is this entry:

> Sunday 28 . . . This day I enter on my eighty-sixth year. I now find I grow old: 1) My sight is decayed, so that I cannot read a small print, unless in a strong light; 2) My strength is decayed, so that I walk much slower than I did some years since; 3) My memory of names, whether of persons or places, is decayed, till I stop a little to recollect them. What I should be afraid of is, if I took thought for the morrow, that my body should weigh down my mind and create either stubbornness, by the decrease of my understanding, or peevishness, by the increase of bodily infirmities. But thou shalt answer for me, O Lord my God.[4]

Many of us find that we can echo that. We can't hear as well as we used to hear. We can't read the small print. We get tired faster. We don't even sleep as well, and we wake up three or four times throughout the night. It is what David is talking about when he tells God, "Do not cast me away when I am old; do not forsake me when my strength is gone" (v. 9).

2. *A continuation of troubles, particularly enemies.* The second problem of old age is that the difficulties we have faced throughout our lives do not go away but instead remain with us. And the trouble they cause is augmented because of our diminishing strength or capacities to deal with them. In David's case this had to do with his enemies, those he has written about in nearly every other psalm. Here he writes of these dangerous people, "My enemies speak against me; those who wait to kill me conspire together" (v. 10). Marvin E. Tate says, "The speaker might have expected mature age to bring exemption from such attacks, but such is not the case."[5] The enemies of the king were present as much at the end of his life as at the beginning.

So also with us. The most disturbing, continuing problems I face are having to support the various ministries I am involved in financially. The Bible Study Hour is usually behind in paying its bills, and at times it is so far behind that I think we are going to have to terminate the ministry. City Center Academy always needs funds. Even Tenth Presbyterian Church goes through regular financial crises, when we have to reduce our staff or curtail some aspects of our outreach. It would be nice if those problems would go away, but they do not. In fact, they are more serious now, more serious because of their greater dimensions, than they were when I began my ministry twenty-eight years ago. I wish somebody else would assume responsibility for these problems, but no one else does. In fact, I even get letters saying that we would not have these problems if we were only more careful about being in the will of God.

Other people have family problems, and these do not get better either. I know one woman who has taken care of her cantankerous octogenarian mother for several decades. The mother is now in a Christian nursing home where she is well cared for. Her finances are well managed. But she doesn't thank her daughter. She is as critical and difficult as ever. In fact, just recently she has brought in a public defender and an unscrupulous lawyer to bring pressure on her daughter to do more. The problem never gets better; that is what is so wearing. The mother doesn't even die.

E. M. Forster, the British novelist, had a mother like that. She lived to her late nineties and didn't die until he was sixty-six.

Some people have health problems all their lives. Some struggle with depression. Others labor against class or ethnic prejudice, and the problems do not go away or even grow lighter as they grow older. In fact, they are often more difficult and certainly more oppressive and hard to bear than when these people were young.

3. *Being alone, no one to help.* The third thing that bothered David is that as he grew older he had fewer people to help him, to solve or help shoulder these burdens. In fact, he describes himself as being utterly alone with none to help but God. His enemies recognized this; they argued that even God had deserted him. "They say, 'God has forsaken him; pursue him and seize him, for no one will rescue him'" (v. 11). Maybe you feel that way too. In your youth you had many friends and coworkers. There were people you could share your burdens with. But now you are old. Those former friends are gone. You have no one.

Looking to the Past: Our Faithful God

You may have no human being with you perhaps, but if you are a Christian, you still have God. And that means that you still have the only one who was really with you and really able to help you all along. It is one advantage of old age to know that experientially.

This leads us to the second important element of this psalm. For the reflections David gives us concerning old age are not so we will wring our hands and complain about how bad it is to grow old, but the contrary. David wants us to see that even old age is given to us by God, is one of his good gifts and should be used for his glory and the blessing and well-being of others. He gets into these points first by pausing to look back over his long life and reflect on what he has learned about God and experienced about him during those former long years. We have spoken about the problems of old age, which are great. But one great advantage is in having a long experience of God's presence, faithfulness, and blessing. There are two things to notice about what David says concerning the past.

1. *David had known God from his youth and even before that.* He says, "You have been my hope, O Sovereign LORD, my confidence since my youth. From birth I have relied on you; you brought me forth from my mother's womb" (vv. 5–6). What this seems to mean is that he remembers how he had come to know God and had trusted God from childhood. We would say that such a person became a "Christian" early in life. But he is also saying that he is aware that God was with him even before childhood, from the moment of his birth, though he cannot remember the years before his early childhood himself. We know that this was true of David. He was a man of God even before he was a man. He was godly even when he was watching the sheep as the youngest and least of Jesse's eight sons (see 1 Sam. 16:1–13).

Have you known the Lord from childhood? If you have, you are fortunate because you can look back over a lifetime of God's faithful care and provision. Spurgeon wrote, "They are highly favored who can like David, Samuel, Josiah, Timothy, and others say, 'Thou art my trust from my youth.'"[6]

I like the testimony of Polycarp, the aged Bishop of Smyrna, who was martyred on February 22, A.D. 156. As he was being driven to the arena where he would be given the choice of worshiping Caesar or, refusing, being offered to the lions, the city officials tried to persuade him to make the gesture of homage to Caesar. They had respect for him because of his age and reputation and argued, "What harm is there in saying, 'Caesar is Lord,' and burning incense . . . and saving yourself?" But Polycarp answered, "For eighty-six years I have been [Christ's] slave, and he has done me no wrong; how can I blaspheme my king who saved me?"[7] Despite his age and undoubted physical weakness, Polycarp was not weak. He was strong in faith. In fact, he was never stronger, because he remembered the strength and faithfulness of God to him throughout the many long years of his service as Christ's slave. So it will be with you if, in your old age, you recall God's love and faithfulness to you over your lifetime.

2. *David had become "a portent" to many.* The word *portent* (v. 7) is hard to define, because it can be taken either in a good or bad sense. In a good sense it would refer to the writer as a marvel of God's protecting care. People would say, "Look how God has protected and blessed David." In a bad sense it would refer to the greatness of his sufferings and the magnitude of his calamities. In that case, people would say, "Has anybody ever suffered as much as David?" Since the word occurs here in the context of remembering God's faithfulness to him in the past, the bad sense should probably be thrown out. But it is possible both might be combined in the sense suggested by J. J. Stewart Perowne, when he says it is best "to understand it as applying to his whole wonderful life of trials and blessings, of perils and deliverances, such as did not ordinarily fall to the lot of man."[8] David

was certainly a portent in this sense, which is why the record of his life is given to us so completely in the Bible.

Looking Ahead: The Next Generation

I suppose there are some people who in their old age only look back to the past and are often quite unhappy as they do. They think of what they have had and lost or what they wish they could have had and never did. The present does not mean much to them except as a basis for complaining about their multiplying aches and pains, and they are afraid to look forward. They are afraid of dying.

David's approach to old age was not like this. For not only did he look to the past to remember God's goodness and faithfulness to him over the many long years of his life, he also looked to the future in terms of the work yet remaining to be done. He knew that if God had left him in life and had not yet taken him home to be with him in glory, it was because there was work to do. This work was testifying to the coming generations about God. This led him to say,

> Since my youth, O God, you have taught me,
>   and to this day I declare your marvelous deeds.
> Even when I am old and gray,
>   do not forsake me, O God,
> till I declare your power to the next generation,
>   your might to all who are to come (vv. 17–18).

Someone has said that the Christian church is always one generation away from extinction, meaning that each generation has the responsibility of passing Christian doctrine to the next. David knew this. It is what he wants to do. But since he is writing about old age, the uniqueness of what he is saying is that older people have a special and peculiar ability to teach the young. This does not mean that they know more than those in middle age. An old deacon or deaconess does not necessarily know more than his pastor about the Bible's content. But the old person has lived with God longer and has seen more of God's faithfulness over more years of life than younger people, however much they may know. Therefore, a person like this is especially well equipped to help the young.

Haven't you noticed that there is a special natural bond between the elderly and children? The secular world has begun to take advantage of this in nursing homes and kindergartens by bringing people from nursing homes to help care for children in day-care centers and other institutions. At Tenth Presbyterian Church we bring older people into the Sunday school to hear the children recite their Bible verses and assist in other ways. The children love these older people and respect them. It is a good arrangement. It is biblical.

The Present: Praising God Now

This brings us to the present, the third way in which David deals with the limitations of old age. He looks to the past to remind himself of God's faithfulness and power. He looks to the future to remind himself of the work yet to be done. Then, having done both of those things, he turns to the present and begins to do exactly what he has been talking about. He bears witness to God now. What he praises God for chiefly is his righteousness (vv. 19–21) and faithfulness (vv. 22–24).

1. *God's righteousness.* The word *righteousness* is used in different ways in the Bible, most notably of that divine righteousness that is imparted to us in justification. That is not the way the word is used here, nor characteristically in the psalms. Here it refers to God's right dealings, to the fact that everything he does is just, that no one can fault him. The word appears in this sense throughout the psalms ascribed to David. Again and again he calls God a "righteous God" and speaks of "your righteousness." (There are not many psalms from which this word or the idea represented by this word is missing.) This is a great testimony, that a person has lived a long time and has found by his or her own experience that God does all things rightly or justly. Therefore, (1) God can be trusted, and (2) it is the part of wisdom to conform one's life to God's will and standards. That is a great and important testimony to pass to the next generation.

2. *God's faithfulness.* In one sense the entire psalm has been about God's faithfulness: his faithfulness in the past, and the prayer of the psalmist that God will remain faithful to him in his old age. Here at the end the theme is the same, for it is the last and chief thing David wants to declare to those who are to come. He wants them to know that God is an utterly faithful God and can be trusted to remain so.

> "Great is thy faithfulness," O God my Father,
> There is no shadow of turning with thee;
> Thou changest not, thy compassions, they fail not;
> As thou hast been thou forever wilt be.
>
> "Great is thy faithfulness! Great is thy faithfulness!"
> Morning by morning new mercies I see:
> All I have needed thy hand hath provided—
> "Great is thy faithfulness," Lord, unto me!

If you have known God at all, you have found that he is indeed a God of great faithfulness and know that this must be your testimony.

Psalm 72

A Song of Solomon

Endow the king with your justice, O God,
*   the royal son with your righteousness.*
He will judge your people in righteousness,
*   your afflicted ones with justice.*
The mountains will bring prosperity to the people,
*   the hills the fruit of righteousness.*
He will defend the afflicted among the people
*   and save the children of the needy;*
*   he will crush the oppressor. . . .*

Praise be to the LORD God, the God of Israel,
*   who alone does marvelous deeds.*
Praise be to his glorious name forever;
*   may the whole earth be filled with his glory.*
*   Amen and Amen.*

verses 1–4, 18–19

At the Republican Convention in the summer of 1988 there was surprise and consternation in the press when George Bush, the Republican nominee for president, chose Dan Quayle as his vice-presidential running mate. Quayle was young, not well known, and quickly declared by many to be incompetent—unjustly in my opinion. Many asked why George Bush would handicap himself by this selection.

599

There were many suggestions, of course. But the most interesting was by Camille Paglia, a Philadelphia-based professor of communication theory and a well-known defender of television. She reminded everyone that television is an image-based medium, that political conventions are television events, and that what occurs at the conventions is not to be explained in rational terms but as symbols and imagery. What happened at the convention was that "George Bush chose a son," she explained. Before this he had been under the shadow of the older Ronald Reagan, sort of a younger son to the older man. Now in order to come into his own and establish his stature as a future president he chose as his running mate the younger, even boyish-looking Quayle.

I mention this to suggest how appropriate it is that a psalm of Solomon, David's son and his successor as king of Israel, should conclude the second book of the Psalter, which ends: "This concludes the prayers of David son of Jesse." The arrangement suggests that the prayers of David are not concluded until the son of David is in place.[1]

David's Son and David's Greater Son

The Hebrew word translated "of Solomon" can also mean "to Solomon," of course, just as the word translated "of David" can mean "to David." It is one ground on which scholars have questioned the traditional authorship of both collections. If this is the meaning here, Psalm 72 could be a psalm of David for the son who succeeded him, which makes the ending ("This concludes the prayers of David son of Jesse") even more appropriate.

Yet the argument does not work out very well. The ending of book two can have only one meaning; that is, most of the preceding psalms were written by David. If that is the case, the titles of those psalms must be read "of David" and not "to David." And if the Hebrew preposition with the noun means "of David" in the case of David's psalms, then it must mean "of Solomon" in the case of Psalm 72. There is no good reason for denying that the last psalm of this collection is by the new king.

However, it is not as a psalm of Solomon that this poem has commended itself so deeply to the synagogue and church. It is because it portrays the ideal king, and in the minds of Christian people this ideal king has always rightly been understood to be the Lord Jesus Christ. Derek Kidner writes that "The New Testament nowhere quotes it as Messianic, but this picture of the king and his realm is so close to the prophecies of Isaiah 11:1–5 and Isaiah 60–62 that if those passages are Messianic, so is this. Language that would otherwise be no more than courtly extravagance makes sober sense with this reference."[2] Charles Hodge wrote in his *Systematic Theology*,

> The Seventy-second Psalm contains a description of an exalted king, and of the blessings of his reign. These blessings are of such a nature as to prove that the subject of the psalm must be a divine person. (1) His kingdom is to

be everlasting. (2) Universal. (3) It secures perfect peace with God and good-will among men. (4) All men are to be brought to submit to him through love. (5) In him all the nations of the earth are to be blessed. . . . The subject of this psalm is, therefore, the Redeemer of the world.[3]

This psalm has given us several well-known hymns. James Montgomery's "Hail to the Lord's Anointed" and Isaac Watts's "Jesus Shall Reign" are two. But we also have Henry Scott Holland's "Judge Eternal, Throned in Splendor" and the Psalter rendering of verses 8–14 and 17–19 that begins "Christ Shall Have Dominion" (sung to the tune "Onward Christian Soldiers" by Sir Arthur Sullivan). The original *Trinity Hymnal* contained seven hymns based on this psalm. The newer *Trinity Hymnal* has four.

The stanzas of Psalm 72 describe five qualities of Christ's kingdom: (1) its character (vv 1–4), (2) its duration (vv. 5–7), (3) its expanse (vv. 8–11), (4) its nature (vv. 12–14), and (5) its blessing (vv. 15–17). The doxology in verses 18 and 19 concludes not only this psalm but also the Psalter's second section.

The Character of the Kingdom: Righteousness

The first four verses of the psalm lift up the essential character of the kingdom being described. It is *righteousness*, a word that occurs three times (in vv. 1, 2, and 3). Verse 1 asks that the king might be endowed with righteousness. Verse 2 predicts that, so endowed, the king will judge the people in righteousness. Verse 3 speaks of the fruit of righteous judgment, which is prosperity, a theme to be developed more fully in stanza five. The first verse also picks up on the ending of the previous psalm, which praised God for his righteousness (v. 19). Righteousness has to do with God doing all things rightly or justly. It is appropriate therefore that Psalm 72 highlight the same quality for the one who is to reign for him on earth.

Did Solomon possess it? Yes, in his early years. Righteousness was a characteristic of Solomon, who, at the commencement of his reign, asked God for wisdom so he might rule justly (see 1 Kings 3:5–28 and 10:1–9).

Unfortunately Solomon did not live up to this high standard. As his reign progressed he turned away from the Lord, followed other gods, and began to oppress the people with high rates of taxation to finance his building projects. That is the way with human kingdoms. They may begin well, but they are always marred by sin and stained with selfishness. We pray that our rulers may be endowed with righteousness, as Psalm 72 does in verse 1. But human rulers always let us down, which is why we look for the only upright, just, and entirely righteous rule of Jesus Christ. Only of him may we say truthfully and with full conviction,

> He will judge your people in righteousness,
> your afflicted ones with justice.

The mountains will bring prosperity to the people,
the hills the fruit of righteousness (vv. 2–3).[4]

In Jesus' case this fruit of righteousness exceeds anything Solomon could accomplish. It was Solomon's duty, like that of all secular rulers, to defend righteous people who were unjustly attacked. But it is Christ's work actually to make people righteous, since he gives them his own perfect righteousness and then, by his Spirit, also renews their minds according to true godliness. Thus he brings back righteousness, which otherwise would be banished from the world.

The Duration of the Kingdom: Endless

The second stanza of the psalm (vv. 5–7) describes the duration of Christ's kingdom, and the idea here is that it is *eternal*. It is a kingdom that will never end. David was a great king. He ruled in Israel for forty years. But at last David died, and the kingdom passed to his successor, Solomon. Solomon reigned another forty years, but he died. So also with all the rulers of this world. No matter how powerful, how just, how good, how beneficial their reigns over their subjects may have been or how loudly their subjects may have cried out, "O king, live forever!" in the end all these earthly rulers die and their kingdoms pass to others. Not so with Jesus Christ! He is an ever-living king and his kingdom an everlasting kingdom.

It is true that the kings of this world have not yet willingly bowed to Christ and acknowledged his sovereignty, though they will one day (Phil. 2:9–11). But Jesus rules nevertheless. By his sovereign power he controls all that is unfolding upon the great world stage, and by the power of his Spirit he calls men and women to loving submission to himself within the fellowship of the church. Charles Haddon Spurgeon wrote, "We see on the shore of time the wrecks of the Caesars, the relics of the Moguls, and the last remnants of the Ottomans. Charlemagne, Maximilian, Napoleon, how they flit like shadows before us! They were and are not; but Jesus for ever is."[5]

One theme that reoccurs throughout the psalm is the blessing that will come to Christ's kingdom because of the nature of his rule. This theme has already been suggested in stanza one, which mentions prosperity and the defense of afflicted people (vv. 3–4). It is developed as a theme to itself in stanza five (vv. 15–17). It is present in this stanza in verses 6–7.

These verses compare the blessing of Christ's rule to "rain falling on a mown field" and to "showers watering the earth." These images find parallels in several places: in Deuteronomy 32:2, where they refer to Moses' teaching about God; Job 29:22–23, where they refer to the way Job says his words were received by others before the beginning of his troubles; and Proverbs 16:15, where they refer to the effect of the king's favor. The most interesting and striking parallel is in David's own, final instruction to Solomon, recorded in 2 Samuel 23:3–4. David said,

> When one rules over men in righteousness,
>> when he rules in the fear of God,
> he is like the light of morning at sunrise
>> on a cloudless morning,
> like the brightness after rain
>> that brings the grass from the earth.

That is true of human rule. Righteousness brings blessing, just as Proverbs 14:34 states: "Righteousness exalts a nation, but sin is a disgrace to any people." Yet among earthly rulers that ideal is realized only from time to time and partially. In Jesus' case it is an ideal that is fully realized and is everlasting. As the hymn based on Psalm 73 and set to music by Sir Arthur Sullivan says,

> Ever and forever shall his name endure,
> Long as suns continue it shall stand secure;
> And in him forever all men shall be blest,
> And all nations hail him King of kings confessed.

The Expanse of the Kingdom: Universal

The third stanza of this psalm (vv. 8–11) speaks of the great expanse of Christ's kingdom, and the point here is that it is *universal*. It is "from sea to sea and from the River to the ends of the earth" (v. 8). The "River" is the Euphrates, of course. But this does not mean that these words are meant to describe only the geographical territory contained in the earthly kingdom of Solomon, though at its fullest extent Solomon's kingdom did extend from the Euphrates to the Mediterranean (1 Kings 4:21; 2 Chron. 9:26). These verses speak of all lands, the Euphrates being the farthest point the writer could think of to the east, Tarshish the farthest city to the west, and Sheba and Seba the farthest kingdoms to the south.[6] In fact, so extensive is this kingdom that, according to the psalmist, even "the desert tribes will bow before him and his enemies will lick the dust" (v. 9). Also, "All kings will bow down to him and all nations will serve him" (v. 11).

So the rule of Jesus extends not only over all times—from age to age—but also embraces all places and all peoples. None can escape his righteous rule. That is why the hymn I just referred to starts,

> Christ shall have dominion over land and sea,
> Earth's remotest regions shall his empire be;
> They that wilds inhabit shall their worship bring,
> Kings shall render tribute, nations serve our King.

In a similar vein the last stanza of James Montgomery's great hymn says,

> O'er every foe victorious, he on his throne shall rest,
> From age to age more glorious, all-blessing and all-blest;

The tide of time shall never his covenant remove;
His name shall stand forever—that Name to us is Love.

This is one of the themes of the songs that will be sung in heaven too. For one of these songs says, "The kingdom of the world has become the kingdom of our Lord and of his Christ, and he will reign for ever and ever" (Rev. 11:15).

The Nature of the Kingdom: Compassionate

The fourth characteristic of the kingdom of Jesus Christ concerns its nature; it is *compassionate*. This is developed in stanza four (vv. 12–14). Most of this world's rulers want to be thought compassionate, and some of them probably genuinely desire to be so. In the 1988 presidential campaign George Bush called repeatedly for "a kinder, gentler America." But America did not become kinder or gentler for all his good will or rhetoric. On the contrary, it is increasingly a harsh, mean, unkind, brutal, and even dangerous place in which to live. It is made so by the sin of the people, who have rejected God. The world is like this everywhere. By nature people are not kind or gentle or compassionate.

Ah, but where Jesus rules his kindness becomes evident, and people are treated gently for his sake. Those who are needy and cry out receive help (v. 12). Those who are weak are pitied, and those in danger of death are saved (v. 13). People who have suffered oppression and have been victimized by violence are rescued by those who love and serve King Jesus. What an unacknowledged debt the world owes to those who are Christ's people!

The Blessing of the Kingdom: Prosperity for All

Each of the preceding stanzas has contributed to the ideal blessing that this kingdom will experience. Because of its righteous character, prosperity will flow from the mountains and the afflicted will be rescued (stanza one). Because of its endless duration, the righteous will flourish and wealth will increase (stanza two). Because of its universal expanse, peace will prevail and treasure will flow to this realm's sovereign (stanza three). Because of its compassionate nature, all who are needy or afflicted or in danger will be helped (stanza four).

All that has been preliminary, however. For now stanza five is given over wholly to the *blessing* that will come from Christ's rule. This blessing will be both material and spiritual.

The material prosperity described in this stanza (vv. 15–17) has to do with gold pouring in from Sheba and grain and fruit thriving even on the tops of the hills, the least productive parts of the land. Gold, grain, and fruit were ancient measures of prosperity. So this is a way of saying that under the reign of Jesus there will be prosperity of every conceivable kind. This does not mean that Christians in every place will all become rich. Riches are not always a blessing. But it does mean that wherever Jesus is honored and served, and wherever righteousness is pursued, there prosperous times will almost inevitably follow. Families will become stable. Parents will care for, educate, and promote the well-being of their children. Unproductive members of society will be reclaimed and assisted in becoming productive. Virtue will permeate the workplace, and wealth will be created through industry and hard work. Christianity has contributed such material blessings to numerous nations, while nations that have persecuted the followers of Christ and repressed Christianity have languished for it.

As for spiritual blessing, the second half of verse 17 certainly refers to the promise of spiritual blessing God gave Abraham when he called him out of Ur of the Chaldees, saying, "All peoples on earth will be blessed through you" (Gen. 12:3). It was not through Abraham that this blessing came to human beings, however. It was through Jesus, Abraham's great descendant, which is why Paul could write to the Galatians, "The Scripture foresaw that God would justify the Gentiles by faith, and announced the gospel in advance to Abraham: 'All nations will be blessed through you.' So those who have faith are blessed along with Abraham, the man of faith" (Gal. 3:8–9).

This is real prosperity, of course. Not to be rich in this world's goods, though Christianity tends to advance people in the direction of material prosperity, but to be rich in those spiritual blessings that are ours because of Christ. The Bible says, "Praise be to the God and Father of our Lord Jesus Christ, who has blessed us in the heavenly realms with every spiritual blessing in Christ" (Eph. 1:3).

Praise to the God of Israel

This brings us to the doxology that ends not only Psalm 72 but also the second book of the Psalter. It corresponds to the parallel but shorter endings to books one and four (Pss. 41:13; 106:48) and to the even shorter endings to books three and five (Pss. 89:52; 150:6).

> Praise be to the LORD God, the God of Israel,
>   who alone does marvelous deeds.
> Praise be to his glorious name forever;
>   may the whole earth be filled with his glory.
>   Amen and Amen (vv. 18–19).

The doxology is a reminder, as G. Campbell Morgan says, that the kingdom described in Psalm 72 is "the Kingdom for which the world still waits."[7] We are to pray for this world's kingdoms (1 Tim. 2:1–2), but we are not to suppose that any earthly ruler will actualize the theocratic kingdom, since it was not achieved even by wise King Solomon or by godly King David. As

Charles Colson reminded delegates to a National Association of Evangelicals convention some years ago after Ronald Reagan had spoken to them and they were all very impressed and cheering wildly, "The kingdom of God does not arrive on Air Force One." Indeed it does not. God's kingdom arrives with God's King, and God's King is Jesus. We wait for his kingdom, not an earthly kingdom. And we pray that it might come (Matt. 6:10), knowing that it alone is truly righteous and that it alone will never pass away.

Book Three of the Psalter

Psalm 73

A Paradigm Shift for Asaph

Surely God is good to Israel,
to those who are pure in heart.

But as for me, my feet had almost slipped;
I had nearly lost my foothold.
For I envied the arrogant
when I saw the prosperity of the wicked. . . .

This is what the wicked are like—
always carefree, they increase in wealth. . . .

When I tried to understand all this,
it was oppressive to me
till I entered the sanctuary of God;
then I understood their final destiny.
verses 1–3, 12, 16–17

There are lots of buzzwords in the English language today—*on-line, downtime, market-driven, politically correct.* One of my favorites is *paradigm shift.* A paradigm is a fully worked out conjugation of a verb or declension of a noun, showing the word in all its forms. It is a complete framework. So a paradigm shift is a radical change from one system or way of looking at something to another, a change in a person's worldview.

Asaph had such a paradigm shift, and Psalm 73 is his record of it.

Asaph was one of the members of the tribe of Levi whom David put in charge of the worship music that was performed at the Tent of Meeting before Solomon built the great temple in Jerusalem (1 Chron. 6:39). In time he seems to have become the leader of this group and then the father of an entire clan of temple musicians. David gave some of his psalms to Asaph, and these were performed by him and his associates (1 Chron. 16:7). Asaph also composed psalms himself. One of these is Psalm 50, from the second book of the Psalter. The other psalms which are said to be by Asaph are Psalms 73–83, which lead off the Psalter's third book (Psalms 73–89). Of the six remaining psalms, four are by the "Sons of Korah," who were also temple musicians.[1]

Telling It Like It Is

One thing that makes Asaph attractive is his honesty about himself and what he saw around him. To use Howard Cosell's phrase, Asaph "tells it like it is."

What he saw and what bothered him so much is that the wicked seem to do very well in this world, much better than the godly, and this is not what we should expect in a moral universe directed by a sovereign God. If God is in control of things, the plans of the wicked should flounder. They should even be punished openly. The godly alone should prosper. But that is not what Asaph saw, and it is not what we see either. We see scoundrels getting rich. Utterly degenerate persons, like particularly vile rock musicians or movie stars, are well paid and sought after. Even criminals get rich selling their crime stories.

Why do the wicked prosper and the godly have such a hard time? This is the same question that was raised in Psalm 37 and in Job. In each of these places a different answer is suggested. In Psalm 37 the answer is to wait, to trust Jehovah, believing that in the end the wrong will be set right even in this world. David says,

> Do not fret because of evil men
> > or be envious of those who do wrong;
> for like the grass they will soon wither,
> > like green plants they will soon die away (vv. 1–2).

In Job there is no answer, at least none given to Job. It is simply that God is above us and we dare not, indeed we cannot, question him. God makes this point in chapters 38–41, demanding in a ruthless and thoroughly exhaustive manner whether Job can explain even one of his manifold works of creation, not to mention God's ways with the righteous and the wicked. Job cannot, and the conclusion comes when he confesses,

> Surely I spoke of things I did not understand,
> things too wonderful for me to know (Job 42:3).

In Psalm 73 the answer is neither ignorance nor trust in the eventual judgment of the wicked in this life. It is a perception of the ultimate end of the wicked, beyond this life, and the blessed reality of God experienced by the righteous here and now. In providing this answer, Psalm 73 is probably the most perceptive treatment of this theme in all literature. But the reason is that Asaph is so honest in his questioning. He looks at the world with open eyes and then comes to God for the answer to his problem.[2]

The Starting Point

Psalm 73 is an example of faith honestly doubting what it does in fact believe. So it is not that kind of boastful doubting we so often hear in the conversation of proud people. Some people think it is clever to be able to raise questions the people of God have trouble answering, but that is not what the psalmist is doing. The proof of this is in the point from which he starts out:

> Surely God is good to Israel,
>> to those who are pure in heart (v. 1).

The next verses are going to record, as a matter of personal testimony, how Asaph was shaken from that fundamental assertion for a time. Nevertheless, the goodness of God is a truth, and for that reason Asaph begins by stating it and finishes by stating it too.

In fact, this is the way the psalm moves forward. Marvin E. Tate in his commentary has a full-page diagram with arrows showing how the psalm begins with the truth of verse 1, descends into personal doubt and turmoil (vv. 2–15), reaches a turning point (vv. 16–17), and then reascends to where the psalm started out (vv. 18–28).[3] Asaph begins with "God is good" and ends with a similar testimony. J. J. Stewart Perowne says rightly, "There is no parade of doubt merely as doubt. He states *first,* and in the most natural way, the *final* conviction of his heart."[4]

A Record of Asaph's Descent

But Asaph did doubt! Having stated that "God is good" in verse 1, he also acknowledges that this was not always a firm conviction with him. Here he contrasts himself with God, saying, "But as for me . . ." God is good, pure, and steadfast. But Asaph confesses his own lack of goodness, admits his personal defilement because of impure thoughts, and acknowledges that for a time at least his "feet had almost slipped" (v. 2).

1. *Envy of the wicked* (vv. 2–3). What Asaph observed was "the prosperity of the wicked," which defies our expectation that virtue should be rewarded and wickedness punished. But that is only one side of the problem and probably the least important. Asaph's real problem, as he acknowledges, was that he had become envious of the wicked, and it was as a result of this

that he had "almost slipped." In other words, his problem was that he compared their health, wealth, and prosperity with his lack of prosperity and was resentful that God would allow such a state to continue.

That is where our problem lies too, isn't it? It is not really the intellectual problems that bother us, though we may express our unhappiness that way. It is that God is not treating us the way we think he should, that other people seem to be doing better than we are, that we have to struggle for a living while they coast along without any obvious trouble. Our problem is envy, and envy is criticizing God. It is sin.

2. *A description of the wicked* (vv. 4–11). Asaph is honest about his sin, however. So the next thing he tells us is what he thought he observed about the wicked during this time of spiritual slippage. They seem to have no problems, to possess near-perfect health, to thrive on pride and be courted by other people, even to the point of being able to dismiss God as having any importance for their lives.

> They have no struggles;
>   their bodies are healthy and strong.
> They are free from the burdens common to man;
>   they are not plagued by human ills.
> Therefore pride is their necklace;
>   they clothe themselves with violence. . . .
>
> They say, "How can God know?
>   Does the Most High have knowledge?" (vv. 4–6, 11).

The wicked seem to get away with their wickedness and even boast about it. That is what is so troubling. Dionysus the Younger, an ancient tyrant of Sicily, plundered the temple of Syracuse, sailed home safely with his loot, and then remarked, "Do you not see how the gods favor those who commit sacrilege?" When we are in an envious state we find such situations galling and wish that God would strike the arrogant person down.

3. *A summary* (v. 12). Verse 12 is a summary of what Asaph has told us about the wicked so far. "This is what the wicked are like," he says. They are "always carefree" and "they increase in wealth." When I think about this summary, it seems to me that what Asaph is talking about is what we call "the lifestyles of the rich and famous."

4. *The psalmist's wrong conclusion* (vv. 13–14). What is the point of being godly then? Asaph asks. Or as we would put it, what is the advantage of being a Christian if those who are not Christians get what I want and I don't get it? Indeed, the situation is even worse than that, for not only do I not get what I want, I have troubles to boot. In fact, it even seems as if I am being punished for trying to be good.

> Surely in vain have I kept my heart pure;
>   in vain have I washed my hands in innocence.

> All day long I have been plagued;
> I have been punished every morning (vv. 13–14).

All of us feel that way whenever we get our eyes off God and begin to compare our condition with the circumstances of the wicked.

Yet even at this low point, when he is oppressed by what he sees and is jealous of those for whom he should have no envy, Asaph is still a believing child of God. One way he shows it is by what he says next. He says that although he felt this way, he did not want to say what he was feeling out loud because he did not want to harm the faith of other people, those he calls "your children" (v. 15). That is an interesting point, because it shows that having doubts like Asaph's is not incompatible with responsible Christian living. It may have been true, as he says, that his feet "had *almost* slipped." But they had not actually slipped, or at least they had not slipped so far as to make him forget his responsibilities as a leader of God's people.

The Turning Point

Suddenly on this downhill path into floundering unbelief there comes a turning point (vv. 16–17). For just when he was about to be swept away, Asaph, the honest doubter, "entered the sanctuary of God" and came to understand the "final destiny" of the wicked.

The destiny of the wicked means their final judgment, that they will perish apart from God in hell. But what is the connection between this important perception and the psalmist's entering into the sanctuary? John Calvin thought that entering the sanctuary meant studying the law of God that was kept there—that is, entering into the Bible's doctrines. Another teacher has suggested that Asaph saw the altar upon which a fire was always burning and where the offerings for sin were consumed. The death of the sacrificial animals symbolized death as the end result of sin, and the fire could have reminded Asaph of this judgment.

I think that each of those views touches on the answer. But the whole answer, in my opinion, is that in the sanctuary Asaph came to see everything from God's perspective rather than from his own limited and sinful worldview. That is, he came to see the lives of the wicked and also his own life from the perspective of eternity. He experienced a paradigm shift.

In an excellent contemporary study of this psalm, Roy Clements, pastor of the Eden Baptist Church in Cambridge, England, links this new perspective to worship, saying, "Worship . . . put[s] God at the center of our vision. . . . It is vitally important because it is only when God is at the center of our vision that we see things as they really are."[5]

The Ascent

We have followed Asaph from his introductory statement of faith in the goodness of God, through his steep descent into doubt and near unbelief, to the important turning point as a result of which he began to see things from God's perspective. Here we see him coming back. This radical reordering of his thinking, described in verses 18–26, touches on three main areas.

1. *A new awareness of the destiny of the wicked* (vv. 18–20). The first new perception is what I have already referred to, the final destiny of the wicked. The wicked seem secure, but they are actually on slippery ground, and it only takes a gentle puff by God to blow them off their proud golden pedestal to ruin. Having learned to look at those he had envied from God's perspective, the psalmist now sees that they are no more stable than a fantasy. They vanish like a dream when we open our eyes from sleep in the morning.

2. *A new awareness of himself* (vv. 21–22). The second area in which Asaph gained a new awareness of the way things really are concerned himself. He saw that in questioning God's just handling of life's circumstances he was not being wise, but was rather being "senseless and ignorant." Indeed, he was behaving as "a brute beast" before God. This is a profound insight, for whenever we fail to learn from God and instead begin to trust our own contrary judgments on anything, we start to think like animals, which have no real awareness of God. And we begin to act like animals too!

This is as far as Job got in his struggles with Asaph's question. For when God finished interrogating Job, Job confessed that God's ways were entirely beyond his understanding, and he despised his pride and repented.

3. *A new awareness of God's presence and thus also of God's genuine blessing on the righteous* (vv. 23–26). Having gone into the sanctuary and having recovered a true spiritual balance with new insight into the destiny of the wicked and his own lack of spiritual understanding, Asaph now also recognized that God has been with him all along and indeed always would be with him. Moreover, he saw that this was a true blessing against which the worldly blessings of the wicked are as nothing.

These verses are the very apogee of his testimony, and they are filled with some of the finest expressions of true spirituality in all the Bible. They deserve to be memorized by every true Christian.

> Yet I am always with you;
>   you hold me by my right hand.
> You guide me with your counsel,
>   and afterward you will take me into glory.
> Whom have I in heaven but you?
>   And earth has nothing I desire besides you.
> My flesh and my heart may fail,
>   but God is the strength of my heart
>   and my portion forever (vv. 23–26).

Verse 25 is a particularly fine expression and has been a blessing to many over the ages. Charles Wesley (1707–1788), the great Methodist hymn writer, was thinking about it on his deathbed and actually composed a hymn based on it as his final testimony. Calling his wife to him, he dictated:

> In age and feebleness extreme,
> What shall a sinful worm redeem?
> Jesus, my only hope thou art,
> Strength of my failing flesh and heart;
> O, could I catch a smile from thee,
> And drop into eternity.

Many Christians have been able to echo the psalmist, confessing that in the final analysis the only thing that really matters for us is God. He is all we have, but he is also all we need. He sustains us here, and afterward he will receive us into glory (v. 24).

Asaph's Final Testimony

The final two verses of this psalm contain Asaph's testimony, a summary of what has been stated previously: first, that the wicked will perish in the end, and second, that God will be with the righteous and they will be with him. In great understatement Asaph declares, "But as for me, it is good to be near God."

Here is a final observation I hope you will remember. It concerns the progression of the dominant pronouns in the psalm. In the first section, as far as verse 12, the emphasized pronoun is *they*, referring to the wicked. The psalmist has his eyes fixed on them. In the second section, verses 13–17, the dominant pronoun is *I*. Having seen the prosperity of the wicked, the psalmist looks at himself and falls into unjustified comparisons. In the third section, verses 18–22, the dominant pronoun is *you*. Here the psalmist has stopped comparing himself to other people and is thinking about God. Then, in the final section of the psalm, verses 23–28, *you* and *I* are combined. Here Asaph says, "you [meaning God] have set your hand upon me" and I for my part want nothing on earth but you.

You and I need to learn that lesson in the deepest possible way, for if we learn it, all life will be transformed and we will find ourselves always content in God. Remember that heaven and earth will pass away (Matt. 24:35) but that those who know God and do his will abide forever.

Psalm 74

Prayer amid the Ruins of Jerusalem

Why have you rejected us forever, O God?
  Why does your anger smolder against the sheep of your pasture?
Remember the people you purchased of old,
  the tribe of your inheritance, whom you redeemed—
Mount Zion, where you dwelt.

verses 1–2

$\mathbf{S}$inging psalms was very important to the Huguenots, those persecuted Protestants who were driven out of France in the late seventeenth and early eighteenth centuries. The power of the psalms to bless and fortify them must have been especially feared by their persecutors, for under Louis XIII and Louis XIV many edicts were passed forbidding their use of the Psalter. Nevertheless, these brave people merely hid their books while carrying on their singing in mountain caves or forests, since they knew the psalms by heart.

One psalm from which they gained particular strength was Psalm 74. In 1686, one year after the revocation of the Edict of Nantes, which removed their protection under the earlier laws of France, the Protestants of Vaud were driven from their homes and dispossessed of their property. They crossed the Alps, some dying on the way, and at last entered Geneva, the City of Refuge. There, their voices choked by exhaustion and misery, they sang the opening verses of this psalm, while scores of refugees who had already reached Geneva as the result of earlier persecutions joined in.

> Why have you rejected us forever, O God?
>> Why does your anger smolder against the sheep of
>> your pasture?
> Remember the people you purchased of old,
>> the tribe of your inheritance, whom you redeemed—
>> Mount Zion, where you dwelt.

Three years later, in 1689, the same psalm was chanted in triumph by seven hundred of these exiles who, led by their pastor, Henri Arnaud, had fought their way back to their homes. When they met at last in their own homeland in one of their own churches the joy and enthusiasm were inexpressible, and once again Psalm 74 was sung.[1]

The Destruction of Jerusalem

Psalm 74 has no historical reference, yet in this case there can be little doubt about the setting—the state of Jerusalem after its fall to the armies of Babylon under King Nebuchadnezzar in 586 B.C. The important point is the destruction of Jerusalem, which is referred to pointedly and poignantly. This fits the time of the Babylonian invasion nicely. Yet some scholars feel that a setting in the time of the Maccabees, when the temple was desecrated by Antiochus Epiphanes, is more likely. One of the arguments for this later period is that Psalm 74:9 says that "no prophets are left, and none of us knows how long this will be." These scholars point out that Jeremiah and Ezekiel were still living after the city's fall and that Jeremiah had prophesied clearly that the captivity would last seventy years (Jer. 25:11; 29:10). In my judgment these are not decisive arguments. After Jerusalem fell Jeremiah was in exile. How many would have known his prophecy about the seventy years?

What should be decisive is that Antiochus Epiphanes did not destroy the temple, but only profaned it, and Psalm 74 is clear about the sanctuary's destruction.[2]

The only thing that is really puzzling about the title of Psalm 74 is that it is called "a *maskil* of Asaph." The Asaph we know of was a contemporary of David, so he obviously did not live until the early sixth century B.C. Therefore, either this is a later Asaph, which is not unlikely since the name might have been perpetuated among the temple musicians, or, more likely, the name was affixed to many psalms produced by this body of musicians. We know that the "descendants of Asaph" were functioning as late as the reign of Josiah (2 Chron. 35:15).

Whoever he was, this writer grieved for the fallen city and its temple and in this psalm cries out passionately to God to hear, answer, and move to reestablish his fallen but covenanted people. For us Psalm 74 is a helpful prayer model. It is direct, passionate, and honest, as the prayers of Asaph tend to be. But the prayer is also respectful and wise. Charles Haddon Spurgeon wrote, "We have here before us a model of pleading, a very rapture of prayer. It is humble, but very bold, eager, fervent and effectual. The heart of God is always moved by such entreaties."[3]

A Painful Inquiry

Verses 1–2 form the first stanza of the psalm and at once strike the sad, wailing tone of this lament. Jerusalem has been destroyed, the temple is in ruins, and the psalmist can see no end to the wretchedness he has experienced and observes. In these verses he asks God if his rejection of his people is going to last forever: "Why have you rejected us forever, O God?" He asks God to remember and therefore help both his redeemed people and Jerusalem: "Remember the people you purchased, . . . the tribe, . . . Mount Zion, where you dwelt."

There is only one other psalm that is quite like this, Psalm 79, which is also identified as a psalm of Asaph. Whoever they are, the two Asaphs must be the same individual, because Psalms 74 and 79 are so much alike. They use similar imagery, and both ask, "Will you be angry forever?" (Pss. 74:1; 79:5).

They are different in tone, but one other psalm (Psalm 137) and parts of Lamentations, especially 2:5–9, also lament the fall of Jerusalem.

Although Psalm 74 is particularly grim, we should not overlook the fact that it too, like Psalm 73, is a psalm of faith and that this is indicated from the beginning, just as Psalm 73 both began and ended by confessing that God is good. In Psalm 74 God is asked to remember his "purchased" and "redeemed" people, those he has already set apart to himself. This reminder of the electing work of God tempers the opening question and lays the groundwork for the petitions still to come.

An Honest Look at the Ruined City

The second stanza, verses 3–8, presents a description of the ruined city, asking God to take a long look at what Israel's enemies have done to it. What chiefly concerns the psalmist here is that they have destroyed the temple, the sanctuary where God met with his worshipers. This is the major difference between Psalm 74 and Psalm 79, which also describes the terrible ruin brought about by Israel's enemies. In Psalm 79 Asaph worries about the people who have been scattered, imprisoned, and killed. In Psalm 74 he is distressed that the house of God has been devastated.

This is very vivid poetry, because we can almost visualize Asaph taking God by the hand to lead him through the twisted rubble left by the invaders. "Look, that is where they broke in," he seems to be saying. "Over there is where they set up their military standards. That is where they attacked the carved paneling, as if they were merely hacking their way through a thicket of trees. Then they burned the temple. Look at those ashes. That is all that is left. And then, as if the damage to the temple itself were not bad enough, they went through the whole land and destroyed every place where you were worshiped. They said, 'We will crush them completely!' And they have! Do you see it? Do you care?" This is a fierce complaint, bordering just possibly on impropriety as an address to God. But we should not miss the fact that it is at least addressed to God. When we complain it is more often the case that we just complain, either to ourselves or to other people. It is better to complain to God.

Verse 8 uses the plural to refer to "all the assemblies," translated "every place where God was worshiped" by the New International Version. This has been used as an argument for dating the psalm from the days of the Maccabees, because we do not know of any synagogues or legalized places of worship in Israel until after the Jews returned from their seventy-year-long Babylonian exile. However, it has also been suggested that the plural might be used to denote the several parts, courts, storehouses, and chambers of the one great temple. Both arguments are probably unnecessary. Although there was only one place appointed for Israel's worship, because it alone housed the altar for the appointed burnt sacrifices, and although the formation of formal synagogues seems to date from a later time, there must, as Perowne says, "surely have been some public worship beyond the limits of the family, and if so, places, houses for its celebration."[4]

This is what the psalmist wanted God to see and points out to him. God had allowed the destruction to be total. How can there be public worship of God if there are no remaining places for worship in the land?

How Long? How Long?

In verses 9–11 Asaph's lament reaches its lowest point in an expression of utter abandonment. Maclaren rightly calls these verses "the kernel of the psalm, the rest of which is folded round them systematically."[5] The psalm seems to descend to this point and then, like Psalm 73 before it, makes a turning point and begins to start back up. Asaph complains,

> We are given no miraculous signs;
>   no prophets are left,
>   and none of us knows how long this will be (v. 9).

It is hard to read this sad confession without thinking of the eighth chapter of Amos, where the preacher from Tekoa prophesied just such a time: "'The days are coming,' declares the Sovereign LORD, 'when I will send a famine through the land—not a famine of food or a thirst for water, but a famine of hearing the words of the LORD'" (Amos 8:11).

It is a desperate thing to be without any word from God. Fortunately, this cannot be said of us in our day. We have the Word of God in Scripture, and we also have many faithful persons to expound it. Today in the United States of America (and in many other parts of the world) a person can turn on a radio at almost any time of day or night and listen to faithful gospel preaching. It is not always profound. It is often stained by strange cultural peculiarities. But it is usually sound. In the same way, we can go into Christian bookstores and pick up scores of books that endeavor to explain the Scriptures. We can find believing churches in nearly every hamlet, town, and city, sometimes in almost every block. No, our problem is not an absence of God's Word or God's teachers. Our problem is that we do not value this Word. We do not cherish it and study it. We do not memorize its important passages. Instead, we allow countless lesser things (like television) to take the Bible's place.

Do you have time for God's Word? Your attitude should be that of John Wesley, the great Methodist evangelist, who wrote, "Give me that book! At any price, give me the book of God!"[6]

The Unchanging God

At the end of the previous stanza the psalmist addressed himself to God, protesting that the offenses he saw were directed not so much against himself and his people, but against God. In their wanton destruction of the temple, Israel's enemies were actually mocking God. This led him to think how great the God of Israel, whom they are mocking, really is (vv. 12–17), and this started him on an uphill path. Earlier he had asked God to remember Israel; here he himself remembers God.

In the commentaries there are two main ways of looking at these verses. Most of the earlier commentators saw them as containing poetic references to God's delivering the Jews from Egypt and bringing them into their own land. The "monster in the waters," Leviathan, was understood to be the crocodile and thus a symbol of Egypt. Many of the modern commentators take a quite different direction, supposing Leviathan to be the mythical monster overcome by Baal in the Canaanite religious legends. They see the psalmist saying that it is Jehovah, not Baal, who has won such victories for his people.

Actually, there are quite a number of diverse poetic images in these verses, and in my judgment the best parallel to what is going on here is the chapters in Job where God questions the patriarch about his mighty acts in heaven and on earth. If we just look over these verses in the psalm, giving them the most natural explanations, they seem to refer to salvation acts in history (v. 12), miraculous delivering interventions (vv. 13–14), provision of life-giving water (v. 15), and the governing of night and day and the seasons

(vv. 16–17). The bottom line of this recitation of God's acts and remembrances of God's power is something like the words of Job after God had questioned him. Job said, "I know that you can do all things; no plan of yours can be thwarted" (Job 42:2).

Not only can God do all things; he has. He ordains and accomplishes whatever comes to pass.

Christians know that! They know that God is in charge of all life, and therefore, even though bad things happen and it might appear that God has forgotten them and no longer shows any interest in their welfare, they discover that they cannot deny what faith assures them they know: "Faith is being sure of what we hope for and certain of what we do not see" (Heb. 11:1). Believers know that God is in charge and that God is good. So they inevitably return to those convictions, even in the midst of great calamity, anchoring their hopes in God, as the psalmist does here.

A Final Urgent Plea

Because God is in charge and because he has acted in the past, why should he not also act powerfully in the present to deliver and restore his people? This is where the psalm has been heading, and it is the question with which it ends. Verses 18–23 voice this final urgent plea.

The new and very powerful idea in these last verses is the covenant (v. 20). A covenant is a formal agreement between two parties, but in the Old Testament the word is usually used of a unilateral relationship with the people entered into by God. In other words, it has to do with God choosing them to be his people and declaring that he will be their God, quite apart from any desires or choices on their part. This is the way God established his covenant with Abraham when he called him out of Ur of the Chaldeans, saying,

Leave your country, your people and your father's household and go to the land I will show you.

> I will make you into a great nation
>   and I will bless you;
> I will make your name great,
>   and you will be a blessing.
> I will bless those who bless you,
>   and whoever curses you I will curse;
> and all peoples on earth
>   will be blessed through you (Gen. 12:1–3).

The reason why the idea of the covenant is so powerful is precisely because the human beings involved have no choice either in its establishment or its terms. If it were up to them, they could opt in or opt out. But since the covenant is not of them and since God is unchangeable, will he not remain faithful to his covenant even though they have broken it and brought upon themselves the judgments that destroyed their city and temple? The strongest of all arguments is that God will remember his covenant, his solemn promises to continue to be the people's God.

Postscript: Pleading with God

I said near the beginning of this study that Psalm 74 is a model for prayer because of the way it pleads with God. Or, as Charles Spurgeon said, it is an example of how we can pray to God with arguments. The psalmist wants God to take his hand out of his pocket and act boldly to rebuke his enemies and reestablish his people in their land (vv. 9–11). But the psalm is not merely a plea that God would do this. It is also a listing of reasons why he should.

1. God should act because the people who are suffering from his harsh but righteous judgment are but sheep (v. 1). That is, they are "poor, silly and defenseless things."[7]

2. God should act because he has already purchased these poor people for himself (v. 2). That is, he has already expended a great deal of effort on them, and they were no better when he first redeemed them than now.

3. God should act not merely because the people have suffered, but because his temple has been devastated and the prescribed formal worship of God by his people has ceased (vv. 3–8).

4. God should act because the people's case is hopeless otherwise (v. 9). Signs and prophetic speaking have to come from God.

5. God should act because the mocking by Israel's enemies is really a mocking of God (vv. 10–11). It is his name that is being reviled, and his name must be honored above all else.

6. God should act because he has acted powerfully and with wonderful compassion in the past (vv. 12–17). It is his nature to make his greatness known. Why should he not do so again? Why should he not do so now?

7. God should act because he has entered into an everlasting covenant with his people, and the terms of that covenant call for God to be with them forever. True, the people have been unfaithful. But "what if some did not have faith? Will their lack of faith nullify God's faithfulness? . . . Let God be true, and every man a liar" (Rom. 3:3). Spurgeon calls this verse "the master key" to Asaph's pleading, for whatever else happens, God does not break his covenants.[8]

8. God should act because it is fitting that his enemies be rebuked and the poor and needy praise his name (v. 21).

9. God should act because it is his cause and not a mere man's that is in jeopardy (vv. 22–23). It is God's purposes that are being opposed by Israel's enemies.

If you are having trouble praying about something important in your life, why not do what Asaph does? Make a list of why God should answer your prayer and plead those reasons. Either God will answer, or you will find that your prayer is not a good one and you will pray for something better.

Psalm 75

Our God Reigns

We give thanks to you, O God,
we give thanks, for your Name is near;
men tell of your wonderful deeds.

You say, "I choose the appointed time;
it is I who judge uprightly.
When the earth and all its people quake,
it is I who hold its pillars firm.   Selah
To the arrogant I say, 'Boast no more,'
and to the wicked, 'Do not lift up your horns.
Do not lift your horns against heaven;
do not speak with outstretched neck.'"

No one from the east or the west
or from the desert can exalt a man.
But it is God who judges:
He brings one down, he exalts another.
In the hand of the LORD is a cup
full of foaming wine mixed with spices;
he pours it out, and all the wicked of the earth
drink it down to its very dregs.

As for me, I will declare this forever;
I will sing praise to the God of Jacob.
I will cut off the horns of all the wicked,
but the horns of the righteous will be lifted up.
verses 1–10

When we were studying Psalm 73 we saw that the complaint of the psalmist was that the wicked seem to prosper ("always carefree, they increase in wealth," v. 12) while the righteous suffer. Asaph confessed that he had become envious of the wicked and that his feet had almost slipped—until he went into the sanctuary of God, where he perceived their true end.

Psalm 75 is also a psalm of faith in God's just rule and judgment, but it comes at this subject from an entirely different point of view. There is no questioning, chafing, struggle, or envy in this psalm. On the contrary, although the psalmist knows that God's way of ruling the universe is often puzzling to us and that his judgments often seem delayed, God nevertheless is near, his judgments are timely, and the wicked will eventually be punished in full for the evil they have done. Whether this punishment is to be effected in this life or in the life to come does not seem to enter into the thinking of the psalmist or the subject matter of the psalm. The psalmist is content merely to know it will be done.

What the psalmist says is that the wicked will be brought down and the humble will be lifted up—because God reigns.

Two Well-Known Parallels

In developing this theme Psalm 75 reminds us of two other well-known portions of Scripture. The first is the song of Hannah when she presented her son Samuel to Eli the priest to work with him in the tabernacle, found in 1 Samuel 2:1–10. Some of it is so close to Psalm 75 that it is possible Asaph borrowed some of his phrasing from Hannah. She says in part,

> Do not keep talking so proudly
> or let your mouth speak such arrogance,
> for the LORD is a God who knows,
> and by him deeds are weighed. . . .
>
> The LORD brings death and makes alive;
> he brings down to the grave and raises up.
> The LORD sends poverty and wealth;
> he humbles and he exalts. . . .
>
> For the foundations of the earth are the LORD's;
> upon them he has set the world (vv. 3, 6–8).

The other well-known parallel to Psalm 75 is Mary's Magnificat, found in Luke 1. Part of that song says,

> He has performed mighty deeds with his arm;
> he has scattered those who are proud in their
> inmost thoughts.

> He has brought down rulers from their thrones
>> but has lifted up the humble.
> He has filled the hungry with good things (vv. 51–53).

In each of these songs the theme is that God reigns over all things; therefore, he brings down the arrogant, and he lifts up the humble. To link Psalm 75 with the one before it, note that at the end of Psalm 74 Asaph asked God to rise up and defend his cause and not to ignore the clamor of his adversaries. In Psalm 75 we are assured both that God does and that he will.

A good outline for this psalm is indicated by the stanzas of the New International Version. In the first (v. 1) the congregation speaks, thanking God that he is always near, present in all places and at all times; in stanza two (vv. 2–5) God speaks, assuring his praying people that he is indeed in control of his universe and warning the arrogant not to be arrogant or fight against heaven; in stanza three (vv. 6–8) the priest or preacher speaks, amplifying what God has said; then in the final stanza (vv. 9–10) the individual worshiper speaks, adding his agreement to everything.

The Congregation Speaks: Thanksgiving

It is natural for the people of God to give God thanks, for there are innumerable blessings for which thanks is due. Here, in verse 1, thanks is given to God for just one thing, and that is that the "Name [of God] is near." The "Name" stands for God himself; so "your Name is near" means that God is near. He is never far away; he is always at hand.

This is true in several senses, and any number of them could have been in the psalmist's mind. For one thing, that God is near could mean that God is everywhere, that he is omnipresent. That would be important for the wicked to know, because it would be a way of reminding them that God knows all about them and that his judgments are inescapable. They may be permitted to sin freely for a time, but they are never able to sin without consequences since judgment always comes. Second, that God is near could mean that God is near to help the righteous, "just around the corner." That would be important for his people to know, because it would be strengthening for upright people who go through hard times. That God is near to help would be an assurance that God will never abandon the righteous and will always step forward to help at just the right moment.

In this context, however, the statement that God is near probably means that he is in charge of his universe; he has not turned his back to it or abandoned its rule to others but is still present and presiding over everything that happens. This is why the words "your Name is near" are followed by "men tell of your wonderful deeds," meaning the things they have themselves witnessed, and why the rest of the psalm dwells on God's ongoing judgments in history. We express similar thoughts when we sing that moving hymn by Maltbie Babcock (1901):

> This is my Father's world, O let me ne'er forget
> That though the wrong seems oft so strong,
> > God is the ruler yet.
> This is my Father's world: The battle is not done;
> Jesus who died shall be satisfied,
> > And earth and heav'n be one.

Are you aware that God really is near at hand, that he is present in all that happens, and that nothing that ever comes into your life or happens to others is accidental? If you can see that and really believe it, it will transform all of life for you. You will never again be "under the circumstances," as we say, but always above them. If you know that God is near, you should thank him for it.

God Speaks: Assurance and Warning

It is not entirely clear from the Hebrew text how much of the following is spoken by God or at what point the writer breaks in to give his own personal comment or reflection on God's words. The New International Version makes as good a judgment as any when it puts verses 2–5 together as being spoken in one way or another by God. But they fall into two parts. In the first two verses (vv. 2–3) God speaks to assure the righteous. These words concern the nature of God's judgments. In the next two verses (vv. 4–5) God addresses the wicked to warn them about their evil actions.

1. *Assurance to the upright.* There is nothing in this psalm to betray turmoil, doubt, or worry on the part of the psalmist, as there is in Psalm 73. But even those who are truly resting in God must sometimes wonder why God does not judge evil in a more timely manner or even whether in this life justice is really done. In verses 2–3, God assures the righteous that whatever might seem to the contrary, his interventions are timely and justice is being done.

The important thing is that it is God who chooses "the appointed time" of his judgments, not other people. If judgment were left in our hands, we would probably let it flash out against anything that displeases us whenever we see it. But God lets evil go unchecked sometimes for a rather long time, knowing that he has appointed a proper time when it will be brought down. In his book *The Treasury of David* Charles Haddon Spurgeon comments on the previous psalm, where God's anger is described as smoldering (Ps. 74:1): "It is a terrible thing when the anger of God smokes, but it is an infinite mercy that it does not break into a devouring flame."[1] That is a blessed truth, of course. But it is equally true that the judgment of God will in time break into flame against evil.

I remember how at summer camp we would try to start a fire without matches. Usually we used a magnifying glass to concentrate the hot rays of the sun on dry tinder. Eventually the tinder would get hot and begin to smoke—usually it took a long time—then suddenly there would be a popping sound, and a small bright flame would leap up from the kindling. That is how it is with the judgments of God. For a long time there is only smoke. But then, suddenly, a flame appears that sweeps everything before it.

It is not wrong to ask at this point why God's judgments are delayed. This is a question the Bible answers clearly. The first reason for the delay of God's judgments is so those who are sinning might have an opportunity to repent of their sin and be saved. Paul wrote of this in Romans, saying, "Do you think you will escape God's judgment? Or do you show contempt for the riches of his kindness, tolerance and patience, not realizing that God's kindness leads you toward repentance?" (Rom. 2:3–4). If you have not yet come to Christ, you should not squander the time you have been given. You should turn from your sin and believe on Jesus now.

The second reason for the delay of God's judgments is so evil might have time to work itself out or come to full fruition. This is harder to understand, but it is a clear teaching of Scripture, the best example being that of the Amorites, who lived in Canaan before the conquest by the Jewish armies under Joshua. Speaking to Abraham, God explained that the conquest with its corresponding judgment would take place in the fourth generation after Abraham and not sooner because "the sin of the Amorites has not yet reached its full measure" (Gen. 15:16). Their case would be like that of Pharaoh, to whom God said, "I have raised you up for this very purpose, that I might show you my power and that my name might be proclaimed in all the earth" (Exod. 9:16; see Rom. 9:17).

2. *Warning to the arrogant.* The last two verses of stanza two are a warning to the arrogant, precisely so they might repent. Here the arrogant are warned against boasting ("Boast no more"), while the wicked are warned not to lift up their horns against heaven or speak with outstretched necks. The horn is a well-known biblical metaphor for strength (see Deut. 33:17; 1 Sam. 2:1, 10). So lifting up one's horn against heaven is the equivalent of shaking one's fist in God's face. The picture of an angry person stretching out his or her neck belligerently is self-explanatory.

The Preacher Speaks: God Is the Judge

God's assurance to the righteous and his warnings to the wicked should be sufficient in themselves. But preachers seem always to like to have the last word, even with God, and Psalm 75 is an example. God has spoken (in vv. 2–5). But now the priest adds his personal observations and applications to God's teaching (vv. 6–8).

He applies God's word in two ways, pointing out that whether a person is lifted up or brought down, exalted or abased, is up to God, and assuring the wicked that God means what he says when he declares that he will judge everyone uprightly and at the appointed time. The first point seems to have to do mostly with the righteous, for it is a way of telling them to stop looking to the world for their advancement. People defer to those in power and sometimes get caught in their wrong ways of doing things, because they want the advancement they think these prominent people can confer. The preacher tells us that advancement of this kind is not worth it; it is not true honor. The only approval or advancement that will ever matter is what comes from God, for "it is God who judges" (v. 7). Therefore, stop looking to other human beings. Learn to look to and live for God alone.

The second point is for those who do evil, and it is a powerful poetic reminder that in due time the wrath of God will be poured out like powerful foaming wine from God's cup and that the wicked will be made to drink it down even to the dregs.

> In the hand of the LORD is a cup
>   full of foaming wine mixed with spices;
> he pours it out, and all the wicked of the earth
>   drink it down to its very dregs (v. 8).

This is not the only place in the Bible where the image of the cup of the wrath of God occurs. It is found in Isaiah 51:17; Jeremiah 25:15–38; 49:12; 51:7; and Revelation 18:6. We know it best for its use in "The Battle Hymn of the Republic," which says of God, "He is pouring out the vintage where the grapes of wrath are stored."

Spurgeon remarks on this verse, "The retribution is terrible, it is blood for blood, foaming vengeance for foaming malice. [If] the very color of divine wrath is terrible, what must the taste be?"[2]

It is not hard to think of examples of the outpouring of the wrath of God against those who have excelled in doing evil. In his book of meditations on the psalms, Murdoch Campbell calls attention to the lifting up and the bringing down of Pharaoh, Nebuchadnezzar, Herod, and, more recently, Adolf Hitler. Campbell writes:

> Pharaoh reacted to God's command to let his people go by saying, "Who is God that I should obey him?" Nebuchadnezzar endeavored to set his throne and kingdom above him whose throne and kingdom are for ever and ever. Herod listened to the adulations of his degenerate admirers: "It is the voice of a god and not of a man." Coming nearer to our own time, we have read of how Adolf Hitler gazed at a picture of himself riding proudly on a white horse, a picture which bore the blasphemous title: "In the Beginning was the Word." Then in a voice that deliberately mocked Christ, the eternal King, he exclaimed, "I am providence."
>
> But Pharaoh and his hosts are swept to destruction; Nebuchadnezzar becomes a companion of "the beasts of the field"; Herod is devoured by

worms; and Hitler becomes a suicide. "Those that walk in pride God is able to abase." "He shall cut off the spirit of princes; he is terrible to the kings of the earth." "All the horns of the wicked will I cut off."[3]

Surely, "the One enthroned in heaven laughs" at such arrogance and will in time terrify the wicked "in his wrath" (Ps. 2:4–5).

The Individual Speaks: A Testimony

The very last verses of Psalm 75 contain a testimony agreeing with all the psalm has been teaching. I take them to be the testimony of the individual, indicated by the pronoun *I* occurring twice in verse 9 and a third time in verse 10. By reciting them, we can add our testimonies to these truths.

Generally speaking, scholars have explained the last verse of the psalm in either of two ways: as an additional oracle from God that is added on to the psalm, somewhat like a musical reprise;[4] or, more commonly, as a promise by the worshiper that he will do what he can to check the influence of the wicked and help the righteous.[5] Either is possible. But I see this verse rather as the substance of the testimony the individual worshiper will be giving: God will do as he says. If we were conveying this idea by printing it according to English style, it would be by a colon after the previous statement and with quotation marks around verse 10. Like this: "As for me, I will declare *this* forever (I will sing praise to the God of Jacob): 'I will cut off the horns of all the wicked, but the horns of the righteous will be lifted up.'"

That is exactly what you and I are called to do, of course. If we have become followers of the Lord Jesus Christ and know him to be the true "King of kings and Lord of lords" (Rev. 19:16), we will want to make this known. We declare him as the rightful king who alone will execute right judgment.

But we say something else as well. Judgment is coming. Jesus is the Judge. We warn people of that coming judgment. There are foretastes of judgment even now, for evil usually does not triumph but is rather brought low. Pharaoh drowns; Nebuchadnezzar is humbled; Herod writhes in agony; Hitler kills himself in his bunker. But we also declare that being forced to drink the cup of the wrath of the God who reigns over all things is not necessary since Jesus has drunk that cup to the bottom for all who will believe on him as their Savior. Jesus drank the cup of God's wrath ("Shall I not drink the cup the Father has given me?" John 18:11) so that you and I might drink from the cup of salvation.

An unidentified later psalmist had it right when he declared, "I will lift up the cup of salvation and call on the name of the LORD" (Ps. 116:13).

Psalm 76

The Fear of the Lord
Is the Beginning

In Judah God is known;
his name is great in Israel.
His tent is in Salem,
his dwelling place in Zion.
There he broke the flashing arrows,
the shields and the swords, the weapons of war. Selah

You are resplendent with light,
more majestic than mountains rich with game.
Valiant men lie plundered,
they sleep their last sleep;
not one of the warriors
can lift his hands.
At your rebuke, O God of Jacob,
both horse and chariot lie still.
You alone are to be feared.
Who can stand before you when you are angry?
From heaven you pronounced judgment,
and the land feared and was quiet—
when you, O God, rose up to judge,
to save all the afflicted of the land. Selah
Surely your wrath against men brings you praise,
and the survivors of your wrath are restrained.

Make vows to the LORD your God and fulfill them;
let all the neighboring lands
bring gifts to the One to be feared.
He breaks the spirit of rulers;
he is feared by the kings of the earth.

verses 1–12

It is not always possible to find a reason for the psalms being placed where they are in the Psalter, but in this case Psalm 76 follows the last psalm nicely. In fact, there are links between Psalms 74, 75, and 76. Psalm 74 looks on the violence and injustice that are in the world and asks the Lord to intervene. In Psalm 75 God speaks to say that in "the appointed time" he will act both to strike down the arrogant and to lift up the meek and afflicted. Psalm 76 celebrates a dramatic incident in which God did exactly that, utterly destroying Israel's enemies. In all three psalms God is viewed as the Judge before whom everyone must one day stand and with whom all must eventually come to terms.

Charles Haddon Spurgeon wrote of this connection, "Faith in the 75th Psalm sung of victories to come, and here it sings of triumphs achieved. The present Psalm is a most jubilant war song, a paean to the King of kings, the hymn of a theocratic nation to its divine ruler."[1]

Like many of the fighting psalms, this too has been a favorite of Christians during religious warfare. The embattled Huguenots sang it as they marched into battle at Cloigny. The Covenanters sang it at Drumclog in 1679 when they defeated the government troops of "Bloody Claverhouse," who came on them suddenly during one of their surreptitious meetings. Psalm 76 was sung in thanksgiving services marking the defeat of the Spanish Armada in 1588. The Pilgrims also loved this psalm, and it was from verse 2 that they derived the name of one of the very first settlements in the New World: Salem, Massachusetts. It was because verse 2 says of God, "His tent is in Salem, his dwelling place in Zion."[2]

Where Is God Known?

The opening stanza of this psalm (vv. 1–3), in which that line occurs, sounds to most people today like the narrowest possible provincialism: that God is known only in Israel. But those who believe the Bible will know this: first, that it is true—that is where God was known—and second, that this is merely the same kind of exclusiveness we also demonstrate when we declare that God has revealed himself uniquely in Jesus Christ.

1. *In Judah God is known.* Until relatively recent times, when atheistic nations such as those of the Communist bloc declared that there was no God, all people everywhere acknowledged God's existence. But they had different ideas about what he was like, and they worshiped him by a variety of names. So the questions were: Which of these various ideas of God is the right one, if any? And how can we be sure?

Clearly there is no way to answer those questions by mere human means. Human beings do not have a perspective from which they can observe God and describe what he is like. We are doomed to ignorance—unless God chooses to reveal himself. But that is exactly what he has done, according to

Judaism and Christianity. God has revealed himself to Israel; that is what the Old Testament is about. And God has revealed himself in Jesus Christ. So at the time of the writing of this psalm—that is, before Jesus was born—it was not only strictly true but also necessary to say that God was known "in Judah" exclusively. In those days, if you wanted to know who God was and what he was like, you had to turn to the Jews and their Bible. The true God was the One who had revealed himself to Abraham and the other patriarchs, later in a special and much fuller way at Mount Sinai, and still later through the prophets.

Jesus was expressing this same truth when he told the Samaritan woman, "You Samaritans worship what you do not know; we worship what we do know, for salvation is from the Jews" (John 4:22).

2. *In Jesus God is known.* But God has also revealed himself in Jesus Christ in a way that now fulfills the Old Testament revelation and amplifies it. There is no one else who does this. No one but Jesus can say, "I and the Father are one" (John 10:30) and "Anyone who has seen me has seen the Father" (John 14:9).

So we preach Jesus! When the apostle Paul was waiting for Silas and Timothy to join him in Athens he was struck by the city's idolatry and began to reason with the wise men of the city about the gospel. A group of Epicureans and Stoics heard him and brought him to a formal meeting of the Areopagus, where he had a chance to speak to the many assembled philosophers. Paul said, "Men of Athens! I see that in every way you are very religious. For as I walked around and looked carefully at your objects of worship, I even found an altar with this inscription: TO AN UNKNOWN GOD. Now what you worship as something unknown I am going to proclaim to you" (Acts 17:22–23). Paul then began to tell them about the Bible's God, who had created all things, including themselves, and he ended with God's revelation of himself in Jesus Christ, whom God raised from the dead.

It is the same today. We see people with their many diverse ideas of who God is, and we say to them, "What you are worshiping in ignorance we proclaim to you." We point them to Jesus Christ. This God is the starting point of all wisdom, for "the fear of the LORD is the beginning of wisdom, and knowledge of the Holy One is understanding" (Prov. 9:10).

What Has God Done?

In spite of the way I have handled this first stanza, using it to ask who God is and where knowledge of the true God may be found, we must not think that the subject matter of the psalm is theoretical. This is not a matter for polite debate with little or no consequences attached. According to this psalm, this true God is a righteous Judge whose wrath is constantly hanging over those who are enemies both of himself and his people.

This is the theme of the psalm, and it is suggested even in the opening stanza, though this is not apparent in the English translation. The word translated "tent" in verse 2 is actually "lair." (It also occurs in Psalm 10:9, where it is rendered "cover.") Similarly, "dwelling" is used in Psalm 104:22 of a "den" of lions. This means that the picture of God in stanza one is of a lion crouching on Mount Zion, ready to pounce. In other words, he is to be reckoned with, to be feared. This led two commentators on Psalm 76 to title it "Lion of Judah" and "The Mighty God of Judgment."

Stanza two (vv. 4–10), which is the main body of Psalm 76, has two overlapping themes: first, a description of a great victory in which a powerful enemy of Israel was defeated, and second, a reflection on that victory suggesting quite possibly the final judgment.

A Dramatic Defeat of Israel's Enemy

The first theme of this main body of the psalm is the defeat of some great enemy of the Jews, a defeat so complete that no one of the enemy was able even to raise a hand against them. The text says,

> Valiant men lie plundered,
>   they sleep their last sleep;
> not one of the warriors
>   can lift his hands.
> At your rebuke, O God of Jacob,
>   both horse and chariot lie still (vv. 5–6).

What great defeat of Israel's enemy was this? The Hebrew title of the poem fails to tell us, and the body of the psalm is not detailed enough to fix the occasion of this defeat with certainty. However, of the events we know about, the one that suits it best is the destruction of the invading armies of Sennacherib by the angel of the Lord, described in 2 Kings 18–19 and Isaiah 36–37.

In the year 701 B.C. Sennacherib, the King of Assyria, invaded Judah and encircled Jerusalem. Hezekiah was Judah's king. Sennacherib sent a message to him, reminding him of all the cities and nations he had already subdued. They all had their gods, but their gods had not saved them, he said. Gozan, Haran, Rezeph, and the people of Eden—all fell before him. Why should the Jews expect their God to deliver them? Why not surrender now? Hezekiah went into the temple and spread this communication before the Lord. "It is true," he said. "The Assyrian kings have laid waste these nations and their lands. They have thrown their gods into the fire and destroyed them, for they were not gods but only wood and stone, fashioned by men's hands. Now, O LORD our God, deliver us from his hand, so that all kingdoms on earth may know that you alone, O LORD, are God" (2 Kings 19:17–19; Isa. 37:18–20).

This was a believing prayer, and God answered Hezekiah. He sent the prophet Isaiah with an announcement that the mighty army of Sennacherib would be overthrown and the king would return to Assyria as he had come. That night, we are told, "The angel of the LORD went out and put to death a hundred and eighty-five thousand men in the Assyrian camp. When the people got up the next morning—there were all the dead bodies! So Sennacherib king of Assyria broke camp and withdrew. He returned to Nineveh and stayed there" (2 Kings 19:35–36; Isa. 37:36–37).

As I mentioned, we are not sure that this is the setting for Psalm 76, but the words fit the account well, and this is the most likely reference. The translators of the Septuagint (LXX) thought this is what was being referred to, because they added as a title to Psalm 76 the words: "concerning the Assyrian," meaning Sennacherib.

So, for that matter, did George Gordon, more commonly known as Lord Byron. He wrote one of his best-known poems on the defeat of the Assyrian armies, part of which draws on the description in Psalm 76:

> For the Angel of Death spread his wings on the blast,
> And breathed in the face of the foe as he passed;
> And the eyes of the sleepers waxed deadly and chill,
> And their hearts but once heaved, and for ever were still!
>
> And there lay the steed with his nostril all wide,
> But through it there rolled not the breath of his pride:
> And the foam of his gasping lay white on the turf,
> As cold as the spray of the rock-beating surf.
>
> And there lay the rider distorted and pale,
> With the dew on his brow, and the rust on his mail.
> And the tents were all silent, the banners alone,
> The lances uplifted, the trumpet unblown.[3]

Reflection on the Assyrian Defeat

It is a natural practice of the psalmists to reflect on the meaning of some great historical event, projecting it onto an even larger screen. That is what happens now in a string of theological comments woven in with the historical descriptions. These deal with the nature and inevitability of God's judgments generally and may even point to the great final judgment of the last days. Derek Kidner calls this a vision of "the end-time" in which "God is foreseen striking the final blow against evil everywhere, as Judge."[4] Whatever the case, verses 7–10 provide us with a helpful theology of God's judgment.

1. *God alone is to be feared* (v. 7). People have all sorts of fears—fear of failure, fear of lacking life's necessities, fear of ridicule, fear of sickness, and ultimately fear of death and dying. This verse tells us that these are ultimately insignificant when measured against a right and proper fear of God's judgment: "You *alone* are to be feared."

Yet sinners ignore God and dismiss all serious thought of his judgment. Why should this be? Possibly because we really do fear judgment and thus bury thoughts of what is too horrible even to contemplate. The Book of Revelation describes the fear of people at the final judgment, saying, "They called to the mountains and the rocks, 'Fall on us and hide us from the face of him who sits on the throne and from the wrath of the Lamb! For the great day of their wrath has come, and who can stand?'" (Rev. 6:16–17).

2. *Every mouth will be silenced by God's judgment* (v. 8). One of the most objectionable characteristics of people who do wrong is that they never seem to admit it and then shut up. On the contrary, they are always making excuses for their wrong behavior, trying to get in the last word of self-serving, self-justifying explanation. There will be no final words from sinners at the last judgment. That is why Paul writes in Romans, "Whatever the law says, it says to those who are under the law, so that every mouth may be silenced and the whole world held accountable to God" (Rom. 3:19). The psalmist captures the same thought when he says that faced with God's judgment "the land feared and was quiet."

3. *God mingles wrath with mercy for the afflicted* (v. 9). Display of God's wrath is only one part of what the final judgment is about, however. The other side of wrath is mercy, and mercy will be shown by God to the meek and afflicted of the earth. In the historical judgment that is the occasion for this psalm it was mercy to Israel. In the judgment of the last days it will be mercy to those who have trusted in Jesus Christ as their Savior and Lord. We saw this theme in the previous psalm, noting that it is also found in Hannah's song, recorded in 1 Samuel 2:1–10, and in Mary's Magnificat, recorded in Luke 1:46–55. Mary's well-known words say,

> He has brought down rulers from their thrones
> but has lifted up the humble.
> He has filled the hungry with good things
> but has sent the rich away empty.
> He has helped his servant Israel,
> remembering to be merciful
> to Abraham and his descendants forever (vv. 52–55).

4. *God is glorified even in his wrath* (v. 10). The last important reflection on God's judgments, looking forward to the final judgment, is that God is glorified and is to be praised even in the outpourings of his wrath: "Surely your wrath against men brings you praise" (v. 10).

This is the answer to why God elects some people to salvation in Jesus Christ while passing by others who are reserved for judgment, as the apostle Paul explains in Romans 9. God's desire is that he might be known and glorified in all his attributes. Therefore, he displays his mercy in saving those he does save, and he displays his power, justice, and wrath in judging those he passes by. Pharaoh is an example: "For the Scripture says to Pharaoh: 'I raised you up for this very purpose, that I might display my power in you and that my name might be proclaimed in all the earth.' Therefore God has mercy on whom he wants to have mercy, and he hardens whom he wants to harden" (Rom. 9:17–18).

What Should I Do?

There are always people who are angry at God's judgments, even at the thought of them. They want to tell God that he is unjust to judge, that he cannot act that way. But that is a futile response. God will do as he will do. If we are wise, we will pursue another line entirely. What should that be? In the final stanza of the psalm (vv. 11–12), the writer makes two suggestions.

1. *"Make vows to the LORD your God and fulfill them"* (v. 11). This is a word to Israel, who alone can claim that God is her God. The point is that because God delivered Israel from the Assyrian invasion, therefore the people owe him their allegiance. The thought is precisely what we find at the start of the Ten Commandments: "I am the LORD your God, who brought you out of Egypt, out of the land of slavery. You shall have no other gods before me" (Exod. 20:2–3). Because God has saved, redeemed, and now delivered his people, they are to worship and serve him only.

Is there any less of a demand upon us who have been saved from sin by the death of Jesus Christ? Hardly! If anything, the obligation is even greater. If you have been saved by Jesus, you must both follow and obey him. Jesus said, "If anyone would come after me, he must deny himself and take up his cross daily and follow me" (Luke 9:23). He also said, "Why do you call me, 'Lord, Lord,' and do not do what I say?" (Luke 6:46).

2. *"Let all the neighboring lands bring gifts to the One to be feared"* (v. 11). This is a word to those whose god is not God but who are answerable to him anyway. It is the equivalent of the way Psalm 2 ends. After describing the arrogant rebellion of the nations of the world and echoing the profound scorn God has for such foolish and inadequate rattling of swords, God turns to the arrogant, saying,

> Therefore, you kings, be wise;
> be warned, you rulers of the earth.
> Serve the LORD with fear
> and rejoice with trembling.
> Kiss the Son, lest he be angry
> and you be destroyed in your way (vv. 10–12).

That applies to you, if you have not yet bowed in faith and obedience before the Lord Jesus Christ. The psalmist says that God "breaks the spirit of rulers," and he will break you too if you resist him. It would be better if you would submit to him now. Then you will find mercy and be able to join with those who sing praise to God in Zion.

Psalm 77

Remembering

I cried out to God for help;
* I cried out to God to hear me.*
When I was in distress, I sought the Lord;
* at night I stretched out untiring hands*
* and my soul refused to be comforted.*

I remembered you, O God, and I groaned;
* I mused, and my spirit grew faint. . . . Selah*

I remembered my songs in the night. . . .

Then I thought, "To this I will appeal:
* the years of the right hand of the Most High."*
I will remember the deeds of the LORD;
* yes, I will remember your miracles of long ago.*
*   verses 1–3, 6, 10–11*

One thing you have to say about Asaph: He tells it like it is. He is respectful. But if he is unhappy or puzzled about what God is doing (or not doing) in the lives of his people, he says so. And he also describes his own state of mind—his doubts and struggles, his questions and his inability to find satisfying answers to life's great problems.

637

In Psalm 77 this honest poet of Israel is remembering the past. His memories are troubling. He has a long historical memory, and he remembers how graciously God used to deal with his people, and with himself as well. He remembers how God cared for him, how he fulfilled his promises and showed him mercy. He even remembers how he used to sing about God during the long hours of the night. But there has not been any mercy for a long time now, at least so far as he can see. God seems to have rejected both him and his people, and the rejection is so complete that it looks as though it is going to go on forever. When he compares his life in the present with the past, his memories of the past drag him down, depress him, and keep him from being comforted.

Have you ever gone through times like that? If so, you will find Asaph's psalm helpful. As he thinks about the past the focus of his remembering shifts from himself and what he experienced and now fails to experience to God, and he begins to move upward to trust and quiet confidence again.[1]

The obvious division of the psalm is into two parts (vv. 1–9 and 10–20), the first part expressing the psalmist's depression, the second part his journey upward again. But each of these parts may be subdivided, perhaps into three stanzas apiece. The *selahs* give meaningful breaks, which would suggest a good four-part outline; this is the division followed by Charles Haddon Spurgeon in his *Treasury of David*. But we can also follow the stanzas of the New International Version, which I will do in this study.

As we go through the psalm, one thing to pay special attention to is the pronouns. In the NIV, in the first six verses of the psalm there are eighteen occurrences of the first person singular pronoun (*I* or *me*), and six references to God by name, title, and pronoun. In the last eight verses (vv. 13–20) there are twenty-one mentions of God and no personal references at all. (There is one first person plural possessive, *our*, in verse 13.) The transition from the poet's thoughts about himself to God comes in the middle section (vv. 7–12).

Cries in the Night

Verses 1–2 are a first expression of the psalmist's plight. God does not seem to be working in his life or in the life of the nation, which would not be so depressing if God had never worked. But he had. The poet remembers it; it is what he will describe in the next stanza. But now all he seems to be able to do is cry out in the night with outstretched hands to God, and his hands are always empty. H. C. Leupold asks the psalmist's question: "Why does God let things go on as long and as tragically as they do without giving any tokens of his interest and concern?"[2]

This is a portion of the psalms that appealed strongly to Charles Haddon Spurgeon, who identified closely with Asaph's physical and spiritual anguish. Spurgeon's studies of the psalms were produced between 1865 and 1885, and during those twenty years he experienced much ill health, which continued to deteriorate until his death in 1892. He had neuralgia and gout, which left him with swollen, red, painful limbs, so that he frequently could not walk or even write. He had debilitating headaches, and with these physical ills came frightful bouts of depression, leading almost to despair. In his later years he was forced to leave London for the sunnier, drier weather in southern France during the months of November, December, and January. In fact, he was in France at the Mediterranean village of Mentone when he died.

This gives us some appreciation for what he was talking about when he wrote on Psalm 77. Spurgeon said, "Some of us know what it is, both physically and spiritually, to be compelled to use these words; no respite has been afforded us by the silence of the night, our bed has been a rack to us, our body has been in torment, and our spirit in anguish. . . . Alas, my God, the writer of this exposition well knows what thy servant Asaph meant, for his soul is familiar with the way of grief. Deep glens and lonely caves of soul depressions, my spirit knows full well your awful glooms!"[3]

Have you ever felt like that? You probably have. And some who will read these words have felt such pains intensely.

Before moving on to stanza two, notice that this stanza is preoccupied with *I*. It occurs five times, and the pronouns *me* or *my* occur twice more. This is all right. If we hurt, there is nothing wrong with expressing it and telling the Lord what we feel. But we must not stop there, rehearsing our disappointments endlessly. We need to move on, as the psalmist does.

Dark Memories of Bright Days

In the second stanza (vv. 3–6) Asaph tells the reader a bit more about his depressed state of mind, explaining in verses 5–6 that what troubled him most in his musings was the memory of former days when he was happy enough in God to sing songs in the night. The important word in this stanza is *remember*, which also reappears in stanza four. Here he is remembering his former happiness. In stanza four he remembers the mighty deeds of God (v. 11), which is a significant shift of his focus.

This is a case where we need to try hard to appreciate the spirit and tone of the verses, if we are to understand what is going on. The first verse says, "I remembered you, O God." So it seems that Asaph is thinking about God, which would be good. The verses go on to show, however, that he is really thinking about himself, that God has been hard with him and has not been as close as he was formerly. He is feeling sorry for himself. His case is not as extreme as that of the Pharisee in Jesus' parable of the Pharisee and the tax collector, for Asaph is a believer and the Pharisee was not. But still, the Pharisee's prayer was much like this. He began with "God" but, as Jesus said, he was really praying "about himself." So the Pharisee continued, "I thank you that I am not like other men—robbers, evildoers, adulterers—or even like this tax collector" (Luke 18:11).

The best we can say about the second stanza of Asaph's prayer is that his focus is beginning to shift, albeit slightly. But there is still an awful lot of *I* (six occurrences) and *my* (four occurrences). In this respect the prayer sounds like many of our prayers.

Six Rhetorical Questions

But at least Asaph has begun to think about God, which is what his memories of past days inevitably led him to do. For regardless of whether he senses the presence of God with him now, at least he did then and he had reason to be happy. Ah, but that is just the problem, isn't it? He was happy with God then. He is not now. God seems to be utterly absent, to have abandoned him. And he is afraid that this apparent abandonment will go on forever. He is afraid that he will never get out of his depressed state and that depression will lead to blank despair.

So he asks a series of questions that give voice to the very root of his dismay. There are six of them (vv. 7–9), and they are all rhetorical.

> Will the Lord reject us forever?
>> Will he never show his favor again?
> Has his unfailing love vanished forever?
>> Has his promise failed for all time?
> Has God forgotten to be merciful?
>> Has he in anger withheld his compassion?

Well, what of it? Does the Lord reject his own forever? Can he ever cease to love those he has once loved? Has his character changed so that he is no longer merciful? Even to ask such questions is to answer them. The answer is, Of course not. God does not change. God does not break his promises. His mercies are new every morning. Therefore, if the psalmist does not believe that God is favorable, it must be because he is seeing things incorrectly. He is the one who is wrong, not God. As the apostle Paul was to write, "Let God be true and every man a liar" (Rom. 3:4).

We have been looking at the pronouns and other references to God in each stanza. Here we can do so usefully again. In the last stanza "God" began to be considered, though in a negative way. In this stanza references to God predominate: "The Lord" (v. 7), "God" (v. 9), and the pronouns *his* or *he* referring to God throughout (six times).

The questions in this stanza are still negative in form. They are asking whether God has forgotten. But even in this form it is better to ask them than not to ask them, because asking them sharpens the issue and pushes us toward the right, positive response. Alexander Maclaren insists that asking such questions is good. He writes, "Doubts are better put into plain speech than lying diffused and darkening, like poisonous mists, in his heart. A thought, be it good or bad, can be dealt with when it is made articulate.

Formulating vague conceptions is like cutting a channel in a bog for the water to run. One gets it together in manageable shape, and the soil is drained."[4] What is impossible to deal with is dissatisfaction that will not express itself openly or submit to reason.

Constructive, Biblical Meditation

Verse 10 is difficult to translate or interpret, because it contains two words that are of doubtful meaning. The word the translators of the New International Version render "appeal" ("To this I will appeal") might be the word for "supplication," hence "appeal." Or it could be the word for "affliction," hence "wound" or "grief." Likewise, the word rendered "years" could be either "years" or "change." Those variations give four possible meanings of the verse.

1. "This is my *appeal:* the *years* of the right hand of the Most High."
2. "This is my *grief:* the *years* of the right hand of the Most High."
3. "This is my *grief:* the right hand of the Most High has *changed.*"
4. "This is my *appeal:* the right hand of the Most High has *changed.*"

Each of these gives a tolerable meaning. If we choose the first, the idea is that in his present depressed state the psalmist will encourage himself by appealing to the merciful acts of God in past years. If we choose the second, he is explaining that his distress comes from remembering what God has done in the past but is not doing now, precisely what we have found in earlier stanzas. The third view is like the second; it would say that Asaph's grief comes from the fact that God is acting differently from what he did in the past. The fourth meaning is not a good one, but it could mean that since God has changed in one direction, from mercy to indifference, he might change back again and be favorable. That would give the psalmist a ground for some hope.[5]

Two factors tip the balance in the direction of the NIV reading. First, the Hebrew word translated "years" in verse 10 also occurs in verse 5, where it must mean "years" since it is parallel to the words *former days.* Second, from verse 10 onward the psalmist reviews what God has done in past years. At this point his review of the past is not a cause for grief but a foundation for spiritual growth and comfort.

In verse 11 the word *remember* comes back after being introduced in verses 3 and 6. Earlier he was remembering the past and how wonderful it was compared to his grim present. In this stanza he is remembering God and his works, which makes all the difference.

Attributes of God

What the psalmist remembers about God when he reflects on the years of his working is in the stanza comprising verses 13–15. This is all about

God, just as the opening stanzas of the psalm were mostly about Asaph. Here, in a manner that makes us think of the musings of Habakkuk in the first chapter of his prophecy, the psalmist muses on the attributes of God as seen in Israel's history. He recalls three matters.

1. *That God is holy*. The holiness of God is a rich concept, having to do more with God's transcendence than his uprightness. Yet it embraces his moral qualities, and here "holy" must refer to the fact that whatever God does is upright. This has been true in the past. Therefore, it must be true in the present too. However matters may seem to the poet from his personal perspective in history, his review of the past teaches him that God can always be trusted to do the right thing. This is true of all his "ways," including those in which the poet himself is called to walk.

2. *That God is great*. In the previous stanza Asaph had reflected on God's "deeds" and "miracles" (v. 11), his "works" and "mighty deeds" (v. 12). This leads him to ask, "What god is so great as our God?" (v. 13), with the implied answer, "No god at all," and to repeat that Israel's God "performs miracles," "display[s his] power" (v. 14) and bares his "mighty arm" (v. 15). This is important because it tells us that God is not only an upright God ("Your ways, O God, are holy," v. 13), but also that he is able and does put all his holy decrees into action. In other words, nothing frustrates him, nothing turns him aside from his perfect, right, and moral path.

3. *That God is caring*. How do we know that God is caring? It is because he "redeemed" the people, meaning that God delivered them from their bondage under the slave lords of Egypt (v. 15). Therefore, if God is caring as well as powerful or sovereign, he can be counted on to work in each detail of history for his people's good. And this means that even allowing the psalmist to fall into the depression with which the psalm began is not carelessness on God's part, but rather a part of his total loving plan. This is practical theology of the best sort, for it reasons from the immutable character of God to purpose for his acts in history and takes comfort from such truths.

God Our Redeemer

The last stanza of Psalm 77 (vv. 16–19, plus verse 20) carries through the theme introduced in stanza five, describing the exodus more fully and in poetic language. Indeed, stanza five calls for it. Not only does it introduce the idea ("you redeemed your people," referring to the exodus), it also echoes words and themes from Moses' great Song of the Exodus after the crossing of the Red Sea (see Exod. 15).

In the account of the Red Sea crossing in Exodus 14, we are told of the cloud that came between the Israelites and the Egyptians and of the strong east wind that drove back the water to make a passage. This is reflected in the description of the water and whirlwind in the psalm. Yet the psalm adds details that are missing in the original account: rain, thunder, lightning, and the shaking of the earth (vv. 17–18). Either these are details missing from the original account but preserved in the historical memory of the people or they are a poetic embellishment of the incident. Whatever the case, there is nothing improbable about these additional manifestations of God's power on that great night of nights for Israel.

The Lord Our Shepherd

The last verse of the psalm has to do with the people's wanderings and God's gentle shepherding of them by the hand of Moses and Aaron. This verse seems abrupt and even an anticlimax to the psalm—some commentators speculate about a lost ending or interpolation—but the ending is intended to be exactly as it is. What it says is that the God who acted in mighty ways in the past to redeem his people also acts in calm, tender, and loving ways; and this is what he is doing at the present time even though it has not been evident to the psalmist before this.[6]

The great German commentator Franz Delitzsch has a wonderful suggestion at this point, namely that the prophecy of Habakkuk, which echoes some of this language, picks up where Psalm 77 leaves off: "The prophet begins with the prayer to revive that deed of redemption of the Mosaic days of old, and in the midst of wrath to remember mercy; and in figures which are borrowed from our psalm, he then beholds a fresh deed of redemption by which that of old is eclipsed."[7] In the meantime, says Habakkuk, in words that could end Psalm 77, "The righteous will live by his faith" (Hab. 2:4).

> Though the fig tree does not bud
> and there are no grapes on the vines,
> though the olive crop fails
> and the fields produce no food,
> though there are no sheep in the pen
> and no cattle in the stalls,
> yet I will rejoice in the LORD,
> I will be joyful in God my Savior (Hab. 3:17–18).

Psalm 78

A Sermon from Israel's History

O my people, hear my teaching;
*   listen to the words of my mouth.*
I will open my mouth in parables,
*   I will utter hidden things, things from of old—*
what we have heard and known,
*   what our fathers have told us.*
We will not hide them from their children;
*   we will tell the next generation*
the praiseworthy deeds of the LORD,
*   his power, and the wonders he has done.*
*   verses 1–4*

D uring the ten years that I was a part of the International Council on Biblical Inerrancy, one of the arguments against the high, historic view of the Bible that we were upholding was that the Scriptures are authoritative and inerrant in matters of faith and morals, but not in matters of history and science. We answered then, as I still do today, that for Christians faith and morals cannot be separated from history or even from science, because Christianity is a historical religion, and attacks on its roots in history inevitably undermine it.

This is clearly true of the New Testament, since Jesus Christ was a historical figure and because our salvation is grounded on what he actually accomplished in history by his atoning death for sins. But this is true for the

Old Testament too. Psalm 78 is a good example. It is one of the great historical psalms: It recounts the history of the people of Israel in order to draw lessons from it—lessons as to who God is, what he has done, how the people responded to him wrongly in the past, and how they should learn from those past failures today. Other psalms that do this are Psalms 105–107, 114, 135, and 136. But there are other examples too, the best known being Stephen's speech before the Sanhedrin recorded in Acts 7. Stephen's point was that the Jewish people had always killed the prophets God sent them and that now they had also killed Jesus.

Psalm 78 is the longest of the historical psalms. Its lesson is that history must not repeat itself. The people must never again be unbelieving. But they were, of course, especially when they rejected Jesus Christ.

The Importance of the Past

The first eight verses of this psalm are a compelling preamble to the history that is to be reviewed. In these verses two very important points are made.

1. *We must learn from the past.* The key word is *parables* (v. 2), which is what the psalmist calls the history he is going to recall. To us the word *parable* means a story, usually a fictitious one; we think of the stories Jesus told. But *parable* actually has more in it than this. *Para* means "alongside of," and *ballein* means "to throw." So a parable is the placing of one incident or story alongside something else so we might learn by the comparison. In this case, the past history of Israel is set alongside the present so that those living today might not repeat the people's past sins.[1]

We must learn from this history too: "For everything that was written in the past was written to teach us, so that through endurance and the encouragement of the Scriptures we might have hope" (Rom. 15:4). If we do not learn from Israel's failures, we are bound to repeat them. And we might anyway!

2. *We must instruct our children.* The second point made in the preamble is that the history of God's dealings with us must be taught to our children. We have a duty to do this because God has commanded us to do it (v. 5), and we should also want to do it because it is the means by which our children may come to "put their trust in God" and "not forget his deeds" (v. 7). Then, says the psalmist,

> They would not be like their forefathers—
> a stubborn and rebellious generation,
> whose hearts were not loyal to God,
> whose spirits were not faithful to him (v. 8).

Actually, in these words Asaph is only echoing for a later generation what God had said clearly to the generation of the exodus. For example, in

Deuteronomy 6, in the chapter immediately following the second listing of the Ten Commandments, Moses wrote,

These commandments that I give you today are to be upon your hearts. Impress them on your children. Talk about them when you sit at home and when you walk along the road, when you lie down and when you get up. Tie them as symbols on your hands and bind them on your foreheads. Write them on the doorframes of your houses and on your gates (vv. 6–9).

And later in the same chapter:

In the future, when your son asks you, "What is the meaning of the stipulations, decrees and laws the LORD our God has commanded you?" tell him: "We were slaves of Pharaoh in Egypt, but the LORD brought us out of Egypt with a mighty hand. Before our eyes the LORD sent miraculous signs and wonders—great and terrible—upon Egypt and Pharaoh and his whole household. But he brought us out from there to bring us in and give us the land that he promised on oath to our forefathers. The LORD commanded us to obey all these decrees and to fear the LORD our God, so that we might always prosper and be kept alive, as is the case today. And if we are careful to obey all this law before the LORD our God, as he has commanded us, that will be our righteousness" (vv. 20–25).

Let me make this relevant to our time by saying that one thing we are to abhor as Christian parents is "values-neutral" education. Our culture wants it. In fact, it fights for it. But then we get a world in which the young avoid hard work, laugh at honesty, steal, and in some cases kill with no apparent conscience. We should not be surprised. We should struggle to make sure that our children are taught morality grounded in the character of God and supported by the life and power of our Savior Jesus Christ. We must teach this in our homes. If necessary we must teach it in our own schools—when the country's schools begin to destroy what we believe and hold dear.

The Case of Ephraim

The second stanza of this psalm begins its review of the historical dealings of God with his people with Ephraim, one of the twelve Jewish tribes (vv. 9–16). This seems a strange place to begin: first, because Ephraim does not seem to us to be a very prominent tribe, and second, because the incident referred to is not known. It was a time when "Ephraim, though armed with bows, turned back on the day of battle" (v. 9). Nothing exactly like this is found anywhere in the Old Testament.

The answer to why Asaph begins here is probably to be found at the end of the psalm, where we are reminded that God rejected Ephraim as the tribe out of which the great and enduring kingship of David should come, choosing Judah instead (vv. 67–68), and that God even "abandoned the tabernacle of Shiloh," which was in Ephraim's territory, and replaced it with Mount Zion (vv. 60, 68). In the early days of this history, at the time of the invasion and conquest of Canaan, Ephraim was the largest and most prominent of the twelve tribes. By the time of the writing of Psalm 78, Judah had eclipsed her. This is important for what Asaph wants to say. For what he is recalling to our minds is that sin brings judgment and that unbelief has consequences.

The problem with Ephraim was that its people forgot God's miracles in bringing them out of Egypt, taking them across the Red Sea, and leading them and providing for them in the desert (vv. 11–16). However, as the rest of the psalm will make clear, this was also a failure of the people as a whole. Therefore, the replacement of Ephraim by Judah is intended as a warning to all. Learn from the past, says Asaph, or you too may be moved aside by God as a result of his onward march in history. Should we not learn from this too? Jesus told the church at Ephesus, "If you do not repent, I will come to you and remove your lampstand from its place" (Rev. 2:5).

Putting God to the Test

When the devil tempted the Lord Jesus Christ, as recorded in Matthew 4 and Luke 4, he invited Jesus to jump from the temple, trusting for his safety to the words of Psalm 91, which say,

> He will command his angels concerning you . . .
> they will lift you up in their hands,
>> so that you will not strike your foot against a stone (vv. 11–12).

Jesus rightly responded by quoting from Deuteronomy 6:16, which says, "Do not test the LORD your God" (cf. Matt. 4:7; Luke 4:12). Not one of us is to tempt God by getting into situations that require him to do a miracle to save us or by demanding of him miracles he has not promised to do. Yet that is what Israel did in the wilderness, says the psalmist in this next stanza (vv. 17–31): "They willfully put God to the test" (v. 18).

What seems to be the problem here is not that the people expected God to provide the necessary food and water for them, since he had brought them into the desert and they needed these necessities lest they perish. The problem was first, that the people were dissatisfied with what God had done, wanting more, and second, that they thought the reason God did not give them everything they wanted was because he could not. In other words, their sins were first, ingratitude, and second, unbelief. In both they "put God to the test," contrary to the law's teaching.

Asaph highlights the base nature of these sins by contrasting them with the abundance of God's blessings. God had "rained down manna" on them (v. 24); it was "all the food they could eat" (v. 25). As for water,

> When he struck the rock, water gushed out,
> and streams flowed abundantly (v. 20).

This food was not poor fare. It was "the bread of angels" (v. 25), and the water was no mere trickle. Still the people complained, "Can God spread a table in the desert?" (v. 19), "Can he supply meat for his people?" (v. 20). The rest of the stanza reminds us that God did exactly that. He gave meat, causing flying birds to descend on their camp so they could eat as many as they could catch and stuff down. But God was angered by the ingratitude and judged them by making them sick on the fowl. The text says, "He put to death the sturdiest among them, cutting down the young men of Israel" (v. 31).

Repentance That Does Not Count

The judgment mentioned at the end of the third stanza of Psalm 78 leads to the subject matter of the fourth stanza (vv. 32–39), repentance. When the people were judged, they repented. Unfortunately, their repentance was seldom true repentance. Therefore, in words that echo Hosea's later description of this sickening hypocrisy (in Hosea 6:1–3), Asaph says,

> Whenever God slew them, they would seek him;
>   they eagerly turned to him again.
> They remembered that God was their Rock,
>   that God Most High was their Redeemer.
> But then they would flatter him with their mouths,
>   lying to him with their tongues;
> their hearts were not loyal to him,
>   they were not faithful to his covenant (vv. 34–37).

A hypocritical repentance like this must be nauseating to God. For as Hosea notes at the end of his prophecy, true repentance involves an honest acknowledgment of sin, a turning from it, and an appeal to God's grace (see Hosea 14:1–3). All this is absent here. Nevertheless, says Asaph, God did not deal with the people as their hypocrisy deserved. Instead of destroying them, God "was merciful" and "forgave their iniquities" (v. 38). "He remembered that they were but flesh, a passing breeze that does not return" (v. 39).

This is precisely how God has dealt with us. If God had not chosen to be merciful to us, we would all have perished long ago. But instead of not being merciful and allowing us to perish, God made atonement for our sins by the death of Jesus Christ. He forgave our iniquities. Certainly a love like this demands a genuine repentance from us and a true following after God in faith and deep gratitude. As Isaac Watts wrote,

> Love so amazing, so divine,
> Demands my soul, my life, my all.

True. But do we actually respond like that? Isn't it more often the case that we only give God lip service while nevertheless continuing to go our own way? J. J. Stewart Perowne seems to be on target when he calls this passage "a most striking and affecting picture of man's heart, and God's gracious forbearance, in all ages—man's sin calling for chastisement, the chastisement producing only temporary amendment, God's goodness forgotten, and yet God's great love never wearied."[2] It is indeed affecting!

Forgetting the Past

There is a sense in which the stanza of Psalm 78 beginning with verse 40 goes back to the beginning and thus starts to tell the story of Israel's base ingratitude to God all over again, beginning with the exodus from Egypt and with the people's failure to remember God's miracles of redemption on their behalf. Some commentators outline the psalm around these two halves.[3] In my judgment, the last half does not exactly repeat the first. But the fresh start is significant, for it is as though Asaph is acknowledging that God had done everything possible to win the people over. They had not responded. Thus, the only thing to do is to tell the entire story all over again, hoping that something about it might stick with them this second time.

Think back on what God has done. In stanza one, we were reminded that he had done miracles but the people had forgotten them. In stanza two, we were reminded that God provided for the people's needs abundantly but they had remained unsatisfied. In stanza three, we were reminded of God's just judgments, which only produced a false repentance. In fact, not even his mercy was effective. In spite of his mercy, the people "often . . . rebelled against him in the desert and grieved him in the wasteland!" (v. 40). Miracles! Provision! Judgment! Mercy! Four great actions. Yet in spite of them, the outcome was rebellion and unbelief.

How is this possible? The answer is in verse 42, which is perhaps the most important verse in the psalm. It says,

> They did not remember his power—
> the day he redeemed them from the oppressor.

They had forgotten God's redemption (v. 42). They had forgotten what God did on their behalf. Do we? I am sure we do, or we would not sin as grievously or as often as we do. Derek Kidner says on this point, "If redemption itself is forgotten, . . . faith and love will not last long."[4] If we forget what it cost God to redeem us from our sins through Jesus' death, we will not long trust him in life's trials or love him enough to obey him in times of temptation.

The cure is to remember, which is what this psalm is about. We need to remember all that God has done.

What Asaph calls to mind particularly in this section are the plagues God brought on the Egyptians, surely one of the greatest single displays of God's power and judgments in history. He does not list all the plagues, but he gives a good description of at least six of them: (1) the turning of the Nile to blood (Exod. 7:14–24); (2) the plague of flies (Exod. 8:20–32, possibly including vv. 16–19); (3) the multiplication of frogs (Exod. 8:1–15); (4) the locusts (Exod. 10:1–20); (5) the hail (Exod. 9:13–35); and finally, (6) the killing of all the firstborn of Egypt (Exod. 11:1–10; 12:29–30). The psalm omits the plague of gnats, the disease inflicted on the livestock, the boils visited on the people, and the days of darkness. There is no discernible reason either for the choice of the six judgments or the omission of the other four. The plagues that are mentioned build forcefully toward the last terrible judgment of God against the firstborn, which is then placed in sharp and beautiful contrast to the way God led his people out of Egypt like a flock of timid but safe and trusting sheep.

Abandoning God and Abandoned

At the end of stanza five there are two verses that bring the people to the borders of the Promised Land and even into it. This causes some writers to join these verses to stanza six. The actual arrangement does not make much difference. What matters is that in stanza six the rebellion of the people once they were in the land was even worse than when they were in the desert. Their rebellion extended to idolatry (v. 58) with the result that God's anger also reached new heights, so that the northern kingdom of Israel, led by Ephraim, was "rejected . . . completely" (v. 59), the ark of the covenant was allowed to go into captivity to the Philistines, and many of the young men of the people were killed.[5]

This is why I wrote earlier that the second half of the psalm is not just a repetition of part one. It repeats the same great themes, but the themes intensify. On the one hand, ingratitude and rebellion lead to outright apostasy. On the other, the anger of God leads to the rejection of the northern kingdom. It is always that way. One sin leads to another, hearts harden, and the end is death and damnation.

Our Merciful God

But there is good news too, and this is where the final stanza and the psalm itself end (vv. 65–72). We have seen that the anger of God builds against entrenched human sin. But his mercy does not end. We saw this at the end of stanza four (vv. 38–39). Here the last stanza is given to it.

One commentator calls this "a new beginning," but it is new only in the sense that there are always new beginnings with God. Ephraim is rejected, but here Judah is chosen. Shiloh is abandoned, but the ark is brought to Mount Zion. Asaph's point is that it was entirely of grace that God chose Judah and elevated its shepherd boy, David, to be a great king.[6] The people did not deserve this, any more than they deserved God's other blessings. But the fact that they received such mercies multiplied their obligations to serve God. It is the same for us, only our mercies are even greater than those experienced by Israel since in Jesus Christ we have been given "every spiritual blessing" (Eph. 1:3). We deserve nothing, yet we have received everything. Don't forget it! Remember God's blessings. Remember his mercy. And remember to tell the next generation too.

Psalm 79

"Where Is Their God?"

O God, the nations have invaded your inheritance;
*   they have defiled your holy temple,*
*   they have reduced Jerusalem to rubble.*
They have given the dead bodies of your servants
*   as food to the birds of the air,*
*   the flesh of your saints to the beasts of the earth.*
They have poured out blood like water
*   all around Jerusalem,*
*   and there is no one to bury the dead.*
We are the objects of reproach to our neighbors,
*   of scorn and derision to those around us. . . .*

Help us, O God our Savior,
*   for the glory of your name;*
deliver us and forgive our sins
*   for your name's sake.*
Why should the nations say,
*   "Where is their God?"*
Before our eyes, make known among the nations
*   that you avenge the outpoured blood of your servants.*
May the groans of the prisoners come before you;
*   by the strength of your arm*
*   preserve those condemned to die. . . .*
*   verses 1–4, 9–11*

It is hard to find perfect scholarly agreement on anything relating to the interpretation of the Bible, including the historical setting for Psalm 79. But the psalm describes the destruction of Jerusalem, the defiling of the temple, and the slaughter of the people, and the most obvious historical setting for this is the period following the destruction of the city by the armies of Nebuchadnezzar in 587 B.C.

There are a few arguments to the contrary, which cause some scholars to date the psalm from the time of the Maccabees and to view the destruction as that caused by Antiochus Epiphanes. I reviewed some of these arguments in the earlier study of Psalm 74, which seems to be about the same period of history and by the same writer. A comparison will show how similar the outlines of the two psalms are and even how many expressions are common to each. In this case the only points that have any real bearing on the matter of dating are the citations of Psalm 79:6–7 in Jeremiah 10:25 and Psalm 79:3 in 1 Maccabees 7:16. Scholars who prefer the later dating argue that the psalm is quoting Jeremiah and that it must be contemporaneous with 1 Maccabees; they refer to the same incidents.

Neither of those arguments holds up well. Jeremiah is in the habit of quoting earlier Scriptures, and in this case his citing of Psalm 79 follows his citation of another verse from the psalms, Psalm 6:1. Besides, the verse in Jeremiah sounds more like a quotation of an earlier source than the other way around. The psalm seems original.

As for the quotation of verse 3 in 1 Maccabees, it is significant that it is introduced by the formal expression, "according to the word that has been written," which is the writer's usual way of quoting Scripture. This probably means that the words were written far enough in the past to have been regarded as Scripture by the time of the Maccabees, which would place the psalm earlier than their age.[1] This would mean they refer to the destruction of the city by Nebuchadnezzar and would have been used by 1 Maccabees only because the earlier destruction had become a pattern of all subsequent judgments on Jerusalem and its people.

The Jews seem to regard the psalm as describing the classic destruction of the city and temple by Nebuchadnezzar, because the psalm is recited at the Wailing Wall in Jerusalem on Friday afternoons even today, as well as being used in the liturgy for the Ninth of Ab, a fast day that commemorates the temple's destruction.[2]

How should the psalm be outlined? A number of writers see it as having two parts: (1) an initial lament in verses 1–4, followed (2) by a prayer for God's deliverance and for judgment on the people's enemies in verses 5–13, some detaching verse 13 as a suitable postscript. The stanzas in the New International Version mark useful units, but verse 12 would be better attached to stanza three, since it is part of the prayer that asks for God's intervention.

The Destruction of Jerusalem

I have already commented on Asaph's distress over the destruction of Jerusalem in the study of Psalm 74. In that psalm Asaph walked God through the ruins of the desolate and abandoned city. "Look, that is where they broke in," he seemed to be saying. "They set up their military standards over there. That is where they attacked the carved paneling. After that they burned the temple. Look at those ashes. That is all that is left. Then, as if the damage to the temple were not bad enough, they went through the whole land to destroy every place where you were worshiped. And they have done it! Do you see? Do you care?"

Both psalms ask how long this terrible state is to continue: Is it to go on forever? Both ask God to rise up and destroy those who have destroyed Judah. Both look forward to a day when the people of God will be able to praise him for his mighty acts of deliverance once again.

But there are differences too. In the earlier psalm Asaph seemed to be chiefly troubled about the temple, that the Babylonians had destroyed the sanctuary where God used to meet with his worshipers. A description of the ruins fills the second stanza. In Psalm 79 Asaph is chiefly concerned for the people: for those who have been killed, whose bodies lie in the street with none to bury them; those who were taken prisoner; and those who have been left desolate after the terrible destruction and slaughter. The first stanza (vv. 1–4) says,

> O God, the nations have invaded your inheritance;
>   they have defiled your holy temple,
>   they have reduced Jerusalem to rubble.
> They have given the dead bodies of your servants
>   as food to the birds of the air,
>   the flesh of your saints to the beasts of the earth.
> They have poured out blood like water
>   all around Jerusalem,
>   and there is no one to bury the dead.
> We are the objects of reproach to our neighbors,
>   of scorn and derision to those around us.

The fact that there would be so many killed and so few survivors that there would be no one to bury the dead had been prophesied by the prophet Jeremiah in 7:33. It was regarded as a terrible calamity and disgrace not to be able to bury the dead, but it had happened.

None of us has been witness to a disaster of this magnitude. Bad things happen to us sometimes. We get sick or someone close to us dies or a fire destroys our home or we lose a job. But here everything that could go wrong has gone wrong. Everything that could possibly be destroyed has been destroyed. The destruction was *political,* because the nation no longer existed. There was no king, no counselors, no people in authority, no army. The destruction was *economic,* because the land was devastated. No one could earn a living, and there was no one to buy anything that might be produced. The destruction was *social,* because entire families were wiped out and there was no one who had not lost a husband, son, father, mother, wife, or children in the conflict. Worst of all, the destruction was *religious,* for there was no temple and the worship of God had ceased throughout the land.

Neither you nor I have ever experienced anything as sweeping as that. But most of us have experienced losses of some sort or another, and the question is, How do we cope with them? This psalm does not set out to find an answer to that question as Psalms 73 and 77 do, for example. Rather it is itself the answer—by hanging on to God, by trusting him.[3] That is exactly what it does from the beginning. We cannot overlook the fact that even when relating details of the disaster that had overtaken them, the psalmist speaks of their enemies as having "invaded *your* [that is, God's] inheritance, . . . defiled *your* holy temple, . . . given the bodies of *your* servants as food to the birds of the air, and the flesh of *your* saints to the beasts of the earth" (vv. 1–2).

In other words, even though the people have suffered a great calamity, they are nevertheless the people of God and can continue to appeal to him, which is what Asaph does. Do you have that confidence? Do you appeal to God? There is nothing like it to get you through difficult times.

Hanging On to God

The next two stanzas (vv. 5–8 and 9–12) are best taken together, for they contain the substance of Asaph's prayer to God following the lament in verses 1–4. They ask different questions. The first asks,

> How long, O LORD? Will you be angry forever?
> How long will your jealousy burn like fire? (v. 5).

This is the same question that was asked in Psalm 74:10. It emphasized the "forever." The next stanza asks,

> Why should the nations say,
> "Where is their God?" (v. 10).

These questions are both actually appeals for God to help his people and punish their enemies, and the stanzas make these points jointly. There are four important questions, confessions, or statements in these verses.

1. *How long will this punishment last?* This is the big question, and it dominated Psalm 74 as well. In fact, it is often the question asked by God's suffering or persecuted people. They do not complain that their treatment by God is unjust. They know they are sinners; they know they have sinned repeatedly in thought, word, and deed. They know that God has been merciful to them even in his judgments. They know they have suffered much less than they actually deserve. God is merciful. Still, they are hurting, and they are hoping that the punishment will not go on much longer. "How long, O LORD?" is their agonizing question.

Those who are innocent victims of persecution ask this question. The martyrs mentioned in Revelation 6 ask, "How long, Sovereign Lord, holy and true, until you judge the inhabitants of the earth and avenge our blood?" (Rev. 6:10).

Saint Augustine asked it during the hours of his deepest soul struggles prior to his conversion, probably quoting this very psalm. He had retired into a far corner of the garden of a friend's estate in Milan, Italy, under great conviction, knowing the truth but yet being unable in himself to break with his old life of sin and commit himself to Jesus Christ. Here is how he describes it: "I cast myself down I know not how, under a certain fig-tree, giving full vent to my tears; and the floods of mine eyes gushed out an acceptable sacrifice to thee. And, not indeed in these words, yet to this purpose, spake I much unto thee: *And thou, O Lord, how long? How long, Lord, wilt thou be angry for ever?* [This is where he quotes Psalm 79.] *Remember not our former iniquities,* for I felt that I was held by them."

It was immediately after this that Augustine heard the voice of a child singing the words *Tolle lege! Tolle lege!* ("Take up and read"), which he did. He picked up a Bible that was there in the garden, opened it at random, and came upon these words from Romans 13: "Let us behave decently, as in the daytime, not in orgies and drunkenness, not in sexual immorality and debauchery, not in dissension and jealousy. Rather, clothe yourselves with the Lord Jesus Christ, and do not think about how to gratify the desires of the sinful nature" (Rom. 13:13–14). Augustine did turn to Christ and was marvelously converted.[4]

The hand of God often does seem heavy upon us, and his workings in our lives seem slow. But it is not forever! Remember that. And it will not be more than you can bear (see 1 Cor. 10:13). So hang on. Trust God. The time will come when you will be able to praise him once again.

2. *It is time to punish those who punished us.* Whenever the psalms ask God to punish the people's enemies, we get uneasy because we have been taught to forgive our enemies and pray for those who use us badly (Matt. 5:38–47). It is right that we should feel uneasy, especially when we come upon language that is intemperate. We *are* told to be forgiving.

But we should remember two things. First, we err on the side, not of being too harsh with those who practice evil, but of being too lax. We treat both virtue and vice lightly, forgetting that virtue should be rewarded and that evil should be punished. So we are not so much more moral than these ancient Jews, as amoral. At least they were concerned about justice; we are not. Second, we need to remember that regardless of the attitude we take, justice is going to be done. God sees the evil, and he will punish it. The blood of the martyrs will be avenged. Every good and every evil deed will receive their different but most appropriate rewards.

Although this is indeed an age of grace, an age in which to proclaim the gospel of God's free salvation from sin through the work of Jesus Christ, we should remember that it is not endless. Judgment will be done. Therefore, we should both warn people of this judgment and be diligent in taking the gospel to those who are without it.

3. *Forgive us our sins.* Every true prayer should have within it a confession of the worshiper's sins. This is not some morbid preoccupation. It is an inevitable result of prayer that is truly prayer to God. This is because God is holy, and we are not. So if we are really praying to him, we will be aware of his holiness, and his holiness will convict us of our sinful state. This is how we know that the prayer of the tax collector in Jesus' parable was a true prayer and the prayer of the Pharisee was not. The Pharisee began his prayer with "God . . . ," but he went on to talk about himself and how good he was. Jesus said he was praying "to himself." The tax collector prayed, "God, be merciful to me, a sinner," and Jesus said that he was heard and went home justified (Luke 18:9–14).

This has bearing on Psalm 79, for one of its most important features is an acknowledgment of sin. There is an acknowledgment of the sins of the fathers, since it was for their sins that Judah was overrun and Jerusalem destroyed (v. 8). But there is also acknowledgment of the people's own and present sins, for the psalmist prays, "Deliver us and forgive our sins for your name's sake" (v. 9).

This is important. The people were suffering the destruction of their entire civilization—politically, economically, socially, and religiously. Yet there is not the slightest suggestion that they did not actually deserve it, or even that they did not deserve having it continue as long as it had. Instead of excusing their sins, the psalmist acknowledges them and pleads for forgiveness (actually "atone for our sins").

What is he thinking of when he mentions atonement? The only atonement he knew was that made at the temple by the high priest when sacrifices were offered up, particularly on the Day of Atonement. That temple was now gone. How could atonement for sin be made? I do not know what the psalmist was thinking of, but I do know how God did it. God did it, not by causing the temple to be rebuilt and the sacrifices to be reinstituted—though the temple was rebuilt in the days of Ezra and Nehemiah, and the offerings were begun again—but rather by sending Jesus Christ to be the perfect and only sufficient sacrifice. That is why, when Jesus died, the veil of the temple was torn in two from top to bottom, indicating that the way into the presence of God was now open for all who would come through faith in his sacrifice, and why, shortly after this, the temple of Herod, which replaced the temple of Ezra and Nehemiah, was destroyed for the final time.

4. *Glorify your name.* In his brief commentary, G. Campbell Morgan notes three great themes in this psalm, one of which is "passion for the glory of the Divine Name."[5] This is wisely noted, for the fourth of the important

questions, confessions, or statements in these verses is the appeal to God on the basis of the glorifying of his name.

> Help us, O God our Savior,
> > for the glory of your name (v. 9).

This is the strongest appeal anyone can make, for God says that he has set his glory above all else. He has declared, "I am the LORD; that is my name! I will not give my glory to another" (Isa. 42:8). Moreover, when we begin this way, with the glory of God as our aim, then other things tend to fall into place naturally and we pray for what is right.

The Lord's Prayer begins, "Our Father in heaven, hallowed be your name" (Matt. 6:9). Petitions follow. Then, in the most quoted version, it ends, "For yours is the kingdom and the power and the glory forever. Amen." Have you made God's glory the number one priority in your life?

Praise from God's Sheep

The last verse of the psalm stands by itself, for this is no longer a case of petition. The prayer has ended. This is rather a faith-filled anticipation of a brighter, future day when God's people will again praise him with full hearts and with fresh memories of what he has done for them (v. 13). It is amazing in its confidence that a day like this will come. Derek Kidner says, "To look back to verse 1 is to wonder at the faith which enabled such a psalm, from such distress, to end, even if only in anticipation, with such a word as *praise*."[6]

The secret of this confidence is in what verse 13 talks about—the people will always be God's people, the sheep of his pasture. In one sense, this brings us back to where the psalm started out, for it began by speaking of "*your* inheritance . . . *your* holy temple . . . *your* servants . . . *your* saints." That is, whatever has happened, it is because the people belong to God and not because they don't. The psalm ends on the same note, because it is still true that "we [are] *your* people."

The closing also links this psalm with the two preceding it and carries their endings forward into the present. Psalm 77 ended with God shepherding the people "like a flock by the hand of Moses and Aaron" at the time of the exodus and desert wanderings. Psalm 78 ended with God shepherding his flock by the hands of David during the time of the monarchy. In Psalm 79 this has extended into the present and beyond, which is a way of saying that God will always be our good shepherd. This is true, which is why the psalm rightly ends with "praise."

Psalm 80

God's Flock and God's Vine

Hear us, O Shepherd of Israel,
*   you who lead Joseph like a flock;*
you who sit enthroned between the cherubim, shine forth
*   before Ephraim, Benjamin and Manasseh.*
Awaken your might;
*   come and save us.*

Restore us, O God;
*   make your face shine upon us,*
*   that we may be saved.*

*   verses 1–3*

Psalm 80 is a psalm with a chorus. It is repeated three times, in verses 3, 7, and 19. So there are also three stanzas to this psalm: Stanza one is in verses 1–2, stanza two is in verses 4–6, and stanza three is in verses 8–18. In its structure Psalm 80 is a lot like Psalms 42 and 43, which belong together and in which the chorus beginning "Why are you downcast, O my soul?" is likewise repeated three times. A repeated chorus sets the tone and provides the theme for the psalm, and in the case of Psalm 80 it does this by asking,

> Restore us, O God;
>   make your face shine upon us,
>   that we may be saved.[1]

What is this restoration for which the psalm is asking? And what does this indicate about its historical setting? The first stanza begins by naming

God as Israel's shepherd, which links it thematically with the earlier two psalms, which also talked about God shepherding his people. But the setting here cannot be that of the earlier psalms. They were written after the destruction of Jerusalem. Here not only the southern kingdom but also the northern kingdom is still in existence. Since Psalm 80 focuses on the northern kingdom—it calls God the "Shepherd of Israel" and speaks of Ephraim and Manasseh, two of the major northern tribes—and since it asks for Israel's deliverance, it is best seen as a plea for the deliverance of the northern kingdom sometime before its fall to the Assyrian armies in 721 B.C. Franz Delitzsch wrote, "The psalmist, as it seems, prays in a time in which the oppression of Assyria rested heavily upon the kingdom of Ephraim, and Judah saw itself threatened with ruin when this bulwark should have fallen."[2]

Like Psalm 76, the Septuagint (LXX) version of Psalm 80 begins with the ascription "a psalm concerning the Assyrian."

The Lord Is Our Shepherd

A second striking feature of this psalm is its effective employment of two great images for God: God as Israel's shepherd, developed briefly in the first stanza (vv. 1–2) and God as the planter and caretaker of a vineyard, which stands for Israel, developed in stanza three (vv. 8–18). The first of these two images, God as Israel's shepherd, is a familiar way the Bible describes God to people who for the most part lived pastoral lives.

There is an important use of the image in Isaiah 40:11.

> He tends his flock like a shepherd:
>> He gathers the lambs in his arms
> and carries them close to his heart;
>> he gently leads those that have young.

There is an extensive development of it by Jesus in John 10, including, for example, verses 14–16: "I am the good shepherd; I know my sheep and my sheep know me—just as the Father knows me and I know the Father—and I lay down my life for the sheep. I have other sheep that are not of this sheep pen. I must bring them also. They too will listen to my voice, and there shall be one flock and one shepherd." Peter called Jesus "the Shepherd and Overseer of [our] souls" (1 Peter 2:25). Hebrews ends, "May the God of peace, who through the blood of the eternal covenant brought back from the dead our Lord Jesus, that great Shepherd of the sheep, equip you with everything good for doing his will, and may he work in us what is pleasing to him, through Jesus Christ, to whom be glory for ever and ever. Amen" (Heb. 13:20–21).

Although appearing frequently elsewhere, the idea of God being Israel's shepherd occurs in the Psalter only twice, here and in Psalm 23.

It is helpful to know that the first use of the shepherding image for God in the Bible is in the farewell words of Jacob, Abraham's grandson, recorded in Genesis 48. Jacob spoke of God as the one "who has been my Shepherd all my life to this day, the Angel who has delivered me from all harm" (Gen. 48:15–16). The reason this is so helpful is that Jacob had been a shepherd himself, and he knew from experience how difficult a shepherd's work was. In his moving confrontation with Laban, after Laban had pursued him on his flight from Haran back to his own country, Jacob aptly described the difficulties of a shepherd's life, saying, "This was my situation: The heat consumed me in the daytime and the cold at night, and sleep fled from my eyes. It was like this for the twenty years I was in your household. . . . If the God of my father, the God of Abraham and the Fear of Isaac, had not been with me, you would surely have sent me away empty-handed" (Gen. 31:40–42).

This is a powerful statement. But it seems to be an understatement as a description of the difficulty of a shepherd's life. Sheep are notoriously helpless, wayward, and even stupid animals, and it is a difficult and full-time job to care for them.

Jacob had also learned a second thing about shepherding, and that was how great a failure he had been when he was trying to shepherd himself. Self-shepherding means trying to run your own life. Jacob was like many Christians today. He acknowledged God. He would have described himself as a believer. But he had followed his own judgment and taken his own paths rather than trusting in the word and wisdom of the divine shepherd. The wonderful thing is that, in spite of Jacob's waywardness, God had been a faithful shepherd to Jacob anyway, which he acknowledges, just as God also is to us.

This, then, is the image we have in the first stanza of Psalm 80. But lest we get the idea that a shepherd is only some gentle, almost helpless soul doomed to care for sheep, the psalm reminds us that this wonderful shepherd of Israel is nevertheless also the God who sits "enthroned between the cherubim." This might refer to God's throne in heaven or to that earthly representation of it within the Most Holy Place of the tabernacle or temple. But whatever the case, it is a reminder of the majesty and power of the true God. In fact, it is on the basis of God's power that the psalm's appeal for salvation from Israel's enemies is made: "Awaken your might; come and save us" (v. 2).

The Aaronic Blessing

The first time the recurring chorus appears is in verse 3, immediately after the appeal to the might of Israel's divine shepherd. It is an obvious prayer based on what has been said. What is unusual about it is that the second line seems to be a reference to the Aaronic blessing found in Numbers 6:24–26:

> The LORD bless you
>> and keep you;
> the LORD make his face shine upon you
>> and be gracious to you;
> the LORD turn his face toward you
>> and give you peace.

The psalmist must have heard this blessing a thousand times. So he prays here, "Make your face shine upon us, that we may be saved."

When the blessing refers to God making his face to shine upon us, this is at the very least a prayer that God might be gracious to us in this life. But it also has overtones of the believer actually seeing God, the specific blessing Moses asked for but was told was impossible for anyone in this life (Exod. 33:18–20). Theologians call this the beatific vision, the ultimate blessing those who love God long for. In Psalm 80 the prayer that God might make his face shine upon the people is that God might be favorable to them again. They are threatened by the Assyrian armies. God's face seems to be turned away. They desperately need him to turn his face back to them, smile on them favorably, and rescue them from the destruction that is about to take place.

If the psalm was written before the fall of the northern kingdom, as it seems to have been, we know that God did not smile favorably. And we know the reason too! The people did not repent of their sins and truly seek after God and his righteousness. So the psalm warns us that restoration is not automatic. God is good—he is the Good Shepherd—but he is also a stern judge of unrepented sin.

Israel's Present Plight

The second stanza of Psalm 80, following the chorus, is a description of Israel's present plight. It is an explanation of why the nation needs to be restored. God is angry and has judged them in his anger. God is so angry, in fact, that his anger is described as smoldering even "against the prayers" of his people (v. 4). What could have caused God to be so angry? There is only one answer—sin for which the people will not repent and in which they stubbornly persist.

Sin has consequences. Thus, the stanza also speaks of these, saying in poetic language that the people have been made to eat and drink tears and that they have become the taunt of their enemies. We have a good example of such taunting from the account of the Assyrian king Sennacherib's challenge to Hezekiah, who was king of the southern kingdom of Judah about the time of the northern kingdom's fall. Sennacherib had his field commander say, "Has the god of any nation ever delivered his land from the hand of the king of Assyria? Where are the gods of Hamath and Arpad? Where are the gods of Sepharvaim, Hena and Ivvah? Have they rescued

Samaria from my hand? Who of all the gods of these countries has been able to save his land from me? How then can the LORD deliver Jerusalem from my hand?" (2 Kings 18:33–35).

Fortunately, Hezekiah was a strong believer who laid the matter before God and sought his aid. God delivered the kingdom by sending his angel to strike down 185,000 Assyrian soldiers in one night. This did not happen in the north. The people persisted in their sin and perished. In this stanza, in just three verses "the psalmist points to an angry God, a weeping nation, and mocking foes, a trilogy of woe," says Alexander Maclaren.[3]

A Second Image: God's Vine

The second great metaphor of this psalm is of God as the planter and keeper of a great vineyard and of Israel as his choice and abundant vine. I have identified this image as filling the third stanza of the psalm (vv. 8–18), but in the New International Version the section is itself divided into three stanzas: verses 8–11, 12–15, and 16–18. These deal with the past, the present, and the future of the vineyard.

Like the image of God as a shepherd, the vine metaphor is also common in Scripture, especially in relation to the northern kingdom. Jacob used this image in his final blessings on the tribes, calling Joseph "a fruitful vine near a spring, whose branches climb over a wall" (Gen. 49:22). The theme is frequent in the prophets. It occurs twice in Isaiah in beautiful and very moving passages: "My loved one had a vineyard on a fertile hillside . . ." (Isa. 5:1–7) and "Sing about a fruitful vineyard . . ." (Isa. 27:2–6). In Jeremiah 2:21, God complains, "I had planted you like a choice vine of sound and reliable stock. How then did you turn against me into a corrupt, wild vine?" Hosea has two important passages: "Israel was a spreading vine; he brought forth fruit for himself . . ." (Hosea 10:1) and "He will blossom like a vine, and his fame will be like the wine from Lebanon" (Hosea 14:7).[4]

Psalm 80 is the only psalm in which the vine is used as a symbol for Israel, and it is almost the only psalm in which the image occurs in any sense. As indicated above, it is in three parts.

1. *The past: brought out of Egypt, planted and prospering.* Set apart as a separate stanza of the psalm by the New International Version (vv. 8–11), the first part describes how God brought Israel out of Egypt as a choice vine, cleared the Promised Land of the nations who were there before her, planted it, and then cared for it so that it grew up to be a mighty vine that covered the mountains and spread from the Mediterranean Sea on the west to the Euphrates River on the east. It is a powerful image, aptly describing what God had done. God had indeed brought Israel out of Egypt, and her present possession of the land was God's doing.

2. *The present: the ruined vineyard.* The second part of the extended image of the vine, marked out as a separate stanza by the New International

Version (vv. 12–15), describes the people's present condition and asks God why he has allowed it to happen.

> Why have you broken down its walls
>   so that all who pass by pick its grapes?
> Boars from the forest ravage it
>   and the creatures of the field feed on it.

The breaking down of the walls and the ravaging of the land have suggested to some commentators that the psalmist is describing the complete over-throw of the kingdom by the Assyrian armies in 721 B.C. But that does not necessarily follow from the words. The walls are not necessarily the literal walls surrounding Samaria, the capital and last northern stronghold. They can also designate the borders or frontiers of the land, and if that is the case, then the stanza is merely describing intrusions into Israel from outside by the pagan nations.

The strongest reason for refusing to place this psalm after the defeat of the northern kingdom is that it is hard to think of anyone asking for its restoration at that point. The overthrow was just too complete. The people of the north were carried away and dispersed, and other peoples were brought in to settle the land.

3. *The future: restoration through "the son of man."* And yet there is hope, at least at this point. For the final section of this extended metaphor, set apart as verses 16–18 by the New International Version, looks to the future and asks for revival and restoration by

> . . . the man at your right hand,
>   the son of man you have raised up for yourself (v. 17).

Who is this "son of man"? It is impossible not to think of Jesus Christ, who used these words of himself and who is undoubtedly the one by whom the fortunes of all God's peoples are to be restored. Yet it is not so clear that this is meant here. There are three possibilities.

First, "the man at your right hand" could be the current king, either of the northern kingdom (if Samaria had not yet fallen) or of the southern kingdom (if Samaria had fallen and the psalm is really for the preservation of Judah). H. C. Leupold writes, "There seems to be no other feasible way of interpreting verse 17 than to think of it as being a prayer for the king that sits upon the throne of Israel."[5] If this is right, the stanza means that if God would bless the king by leading him in the way of righteousness, then the people would remain faithful to God too, and would be revived and would not perish. The king would point the way to the desired restoration.

Second, the reference could be to the people themselves. The best rea-son for thinking this is that verse 15 also uses the word *son,* and in that verse the reference is certainly to Israel, since it is parallel to "the root your right hand has planted." This led no less a scholar and careful exegete than John Calvin to identify "the son of man" as Israel. It is also the position taken by J. J. Stewart Perowne.[6] It fits this view that Israel is called God's "firstborn son" in Exodus 4:22 (see Hosea 11:1).

The third view is that "the son of man" is the Messiah. This was the interpretation given to the text by the later rabbis. It is also the interpretation adopted by Charles Haddon Spurgeon, who wrote, "There is no doubt here an outlook to the Messiah, for whom believing Jews had learned to look as the Savior in time of trouble."[7] And later, quoting other commentators in the section on "Quaint Sayings," Spurgeon says, "To whom can the title apply but to him? For 'to which of the angels said God at any time, Sit on my right hand?' (Heb. 1:5); and much less has he said this of any Jewish king. . . . Though the phrase, 'man of thy right hand,' may have an immediate reference to the King who ruled in Judah when this psalm was penned, it must ultimately and most properly intend Jesus Christ, the great antitype of all the kings of David's line."[8]

"I Am the True Vine"

I think Calvin was right as to the setting of the psalm. The prayer is that God would bless Israel by turning this "son of man" back to God again. It is how we should all pray. At the same time, from our perspective on this side of the earthly ministry of Jesus Christ, we cannot forget that Jesus applied the image of the vine to himself, calling himself the "true vine"—the one, essential, and enduring vine before whom all other vines are but types. Jesus said, "I am the true vine and my Father is the gardener" (John 15:1). He also said, "You are the branches. If a man remains in me and I in him, he will bear much fruit; apart from me you can do nothing" (John 15:5).

Without God Israel herself could do nothing. At least she could do nothing but sin, which she did abundantly, eventually falling away into the Lord's terrible national judgment. To survive, to prosper, even to live—the people of the old covenant had to abide in God.

No less do we! Without Jesus Christ and his power, we cannot come to faith, trusting him as our Savior. Without Jesus Christ and his power, we cannot live a righteous life, turning our backs on sin and cleaving to our master. Without Jesus Christ and his power, we cannot achieve any spiritual victory or produce any spiritual fruit. Spurgeon wrote, "Without the Lord you will do nothing. Immeasurable cloudland of proposals and not a spot of solid doing large enough for a dove's foot to rest on."[9] On the other hand, as Paul wrote, in Christ we can do "everything" (Phil. 4:13).

Psalm 81

"If My People . . ."

Sing for joy to God our strength;
*   shout aloud to the God of Jacob!*
Begin the music, strike the tambourine,
*   play the melodious harp and lyre. . . .*

"Hear, O my people, and I will warn you—
*   if you would but listen to me, O Israel!*
You shall have no foreign god among you;
*   you shall not bow down to an alien god.*
I am the LORD your God,
*   who brought you up out of Egypt.*
*   Open wide your mouth and I will fill it.*

"But my people would not listen to me;
*   Israel would not submit to me.*
So I gave them over to their stubborn hearts
*   to follow their own devices.*

"If my people would but listen to me,
*   if Israel would follow my ways,*
how quickly would I subdue their enemies
*   and turn my hand against their foes!*
Those who hate the LORD would cringe before him,
*   and their punishment would last forever.*
But you would be fed with the finest of wheat;
*   with honey from the rock I would satisfy you."*
*   verses 1–2, 8–16*

Some time ago some members of Tenth Presbyterian Church developed an advertising campaign that was intended to appeal to young, secular, inner-city people. One ad contained the headline "Jesus Hated Church Too," which was a confession that there is often much about the institutional church that is rightly offensive to any thinking person—hypocrisy, sin, political scrambling for power, and such things. But it went on to observe that Jesus didn't stop going to church because of the church's failures. It suggested that he might have known something today's secular people do not know, and it invited them to visit Tenth.

We delayed moving on the campaign for a while because a few people objected that the ad made fun of the true church, Christ's body. The people who were objecting could not (or perhaps would not) see that hating "church" is not the same thing as hating "the true church" and that sometimes you have to hate one to love the other.

What was really surprising to me was the failure of these critics to remember that nobody spoke out against the hypocrisy and sin of the church more than Jesus Christ. Or God the Father, for that matter! After all, the church of Jesus' day was a Judaism directed by religious leaders whom Jesus denounced in sharp terms. He called them "hypocrites," "blind guides," and "fools." He said of them, "You shut the kingdom of heaven in men's faces. You yourselves do not enter, nor will you let those enter who are trying to" (Matt. 23:13; see vv. 15–17). Similarly, in the book written by Amos, God told the people,

> I hate, I despise your religious feasts;
>   I cannot stand your assemblies.
> Even though you bring me burnt offerings and grain
>   offerings,
>   I will not accept them. . . .
> Away with the noise of your songs!
>   I will not listen to the music of your harps
>   (Amos 5:21–23).

These are reminders that just because we go to church and practice what we call worship does not mean that we are actually worshiping the true God or even doing anything at all that might please him.

An Invocation: The Call to Worship

This is precisely the problem with which Psalm 81 deals. It begins with a wonderful stanza calling for the joyful worship of God, who delivered the people of Israel from the power of the Egyptians (vv. 1–5). In fact, it calls all Israel to worship, much like a minister in one of today's churches who might begin a service with a call to the entire congregation to join in worshiping God. Franz Delitzsch, one of the great German commentators, points out that the summons in verse 1 is to the whole congregation; the summons in verse 2 is to the Levites, who were the appointed temple singers and musicians; and the summons in verse 3 is to the priests who had the specific task of blowing the trumpets.[1] This gives the impression that all is well with the people and that they are all completely right in their worship.

But from this point on the psalm continues with the words of God, who reminds the people of what he has done for them in the past and warns them to repent of their sin, particularly their worship of the false gods of the surrounding nations, in order that their enemies might be subdued and that they might be blessed. It protests that they will not do this.

What a strange anomaly: a happy, joyfully worshiping congregation and a neglected and offended God. Strange? Yes, but all too characteristic of religious people. Isaiah wrote, in words quoted approvingly by Jesus,

> These people come near to me with their mouth
> and honor me with their lips,
> but their hearts are far from me (Isa. 29:13;
> see Matt. 15:8).

We have to ask ourselves: Is our worship like that? Do we please God? Or are we merely worshiping God outwardly while our hearts are set on sin?[2]

A Reminder: What God Had Done

God's rebuke in this psalm begins with a reminder of what he had done in delivering the Jews from Egypt (vv. 6–7). The people had called to him in their distress, and he had heard, answered, and rescued them, lifting the burdens from their shoulders and freeing their hands from the baskets with which they had carried the bricks for Pharaoh's massive building projects. This last note (in v. 6) is a historical remembrance of what the deliverance from bondage actually entailed. Derek Kidner calls the mention of baskets "an independent memory, not mentioned in the record, but confirmed by many pictures."[3] They can be seen in the tomb paintings of Luxor from the Valley of the Kings, as well as in other places.

God had seen this, and he cared. In these words we find an echo of what God told Moses when he appeared to him at the burning bush: "I have indeed seen the misery of my people in Egypt. I have heard them crying out because of their slave drivers, and I am concerned about their suffering. So I have come down to rescue them from the hand of the Egyptians and to bring them up out of the land into a good and spacious land, a land flowing with milk and honey" (Exod. 3:7–8).

Many such echoes of the Pentateuch, particularly from Deuteronomy and Exodus, occur in Psalm 81.

A Warning: Ears to Hear?

There are two main parts to this psalm, the opening invocation or call to worship and God's rebuke of the people in the words we have already begun to study. But pressed further, the second part can also be divided into sections along the lines of the New International Version's stanzas. By this arrangement there is: (1) the reminder of what God had done (vv. 6–7); (2) a warning because of the people's idolatry (vv. 8–10); (3) a record of the people's disobedience, followed by a description of its sad result (vv. 11–12); and (4) a jump to the present to indicate that the situation is still continuing, because the hearts of the people were unchanged. We are at the second of these last four sections now.

This is the most important part of the psalm, its very heart, and not just because it is the middle stanza, though the poem has intentionally been written that way. It is because it has to do with the worship of the one true God and him only, which is the heart of true religion.

This warning is right out of the start of the Ten Commandments, but it also draws in reminiscences of other key texts. For instance, it begins with the first three words of the well-known and often recited *shema* of Deuteronomy 6:4 ("Hear, O Israel: The LORD our God, the LORD is one"). The words "if you would but . . ." (later, "if my people") echo similar phrases in Deuteronomy 5:29, 32:29, and elsewhere. Other phrases seem to be borrowed from the Song of Moses in Deuteronomy 32; for example, "foreign gods" (in vv. 12, 16). In fact, though it is shorter, the outline of Psalm 81 is more or less the same as that of Moses' Song.

However, the most obvious and important reference to the earlier books of the law is the borrowing from the start of the Ten Commandments: "I am the LORD your God, who brought you out of Egypt, out of the land of slavery. You shall have no other gods before me" (Exod. 20:2–3). This is the law above all laws, the earliest equivalent of Deuteronomy 6:5, which Jesus called the first and greatest commandment: "Love the LORD your God with all your heart and with all your soul and with all your strength" (see Matt. 22:37–38). From it all the other commandments follow naturally.

The importance of this for us is that this is also the greatest issue of all time and therefore also a critical command and warning that we need to pay attention to today. For the great issue in religion—indeed, the great issue of life—is not whether or not we worship "a" god, that is, whether or not we are religious rather than being atheists, but whether we know the true God who has revealed himself in history: (1) in the Old Testament to the Jews at the exodus and at Sinai, and (2) in the New Testament to us in the person of Jesus Christ. And whether we obey him! In other words, the great issue today, as always, is the truth or falsity of the statement: "I am the LORD your God, who brought you out of Egypt, out of the land of slavery" (Exod. 20:2–3).

While writing this study I came across an article in the magazine *First Things* by Robert L. Wilken, a professor of the history of Christianity at the University of Virginia. Titled "No Other Gods," it is a moving attempt to apply the first commandment to our times.

Wilken begins with an analysis of our current Western culture, which he accuses of undermining the beliefs, attitudes, and conventions that have nurtured our civilization for centuries. In fact, he says, its explicit goal is "to dismantle the common Western culture, to turn everything into a subculture. Secularism wants religious practice, especially Christian practice, banished to a private world of feelings and attitudes, while at the same time the realm of the public is to be expanded to include every aspect of one's life."[4]

Christianity stands against this goal, of course. It does so because it is committed to the truth that the true God has revealed himself in history and that those who have come to know him must witness to this fact. In other words, Christians must bear witness to the truth of the first commandment, though they are usually hated for it.

Wilken refers to Origen of Alexandria, the great Christian apologist of the third century, who insisted that Christianity is strong because it is confident of what it knows. It knows that God has revealed himself in the Old Testament in the history of Israel and in Jesus Christ. Of course, the knowledge of God possessed by Christians is different from secular forms of knowledge because secularism begins with man and man's reason and Christianity begins with God and God's revelation. But Christianity is not less rational or less sure because of that. On the contrary, it is more rational and even more sure because it begins with these historical facts. Origen and the other early apologists often and rightly referred to John 1:18 in support of their position: "No one has ever seen God, but God the One and Only, who is at the Father's side, has made him known."

Wilken also brings in some observations by T. S. Eliot, author of "The Waste Land" and other poems and dramas, such as *Murder in the Cathedral.* Eliot did his most significant work between the two world wars, when he perceived Western society to be crumbling into a new paganism, and he voiced the challenge he saw in lectures later published as *Christianity and Culture.* "The choice before us is between the formation of a new Christian culture, and the acceptance of a pagan one," he said. Instead of showing that "Christianity provides a foundation for morality" we must show "the necessity of Christian morality from the truth of Christianity. It is not enthusiasm, but dogma, that differentiates a Christian from a pagan society."[5] All this was a way of saying that we must return to the first of the Ten Commandments.

Wilken concludes that "Christians are . . . called to persuade others (including many within the churches) that our first duty as human beings is to honor and venerate the one true God, and that without the worship of God, society disintegrates into an amoral aggregate of competing, self-centered interests destructive of the commonweal."[6] "Only God can give ultimate purpose to our lives and direction to our society," he says. "The First Commandment is not just a text to be memorized in catechism class; it is the theological basis for a just and humane society."[7]

The Result in Past Days

This is something the people of God should know and practice. But often they do not, which is what the fourth stanza of Psalm 81 is about (vv. 11–12). Looking to their actions in the past, God says that he heard them, delivered them, instructed them, and warned them.

> But my people would not listen to me;
> Israel would not submit to me (v. 11).

The remarkable thing about this rejection is that it is by "my [that is, God's] people," not the world. This is emphasized, because the words "my people" are repeated in verses 8, 11, and 13, at the start of each of the last three stanzas. Alexander Maclaren says, "There is a world of baffled tenderness and almost wondering rebuke in the designation of the rebels as 'my people.' It would have been no cause of astonishment if other nations had not listened; but that the tribes bound by so many kindnesses should have been deaf is a sad marvel."[8]

Isn't this exactly the problem we face today? The problem is not that the world does not know God. How can we expect it to? The problem is that the people of God do not know God, or at least they do not act like they do. Instead of worshiping the Lord and him only, Christians seem to be worshiping the gods of the secular culture—gods of wealth, pleasure, fame, status, and self-absorption.

When I travel around the country and speak in so-called evangelical churches, the thing that strikes me the most is how little awareness of the presence of God there seems to be, even on a Sunday morning. The services are relevant in the sense that they deal with supposed human needs. They are lively, often entertaining. Like the worship described at the beginning of this psalm, they are often loud, joyful, and boosted by musical instruments. But there is almost no serious mention of God. The hymns are increasingly man-centered, dealing with who we are rather than with who he is, and there are almost no prayers. To judge from what I hear, Christianity has become a form of Sunday entertainment, a political pressure group, or a twelve-step recovery process, rather than a community of those who know and are learning to obey God.

This is what we have to offer our culture, however. And it is what our culture needs. In a recent book exploring these evangelical weaknesses and our true opportunities, Michael Scott Horton says, "What is required in our day, as even many non-Christian thinkers are saying, is nothing less than a spiritual quest. Will we be there, ready for the ultimate questions with answers from the personal God of biblical revelation, who is the source of all truth, or will we still be entangled in the ideological movements and draw our water from streams which have run their course, progressing from a mighty ocean to a stagnant pond?"[9]

The Result to Be Anticipated Now

At the end of the fourth stanza of this psalm, God indicates the result of his people's refusing to hear his voice and worship and proclaim him only. He gives them up to their own devices, precisely as, in Romans, Paul indicates that he gives up the unbelieving world to its devices (see Rom. 1:24, 26, 28). In the case of the world, this abandonment by God is to moral perversion and to spiritual insanity. In our day evangelicals are being abandoned to materialism and secularism, the very things they rail against and deplore.

But what is the alternative? Suppose the people of God return to God and actually listen to him and follow in his ways. Then, says God, he will bless them by defeating their enemies and satisfying them with the best of all spiritual and physical things, here poetically called "the finest of the wheat" and "honey from the rock" (v. 16). This is the point of the psalm's last stanza (vv. 13–16).

What God says reminds me of that well-known and frequently quoted text from 2 Chronicles 7:14: "If my people, who are called by my name, will humble themselves and pray and seek my face and turn from their wicked ways, then will I hear from heaven and will forgive their sin and will heal their land." The trouble with us is that we want to straighten out the other people. We want *them* to be humbled, to pray (witness our concern to get prayer back into the public schools, even prayer to "an unknown god"), to seek God's face and to turn from *their* wicked ways. But the world can't do that, not by itself. What the world needs is the gospel, which we must bring to it. Second Chronicles 7:14 and Psalm 81 are for us. It is for us to humble ourselves, repent, and seek God. Then by grace the Lord may indeed hear from heaven, forgive our sin, and heal our land.

Psalm 82

All "Gods" Judged by God

God presides in the great assembly;
he gives judgment among the "gods":

"How long will you defend the unjust
and show partiality to the wicked? Selah
Defend the cause of the weak and fatherless;
maintain the rights of the poor and oppressed.
Rescue the weak and needy;
deliver them from the hand of the wicked.

"They know nothing, they understand nothing.
They walk about in darkness;
all the foundations of the earth are shaken.

"I said, 'You are "gods";
you are all sons of the Most High.'
But you will die like mere men;
you will fall like every other ruler."

Rise up, O God, judge the earth,
for all the nations are your inheritance.
verses 1–8

On one occasion Jesus' enemies came to him with a trick question: "Is it right to pay taxes to Caesar or not?" (Matt. 22:17). They thought that if he said it was right to pay taxes, they could discredit him in the eyes of those who hated Rome and for whom taxes were a

673

much-resented burden. On the other hand, if he said that the Jews should resist Rome by refusing to pay taxes, then they could denounce him to the Roman authorities as an insurrectionist who was trying to overthrow Caesar.

Jesus asked for a coin. When they produced it, he asked whose portrait was on it, probably holding it out so they could see it.

"Caesar's," they replied.

"Give to Caesar what is Caesar's," Jesus said.

Then, probably turning the coin over so they could see the portrait of the Roman god or goddess that would have been on the reverse side, he added, "and to God what is God's" (Matt. 22:21).

The first part of Jesus' answer reinforced Caesar's authority, even in such an unpopular matter as taxes. His second part drew limits since, although the state has a God-given and therefore legitimate authority, the authority of God is greater. Jesus' words were a reminder that those who exercise authority are responsible to God for what they do.

Who Are the "Gods"?

This is the precise situation we are dealing with in Psalm 82, for it is a psalm in which the earthly judges of Israel are being called to account by God. The opening verse says,

> God presides in the great assembly;
>   he gives judgment among the "gods."

There are two possibilities as to the meaning of "gods" in this verse and verse 6 ("I said, 'You are "gods"; you are all sons of the Most High'").[1]

1. *Human judges, particularly the judges of Israel.* The oldest and, in fact, almost universal view among the earlier commentators is that "gods" refers to human judges, particularly the judges of Israel.[2] To call a human judge a "god" may seem strange to us, even when we know that the word for "gods" is the broad term *elohim.* But it does not seem to have been strange for ancient Israel. For example, in Exodus 21:6, as part of the Jews' civil law, the people were told that if a man who had been a slave for six years and was to be set free in the seventh year should nevertheless have come to love his master and want to remain with him, he was to be brought to the *elohim,* who should pierce his ear as a sign that he had chosen to be a servant for life. The New International Version (and some others) rightly translates this verse: "then his master must take him before the *judges.*" The same usage occurs several more times in Exodus 22.[3]

The best argument for this view is the way Jesus referred to this psalm in John 10:34–36. The leaders had accused him of blasphemy because he habitually called himself "God's Son." Jesus answered, "Is it not written in your Law, 'I have said you are gods'? [This is where he referred to Psalm 82.] If he called them 'gods,' to whom the word of God came—and the

Scripture cannot be broken—what about the one whom the Father set apart as his very own and sent into the world? Why then do you accuse me of blasphemy because I said, 'I am God's Son'?"

Some have accused Jesus of trying to escape on a technicality regarding the use of words, but he was not doing this. He did not downplay his unique relationship to God, for his reply asserted that the Father had set him apart as his very own and sent him into the world. What he was doing was replying to their specific accusation, which was his use of the phrase "Son of God" for himself, and his point was that God had used even stronger language than this of human judges in the Old Testament. Jesus' reply shows that he regarded Psalm 82 as being about Israel's civil rulers.

His reply does something else also important: It gives one reason why the judges of Israel could be called "gods." It is because "the word of God came" to them. That is, they were God's spokesmen. When they acted justly and rendered just judgment it was as if God himself had acted, by acting through them. J. J. Stewart Perowne adds, "They were sons of the Highest, called by his name, bearing his image, exercising his authority, charged to execute his will, and they ought to have been in their measure his living representatives."[4] They did not do this, of course, which is what the remainder of the psalm is about.

2. *Demons, the "principalities and powers."* In the last hundred years or so a second view has gained ground in scholarly circles, and that is that the "gods" in Psalm 82 are minor deities. We would call them demons, or at least the "principalities and powers" about which Paul speaks when he writes that the Christian's struggle "is not against flesh and blood, but against the rulers, against the authorities, against the powers of this dark world and against the spiritual forces of evil in the heavenly realms" (Eph. 6:12). This is the view of Derek Kidner, who has written two volumes on the psalms for InterVarsity Press, and of Marvin E. Tate, who has contributed his studies to the *Word Biblical Commentary.*[5]

There are two arguments for this view. First, the Old Testament speaks of such powers, occasionally referring to them as "gods" (sometimes translated "angels"). Examples are Isaiah 24:21 ("the LORD will punish the powers in the heaven above") and Daniel 10:13 ("the prince of the Persian kingdom" who resisted Michael, the archangel). As far as God presiding over an assembly of such "gods" is concerned, an excellent example is Job 1, where "the sons of God" ("angels," NIV), including Satan, present themselves before God in heaven.

The second argument is the way in which Psalm 82 speaks of the judgment of God on these "gods." He says they will "die like mere men." If they are to die "like" men, the argument goes, then they cannot be men; they must be something else, and the only other thing they can be are demonic powers.

Yet that is an argument that cuts two ways. For isn't it true that the demons (and angels) are spirits, who have no bodies and who therefore cannot die? The demons will be punished. They will be punished in hell forever, but they will not die. On the other hand, if these "gods" are human judges, then the words are appropriate. For they mean that in spite of the fact that these wicked men have considered themselves to be virtually invincible because of their high office, they will die just like anybody else. They will fall just like any other ruler.

The bottom line is that either view is possible, but the first should be preferred, above all because it is the interpretation given to the psalm by Jesus Christ. He tells us that it is about human beings.

Convening the Court

We need to return to the first verse briefly because it sets the scene for what follows. The setting is a convening of the court. It is God calling the "gods" before him for him to render judgment.

This verse meant a great deal to Martin Luther, who spent many pages on it in his lectures on the psalms. At the time he wrote his study of Psalm 82 he was reacting to the Peasants Revolt, which in his judgment threatened to sidetrack or even undermine the Reformation. This revolt, which erupted in 1525, was an attempt at political revolution, and the peasants expected the great Reformer's support. Luther did not give it, because he knew that spiritual goals cannot be advanced by political means and also because he knew the value of civic order and rightly feared anarchy. He had been protected from death from the Roman church by the Elector of Saxony, his prince. So he pointed out that Psalm 82:1, 6 both establishes and limits the authority of princes. It establishes it, because it is God who appoints the authorities; it is he who calls them "gods." It limits their authority because they are accountable to him, as the psalm shows.

This is exactly what Jesus said when he appeared before Pilate, for he recognized Pilate's authority to preside over him at his trial while at the same time he reminded him that he was responsible to God for what he did. Jesus told Pilate, "You would have no power over me if it were not given to you from above. Therefore the one who handed me over to you is guilty of a greater sin" (John 19:11). Paul taught the same thing in Romans 13, when he spoke of rulers as "God's servants." Paul said, "Therefore, it is necessary to submit to the authorities" (Rom. 13:5).

Luther struck a wonderful balance, though he has been criticized for not joining the peasants' cause as a revolutionary. On the one hand, he argued that the rulers must be obeyed: "For where there is no government, or where government is not held in honor, there can be no peace. Where there is no peace, no one can keep his life or anything else in the face of another's outrage, thievery, robbery, violence and wickedness. Much less will there be room to teach God's Word and to rear children in the fear of God and his discipline (Eph. 6:4)." On the other hand, God "keeps down the rulers, so that they do not abuse his majesty and power according to their own self-will. . . . For they are not gods among the people and overlords of the congregation in such a way that they have this position all to themselves and can do as they like. Not so! God himself is there also. He will judge, punish, and correct them; and if they do not obey, they will not escape."[6]

The Indictment

In the New International Version the next three verses are set apart as a separate stanza, and rightly so, for they constitute God's indictment of the injustice practiced by Israel's judges. Technically, the first part is a question: "How long will you defend the unjust and show partiality to the wicked?" (v. 2). The second part is a command:

> Defend the cause of the weak and fatherless;
> maintain the rights of the poor and oppressed.
> Rescue the weak and needy;
> deliver them from the hand of the wicked (vv. 3–4).

These verses are an indictment of the judges, saying that they have not punished wickedness; defended the weak or orphans, the poor or the oppressed; or intervened to save the weak from those who are more powerful. The duties of the civil rulers are twofold: (1) to establish, promote, and maintain justice and (2) to defend citizens from aggression, both from within and from without, from enemies. These judges had done neither. They had failed on both counts.

Continuing his challenge to the rulers, Luther wrote, "These . . . three verses, indeed the whole psalm, every prince should have painted on the wall of his chamber, on his bed, over his table, and on his garments. For here they find what lofty, princely, noble virtues their estate can practice, so that temporal government, next to the preaching office, is the highest service to God and the most useful office on earth."[7]

Extolling the value of these secular princes, Luther declared, "I would rather be a pious secretary or tax collector for one of these 'gods' than twice a Hilary [the founder of the monastic life in Palestine] or a Jerome among the angels."[8]

What Can the Righteous Do?

Can justice like this ever be established and maintained in the ongoing flux of sinful human affairs? Well, Job claimed to have done it. Job was a "prince" in his day, a ruler among the people. He sat in the gate and gave justice. He said of himself,

> I rescued the poor who cried for help,
>> and the fatherless who had none to assist him.
> The man who was dying blessed me;
>> I made the widow's heart sing. . . .
> I was a father to the needy;
>> I took up the case of the stranger.
> I broke the fangs of the wicked
>> and snatched the victims from their teeth
>> (Job 29:12–13, 16–17).

This is exactly what is required of the judges of Israel (and indeed of all civil rulers) in Psalm 82. But the point of the psalm is that they had not done it. Hence, the consequence, following on the indictment of verses 2–4, is that "they know nothing. . . . They walk about in darkness; all the foundations of the earth are shaken" (v. 5).

This is a right description of all godless governments, whether overt godless governments like that of the former Soviet Union and the Communist bloc, or more subtle godless governments like our own. A government that does not acknowledge God and try to govern according to the responsibilities for it that God has laid down will inevitably succumb to the three perils listed in this verse. First, *ignorance.* It will not perceive what is happening or what to do about it; events will outstrip its ability to cope. Second, *inept action.* When it does act, it will operate "in darkness," and its programs and policies will be ineffective. Third, *the foundations of common life will be shaken.* That is exactly what happened in the Communist countries when their governments collapsed in the late fall of 1989, and it is what seems to be happening in our own country in a less obvious but nonetheless steady and insidious way even now. Our most basic institutions, like the courts, public schools, and even government itself, are in turmoil, and it is increasingly unsafe even to walk on our streets.

> When the foundations are being destroyed,
>> what can the righteous do? (Ps. 11:3).

Passing Sentence

In a judicial setting as significant as this one seems to be, we might anticipate a thunderous judgment of eternal death being passed upon Israel's unjust judges. There are some who take the sentence of verses 6–7 in this way, death being understood as eternal death or damnation. Yet the psalm does not actually say this, though it might be inferred as a final consequence of the rulers' sin. Instead it seems to speak temporally only, reminding the rulers that they are human after all, that they will die in time, just like anybody else, and that they will fall from their exalted position just like any other ruler.

That doesn't seem enough somehow. And yet it probably is! For what people in high office need to know is that, although they may have been called to a position in which they have functioned as "gods," and are almost regarded as gods, they are not actually "gods" but only men and women after all. They will die. In time they will be replaced by others. In the meantime, while they still hold and exercise their high office, they need the wisdom of God to function even minimally. As for those like us who are not in government but who are Christians, we need to remind people who are in authority of these truths and pray for them (1 Tim. 2:1–2).

Judge of All the Earth

And one thing more: We need to practice justice and come to the defense of the poor and oppressed ourselves, as Job did. I say this because of the way the psalm ends and because of the way some commentators have handled it. The psalm ends:

> Rise up, O God, judge the earth,
>   for all the nations are your inheritance.

This last verse matches verse 1 in describing God's judgment, the two verses being what Marvin Tate calls "framing verses for the speech in between."[9] It extends the judgment scene in heaven to earth, like the words "your will be done on earth as it is in heaven" from the Lord's Prayer (Matt. 6:10).

Is this a prayer for God's intervention in history in what we call the Last Judgment, when he will pour out his wrath upon all evildoers? Probably. But it is also a prayer that justice might be done by God through his people, who, whatever the failure of the civil rulers may be, nevertheless are called to show mercy and exercise justice in the sphere of their more limited influence and to the extent of their responsibility.

This is a challenge for what each of us can do. We must not avoid it. One commentator wrote wrongly, "There will be no universal betterment of human existence till the right judge appears and saves the poor and needy. . . . The true Church does not pray this prayer."[10] I say that we had better pray it, and we had better act justly and for justice too.

Psalm 83

The Encircling Foe

O God, do not keep silent;
*   be not quiet, O God, be not still.*
See how your enemies are astir,
*   how your foes rear their heads.*
With cunning they conspire against your people;
*   they plot against those you cherish.*
"Come," they say, "let us destroy them as a nation,
*   that the name of Israel be remembered no more."* . . .

Do to them as you did to Midian,
*   as you did to Sisera and Jabin at the river Kishon,*
who perished at Endor
*   and became like refuse on the ground.*
Make their nobles like Oreb and Zeeb,
*   all their princes like Zebah and Zalmunna,*
who said, "Let us take possession
*   of the pasturelands of God."* . . .

May they ever be ashamed and dismayed;
*   may they perish in disgrace.*
Let them know that you, whose name is the LORD—
*   that you alone are the Most High over all the earth.*
*   verses 1–4, 9–12, 17–18*

Edmund Burke was an Irishman who was a member of the English House of Commons from 1766 to 1794. He was known as an outstanding intellect and effective writer, and he was admired among other things for his brilliant essay on the French Revolution ("Reflections on the Revolution in France") and his passionate speech on behalf of American liberties ("On Conciliation with America"). It is interesting, Burke being a writer, that the sentence he is best remembered for is one that does not appear in his writings but which he is credited with by several sources. Burke said, "All that is necessary for evil to triumph is for good men to do nothing."

We can think of historical examples to prove this truth. One that comes to mind immediately is the lack of resolve and blindness of the democratic nations in the years prior to World War II, which allowed Germany under Hitler to rearm. Winston Churchill described it in *The Gathering Storm.* In the face of such a threat we rightly deplore "doing nothing."

But here is an even greater problem. How about when God does nothing? What should we think when he is silent when his people call to him in trouble, as they do and he often seems to be? This is no small matter. It is a terrible problem, and it is what Psalm 83 is about. It tells God, "Do not keep silent; be not quiet . . . be not still" when we are surrounded by enemies.

This is the last of the psalms of Asaph (Psalms 50, 73–83), a writer who consistently seems troubled by the wicked and who regularly calls on God to rise up and defeat their evil plans.

The Immediate Problem

Asaph's psalms are not all alike, of course. Some are personal, like Psalm 50. Others have a wider scope and deal with evil in general or with the dangers evil people present to the nation. This psalm is in the latter category. It deals with a time when the nations that surrounded Israel had united against her and threatened her survival.

Verses 2–8 describe it. After asking God to speak up and act in verse 1, the psalm continues:

> See how your enemies are astir,
>   how your foes rear their heads.
> With cunning they conspire against your people;
>   they plot against those you cherish.
> "Come," they say, "let us destroy them as a nation,
>   that the name of Israel be remembered no more."
>
> With one mind they plot together;
>   they form an alliance against you—

It does not seem possible to identify this conspiracy. There is an example of what it might have been like in 2 Chronicles 20, when Jehoshaphat was king and Israel was threatened by a coalition of Edom, Moab, and Ammon. God saved the people by causing the three nations to fight among themselves. There was great destruction and a great deliverance. Some commentators have suggested that Jahaziel, a descendant of Asaph who is mentioned in 2 Chronicles 20 as having uttered a prophecy of the Jews' victory, may be the actual author of this psalm. But this is mere conjecture.

What is significant about the specific peoples listed in the ongoing flow of the psalm (vv. 6–11) is that they form an almost complete circle of entrapment around Israel. The Edomites (v. 6) were descendants of Esau, the twin brother of Jacob, Abraham's grandson. The Ishmaelites (v. 6) had descended from Ishmael, Abraham's son by Hagar. The Hagarites (v. 6) were a tribe against whom the Transjordanian tribes of Reuben, Gad, and Manasseh fought at the time of the Jewish conquest of Palestine. These peoples, plus the tribal nations of Moab (v. 6) and Ammon (v. 7), were situated to the east of the Jews' territory.

Identification of Gebal (v. 7) is uncertain. It might be a tribal area south of the Dead Sea linked with Edom, Moab, Ammon, and Amalek. The Amalekites (v. 7) also lived in the area. Or Gebal might be a Canaanite and Phoenician port about twenty miles north of modern Beirut, known to the Greeks as Byblos. The modern site of ancient Byblos is called Jebeil (a variant of Gebal). As for Philistia and Tyre (v. 7), these areas were to the west of Israel on the Mediterranean coast. Philistia was south, roughly what we today call the Gaza Strip. Tyre was to the north.

The tenth and last tribal or national power mentioned is Assyria (v. 8), the great and later very formidable power that always came down into Jewish territory from the north. It was Assyria under the leadership of Shalmaneser that besieged, captured, and destroyed Samaria, overthrew the northern kingdom of Israel, and deported its people in 721 B.C.

But that was later than when Psalm 83 was written. We know of no time in Israel's history when these ten powers were actually arrayed against her, so the listing in verses 6–8 is probably a generalization. It is a way of saying that the Jews always seemed to be surrounded by enemies and in danger of being liquidated.

Anti-Semitism throughout History

This has been the actual condition of Israel throughout history as many peoples and nations have arrayed themselves against her. We can start with Egypt. The fierce efforts of the pharaoh of the generation immediately prior to the birth of Moses to enslave and then kill the Jews is the first expression of anti-Semitism in world history and supplies a pattern that has been repeated again and again. God had blessed the Jewish people in faithfulness to his ancient promises to Abraham. He had said,

> I will make you into a great nation
>   and I will bless you;
> I will make your name great,

> and you will be a blessing.
> I will bless those who bless you,
>   and whoever curses you I will curse;
> and all peoples on earth
>   will be blessed through you (Gen. 12:2–3).

This resulted in the nation's striking numerical growth so that the people literally became like "the stars in the sky and as the sand on the seashore" (Gen. 22:17). This growth created fear in Pharaoh, and he instigated a pattern of abuse and oppression that extended to the murder of the Jewish male children. The end of the persecution was not the destruction of the Jews, however, but rather the destruction of Egypt by the plagues effected through Moses and eventually the death of Pharaoh and his soldiers when they tried to cross the waters of the sea that had parted to allow the Jews to pass over but had returned on their pursuers.

Even after the overthrow of their nation by the Assyrians in 721 B.C. and by the Babylonians in 586 B.C., persecutions continued. We know from the New Testament that the Jews were expelled from Rome in the days of the Emperor Claudius (Acts 18:2).

Jews were persecuted during the Middle Ages, both before the Crusades and during them. Thousands were abused, attacked, and murdered in Germany, France, Italy, and England.[1] In the fifteenth and sixteenth centuries these earlier pogroms were repeated, only with greater intensity. In the fifteenth century, 510 Jewish communities were exterminated in Europe and more were decimated. When the Jews were driven out of Spain at the end of that same century, they relocated to Italy, Holland, Egypt, and Turkey. But they were not allowed to stay longer than a few weeks or months in some places, and in others they were confined to a ghetto or Jewish quarter, as in Venice and Rome.[2]

Coming to more modern times, we remember with horror the systematic attempt to exterminate the Jews of Nazi Germany and German-dominated states in the period leading up to and during World War II. More than six million Jews perished in Adolf Hitler's death camps.

In all the annals of recorded history there has never been a people so encircled by foes or as persecuted as the Jews have been. Yet surprisingly, the Jews have prospered. In 1836 a world census indicated that there were then three million Jews living in many countries. A century later, in 1936, in spite of severe persecutions in which many Jews were killed, particularly in Russia, a second census indicated that the Jewish world population had risen to sixteen million, an increase of thirteen million in a century. The Nazis killed more than six million Jews, but today there are more Jews in the world than before the Nazi era. The only explanation for this growth is that the hand of God has been on this people and that he has blessed them.

Why has there been so much hatred? The Egyptians feared and hated the Jews because of their numbers. Europeans hated them because they were prosperous, because they were different, and because of warped religious sentiments. Hitler hated them because they were not of Aryan stock, and because he needed an enemy to focus the aggressive passions of his people.

Yet these are not adequate explanations in themselves. The ultimate and only full explanation must be found in God's words to the serpent in the Garden of Eden, when he said, "I will put enmity between you and the woman, and between your offspring and hers; he will crush your head, and you will strike his heel" (Gen. 3:15). Satan hates the Jews because God promised to send the Messiah through them, which is why he stirred up Pharaoh and his court, why he caused Herod to strike out against the Jewish babies at the time of Christ's birth, and why he used Adolf Hitler later. In the face of such hatred, the preservation of the Jews throughout history, in spite of their persecutions and scattering, has been both a mystery and a miracle.

This section of the psalm ends with a *selah,* or pause (v. 8). We cannot always tell why these *selahs* occur where they do, but this is an example of a pause well placed, for it is important for us to reflect on the terrible persecutions of these ancient people of God before going on to the prayer that God might judge their enemies.

An Appeal to Past Victories

The outline of Psalm 83 is easy. It consists of two main parts, the first describing the desperate situation in which the Jews found themselves (vv. 1–8), the second an impassioned appeal to God to overthrow and destroy their enemies (vv. 9–17). If we want to be fussy, it is possible that the first and last verses should be separated out, the first as an introduction and the last as a conclusion.

It is the second part, the appeal to God to overthrow and destroy the people's enemies, that bothers us, of course. The prayer is vindictive, and we have been taught to forgive our enemies rather than call down judgment on them. Because an ethic of forgiveness is part of our culture, most of us think of ourselves as being too nice to have such thoughts or to utter such a prayer, even though that is probably not the case.

What are we to say about this? The first thing is an observation on the psalm itself, and it is that God had destroyed Israel's enemies in this way from time to time in the past. Thus, whatever else the psalmist may be doing, he is at least appealing to a historical precedent. Two of these judgments are referred to in verses 9–12.

1. *A victory over Midian recorded in Judges 6–8.* The psalmist refers to this victory in verse 9 and amplifies on it in verse 11, where four of the Midianite rulers are mentioned: Oreb, Zeeb, Zebah, and Zalmunna. This was a striking victory, because it was won by Gideon and only three hundred eager men. The Midianites had been harassing the land and carrying off the harvests and were at this time encamped in large numbers in a nearby valley. Gideon started out with thirty-two thousand soldiers.

God said these were too many for him to use to defeat the Midianite armies. So Gideon told all who were afraid to go home. Twenty-two thousand went back. Gideon was left with only ten thousand men. God said this was still too many. So the numbers were pared down even further to only three hundred, "Gideon's band." With these fearless men Gideon then surrounded the Midianite camp by night, had each of his men blow a trumpet and suddenly expose a torch that had been hidden in an earthen jar, and shout, "A sword for the LORD and for Gideon" (7:20). The enemy soldiers were so startled and so frightened that they jumped up in the darkness and fled for their lives, drawing their swords and killing thousands of their own men in the rout. Thus the soldiers that had encircled Israel were themselves encircled by the three hundred daring men and were destroyed.

2. *The victory over Sisera recorded in Judges 4–5.* The second example of a sudden and thorough judgment on Israel's enemies referred to by the psalmist is the victory over Sisera recorded in Judges 4–5. Sisera was the commander of an army fortified by nine hundred iron chariots, and he had terrorized the land for twenty years. The Israelite commander was Barak, who defeated Sisera's army with ten thousand of the men of Israel.

In the rout Sisera was forced to abandon his chariot and flee on foot. He came to the tent of a man named Heber, whose wife was Jael. Sisera was exhausted and asked to be taken in so he could rest. While he was sleeping, Jael, Heber's wife, took a tent peg and a mallet, went to where he was lying, and drove it through Sisera's temple into the ground so he died. Thus Israel was delivered by the armies of Barak and by a courageous woman. The triumphs of Barak and Jael are celebrated in the Song of Deborah, the prophetess, in Judges 5:

> So may all your enemies perish, O LORD!
> But may they who love you be like the sun
> when it rises in its strength (Judg. 5:31).

Clearly Asaph was drawing on this and other victory stories of Israel when he composed his psalm. He was saying, "O Lord, as you have delivered us in the past, so deliver us again. Show yourself to be as powerful in our day as you have been for the generations that have preceded us." We may not pray exactly this way ourselves, but we can understand and sympathize with the prayer when we remember it in the context of Israel's many and bitter persecutions throughout history. Would we not pray for the destruction of our enemies ourselves in such circumstances?

"They're Attacking Your Property"

The second thing we should notice about the way the psalm handles its desire for judgment on the Jews' enemies is that it does not speak of them as the Jews' enemies so much as the enemies of God. Notice verse 2: "your enemies" and "your foes"—that is, the enemies and foes of God. Even when it mentions the people themselves, as it does in verse 3, it is "your people" and "those you cherish." When the plots of enemies are mentioned, as they are in verse 5, these plots are "against you." In verse 12 the enemies of Israel are cited for trying to steal their land; but again, these are called "the pasturelands of God." In every case, the psalmist says that it is God's cause that is in danger, and therefore that it is God's battle—not that of the people.

This perspective makes a tremendous difference in how one thinks of judgment. If the evil is thought of as being against one's self, then the call is for revenge. But if it is thought of as being against God, then our response is to leave justice in God's hands and trust him for whatever he sees fit to do. And we can trust him! God is not indifferent! He himself says, "It is mine to avenge; I will repay" (Deut. 32:35; cf. Rom. 12:19). When we understand that, we can be like the man who always turned to God whenever he was attacked and said, "They're attacking your property, Lord." He left judgment to God.

That They Might Know You

The final observation on the way the psalm handles the encircling danger and the need for God's timely intervention and judgment is the most important of all. It is the way it ends. It calls for judgment—that is true—but it ends by stating the purpose for that judgment: "so that men will seek your name, O LORD" (v. 16). And in the last verse,

> Let them know that you, whose name is the LORD—
> that you alone are the Most High over all the earth (v. 18).

In other words, although desiring deliverance and judgment, the ultimate desire of the psalmist is that other people, even the Jews' enemies, might come to know and obey the true God.

That is precisely why we do not rush to calls for judgment. Judgment will come. The God of all the universe will do right (see Gen. 18:25). But this is still a day of grace, when men and women may still repent of their sin and seek after God that they might find him and be rescued from the wrath to come.

Let me end by going back to the beginning of the psalm and reminding you of the greatest "non-answer" to that prayer in all history. The first verse of Psalm 83 says, "O God, do not keep silent; be not quiet, O God, be not still." One day many centuries after this was written the Son of God was hanging on a cross outside the city of Jerusalem, where he had been encircled and condemned by his cruel enemies, and he in a sense prayed this prayer. He cried to God, "My God, my God, why have you forsaken me?" (Matt. 27:46; Mark 15:34). God did not answer. He did not intervene to save Jesus from his enemies or rescue him from the cross.

It was good God did not answer, for God's silence to Christ's forsaken cry meant our salvation from the Father's wrath, and it meant that we have the gospel and not just judgment to proclaim.

Psalm 84

The Psalm of the Janitors

How lovely is your dwelling place,
*O L*ORD *Almighty!*
My soul yearns, even faints
*for the courts of the L*ORD;
my heart and my flesh cry out
for the living God.

Even the sparrow has found a home,
and the swallow a nest for herself,
where she may have her young—
a place near your altar,
*O L*ORD *Almighty, my King and my God.*
Blessed are those who dwell in your house;
they are ever praising you. Selah . . .

Better is one day in your courts
than a thousand elsewhere;
I would rather be a doorkeeper in the house of my God
than dwell in the tents of the wicked.
*For the L*ORD *God is a sun and shield;*
*the L*ORD *bestows favor and honor;*
no good thing does he withhold
from those whose walk is blameless.

*O L*ORD *Almighty,*
blessed is the man who trusts in you.
verses 1–4, 10–12

A ll the Psalter's psalms are beautiful and poignant, but some stand out above the rest, and Psalm 84 is one of them. For its high and uplifting sentiment, the simplicity and exquisite beauty of its images, and its moving aspirations it may be unequaled anywhere. Charles Haddon Spurgeon called Psalm 84 "one of the choicest of the collection." He wrote, "If the twenty-third be the most popular, the one-hundred-and-third the most joyful, the one-hundred-and-nineteenth the most deeply experimental, the fifty-first the most plaintive, this is one of the most sweet of the Psalms of Peace."[1]

Psalm 84 is a psalm of longing, longing for God's house, and it is by the Sons of Korah, as the title indicates. This is very important, as we will see. Psalm 84 is one of four Korahite psalms found in book three of the Psalter (Psalms 84, 85, 87, 88). There are seven in book two (Psalms 42, 44–49).

At Parbar, Westward

When Donald Grey Barnhouse, one of my predecessors as a pastor of Tenth Presbyterian Church, was in seminary early in this century, he knew a student who seemed unable to take anything spiritual seriously. This student was with him at a prayer meeting at which the leader asked each person to give a Bible verse that had been a special blessing. When his turn came this student said quite solemnly, "First Chronicles 26:18." There was a pause while the others looked it up. Then, just as they were finding it, the young man blurted it out so rapidly that the words almost ran together: "At Parbar, westward, four at the causeway, and two at Parbar" (KJV). Everyone was a bit puzzled. Then the seminarian quipped, "If you believe in the inspiration of the Bible, find some inspiration in that verse." Fortunately he later dropped out of seminary and took a secular position.

Years went by, and from time to time Barnhouse remembered that remark. Then one day, when he was studying the Bible and came across 1 Chronicles 26:18, Barnhouse decided to find out what the verse meant. He looked at the context and found that it was a record of the assigning of the sons of Levi to various places of service in the Lord's house. Aaron was of this tribe, and his sons were divided into twenty-four groups to maintain the sacrifices at the altar (1 Chron. 24). The descendants of Aaron's cousins Asaph, Heman, and Jeduthun were divided into similar groups to conduct the music that was to be sung at God's house, "accompanied by harps, lyres and cymbals" (1 Chron. 25:1). The next chapter, from which this strange verse had been lifted, was a record of the assignments given to a third branch of Levi's tribe, that of the Sons of Kore (Korah), who were called Korahites. These men were chosen to be "gatekeepers," or doorkeepers—janitors, if you like. It was humble work, but the Bible takes approving notice of it, saying, "They were very capable men . . . men with the strength to do the work" (1 Chron. 26:6, 8). The chapter then goes on to record where each should serve. Some were stationed to the north, others to the east, south, and west. It is at this point that the verse concerning Parbar and the causeway occurs.

Parbar is merely the Hebrew word, of course. It is uncommon. So when the translators of the King James Bible came to render this into English they had no way of determining what the word meant and so transliterated it, taking it as a place name. It turns out that Parbar was the name for the temple's western colonnade, which is how the newer versions render it. For example, the New International Version says, "As for the court to the west, there were four at the road and two at the court itself." What this chapter teaches is that God took pains to appoint specific men to be the gatekeepers or janitors of the temple and honored them for rendering that service.

Here is where Barnhouse's story has bearing on the psalm. Those who were appointed gatekeepers were the Sons of Korah, among others, and in time they wrote our beautiful eighty-fourth psalm as an expression of their joy in their work. Read it now in this light.

> How lovely is your dwelling place,
>   O Lord Almighty!
> My soul yearns, even faints
>   for the courts of the Lord;
> my heart and my flesh cry out
>   for the living God.
>
> Even the sparrow has found a home,
>   and the swallow a nest for herself,
>   where she may have her young—
> a place near your altar,
>   O Lord Almighty, my King and my God.
> Blessed are those who dwell in your house;
>   they are ever praising you. . . .
>
> Better is one day in your courts
>   than a thousand elsewhere;
> I would rather be a doorkeeper in the house of my God
>   than dwell in the tents of the wicked (vv. 1–4, 10).

Years later Barnhouse wrote, "Many times I have thanked God for the cynical twist in the mind of that fellow who tossed a seemingly nonsensical verse into the midst of a prayer meeting. He meant it for confusion, but the Lord meant it to me for good. For I learned later, as I probed into the depths of the Word of God, that God is interested in the simplest tasks of the simplest men."[2]

Sparrows and Swallows

As I have read over the various commentaries on this psalm I sense that the understanding of it that I have just shared eliminates a lot of the scholarly barnacles that surround it and opens it up to us in fresh ways.

For this is not a song of pilgrims making their way up to Jerusalem for one of the three annual feasts, as many commentators argue. There are other psalms that do that (Psalms 120–134). Nor is it an allegory in which the sparrows and swallows of verse 3 represent the psalmist, even less their "young" referring to his children, which others have suggested. It is not even a psalm of a person who has been separated from the temple, as David was on at least several occasions, though it would be appropriate for such a person. It is a psalm of people who were present in the temple, who served in God's house, and who are expressing here how intensely their very souls yearned and even fainted for God. They are saying that their souls yearned for God's house not because they were separated from it, but because that is where they were and wanted to be. It was why they were serving.

This throws light on the most beautiful language of the psalm, the part having to do with the sparrows and swallows. People have tried to read hidden meanings into this, but it is best taken as a simple observation, as H. C. Leupold suggests: "The statement is not to be thought of as being a kind of allegory in which the birds represent the writer or any worshiper. Nor do the 'young' in this case symbolize the children of the writer. Nor is the term 'altars' to be understood in absolute literalness as though the writer were trying to indicate that birds actually built their nests upon the altars which were in use every day."[3] The poet simply saw birds at the temple, and his point was that as the birds made their home at the temple and were secure there with no fear of enemies, so may the people of God make their home in God and find their security in him.

And yet there probably are some poetic overtones to the mention of the sparrows and swallows, which is only to say that the imagery supports the writer's message, as it should.

1. *Sparrows.* In the Bible sparrows are a symbol for something that is almost worthless. In Jerusalem the boys that caught sparrows to get a little bit of spending money sold two for a farthing and five for two farthings (Matt. 10:29; Luke 12:6). A farthing *(assarion)* was the smallest and least valuable copper coin. Yet the sparrow found a home near God's altar (Ps. 84:3). Will God not also provide a home for you, who are worth much more than sparrows? When he was referring to a sparrow's value Jesus said, "Are not two sparrows sold for a penny? Yet not one of them will fall to the ground apart from the will of your Father. . . . So don't be afraid; you are worth more than many sparrows" (Matt. 10:29, 31).

Donald Grey Barnhouse wrote about sparrows thoughtfully, comparing them to the people of God: "I look down some little street and see a humble chapel where a group of simple people worship the Lord in the beauty of holiness, despised and rejected of men, even as was their Lord, and I know that this is the rich reality of spiritual truth. Here are the sparrows who find their nest at the cross of Jesus Christ. Here is worthlessness that finds its worth because the Savior died."[4]

2. *Swallows.* Just as the sparrow is a symbol of worthlessness, so is a swallow the Bible's symbol of restlessness. It is a bird that is always in the air, winging its way from point to point from the earliest glimmer of dawn to after sunset. It wearies the watcher who is trying to keep it in view. But then the time comes for it to mate and raise young, and the swallow builds a nest and settles down upon it to rest peacefully. This is a picture of the soul apart from God and then in God, when at last it comes to rest in him. Alexander Maclaren said, "There is only one being in this world that does not fit the world that he is in, and that is man, chief and foremost of all. Other beings perfectly correspond to what we now call their 'environment.'"[5] He meant what Saint Augustine meant when he wrote in words much better known, "Our hearts are restless till they rest in thee."[6]

Have you found rest in God, or are you still wandering and restless, as so many people are? God offers you peace. Even the swallow found "a nest for herself, where she may have her young—a place near your altar."

Three Blessings

There are a number of ways of outlining Psalm 84, or parts of it. It can be done by the *selahs,* which divide the psalm into three parts, by the stanzas of the New International Version, which would give us six parts, or in other ways. I have avoided expounding the psalm by means of its outline, considering that a far better way to get into it is by dealing with its authorship and images, as I have done. However, at this point a three-part outline encompassing the three blessings, or beatitudes, found in verses 4, 5, and 12, can move us forward. The first is for those who live and work in the temple. The second is for those who are on their way to it, for pilgrims. The third is for those who cannot get to the temple but who place their faith in God.

1. *Those who dwell in God's house* (v. 4). We should be prepared for this blessing now, since it is what the psalm has been about almost entirely up to this point. The psalmists were aware that "the Lord of heaven and earth does not live in temples built by hands," as the apostle Paul would later tell the Athenians (Acts 17:24). But there had been a special manifestation of God at the temple, when God descended in the form of the Shekinah glory to dwell within the Most Holy Place. And even though that visible glory at some point had departed or would depart, the ancient worshipers nevertheless felt the presence of God in the temple and even in Jerusalem, as nowhere else. It is why David wrote, in Psalm 27,

> One thing I ask of the LORD,
>   this is what I seek:
> that I may dwell in the house of the LORD
>   all the days of my life,
> to gaze upon the beauty of the LORD
>   and to seek him in his temple (v. 4).

It is why the Sons of Korah speak of yearning and even fainting for the courts of the Lord in Psalm 84.

Because God dwelled in Zion, the most favored of all human beings were those who lived there too, especially those who, like the priests, actually worked in the temple, whether making the sacrifices, conducting the music, or attending to the inevitable custodial work. "Blessed are those who dwell in your house," says the psalmist. "They are ever praising you."

2. *Those who are making their way to God's house* (v. 5). Everyone was not able to live in Jerusalem, of course. The majority of the people were scattered throughout the country in small villages or family farms. The psalmist does not forget these people and, in fact, has a blessing for them too.

> Blessed are those whose strength is in you,
>   who have set their hearts on pilgrimage (v. 5).

The remainder of this stanza (vv. 6–7) describes the blessings of those who would be making their way up to Jerusalem for the feasts.

It is because of this stanza that so many of the commentators consider this a pilgrim psalm. It is not, as I have indicated. Nevertheless, there are blessings for these pilgrims. They are: (1) that they bless every area they pass through, even the Valley of Baca ("valley of weeping"), turning it into "a place of springs"; and (2) that they "go from strength to strength till each appears before God in Zion."

What a wonderful picture of the Christian life! Those who have come to know God in Jesus Christ are not seeking an earthly temple. We are seeking a heavenly temple and a city that has heavenly foundations (Heb. 12:22–24). As we press forward to that goal we pass through many Valleys of Baca and many autumns with falling brown leaves and cold, slashing rains. But we are not disheartened by these things. On the contrary, we rise above them and go on from strength to strength, strengthening one another along the way, and blessing all we meet. I have been encouraged and helped and blessed by scores of people like this. You and I need to be exactly that for other people.

3. *Those who trust God* (v. 12). The third blessing occurs at the end of the psalm and is for those who trust God: "O LORD Almighty, blessed is the man who trusts in you" (v. 12).

Perhaps the greatest mistake we can make in looking at this psalm or any of the psalms that are like it (for example, Psalms 27, 42, 43) is to suppose that when the writers express their passionate longing for the house of God all they are thinking of is the building or possibly the festivals that occurred there. The ancient writers did give more importance to buildings and festivals than we usually do, so this idea is a bit foreign to us. We cannot associate the worship of God with our particular church structure, as they seem to have done. But we misunderstand these writers if we suppose that all they were thinking about was the building. Actually, their true delight was in God. This is why, in spite of the earlier open passionate pining for God's house, the psalm ends with blessing for the person who simply trusts God. It is a way of saying that in the final analysis this is what truly matters and what life is about.

It is why the verse immediately before this does not speak about the temple, even though the writer says he would rather be a doorkeeper there than dwell in the tents of the wicked, just a verse before that. The verse is about God and his attributes.

> For the LORD God is a sun and shield;
>   the LORD bestows favor and honor;
> no good thing does he withhold
>   from those whose walk is blameless.

This is the only place in the Bible where God is explicitly called "a sun." It is because he shines on us and is the brightness of our days. Moreover, he is a shield from our foes and the only possible source of favor and true honor. The last phrase ("no good thing does he withhold from those whose walk is blameless") is a close equivalent of Romans 8:28 ("And we know that in all things God works for the good of those who love him").

Trust in God Alone

So let us learn to seek God—in the company of his people, the church, and by looking toward heaven. I mention the church first, because God has promised to meet us there. Jesus said, "Where two or three come together in my name, there am I with them" (Matt. 18:20). If you want to learn about God and come to know God personally, start with church. It is why we meet together. But I also say heaven, because ultimately it is God himself we long for and in whom alone we will be satisfied, not the fellowship of God's people, however rewarding that may be. Maclaren says, "If we want rest, let us clasp God as ours; if we desire a home warm, safe, sheltered from every wind that blows, and inaccessible to enemies, let us, like the swallows, nestle under the eaves of the Temple. Let us take God for our hope."[7]

Psalm 85

When Righteousness and Peace Meet

You showed favor to your land, O LORD;
*   you restored the fortunes of Jacob.*
You forgave the iniquity of your people
*   and covered all their sins.   Selah*
You set aside all your wrath
*   and turned from your fierce anger.*

Restore us again, O God our Savior,
*   and put away your displeasure toward us.*
Will you be angry with us forever?
*   Will you prolong your anger through all generations?*
Will you not revive us again,
*   that your people may rejoice in you?*
Show us your unfailing love, O LORD,
*   and grant us your salvation.*

I will listen to what God the LORD will say;
*   he promises peace to his people, his saints—*
*   but let them not return to folly.*
Surely his salvation is near those who fear him,
*   that his glory may dwell in our land.*

Love and faithfulness meet together;
*   righteousness and peace kiss each other.*
Faithfulness springs forth from the earth,
*   and righteousness looks down from heaven.*

694

The LORD will indeed give what is good,
and our land will yield its harvest.
Righteousness goes before him
and prepares the way for his steps.
verses 1–13

H̲ave you ever been discouraged be-
cause the life you are living now does not seem to be as real or as joyful as
your life was after you first became a Christian? John Wesley knew times
like this and wrote about them poetically, asking,

Where is the joy I knew
When first I saw the Lord?

It is a good question. In such times we long for the spiritual vitality and
fruitfulness of earlier days. And if we are not too discouraged to pray about
it, our prayer is often that God might revive us or restore us to what we once
knew. Psalm 85 is precisely this kind of prayer.

A Downcast People

There is nothing in the title to show what historical setting Psalm 85
might have come out of. It is introduced only as another of the songs of the
"Sons of Korah" (Psalms 42, 44–49), which we encountered first at the
opening of book two of the Psalter and are reencountering now (Psalms 84,
85, 87, 88). Yet it is likely, to judge from the contrast between the opening
verses, which speak of a recent restoration of the people, and the prayer in
verses 4–7, which asks for a new restoration or revival, that the psalm is from
the time shortly after the return of the Jews from their seventy-year-long
captivity in Babylon.[1]

This may not be the right setting for this psalm. A number of key inter-
preters doubt it. But even if it is not, the condition of the exiles shortly after
their return from Babylon is an illustration of the kind of discouragement
out of which the psalm comes.

The first Jews to return to Jerusalem did so in response to the decree of
Cyrus, the king of Persia, in 538 B.C. The account is in Ezra 1–6. The foundations of the temple were laid immediately, and the temple itself was completed between 520 and 515 B.C. to judge from the prophecies of Haggai
and Zechariah. Somewhere along the way the Jews also tried to rebuild the
city's walls. This was hard and the work was abandoned, probably after their
enemies destroyed what little rebuilding work had been done and burned
the city's gates (Neh. 1:3). At first the people must have felt joy at being
able to return to their homeland. They would have confessed with gratitude

that God had indeed restored their fortunes, forgiven their sin, and turned aside his wrath (Ps. 85:1–3). But when these first excellent beginnings broke down and the forward motion to rebuild the city and nation ceased, discouragement and even despair set in. According to the opening chapter of Nehemiah, the people acknowledged frankly that they were "in great trouble and disgrace."

What do God's people do in such circumstances? They pray and wait for God to answer. Psalm 85 is this kind of prayer. If the return from exile is the true historical setting, God answered the prayer by sending Nehemiah to rebuild the walls, reconstitute the nation, and lift the people to new levels of spirituality and rejoicing.

So let's look at our psalm that way. Let's look at it for the pointers or steps it gives by which a discouraged Christian, maybe you, can be lifted from spiritual depression to new levels of rejoicing. I suggest that there are four steps, clearly marked by the four stanzas of the New International Version translation.

Reflection on Past Mercies

The place we have to start to overcome discouragement is by reflecting on the goodness of God toward us in past days (vv. 1–3). This is part of the problem, of course, because it is the unfavorable contrast between these past experiences of God's mercies and the lack of them now that has caused us to become discouraged. Yet it is part of the solution too, since the goodness of God is real goodness—it is worth remembering—and it is because God is good that we have hope of recovering what we've lost.

The first verse deals with the land and with the people's reversal of fortune, which is why we think of this as applying to the period following the exile. But what is striking about this opening stanza is that it dwells not on the restoration to the land but rather on the forgiveness of sins and the removal of the wrath of God, which preceded it.

> You forgave the iniquity of your people
>   and covered all their sins.
> You set aside all your wrath
>   and turned from your fierce anger (vv. 2–3).

The greatest of all mercies that we can receive from God is forgiveness of sins, and it is from this foundation that all other covenanted mercies flow. Yet how little we value it! If God gives us good health, a happy and supportive family, a good job, and praise from our employer and friends, we think we are blessed. If we lack any one of these things, we begin to suppose that God has somehow forgotten us or does not care. We do not think how blessed we are to have our sins forgiven and to be delivered from the judicial wrath of God through the atoning death of his Son, the Lord Jesus

Christ. Some of the strongest salvation language in Scripture is present in these verses. "Covered their sins" describes what is meant by *atonement.* "Set aside your wrath" is what is meant by the word *propitiation.*

If we would remember God's mercy to us in the forgiveness of our sins, it might not be necessary for us to go any farther along the four-step path suggested by this psalm. By taking this step alone we might find that we are already rising out of our discouragement and will soon be praising God again rather than complaining to him.

Pointed Prayer for Restoration

Remembering the past does not always provide victory in the present, however. Therefore, in the second stanza of this gentle, perceptive psalm the writer moves to direct petition (vv. 4–7). That is, he moves to prayer. On the people's behalf, he asks God to (1) restore us again (v. 4), and (2) revive us again (v. 6).

1. *Restore us again.* There is some question as to how the Hebrew of this prayer should be translated, for the root word means "turn" and can be thought of in at least three ways. It can refer to the people, which is what the New International Version suggests. That is, it can mean "turn us" or "turn us back," with the idea of restoration. Second, it can refer to God in the sense that God is being asked to turn from his wrath, a repeat of what is said in verse 4. Or third, it can refer to God with the sense that he is being asked to turn back to the people again, since he seems to have turned from them in his displeasure. That would mean that the idea gets repeated again almost exactly in the second half of the verse.

The best translation is probably what the NIV gives us, since the other two ideas are redundant and since the prayer "restore us again" is thereby matched by "revive us again" two verses later. It is what the people needed. It is what we need whenever we seem to have lost the joy of our salvation. Fortunately God is the great restorer. He can restore what apart from him could never be made good.

We may think of the promise in the Book of Joel in which God pledges himself to restore what the locusts have eaten. There had been a devastating locust invasion in Joel's day, and Joel explained it as being God's judgment for the people's sins as well as a warning of a greater final judgment yet to come. Nevertheless, if the people will repent, says God,

> I will repay you for the years the locusts have eaten—
>> the great locust and the young locust,
>> the other locusts and the locust swarm—
> my great army that I sent among you.
> You will have plenty to eat, until you are full,
>> and you will praise the name of the LORD your God,
>> who has worked wonders for you (Joel 2:25–26).

Sin causes us to lose many blessings. These cannot be recovered; they are gone. But God can give new opportunities and new blessings. If you are one whose life has been ruined by the locusts of sin, making it a spiritual desert, you need to return to the one who can make your life fruitful again. If you will turn to God, he will return to you and restore what "the locusts have eaten."

2. *Revive us again.* The second prayer is that God would revive the people. *Revive* means to resurrect or make alive. It implies that the people were alive once, have died in a spiritual sense, and now need to be given spiritual life again. This is what the church almost always needs, and it is how revivals come. We think of revivals as being a movement of God in the world so that unchurched unbelievers come to Christ. But revivals do not start in the world. They start in the church, since it is the church that needs to live again.

Historically revivals have followed three stages. First, under strong biblical preaching by people like Martin Luther, Jonathan Edwards, Gilbert Tennent, or George Whitefield, the members of the church, who beforehand had thought they were Christians and that all was well with their souls, wake up to the fact that they are not Christians at all. In the American revivals under Edwards and his contemporary preachers, this was called the Great Awakening. Second, there is the revival itself, which means that those who had thought they were alive but were actually spiritually dead are revived. That is, they repent of their sin and become Christians. The third stage is when these churchgoing people who are now converted begin to live for Christ so openly and consistently, with noticeable changes of conduct, that the world outside takes notice and begins to press into the church to see what is happening. This is revival. We have had them in the past, but we have not had one in the United States for many years.

We need to notice one more thing about this stanza, and that is the reference to God's "unfailing love" in verse 7, used as an argument for the two prayers. The psalmist does not plead the people's goodness or even their intentions to reform. On the contrary, he acknowledges the justice of God's displeasure. Nevertheless, God is unfailing in his love, and it is to this, the mercy of God, that the writer pleads. Never plead your merits before God. Plead mercy. It is mercy we need. We need it from first to last, and we need it every single day.

Waiting on God

Having reminded himself of God's past mercies and having prayed for a renewal of those mercies in his own day, the psalmist does what Habakkuk did in a nearly identical situation. He waits for God to answer (vv. 8–9). The text says, "I will listen to what God the LORD will say."

Habakkuk was a minor prophet who lived in a time when Israel was far from the Lord, and he asked God to send a revival, which is exactly what the author of Psalm 85 is doing. Unfortunately, God told Habakkuk that he was going to send judgment by allowing the Babylonians to invade Judah and carry the people into captivity instead. This raised tremendous anxiety and fear in Habakkuk, and he asked God a number of questions about it. He could not understand how God could use an ungodly nation to punish people who, though they were not very godly at this time, were nevertheless at least more godly than the Babylonians. Habakkuk asked his questions, then said,

> I will stand at my watch
> and station myself on the ramparts;
> I will look to see what he will say to me,
> and what answer I am to give to this complaint (Hab. 2:1).

When God answered, it was to say that in time the Babylonian nation would itself be judged and that, in the meantime, the righteous were to live by faith (Hab. 2:4). This is the great verse that, carried over into the Book of Romans, was used by God in the conversion of Martin Luther and thus became the theme verse of the Protestant Reformation.

It is never foolish to wait upon God, for God is not slow to answer. Our problem is that we are impatient and do not wait for him at all. In fact, it is often the case that we do not even lay our requests before him. We do not pray.

A Hopeful Looking to God's Promises

While he had been waiting for God to answer the psalmist found his mind turning expectantly to what God would do. He remembered that God had promised "peace" *(shalom)* to his people. He reminded himself that the Lord's "salvation is near those who fear him, that his glory may dwell in our land" (v. 9). This leads him to look ahead in the last stanza (vv. 10–13) to that brighter promised day, and thus to encourage his spirits by what was surely coming, though it might be delayed. Looking ahead to this bright future is the fourth and last step by which the writer shows us how to rise out of our discouragements into a more faithful frame of mind.

Verse 10 is one of the great poetic sections of the Psalms. It is best known in the King James Version: "Mercy and truth are met together; righteousness and peace have kissed each other."

This is generally understood as pointing to the work of Jesus Christ in making atonement for our sins by which alone God is able both to satisfy the demands of his righteousness or justice and at the same time to show mercy to those who have fallen short of his just standards. This may be part of what is involved. But the picture painted by these verses is larger and more comprehensive than that. They are actually looking forward to an ideal state and time when the harmony that is in God will also pervade and dominate God's creation. Derek Kidner says of this stanza, "The climax is one of the most satisfying descriptions of concord—spiritual, moral and material—to be found anywhere in Scripture."[2]

The devil is the great disrupter. He has brought disharmony to the universe. God brings harmony. In these verses four great attributes of God meet together—love, faithfulness, righteousness, and peace—and then, like conquering generals, they march side by side to a victory that is the sure and certain hope of God's people. The stanza suggests three harmonies.

1. *The harmony in God.* When we speak of mercy and truth as well as righteousness and peace being reconciled in God because of the work of Jesus Christ, we imply that somehow they are in conflict. But the qualities in God are never in conflict, and the psalm is certainly not speaking of a conflict. On the contrary, love and faithfulness, righteousness and peace are always at home in God, and it is from this divine harmony that all other harmonies come. We have peace only when we rest in him.

2. *Harmony between heaven and earth.* The second harmony is between God and man, which is what verse 11 suggests when it speaks of faithfulness springing from the earth and righteousness looking down from heaven. We may see this as God's gift of righteousness from above and our response of faith reaching up to receive God's righteousness and then issuing in faithfulness. But the picture is probably not as specific as this. The verse is better seen as pointing to a state in which God's people live in faithful obedience to God and are blessed by him. When that happens salvation has indeed come to a people and the glory of God dwells in their land.

3. *A harmony in man.* The third harmony is in man himself. For these qualities—love, faithfulness, righteousness, and peace—are not among the incommunicable attributes of God, meaning that they are uniquely God's and cannot be shared with man. They are communicable qualities. They can be shared and therefore can and must appear in those who are God's people. Moreover, when they appear in us, we find that we are at peace not only with God but also with ourselves and one another. In fact, we become peacemakers in an otherwise cruel, warring, and disharmonious world.

Oliver Cromwell, the Lord Protector of England between the execution of Charles I and the reestablishment of the monarchy under Charles II, loved the psalms.

On September 16, 1656, the day before the meeting of the second Parliament of the Protectorate, he was reading Psalm 85 in Whitehall. It was a Tuesday. On Wednesday Parliament was opened, and Cromwell addressed the members with a talk based in part on these verses: "Yesterday I did read a psalm, which truly may not unbecome both me to tell you of and you to observe. It is the 85th Psalm; it is very instructive and significant; and though I do but a little touch upon it, I desire your perusal and pleasure." He then expounded on these verses as an expression of his vision and hope that by their faithfulness to God righteousness might reign in England and a better, finer, happier, and more harmonious age might come.[3] That was never perfectly achieved, of course. But it was in part and still is wherever the people of God turn from their folly and are revived by him.

Psalm 86

An Appeal
to the Compassionate God

Hear, O LORD, and answer me,
for I am poor and needy.
Guard my life, for I am devoted to you.
You are my God; save your servant
who trusts in you.
Have mercy on me, O Lord,
for I call to you all day long.
Bring joy to your servant,
for to you, O Lord,
I lift up my soul.

You are kind and forgiving, O Lord,
abounding in love to all who call to you.
Hear my prayer, O LORD;
listen to my cry for mercy.
In the day of my trouble I will call to you,
for you will answer me.

verses 1–7

Psalm 86 is by David, the only such psalm in this section. Characteristic of David, it is an appeal for mercy based on the character of God.

The psalm is filled with petitions, at least fifteen of them, but they are variants of this one idea. It is found throughout, explicitly in verses 3, 6, and

16. Verse 3 says, "Have mercy on me, O Lord, for I call to you all day long."
Verse 6 reads, "Hear my prayer, O LORD; listen to my cry for mercy." Verse
16 pleads, "Turn to me and have mercy on me; grant your strength to your
servant and save the son of your maidservant." Nothing is more important
to sinful men and women than finding mercy with God. Charles Haddon
Spurgeon said, "The best of men need mercy and appeal to mercy, yea to
nothing else but mercy."[1] Yet we do not appeal to mercy naturally, and we
do not show it to others very often.

Do you remember that magnificent speech in praise of mercy from
William Shakespeare's *Merchant of Venice*? The speaker is Portia, who is acting as a lawyer in order to plead a case before the court of Venice. She says,

> The quality of mercy is not strained:
> It droppeth as the gentle rain from heaven
> Upon the place beneath. It is twice blest;—
> It blesseth him that gives, and him that takes.
> 'Tis mightiest in the mightiest: it becomes
> The throned monarch better than his crown (Act IV, Scene 1).

These are beautiful words. But in practice most human beings neither
seek nor give mercy. We want to be treated on our merit, and what we
demand from other human beings we demand from God. David was spiritually wiser than we are. He knew that what he needed was mercy, not his just
due, and here he pleads for it.

The outline of the psalm is fairly straightforward. It consists of a lament
(vv. 1–7), praise (vv. 8–10), prayer (vv. 11–13), and final petition (vv. 14–17).
Yet these elements overlap in the psalm's four sections, and for that reason
the best way to get into the psalm is by focusing on its most important ideas.
These are (1) David's relationship to God, (2) David's requests of God,
(3) the reasons God should answer his requests, and (4) the most important characteristic of God from the point of the psalmist's need, mercy.

David's Relationship to God

It is consistent with David's appeal to God's mercy, which becomes
explicit for the first time in verse 3, that Israel's king does not begin his
prayer by arguing that God owes him anything. On the contrary, he is "poor
and needy" (v. 1), God's "servant" (v. 2), one who looks to God for help.
These themes are repeated later, in verse 7, where he speaks of his "trouble"; verse 14, where he speaks of "the arrogant" who are attacking him;
verse 16, where he again describes himself as God's "servant"; and verse 17,
where he again draws attention to his "enemies."

We find it hard to pray this way. By nature we want to plead our rights or
accomplishments before God. To confess that we are poor and needy seems

demeaning. To be a servant seems unworthy. We want to be people who deserve something from God because of who we are.

Of course, it is true that we have become something of value because of God's favor to us. But it is only because of God; that is the point. And the only reason why he has been favorable to us is because he is merciful, not because we deserve it. Therefore, when David refers to himself as God's servant he is already developing his most important theme and is speaking consistently with it. It is only because God has been merciful to him that he has a relationship to God, and it is only because God has shown himself to be merciful that David can make this appeal.

David's Requests of God

David makes fifteen requests, as I mentioned earlier. He asks God to: "hear" and "answer" (v. 1), "guard" and "save" (v. 2), "have mercy" (v. 3), "bring joy" (v. 4), "hear" and "listen" (v. 6), "teach me" and "give me an undivided heart" (v. 11), "turn," "have mercy," "grant . . . strength," and "save" (v. 16), and "give me a sign of your goodness" (v. 17).

Most of these requests have to do with his perilous circumstances, which he develops in the last stanza. We may remember that there is hardly a psalm of David's that does not mention his enemies and ask God's help in delivering him from their attacks and stratagems.

But in the midst of these many requests for deliverance from his ever-present enemies there is a remarkable stanza in which David also prays that God will teach him his "way" and give him an "undivided heart" (vv. 11–13). This is the key to David's greatness. Most of us, when we pray, are concerned about deliverance and help and guidance and such things. But we are not nearly as concerned to be taught God's way and to be helped to serve him with an undivided heart. In other words, we want the blessings of salvation without the duties. We want prosperity and personal safety while we nevertheless go our own way. David was not like this. He knew his heart, how prone he was to wander from God. But he also knew he needed to go in God's way if he was to prosper spiritually. So he asks God for this great blessing.

Praying with Arguments

One of Charles Haddon Spurgeon's great themes when he was writing or speaking about prayer was that we should learn to pray with arguments. That is, that we should sharpen our thinking by learning to express the reasons why God should answer our prayers affirmatively. It should be clear that this is not so much for God's benefit as for ours. If we cannot think of reasons why God should answer our prayers, it is probably the case that our requests are wrong and need to be revised or redirected.

Notice how David buttresses his prayers with sound arguments. They are easy to find because they are highlighted by an eightfold repetition of the word *for,* which means "because." He begins with reasons based on who he is and his need. As he prays his thoughts shift to God, and his later reasons therefore have to do with who God is, with his power and great grace.

First, there are four reasons based on David and his need.

1. *"For I am poor and needy"* (v. 1). The first reason is based on David's sad plight. He is not mighty or self-sufficient. On the contrary, he is poor and needy. So if God will not help him, there is no real help to be found anywhere. This argument presupposes God's mercy. It is because God is merciful that he helps the poor and needy.

2. *"For I am devoted to you"* (v. 2). The second reason is that the psalmist stands in a covenant relationship to God. In other words, he is God's servant and God is his master. As a servant he has duties toward God, but God also has duties toward him. This seems to have meant a lot to David at this point in his life, for he calls God *Adonai* (translated "Lord" but meaning "master") seven times.[2]

3. *"For I call to you all day long"* (v. 3). The third reason God should answer his prayer is that he is asking God to do it. God is not obliged to answer. Even this is of grace. Nevertheless, David is not like one who does not know God or is indifferent to God. He does know God, and he knows God can help. God is a prayer-answering God, so David asks him to take note of the fact that he is praying.

4. *"For to you, O Lord, I lift up my soul"* (v. 4). The fourth reason is that David is calling on God and on no other. A pagan might have many gods and call on all of them, but that would only show that he has no real confidence in any. David is praying to God only, because he knows that only the one true God can help him.

Second, there are four reasons based on God and God's character.

1. *"For you will answer me"* (v. 7). Earlier (in v. 1) he had asked God to hear and answer him, but here he asserts his confidence that God will answer. In other words, he is praying because he knows that "the prayer of a righteous man is powerful and effective" (James 5:16). Prayer is not an empty exercise. It works.

2. *"For you are great and do marvelous deeds"* (v. 10). Sixth, not only is God a prayer-hearing and prayer-answering God, he is also a God who is able to do what the one who is praying asks. God is great and powerful and consistently does great deeds. Many of the psalms recount these deeds, though David does not take time to do so here.

3. *"For great is your love toward me"* (v. 13). The seventh of these requests gets near the heart of the psalm's major theme, which is God's mercy, for it pleads as a reason for God to answer prayer the fact that God in his mercy has already set his love upon the one praying. In Hebrew the word translated "love" is the powerful word *hesed,* which refers to covenanted love, love that is promised in a covenant relationship. God had established a covenant

like this with David. Our equivalent would be the fact that God has made us his sons and daughters by the new birth.

Family relationships have family privileges, which is why Jesus said, "Which of you, if his son asks for bread, will give him a stone? Or if he asks for a fish, will give him a snake? If you, then, though you are evil, know how to give good gifts to your children, how much more will your Father in heaven give good gifts to those who ask him!" (Matt. 7:9–11).

4. *"For you, O LORD, have helped me and comforted me"* (v. 17). The final argument for why God should answer David's prayer is that God helped David in the past, perhaps even as he had been praying. It is consistent with our every past experience of God to ask for mercy now.

The Merciful God

That brings us to the major theme of the psalm. It is the mercy of God to which David is appealing in virtually everything he says. David knows that God is merciful because God himself had revealed it clearly. David is appealing to that clear revelation.

After Moses had interceded for the people of Israel so that God would not destroy them because of their having made the golden calf, Moses made three great prayers, which are recorded in Exodus. God had said that he would send his angel to lead the people to the Promised Land (Exod. 33:2). But this was not enough for Moses. As Moses looked at things, to be led by an angel was less than being led by God, and he did not want any lessening of the special relationship between God and the people that they had enjoyed previously. They were sinners—Moses as well as the others. Any relationship between them and God would have to be on the basis of the mercy of God and not their deserving. Still, they must be led by God or not at all. So Moses began to pray.

His first request was that he might know God. He had been with God in the mountain twice for forty days at a time, but he still yearned to know God better. "If you are pleased with me, teach me your ways so I may know you and continue to find favor with you" (Exod. 33:13). This is a petition every Christian should make often. If we are Christians, we know God partially already. But every one of us needs to know God better. This is what David was praying about when he asked God to teach him his "ways."

Moses' second petition expressed his most pressing concern, which had to do with God's sending an angel with the people. Moses judged it impossible that he should lead the people without the Lord's very own presence. So he prayed, "If your Presence does not go with us, do not send us up from here" (Exod. 33:15). The Lord heard this request and granted it. "I will do the very thing you have asked, because I am pleased with you and I know you by name," God replied (v. 17).

It would be good if all who are in a position of Christian leadership should think as Moses did. We ought to be afraid to take a single step without the assurance of God's presence. As it is, we are often so self-confident that we think we can execute great projects without first asking God what we should do and then how we should do it. It is why so many of our projects fail and there is so little blessing.

At this point Moses had achieved what most concerned him. God had promised to go with the people. But Moses was a remarkable man, and one of his remarkable characteristics emerged now as he added a third petition to the two that had already been granted. "Now show me your glory," he said (Exod. 33:18). As God's answer makes clear, this was nothing less than a request to see God face-to-face in all his splendor, to see him unobscured by clouds or devices like the burning bush.

God replied that he could not show his face to Moses, because no human being can see the face of God and live. But he would reveal his goodness and proclaim his name to Moses, which he did by placing him in the cleft of a rock, covering the opening with his hand, and then causing his goodness to pass by. The text says, "Then the LORD came down in the cloud and stood there with him and proclaimed his name, the LORD. And he passed in front of Moses, proclaiming, 'The LORD, the LORD, the compassionate and gracious God, slow to anger, abounding in love and faithfulness, maintaining love to thousands, and forgiving wickedness, rebellion and sin'" (Exod. 34:5–7). These words unfold the meaning of "the name" of God, expressed in his mercy to all who confess their sin and come to him.

This is one of the greatest revelations of God in the Bible, and it meant a lot to Israel. Exodus 34:6 is one of the most frequently quoted passages in the Old Testament. For example, it is referred to in Nehemiah 9:17, Psalms 103:8 and 145:8, Joel 2:13, and Jonah 4:2. And here is the point: It is referred to by David in our psalm. In fact, it is referred to twice. It is mentioned briefly in verse 5 ("You are kind and forgiving, O Lord, abounding in love to all who call to you"). It is cited extensively in verse 15 ("But you, O Lord, are a compassionate and gracious God, slow to anger, abounding in love and faithfulness").

This is where David learned that God was merciful. He learned it from this great story in the Bible. Moreover, he was wise enough to base his prayer requests on it. So should we! Indeed, we have even more cause to do it, because we know how merciful God has been to us through the death of Jesus Christ.

Four Points of Application

The mercy of God is such a tremendous and all-embracing theme that it applies to virtually every area of life. There are four applications that we cannot afford to miss.

1. *We need mercy if we are to be saved.* This can never be said enough, simply because we do not think this way naturally. We think in terms of justice, supposing ourselves to be deserving. But we are not deserving. If we are to be saved,

we must not plead our desserts but God's mercy. Israel needed mercy. Moses and David needed mercy. We need mercy. Apart from mercy we will perish.

2. *God is a God of mercy.* Here is the good news. God is a God of mercy. True, he is also a God of justice and wrath. Sin will be punished. The wrath of God will be made known along with his other great attributes. But God emphasizes mercy. He offers mercy. To find mercy we must come to him on the basis of the shed blood of his Son, the Lord Jesus Christ, who died to be our Savior. The mercy of God is seen at the cross of the Savior more than at any other place. It is the ultimate expression of mercy and the means by which God saves.

3. *We can appeal to mercy.* The mercy of God is not compelled in any way. Otherwise it would not be mercy. But that does not suggest that we cannot appeal to it. We can. Indeed, the Scriptures are full of such appeals. Our psalm is one example. The Scriptures even tell us that it is through appeals to mercy that mercy may be found.

Remember the tax collector in Jesus' story. He knew he was a sinner. So he did not come to God to remind God of his ethical attainments, as the Pharisee did. He stood at a distance and would not even look up to heaven. Instead he beat his breast, a sign of genuine remorse or repentance, and prayed, "God, have mercy on me, a sinner." Jesus' judgment was that "this man, rather than the other, went home justified before God. For everyone who exalts himself will be humbled, and he who humbles himself will be exalted" (Luke 18:13–14). Who are those who receive mercy? They are those who ask God for it. They are those who turn from their own self-sufficiency and trust Jesus. This is the only way the children of God are made known.

4. *We can proclaim God's mercy to others.* God is sovereign in salvation. He has mercy on whom he wills to have mercy and has compassion on whom he wills to have compassion. But God is also a merciful God, and there is nothing in the Bible to hinder us from saying this as forcefully as we can. His very name is Mercy. Because his name is Mercy, we can assure others that if they will come to him through faith in Jesus Christ, which is how he has made his mercy possible as well as known, they will find it. God has never turned a deaf ear to one who has truly asked for mercy. He has never rejected anyone who has believed on Jesus Christ.

> Come, every soul by sin oppressed,
> There's mercy with the Lord,
> And he will surely give you rest,
> By trusting in his Word.
> Only trust him, only trust him,
> Only trust him now.
> He will save you, he will save you,
> He will save you now.

If a person believes that and comes to Jesus, he will find God to be exactly what the Bible declares him to be: the merciful God who has reached out to save many through his Son. He will hear and save you.

Psalm 87

Zion, City of Our God

He has set his foundation on the holy mountain;
*   the LORD loves the gates of Zion*
*   more than all the dwellings of Jacob.*
Glorious things are said of you,
*   O city of God:*   Selah
"I will record Rahab and Babylon
*   among those who acknowledge me—*
Philistia too, and Tyre, along with Cush—
*   and will say, 'This one was born in Zion.'"*

Indeed, of Zion it will be said,
*   "This one and that one were born in her,*
*   and the Most High himself will establish her."*
The LORD will write in the register of the peoples:
*   "This one was born in Zion."*   Selah
As they make music they will sing,
*   "All my fountains are in you."*
*   verses 1–7*

I read some time ago in an article critical of former President Jimmy Carter, who remains politically active through his Georgia-based political think tank, that he has only one objective, "peace among nations at any cost." The last part of that judgment seems an unjustified slander to me. But whether it is or not, the idea of world peace issuing in a true brotherhood of people and nations is a good one and well worth pursuing.

Many have expressed this, of course. Socrates voiced the idea when he called himself "a citizen of the world." The philosophers who were known as Stoics dreamed openly of a worldwide brotherhood of peoples. Rome imposed a harsh kind of unity by force of their arms. In our day the vision has been embodied in such dreams as Woodrow Wilson's League of Nations or the United Nations. Yet brotherhood does not come about that easily, as the many wars of history, both ancient and modern, testify. Most nations want to achieve unity by conquest, trying to force others into one all-embracing government, their own. Even the ancient Israelites thought along these lines. They looked for a day when their enemies would be subdued and be brought under the rightful sway of God's own king in Zion.

Yet sometimes the Jews rose to greater heights of vision and saw the goal of peace as something God himself would achieve and by means very different from those of godless nations. Psalm 87 embraces such a vision. It is a prophecy that anticipates a day when the heathen nations of Egypt, Babylon, Philistia, Tyre, and Cush, and no doubt many others, since these are clearly representative, will be received as citizens of Zion, the poetical name for God's rule over God's people from Jerusalem.

This prophecy is a great advance over psalms that call for the utter destruction of Israel's enemies. But we cannot read it without thinking of an even greater advance provided by the New Testament, since in the writings of the apostles, Zion of Israel becomes Zion, which is the church of God, and the unity of the peoples described in the psalm becomes the unique and truly amazing fellowship of Christian brothers and sisters in the spiritual family and under the reign of Jesus Christ. In other words, the vision of Psalm 87 is achieved in the church, where, writes Paul, "There is neither Jew nor Greek, slave nor free, male nor female," since we "are all one in Christ Jesus" (Gal. 3:28).

This is the psalm that led John Newton, the former slave trader turned preacher, to write "Glorious Things of Thee Are Spoken, Zion, City of Our God," the first line coming from verse 3. The lines of this well-known hymn provide apt titles for some of the psalm's themes and sections.

> Glorious things of thee are spoken,
> Zion, City of our God;
> He whose word cannot be broken,
> Formed thee for his own abode.
> On the Rock of Ages founded,
> What can shake thy sure repose?
> With salvation's walls surrounded,
> Thou may'st smile at all thy foes.

Psalm 87 follows nicely on Psalm 86, which prophesied that "all the nations you have made will come and worship before you, O Lord; they will bring glory to your name" (v. 9). That was a prophecy, and this is also, though Psalm 87 is more fully developed. The vision of Gentiles joining Jews in Jerusalem to worship the true God is also expressed in Isaiah 2:2; 19:23–25; 56:6–7; Micah 4:1; Zechariah 2:11; 8:22–23; 14:16–19; Malachi 1:11; and other places.

"On the Rock of Ages Founded"

There are any number of ways to partition this psalm, short as it is. The New International Version divides it into two stanzas (vv. 1–4 and vv. 5–7). But the psalm's themes unfold almost verse by verse, and I think it best merely to take the ideas in sequence. The first occurs in verses 1–2, which are the theme verses of the psalm. Their point is that God has chosen and established Zion. Therefore, by inference, Zion cannot be shaken even though the entire world should unite in arms against it. This caused Newton to write,

> On the Rock of Ages founded,
> What can shake thy sure repose?

In the Hebrew text, verse 1 begins with "his foundation," no doubt for emphasis. We can hardly read this without thinking of Hebrews 11:10, which praises Abraham because "he was looking forward to the city with foundations, whose architect and builder is God." The Hebrews chapter makes clear that it was a heavenly city rather than an earthly residence that Abraham was seeking. So we learn at once that even in Old Testament days the greatest saints did not set their affections on earthly Jerusalem alone, but loved it rather only as a symbol of the greater glories they knew they would enjoy in heaven.

Should we not say that believers today can love their local church in nearly the same way? It should be something very precious to them, and they should pray for its welfare. But the earthly is only a small foretaste of the heavenly, and we should be looking from the earthly to those invisible glories that will never pass away.

"Glorious Things of Thee Are Spoken"

The next verse of the psalm (v. 3) is a cryptic statement of praise for Zion and is the verse Newton began with in his hymn. It says,

> Glorious things are said of you,
> O city of God.

What is it that God (or others) have said in praise of Zion? A few representative statements are these: "It is beautiful in its loftiness, the joy of the whole earth. Like the utmost heights of Zaphon is Mount Zion, the city of the Great King" (Ps. 48:2); "The LORD has chosen Zion, he has desired it for his dwelling" (Ps. 132:13). Isaiah 2:2–3:

In the last days

the mountain of the LORD's temple will be established
    as chief among the mountains;
it will be raised above the hills,
    and all nations will stream to it.

Many peoples will come and say,

"Come, let us go up to the mountain of the LORD,
    to the house of the God of Jacob.
He will teach us his ways,
    so that we may walk in his paths."
The law will go out from Zion,
    the word of the LORD from Jerusalem.

Not only did Newton choose verse 3 as the theme of his great hymn on the church, Saint Augustine also chose it as the theme verse for his great masterpiece of Christian historical philosophy, *The City of God*. He wrote that "two cities have been formed by two loves: the earthly by the love of self, even to the contempt of God; the heavenly by the love of God, even to the contempt of self."[1] Augustine's use of the term, like Newton's use of it, reminds us that even greater things have been spoken of the church than have been said of earthly Jerusalem.

The author of Hebrews makes this point explicitly, referring to this psalm:

You have come to Mount Zion, to the heavenly Jerusalem, the city of the living God. You have come to thousands upon thousands of angels in joyful assembly, to the church of the firstborn, whose names are written in heaven. You have come to God, the judge of all men, to the spirits of righteous men made perfect, to Jesus the mediator of a new covenant, and to the sprinkled blood that speaks a better word than the blood of Abel (Heb. 12:22–24).

Charles Haddon Spurgeon said that although "glorious things were taught in [Jerusalem's] streets, and seen in her temples," yet this is "more true of the church: she is founded in grace, but her pinnacles glow with glory. . . . Whatever glorious things the saints may say of the church in their eulogies, they cannot exceed what prophets have foretold, what angels have sung, or what God himself has declared. Happy are the tongues which learn to occupy themselves with so excellent a subject."[2]

"Gentiles and Jews in Jesus' Fold"

The title I have used for verses 4–6 comes from a hymn by William Shrubsole written in 1795, about sixteen years after Newton's hymn, beginning "Arm of the Lord, awake, awake!" It is the theme of these verses, and the chief idea of the psalm. In the latter days envisioned by the psalmist, the Gentile nations will join the sons and daughters of Israel in acknowledging and worshiping the true God. It is from this that the psalmist gets his vision of a true brotherhood of nations and world peace.

To show what he means the writer mentions five representative nations: (1) *Rahab.* The psalm does not indicate what Rahab stands for, but other texts show that it was a name for Egypt, the great power to the south of Israel (see Isa. 30:7; 51:9–10). The word itself denotes pride or ferocity. (2) *Babylon* is next, the great power to the east. Since Babylon did not emerge to prominence until after the decline of Assyria, this reference probably dates the psalm from the time of the later kings of Judah, perhaps during the reign of Hezekiah. (3) *Philistia.* The first two names pointed to major world powers, the first to the south, the second to the east. Philistia was a closer, more immediate threat. It was located to the west. (4) *Tyre* was a powerful city-state to the north. With these four names all four points of the compass—north, east, south, and west—are covered. (5) *Cush* stands for Ethiopia, often used as a representative, far-distant nation. Thus, in a very short space, the psalmist indicates that in the day of God's future blessing all the nations of the world (or at least representatives of all the nations of the world) will come to know and praise the true God.

It is hard to read this without thinking of the coming of the Holy Spirit on the Day of Pentecost, after the resurrection of Jesus Christ, and of how God began to draw people from diverse backgrounds and races to faith in Christ on that occasion (see Acts 2:9–11). The names of the nations had changed from the psalmist's day, but many from all the points of the compass are mentioned: "Parthians, Medes and Elamites; residents of Mesopotamia, Judea and Cappadocia, Pontus and Asia, Phrygia and Pamphylia, Egypt and the parts of Libya near Cyrene; visitors from Rome . . . ; Cretans and Arabs."

The vision of Gentiles and Jews together knowing and praising God is frequent in the New Testament. It is found, for example, in Romans 11; Ephesians 3:3–9; Hebrews 12:22–23; and Revelation 7:9; 14:1–5; as well as in other less explicit passages.

Noticing the parallel between Psalm 87 and the Christian church, one of the ancient writers said, "This is the glory of the church, that into her the fullness of the nations shall enter—the proud from Egypt, who for her haughtiness is called Rahab; the worldly from Babylon, the city of confusion; the wrathful from Philistia, so long the enemies of Israel; the covetous from Tyre, the rich city of the traders; and the slaves of ignorance from Cush, and from the land of Ham."[3] It is true that we do not yet see all the peoples of the world bowing in grateful submission to Jesus Christ, as we will one day. But we do have a foretaste of this in the joy and wonderful unity of purpose the people of God have within the fellowship of Christ's church.

Two things are said of those who will be brought to the worship of God in the days the psalmist envisions.

1. *The people will acknowledge God.* The word *acknowledge* in verse 4 is a translation of the Hebrew verb *yadah,* which has a rich variety of meanings. It can mean "know," "acknowledge," "understand," "be sure," "know about," "experience," and other variations. In the New International Version it is translated no fewer than 190 different ways to get as close as possible to the meaning. Here it means more than merely admitting that there is such a God as Jehovah or even acknowledging him as the one true God. It means coming to him in a saving relationship, bowing before him, and seeking to know him better. It is exactly what Jesus meant when he said in the great prayer recorded in John 17, "This is eternal life: that they may know you, the only true God, and Jesus Christ, whom you have sent" (v. 3).

Therefore, to those who consider themselves wise or strong or rich, the very categories suggested by the names Egypt, Babylon, Philistia, Tyre, and Cush, we say with Jeremiah,

> "Let not the wise man boast of his wisdom
> or the strong man boast of his strength
> or the rich man boast of his riches,
> but let him who boasts boast about this:
> that he understands and knows me,
> that I am the LORD, who exercises kindness,
> justice and righteousness on earth,
> for in these I delight," declares the LORD (Jer. 9:23–24).

The greatest blessing that can come to any person or nation is that those involved might know and worship God.

2. *The people will be born again.* The second thing recorded of the nations is that it will be said of them, "This one was born in Zion" (vv. 4, 6), and "This one and that one were born in her" (v. 5). Since this is repeated three times in such a short psalm it is clear that it is very important.

But what does it mean? It cannot mean that all the people of the world will one day literally be born in Jerusalem. It can only mean that it will be set down in the official records as if they had been born there, meaning that they will be given the status of true citizens. H. C. Leupold says, "More than submission is involved. Though the New Testament doctrine of the new birth does not appear clearly in the Old Testament, the expression here used surely implies some deeper kind of transformation that is to take place. These people will be natives in the sense of native-born."[4]

Yes, but probably more than this too. For if the vision of Psalm 87 is being fulfilled in the church, as I believe it is, then being "born again" is exactly what is involved and is necessary. Being "born in Zion" is to become a spiritual Jew—that is, a member of the people of God—and this is exactly what the new birth signifies.

Here is a confirming piece of evidence. In the Septuagint version of verse 5, which the apostle Paul knew and from which he frequently draws in his epistles, the additional word *mother* appears, which gives the sense captured by the New English Bible's translation: "and Zion shall be called a mother in whom men of every race are born." This lies behind Paul's saying in Galatians 4:26, "The Jerusalem that is above . . . is our mother," which means that he interpreted Psalm 87 as pointing to spiritual rebirth.

"Fount of Every Blessing"

The last verse of this short but very beautiful psalm is about those who have been reborn and who praise God for it, singing, "All my fountains are in you." This lovely image is echoed elsewhere. It occurs in Psalm 46:4, for instance, where we read of "a river whose streams make glad the city of God." Or Ezekiel 47:1, which describes "water coming out from under the threshold of the [heavenly] temple," which became a great river of blessing. John Milton referred to these springs in the preface to *Paradise Lost,* asking the Holy Spirit to inspire him as he composed his epic:

> . . . or, if Sion's hill
> Delight thee more, or Siloa's brook that flowed
> Fast by the oracle of God, I thence
> Invoke thine aid to my adventurous song.

What all these references are saying is that "every good and perfect gift is from above"—that is, from God. All we are or hope to be, all we have or ever hope to have, all we attain or ever hope to attain is from him. The people of God acknowledge this and praise God for it.

Do you do that? Or do you take credit for what you are or accomplish yourself? May I suggest that if you acknowledge that "all your fountains are in God," as they truly are, then you will have joy in your salvation and, what is more, you will be encouraged to keep on serving God, since you know that he will sustain your effort. You will know that "he who began a good work in you will carry it on to completion until the day of Christ Jesus" (Phil. 1:6).

Newton put it in the second verse of his hymn:

> See, the streams of living waters,
> Springing from eternal love,
> Well supply thy sons and daughters,
> And all fear of want remove:
> Who can faint while such a river
> Ever flows their thirst to assuage—
> Grace which, like the Lord the Giver,
> Never fails from age to age?

That grace has not failed yet, and it will never fail, because it comes from the inexhaustible supply of the infinite and eternally merciful and gracious God. We are eternally blessed if we know, worship, and serve him.

Psalm 88

The Dark Night of the Soul

O LORD, the God who saves me,
day and night I cry out before you.
May my prayer come before you;
turn your ear to my cry.

For my soul is full of trouble
and my life draws near the grave.
I am counted among those who go down to the pit;
I am like a man without strength.
I am set apart with the dead,
like the slain who lie in the grave,
whom you remember no more,
who are cut off from your care.

You have put me in the lowest pit,
in the darkest depths.
Your wrath lies heavily upon me;
you have overwhelmed me with all your waves. Selah . . .

Why, O LORD, do you reject me
and hide your face from me?

verses 1–7, 14

The powerful, descriptive phrase "dark night of the soul" is not much used today, but it was in the Middle Ages, where it was found in the writings of the European mystics. It is a translation

715

of the title of a book by the Spanish monk St. John of the Cross known in English as *The Ascent of Mount Carmel* (1578–1580). What is the dark night of the soul? It is a state of intense spiritual anguish in which the struggling, despairing believer feels he is abandoned by God.

This is what Psalm 88 describes. It is not unlike other psalms in which the writers complain of their wretched circumstances and lament their misery. But these others all move toward some state of resolution, maturing faith, or hope by the end of the psalm. This is not the case with Psalm 88. It begins with God, but it ends with the words "darkness is my closest friend," and there seems to be no hope anywhere. Derek Kidner says, "This is the saddest prayer in the Psalter."[1] H. C. Leupold wrote, "It is the gloomiest psalm found in the Scriptures," adding, "The psalmist is as deeply in trouble when he has concluded his prayer as he was when he began it."[2] J. J. Stewart Perowne said, "This is the darkest, saddest Psalm in all the Psalter. It is one wail of sorrow from beginning to end."[3]

It is good that we have a psalm like this, but it is also good that we have only one. It reminds us that life is filled with trouble, even to the point of despair, even for mature believers. Psalm 88 is by an inspired writer, after all. He is identified as Heman the Ezrahite, one of the "Sons of Korah."[4]

Once when I was discussing Christian contributions to modern literature, a friend and I asked each other why there is so little outstanding Christian fiction today. We concluded that it is because we are not true enough to life. Christians feel that in order to be Christian a composition has to work out right in the end and that there has to be a clear lesson or moral. Psalm 88 is a reminder that life is not always like that. There may be a perfectly good moral from God's point of view; I believe that all life does have a divine purpose. But that does not necessarily mean that we can see it or that it will ever become clear in our lifetimes.

Marvin Tate says, "Psalm 88 stands as a witness to the intent of the psalms to speak to all of life, to remind us that life does not always have happy endings."[5] Historian and Christian social critic Martin Marty wrote, "The psalm is a scandal to anyone who isolates it from the biblical canon, a pain to anyone who must hear it apart from more lively words. Whoever devises from the Scriptures a philosophy in which everything turns out right has to begin by tearing out this page of the volume."[6]

Commentators on the psalms propose many different outlines for this psalm, which suggests that no one outline is necessarily to be preferred. In fact, not much of an outline is needed, because the verses simply move along from one expression of profound misery and despair to another. My plan is to take the ideas in sequence, following (for convenience) the stanzas laid out by the New International Version.

By Day and by Night

The only hopeful line in this prayer is the first, the beginning, which reads, "O LORD, the God who saves me." This is not to be dismissed lightly, for no person who knows that God is his Savior can ever utterly despair. The line is used as a mere address, however, a designation, and the psalm immediately passes to the fact that the writer has been crying to God "day and night"—that is, unrelentingly and (as becomes apparent very quickly) without an answer. The writer has also been calling to God for a very long time—he has been afflicted from his youth (v. 15)—but God has not removed the cause of his suffering.

This next-to-the-last of the Korahite psalms may echo the first, Psalm 42. Psalm 42 is not nearly as sad as this gloomy composition, but verse 3 of that psalm says, "My tears have been my food, *day and night,* while men say to me all day long, 'Where is your God?'"

We cannot fault the psalmist for failing to cling to promises he did not have. But also we cannot help remembering how Jesus insisted that in spite of God's seeming indifference, God actually does hear prayer and will act "quickly." He made this point in the story of the persistent widow and the unjust judge who concluded that although he did not care for justice he would see that the widow got justice so she would not wear him out with her coming. Jesus said, "And will not God bring about justice for his chosen ones, who cry out to him day and night? Will he keep putting them off? I tell you, he will see that they get justice, and quickly" (Luke 18:7–8). The problem is merely that God's timing differs from our own.

The Shadow of Death

The coloring of the psalm grows darker as it moves along. For what is staring the writer in the face is death's dark shadow (vv. 3–5). Notice how the darkness builds. First, the writer's "soul is full of trouble." Next he is "drawing near the grave"—that is, dying. Third, he is "counted among" the dead, "those who go down to the pit," perhaps even by his friends. Fourth, he is "without strength." Finally, he is even

> . . . set apart with the dead,
>> like the slain who lie in the grave,
> whom you remember no more,
>> who are cut off from your care (v. 5).

In this last sentence the psalmist sees himself almost being laid out in the mortuary or charnel house, and his most faith-destroying terror is that in that place God, who lives for the living, will "remember [him] no more." Speaking of verse 5 particularly, Marvin Tate says, "The description of the dead [in v. 5] is the central focus of the first part of the psalm."[7]

In his perceptive book *Reflections on the Psalms,* the great Christian apologist C. S. Lewis has a chapter called "Death in the Psalms," in which he faces the apparent Jewish lack of faith in a blessed afterlife for those who are God's. They spoke of the grave as Sheol, the actual word behind the psalmist's word "grave" in verse 3. Lewis wrote,

> They speak of Sheol (or "hell" or "the pit") very much as a man speaks of "death" or "the grave" who has no belief in any sort of future state whatever—a man to whom the dead are simply dead, nothing, and there's no more to be said.
>
> In many passages this is quite clear, even in our translation, to every attentive reader. The clearest of all is the cry in [Psalm] 89:47: "O remember how short my time is: why hast thou made all men for nought?" We all come to nothing in the end. Therefore "every man living is altogether vanity" (39:6). Wise and foolish have the same fate (49:10). Once dead, a man worships God no more; "Shall the dust give thanks unto thee?" (30:10); "for in death no man remembereth thee" (6:5). . . . Death is "the land" where, not only worldly things, but all things, "are forgotten" (88:12).[8]

This is exactly how the psalmist is speaking, perhaps more than he might otherwise have done were it not for his depression. We cannot think this way, because we stand on this side of the resurrection of Jesus Christ and know his promises concerning heaven. However, we also remember that Psalm 88 is not the only reflection on death to be found in the Old Testament or even in the Book of Psalms. David looked at death's shadow and said, "Even though I walk through the valley of the shadow of death, I will fear no evil, for you are with me" (Ps. 23:4). And again,

> Surely goodness and love will follow me
>   all the days of my life,
> and I will dwell in the house of the Lord
>   forever (v. 6).

God has never left his people entirely without hope, even though that hope was dimmer in the Old Testament period than it can be today. God tests our faith, but he does not leave it without a sure foundation in his Word.

This Present Darkness

I used the word *darkness* to describe the tone of the last stanza, but the word actually occurs for the first time in verse 6, in a stanza that takes us even farther into the abyss. What makes this darkness so dark and this stanza so depressing is that here God is thought of as having caused the psalmist's problems. In verse 1 the writer called God the one "who saves me." In verses 3–5 he described his actual, present state. But here, in verses

6–9a, he says, contrary to his opening statement, that God is the cause of his misery. Notice the repeated complaints about God's actions:

> *You* have put me in the lowest pit (v. 6).
> *Your* wrath lies heavily upon me (v. 7).
> *You* have overwhelmed me with all *your* waves (v. 7).
> *You* have taken from me my closest friends
>   and have made me repulsive to them (v. 8).

The psalmist does nearly the same thing later (in v. 16), complaining, "*Your* wrath has swept over me; *your* terrors have destroyed me."

It is worth noticing the similarities between Psalm 88 and Job. Job was a godly man whom God blessed with a large family and many possessions. Suddenly these were all taken from him. His life became so miserable that he condemned the day he was born, stared death in the face, and prepared to perish miserably. This is a close echo of what the psalmist seems to be saying of himself in Psalm 88. Yet the most important similarity is that God had caused Job's suffering, if not directly, at least by permitting Satan to afflict him—Job was unable to imagine why—and this is what the psalmist is claiming too. These similarities are so great, including even certain echoes of language that Franz Delitzsch has suggested that Job and the psalm might even be by the same author, Heman the Ezrahite.[9]

We know from the beginning and ending of Job that God had a purpose in Job's suffering. It was to demonstrate before Satan, the demons, and the watching angels that a man will serve God for love's sake quite apart from what God may do for him materially. But the point of Job is that this great patriarch did not himself know what was going on. And neither apparently did the psalmist. Both works are present in Scripture to remind us that we do not necessarily know what God is accomplishing by our suffering, either.

No Praises from the Dead

The next stanza (vv. 9b–12) is where C. S. Lewis got one of his quotations showing that the ancient Jews did not reflect very much on life beyond the grave, if indeed they believed in it at all. Verse 10 seems to deny the resurrection, and verses 11–12 seem to say that the dead are not even awake or conscious enough to remember God.

This is not true, of course. But it is from the perspective of what we can see on earth unaided by specific revelation about the afterlife, which the psalmist did not have. Derek Kidner says, "From the standpoint of God's congregation and his glory in the world, all that is said here is true. It is among the living that his miracles are performed, his praises sung, his constancy and acts of deliverance exhibited. Death is no exponent of his glory. Its whole character is negative: it is the last word in inactivity, . . . silence, . . . the severing of ties, . . . corruption, . . . gloom, . . . oblivion. The New

Testament concurs, calling it the last enemy."[10] Nothing is to be gained by denying this. It is not the whole truth; we know much more because of the New Testament and its revelation. But it is at least part of the truth and therefore rightly has its niche in Scripture.

The Silent God

Not only are the dead silent, since they unable to rise up and make God's wonders known. God is also silent toward them, so far as the psalmist knows (vv. 13–14). One reason why he feels so close to death, "as good as dead," we might say, is that God is not speaking to him now. He tries to speak to God; he is praying. But God rejects him and seems to hide his face. Have you ever felt like that? Most of us have times when the heavens seem made of brass and the prayers we throw upward fall back upon our heads unanswered. When that happens it is no wonder that we feel dead or almost dead spiritually. If "man does not live on bread alone, but on every word that comes from the mouth of God" (Matt. 4:4; from Deut. 8:3), it is no surprise that we feel nearly dead when God is silent.

A Lifetime of Sorrows

This is the point where we have learned to expect that a lament like this should become positive, however dim that positive hope might be. We expect it to say something like, "Nevertheless, I know that you hear me and will answer before very long" or "I will wait to see what wonderful things you will do." We do not find that here. Instead of optimism we find the gloomiest and darkest words of all. It is as though the psalmist looks about in every direction and sees nothing but misery, despair, death, terror, and loneliness everywhere.

First, he looks back. Sometimes when things are going bad, we are able to look to the past and remember better days and be encouraged by them. But when the psalmist looks back all he can remember is that "from my youth I have been afflicted and close to death" (v. 15). He cannot recall any happy or brighter days to cheer him up.

Second, he looks forward. It is even worse when he does this, for all he can see there is death, made horrible by his present experiences of the terror and wrath of God (vv. 15–16). He has every reason to suppose they will continue. This has plunged him into the very pit of "despair" (v. 15).

Third, he looks around at the present. These are his last words, and they are no better. In fact, they are the worst description yet. The present leads to blank despair. He sees himself as having been "destroyed" (v. 16) by God; "surround[ed]" and "engulfed" by God's terror (v. 17); separated from his "companions and loved ones," whom God has taken from him; and, without God, to be all by himself in the "darkness" (v. 18). In the Hebrew text *darkness* is the psalm's very last word. So it is as though the writer reaches up and with a final, despairing effort of his will snuffs out the already fading light. Thus the psalm ends.

Is Darkness the Final Word?

Well, Heman's last word may be *darkness*. But it does not have to be the last word for us. If we do not repent of sin and come to God through faith in the atoning death of Jesus Christ, the darkness of death, hell, and judgment is all we can anticipate. Jesus described hell as a place of outer darkness, after all (Matt. 25:30). On the other hand, if we believe the gospel and receive Jesus as our Savior, not only is the future changed from darkness to brightness and from death to life, but the past is changed also; it need no longer rise up to haunt us. And the present is changed too.

Let me quote Derek Kidner again as he takes a final look at this sad psalm: "With *darkness* as its final word, what is the role of this psalm in Scripture? For the beginning of an answer we may note [the following]."

1. "Its witness to the possibility of unrelieved suffering as a believer's lot. The happy ending of most psalms of this kind is seen to be a bonus, not a due." Even after we become Christians and should know better, most of us still feel that God owes us a happy or easy life. But we are not owed an easy life. Therefore, the withholding of such a life from God's people is no proof of his displeasure, just as a happy life or the possession of riches is no sure proof of his approval.

2. "The psalm adds its voice to the 'groaning in travail' which forbids us to accept the present order as final." In spite of the kind of suffering described in this psalm, the Bible teaches that there is a moral order to the universe and therefore we look forward to a balancing out of good and evil and to a final redemption at the end. Kidner says that Psalm 88 is "a sharp reminder that 'we wait for adoption as sons, the redemption of our bodies' (Rom. 8:22f.)."

3. "This author, like Job, does not give up. He completes his prayer, still in the dark and totally unrewarded. The taunt, 'Does Job fear God for naught?' is answered yet again." Like Job, the author has received no satisfactory answer for why his life has turned out as miserably as it has. But also, like Job, he does not "curse God and die" (Job 2:9). Rather, he is seen clinging to God, praying to him, even to the end. This is beyond human explanation, but it is the full faith-victory of the saints.

4. "The author's name allows us, with hindsight, to see that his rejection was only apparent. . . . His existence was no mistake; there was a divine plan bigger than he knew, and a place in it reserved most carefully for him."[11] Thus, probably to his surprise, this painful psalm of lament is included, along with all the happier songs, in sacred Scripture.

Psalm 89

Our Covenant-Keeping God: Part 1

Great Is Your Faithfulness

I will sing of the LORD's great love forever;
*   with my mouth I will make your faithfulness known through all*
*   generations.*
I will declare that your love stands firm forever,
*   that you established your faithfulness in heaven itself.*

You said, "I have made a covenant with my chosen one,
*   I have sworn to David my servant,*
'I will establish your line forever
*   and make your throne firm through all generations.'"*   Selah

The heavens praise your wonders, O LORD,
*   your faithfulness too, in the assembly of the holy ones.*
For who in the skies above can compare with the LORD?
*   Who is like the LORD among the heavenly beings?*
In the council of the holy ones God is greatly feared;
*   he is more awesome than all who surround him.*
O LORD God Almighty, who is like you?
*   You are mighty, O LORD, and your faithfulness surrounds you.*

verses 1–8

There are as many attributes of God as there are names of God, one for each day of the year, according to one writer's collection. But of all these divine attributes it would be hard to find one as important to us as faithfulness. Men and women are unfaithful. We make promises and break them. We want people to rely on us, but we cannot be relied on ourselves. God is utterly faithful. What he promises, he performs. This is what Psalm 89 is about. Yet with an honesty found consistently in the psalms but often lacking in ourselves, it also describes a situation in which God has not seemed to be faithful, and it asks, "Where is your faithfulness?"

> Great is thy faithfulness, O God my Father;
> There is no shadow of turning with thee. . . .

That is what we sing, and it is true. God is faithful! But it is also true that there are times when he does not seem to be. We are going to look at God's faithfulness in this study of Psalm 89 (vv. 1–37), and the question "Where is your faithfulness?" in study two (vv. 38–52).

God's Covenant with King David

Psalm 89 is an unusual psalm in that the first part of it (vv. 1–37) is an exposition of an Old Testament story. In 2 Samuel 7, after King David was at peace with the neighboring warring kingdoms, we are told that he had the idea of building a temple for God in Jerusalem. "Here I am, living in a palace of cedar, while the ark of God remains in a tent," he said (v. 2). The prophet Nathan told David that whatever he had in mind to do he should do. But that night the Lord spoke to Nathan, giving him a word for David in which God said that instead of David building a house for God, God would build a house for David—that is, a dynasty.

> This is what the Lord says: Are you the one to build me a house to dwell in? . . .
> The Lord declares to you that the Lord himself will establish a house for you: When your days are over and you rest with your fathers, I will raise up your offspring to succeed you, who will come from your own body, and I will establish his kingdom. He is the one who will build a house for my Name, and I will establish the throne of his kingdom forever. I will be his father, and he will be my son. When he does wrong, I will punish him with the rod of men, with floggings inflicted by men. But my love will never be taken away from him, as I took it away from Saul, whom I removed from before you. Your house and your kingdom will endure forever before me; your throne will be established forever (2 Sam. 7:5, 11–16).

This important Old Testament passage is the account of God's making a covenant with David, according to which David's throne was to be established in the line of his descendants. *Forever* is the critical word, and it is one of the words from 2 Samuel 7 that occurs again and again in Psalm 89. It occurs eight times (in vv. 1, 2, 4, 28, 29, 36, 37, 46). Similarly, *faithfulness* occurs seven times (in vv. 1, 2, 5, 8, 14, 33, 49; see also v. 24). *Covenant* is found in verses 3, 28, and 34.

Psalm 89 is said to be by Ethan the Ezrahite, who is mentioned in 1 Kings 4:31 and probably 1 Chronicles 2:6. This is the only psalm that has his name affixed to it. But, like some or all of the psalms of Asaph, this must mean that the psalm was by Ethan's school of composers or descendants, since the problems expressed in the poem's second half did not develop until after David's time, when the original Ethan lived.

The Mercies of the Lord Forever

The theme of the psalm is established in the first stanza (vv. 1–4) by the repeated use of *faithfulness* and *forever* and by one use of the word *covenant*. These words occur throughout the psalm, but they are particularly prominent here. *Forever* occurs three times, the word *faithfulness* twice, and *covenant* once.

The New International Version's rendering of verse 1 loses something, at least for people who are familiar with the hymn beginning, "I will sing of the mercies of the Lord forever," for that is what the verse literally says. That is, the word translated "great love" is actually "mercies," and it is plural. It seems to me that "mercies" suggests two things that "great love" does not. First, it suggests specific tangible blessings, not merely a favorable attitude. Second, it emphasizes that there are many of these mercies. The hymn "Great Is Thy Faithfulness" claims, "Morning by morning new mercies I see." And what are they?

> Pardon for sin and a peace that endureth,
> Thine own dear presence to cheer and to guide,
> Strength for today and bright hope for tomorrow,
> Blessings all mine, with ten thousand beside.

That is the way it is with Christians, and it is one thing that makes God's faithfulness not merely an "attribute," but a tangible reality. The mercies of God are innumerable and unending. It is why we sing about them joyfully.

I wrote earlier that Psalm 89 is a poetic exposition of 2 Samuel 7, in which God established an everlasting covenant with David. There are echoes of that chapter throughout the psalm. But lest we miss what is happening, the author specifically cites the words of God from 2 Samuel 7 in verses 3–4.

> You said, "I have made a covenant with my chosen one,
> I have sworn to David my servant,

'I will establish your line forever,
and make your throne firm through all generations.'"

We are going to see the problems of living with that assurance later on, but it is significant that the author begins with God's words—and ends by going back to them too (v. 49). For that is his foundation, the only possible foundation in troubled times. That should be our foundation too. The one who builds on the Word of God is building on a rock.

God's Faithfulness Praised in Heaven

The first four verses, ending with God's words from 2 Samuel 7, have been a sort of introduction to the psalm, setting its theme. But starting with the second stanza (vv. 5–8) the exposition begins. The point at which it begins is at the highest peak, with God in heaven accompanied by the holy angels. The angels are called an "assembly" or congregation, because, like the church on earth, they live to worship and praise God.

For what do they praise him? It should be no surprise in view of the psalm's theme that the angels are said to be praising God for his faithfulness. The word occurs at the beginning of the stanza (in v. 5) and again at the end (in v. 8). But it is a mighty faithfulness, which leads the angels to ask, "Who in the skies above can compare with the LORD? Who is like the LORD among the heavenly beings?" (v. 6). Again, "O LORD God Almighty, who is like you?" (v. 8). The answer: "You [alone] are mighty, O LORD, and your faithfulness surrounds you" (v. 8). Isn't it interesting to think that the angels are praising God in heaven for the very characteristic we are tempted to question him about below? Isn't it a rebuke to our weak faith? If we thought as the angels, we would be praising God for his great faithfulness constantly.

God's Faithfulness on Earth

Having spoken of the faithfulness of God in heaven and of the strength that is one of its characteristics, the psalmist next moves to earth, where the power of God is particularly evident (vv. 9–13). Faithfulness itself is not mentioned here, since the writer seems to be concentrating on the power of God. The reason for this becomes clear in the next stanza; it is the power of God that enables God to be effective in his faithfulness to his people. He is effectively faithful because he is his people's "shield" and sure defense against enemies (see v. 18).

There seem to be two spheres in which the writer praises God's power.

First, he praises God's power in creation, particularly the manner in which he governs it providentially. He thinks of heaven and earth, the world, even the north and the south (vv. 11–12). The two mountains, Tabor and Hermon, are probably selected because they stand to the east and west of the Jordan River. Tabor is not very high (1,843 feet). Hermon is much more imposing (9,100 feet). They are in the middle of the land.

The sea attracts special attention, perhaps because it is so vast and so uncontrollable by man. Storms at sea are terrifying. But "when its waves mount up, you still them" (v. 9). The inspired writer may not have had any specific stilling in mind when he wrote this, but we can hardly read it without thinking of how Jesus stilled the waves on the Sea of Galilee. The disciples and Jesus were at sea in a small boat. Jesus was sleeping. While he was sleeping a storm arose that was so fierce that the disciples, many of whom were seasoned fishermen, were afraid they were going to perish. They woke Jesus up, crying, "Teacher, don't you care if we drown?"

Jesus rebuked the wind and said to the waves, "Quiet! Be still!" The wind died down and it was completely calm. The disciples were so impressed that they were more terrified now of Jesus and his power than they had been by the storm. The story ends by their asking one another, "Who is this? Even the wind and the waves obey him" (Mark 4:35–41). Who indeed but the Lord of glory? Who but God?

The second sphere in which the writer praises God's power is his rule over the events of history. This is a small reference, but an important one. It concerns "Rahab," a name used for Egypt (see Ps. 87:4), and the historical events in view are the miracles of God in delivering the Jews from their slavery by that country. For our part, we can look back to the power of God in delivering us from our slavery to sin. Indeed, these two events are parallel, which is why Derek Kidner calls the exodus a victory "as central to the Old Testament as Calvary to the New."[1]

God's Faithfulness with His People

Having moved from heaven to earth and from nature to the specific event of the Jewish exodus from Egypt, the writer now turns to the faithfulness of God to his people generally (vv. 14–18). At this point he brings in many other attributes of God that his people have experienced and for which they praise him. These attributes are added to faithfulness as basic to God's character and as a foundation for faith in his faithfulness. God has the power to be faithful, but does he want to be? Is God willing? These attributes assure us that the answer is Yes.

The first new attribute of God is *righteousness*. Righteousness is the underlying principle of justice, which is mentioned next, for without righteousness there can be no justice. *Justice,* the next term, is giving to everyone what is due to him or her, acquittal for those who are innocent, condemnation for those who are guilty. Justice is the application of righteousness. *Love* has already been mentioned in verses 1–2, where, as in verse 14, it is linked to faithfulness. The Hebrew word *(hesed)* actually means steadfast, faithful, or covenant love. *Faithfulness* is the attribute of God we have been looking at all along. It means that he can be counted on to do what he has promised to do. The final three attributes are introduced as possessions of God's people: *glory, strength,* and *favor* (that is, "grace"). But these are the people's only because they are first of all God's. He alone is glorious, strong, and gracious; it is because he is that we, his people, experience these graces ourselves.

What is the proper response of people who have come to know and partake of the blessings of such a great God? The answer is, To praise God and rejoice in him. This is what verses 15–16 say: "Blessed are those who have learned to acclaim you. . . . They rejoice in your name all day long."

God's Faithfulness to His Covenant

In verses 19–29, the fifth stanza, the covenant introduced initially in verse 3 begins to be discussed explicitly, for these verses are essentially a commentary on 2 Samuel 7. Or to look at it in terms of the psalm, they are a commentary on the summation of the covenant that appeared as verses 3 and 4 of the introduction. Verses 19–29 contain explicit references to the historical passage.[2] They highlight six critical features of God's covenant with David.

1. *God's choice of David to be king* (vv. 19–20). God's covenants are established according to his own good pleasure and not on the basis of anything in the people who benefit by them. In this case, we are reminded that God chose David as king when he was just a young man without any claim on the throne or pretensions to kingship. The story of his choice by God and his anointing by Samuel is told in 1 Samuel 16:1–13. We remember that God chose us for salvation when there was no good in us. He saved us only according to his own good pleasure.

2. *God's strengthening of David for his work as king* (v. 21). God does not abandon to their own strength or devices those upon whom he has set his love. In David's case the covenant meant that God would equip him and strengthen him for his work as king. In the same way God will also equip us for whatever work he has for us to do. Jesus said, "Apart from me you can do nothing" (John 15:5). But Paul added the other side of the truth when he wrote to the Philippians, "I can do everything through him who gives me strength" (Phil. 4:13).

3. *God's protecting David from his enemies* (v. 22). David had many enemies, but God promised to protect him from them. And he did! So also does God protect us. Jesus told Peter, "Satan has asked to sift you as wheat. But I have prayed for you, Simon, that your faith may not fail. And when you have turned back, strengthen your brothers" (Luke 22:31–32).

4. *God's granting David victory over his enemies* (v. 23). Not only did God protect David from his enemies, he also promised him victory over them. In a similar way, Paul said of those who benefit from God's covenant of salvation today, "The sting of death is sin, and the power of sin is the law. But thanks be to God! He gives us victory through our Lord Jesus Christ" (1 Cor. 15:56–57).

5. *God's exalting David to prominence among the kings of the nations* (vv. 24–27). These verses elaborate David's prominence as a king among the world's rulers. But the greatest thing they tell about David's prominence is that he was given a special relationship to God. For his part, David would call out, "You are my Father, my God, the Rock my Savior" (v. 26). For his part, God would appoint David his "firstborn" (v. 27). Our great claim to prominence is that we have been made sons and daughters of God, "heirs of God and co-heirs with Christ" (Rom. 8:17).

6. *God's extending the blessing to David's sons* (vv. 28–29). The final and critical part of God's covenant with David is that he promised to extend the blessings of the covenant to David's descendants forever. This was fulfilled in Jesus Christ, for he alone will rule forever on David's throne.

The Faithfulness of God in Discipline

The final stanza of this first half of the psalm (vv. 30–37) is also a commentary on the covenant established in 2 Samuel 7, particularly the part dealing with David's human descendants and what should be expected if they should drift into sin. The answer is that they will be disciplined, as a father disciplines his son (vv. 30–32). This is repeated in Hebrews 12:4–11, particularly verse 6: "The Lord disciplines those he loves, and he punishes everyone he accepts as a son" (quoting Prov. 3:11–12). The covenant will remain intact even in that case (vv. 33–37), for it is an eternal covenant; it will never be broken.

Yet the faithfulness of God is in the discipline too. In one of his writings the great Bible teacher Harry Ironside tells of something that happened to him early in his ministry. He had been preaching in Fresno, California, and the day came when he was entirely out of money. He had to check out of his hotel. That evening, hungry, having had no supper, he settled himself under a tree on the lawn of the courthouse for the night. He thought of Philippians 4:19, "My God will meet all your needs according to his glorious riches in Christ Jesus." He complained. Why doesn't God do it, then? Why isn't he faithful to his promise?

As he prayed that night, God brought to his mind things about which he had grown careless and renewed him spiritually. And later God did provide for his needs. Old friends appeared to provide housing. The meetings went well. The people even took up a collection that helped him get home.

But here is the interesting thing. As he left Fresno, Ironside stopped by the post office, where he found a letter from his father. He wasn't expecting it, so it surprised him. In it his father had written, "God spoke to me through Philippians 4:19 today. He has promised to supply all our need. Some day he may see I need a starving, and if he does, he will supply that." Ironside saw then that God had been putting him through a time of deprivation for discipline, to bring him closer to himself.[3]

Arthur Pink wrote,

Unfaithfulness is one of the most outstanding sins of these evil days. In the business world, a man's word is, with rare exceptions, no longer his bond. In the social world, marital infidelity abounds on every hand. . . . In the ecclesiastical realm, thousands who have solemnly covenanted to preach the truth have no scruples about attacking and denying it. Nor can reader or writer claim complete immunity from this fearful sin. . . . How refreshing, then, and how blessed, to lift our eyes above this scene of ruin, and behold One who is faithful, faithful in all things, at all times.[4]

Psalm 89

Our Covenant-Keeping God: Part 2

Where Is Your Faithfulness?

But you have rejected, you have spurned,
  you have been very angry with your anointed one.
You have renounced the covenant with your servant
  and have defiled his crown in the dust.
You have broken through all his walls
  and reduced his strongholds to ruins.
All who pass by have plundered him;
  he has become the scorn of his neighbors.
You have exalted the right hand of his foes;
  you have made all his enemies rejoice.
You have turned back the edge of his sword
  and have not supported him in battle.
You have put an end to his splendor
  and cast his throne to the ground.
You have cut short the days of his youth;
  you have covered him with a mantle of shame.   Selah

How long, O LORD? Will you hide yourself forever?
  How long will your wrath burn like fire?
Remember how fleeting is my life.
  For what futility you have created all men!
What man can live and not see death,

> *or save himself from the power of the grave?*   Selah
> *O Lord, where is your former great love,*
> *which in your faithfulness you swore to David?*
>
>   *verses 38–49*

P salm 89 has the distinction of being one of the greatest passages in the Bible dealing with the faithfulness of God. But it does it in two ways. The first half praises God for his faithfulness exuberantly and without any qualifications. It particularly praises him for his faithfulness in keeping his covenant with King David (2 Sam. 7). The second half expresses the gap between the promise and reality. It is as though we should sing our great hymn dealing with God's faithfulness, beginning,

> Great is thy faithfulness, O God my Father,
> There is no shadow of turning with thee . . . ,

but then have a final stanza that goes,

> Where is thy faithfulness, O God my Father?
> There is no truth in your dealings with me; . . .

We would be wrong to believe this, of course, and so is the psalmist. But it is a mark of the poet's stark honesty that he freely tells God what he thinks he sees.

More Than the End of an Era

Psalm 89 has eight stanzas, but this stanza, the seventh (vv. 38–45), contains the first hint we have had of the disaster that lies behind the psalm's composition. We do not know precisely what it was, but it must have involved the breakup, collapse, or possibility of collapse, of the Davidic dynasty, for that is the only thing that would give meaning to the author's complaint about the breaking of the covenant with David: "You have renounced the covenant with your servant" (v. 39).

We know of a number of situations that could explain the psalmist's words. The one closest to the time of David was the breakup of the united monarchy of David and Solomon into the two kingdoms of Judah and Israel in the reign of Rehoboam.[1] The strength of this view is that it fits an early dating of the psalm. It would even make it possible for Psalm 89 to have been written by the Ethan who was appointed to the role of temple musician by David. He could have lived through the latter part of David's reign, the entire reign of Solomon, and have written the psalm in the early days of Rehoboam, though as an old man.

At the other extreme, some writers believe that verses 38–45 more aptly describe the end of the monarchy in the deportation of Jehoiachin (Jeconiah), one of the last descendants of David to actually sit upon his throne. Verses 40–41 seem to reflect this later situation, for they describe the breaking up of the city's walls and reduction of the king's stronghold to ruins. If they do not describe this, they must be understood figuratively. The deportation of Jehoiachin at the age of eighteen after a reign of only three months may also be reflected in verse 45.

Leupold thinks "the days of Josiah or even of Zedekiah just before the fall of Jerusalem" fit the situation better.[2]

Whatever the exact circumstances behind this psalm, they seemed sufficiently grim to the psalmist to make him question God's faithfulness in regard to his keeping of the covenant. How could God be faithful when the king's crown has been "defiled . . . in the dust" (v. 39), the walls have been "broken through" (v. 40), the city "plundered" (v. 41), the enemies of the king "exalted" (v. 42), the edge of the king's sword "turned back" in battle (v. 43), and his royal "splendor" terminated (v. 44)? And not only that, "You have cut short the days of his youth" (v. 45). The meaning is not that the king died young, but that he was made to grow old before his time.

God or Despair

What is most striking about the phrasing of this list of accusations is that God is held to be responsible. Notice the pronoun *you,* meaning God. It is the subject of nearly every sentence in this section (eleven times in the New International Version). The only sentences that do not have God as their subject are in verse 41.

> But *you* have rejected, *you* have spurned,
>   *you* have been very angry with your anointed one.
> *You* have renounced the covenant with your servant
>   and have defiled his crown in the dust.
> *You* have broken through all his walls
>   and reduced his strongholds to ruins.
> All who pass by have plundered him;
>   he has become the scorn of his neighbors.
> *You* have exalted the right hand of his foes;
>   *you* have made all his enemies rejoice.
> *You* have turned back the edge of his sword
>   and have not supported him in battle.
> *You* have put an end to his splendor
>   and cast his throne to the ground.
> *You* have cut short the days of his youth;
>   *you* have covered him with a mantle of shame (vv. 38–45).

No wonder the psalmist adds a *selah* at this point. This is a situation that ought to give us pause. For this is not just a random or meaningless event—it is something that has been caused by God. And that is the real problem; the problem is that God has caused it.

But God's involvement is the only possibility of a solution too. If God is not behind the disaster, then the tragedy of the king's defeat and overthrow, as well as any other disaster in life, really is a random and therefore meaningless event. Therefore, by definition there is not and never can be a solution. Likewise, whatever tragedies come into your life have no meaning and no solution. If there is no God, sickness, death, the loss of friends, jobs, reputation, or anything else just happens. And the good things have no meaning either! All you can do is go with the flow, take it as it comes, and die knowing that no matter what you have accomplished in life it means nothing.

On the other hand, if God is behind what happens, then although we may not understand what God is doing we can know that there is a purpose somewhere and that a solution to the problem will be found, if not in this life, then in the next.

Some will consider this to be hiding one's head in the sand, failing to face up to reality. But the choice is not between an unfounded optimism and a bold facing of reality. It is between faith and despair. The psalmist is no Pollyanna. He faces reality, but he faces it with God.

The Saints' Cry: "How Long, O Lord?"

In case we have any question about the tone in which the psalmist is making the statements in verses 39–45, we find ourselves pointed in the right direction in the eighth and final stanza (vv. 46–51). Here we have his appeal, focused on the question: "How long, O Lord?" (v. 46). It is a common question of the saints, arising out of what seems to be a breaking of the covenant. In Revelation the saints ask God, "How long, Sovereign Lord, holy and true, until you judge the inhabitants of the earth and avenge our blood?" (Rev. 6:10). Believers ask this when they feel abandoned and when God does not seem to act. The cry is not unbelief. On the contrary, it is the cry of faith; for it is to God, and it is looking for an answer.

In other words, in the final analysis the saints know that the problem they are dealing with is not God's faithlessness, but rather his timing or delays, or their own limited and mistaken impressions. So what Marvin Tate says, based on the earlier verses, is not quite the case. Tate says, "Yahweh is charged with having broken his covenant-obligations to David by his rejection of the Davidic kingship and by giving victory to the foes of the king."[3] It is true that the language reads this way, for the psalmist is not afraid to describe the king and the people's circumstances to God as he sees them. Yet when all is said and done, he knows that God is faithful to his covenant, he will not break his promises, and the problem becomes one merely of God's timing. "When are you going to show that you are faithful?" he asks.

Two Pleas for God to Act

There is something here that is more than a mere asking of the question "How long?" however. For this is not a passive man who is writing. He is not interested in a theoretical answer, as if he would be satisfied if God were to say, "I will act to restore the fallen throne of David in ten years' time (or a hundred years' time)." Or "I will rebuild the city in the days of Nehemiah." No. The psalmist wants God to act now, while he is still alive. Therefore, the last stanza of the psalm is an appeal to God to act in the psalmist's lifetime.

There are two appeals, each of three verses.

1. *The shortness of human life* (vv. 46–48). The psalmist knows that God's timing is his own. He can take a thousand years to work out his promises to David, if he wants to. But the writer is only a human being, and human beings don't live long. Human life is "fleeting" (v. 47), and the writer of the psalm cannot keep himself from the grave long enough to see and enjoy God's blessing, if God does not hurry (v. 48). That is true for us too. We may not be here long enough to see everything God has in mind for his people, but if we are going to see anything, it has to be now.

2. *The dishonoring of God by his enemies* (vv. 49–51). This is the same argument Moses used when God was threatening to destroy the people in the wilderness after they had rejected him by making the golden calf: "Why should the Egyptians say, 'It was with evil intent that he brought them out, to kill them in the mountains and to wipe them off the face of the earth'?" (Exod. 32:12). In these verses the writer seems to combine mockery against God, mockery of the king, and mockery directed at himself.

> Remember, Lord, how your servant has been mocked,
>   how I bear in my heart the taunts of all the nations,
>   the taunts with which your enemies have mocked, O LORD,
>   with which they have mocked every step of your anointed
>   one (vv. 50–51).

If we are praying selfishly, our pleas have little force with God. But we are on firm ground when we can say, as Paul did in Romans, "The insults of those who insult you have fallen on me" (Rom. 15:3; cf. Ps. 69:9).

God's Irrevocable Covenant

I cannot end this treatment of God's faithfulness and the way in which God seemed to have broken his covenant by allowing the throne of David to be overthrown without calling attention to Paul's handling of the same problem in Romans 9–11. Paul's concern is not identical; he knew that the kingdom of David has been established forever in the reign of Jesus Christ. He is concerned with the salvation of Israel instead. Nevertheless, the covenant is the matter in question, and he introduces it explicitly when he combines the coming of Jesus with the Jews' salvation, quoting from Isaiah.

> The deliverer will come from Zion;
>   he will turn godlessness away from Jacob.
> And this is my covenant with them
>   when I take away their sins (Rom. 11:26–27;
>   from Isa. 59:20–21; 27:9).

Paul's argument in Romans is that in time "all Israel will be saved" (Rom. 11:26), precisely because God made a covenant with them and God is faithful to his covenants.

We also are party to a covenant, if we have believed on Jesus Christ. The Jews are to be brought to faith in the last days. But we stand in a like covenant today, and the attributes of God that formed the earlier covenants are for our encouragement. When we talk about God's irrevocable covenant we are speaking about God's immutability. Immutability means that God does not change, and because he does not change he can be counted on. In what ways does God not change? In his popular book, *Knowing God,* English theologian J. I. Packer lists six areas:[4]

1. *God's life does not change.* Created things have a beginning and an end, but God does not. His life is a constant datum. God does not grow old or mature or weaken or grow stronger. God cannot change for the better, because he is already perfect, and he certainly cannot change for the worse.

2. *God's character does not change.* One of the most repeated passages in the Bible is Exodus 34:6–7, in which God reveals himself to Moses, saying, "The LORD, the LORD, the compassionate and gracious God, slow to anger, abounding in love and faithfulness, maintaining love to thousands, and forgiving wickedness, rebellion and sin. Yet he does not leave the guilty unpunished; he punishes the children and their children for the sin of the fathers to the third and fourth generation." That is what God was like in the days of the Jewish exodus, and that is what he is like today. Sickness, old age, or adverse circumstances can destroy our good traits, but nothing like this ever happens to God. He can be counted on to be as kind, gracious, forgiving (and holy) as he always was.

3. *God's truth does not change.* This means that the truths of the Bible do not change. What we read in the pages of holy Scripture is as right and true today as ever.

4. *God's ways do not change.* Packer writes,

He continues to act towards sinful men in the way that he does in the Bible story. Still he shows his freedom and lordship by discriminating between sinners, causing some to hear the gospel while others do not hear it, and moving some of those who hear it to repentance while leaving others in their unbelief. . . . Still he blesses those on whom he sets his love in a way that humbles them, so that all the glory may be his alone. Still he hates the sins of his people, and uses all kinds of inward and outward pains and griefs to wean their hearts from compromise and disobedience. . . . Man's ways, we know, are pathetically inconstant—but not God's.[5]

5. *God's purposes do not change.* The ups and downs of history do not frustrate God or cause him to alter what he has determined beforehand to do. Has he planned to bring many sons and daughters into glory through faith in Jesus? Then he will do it. Has he purposed to bless Israel nationally? Then it will come to pass. What God does he has planned in eternity, and what he has planned in eternity will be carried out in time.

6. *God's Son does not change.* Most blessed of all for Christians is the fact that the Lord Jesus Christ does not change. Thus it remains true that "he is able to save completely those who come to God through him" (Heb. 7:25). When the great protector Oliver Cromwell was dying, he was overcome with spiritual darkness and depression, and in his despair he asked his chaplain, "Tell me, is it possible to fall from grace?"

"No," said his minister. "It is not possible."

"Then I am safe," said Cromwell, "for I know that I was once in grace. I am the poorest wretch that ever lived, but I know that God has loved me."

The Heidelberg Catechism poses this question: "What is thy only comfort in life and in death?" Answer: "That I, with body and soul, both in life and in death, am not my own, but belong to my faithful Savior Jesus Christ, who with his precious blood has fully satisfied for all my sins, and redeemed me from all the power of the devil; and so preserves me that without the will of my Father in heaven not a hair can fall from my head; yea, that all things must work together for my salvation. Wherefore, by his Holy Spirit, he also assures me of eternal life, and makes me heartily willing and ready henceforth to live unto him."

Praise through God's Anointed

There is one last point. In the Targums the Jewish rabbis interpreted verse 51 as a reproach to God because of his delay in sending the Messiah: "He delays so long in coming that they say he will never come."[6] I am not at all sure this is what the psalmist had in mind. For him "your anointed one" probably meant the reigning or last reigning Davidic king. But whether Ethan had the Messiah in view or not, it is certainly the Messiah who is the fulfillment of the covenant with David and for whom we look.

Do you remember the cry of the saints in Revelation 6:10, "How long, Sovereign Lord?" That question hangs in the air throughout Revelation. It is there at the end. But at the end we also have the answer of Jesus, who says, "Behold, I am coming soon! My reward is with me, and I will give to everyone according to what he has done. I am the Alpha and the Omega, the First and the Last, the Beginning and the End" (Rev. 22:12–13; see vv. 7, 20). To this we reply, "Amen. Come, Lord Jesus" (v. 20). The editor who closed out this third book of the Psalter had a like faith when he followed Ethan's cry with the faith-filled ascription: "Praise be to the LORD forever! Amen and Amen" (Ps. 89:52).

Book Four of the Psalter

Psalm 90

A Somber "Song of Moses"

Lord, you have been our dwelling place
throughout all generations.
Before the mountains were born
or you brought forth the earth and the world,
from everlasting to everlasting you are God.

You turn men back to dust,
saying, "Return to dust, O sons of men."
For a thousand years in your sight
are like a day that has just gone by,
or like a watch in the night.
You sweep men away in the sleep of death;
they are like the new grass of the morning—
though in the morning it springs up new,
by evening it is dry and withered. . . .

The length of our days is seventy years—
or eighty, if we have the strength;
yet their span is but trouble and sorrow,
for they quickly pass, and we fly away. . . .

Teach us to number our days aright,
that we may gain a heart of wisdom. . . .

May the favor of the Lord our God rest upon us;
establish the work of our hands for us—
yes, establish the work of our hands.
verses 1–6, 10, 12, 17

Psalm 90 is the only psalm in the Psalter that is attributed to Moses, but it is not the only piece of poetry Moses wrote.[1] There are two other songs of Moses in the Bible, one of them the hymn the Jews sang after their deliverance from Egypt and the drowning of Pharaoh and his army in the Red Sea (recorded in Exod. 15:1–18), the other the song Moses recited to the people before his ascension of Mount Nebo, where he died (recorded in Deut. 32:1–43). The first song is pure praise, a joyful celebration. The second is a reminder of Israel's past rebellion against God and of God's resulting judgments. Psalm 90 is the most somber and also the most personal of these poetic compositions.

If the psalm really is by Moses, as I believe (though this is doubted by many scholars), the historical setting is probably best understood by the incidents recorded in Numbers 20: (1) the death of Miriam, Moses' sister; (2) the sin of Moses in striking the rock in the wilderness, which kept him from entering the Promised Land; and (3) the death of Aaron, Moses' brother.

These sad events are reflected throughout the psalm. Yet Psalm 90 does not have a defeated or bitter tone, only the recognition that man is frail and sinful and that he needs the eternal God as his only possible hope and home. H. C. Leupold wrote of Psalm 90, "There does not appear to be any trace of bitterness or of undue pessimism. Just plain, realistic thinking marks these words."[2]

Psalm 90 has given us one of our best loved hymns, "Our God, Our Help in Ages Past," by Isaac Watts, a hymn frequently sung at the closing of the year and even at funerals. The first verse goes,

> Our God, our Help in ages past,
> Our Hope for years to come,
> Our Shelter from the stormy blast,
> And our eternal Home.

Like Moses, Watts recognized that our lives are insubstantial and fleeting. After a short duration we fly away "forgotten as a dream." But he also knew that believers have an eternal home in God.

The Deaths of Miriam and Aaron

If Numbers 20 is the background for this psalm, as I suggested, we can find important light shed on the psalm from that chapter. Miriam and Aaron have died. Soon Moses will die. In the meantime, Moses' sin has kept him from entering the land of promise. The themes of the psalm suggest that it is probably an inspired reflection on these circumstances.

1. *The death of Miriam.* The death of Miriam is reported briefly—in one verse and with just six words in English (Num. 20:1). This must have been a terrible

loss for Moses. Miriam was the leading female character at the time of the exodus, and although she was not perfect—she led Aaron in the unwarranted rebellion against Moses' unique authority recorded in Numbers 12—she must have been close to Moses and was one of the few (with Aaron) with whom he could reminisce about their former life in Egypt. By this point Moses, Aaron, Miriam, Caleb, and Joshua were the only survivors of the generation that had come out of Egypt, met with the Lord at Sinai, and been turned back before being able to enter Canaan. Miriam's death was a reminder of God's judgment on that generation, that none should enter Canaan, and a sad anticipation of the deaths of Aaron and Moses, which were soon to come.

Death is inescapable. God has declared, "Man is destined to die once, and after that to face judgment" (Heb. 9:27). Because death is inescapable, it is important that we prepare for it.

2. *Moses' sin in striking the rock.* The next section of Numbers 20 (vv. 2–13) tells of Moses' sin in striking the rock. We can sympathize with Moses, even to the point of thinking that God's judgment was unfair. Moses was almost 120 years old at this time. For 38 years he had looked forward to the conquest of Canaan, which could have taken place four decades earlier. He had been patient all this time, but at last his patience broke. No wonder! We are not surprised that he denounced the complainers among the people as being no different than their forefathers. We would have done the same.

Nevertheless, this was a sad failure on Moses' part, and God took it seriously. God always takes sin seriously. With God no sin is unimportant.

3. *The death of Aaron.* The third incident is the death of Aaron (Num. 20:22–29). This was a transitional moment marked by a month of formal mourning by all the people. Aaron's death must also have been a terrible loss for Moses, for he had worked with Aaron for forty years and Aaron was the last of his father's family.

The Eternal Grandeur of God

Like Numbers 20, Psalm 90 is a reflection on human mortality and the brevity of life, plus quiet confidence in God who is the steadfast hope of the righteous. This psalm is probably the greatest passage in the Bible contrasting the grandeur of God with man's frailty.

Few people on earth, perhaps none, have had as strong a sense of the greatness and eternal grandeur of God as did Moses, for Moses knew God intimately and conversed with him "face to face" (Num. 12:8). It is not surprising then that he should begin with a reflection on God's being a sure eternal refuge for his people.

> Lord, you have been our dwelling place
> throughout all generations.
> Before the mountains were born
> or you brought forth the earth and the world,
> from everlasting to everlasting you are God (vv. 1–2).

Moses was aware, probably more than most of us, that life is uncertain at best. There is no permanence to be found in it. Nevertheless, he was also profoundly aware of God's existence, and he knew that God is the one foundation for everything. Therefore, the person who is anchored in him is eternally secure. Moreover, the one who trusts God has a secure "dwelling place" in him. The Hebrew word for "dwelling place" may also be translated "refuge," which is how it appears in Deuteronomy 33:27, one of the other songs of Moses. It is one of several allusions to Moses' other writings, which may be evidence of his authorship of the psalm.[3]

Here we have no fixed home, but like Moses, Abraham, and the other Old Testament patriarchs, we look "forward to the city with foundations, whose architect and builder is God" (Heb. 11:10). Do you look forward to such a dwelling? Or are you putting your hope and all your earthly efforts into perishable things that will soon pass away? Paul said, "We fix our eyes not on what is seen, but on what is unseen. For what is seen is temporary, but what is unseen is eternal" (2 Cor. 4:18).

The Frailty of Man

In contrast with the stability and eternity of God, Moses directs our attention next to the weakness of man and to the brevity of his earthly life (vv. 3–6).

> You turn men back to dust,
>   saying, "Return to dust, O sons of men."
> For a thousand years in your sight
>   are like a day that has just gone by,
>   or like a watch in the night.
> You sweep men away in the sleep of death;
>   they are like the new grass of the morning—
> though in the morning it springs up new,
>   by evening it is dry and withered.

In the arid climate of the Near East a night rain will often cause a carpet of green grass to spring up in the morning on the otherwise brown hills. But the blazing daytime sun will frequently also scorch it out by nightfall. Moses is saying that our lives are like that.

The apostle Peter picks up on verse 4 in 2 Peter 3:8, writing, "With the Lord a day is like a thousand years, and a thousand years are like a day." His point is that God is not slow in bringing about the return of Jesus Christ and the final judgment but delays his judgment to give people time to repent of sin and come to faith. Moses' point is not that time passes quickly for God, but rather that it passes quickly for us. Even if we should live a thousand years, as Methuselah almost did (see Gen. 5:27), it is still only as "a day that has gone by" or "a watch in the night."

Later in the psalm Moses will speak of "the length of our days" being "seventy years—or eighty, if we have the strength" (v. 10). I have noticed when I have been visiting very elderly people on their birthdays that there are usually two things of which they seem proud: first, that they have lived as long as they have, and second, that so many people have remembered their birthdays by sending them cards. I am pleased for them, but we must remember that however long we live, death comes in the end and that what we accomplish will eventually be forgotten by everyone. Only God does not forget. Only what we do for him will remain as an everlasting accomplishment.

Man's Sin and God's Wrath

The third section of Psalm 90 (vv. 7–12) recognizes that man's greatest problem is not just his frailty—that is, that he exists for only a short bit of time and is then no more. It is that he is also a sinner and is subject to the just wrath of God. In fact, it is sin that is the cause of his death and misery. Moses must have been thinking of the fall of Adam and Eve when he wrote this (remember that he also wrote Genesis 3), as well as of his own sin in striking the rock and of God's judgment, which kept him from the Promised Land.

> We are consumed by your anger
>   and terrified by your indignation.
> You have set our iniquities before you,
>   our secret sins in the light of your presence. . . .
>
> Who knows the power of your anger?
>   For your wrath is as great as the fear that is due you
>   (vv. 7–8, 11).

This is a profound set of statements. Not only has Moses set the weakness of man and the shortness of his life against the grandeur and eternity of God, he has also traced man's mortality to its roots, seeing death as a judgment for sin. We might think that he would contrast man's sin with God's holiness, just as he has contrasted man's mortality with God's eternity. Instead, he is trying to show that death is linked to sin and is caused by it. We die because Adam sinned (see Rom. 5:12–21), and because we sin ourselves.

Are you aware that sin always leads to death? To the death of dreams, hopes, plans, relationships, health, and eventually even to that ultimate spiritual death that is a separation from God forever? If you are aware of this, you will not treat sin lightly, as many do. You will say with David, "Who can discern his errors? Forgive my hidden faults" (Ps. 19:12). You will pray, "Keep your servant also from willful sins; may they not rule over me" (v. 13). You will strive to live an upright life before God.

Man's Need of God's Grace

The fourth section of Psalm 90 (vv. 13–17) is an appeal to God for an outpouring of his grace—that we may be satisfied with God himself and that our work might endure as something of lasting value even though we ourselves quickly pass away.

> Relent, O LORD! How long will it be?
>   Have compassion on your servants.
> Satisfy us in the morning with your unfailing love,
>   that we may sing for you and be glad all our days.
> Make us glad for as many days as you have afflicted us,
>   for as many years as we have seen trouble.
> May your deeds be shown to your servants,
>   your splendor to their children.
>
> May the favor of the Lord our God rest upon us;
>   establish the work of our hands for us—
>   yes, establish the work of our hands (vv. 13–17).

Backing up to verse 12, we find three petitions in this closing section of the psalm.

1. *"Teach us to number our days aright, that we may gain a heart of wisdom"* (v. 12). This is not a request that we might know that each day is from God and thus be able to check it off as we go along, subtracting it from our allotted "seventy years—or eighty," as it were (v. 10). It is a prayer that God will help us to live holy lives, which is the path of true wisdom. How do we make each day count for God?

First, by recognizing life's brevity, which is what Moses has been chiefly writing about in this psalm. If Moses had been a lesser poet, he might have written,

> Only one life! 'Twill soon be past.
> Only what's done for Christ will last.

Second, by living each day for God. One Bible student wrote wisely, "We cannot apply our hearts unto wisdom, as instructed by Moses, except we number every day as our possible last day."[4] We remember that in Jesus' parable the fool wanted to build bigger and better barns to store his surplus crops so he could settle down and take life easy. But Jesus said of him, "You fool! This very night your life will be demanded from you. Then who will get what you have prepared for yourself?" (Luke 12:20; see vv. 13–20). Of all the mathematical disciplines this is the hardest: to number our days. We count everything else, but we do not seem able to use our days rightly and with wisdom.

2. *"Satisfy us in the morning with your unfailing love, that we may sing for joy and be glad all our days"* (v. 14). Alexander Maclaren said, "The only thing

that will secure life-long gladness is a heart satisfied with the experience of God's love."[5] This means that nothing will satisfy the human heart ultimately except God. So forget trying to fill your life with mere things. They will perish. Do not even put your hope in other people. They will die. Saint Augustine prayed, "You made us for yourself, and our hearts find no peace until they find rest in you."[6]

3. *"Establish the work of our hands for us—yes, establish the work of our hands"* (v. 17). At last, with his weakness and sin before him, Moses appeals to the grace of God to make what he had been trying to do for God worthwhile. God needs nothing from us, being able from stones to raise up children to Abraham. But if God has put us in this life to do something good for him, then it is important that we do it and do it well. William M. Taylor wrote, "So long as we are here . . . we are required by him for something. Let us therefore find out what that is, and do it; and while we do it, let us pray that God may establish it so that it may remain to bless posterity."[7]

Moses did what God had called him to do, and God established his work. We see it in the ongoing history of Israel, of which he was so large a part, in the first five books of the Bible, which he wrote, and even in the psalm we have been studying.

One more thing. For centuries this somber song of Moses has been read at funeral services. It is easy to see why. It recognizes the shortness of life but also the truth that God is able to establish the work of our hands, making what we do for God count eternally.

Do you want God to do that? Do you want your life here and what you do here to have meaning? Do you want to be a blessing to others? The only way that can happen is if God establishes your work. May he do that so that others who come after you will be blessed because of you, and so, when you die and appear before God the Father, you will hear him say, "Well done, good and faithful servant! You have been faithful with a few things; I will put you in charge of many things. Come and share your master's happiness!" (Matt. 25:21, 23).

Psalm 91

Under the Shadow of God's Wings

He who dwells in the shelter of the Most High
*   will rest in the shadow of the Almighty.*
I will say of the LORD, "He is my refuge and my fortress,
*   my God, in whom I trust."*

Surely he will save you from the fowler's snare
*   and from the deadly pestilence.*
He will cover you with his feathers,
*   and under his wings you will find refuge;*
*   his faithfulness will be your shield and rampart.*
You will not fear the terror of night,
*   nor the arrow that flies by day,*
nor the pestilence that stalks in the darkness,
*   nor the plague that destroys at midday.*
A thousand may fall at your side,
*   ten thousand at your right hand,*
*   but it will not come near you.*
You will only observe with your eyes
*   and see the punishment of the wicked.*
If you make the Most High your dwelling—
*   even the LORD, who is my refuge—*
then no harm will befall you,
*   no disaster will come near your tent.*
For he will command his angels concerning you
*   to guard you in all your ways.*

verses 1–11

All the psalms are from God and are wonderful. But some have commended themselves to God's people as being especially rich and comforting and to which they have repeatedly turned in times of sickness, loneliness, and trouble. Psalm 91 is one of these special psalms. It has been committed to heart by thousands of people, and millions have turned to it with thankfulness in the midst of life's calamities.

Psalm 91 may be compared with Psalm 46, which calls God "our refuge and strength, an ever-present help in trouble" (Ps. 46:1). Martin Luther loved that psalm and turned to it often because he had so many troubles. Psalm 91 may also be compared with Psalm 90. Both call God the "dwelling place" of his people, which is probably why they have been placed together in the Psalter. There are verbal similarities between the two psalms, which has led some commentators to conclude that Psalm 91, as well as Psalm 90, was written by Moses, though there are no other truly substantial reasons for thinking that. Besides, the psalms differ greatly in their tones. As H. C. Leupold says, "The latter [Psalm 90] is somber and stately; this is bright and simple. The one breathes deep insight; the other cheerful trust."[1]

Charles Haddon Spurgeon was not overstating the case when he wrote, "In the whole collection there is not a more cheering psalm; its tone is elevated and sustained throughout, faith is at its best and speaks nobly."[2]

Psalm 91 has given us two great hymns as well as some additional verses by well-known writers such as Edmund Spenser ("And Is There Care in Heaven") and Horatius Bonar ("He Liveth Long Who Liveth Well"). The hymns we sing are "Under the Care of My God, the Almighty" from the *Bible Songs Hymnal* of 1927 and "The Man Who Once Has Found Abode" from the Reformed Presbyterian *Book of Psalms* of 1940.

One striking feature of Psalm 91 is that it consists of three clear movements marked by a change in pronouns. The first movement is marked by the pronoun *I* (vv. 1–2). It expresses the psalmist's personal faith in God. The second movement is marked by the pronoun *you* (vv. 3–13). It is a word from the psalmist to the reader or listener, his word to us. The final stage is marked by the divine pronoun *I* (vv. 14–16). Here God speaks to the reader to declare what he will be and do for the one who loves him and calls upon him. In the New International Version the second of these two major movements is divided into separate stanzas (vv. 3–8 and 9–13). The first speaks of God's protection from many kinds of dangers. The second expresses the condition for such protection by God and the results if the condition is met.

The Psalmist's Personal Faith in God

The first verse of the psalm is a thematic statement, expressing what the remainder of the psalm will be about:

> He who dwells in the shelter of the Most High
> will rest in the shadow of the Almighty.

However, as soon as the psalmist makes that statement he immediately breaks in to confess his own faith before commending it to us: "I will say of the LORD, 'He is *my* refuge and *my* fortress, *my* God, in whom *I* trust'" (v. 2). This is the equivalent of the apostle Thomas's confession of faith after Jesus had appeared to him following the resurrection and Thomas fell at his feet, exclaiming, "*My* Lord and *my* God!" (John 20:28).

So here is a first point of application: Is Jesus Christ your Lord and God? Is the God of the Bible your refuge in times of trouble? The psalm's promises are for you only if he is.

What promises they are! And with what force they are commended to us! There are four metaphors for the security we can have in God. God will be our "shelter" and "shadow" (v. 1) and our "refuge" and "fortress" (v. 2). There are also four names for God, which give substance and strength to the metaphors. He is "the Most High," "the Almighty" (v. 1), "the LORD," and "my God" (v. 2). When the psalmist identifies God as his God in the last expression, it is a way of saying that the shelter, shadow, refuge, and fortress are for those who really do dwell in God and trust him. Spurgeon wrote, "The blessings here promised are not for all believers, but for those who live in close fellowship with God. Every child of God looks towards the inner sanctuary and the mercy-seat, yet all do not dwell in the most holy place; they run to it at times, and enjoy occasional approaches, but they do not habitually reside in the mysterious presence."[3]

So here is a second application: Do you live in close fellowship with God? Do you rest in the shadow of the Almighty? Is he your place of habitual dwelling? The psalm is written to urge you to trust and cling to God in all circumstances.

Trust in God Commended

Having stated his own personal faith in God, the psalmist now commends that faith to us, taking six verses to explain what God will do for the one who trusts him. The most striking feature of this section (and the one following) is the use of the singular *you* throughout, which is a way of saying that these truths are for each person individually. They are for you if you will truly trust or abide in God.

Verse 3 sets the tone for this section by saying that God will save the trusting soul from two kinds of dangers: first, the subtle snare of enemies, described as the trap a fowler used to catch birds, and second, death by disease or pestilence. This does not mean that those who trust God never die from infectious diseases or suffer from an enemy's plot, of course. It means that those who trust God are habitually delivered from such dangers. What Christian cannot testify to many such deliverances? Indeed, our entire lives are filled with deliverances from many and manifold dangers, until God finally takes us to be with himself.

The words "deadly pestilence" (v. 3) and later "the pestilence that stalks in the darkness" and "the plague that destroys at midday" (v. 6) help us recall many instances of such protection.

Lord Craven, a Christian, was a nobleman who was living in London when plague ravaged the city in the fifteenth century. In order to escape the spreading pestilence Craven determined to leave the city for his country home, as many of his social standing did. He ordered his coach and baggage made ready. But as he was walking down one of the halls of his home about to enter his carriage, he overheard one of his servants say to another, "I suppose by my Lord's quitting London to avoid the plague that his God lives in the country and not in town." It was a straightforward and apparently innocent remark. But it struck Lord Craven so deeply that he canceled his journey, saying, "My God lives everywhere and can preserve me in town as well as in the country. I will stay where I am." So he stayed in London. He helped the plague victims, and he did not catch the disease himself.[4]

There is a similar story from the life of Charles Haddon Spurgeon. In 1854, when he had been in London only twelve months, the area of the city in which the young preacher lived was visited by Asiatic cholera. Many in Spurgeon's congregation were affected, and there was hardly a family in which someone did not get sick, and many died. The young pastor spent most of every day visiting the sick, and there was hardly a day when he did not have to accompany some family to the graveyard.

Spurgeon became physically and emotionally exhausted and sick at heart. He was ready to sink under this heavy load of pastoral care. But as God would have it, one day he was returning home sadly from a funeral when he noticed a sign in a shoemaker's shop on Dover Road. It was in the owner's own handwriting, and it bore these words: "Because thou hast made the LORD, which is my refuge, even the Most High, thy habitation, there shall no evil befall thee, neither shall any plague come nigh thy dwelling," a quotation from Psalm 91:9–10 (KJV).

Spurgeon was deeply and immediately encouraged. He wrote, "The effect upon my heart was immediate. Faith appropriated the passage as her own. I felt secure, refreshed, girt with immortality. I went on with my visitation of the dying in a calm and peaceful spirit; I felt no fear of evil, and I suffered no harm. The providence which moved the tradesman to put those verses in his window I gratefully acknowledge, and in the remembrance of its marvelous power I adore the Lord my God."[5]

Verse 4 contains two appealing images of God's protection: first, that of a mother bird, sheltering and protecting her young ("He will cover you with his feathers, and under his wings you will find refuge") and second, that of a warrior's armor ("his faithfulness will be your shield and rampart"). The exact meaning of the word *rampart* (NIV) is uncertain. The Hebrew word signifies something that is wrapped around a person for his or her protection; hence, it can mean "buckler," "armor," or, as in the NIV, a "rampart" or fortress. It may be that something of each of these ideas is in the Hebrew word.

Jesus appropriated the first of these two images for himself, saying as he looked out over the city of Jerusalem, "O Jerusalem, Jerusalem, you who kill the prophets and stone those sent to you, how often I have longed to gather your children together, as a hen gathers her chicks under her wings, but you were not willing" (Matt. 23:37). Jesus would have saved and sheltered Jerusalem and its inhabitants, but the people were not willing. They would not come to him. They would not "dwell" in the shelter of the Most High. They cried out for his crucifixion instead.

As for the second image, we may recall God's words to Abraham when he was returning from his attack on the kings who had raided Sodom and Gomorrah and carried off Abraham's nephew Lot. Abraham had won the battle, recovering Lot, the women, and their possessions. But Abraham was in danger of retaliation by these kings. It was then that God spoke to him in a vision, saying, "Do not be afraid, Abram. I am your shield, your very great reward" (Gen. 15:1). That is what God will be to us, if we will trust him.

Here is an important question: What exactly is it that is said to be the believer's "shield and rampart" (v. 4). God, of course! But in what respect? The King James Version says, "His *truth* will be your shield and buckler." In my view, the New International Version is richer at this point, for the Hebrew word means more than mere truth. It has to do with God's entire character, described as faithfulness. Still something is lost if we do not also realize that the Hebrew word for faithfulness is based on the word for truth and that what is involved here is God's faithfulness to his promises—that is, to his word. In other words, it is when we believe God's Word and act upon it that we find him to be faithful to what he has promised and learn that he is in truth our shield from dangers and our rampart against enemies.

Verses 7–8 describe thousands falling on either side of those who trust God, noting, "You will only observe with your eyes and see the punishment of the wicked." This interprets the death of the thousands as God's punishment for sin and places the deliverance of God's people in that context. In other words, it is not a promise that those who trust God will never die of disease or even in some military conflict, but that they will not suffer those or any other calamities as God's judgment against them for their sin. Their sin has been atoned for by the blood of Jesus Christ.

Protection from Dangers: The Condition

Much of what is found in the third stanza of this psalm (vv. 9–11) is like what we have seen already. It tells us that "no harm will befall" us and that "no disaster will come near your tent" (v. 10). But there are a few new elements.

One of them, probably the chief idea because it comes first, is that there is a condition to the kind of protection the psalm has been promising—that the individual "make the Most High [his] dwelling" (v. 9). This is more than merely believing in God or coming to God occasionally when danger threatens. It means resting in God continually and trusting him at all times. It means living all of life "in God." Martin Luther wrote that this refers to "one who really dwells and does not merely appear to dwell and does not just imagine that he dwells" in God.[6]

The second new element reinforces the first and, by means of its use in the New Testament, is an illustration of it. It is the reference to angels, the psalmist saying,

> For he will command his angels concerning you
>   to guard you in all your ways;
> they will lift you up in their hands,
>   so that you will not strike your foot against a stone
>   (vv. 11–12).

This is the verse the devil quoted as part of his temptation of Jesus Christ, recorded in Matthew 4:1–11 and Luke 4:1–13. It is the only verse of Scripture actually quoted by the devil, at least that we have a record of. But he misquoted it! He left out "in all your ways"—that is, in the ways marked out for us by God and not our own willful ways. For that was the very essence of the temptation; he wanted Jesus to go his own way rather than trusting God and being contented with God's way, even if it meant going to the cross. The devil wanted Jesus to test God by jumping off a pinnacle of the temple, trusting his Father to send angels to bear him up so he would not be dashed to pieces when he fell and thus impress the people. Jesus replied rightly, saying, "It is also written: 'Do not put the Lord your God to the test'" (Matt. 4:7, quoting Deut. 6:16). Testing God by jumping off a pinnacle of the temple would not be going in the way God had given him to go. It would be the very opposite of trusting God; it would be "baiting" him or "putting him to the test."

The Lord's trust in his Father also resulted in Satan's defeat, another part of the psalm the devil omitted (v. 13). The psalm tells us that if we go in God's way, trusting him to uphold us, then we will "tread upon the lion and the cobra"; we will "trample the great lion and the serpent." The Bible elsewhere describes Satan as "a roaring lion" (1 Peter 5:8) and that "ancient serpent" (Rev. 12:9; 20:2). Jesus triumphed over him by trusting God. Likewise, in Christ the righteous will be victorious over Satan too.

Here is one more thought about this incident. When Jesus replied to Satan, he rejected the temptation to jump from the temple, trusting the angels of God to keep him from being killed. But the angels were there anyway, though invisibly. For after Satan had completed his temptation we are told God's "angels came and attended him" (Matt. 4:11). In other words, God was upholding Jesus even in the temptation.

God's Promises for Those Who Trust Him

The last three verses of this psalm contain a confirming oracle of God in which the controlling pronoun switches from *you,* which dominated in verses 3–13, back to *I,* as in verse 2. Only here the *I* is God himself. In these verses God adds his seal to what the psalmist has been saying. God promises three things to those who trust him.

1. *Protection for the one who is in danger* (v. 14). The psalm speaks throughout of the many dangers that threaten God's people, but its central message is that God will rescue and protect from all such dangers those who trust him. Those who have trusted God know this and praise God constantly for his help and protection.

2. *An answer for the one who is in trouble and prays to God about it* (v. 15). One of the great blessings of following hard after God is knowing that when we call upon him he will hear and answer us. These verses say that God will deliver and honor such a person. They also say that God will be with the believer "in trouble," which is a way of acknowledging that God does not always lift a Christian out of troubles. Sometimes it is his will that we endure them and profit from them. We are told in Romans that we acquire hope, develop character, and learn perseverance from what we suffer (Rom. 5:3–4). When we go through such circumstances, God goes through them with us. He sustains us in our sufferings.

3. *Long life and salvation for the one who seeks God's satisfaction* (v. 16). Long life is a blessing frequently promised to the righteous in the Old Testament (Exod. 20:12; Deut. 30:20; Pss. 21:4; 23:6; Prov. 3:2, 16), but the promise is not necessarily for a prolongation of days but rather for a complete or full life. Here there is the added promise of a "salvation" in heaven, yet to come.

These verses also make a point that has been developed several times already—the promises are for those who trust in or love God. Therefore, they are blessings that some believers miss out on, simply because they are always fretting and do not trust God as they should. Here the psalmist quotes God as saying that the blessings are for those who love God and acknowledge his name (v. 14), call upon him (v. 15), and seek satisfaction in what he alone can provide.

Do you do that? Or are you still trying to find satisfaction in the world? Do you love the world more than you love Jesus? John R. W. Stott reminds us of Romans 8:28, observing that "God is the supreme object of the believer's love as well as faith, and it is to those who love God that the assurance is given that 'in all things God works for their good.'"[7]

Psalm 92

A Psalm for the Sabbath

It is good to praise the LORD
and make music to your name, O Most High,
to proclaim your love in the morning
and your faithfulness at night,
to the music of the ten-stringed lyre
and the melody of the harp. . . .

The righteous will flourish like a palm tree,
they will grow like a cedar of Lebanon;
planted in the house of the LORD,
they will flourish in the courts of our God.
They will still bear fruit in old age,
they will stay fresh and green,
proclaiming, "The LORD is upright;
he is my Rock, and there is no wickedness in him."

verses 1–3, 12–15

In most Reformed circles and in some others there is an ongoing debate about the right way to observe Sunday. Some see it as an extension of the Jewish Sabbath and call for an end to all work, except what are called works of necessity, like emergency medicine and fire fighting. This is called the Puritan view. Others regard Sunday as

753

a day for Christian worship but do not forbid other positive activities. This view is sometimes called the continental understanding of the Sabbath.

I side with the continental view on grounds of the activity associated with the first Lord's Day as recorded in the Gospels. But whatever the right answer to this ongoing debate may be, there can be little disagreement among Christians that Sunday is at least a day to worship God. The psalm we are to study now is the only one in the Psalter specifically designated "for the Sabbath," and it tells us something that it is certainly good to do—to "praise the LORD" and to do so throughout the day from morning until night. So I ask as we start: *How do you approach Sunday?* Do you think of it as a day in which you have to go to church, but the duties of which you try to get over as soon as possible so you can spend the rest of the time with your family or get on to other more enjoyable things? Or do you think of it as a precious day given to you by God in which you can learn about him and so praise him? Is Sunday a trial or a treat? Is it a delight or a deadly duty?

Derek Kidner says, "This *Song for the Sabbath* is proof enough, if such were needed, that the Old Testament sabbath was a day not only for rest but for corporate worship ('a holy convocation,' Lev. 23:3), and intended to be a delight rather than a burden."[1] The rabbis made it into a burden, of course, but Jesus opposed their error, reminding them that "the Sabbath was made for man, not man for the Sabbath" (Mark 2:27). Sunday should be a time for thanksgiving and joyful celebration.

A Psalm for Every Day

This does not mean that we are not to praise God on other days of the week too, for of course we are. The Masoretes had an interesting way of asserting this, for they assigned a specific psalm to each day of the week, every one of which was written to help us praise God—for different things. The specific assignments were as follows:

On the first day, Sunday: Psalm 24

On the second day, Monday: Psalm 48

On the third day, Tuesday: Psalm 82

On the fourth day, Wednesday: Psalm 114

On the fifth day, Thursday: Psalm 81

On the sixth day, Friday: Psalm 93

On the seventh day, Saturday: Psalm 92

If we wanted to do it, we could follow the assignment for Saturday at least, for we have an excellent hymn based on Psalm 92. It is the hymn "How Good It Is to Thank the Lord" by Isaac Watts.

> How good it is to thank the Lord,
> And praise to you, Most High, accord,
> To show your love with morning light.
> And tell your faithfulness each night;
> Yea, good it is your praise to sing,
> And all our sweetest music bring.

Watts's hymn stresses the goodness of praising God constantly.

It is not easy to outline this psalm. Some see it as following a chiastic pattern, keying on verse 8, which stands alone in the middle of the poem. The pattern would be A, B, C, D, C, B, A, in which the first and seventh stanzas have to do with praising God, the second and sixth with the works of God for which he is to be praised, and the third and fifth with the failure of "senseless" men to praise him. The New International Version has four stanzas, with verse 8 treated as an additional one-line center stanza. However, to judge by the subject matter, the three-part outline Kidner proposes is probably better: (1) Tireless Praise (vv. 1–4), (2) Heedless Arrogance (vv. 5–9), and (3) Endless Vitality (vv. 10–15). I am following that division, but I am phrasing the titles of the sections differently.

It Is Good to Praise God

The first verse establishes the theme for the entire psalm, that it is good to praise God:

> It is good to praise the LORD
> and make music to your name, O Most High.

Why is it good to praise God? There are various ways of answering this question. We might reply that it is good because God declares worship to be good, as he does in this psalm. The phrase "it is good" reminds us of God's verdict on his creation found in Genesis 1 (seven times in verses 4, 10, 12, 18, 21, 25, 31). Indeed, the psalm speaks of the created works of God (vv. 4–5) and may even be reflecting on the first chapter of the Bible. Again, praising God is good because it is good for us. It "makes me [us] glad" (v. 4).

Spurgeon had an interesting way of putting this. He said that praise of God is good "ethically, for it is the Lord's right," "emotionally, for it is pleasant to the heart," and "practically, for it leads others to render the same homage."[2]

Yet "good" is too weak in this context, for worshiping God is more beneficial than what we usually imply when we use the word *good*. Some writers call the praise of God "salutary" or "delightful." Luther called it "precious." He said, probably on more than one occasion, "Come, let us sing a psalm and drive away the devil." Worshiping God is a glorious, splendid, delightful, and most reasonable thing to do.

And Enjoy Him Forever

So let me ask: *Does the thought of praising God seem boring to you?* If it does, you should recall that it is for this we were created. The Westminster Shorter Catechism asks as its first question, "What is the chief end of man?" It answers: "Man's chief end is to glorify God and to enjoy him forever."

And the enjoyment of God is important also, for the two go together! In fact, our enjoyment of God is expressed in our praise of God, and when we praise God we do indeed enjoy him. If you do not find the worship of God on Sunday (or at any other time) to be enjoyable, it is not because you have come to know God and have found that he is boring. It is because you do not know him much at all. For the more you know him, the more enjoyable the praise of God will be.

Dr. John Piper is the senior pastor of Bethlehem Baptist Church in Minneapolis, Minnesota, and he has written a book on the enjoyment of God called *Desiring God: Meditations of a Christian Hedonist.* Picking up on the first answer of the Westminster Shorter Catechism, Piper urges Christians to glorify God *by* enjoying him, for that is what God wants and it is both our greatest duty *and* pleasure.

Piper asks,

> Does Christian hedonism put man's pleasure above God's glory? No. It puts man's pleasure in God's glory. Our quest is not merely joy. It is joy *in* God. And there is no way for a Christian to consciously manifest the infinite worth and beauty of God without delighting in him. It is better to say that we pursue our joy *in* God than to simply say that we pursue God. For one can pursue God in ways that do not honor him. . . . The enjoyment of God and the glorification of God are one.[3]

The psalmist would have understood that perfectly, even if we do not, for he reminds us wisely that "it is *good* to praise the LORD and make music to [his] name." Do you understand that? Do you know how good it is?

Here is another question based on these first verses of Psalm 92: *What should we praise God for?* The psalm suggests two things: (1) the steadfast love of God, for that is what the Hebrew word translated "love" in verse 2 *(hesed)* actually means, and (2) God's faithfulness. There are other things for which we will also want to praise God, of course, but those two alone are enough to keep us busy. It is God's steadfast, covenant love that reaches out to us initially to redeem us from sin, and it is his faithfulness that keeps us in that love relationship. As Christians we know both of these to the highest degree in Jesus Christ.

Here is still another question based on these first verses: *How should we praise God?* The psalm answers: joyfully (v. 4) and with instruments (v. 3). In fact, it specifies two of the instruments of that day: "the ten-stringed lyre" and "the harp." I know that there is a tradition in the church that opposes the use of musical instruments in worship, but I do not see how it can stand in the light of these and other Bible passages.

Spurgeon's congregation used only unaccompanied hymns. So it is not surprising that he quotes some who were opposed to instruments. He quotes John Calvin, who said, "From this it appears that the Papists, in employing instrumental music, cannot be said so much to imitate the practice of God's ancient people, as to ape it in a senseless and absurd manner, exhibiting a silly delight in that worship of the Old Testament which was figurative, and terminated with the gospel." Calvin believed that our spiritual worship of Christ today displaces musical instruments.

Spurgeon also quotes John Chrysostom: "Instrumental music was only permitted to the Jews, as sacrifice was, for the heaviness and grossness of their souls." He quotes Andrew Fuller, who wrote, "Instrumental music . . . appears with increasing evidence to be utterly unsuited to the genius of the gospel dispensation."[4] That may be their opinion, but I regard this as merely special pleading to uphold a personal dislike of instrumental music and a preference for unaccompanied singing. For what can possibly be wrong with making a loud noise to the Lord, as the ancients did, as long as we understand what we are doing and are truly praising God? Indeed, how can we fail to worship loudly and with instruments? We should worship God with every possible tool at our disposal.

The Silence of the Senseless

Having said a great deal about the value, reasons for, and methods of worshiping God, the psalm next introduces a contrast, the case of those who, unlike the psalmist, do not know or praise God (vv. 5–9). There are two things wrong with them.

1. *They are like brute beasts.* This is the literal meaning of the phrase "the senseless man." The words mean "the brute man," a man who knows no more of reality than an animal. According to the Bible, men and women are made to know and enjoy God, but when they turn their backs on God, as the unregenerate do, they isolate themselves from all that is spiritual in life and operate on a physical level only. Derek Kidner quotes Samuel Johnson's comment on people who are like this. "It is sad stuff," he said. "It is brutish. If a bull could speak, he might as well exclaim—Here am I with this cow and this grass; what being can enjoy better felicity?"[5]

On a slightly higher note we should remember that this is the inference of Psalm 8, which places man at a mediating point in creation, saying, "You made him a little lower than the heavenly beings and crowned him with glory and honor" (v. 5). By calling him "a little lower than the heavenly beings" rather than "a little higher than the beasts," it indicates that it is man's calling to look up to God and become like God, in whose image he is made. But if he will not look up, the only place he will be able to look is down, and he will begin to behave like an animal. Someone said, "God made man a little lower than the angels, and he has been trying to get lower ever since."

2. *They are wicked in their beastlike behavior.* The second thing that is wrong with those who do not know or praise God is that they are also wicked. This is what the psalmist calls them in verses 7 and 9 and why he writes of their judgment.

> . . . though the wicked spring up like grass
>   and all evildoers flourish,
> they will be forever destroyed. . . .
>
> For surely your enemies, O LORD,
>   surely your enemies will perish;
>   all evildoers will be scattered.

This means that the failure of the "senseless" to worship God is not merely a case of their being blind to spiritual realities, though they are. Theirs is a willing blindness; they are blind because they choose not to see. The reason they do not know and will not praise God is that they do not want to know or praise him. They actually hate him because *he* is God, and they are not.

The Psalmist's Final Testimony

Having made a contrast between himself and those who do not know and worship God and having shown the destiny of the latter, the psalmist now picks up on the destiny of these wicked persons and makes a still further contrast between the destiny of the wicked, which he has just mentioned, and the end of the righteous (vv. 10–15). The wicked will wither like grass, but the righteous will flourish like a palm tree and a cedar of Lebanon.

But first a testimony! God has blessed the psalmist with anointing and with preservation from his enemies. He wants to say this. He does not want to forget it, and he does not want others to miss knowing about it, either: "You have exalted my horn like that of a wild ox; fine oils have been poured over me. My eyes have seen the defeat of my adversaries; my ears have heard the rout of my wicked foes" (vv. 10–11). But what is true of him is true for all the righteous (vv. 12–15), and it is on this encouraging note that he brings his composition to a close. He states three things about those who truly know and worship God.

1. *They will flourish like a palm tree and grow strong like a cedar of Lebanon* (vv. 12–13). This was true of Moses in a physical sense, for although he lived to be 120 years old, "yet his eyes were not weak nor his strength gone" (Deut. 34:7). Not all are blessed with physical strength to the end of their lives, of course. David became feeble in his old age. But that is not what these verses are about primarily. They are talking about what we would call "strength in the Lord," spiritual strength. It is what Paul was writing about when he said, "Though outwardly we are wasting away, yet inwardly we are being renewed day by day" (2 Cor. 4:16). That is an internal, spiritual strength that only those who have grown old walking with Jesus and trusting Jesus know. It goes beyond all human understanding.

2. *They will be fruitful even into old age.* Not only will believers such as this be spiritually strong, they will be fruitful too (v. 14). That is, they will testify to the greatness and goodness of God, and God will use their testimonies to bring others to faith in Jesus Christ. When we are young we are often caught up with this world's concerns and miss many opportunities to bear fruit for our Lord. But as we grow old and the time when we shall meet him face-to-face and give an accounting for the deeds done in the body grows ever closer, we focus our strength and make our more limited energies count all the more strongly for him.

3. *Their testimony will remain firm to the very end of their lives.* Finally, says the psalmist, the righteous will maintain their testimony to the very end, proclaiming, "The LORD is upright; he is my Rock, and there is no wickedness in him" (v. 15). J. J. Stewart Perowne says, "The flourishing of the workers of iniquity has been but for a moment (vv. 7, 9, 11); the joy and prosperity of the righteous is forever."[6]

At this point the psalm comes full circle, ending on the idea of the righteous praising God. It has been introduced as a song "for the Sabbath day." So let me combine these ideas, asking: If you cannot praise God on the Lord's day, if you find it tedious and troublesome, how are you going to keep on doing it into old age?

Earlier I wrote of Moses, whose "eyes were not weak, nor his strength gone" (Deut. 34:7), even though he lived to be 120 years old. He praised God in his old age, finishing the last book of the Pentateuch with both a song and a sermon (Deuteronomy 32–33). Jacob also praised God in his old age. In fact, what he spoke in his old age were probably the most spiritual and helpful words he ever uttered (Genesis 49). Joseph too gave a strong old-age testimony. He spoke of God's sovereignty, telling his brothers, "You intended to harm me, but God intended it for good" (Gen. 50:20). Paul wrote some of his most helpful epistles not long before he died. The Book of Revelation was written from exile on the island of Patmos by John when he was a very old man.

Will that be your experience, assuming God will allow you to live so long? Will you be able to praise God then? Much of the answer depends on what you are willing to do now. What is your testimony now? Can you say what the righteous of the Lord do at the end of Psalm 92?

> The LORD is upright;
> he is my Rock, and there is no wickedness in him.

I hope you will be able to say that, for it is a strong and very much needed testimony. Unfortunately, it is far from the kind of carping words I hear from many Christians today. Maybe they do not know God very well. Maybe they do not know how to praise him. Probably they need practice.

Psalm 93

A Psalm to God as King

The LORD reigns, he is robed in majesty;
the LORD is robed in majesty
and is armed with strength.
The world is firmly established;
it cannot be moved.
Your throne was established long ago;
you are from all eternity.

The seas have lifted up, O LORD,
the seas have lifted up their voice;
the seas have lifted up their pounding waves.
Mightier than the thunder of the great waters,
mightier than the breakers of the sea—
the LORD on high is mighty.

Your statutes stand firm;
holiness adorns your house
for endless days, O LORD.

verses 1–5

Psalm 93 is the first of a group of eight psalms dealing with the kingly reign of God, a "theocracy." The word *theocracy* was coined by Josephus, the Jewish historian, not long after the birth, death, and resurrection of Jesus Christ (*Against Apion*, 2, 17) to describe the distinct quality of Israel's government. Governments of other nations were monarchies, oligarchies, or democracies, but Israel was a theocracy, said Josephus. Monarchy is a form of government in which rule is in the hands of a single individual, a king. Oligarchy is government by an elite few, which is what the Greek word *oligoi* ("few") means. Democracy is government by the *demos,* or people. *Theos* means "god." So a theocracy is the direct rule of a people by God as king.

Franz Delitzsch gave theocracy a formal biblical definition when he wrote, "Theocracy . . . is a reciprocal relationship between God and men, exalted above these intermediary forms [monarchies, oligarchies, or democracies], which had its first manifest beginning when Jahve became Israel's King (Deut. 33:5; cf. Exod. 15:18), and which will be finally perfected by its breaking through this national self-limitation when the King of Israel becomes King of the whole world."[1] The ultimate fulfillment of the promise inherent in the word *theocracy* is the present and coming reign of our great Lord and King, Jesus Christ.

Psalm 93 describes a theocracy, as do the seven psalms that follow it.[2] The words *Yahweh melek* ("Jehovah reigns" or "Jehovah is king") are the watchwords of these theocratic psalms. But the theocracy they describe is more than Josephus had in mind when he invented the word. He meant the direct rule of Israel by Israel's God. The psalms describe God's rule of the entire earth and indeed the universe.

H. C. Leupold wrote, "This brief psalm is mighty in utterance, colorful in language, and a strong incentive to faith."[3] In one sense, Psalm 93 is an unfolding of the truth in just one verse of Psalm 92: "But you, O LORD, are exalted forever" (v. 8). Yet what does that mean? How is God exalted? The answer is in the psalms we are to study now.

Psalm 93 has three parts, well marked by the stanzas of the New International Version: (1) the reign of the sovereign God (vv. 1–2), (2) the turmoil of the world over which God reigns (vv. 3–4), and (3) two important characteristics of God's kingdom (v. 5).

The Reign of the Sovereign God

The first two verses of the psalm speak of the nature of God's reign, introducing four characteristics of God's kingly rule, which are at the same time four important attributes of God. These are stated in strong poetic language, involving blatant repetitions in nearly every case, a particularly bold form of Hebrew parallelism.

1. *The majesty of God.* The first characteristic of God's kingdom and indeed of God himself is majesty. Majesty is a hard idea to define, but it has to do with dignity, authority of sovereign power, stateliness, and grandeur. It is the proper characteristic of earthly monarchs, who have often gone to great lengths to enhance the impression of their majesty by multiplications of trap-

pings of power. But it is supremely the attribute of him who is the Monarch over all and who does not need to multiply the trappings of his power.

Majesty is the dominant element in the visions of God in his glory seen in both the Old and New Testaments. It inspires awe in mere human beings and often leaves them speechless or nearly dead. Isaiah saw the majesty of God in the vision recorded in chapter six of his prophecy:

> In the year that King Uzziah died, I saw the Lord seated on a throne, high and exalted, and the train of his robe filled the temple. Above him were ser- aphs, each with six wings: With two wings they covered their faces, with two they covered their feet, and with two they were flying. And they were calling to one another:
>
> > "Holy, holy, holy is the LORD Almighty;
> >   the whole earth is full of his glory."
>
> At the sound of their voices the doorposts and thresholds shook and the temple was filled with smoke (Isa. 6:1–4).

Isaiah was so overcome with a sense of God's majesty that he cried out, "Woe to me! . . . I am ruined! For I am a man of unclean lips, and I live among a people of unclean lips, and my eyes have seen the King, the LORD Almighty" (v. 5). Majesty is an attribute that links God's holiness and God's sovereignty.

2. *The power of God.* The author of Psalm 93 was so impressed with majesty as a characteristic of God's kingdom that he repeated the idea twice: first, "the LORD reigns, he is robed in majesty"; second, "the LORD is robed in majesty." But even that did not seem to satisfy him, so he adds in a third par- allel statement in this verse, "and is armed with strength." He means that the majesty of God is also a majesty of power. It is not a mere show of sovereignty, as has often been the case with human rulers. It is an actual sovereignty, as the psalmist will show more completely in the next stanza. In other words, when he says, as he does at the start of the psalm, "The LORD reigns," he means that he does actually reign, not merely that he seems to. He really is sovereign.

3. *The immutability of God.* The third characteristic of God's rule, which is also an attribute of God, is immutability. That is the proper term for what the writer means by "established" in verses 1–2. The second part of verse 1 says that "the world is firmly established." That is, "it cannot be moved." Despite appearances, nothing is able to move or, even less, destroy God's creation but God himself. However, the only reason why the world is estab- lished is because God himself is established or immutable, which is what verse 2 is about.

> Your throne was established long ago;
>   you are from all eternity.

This quality is one that separates God from even the highest of his creatures. God is unchangeable, but no other part of creation is. If we think of the material universe, it is clear that it is in a state of constant change, and not merely in the cyclical sense envisioned by the Greeks—that is, that all things eventually return to what they were. The universe changes in the sense that it is constantly decaying or running down. Its decay may be spread over so long a time span that it is almost unnoticed by us, but it is nevertheless running down. The sun is cooling and will eventually die out. The varied and abundant resources of the earth are exhaustible and will run out. Species have become extinct. Each of us matures, grows old, and dies.

Nor is human nature immutable. On the contrary, it is restless and constantly changing. Jude speaks of the wicked as "clouds without rain, blown along by the wind; autumn trees, without fruit and uprooted . . . wild waves of the sea, foaming up their shame; wandering stars, for whom the blackest darkness has been reserved forever" (Jude 12–13). No better illustration of the variableness of human nature exists than the inhabitants of Jerusalem who one week were hailing Jesus as their king ("Hosanna! . . . Blessed is the King of Israel!") and the next week were calling out for his crucifixion (John 12:13; 19:15).

Ah, but God is unchangeable. And the characteristics of his kingdom do not change either. He rules as well today as he ever did, and he will rule forever.

4. *The eternity of God.* That leads to the fourth of the attributes of God mentioned in the opening stanza of Psalm 93, God's eternity. This is a difficult idea to put into a single English word, but it means that God is, that he has always been and that he will always be, and that he is everywhere the same in his eternal being. We find this idea throughout the Bible, from the Book of Genesis to the very end. Abraham called God "the Eternal God" (Gen. 21:33). Just three psalms before this Moses wrote:

> Lord, you have been our dwelling place
> > throughout all generations.
> Before the mountains were born
> > or you brought forth the earth and the world,
> > from everlasting to everlasting you are God (Ps. 90:1–2).

Revelation describes God as the "Alpha and the Omega, the beginning and the end" (Rev. 21:6; see 1:8; 22:13). The angels that are before his throne cry out continually, "Holy, holy, holy, is the Lord God Almighty, who was and is and is to come" (Rev. 4:8).

This means two things for us. First, God can be trusted to remain as he reveals himself to be. He will be at the end of our days what he was at the beginning. He will not change his character or break his word. Second, God is inescapable. We may try to ignore him, but ignoring him will not work. One day we will have to give an accounting to him before whom all hearts are open and all desires known.

The Surging World

When he was introducing the idea of God's immutability in verses 1–2, the psalmist said that "the world is firmly established" because the throne of God is established. But is it really the case that the world is established? It does not seem to be. In fact, when I was writing about God's immutability, I pointed out that everything changes but God. That thought must have occurred to the psalmist too. For immediately after writing about the immutability of God's throne in verse 2, he writes a stanza about the surging, pounding, changing character of this world.

The image he uses is a common one, but it is one that has led to several different interpretations. It is that of the sea, which is always in a state of fluctuation.

> The seas have lifted up, O LORD,
>   the seas have lifted up their voice;
>   the seas have lifted up their pounding waves (v. 3).

There is a popular theory among Old Testament scholars that this image has to do with Yahweh's triumph over the primordial powers of chaos. They say this not because of anything in the psalm itself but because of parallels in Ugaritic and Babylonian poetry. In the Babylonian creation myth there is an account of a cosmic struggle between the god Marduk and Tiamat, the old sea-water goddess.[4] The problem with this theory is that it has almost no foundation in anything Jewish. The Jewish Scriptures just do not contain mythological elements of this type.

In all probability verse 3 has to do either with God's sovereignty over nature itself or with his sovereignty over the nations and world history. If it is the first of these two possibilities, the thought would follow naturally on verse 1, which spoke of the world being "firmly established" by God. It would be a way of acknowledging that the world of nature is indeed in constant turmoil but that God is sovereign over even this change. It would be an Old Testament answer to the fundamental question of Greek philosophy: Why is there order in the universe even though all things are in a state of constant change? The Greeks got close to the answer when they said that it is because the change is not random but is instead ordered change and that it is ordered because an ordering law or word (*logos*) of God stands behind it. The psalmist would be saying that it is because Jehovah himself stands behind it. In other words, the biblical answer is not the philosophical idea of law or order, but of providence. God is involved in his creation. He sustains and controls it moment by moment. He is never the absentee landlord. He is always in charge.

On the other hand, it is hard to think that this is all the psalmist has in mind when he writes of the surging, pounding seas, particularly when we remember that in the Old Testament the ocean with its restless waves is often a symbol of the vacillating world of the surrounding Gentile nations. Examples would be Isaiah 17:12 ("Oh, the raging of many nations—they rage like the raging sea!") and Jeremiah 6:23 and 50:42 ("They sound like the roaring sea as they ride on their horses").[5] Franz Delitzsch argues for this view: "The sea with its mighty mass of waters, with the constant unrest of its waves, with its ceaseless pressing against the solid land and foaming against the rocks, is an emblem of the Gentile world alienated from and at enmity with God."[6] Tate also sees this as a possibility: "If the 'floods' are translated into historical reference, they could refer to the 'roaring' of hostile nations against Yahweh and Israel."[7]

If the seas represent the Gentile nations, as I think they do, then the second stanza is an assertion of God's sovereignty over every historical development. He is king not just of the cosmos, which has been asserted earlier, but of human beings too.

Two Characteristics of God's Rule

One of the greatest things about the Bible is its unexpected character, for often just when we think things are coming to an end we suddenly come to something that is quite fresh and that stretches our thinking a bit further than we had expected to go. That is the case with verse 5, which is the final stanza of the psalm. What we might have expected is an encouragement to the believer in God to stand firm, or perhaps a repeated word of praise to God as king. Instead we find two more unanticipated characteristics of God's kingly rule: that it is a kingdom of law and that it is a kingdom of holiness or justice.

1. *A rule of law.* Thus far we have been thinking of the theocratic rule of God as being a rule of power. But God's rule is not a rule of power alone. The Greek word for power is *kratos,* which is where the words *democracy* ("power in the hands of the people") and *theocracy* ("power in the hands of God") come from. It is also a rule of law, which is what the important word *statutes* in verse 5 refers to. God's statutes are his decrees, above all his laws, as in Psalm 119:2.

> Blessed are they who keep his statutes
> and seek him with all their heart.[8]

What this means is that God rules his people by his Word. It is true that he rules over the world and history. But that is a sovereign rule, independent of and somewhat removed from us or what we do. By reminding us that the statutes of God "stand firm," like the world and even the throne of God itself, the psalmist is saying that those of us who profess to know God and confess him as our God must know and obey his statutes too—if we would be actually ruled by him.

Let me put it another way. The Lord Jesus Christ rules his church by guiding its destiny sovereignly, of course. But the way he specifically rules his people within his church is by the teaching of the Scriptures. It is there that we learn what he would have us do and what he would have us be.

There is an important general sovereignty possessed by Jesus. Revelation says, "The kingdom of the world has become the kingdom of our Lord and of his Christ, and he will reign for ever and ever" (Rev. 11:15). There is also a specific rule of Jesus over his people, which has to do with his direct commandments for us. When the apostle Paul met Jesus Christ on the way to Damascus, the first thing that happened after he discovered that Jesus was the one he had been persecuting was that Jesus told him what to do: "Get up and stand on your feet. I have appeared to you to appoint you as a servant and as a witness of what you have seen of me and what I will show you" (Acts 26:16). We cannot claim to be ruled by Jesus Christ unless we know what he has told us to do in the Bible and are doing it.

2. *A rule of justice.* There are two obvious ways that human rule can be perverted. It can be by the whim of those in power and not by law. Or even if it is by law, it can be by unjust laws that exist only to legitimize the oppression of the weak by those more powerful. God is guilty of neither of those perversions. First, his rule is by law. Second, it is according to holiness or justice, for the law of God is perfectly upright, which is what the last sentence of the psalm asserts: "Holiness adorns your house for endless days, O LORD" (v. 5).

Everything associated with God is holy, from which it follows that we must be holy too. If we are not holy, how can we adorn the house of God? We cannot! We do the very opposite. We dishonor it—and the God we profess to serve. If we strive to live holy lives, as we must, then we honor God and prove that he is indeed ruling us as his holy people. Peter wrote, "But you are a chosen people, a royal priesthood, a holy nation, a people belonging to God, that you may declare the praises of him who called you out of darkness into his wonderful light" (1 Peter 2:9).

Psalm 94

All Hearts Open, All Desires Known

O Lord, the God who avenges,
    O God who avenges, shine forth.
Rise up, O Judge of the earth;
    pay back to the proud what they deserve.
How long will the wicked, O Lord,
    how long will the wicked be jubilant?

They pour out arrogant words;
    all the evildoers are full of boasting.
They crush your people, O Lord;
    they oppress your inheritance.
They slay the widow and the alien;
    they murder the fatherless.
They say, "The Lord does not see;
    the God of Jacob pays no heed."

Take heed, you senseless ones among the people;
    you fools, when will you become wise?
Does he who implanted the ear not hear?
    Does he who formed the eye not see?
Does he who disciplines nations not punish?
    Does he who teaches man lack knowledge?
The Lord knows the thoughts of man;
    he knows that they are futile.

verses 1–11

767

There are times when the wicked seem to have things all their own way," says Charles Haddon Spurgeon in a sermon on Psalm 94.[1] That is never entirely the case, of course. The wicked have their troubles too, including problems dealing with one another. But they do seem to prosper, and they certainly oppress those who are weaker than they are and take advantage of them. The earth is not a place for perfect justice.

Believers should not be shocked by this situation. Spurgeon said,

> The righteous need not wonder that they suffer now, for that has been the lot of God's people all along, and there have been certain times in human history when God has seemed to be altogether deaf to the cries of his suffering people. Remember the martyr-age, and the days of the Covenanters, who were hunted upon the mountains like the partridge. You must not wonder if the easy places of the earth are not yours, and if the sentinel's stern duties should fall to your lot. It is so, and it must be, for God has so ordained it.[2]

Nevertheless, we should not be indifferent to the evil. We should ask God to punish sin and avenge the righteous, which is what Psalm 94 does—at length and in memorable language.

Psalm 94 is thought to be an interruption in the block of eight psalms dealing with Jehovah as king, but this is probably not right. Although the psalm does not call God king specifically, it does deal with one aspect of a king's work, which is to render righteous judgment. In the ancient world the offices of king and judge were frequently one. Recognizing this as true, Marvin E. Tate includes Psalm 94 in this block along with Psalm 92, saying, "Both psalms seem to deal with a current situation among the people which is keeping them from recognizing the kingship of Yahweh, set forth in Psalms 93, 95–99."[3]

The outline is exceptionally easy, and the New International Version has it right except for the possible reassignment of verse 3 to the second rather than the first stanza. There are six stanzas in all.

Here Comes the Judge

The first stanza is a call for God to arise in judgment against the "proud" who crush or oppress God's people (vv. 1–2). If verse 3 belongs with this stanza (probably even if it does not), the complaint is not that God is unjust or uncaring but only that he is apparently slow to act. As Derek Kidner puts it, "There is no room for the crippling suspicion that God, perhaps, is blind (7) or has done a deal with darkness (20). Nothing has changed the Sun or corrupted the Judge: it is simply that the night is long (1b, 2a)."[4] In other words, it is the problem with which we began: In this world, for now, there often seems to be very little justice.

The problem some people will have with these verses is that they invoke the idea of vengeance.

> O LORD, the God who avenges,
>   O God who avenges, shine forth.
> Rise up, O Judge of the earth;
>   pay back to the proud what they deserve.

The reason such people have this problem is that they do not distinguish between vengeance and revenge. Dr. Samuel Johnson, the maker of the first great English dictionary, made the distinction well when he said, "Revenge is an act of passion, vengeance of justice; injuries are revenged, crimes are avenged."[5] In other words, revenge is a response to personal injury while vengeance is a function of legitimate judicial authority. This is why Paul writes about both as he does in Romans 12: "As far as it depends on you, live at peace with everyone. Do not take revenge, my friends, but leave room for God's wrath, for it is written: 'It is mine to avenge; I will repay,' says the Lord" (Rom. 12:18–19; quoting Deut. 32:35). The reason why vengeance belongs to God and not man is that in man our emotions usually cause it to degenerate into mere revenge.

Vengeance is proper to God. It is a function of his perfect justice. Alexander Maclaren writes, "There are times when no thought of God is so full of strength as that he is 'the God of recompenses,' as Jeremiah calls him (51:56). . . . They who have no profound loathing of sin, or who have never felt the crushing weight of legalized wickedness, may shrink from such aspirations as the psalmist's, and brand them as ferocious; but hearts longing for the triumph of righteousness will not take offence at them."[6]

Even more, avenging justice from God is what everyone should *desire* when they observe terrible wrongs being done. John Milton heard about the massacre of entire Protestant families at Piedmont in northern Italy in the seventeenth century and wrote about it, drawing on Psalm 94. The poem began:

> Avenge, O Lord, thy slaughtered Saints, whose bones
>   Lie scattered on the Alpine mountains cold. . . .

Even closer to Psalm 94 is a hymn that we sometimes sing. The first stanza goes:

> O Lord, thou Judge of all the earth,
> To whom all vengeance doth belong,
> Arise and show thy glories forth,
> Requite the proud, condemn the wrong.

It is a way of confessing rightly that we stand on the side of justice with God and long for the day when the arrogant people of the world will be punished for their crimes against the weak.

The Boast of the Arrogant

If verse 3 belongs with the second stanza, as I believe it does, then the problem that is disturbing the psalmist is the jubilant boasting of the arrogant, who do not believe God sees what they are doing (vv. 3–7).

They are oppressing the weak, defined specifically as the widow, the alien, and the fatherless. In each case, these are people who have little means of self-defense. The widow has no husband to provide for her. The alien has limited rights in a foreign country under foreign laws. The orphan has no father to protect him. These were all weak, so they became the prey of the arrogant. And the arrogant were not even ashamed of what they were doing! On the contrary, they were proud of being able to do it. They were also convinced that God did not even see their wickedness. They stole and got away with it, so they concluded that God had not observed them. They said, "The LORD does not see; the God of Jacob pays no heed" (v. 7).

It is true that the Lord does not seem to see, at least in the short run. This is what the psalm is dealing with when it asks God to intervene and take vengeance.

A Warning for Fools

In the meantime, the psalmist boldly warns the arrogant oppressors of this world, whom he calls fools (vv. 8–11). He does it by a sharp series of rhetorical questions that remind us of Amos's questions in chapter 3 of his prophecy ("Do two walk together unless they have agreed to do so? Does a lion roar in the thicket when he has no prey? . . . When disaster comes to a city, has not the LORD caused it?" vv. 3–4, 6). Psalm 94 asks,

> Does he who implanted the ear not hear?
> Does he who formed the eye not see?
> Does he who disciplines nations not punish?
> Does he who teaches man lack knowledge? (vv. 9–10).

The conclusion of the psalmist's rhetorical questions is that "the LORD knows the thoughts of man" (v. 11). God is omniscient. He has to be if he is God. Therefore, anyone who thinks that he or she is getting away with anything just because judgment is not immediate is like a senseless brute, a fool. A man would have to be a fool to think that the all-seeing God does not see or that the Judge of all the earth will not judge justly at the proper time.

Moreover, according to verse 11, God does not only know the thoughts of man, he also "knows that they are futile." This is not a statement against the value of human thought itself, for the psalmist has just appealed to the arrogant to think rightly by his questions. It is a comment on the folly of supposing that God does not see or care what one is doing. It is the folly of acting as though there is no God (see Psalms 14 and 53). Paul quotes this verse in 1 Corinthians 3:20 to prove that "the wisdom of this world is foolishness in God's sight" (1 Cor. 3:19).

H. C. Leupold says, "There has, perhaps, never been a more devastating demonstration of the foolish thinking which men occasionally become guilty of when they imagine that the Lord is not aware of what they are doing."[7] He is right. But how often we all make that very foolish error.

The rabbis said that the three best safeguards against falling into sin are to remember: (1) that there is an ear that hears everything, (2) that there is an eye that sees everything, and that (3) there is a hand that writes everything into the Book of Knowledge which shall be opened at the judgment.[8]

The Blessing of God's Discipline

In the meantime, what are the righteous to think? The psalmist has asked God to rise up and execute justice. He has described the crimes of the arrogant that he is asking God to avenge. He has warned the arrogant. But what of those who are oppressed? What about the righteous? In this stanza the tone of the psalm becomes quieter as the psalmist addresses these people (vv. 12–15), assuring them that the evils they endure are for their discipline in the school of faith and that righteous judgment of oppressors will surely be provided by God in the end.

Verse 12 speaks of "discipline," but this is not discipline that is a punishment for sin. It is the discipline of a hard life that causes us to turn to God to learn more about him, which is why the psalm links discipline with being taught from God's law. Four things are promised to God's people in these verses.

1. *Relief from days of trouble* (v. 13). The upright do have trouble, as the psalm and common experience both teach. But the trouble is never utterly unmitigated or unrelieved. God provides relief from trouble in his time, and in any case he is always with his people when they are called upon to go through it. Jesus foretold trouble for the preachers of the gospel, but he also said, "Surely I am with you always, to the very end of the age" (Matt. 28:20).

2. *Eventual punishment for the wicked* (v. 13). Then too, not only does God provide relief for the righteous, he also assures them that those who oppress them will be punished in due time. In other words, "a pit" is being dug for them, and they will surely fall into it. Elsewhere in the psalms it is said that the wicked dig the pit themselves—for others, but that they themselves fall in (Pss. 7:15; 9:15; 35:7–8).

3. *The steadfast faithfulness of God* (v. 14). The third promise is that God will not reject his people or forsake his inheritance. He may seem to do this at times, when deliverance is delayed. But his people are never abandoned in actuality. Paul told the Romans, "We know that in all things God works for the good of those who love him, who have been called according to his purpose" (Rom. 8:28).

4. *The final triumph of righteousness* (v. 15). Finally, there is a promise that judgment will again be established in righteousness. This may refer to times

of moral renewal in Israel or in some other nation, for times like this do come. But in the ultimate sense it must refer to the day when the righteous kingdom of the Lord Jesus Christ will be set up. It will be when the Almighty God will "make the nations [his] inheritance, the ends of the earth [his] possession" (Ps. 2:8), when

> . . . at the name of Jesus every knee should bow,
> in heaven and on earth and under the earth,
> and every tongue confess that Jesus Christ is Lord,
> to the glory of God the Father (Phil. 2:10–11).

Where do the righteous learn about these things? Where do they find such precious promises? In God's law (v. 12). They are sustained in life's troubles by the Bible. Is that where you go when life becomes difficult for you or when you are called to endure something hard for Jesus Christ? The author of Psalm 119 wrote, "Though rulers sit together and slander me, your servant will meditate on your decrees. Your statutes are my delight; they are my counselors" (vv. 23–24). God will provide wonderful comfort for you through Scripture if you read it.

God Is the Answer

Having assured the righteous of things God will do for them, the writer now adds a word of personal testimony as if to say that what he has been promising to others he has proved true himself (vv. 16–19). In words that recall Psalm 73, he says that his foot was slipping (v. 18; see Ps. 73:2) but that God reached out to support him at nearly the last possible moment and provided comfort.

> When I said, "My foot is slipping,"
> your love, O LORD, supported me.
> When anxiety was great within me,
> your consolation brought joy to my soul (vv. 18–19).

What is special about this stanza is the psalmist's insistence that God was the only one who did this. It is not that he did not look for others. He did. He looked around for someone who would "take a stand for me against evildoers" (v. 16). But there was no one.

Have you ever felt like that? I am sure you have. It is not the way it is meant to be. Christians are to stand alongside one another to help one another and oppose wrongdoing together. But that does not always happen. When Paul was in his last imprisonment he wrote that everyone had abandoned him: all those in Asia (2 Tim. 1:15) and Demas, "because he loved this world" (2 Tim. 4:10). Indeed, "At my first defense, no one came to my support, but everyone deserted me" (v. 16). Nevertheless, he said, "The

Lord stood at my side and gave me strength" (v. 17). If you feel abandoned, you should know that God will do exactly that for you.

The Just Shall Live by Faith

The last stanza of Psalm 94 gets back to where it started, with God as the Judge of all the earth (vv. 20–23). The corrupt judgment thrones of this earth cannot be allied with the upright throne of heaven. Thus the psalmist looks for the day when the Judge of the earth will rise to destroy the wicked for their sins against the righteous.

In the meantime, what shall the righteous do? The answer here is the same as it is everywhere in Scripture: The righteous shall live by faith in God. This is what the psalmist is affirming when he says as a further word of personal testimony, "The LORD has become my fortress, and my God the rock in whom I take refuge" (v. 22).

It is hard to reach this point of the psalm without thinking of the minor prophet Habakkuk, from whom the words "the righteous will live by his faith" come (Hab. 2:4). Habakkuk lived in an age of moral and spiritual decline, and God answered his prayers for Israel by saying that he was going to judge the people for their sins. Moreover, he was going to judge them by sending ruthless hordes of Babylonians to invade the land and overthrow the kingdom. This was a terrible thing to be told, and it was very frightening for Habakkuk. Many would be killed in this invasion. Women would be violated, infants slaughtered. How could those who acknowledged God survive such terrifying times?

The answer God gave to Habakkuk was, "The righteous will live by his faith." And that is exactly what Habakkuk learned to do. Disturbed and fearful as he was—so much so that his "heart pounded," his "lips quivered," "decay crept into [his] bones," and his "legs trembled" (Hab. 3:16)—he learned to fix his soul in God and so pass through the trouble. Habakkuk's final glorious testimony is in these words:

> Though the fig tree does not bud
>   and there are no grapes on the vines,
> though the olive crop fails
>   and the fields produce no food,
> though there are no sheep in the pen
>   and no cattle in the stalls,
> yet I will rejoice in the LORD,
>   I will be joyful in God my Savior (Hab. 3:17–18).

The wicked rejoice in their sin, saying, "The LORD does not see" (Ps. 94:7). The righteous rejoice in God, who does see and who will both punish sin and vindicate the righteous.

Psalm 95

How to Worship God

Come, let us sing for joy to the LORD;
  let us shout aloud to the Rock of our salvation.
Let us come before him with thanksgiving
  and extol him with music and song.

For the LORD is the great God,
  the great King above all gods.
In his hand are the depths of the earth,
  and the mountain peaks belong to him.
The sea is his, for he made it,
  and his hands formed the dry land.

Come, let us bow down in worship,
  let us kneel before the LORD our Maker;
for he is our God
  and we are the people of his pasture,
  the flock under his care.

Today, if you hear his voice,
  do not harden your hearts as you did at Meribah,
  as you did that day at Massah in the desert,
where your fathers tested and tried me,
  though they had seen what I did.
For forty years I was angry with that generation;
  I said, "They are a people whose hearts go astray,
  and they have not known my ways."
So I declared on oath in my anger,
  "They shall never enter my rest."

verses 1–11

Ｉt is time to rediscover worship. John R. W. Stott, the former rector of All Souls Church in London, writes that "true worship is the highest and noblest activity of which man, by the grace of God, is capable."[1] But much of what takes place in our churches today is not worship at all, and many who sincerely desire to worship God do not know how to go about it.

A. W. Tozer pondered the problem:

> Thanks to our splendid Bible societies and to other effective agencies for the dissemination of the Word, there are today many millions of people who hold "right opinions," probably more than ever before in the history of the church. Yet I wonder if there was ever a time when true spiritual worship was at a lower ebb. To great sections of the church the art of worship has been lost entirely, and in its place has come that strange and foreign thing called the "program." This word has been borrowed from the stage and applied with sad wisdom to the type of public service which now passes for worship among us.[2]

Today many do not even hold those "right opinions." So the situation is worse than it was when Tozer wrote about it fifty years ago.

Psalm 95 tells us how to worship. Indeed, it does more. It is a call to worship; it explains how and why we should worship; and it warns of what can happen if we do not worship but harden our hearts instead. Charles Haddon Spurgeon wrote, "It has about it a ring like that of the church bells, and like the bells it sounds both merrily and solemnly, at first ringing out a lively peal, and then dropping into a funeral knell as if tolling at the funeral of the generation which perished in the wilderness."[3]

The church has used the first part of the psalm as a call to worship from at least the fourth century. In many circles it is known as the *Venite,* from the Latin word for "come" with which it begins.

The Joy of Worship

This bright psalm starts with a call to joyful worship (vv. 1–2), appropriately so, since, as it says, God is the "Rock of our salvation."

> Come, let us sing for joy to the Lord;
>   let us shout aloud to the Rock of our salvation.
> Let us come before him with thanksgiving
>   and extol him with music and song.

There are other ways to worship, of course. We can worship silently or even with sighs or tears. But a natural and proper way to worship is with joy and enthusiasm.

Already in these studies I have had occasion to refer to C. S. Lewis's help-ful insights into the exuberance of Jewish worship. Lewis does not suppose that these exuberant forms of worship were necessarily better than ours, but they did have something we lack or at least attain to only in very special moments. He calls it the ancient Jews' "appetite" for God:

> These old poets do not seem to think that they are meritorious or pious for having such feelings; nor, on the other hand, that they are privileged in being given the grace to have them. They are at once less priggish about it than the worst of us and less humble—one might almost say, less sur-prised—than the best of us. It has all the cheerful spontaneity of a natural, even a physical desire. It is gay and jocund. They are glad and rejoice (Ps. 9:2). Their fingers itch for the harp (Ps. 43:4), for the lute and the harp—wake up, lute and harp!—(Ps. 57:9); let's have a song, bring the tam-bourine, bring the "merry harp with the lute," we're going to sing merrily and make a cheerful noise (Ps. 81:1, 2). Noise, you may well say, mere music is not enough. Let everyone, even the benighted gentiles, clap their hands (Ps. 47:1). Let us have clashing cymbals, not only well tuned, but *loud,* and dances too (Ps. 150:5).[4]

Psalm 95 suggests some of the forms of worship we can enjoy.

1. *Singing.* There are many kinds of worship, just as there are many styles of music. But it is no accident that biblical worship, in its Old Testament, New Testament, and subsequent church forms, includes much singing. Singing expresses human thought emotionally, and Christianity is a feeling religion. More particularly, singing expresses joy, and the Bible's religion at its heart is joyful. True, there is sorrow for sin. There is empathy for those who are deprived or suffering. But there is also joy in our salvation and enthusiastic praise of God, who has provided it for us.

2. *Shouting.* Most of us probably have more trouble with shouting than with anything else in this list, and it is fine if we do not shout. But we should remember that some ecclesiastical traditions do shout, like charismatics, for instance. In other services people at least say, "Amen."

3. *Music.* Unaccompanied singing is music, but that is not what the psalmist has in mind here, since he writes of extolling God both "with music and song." This psalm does not mention the instruments that might have been used to make such worship music, but other psalms do. Psalm 150, for example, lists trumpets, harps, lyres, tambourines, strings, flutes, and cymbals. If the ancients had guitars, organs, and electronic keyboards, I am sure they would have been included. No one has to use musical instruments, and worship without instruments is worship too. Also, instru-mental music can degenerate into mere performance, just as singing can. But the point both I and the psalm are making is that it is right and natu-ral to use every musical means to extol God. If we can have a whole orches-tra, let's use the orchestra.

4. *Words.* And don't forget words! First, we must hear God's words, so we might know who it is we are worshiping and why. Then we can use words to express our adoration of him. Indeed, words are the first and crucial thing apart from which other forms of adoration are mere sounds. Psalm 95 has both kinds of words. The last phrase of verse 7 speaks of "hear[ing] his [God's] voice," which has to do with God's revelation. The proper response to this is obedience. On the other hand, the first stanza speaks of "thanksgiving," which is one important way we use words to worship God.

And if we have been able to worship God joyfully, it is natural that we should invite others to do the same. The psalm itself is doing that, when it begins: "Come, let us sing for joy to the LORD" (v. 1) and later, "Come, let us bow down in worship" (v. 6). When the great pioneer missionary William Carey reached India in 1792, he found that his predecessor, Christian Friedrich Schwartz, had inscribed over the portal of the Mission Church at Tranquebar these words from Psalm 95: "O come, let us worship and fall down, and kneel before the LORD our Maker." What an appropriate invitation to those Schwartz was trying to win to faith in Jesus Christ.

Why We Should Worship God

We have seen a few ways in which we can worship God. The next stanzas give two important reasons we should worship him.

1. *Because God is such a great God* (vv. 3–5). Appreciation can be shown to many people, praise to others. Worship belongs to God only. Yet we cannot worship God until we have a proper sense of who he is. "Not until we grasp who the Lord is, are we inwardly moved to worship him," writes John Stott.[5] Verses 4–5 begin by teaching that he is the Creator of all things.

> In his hand are the depths of the earth,
>   and the mountain peaks belong to him.
> The sea is his, for he made it,
>   and his hands formed the dry land.

This is the starting place. That God is the Creator of everything is the first reason for the call to worship in verses 1–2.

2. *Because God is our own dear Shepherd* (vv. 6–7). This stanza uses God's relationship to his people as a second reason why we should worship God and as a reason for the psalm's second call to worship in verse 6. Here the worship of God is made personal, for we are reminded that God not only made the caves and the mountains, the seas and the dry land; he made us too. What is more, he cares for us, if we are numbered among his people. Using a common but beautiful pastoral image, the psalm says that we are God's sheep, "the flock under his care" (v. 7).

What Christian can read this without thinking of Jesus' use of the same image in John 10: "I am the good shepherd. The good shepherd lays down his life for the sheep. . . . I know my sheep and my sheep know me—just as the Father knows me and I know the Father—and I lay down my life for the sheep. . . . My sheep listen to my voice; I know them, and they follow me. I give them eternal life, and they shall never perish; no one can snatch them out of my hand" (vv. 11, 14–15, 27–28). We owe God worship because he is God and has created us. But even more, we owe him worship because he has given his life for us, has called us to faith, and now keeps and preserves us with a power that nothing either in heaven or earth can shake. We are the sheep of Jesus' hand, and nothing will ever snatch us out of Jesus' hand.

The new idea in this stanza, besides the second reason why we should worship God, is reverence. It is important that we use it to balance the call to exuberant worship in stanza one, because noise can be mere noise and true worship is the opposite of noise for its own sake. What is important in verse 6 is that each of the three Hebrew verbs involves the thought of humbling oneself before God: bowing and kneeling obviously, but also worshiping, which in Hebrew means "to prostrate oneself." Ascribing worth to God, which we often explain worship as being, is the idea behind the English word but not the Hebrew, though the Old Testament does invite us to ascribe to the Lord the glory due him (see Ps. 96:8). The Hebrew text uses the verbs in direct sequence of one another so that the text literally reads, "Come, let us prostrate ourselves, let us bow down, let us kneel."

An Unexpected Warning

Suddenly in the midst of these strong calls to joyful personal worship, we find an unexpected warning (vv. 7–11). It is so sudden that some of the more liberal commentators speculate on this being an entirely separate psalm that somehow got attached to the earlier portion. There is no good reason for such speculation. Abrupt changes like this are not infrequent in the psalms, and the warning to hear the voice of God and obey it is actually a critical part of what needs to be said about the worship God accepts. Worship without obedience is mere sham. It calls down the judgments of God the Father and Jesus, who once said,

> These people honor me with their lips,
>   but their hearts are far from me.
> They worship me in vain (Matt. 15:8–9, quoting Isa. 29:13).

Here I come back to what I said earlier: Worship begins with listening rather than speaking, still less singing or shouting. It requires listening to God as he speaks to us in his Word. Worship must be based on the preaching of the Word of God. First, we must hear God's Word. Second, we must obey it. Only then can we praise God joyfully for what we have heard.

Obedience is the sticking point, of course. So this is what God breaks in to talk about in the psalm's final stanza. It is an oracle in which God refers to something that happened during the years of Israel's desert wanderings. After the people had come out of Egypt and had passed through the Desert of Sin they came to a place called Rephidim, where there was no water. This was a serious matter for so large a company of people in so inhospitable an environment. The people had just seen the miracles God did in Egypt to free them from the Egyptian yoke. They should have trusted God to provide for them implicitly. But instead they quarreled with Moses and were almost ready to stone him. God told Moses to take the staff he had used to turn the Nile to blood and use it now to strike a great rock, called the rock at Horeb. When he did this a stream of water came forth from the rock and the people's thirst was quenched. However, a double name was given to the place. It was called Massah, which means "testing," because the people tested God by their sinful unbelief, and Meribah, which means "quarreling," because they quarreled with Moses about the lack of water (see Exod. 17:1–7).

Years later a similar incident occurred at Kadesh. God provided water there too. But it was said, "These were the waters of Meribah, where the Israelites quarreled with the LORD and where he showed himself holy among them" (Num. 20:13; see vv. 1–13). The two place names occur together in Deuteronomy 33:8.

This is what God brings forward in the psalm as an illustration of the disobedience of the people, as a result of which not one of them was allowed to enter the Promised Land. In the unfolding of the story in Exodus and Numbers, it was the refusal of the people to believe the report of Joshua and Caleb about entering and possessing the land that led to the actual judgment of God, according to which every one of that generation except Joshua and Caleb were to die in the wilderness. But the spirit that led to the later unbelief was already present at the place called Massah and Meribah. Testing and unbelief were typical of the people, and they were present during the entire desert journey.

So the warning is this. If you want to worship God, make sure you do not harden your heart against God's Word, or quarrel with him or test him, as the ancients did. On the contrary, true worship is: (1) hearing the Word of God, (2) obeying the Word of God, and (3) praising God for it.

The Urgency of Worship: Today!

There is an inspired commentary on this psalm in the New Testament, in Hebrews 3:7–4:13. These two chapters of Hebrews quote Psalm 95 four times, beginning with an extensive citing of the entire last stanza (Heb. 3:7–11). Psalm 95:7–11 is introduced as a text to be expounded, just as the words of a Bible text appear at the start of one of my studies. After this, verses 7–8 are cited again in Hebrews 3:15, verse 11 in Hebrews 4:3, and verses 7–8 for a final time in Hebrews 4:7. This is probably the most thorough citing of an Old Testament passage in the New Testament.

There are several things to note.

1. *The verses are applied to salvation through faith in Christ.* In their Old Testament context they have to do with entering the Promised Land, and under normal circumstances we would have no warrant for applying them to anything else, except perhaps as an illustration of some spiritual truth. But here we have an inspired New Testament commentary on the psalm that tells us that the meaning of the psalm is not exhausted by the entry of the people into Canaan, or by their failing to enter, but is to be seen in the far more important matter of entering the promised rest of God, which is in heaven. Derek Kidner says that Hebrews "forbids us to confine [the psalm's] thrust to Israel. The 'Today' of which it speaks is this very moment; the 'you' is none other than ourselves, and the promised 'rest' is not Canaan but salvation."[6]

Hebrews says, "If Joshua had given them rest, God would not have spoken later about another day" (4:8). This means that the psalm, which came later than the conquest, would not have been written; but it was written because the rest about which it speaks is more than the rest the people had after occupying Canaan and defeating its inhabitants. The writer of Hebrews continues, "There remains, then, a Sabbath-rest for the people of God; for anyone who enters God's rest also rests from his own work, just as God did from his" (4:9–10).

2. *The warning is for those who have heard the gospel and who seem to have responded to it.* Others should be warned too, of course. But the uniqueness of Hebrews is that it is written to those who have heard the gospel, have even seemed to respond to it by attending Christian worship services, but who have never actually surrendered to Jesus Christ and are in danger of falling away from Christ entirely. The author of Hebrews traces this to unbelief, just as the psalm traces the rebellion in the desert to "testing" and "quarreling." Hebrews says, "See to it, brothers, that none of you has a sinful, unbelieving heart that turns away from the living God. But encourage one another daily, as long as it is called Today, so that none of you may be hardened by sin's deceitfulness" (Heb. 3:12–13).

This is a good equivalent of Jesus' parable about the five wise and five foolish young women who were waiting for the bridegroom. All seemed to be Christians. But in the end five were shut out. The master said, "I tell you the truth, I don't know you" (Matt. 25:12).

3. *It is important to believe on Jesus Christ now, while it is still "today."* The psalm says, "Today, if you hear his voice . . ." (v. 7), and Hebrews repeats "today" five times (once each in 3:7, 13, and 15, and twice in 4:7). The point is that "today" is the day of gospel invitation, and it is a day that will not last forever. Now is the time to turn from sin. Now is the time to believe and follow Jesus Christ. Have you? Have you trusted Jesus Christ for your salvation? Don't put it off. Others have delayed and perished.

Psalm 96

Worship in the Splendor of God's Holiness

Sing to the LORD a new song;
sing to the LORD, all the earth.
Sing to the LORD, praise his name;
proclaim his salvation day after day.
Declare his glory among the nations,
his marvelous deeds among all peoples.

For great is the LORD and most worthy of praise;
he is to be feared above all gods.
For all the gods of the nations are idols,
but the LORD made the heavens.
Splendor and majesty are before him;
strength and glory are in his sanctuary.

Ascribe to the LORD, O families of nations,
ascribe to the LORD glory and strength.
Ascribe to the LORD the glory due his name;
bring an offering and come into his courts.
Worship the LORD in the splendor of his holiness;
tremble before him, all the earth.

Say among the nations, "The LORD reigns."
The world is firmly established, it cannot be moved;
he will judge the peoples with equity.

Let the heavens rejoice, let the earth be glad;
let the sea resound, and all that is in it;
let the fields be jubilant, and everything in them.
Then all the trees of the forest will sing for joy;
they will sing before the LORD, for he comes,
he comes to judge the earth.
He will judge the world in righteousness
and the peoples in his truth.

verses 1–13

There must have been many joyful moments in the lifetime of King David, but to judge from the narratives the brightest of all must have been when the ark of God was brought to Jerusalem from its temporary resting place in the house of Obed-Edom. Thousands of people were assembled, led by hundreds of priests clothed in white linen. There were choirs and an orchestra. And when the priests set out with the ark, their advancing steps were heralded by the sounding of rams' horns and trumpets, the clash of cymbals, and the happy plucking of myriads of lyres and harps. David was so delighted that he threw decorum aside and danced among the people before the Lord.

He also composed a psalm for the occasion, found in 1 Chronicles 16. The middle verses of that psalm (vv. 23–33) also appear as Psalm 96. Other portions are Psalms 105:1–15 and 106:1, 47–48.

Not all commentators agree that David wrote Psalm 96. Since Psalm 96 has echoes of other psalms as well as similarities to portions of Isaiah,[1] it is possible that the Chronicler used psalms written later to express the type of praise David must have offered to God on this occasion. Regardless, the important thing about Psalm 96 is that it is a joyful hymn to the God of Israel as king and an invitation to the nations of the world to join Israel in praising him. It is also a prophecy of a future day when God will judge the entire world in righteousness.

What this means is that the coming of the ark of God to Jerusalem was viewed by David as a pledge of the future coming of God to rule as king over all the earth. Against this background, H. C. Leupold says that the psalm literally "throbs with the hope of the Lord's coming." He adds that it "is definitely of a Messianic cast."[2]

A Call to Worship God

In the last third of the Psalter, which we are approaching, there are numerous psalms that begin with a call to worship God. Psalm 95 began this way, starting with the words: "Come, let us sing for joy to the LORD; let us shout aloud to the Rock of our salvation" (v. 1). Psalm 96 does the same. It begins:

> Sing to the LORD a new song;
>   sing to the LORD, all the earth.
> Sing to the LORD, praise his name;
>   proclaim his salvation day after day.
> Declare his glory among the nations,
>   his marvelous deeds among all peoples (vv. 1–3).

There are six imperatives in these verses, three calls to "*sing* to the Lord" (twice in verse 1 and a third time in verse 2) and one call each to "*praise* his name," "*proclaim* his salvation day after day," and "*declare* his glory among the nations." We are being told to do this. The psalm itself is doing this, of course, so it is a model of how we can praise God properly.

There are a couple of things to notice especially.

1. *A new song.* When we read the words "a new song," we are disposed to think of the psalm itself, as if the psalmist were saying, "I have just composed a new song that I would like you to hear; and then if you like it, I would like you to join me in singing it." Most commentators agree, however, that this is not what the psalmist is thinking of, simply because these writers are usually not thinking of themselves or what they are able to accomplish. They are thinking about God. So the call to sing a new song is actually a call to sing about some new thing God has himself done. In 1 Chronicles, where the words of the psalm occur for the first time, the new thing was God's coming to Jerusalem by the symbolism of the moving of the ark. From this time forward he was to be especially honored there, which is what the psalm does. It was also expected that he would now rule over his people as well as the Gentile nations from Mount Zion.

When we read about "a new song" today we also think of the new song of Revelation 5. There we are told of four living creatures and twenty-four elders who fall down before God's Lamb and sing "a new song," saying,

> You are worthy to take the scroll
>   and to open its seals,
> because you were slain,
>   and with your blood you purchased men for God
>   from every tribe and language and people and nation.
> You have made them to be a kingdom and priests to serve our God,
>   and they will reign on the earth (Rev. 5:9–10).

The new thing here is Christ's atonement, and the "new song" is a joyful acknowledgment of it. It is possible that John, the author of Revelation, was even thinking of Psalm 96, for his emphasis is on the universal reign of Christ, which is what Psalm 96 anticipates.

2. *Praise plus proclamation.* The second thing to notice about this stanza is the way the declaration of God's glory among the nations follows upon praising him. The psalm teaches that worship should never be merely a private thing, something between ourselves and God only, but should also be that which leads to a missionary witness. We should never be satisfied to worship God alone. G. Campbell Morgan wrote of these verses, "If the song of the Lord begins in the heart, it always grows into the chorus in which others are included in its music."[3]

The King's Glory

Derek Kidner joins the first three verses of the psalm to verses 4–6, giving them one title, "The King's Glory." He calls verses 7–9 "The King's Due" and verses 10–13 "The King's Coming."

The first point the psalmist makes about God's glory—why he is "most worthy of praise"—is that "he is to be feared above all gods" (v. 4). Some commentators spend significant time discussing whether the writer thought of the heathen gods as actual (demon) gods or not. But it is hard to imagine why there should be any question about this since the next sentence goes on to state: "for all the gods of the nations are idols." In Hebrew the word *idol* means "a no-thing," that is, a nonentity or nothing. So verse 4 can only mean that God is to be praised and feared above those who are only thought to be gods by the heathen nations. Actually, there is a play on words in this stanza. The word for "gods" is *elohim,* and the word for "idols" is *elilim.* So what the writer is saying is that the *elohim* of the Gentiles are *elilim.* This word occurs only two places in the psalms, here and in Psalm 97:7.

It also occurs in two classic passages in Isaiah, which is one of several reasons some of the commentators think the psalm is from Isaiah's time or later. In one of these passages Isaiah mocks the "no gods" of the heathen by describing how an artisan makes an idol with one part of a piece of wood while he uses the other to make a fire and cook his dinner. Then he falls down and worships the manufactured idol (Isa. 44:9–20). In the other passage Isaiah challenges the handmade heathen "gods" to do something, something either good or evil, that one might fear them:

> "Present your case," says the LORD.
> "Set forth your arguments," says Jacob's King.
> "Bring in your idols to tell us
>   what is going to happen.
> Tell us what the former things were,
>   so that we may consider them
>   and know their final outcome.
> Or declare to us the things to come,

> tell us what the future holds,
> so that we may know that you are gods.
> Do something, whether good or bad,
> so that we will be dismayed and filled with fear.
> But you are less than nothing
> and your words are utterly worthless;
> he who chooses you is detestable" (Isa. 41:21–24).

Paul expressed the same thought when he declared, "We know that an idol is nothing at all in the world and that there is no God but one" (1 Cor. 8:4).

This is a very important point, of course. For it is a repudiation of the other world religions; it means that Christianity is an exclusive faith. This is an unpopular, even a so-called "hateful" idea in an age of political correctness. But it follows directly from who God is and what the Bible says about him. If, as the psalm says, Jehovah "made the heavens" and if "splendor and majesty," "strength and glory" belong to him alone, then it is not only wrong but also a sin to worship any other. If you are not worshiping the God of the Bible exclusively, as God says you must do, you are not worshiping God. You are not a Christian.

The King's Due

Kidner calls the third stanza of this four-part poem "The King's Due," which is a good title since it is about the glory due God for his greatness (vv. 7–9).

It is interesting to compare this stanza with the opening two verses of Psalm 29. Those verses are the same as verse 7 and the first lines of verses 8 and 9 of Psalm 96. Or to put it another way, Psalm 96 borrows verses 1 and 2 of Psalm 29 but adds the lines about bringing an offering and trembling before God. Yet there is this major difference: Psalm 29 calls on the angels ("O mighty ones") to worship God, while here the appeal is to the "families of nations." That is, it is the Gentiles, whose gods have been dismissed as mere idols in stanza two, who are here called on to "ascribe to the LORD the glory due his name." The threefold "ascribe to the LORD" in this stanza corresponds to the repeated "sing to the LORD" in stanza one.

The meaning of the Hebrew word for worship is to prostrate oneself, not to praise God for his attributes, which is what the English word *worship* means. But here we must note that although the meaning of the Hebrew word differs from the English word, the Hebrew understanding of worship nevertheless also involves giving God praise for his attributes. That is what is being said here. Here the nations of the world are told to give God glory.

Glory is a difficult word to define. It refers to the majestic aura of the divine presence, which is why the stanza speaks of "the splendor of his holiness." But it is also more than that. *Kabod,* the Hebrew word, refers to something that is impressive or weighty. Thus, in Genesis 31:1 the possessions of

Jacob are said to have been his "glory" (translated as "wealth" in the NIV), that is, something that impressed people or made Jacob impressive. Similarly, Jehovah's glory is the manifestation of his presence (as in Num. 16:19, 42; Ps. 102:16; Isa. 8:7; 40:5; 60:1–2). It is seen in the "work of his hands" (Ps. 19:1) and in his "marvelous deeds" (Ps. 96:3). Marvin E. Tate, who lists these and other texts, concludes, "The whole of the created world is filled with the 'glory' of Yahweh (Isa. 6:3), and his power over the processes of creation is acclaimed as 'Glory!' in Ps. 29:9. His glory also manifests itself in history (cf. Exod. 14:4, 17, 18; Ezek. 28:22 . . .). Thus the 'glory' of Yahweh is an active, not a static, concept. It is his presence, power and action in the world."[4]

And one more idea about worship. In this stanza the worship of God is described as our bringing something to God rather than our coming to God to get something from him. We usually think of it the other way around. We think of coming to church to receive either: (1) knowledge through the teaching or (2) specific gifts from God as his answers to our prayers. But here worship is chiefly our bringing praise and offerings to God. J. J. Stewart Perowne rightly reminds us that "we go into God's courts . . . to *give* rather than to *get*."[5]

The King's Coming

The last stanza begins with verse 10, which is a command to proclaim the universal reign of God "among the nations."

> Say among the nations, "The LORD reigns."
> > The world is firmly established, it cannot be moved;
> > he will judge the peoples with equity.

H. C. Leupold includes verse 10 with the previous stanza, noting that "the whole piece then becomes a summons to praise Yahweh's kingship."[6] But this is not quite right. The earlier stanza is addressed to the nations, calling on them to praise God. Here the people of Israel are addressed, as in stanza one (cf. vv. 3, 10), and a new idea is brought in—the reign of God by which righteous judgment will come to this earth. In fact, verse 10 is the climax of the psalm: *Yahweh malak* ("The LORD reigns"). The verses that follow are chiefly a commentary on and a response to this statement.[7]

There are two ways in which this stanza speaks of God's reign.

1. *God rules all history now.* It is difficult to appreciate this fact sometimes because there is so much unrighteousness and violence in the world. Nevertheless, God does rule in the sense that he both holds the evil in check and also intervenes to judge it in history from time to time.

One striking contemporary example of God's intervention is the fall of Communism in eastern Europe toward the end of 1989. The overthrow of the Communist states was perceived as a purely political matter by the secular world press, but the true instrumental cause was the prayers of God's people beforehand and the revivals that led up to it. This was especially obvious in Germany, where a prayer meeting at the St. Nikolai Church in Leipzig grew from a small group of people in the early 1980s to hundreds of thousands by the end of 1989. News of what was happening in Leipzig spread to the people of East Berlin, and on November 9 the hated wall was torn down and the East German government collapsed.

Bud Bultman, a producer and writer for CNN, wrote later,

> We in the media watched in astonishment as the walls of totalitarianism came crashing down. But in the rush to cover the cataclysmic events, the story behind the story was overlooked. We trained our cameras on hundreds of thousands of people praying for freedom, votive candles in hand, and yet we missed the transcendent dimension, the explicitly spiritual and religious character of the story. We looked right at it and could not see it.[8]

2. *God will rule the world's nations in perfect righteousness in the future.* Victories like that over Communism are infrequent, however, which is why Psalm 96 also looks forward to the day when God will judge the people with equity and rule in perfect righteousness.

The striking thing for most of us is the way these verses look forward to God's judgment joyfully. It is striking because we usually think of the judgment of God differently. We have been taught to have an acute sense of sin and to be thankful that we will be spared God's judgment because of the death of Jesus Christ on our behalf. But, as C. S. Lewis points out, the ancients lived in a world where judges usually needed to be bribed and right judgment was exceedingly hard to come by, especially for weak, poor, or disadvantaged persons. In such a climate, the disadvantaged did not fear judgment but rather longed for it, because it meant a day when evil would be punished and those who did the right things would be vindicated.[9]

Without losing our joy in the atonement, by which we have escaped God's just judgment for our sins, we who trust Christ should nevertheless also be looking forward to that day of perfect righteousness, which will come when he returns to rule the world justly. In that coming day we shall sing with the glorified saints in Revelation, "Hallelujah! For our Lord God Almighty reigns. Let us rejoice and be glad and give him glory!" (Rev. 19:6–7).

Psalm 97

The Awesome God

The LORD reigns, let the earth be glad;
   let the distant shores rejoice.

Clouds and thick darkness surround him;
   righteousness and justice are the foundation of his throne.
Fire goes before him
   and consumes his foes on every side.
His lightning lights up the world;
   the earth sees and trembles.
The mountains melt like wax before the LORD,
   before the Lord of all the earth.
The heavens proclaim his righteousness,
   and all the peoples see his glory.

All who worship images are put to shame,
   those who boast in idols—
   worship him, all you gods!

Zion hears and rejoices
   and the villages of Judah are glad
   because of your judgments, O LORD.
For you, O LORD, are the Most High over all the earth;
   you are exalted far above all gods.

Let those who love the LORD hate evil,
   for he guards the lives of his faithful ones
   and delivers them from the hand of the wicked.
Light is shed upon the righteous
   and joy on the upright in heart.
Rejoice in the LORD, you who are righteous,
   and praise his holy name.

verses 1–12

Psalm 97 begins with two sentences from Psalm 96: "The LORD reigns" (from verse 10) and "let the earth be glad" (from verse 11). It is a way of reminding us that these two psalms, as well as Psalms 93–100, belong together and that their theme is the kingly rule of God. The words "Jehovah reigns" (or "Jehovah is King") are found in nearly all of them.

The psalms have different emphases, but they develop complementary aspects of God's kingship. Psalms 96, 97, and 98 each hail God's coming as the world's King. But Psalms 96 and 98 soar with delight at what is in store for the world when God returns, while in Psalm 97 the frightening, awesome side of God's kingly rule is emphasized. God's rule is still something to be joyful about, but we are to be under no illusions as to what is involved. God's rule will mean the confounding of all evil and the rule of perfect righteousness.

It is surprising how differently the psalm has been outlined. Marvin Tate divides it into two sections: verses 1–9 and 10–12. Derek Kidner has three sections: verses 1–5, 6–9, and 10–12. H. C. Leupold and J. J. Stewart Perowne each have four: verses 1–3, 4–6, 7–9, and 10–12. Franz Delitzsch has five: verses 1–3, 4–6, 7–8, 9, and 10–12. The New International Version also has five divisions, but they are different: verses 1, 2–6, 7, 8–9, and 10–12. I will be following the New International Version arrangement in this study.

The Sovereign God

One reason I am following the NIV is that I think it is right in setting the first verse off by itself as a sort of theme statement for the psalm. It could be a theme verse for the entire block of kingly psalms.

> The LORD reigns, let the earth be glad;
> let the distant shores rejoice.

God's "reign" here means his sovereignty. He has absolute authority and rule over his creation, and it is an attribute of deity without which God could not be God. Sovereignty involves other attributes too. In order to be sovereign, God must also be all-knowing, all-powerful, and absolutely free. If he were limited in any one of these areas, he would not be completely sovereign. If he did not know what was going on, he would be constantly taken by surprise. If he were not omnipotent, he would not be able to control events. If he were not absolutely free, his actions would be predetermined by some other will or by unavoidable circumstances. Yet the sovereignty of God is greater than any of the attributes it contains.

A little thought will show why this is so. We might think of love as being a greater attribute than sovereignty. But if God were not sovereign, he might love but circumstances would arise to thwart his love, making it useless to us. It is the same with matters involving justice. If God were not sovereign, justice would be frustrated and injustice would prevail.

This means that God's rule gives substance to all the other doctrines. It is, as Arthur W. Pink wrote, "the foundation of Christian theology . . . the center of gravity in the system of Christian truth—the sun around which all the lesser orbs are grouped."[1] It is also, as Psalm 97 is going to show, the believer's strength and comfort amid the storms of this life.

Here is a story of someone who was comforted by being reminded of God's sovereignty. His name was Bulstrode Whitelock, and he was an envoy of Oliver Cromwell to Sweden in 1653. He was resting at the village of Harwich the night before he was to sail to Sweden, and he was so distracted by the perilous state of England that he could not sleep. He had a servant who was accompanying him, and this man, discovering that Whitelock could not sleep, said, "Sir, may I ask you a question?"

"Of course," said Whitelock.

"Pray, sir, do you think God governed the world very well before you came into it?" he asked.

"Certainly."

"And do you think he will govern it quite as well when you are gone out of it?" he continued.

"Undoubtedly."

"Then pray, sir, excuse me, but do you not think that you may trust him to govern it quite as well while you are living?"

Whitelock had no answer to this question. But he rolled over quietly in his bed and was soon asleep.[2]

The great Reformer and friend of Martin Luther, Frederick Myconius, once wrote to Calvin about the church's enemies: "I am glad that Christ is Lord of all, for otherwise I should utterly have been out of hope."[3] Indeed! In this world we see much injustice and look hopefully for the personal return of our Sovereign. But in the meantime, the fact that God is sovereign is an immense source of comfort to God's people.

The Awesome God

The second stanza of this psalm (vv. 2–6) is its most unique feature in comparison with the others of this group. But the language itself is not unique. It is taken from accounts of various theophanies, or manifestations of God, from past Jewish history.

We think first of God's appearance to the people of Israel at Mount Sinai. It was terrifying to them. The text says,

> On the morning of the third day there was thunder and lightning, with a thick cloud over the mountain, and a very loud trumpet blast. Everyone in the camp trembled. Then Moses led the people out of the camp to

meet with God, and they stood at the foot of the mountain. Mount Sinai was covered with smoke, because the LORD descended on it in fire. The smoke billowed up from it like smoke from a furnace, the whole mountain trembled violently, and the sound of the trumpet grew louder and louder (Exod. 19:16–19).

The same phenomena occurred when God appeared to Moses sometime later (Exod. 34:5) and still later to Isaiah (Isa. 6:1–4) and other prophets, such as Ezekiel (Ezek. 1:4–28), Daniel (Dan. 7:9–14), and Micah (Micah 1:3–4). Psalms 18:7–15 and 50:3 and Habakkuk 3:3–15 also contain this language.

The point of these passages is that a manifestation of the true God is awe inspiring to the point of bone-shattering fear and trembling on the part of the worshiper. When God appeared at Sinai, all the people trembled (Exod. 19:16). Even Moses said, "I am trembling with fear" (Heb. 12:21). Isaiah cried, "Woe is me! I am ruined! For I am a man of unclean lips, and I live among a people of unclean lips, and my eyes have seen the King, the LORD Almighty" (Isa. 6:5). Ezekiel "fell facedown" (Ezek. 1:28). Daniel "turned pale" (Dan. 7:28). Habakkuk wrote,

> I heard and my heart pounded,
>   my lips quivered at the sound;
> decay crept into my bones,
>   and my legs trembled (Hab. 3:16).

"Our God is a consuming fire," said the author of Hebrews (Heb. 12:29). And again, "See to it that you do not refuse him who speaks" (v. 25). This means that we must never take God lightly, as if he were nothing more than some great heavenly buddy or pal. In fact, the common lightness of many in approaching God is not a sign of their close acquaintance with him, as they probably suppose, but of the fact that they hardly know God at all. Those who know God approach him joyfully but reverently and with the greatest awe. Two psalms before this we read, "Come, let us *bow down* in worship, let us *kneel* before the LORD our Maker" (Ps. 95:6).

The Only God

The translators of the New International Version are the only scholars I know who have set verse 7 apart by itself. But I think they are right in this, just as they are also right in setting verse 1 apart. The point of verse 7 is that if Jehovah really is as the previous stanza has described him, then he is unique in these qualities and is in fact the only true God. There is a problem with verse 7, however: How can the psalmist call upon the gods of the heathen, the idols presumably, to worship God ("Worship him, all you gods!")? Mere idols are nothing; they cannot worship. Even if the psalmist is thinking of the demon gods and goddesses that stood behind the pagan idols, how can he suppose that they, the demons, would ever praise the God against whom they have rebelled? This question is discussed at length by the great Puritan theologian John Owen.[4] He suggests three options.

First, the appeal could be to the nations that worship idols with the meaning, "Worship him, all you who serve idols. Turn from these false gods to the true God." This is the meaning given to verse 7 by the rabbis whose thoughts are preserved in the Jewish Targums. They understood that the gods of the heathen were nothing and therefore reinterpreted the psalm to have a missionary meaning.

Second, the appeal could be to the magistrates or rulers of the people, for the word *elohim* that occurs here (translated "gods") sometimes has that meaning in other places. This was the way Jesus interpreted *elohim* when he was accused of blasphemy because he had called himself the Son of God. He referred his accusers to Psalm 82:6, saying, "If he called them 'gods,' to whom the word of God came—and the Scripture cannot be broken—what about the one whom the Father set apart as his very own and sent into the world? Why then do you accuse me of blasphemy because I said, 'I am God's Son'?" (John 10:35–36).

The third possibility, which Owen preferred and the New International Version probably also favors by its straightforward translation, is that "gods" refers to angels. This makes good sense, and it may even be the case that this is the verse referred to by Hebrews 1:6, which says, "When God brings his firstborn into the world, he says, 'Let all God's angels worship him.'" However, that verse is usually assumed by scholars to be a citation of Deuteronomy 32:43 in the Septuagint, which speaks of angels although the Hebrew and English texts do not.

The angels do worship God, of course. At least the holy angels do. They praise God without ceasing. The problem is not there. The problem is with people who worship idols, even though they know idols are "nothing at all in the world" (1 Cor. 8:4) and that there is only one true God. What are these idols? Self, power, fame, sex, and money. The people of the world sell their souls to these idols constantly.

Christians sometimes appear to serve them too. Why do we appear to serve these "lesser gods"? Probably it is because we know so little of the true God! And the reason we know so little of the true God is that we spend so little time with him. How foolish for us who have the Word of God, the Bible, and who possess the Holy Spirit, who has been given to us to help us understand the Bible and obey it. Psalm 119 says, "I have hidden your word in my heart that I might not sin against you" (v. 11), and "I gain understanding from your precepts; therefore I hate every wrong path" (v. 104).

The Righteous God

The fourth of these five stanzas returns to the theme introduced at the end of the preceding psalm, the righteous judgment of God. Zion and the surrounding villages are rejoicing because God has intervened in history to establish his righteous kingly rule over the entire earth. This probably refers to some special act of God for the salvation of his people, though we are not told enough in the psalm to figure out what it might be. Some scholars suggest the return of the Jews from Babylon and the rebuilding of their country.

Whatever the immediate historical reference might be, the only complete fulfillment of this vision must be the eventual return of Jesus Christ and the reign of Jesus in his millennial kingdom at the end of this age. Only then will perfect justice come to this earth. There is no such thing as perfect justice now. Now those who are strong oppress the weak. The unscrupulous cheat the innocent. Murderers go free, and the perpetrators of other horrible crimes go unpunished. But when Jesus returns there will be perfect righteousness. The helpless will be defended, liars confounded, and the guilty judged. This will be grounds for great rejoicing by the righteous, as is the case in this psalm.

> Zion hears and rejoices
> > and the villages of Judah are glad
> > because of your judgments, O LORD (v. 8).

In Revelation joy is expressed over the fall of "Mystery Babylon," a symbol of the earth's great godlessness and wickedness, and praise is given to God, who judged the city righteously.

> Hallelujah!
> Salvation and glory and power belong to our God,
> > for true and just are his judgments.
> He has condemned the great prostitute
> > who corrupted the earth by her adulteries.
> He has avenged on her the blood of his servants. . . .
>
> Hallelujah!
> The smoke from her goes up for ever and ever (Rev. 19:1–3).

Is This Your God?

The final stanza of this psalm is an encouragement to those who are still living in bad times to hold fast to their profession, knowing that God will remain faithful to them and protect them as they do. They are told to do two things. First, "hate evil" (v. 10), and second, "rejoice in the LORD" (v. 12), which is exactly what we see at the end of Revelation. And the first leads to the second! Note the sequence of Psalm 97:10–12. If we hate evil, God will provide us with: (1) protection, (2) deliverance, (3) light on our path through life, and (4) joy. So hatred of evil leads to rejoicing, which we are also told to do. We will do both if we truly know and love God. Do you know God? Is this righteous, awesome God of the psalm your God?

We do not naturally hate evil. In fact, the opposite is the case. We naturally love sin. We are intrigued by wrong in other people, and we do not want to part with the sins we ourselves are practicing. We must learn to hate sin, and we will, if we are getting to know God. If we do not, we will increasingly hate God. We see an illustration of this in the way the masses reacted to Jesus Christ during his time on earth. Some people saw his holiness, learned to hate sin, and became his disciples. Others saw him, hated him for exposing their sin as sin, and eventually crucified him. If you love God and are coming to know him, you will hate sin simply because it is contrary to the character of the one you now love.

How do you know if you are really coming to hate evil? That is a good question and one well worth pondering, since we are prone to think better of ourselves than we should, and we deceive ourselves. Richard Sibbes was one of the great Puritan divines, and like many of them he often thought about the nature of human personality and how we can examine ourselves profitably. When he turned to this question he observed that since hating sin is a proof of our conversion, it is important that we know if we truly hate it. The way to know that we hate evil is this:

1. *If our hatred of sin is universal.* That is, the one who hates sin truly, hates all kinds of sin.

2. *If our hatred of sin is fixed.* There should be no appeasing of sin but rather an abolishing of the thing hated.

3. *If our hatred of sin is a more rooted affection than anger.* Anger may be appeased, but hatred remains and opposes the hated object.

4. *If we hate sin wherever it is found.* We must hate sin in others but especially in ourselves. "He that hates a toad would hate it most in his own bosom," said Sibbes. "Many, like Judah, are severe in censuring others (Gen. 38:24) but partial to themselves."

5. *If we hate the greatest sin in the greatest measure.* That is, if we hate all sins in a just proportion, not being offended by the slight flaw in another while overlooking a much greater offense in ourselves.

6. *If we can be reproved for sin and not get angry.* If we truly hate sin, we will welcome whatever help we may get in dealing with it and driving it from our lives. "Those that swell against reproof do not appear to hate sin," wrote this great Puritan.[5]

> Rejoice in the LORD, you who are righteous,
> and praise his holy name.

This is where the psalm ends. It began by calling upon the people of the whole earth to rejoice in God's rule (v. 1). It ends by calling upon us to lead the way in this worship. Shall we not do it? If we do not praise God joyfully, who will? If we do not praise him now, when will we?

Psalm 98

An Exuberant Praise Song

Sing to the LORD a new song,
  for he has done marvelous things;
his right hand and his holy arm
  have worked salvation for him.
The LORD has made his salvation known
  and revealed his righteousness to the nations.
He has remembered his love
  and his faithfulness to the house of Israel;
all the ends of the earth have seen
  the salvation of our God.

Shout for joy to the LORD, all the earth,
  burst into jubilant song with music;
make music to the LORD with the harp,
  with the harp and the sound of singing,
with trumpets and the blast of the ram's horn—
  shout for joy before the LORD, the King.

Let the sea resound, and everything in it,
  the world, and all who live in it.
Let the rivers clap their hands,
  let the mountains sing together for joy;
let them sing before the LORD,
  for he comes to judge the earth.
He will judge the world in righteousness
  and the peoples with equity.

verses 1–9

There is a well-known and frequently quoted passage in Ecclesiastes that asserts, "There is a time for everything, . . . a time to weep and a time to laugh, a time to mourn and a time to dance" (Eccles. 3:1, 4). It is familiar and frequently quoted because it applies to so many experiences of life. It also applies to Psalm 98. As we have made our way through the Psalter, there have been many psalms that have expressed reasons why we or somebody else might mourn, psalms that have dealt with sin, defeat, despair, or loneliness, for instance. But it is not a time for weeping now. This is a time to laugh. For we have come to one of the most joyful songs in the Bible, a psalm that I have titled "An Exuberant Praise Song." It is a noisy, effervescent song from its beginning to the end.

In the church Psalm 98 is known as the *Cantate Domino,* from its first words ("Sing to the Lord"). In the Book of Common Prayer, which is used in the Anglican and Episcopal churches, it follows the reading of the first lesson for the evening service, which means that it is familiar and probably committed to memory by many in that tradition. It is much like Psalm 96. Both psalms begin and end in nearly the same way. But Psalm 98 is wholly given to praise. In this psalm there are no comparisons with the heathen, no lessons about how we should worship. Instead, all is pure joy and celebration. It is a minor curiosity that this is the only psalm that has as its heading the single word *mizmor,* meaning "psalm," which may signify that the best of all praise psalms should be like it.

John R. W. Stott has a useful description of the psalm's three parts: (1) "God the Savior" (vv. 1–3), (2) "God the King" (vv. 4–6), and (3) "God the Judge" (vv. 7–9). But the stanzas can also be looked at as a swelling expansion of the worship being offered. Stanza one is directed to Israel, stanza two to the whole earth, and stanza three to nature. The force of the last section is captured beautifully in the sixth verse of the hymn "Come, Let Us Sing unto the Lord," which is a rendering on Psalm 98.

> Let earth be glad, let billows roar
> And all that dwell from shore to shore;
> Let floods clap hands with one accord,
> Let hills rejoice before the Lord.

We have three well-known hymns based on this psalm: "New Songs of Celebration Render" by Eric Routley; "Come, Let Us Sing unto the Lord," which I have just quoted (from the Associate Reformed Psalter of 1931); and, best known of all, "Joy to the World!" by Isaac Watts (1719). There is no better way of proving that Psalm 98 is "An Exuberant Praise Song" than to indicate that Watts's hymn, which is probably the most joyful and exuberant of all our hymns or Christmas carols, is based on it. The psalm is a great one with which to praise God.

God the Savior

Each of the three stanzas of this psalm calls on one part of creation to praise God, and in the first stanza this is Israel (vv. 1–3), because, "He [God] has remembered his love and his faithfulness to the house of Israel" (v. 3).

Since the verb is in the past tense ("has remembered") we are probably to understand that the psalmist is thinking of some great act of deliverance of the people by God. We are not told what this was and have no sure way of finding out, though commentators who believe that the psalms in this section are late compositions generally suppose that it was God's deliverance of the people from their Babylonian captivity, bringing them back to their own land. What is certain is that the deliverance was a victory in some sense. The word translated "salvation," which occurs in each of the first three verses, includes the idea of "victory" and is so translated in verse 1 in the King James Version. It is because of this new act of deliverance or new victory that the people are to sing "a new song."[1]

It is probably good that we do not know what this deliverance was, because if we did we would spend our time discussing it. It is far more important that we think of deliverance in terms of the victories God has provided for us through Jesus Christ. The New Testament reveals three kinds of deliverance.

1. *Deliverance from sin.* The single greatest problem you and I have is our sin, not a lack of self-esteem or accomplishment or anything else. Sin both separates and destroys. It separates us from God, who is the source of all good, and it destroys relationships. In the end it will bring us to that final place of all separation, hell.

Who is to save us from sin? We look to the world, and we find no help there. The world is unable to solve its own problems, and even if it could, this would mean nothing in terms of deliverance from the punishment of God due to each of us for our many transgressions of God's law and the harm we have done to other people. We look to ourselves, and we find no help there either. If we could conquer sin, we would do it. But we cannot. Sin lives in us and drags us down. The apostle Paul wrestled with sin, crying, "When I want to do good, evil is right there with me. . . . What a wretched man I am! Who will rescue me from this body of death?" (Rom. 7:21, 24).

The next verse gives the answer: "Thanks be to God—through Jesus Christ our Lord!" (v. 25).

How does God do it? Paul explains:

Therefore, there is now no condemnation for those who are in Christ Jesus, because through Christ Jesus the law of the Spirit of life set me free from the law of sin and death. For what the law was powerless to do in that it was weakened by the sinful nature, God did by sending his own Son in the likeness of sinful man to be a sin offering. And so he condemned sin in sinful man, in order that the righteous requirements of the law might be fully met in us, who do not live according to the sinful nature but according to the Spirit (Rom. 8:1–4).

This deliverance is in three stages. First, there is deliverance from sin's penalty. Jesus died for our sin, in our place. So there is now "no condemnation for those who are in Christ Jesus." Second, we are delivered from sin's power. Jesus saved us so that now "the righteous requirements of the law might be fully met in us." Finally, as Paul says later in the chapter, there is deliverance even from sin's presence. For the end of all God's working for us and in us is that we might be "glorified" (v. 30). We, above all people, can sing "a new song" for this deliverance (see Rev. 5:9–10).

2. *Deliverance from death.* Glorification embraces the second kind of deliverance emphasized in the New Testament, deliverance from death. Death is a great enemy. But though we are appointed to die once, we look forward to our resurrection from the dead because of the victory over death by our great Savior Jesus Christ. Paul wrote about Christ's resurrection and ours extensively in 1 Corinthians 15, concluding, "Death has been swallowed up in victory" (v. 54; cf. Isa. 25:8) and, "He gives us the victory through our Lord Jesus Christ" (v. 57). Because of Christ's victory we no longer fear death but live our lives obediently and to the full, knowing that when we die we will be with Jesus: "To be away from the body [is to be] at home with the Lord" (2 Cor. 5:8).

3. *Deliverance from Satan.* The third deliverance emphasized in the New Testament is deliverance from Satan and his power. In Genesis 3:15, in the first of all the many announcements of the gospel, it is said that the coming of Christ will accomplish the defeat of Satan.

> He [that is, Jesus] will crush your head,
> and you [Satan] will strike his heel.

Jesus did that at the cross. He defeated Satan, though Satan wounded him (temporarily) in the process. The atonement broke Satan's power, which was the power of sin and death. Jesus' victory over Satan enables us to be victors too. In the power of Christ we need not fear him. James says, "Submit yourselves, then, to God. Resist the devil, and he will flee from you" (James 4:7). Likewise, we read in Revelation, "I saw what looked like a sea of glass mixed with fire and, standing beside the sea, those who had been victorious over the beast and his image" (Rev. 15:2).

There are striking parallels between the first part of Psalm 98 and Mary's Magnificat (Luke 1:46–55), which may mean that the mother of Jesus had the psalm in mind as she composed her hymn and that she rightly saw that the promises of the psalm were to be fulfilled in the spiritual victories to be achieved by Jesus Christ.[2]

Psalm 98	The Magnificat
"Sing to the LORD a new song."	"My soul glorifies the Lord."
"For he has done marvelous things."	"The Mighty One has done great things for me."

"His right hand and his holy arm
   have worked salvation for him."
"The LORD has made his salvation known
   and revealed his righteousness
   to the nations."
"He has remembered his love and his
   faithfulness to the house of Israel."

"He has performed mighty deeds
   with his arm."
"His mercy extends to those who
   fear him, from generation to
   generation."
"He has helped his servant Israel,
   remembering to be merciful."

In *The Treasury of David* Charles Spurgeon tells of a little church in the county of Tyrone where a small, ragged boy came every Sunday, placing himself in the very center of the pews opposite the pulpit. The minister frequently tried to speak to him after the service because he seemed so attentive, but the boy always slipped away quietly and the minister was never able to find out who he was. The lad was missing for some weeks, and one day a man came to the church to see the minister. He wanted him to visit his son, who was dying. "I am really ashamed to ask you to go so far," he said, indicating that his home was about six miles distant. "But he is an extraordinary boy, and he is refusing to see anyone but you. He talks about things I do not understand."

The minister started out, trudging along the rural road in drenching rain, and at last came to the home, a poor hovel tucked into a desolate mountain valley. The man who had come for him was waiting at the door, and when the minister went in he found the boy lying in the corner on a straw mat. When he saw the minister he raised himself up, stretched out his frail little arms and said, "His own right hand and his holy arm hath gotten him the victory" (from v. 1 of our psalm). Shortly afterward he died.

How great a victory has been achieved for us by Jesus! How great that it produces conquering faith even in a child.

God the King

The second stanza of Psalm 98 praises God as King, which is why it is included in the block of royal psalms that we are currently studying (Psalms 93–100). The first stanza praised God as Savior and called on the people of Israel to sing a new song to him. This stanza views him as King not only of Israel but of the whole earth. Therefore, it broadens its call to worship by engaging the whole earth in singing his well-deserved praises.

Shout for joy to the LORD, all the earth,
   burst into jubilant song with music;
make music to the LORD with the harp,
   with the harp and the sound of singing,
with trumpets and the blast of the ram's horn—
   shout for joy before the LORD, the King (vv. 4–6).

The most striking feature of this stanza is something we have seen before and will see again, the desire of the psalmist that the worship of God be joyful and above all, loud. "The noise of temple worship was legendary," according to Marvin E. Tate.[3] He points to the accounts of Israel's worship in 2 Chronicles 29:25–30 and Ezra 3:10–13, where in the second passage the sound of the instruments and the shouts of the people are said to have been "heard far away" (Ezra 3:13).

Should the worship of God's people be any less exuberant today? Should we be quiet when we have come to know him who is the great King above all kings and the great Lord above all lords? Shame on us for all lackluster worship and all halfhearted praise.

The Methodists have always been noted for their hearty singing of God's praises, and one reason for it is what John Wesley told his followers: "Sing lustily, and with good courage. Beware of singing as if you were half dead or asleep; but lift up your voice with strength. Be no more afraid of your voice now, nor more ashamed of its being heard, than when you sang the songs of Satan."[4] Not all of us have good voices. But I do not think the angels find poor voices offensive when hearts are full of gratitude to God.

God the Judge

The final stanza is poetic and in some ways the most unexpected. For in it, in beautiful language, the psalmist calls upon the entire creation to praise God. In the first stanza the appeal is to Israel. In the second stanza the appeal is to the nations of the earth. In this last stanza the call is to creation, the cosmos. The reason for it is that God is coming to "judge the world in righteousness and the peoples with equity" (v. 9). The psalm closes by looking ahead to that future day when the ills of this suffering world will be set right. We know this as the day of the return of Jesus Christ.

This joyful future liberation of the cosmos to join in praise to God is explained further by Paul in Romans 8: "The creation waits in eager expectation for the sons of God to be revealed. For the creation was subjected to frustration, not by its own choice, but by the will of the one who subjected it, in hope that the creation itself will be liberated from its bondage to decay and brought into the glorious freedom of the children of God" (vv. 19–21). In these verses Paul is personifying nature. He does not mean that nature has personal feelings that correspond to ours, only that nature is not yet all that God has predestined it to be and is in a sense waiting for its true fulfillment. This is what the psalmist is suggesting too.

This understanding of creation is radically different from the way the world looks at nature. The world makes either one of two errors where the cosmos is concerned. Either it deifies nature, virtually worshiping it, which is why some people think it is worse to harm the environment for spotted owls than to abort babies. Or the world regards nature as evolving toward perfection, accompanied by the human race, which is also evolving.

Many of us can recall that powerful television image of Carl Sagan on the *Cosmos* series standing before a large screen on which there was a display of the night sky in all its starry splendor and saying in nearly mystical tones, "The cosmos is all that is or that ever was or that ever will be." Sagan is the image of unbelieving man, standing on the very tips of his toes, peering into the distant heavens as far as his telescopes will allow and declaring with blind arrogance, "The world is all that is."

Paul gives us a very different picture. He also pictures something staring off into the distance. But it is not man who is on tiptoe looking off into the distance. It is creation itself, and what creation is earnestly looking for, as it looks beyond itself, is the "glorious freedom of the children of God," which it will share. Creation wants to praise God, and will, according to Paul's teaching and this psalm.

The world makes another error that is not entirely different from the first error. It sees in nature some kind of perfecting principle, almost like saying, "The world is not God yet, but it is on the way." In cosmic terms this is the principle of evolution. In human terms it is the principle of inevitable perfection: "Every day in every way I am getting better and better." In other words, I may not be God yet, but I will be, given time. Of course, a lot of time has gone by—millions of years, according to L. S. B. Leakey and other evolutionists—and man seems to be as much unlike God as he ever was.

The Christian's perspective is far more balanced and more mature than this or anything the world can devise. The Christian doctrine of creation has three parts.

1. *This is God's world.* God made it, and it is his. As a result, we must respect the world and not abuse it. We must treat it responsibly.

2. *The world is not what it was created to be.* It has been subjected to troubles as the result of God's judgment on man at the time of the Fall. It has been subjected to frustration, bondage, and decay, according to Paul's teaching in Romans.

3. *The world will one day be renewed.* I think of the way C. S. Lewis developed this idea in *The Lion, the Witch, and the Wardrobe.* In the first section of that book, when Narnia was under the power of the wicked Witch of the North, the land was in a state of perpetual winter. Spring never came. But when Aslan rose from the dead the ice began to melt, flowers bloomed, and the trees turned green. It is poetical writing, but it describes something that will happen. The rivers will indeed clap their hands. The mountains will indeed sing. And we will all join in. Hallelujah!

Psalm 99

Holy, Holy, Holy

The LORD reigns,
    let the nations tremble;
he sits enthroned between the cherubim,
    let the earth shake.
Great is the LORD in Zion;
    he is exalted over all the nations.
let them praise your great and awesome name—
    he is holy.

The King is mighty, he loves justice—
    you have established equity;
in Jacob you have done
    what is just and right.
Exalt the LORD our God
    and worship at his footstool;
    he is holy.

Moses and Aaron were among his priests,
    Samuel was among those who called on his name;
they called on the LORD
    and he answered them.
He spoke to them from the pillar of cloud;
    they kept his statutes and the decrees he gave them.

O LORD our God,
    you answered them;
you were to Israel a forgiving God,
    though you punished their misdeeds.
Exalt the LORD our God
    and worship at his holy mountain,
    for the LORD our God is holy.

verses 1–9

P salm 99 is about the holiness of God. It is about his kingly reign too, since it begins with the words "the LORD reigns" (it is the third psalm to do so; the others are Psalms 93 and 97), and it is the next to last in the series of eight royal psalms, beginning with Psalm 93 and ending with Psalm 100. But chiefly Psalm 99 is about God's holiness, which is important for us to understand if we are to appreciate the character of this supreme and reigning Monarch. It is almost impossible to miss this emphasis because the point is made three times in the psalm: in verse 3 ("he is holy"), in verse 5 ("he is holy"), and in verse 9 ("the LORD our God is holy").

It is also hard to miss the importance of holiness as an attribute of God in the Bible generally. To begin with, the Bible calls God holy more than anything else, more than sovereign, more than just, more than merciful or loving. In fact "holy" is the only epithet of God that is repeated three times for emphasis, like this: "Holy, holy, holy" (Isa. 6:3; Rev. 4:8).

Since the ancients did not have our ways of emphasizing something in print, either by capitalizing or printing in boldface or color, they achieved their emphasis by repetition. Jesus did it when he prefaced many of his sayings by "verily, verily" or "truly, truly." It was a device for calling special attention to what followed. But if saying something twice gives it emphasis, how about if the idea is repeated three times, as "holy" is? Obviously this makes it of superlative importance.

As we read the Bible we discover that God alone is holy: "Who will not fear you, O Lord, and bring glory to your name? For you alone are holy" (Rev. 15:4). God is said to be majestic in his holiness, which is the precise theme of Psalm 99. Exodus 15:11 says, "Who among the gods is like you, O LORD? Who is like you—majestic in holiness, awesome in glory, working wonders?" This attribute of God is celebrated before his throne day and night by the seraphim. Isaiah heard them sing:

> Holy, holy, holy is the LORD Almighty;
>   the whole earth is full of his glory (Isa. 6:3).

So did John in Revelation:

> Holy, holy, holy
> is the Lord God Almighty,
> who was, and is, and is to come (Rev. 4:8).

God's people are called on to join these praises. For example, "Sing to the LORD, you saints of his; praise his holy name" (Ps. 30:4).

The Holy, Holy, Holy Psalm

Psalm 99 is hard to outline because it can be divided in so many ways. Verses 5 and 9 are nearly identical, which divides the psalm into two fairly equal parts (vv. 1–5 and 6–9). But the psalm can also be given three parts, each ending with the words "he is holy" (vv. 1–3, 4–5) or "the Lord our God is holy" (vv. 6–9). Again, there are four locations where God is seen to be reigning, and these correspond to the stanzas of the New International Version: (1) "between the cherubim" (vv. 1–3), (2) "at his footstool" (vv. 4–5), (3) "from the pillar of cloud" (vv. 6–7), and (4) "at his holy mountain" (vv. 8–9). Each of these is uniquely associated with God's holiness and therefore teaches some essential truth about it.

In my judgment, the best way to outline the psalm is by the three parts ending with the words "he (or 'the LORD our God') is holy." Charles Haddon Spurgeon saw this and called Psalm 99 "The Holy, Holy, Holy Psalm."[1] J. J. Stewart Perowne wrote rightly, "In this psalm not only the righteous sway of the King, but his awful holiness forms the subject of praise."[2]

Holy Is the Lord Almighty

"His awful holiness!" That is a good phrase of Perowne's, because it is exactly what the first stanza is intended to impress on the worshiper. It begins by picturing the Lord sitting on his throne in heaven, much like an earthly monarch might receive visitors to his court while sitting on an earthly throne. But this is no ordinary throne room and no ordinary throne. This is heavenly Zion, and God is enthroned not between some brass ornaments or even the legendary gems on India's famous "Peacock Throne," but between the awe-inspiring figures of the cherubim. Before this "holy, holy, holy" God the nations might well "tremble" and the earth "shake" (v. 1).

Visions similar to this are found elsewhere in Scripture, in Psalm 18 and Ezekiel 1 and 10, for instance. The best known of these is in Isaiah 6. Isaiah says that he received this vision "in the year that King Uzziah died." Uzziah was a good king who had reigned for fifty-two years. So his passing must have been a great blow to the people and have ushered in a time of anxiety about the future. What would happen to them now that this good king was gone? It was at this fateful time that God gave Isaiah a peek into heaven, which was a way of assuring Isaiah and others that although the earthly king was gone, the heavenly King was nevertheless still reigning on his throne.

Isaiah says that he saw

the Lord seated on a throne, high and exalted, and the train of his robe filled the temple. Above him were seraphs, each with six wings: With two wings they covered their faces, with two they covered their feet, and with two they were flying. And they were calling to one another:

"Holy, holy, holy is the LORD Almighty;
the whole earth is full of his glory."

At the sound of their voices the doorposts and thresholds shook and the temple was filled with smoke (6:1–4).

This is close to what the psalmist describes in his vision of the Lord in verses 1–3.

The important idea in each of these visions is holiness, of course. But holiness is not an easy concept to understand or define. In fact, it is impossible to define it adequately. The most common mistake we make is to think of it primarily in terms of human righteousness. That is, we think of it as moral perfection, purity, or right conduct. Holiness involves this element, but it is far more than this. At its root, "holy" is not an ethical concept at all. Rather it is the very nature of God and what distinguishes him from all else. It is what sets God apart from his creation. It concerns transcendence.

We see this root meaning of *holy* in the meaning of the words *saint* and *sanctify*, which are nearly identical to it. *Holy* comes from the Germanic languages. *Saint* comes from the Romance languages. But both have to do with separation. In the biblical sense, a saint is not a person who has achieved a certain level of goodness (as most people think), but rather one who has been "set apart" by God. That is why all Christians are saints. They are the "called-out ones" who form God's church. Similarly, "to sanctify" something is to set it apart for God's service.

Holiness, then, is the characteristic of God that sets him apart from his creation. It has at least four contributing elements.

1. *Majesty.* Majesty means "dignity," "authority of sovereign power," "stateliness," or "grandeur." It is the characteristic of strong rulers and of God, who is ruler over all. Majesty links holiness to sovereignty, which is why in Psalm 99 the stanza that begins with a statement about God's rule ("The LORD reigns") ends with a reference to his holiness ("he is holy").

2. *Will.* A second element in holiness is will, that of a sovereign personality. This makes holiness personal and active, rather than abstract and passive. The will of God is primarily set on showing himself to be the "Wholly Other," the one whose glory must not be tarnished by the wickedness of men. This element of holiness comes close to what the Bible speaks of when it refers to God's "jealousy." It means that God is not indifferent to how we regard him.

3. *Wrath.* Wrath is part of holiness, because it is the natural and proper stance of the holy God against all that opposes him. It means that God takes the business of being God so seriously that he will permit no one else to usurp his place. When Satan tried to do it he was judged (and will yet be judged). When men and women refuse to take the place God has given them, they will suffer the outpouring of God's righteous wrath also.

4. *Righteousness.* This is the matter mentioned earlier. It is involved in holiness not because it is the term by which holiness may best be understood but because it is what the holy God wills in moral areas. What is right? What is moral? We can answer that not by appealing to some abstract, independent moral standard, but by appealing to the character and will of God himself. The right is what God is and reveals to us.

But here is our problem. We are not holy, even in the strictly moral sense. Therefore, and precisely because holiness is not an abstract or passive concept but is instead the active, dynamic will of God at work to punish rebellion and establish righteousness, the experience of confronting the holy God is profoundly threatening to us. Holiness intrigues us, as the unknown always does. We are drawn to it. But at the same time we are in danger of being undone, and fear being undone, by the confrontation. When Isaiah had his encounter with the holy God, he reacted in terror, saying, "Woe to me! I am ruined! For I am a man of unclean lips, and I live among a people of unclean lips, and my eyes have seen the King, the LORD Almighty" (Isa. 6:5).

Similarly, when God revealed himself to Habakkuk, the prophet described the experience by saying, "I heard and my heart pounded, my lips quivered at the sound; decay crept into my bones, and my legs trembled" (Hab. 3:16).

Job said, "I despise myself and repent in dust and ashes" (Job 42:6).

Peter caught only a brief glimpse of Jesus' holiness, but he cried out, "Go away from me, Lord; I am a sinful man!" (Luke 5:8). These encounters show that the experience of confronting the holy is awe inspiring, even life threatening, which is exactly what the psalmist is indicating in verses 1–3.

Worshiping the Holy God

The fourth element of holiness, the moral uprightness or righteousness of God, is developed in the second stanza of Psalm 99 (vv. 4–5), especially in terms of God's righteous rule among his people and over the nations. He is said to love justice, to have established equity, and to have done always what is just and right (v. 4). Therefore, says the writer, we must

> Exalt the LORD our God
> and worship at his footstool (v. 5).

If the psalmist's description were only of an earthly king and earthly throne, "his footstool" would indicate the platform or dais on which the king's throne rests. But this is a divine king and a divine throne. God's footstool in this case could be several things. It could be the earth, as in Isaiah 66:1 ("Heaven is my throne and the earth is my footstool"), or more particularly, Mount Zion (as probably in Isa. 60:13). What is most likely here is the ark of the covenant.

The ark was a box about a yard long and a foot and a half wide and deep. It was covered with gold, and it had a lid called the mercy seat, on either end of which were figures of cherubim, between whose wings God was understood to dwell. The box contained the law of God, the stone tablets on which were written the Ten Commandments. All these features fit the psalm, especially since the ark was an earthly picture of the heavenly scene where God was understood to be "enthroned between the cherubim." The enthronement between the cherubim fits stanza one, and the reminder of the law, which the ark contained, fits the emphasis on God's just and equitable rule in stanza two. In 1 Chronicles 28:2 David refers to "the ark of the covenant" explicitly as "the footstool of our God."

This "footstool" was a terrible, awe-inspiring element in the religious experience of Israel. It was kept in the Most Holy Place of the temple and could be approached by the high priest only once a year on the Day of Atonement, and only then after first having made a sacrifice for himself and the people in the adjoining courtyard. To approach the ark at any other time or in any other way would result in immediate death for the one who had thus violated God's holiness. This is how some who did this were judged: Nadab and Abihu, for example (see Lev. 10:1–3).

But the ark of the covenant was a picture of God's mercy too, for it was there, on the mercy seat, that the high priest was able to make atonement for the people's sins. He did it by sprinkling the blood of the sacrifice on the covering, which meant that the blood, which testified to the death of an innocent sacrificial victim, now came between the presence of the holy God, who was understood to dwell between the wings of the cherubim, and the law contained in the ark, which all of us have broken.

This is the only way we can approach God to worship him. We "worship at his footstool" because it is only on the basis of the shed blood, pointing to the poured-out blood of Jesus Christ, that we can approach the holy God. Have you come to God in that way? If you have not come through faith in Jesus and his atoning death for your sins, you have not really come to God at all and you will be sent away from him into outer darkness at the final day.

Answered Prayer and Forgiveness

The final section of this three-part psalm (the last two stanzas in the New International Version) breaks away from heaven to speak of three past leaders of Israel—Moses, Aaron, and Samuel—and of the wilderness experience of the people, when God "spoke to them from the pillar of cloud" (vv. 6–7).

A change like this usually seems abrupt to us and even causes some commentators to begin speculating about two separate psalms that have somehow been wrongly joined together. But such changes are common in the psalms, and in this case the purpose seems to be to remind us that worship of the high and holy God is not for angels alone, though angels do worship him, but for human beings like us. It is we who are being called to "exalt the LORD our God and worship at his footstool" (v. 5) or "worship at his holy mountain" (v. 9).

If we come to God on the basis of the shed blood of Jesus Christ, as God requires, we will discover two things. First, God answers prayer. Moses, Aaron, and Samuel "called on the LORD and he answered them" (v. 6).

Second, God forgives our sins. "You were to Israel a forgiving God, though you punished their misdeeds" (v. 8).

Be Holy, as God Is Holy

Our study of the holiness of God, as it is developed in Psalm 99, leads to three important consequences:

1. *If God is holy, we must be holy.* Peter wrote, "But just as he who called you is holy, so be holy in all you do; for it is written: 'Be holy, because I am holy'" (1 Peter 1:15). Holiness is no option for a Christian.

2. *If we are not holy (and we are not), we must flee to Christ for forgiveness and cleansing.* Notice that at the end of the psalm "he is holy" is changed to "*our* God is holy," which is surely significant. God needs to be our God. But how does the holy God become our God since we are not holy? The answer is by atonement and forgiveness (v. 8). It is only the forgiven who can worship at God's holy mountain.

3. *If we know God, we must worship him.* At the beginning of Psalm 99 the nations are exhorted to praise God, which they may or may not do. But regardless of how the nations respond, God is great in Zion, and this means that he is praised by his people. Charles Haddon Spurgeon wrote, "The ignorant forget him, the wicked despise him, the atheistical oppose him, but among his own chosen he is great beyond comparison. He is great in the esteem of the gracious, great in his acts of mercy, and really great in himself: great in his mercy, power, wisdom, justice and glory."[3]

Let me close with the way this is handled in Hebrews. The author of that book wrote:

> You have not come to a mountain that can be touched and that is burning with fire; to darkness, gloom and storm; to a trumpet blast or to such a voice speaking words, so that those who heard it begged that no further word be spoken to them, because they could not bear what was commanded: "If even an animal touches the mountain, it must be stoned." The sight was so terrifying that Moses said, "I am trembling with fear."
>
> But you have come to Mount Zion, to the heavenly Jerusalem, the city of the living God. You have come to thousands upon thousands of angels in joyful assembly, to the church of the firstborn, whose names are written in heaven. You have come to God, the judge of all men, to the spirits of righteous men made perfect, to Jesus the mediator of a new covenant, and to the sprinkled blood that speaks a better word than the blood of Abel. . . .
>
> Therefore, since we are receiving a kingdom that cannot be shaken, let us be thankful, and so worship God acceptably with reverence and awe, for our God is a consuming fire (Heb. 12:18–24, 28–29).

Indeed he is! Yet worship him is what each of us must do.

Psalm 100

The Psalm for Giving Thanks

Shout for joy to the LORD, all the earth.
Worship the LORD with gladness;
come before him with joyful songs.
Know that the LORD is God.
It is he who made us, and we are his;
we are his people, the sheep of his pasture.

Enter his gates with thanksgiving
and his courts with praise;
give thanks to him and praise his name.
For the LORD is good and his love endures forever;
his faithfulness continues through all generations.
verses 1–5

It is a striking fact about the one hundredth psalm that it is the only one in the Psalter explicitly identified as "a psalm for giving thanks." This does not mean that this is the only psalm of the 150 in the Psalter that is to be used to give thanks, of course. Expressions of thanks and exhortations to give thanks occur many places in the psalms, and there are other psalms of specific thanksgiving besides this one. Psalm 107 is one. It has been called "The Pilgrims' Psalm" because it was cherished by our Puritan forebears as an appropriate and moving description of their experiences in coming to the New World. It describes their deliverance from homeless wanderings, imprisonment, and persecutions, which they endured in Europe before coming to America, and then their perils at sea, starvation, and the deaths of family and friends, which they experienced once they had departed. It concludes,

> Whoever is wise, let him heed these things
> and consider the great love of the LORD (v. 43).

The pilgrims undoubtedly read this psalm with tears both of sorrow and joy on the first Thanksgiving.

Also, Psalm 118 uses the word *thanks* more than any other psalm, beginning and ending with the challenge:

> Give thanks to the LORD, for he is good;
> his love endures forever (vv. 1, 29).

Yet Psalm 100 is the only psalm that is explicitly identified as "a psalm for giving thanks." And what a psalm it is! It is the very quintessence of thanksgiving. Christians have clearly felt this throughout many generations of church history, because numerous poets have rendered it in verse and it has been sung to several well-known tunes. We know Psalm 100 significantly as "Old Hundredth." The words are by William Kethe (1561), and the tune is by Louis Bourgeois from the Genevan Psalter.

> All people that on earth do dwell,
> Sing to the Lord with cheerful voice;
> Him serve with fear, his praise forthtell,
> Come ye before him and rejoice.

Isaac Watts also wrote a hymn based on Psalm 100. It begins,

> Before Jehovah's awful throne,
> Ye nations, bow with sacred joy;
> Know that the Lord is God alone,
> He can create, and he destroy.

Charles Haddon Spurgeon, the great Baptist preacher of the nineteenth century, declared, "Nothing can be more sublime this side of heaven than the singing of this noble Psalm by a vast congregation."[1]

The psalm is not hard to analyze. It contains seven great imperatives, plus two explanations of why we should give thanks, the first halfway through the psalm and the other at the end. Psalm 100 contains: (1) a statement of how to give thanks, (2) an explanation of why God's people must

give thanks, (3) an invitation to give thanks, and (4) a final great expression
of praise or thanksgiving.

Three Ways to Give Thanks

Occasionally, when someone has done something special for us, we find
ourselves asking, "What can I do for so-and-so to show my appreciation?" It
is a valid question and not always an easy one to answer. But think: If it is
hard to know how to show appreciation to another human being, how
much more difficult must it be to show appreciation to God? How should
we show appreciation to God? We cannot thank God by giving him something. He needs nothing from us. What can we do? The opening verses suggest three things.

1. *We can "shout."* That seems a strange place to begin, particularly since
the psalm envisions the people of God giving thanks together in God's
house. Is that really what we are to do? Are we to come to church in order
to shout? It is helpful to know that the Hebrew word originally meant a glad
shout, such as loyal subjects might utter when the king appears among
them, the emphasis being on the gladness. This should be clear from the
first two verses since the idea of joy appears there three times: "joy," "gladness," "joyful." Still the text does say "shout." It would be accurate to express
this idea by saying that the people of God are to praise God loudly because
they are happy with him.

Spurgeon said of this verse, "Our happy God should be worshipped by a
happy people; a cheerful spirit is in keeping with his nature, his acts, and
the gratitude which we should cherish for his mercies."[2]

2. *We can "serve."* Verse 2 says, "Worship [literally, "serve"] the LORD with
gladness." The psalm suggests that we serve God by our worship: "Enter his
gates with thanksgiving and his courts with praise" (v. 4). Yet we need to
remember the words of Jesus in which the righteous are praised in the day
of judgment because, when the Lord was hungry they gave him something
to eat, when he was thirsty they gave him something to drink, when he was a
stranger they invited him in, when he needed clothes they clothed him,
when he was sick they looked after him, and when he was in prison they visited him (Matt. 25:35–36).

When the righteous protest, "Lord, when did we see you hungry and
feed you, or thirsty and give you something to drink? When did we see you
a stranger and invite you in, or needing clothes and clothe you? When did
we see you sick or in prison and go to visit you?" (vv. 37–39), the Lord
replies, "I tell you the truth, whatever you did for one of the least of these
brothers of mine, you did for me" (v. 40). How can we give thanks? Jesus
said that we give thanks when we meet the needs of others.

We thank God *by feeding the hungry.* We do this at Tenth Presbyterian
Church through our community dinner programs. We can also do it by
inviting those who are alone or impoverished to have dinner with us.

We thank God *by welcoming strangers.* There are many people who are utterly alone. They need to be included in family times by church people. The Bible says, "God sets the lonely in families" (Ps. 68:6). How? By having his families include them, of course. That is something nearly every family can do.

We thank God *by clothing those who lack adequate clothing* and *by caring for those who are sick and lack adequate care.* Christians should not only care for but even stay with those who are sick or dying. We do this through our ministry to people who have AIDS. Others do it simply by visiting the ill or dying and by various hospital and nursing home visitation programs.

We thank God *by visiting those who are in prison.* In recent years, thanks to the work of Prison Fellowship, many Christians have rediscovered this important ministry.

3. *We can "come."* The third imperative at the beginning of Psalm 100 is "come." This refers to formal worship, since the psalm describes the coming of the people of God to Jerusalem and its temple enclosure. Are we to thank God by serving others? Yes, but we are to worship God too. In other words, faith and works go together. A social gospel alone is not enough. In fact, silent belief is not enough. I am struck by the well-rounded nature of these terms—shout, serve ("worship"), and come—for they embrace our verbal witness, our humanitarian activity, and worship, three necessary parts of Christianity.

Why We Must Give God Thanks

The fourth imperative in this psalm is "know" (v. 3). It is very important, which is why I have set it apart to mark a second section. By including this word the psalm tells us that our thanksgiving to God must be intelligent; we must know whom we are thanking. The Athenian Greeks had been worshiping "an unknown God." But when Paul stood on Mars hill to address them, he said, "What you worship as something unknown I am going to proclaim to you" (Acts 17:23). We cannot rightly thank or worship a God who is unknown to us.

So we ask, What is it about God we should know? Verse 3 gives two answers: (1) He is our Creator, and (2) he is our Redeemer. The words are:

> It is he who made us, and we are his;
> we are his people, the sheep of his pasture.

The first thing we should notice about this verse is the connection between knowing God as Creator and knowing ourselves as his creatures. This is the point John Calvin made in the opening chapter of his *Institutes of the Christian Religion* when he pointed out that the natural result of knowing God is to know ourselves, and that the only way we really know ourselves is by knowing God. Knowing God and knowing ourselves always go together.

But there are two specifics:

1. *Knowing God as Creator.* What happens to us when we do not know God as Creator? We imagine that we are our own creators. Sometimes we do this scientifically. This is what lies behind the surprising persistent appeal of evolution, a theory that has very little if any true evidence in its support. The appeal of evolution is that it does away with the need for God. It explains how things got to be as they are without any divine creative force behind them. Of course, if we do not need God as our Creator, then we do not need to be thankful. Why should we? We got here by ourselves, thank you. We have no one but ourselves to thank.

Another way we imagine that we are our own creators is by an inordinate admiration of our abilities or achievements. This is what the humorist meant when he described the Englishman as "a self-made man who worships his creator." It is only when we know God as our Creator that we know ourselves as his creatures and find ourselves appropriately thankful to him.

2. *Knowing God as Redeemer.* Even more important than knowing God as Creator is knowing him as Redeemer, which is what the words "his people" and "the sheep of his pasture" ultimately refer to. It is hard at this point not to think of David's moving, personal expression of faith in God as his shepherd in Psalm 23: "The LORD is my shepherd, I shall not be in want" (v. 1).

Or we think of the way the Lord explained it to the disciples in his extensive discourse on himself as the Good Shepherd, recorded in John 10:

> I am the good shepherd. The good shepherd lays down his life for the sheep. The hired hand is not the shepherd who owns the sheep. So when he sees the wolf coming, he abandons the sheep and runs away. . . .
> I am the good shepherd; I know my sheep and my sheep know me—just as the Father knows me and I know the Father—and I lay down my life for the sheep. I have other sheep that are not of this sheep pen. I must bring them also. They too will listen to my voice, and there shall be one flock and one shepherd (John 10:11–12, 14–16).

If there is no other reason why we must be thankful to God it is because he has both made us and redeemed us. No one should be more thankful to God than the sheep who are cared for by the Good Shepherd.

The second thing we need to notice about this verse is the implication of the words "he . . . made us." If it is really *God* who has made us, not ourselves, and if we are his *because* he made us, then we are his to do with as seems best to him.

Has he given us days of unusual prosperity? If so, it has pleased him to do it; we must be thankful to him for being the good and generous God he is. Has he given us days of troublesome trials or sorrow? If this is the case, we must thank him for that, knowing that he is wise and gracious even in allowing such hard times. The apostle Paul said, "I have learned to be content whatever the circumstances. I know what it is to be in need, and I know what it is to have plenty. I have learned the secret of being content in any and every situation, whether well fed or hungry, whether living in plenty or in want. I can do everything through him who gives me strength" (Phil. 4:11–13). Paul was in prison when he wrote that, but the letter in which it occurs, the letter to the Philippians, is overflowing with thanksgiving.

There is one more important point in this verse, in the phrase "we are his." Regardless of what may happen to us, we are *still* his. Troubles inevitably will come. But it is no matter. We are his.

Sickness may come. We are his.

We may lose a job. We are his.

Suppose death should come into our immediately family. We are still his, and we will always be his. God the Father said,

> Never will I leave you;
> never will I forsake you (Heb. 13:5).

Likewise, Jesus said, "Surely I am with you always" (Matt. 28:20). The apostle Paul said he was convinced that "neither death nor life, neither angels nor demons, neither the present nor the future, nor any powers, neither height nor depth, nor anything else in all creation, will be able to separate us from the love of God that is in Christ Jesus our Lord" (Rom. 8:38–39).

An Invitation to Thank God

The third part of the psalm is an invitation to thank God, and once again there are three strong imperatives: "enter," "give thanks," and "praise." Earlier I emphasized that our thanks to God should be expressed by what we do for others. But when we get to verse 4 the emphasis is clearly upon the gathering of God's people to the temple to thank and praise God together. This is not just a way of saying that it is good to go to church, though that is true enough. It teaches that there is a special aspect of thanksgiving that involves the whole people of God together and not just the private prayers of individuals.

This is what we should expect, of course. For when God called us to Christ he did not call us in isolation but to be his elect people together, participating in a common heritage. This means that those among whom, for whom, and with whom we should give thanks are other believers. Moreover, we should exercise responsibility toward these others by encouraging a thankful response in them toward God. I can imagine that this psalm was often used as an invitation from one Jewish worshiper to another to come to the holy city or to the temple to thank God for his benefits.

How do we thank God? One way is by inviting others to join us in the thanksgiving. We can ask others to go to church with us. I notice that the psalm begins this way: "Shout for joy to the Lord, *all the earth*" (v. 1). It is an invitation to all the people of all the world to praise God.

The Character of God

The final verse of the psalm, like verse 3, explains why you and I should thank God. But it is not just a repetition of the first explanation. The third verse said that we should thank God because of what he has done; he has both made and remade us. That is, he is both our Creator and Redeemer. The final verse invites us to thank God because of who he is. It tells us three things about him.

1. *God is "good."* The gods of the heathen were not good. They were selfish and capricious. You could never know when they might turn against you and do you harm. Not so our God. The God of the Bible is and has always been good. When he created the world and all that is in it, he saw that it was "good" (Gen. 1:4–31). When he gave us his law, that law was "good" (Rom. 7:12). When he reveals his will to us, his will is "good, pleasing and perfect" (Rom. 12:2). The word *gospel* means the "good news." The very word *God* is a shortened form of "good." No wonder the psalmist cried out:

> Taste and see that the LORD is good;
>   Blessed is the man who takes refuge in him (Ps. 34:8).

2. *God is "love."* This love "endures forever." God is many things. He has many attributes. But nothing lies so much at the very heart of God as love. Nothing so endears him to his people.

3. *God is "faithful."* We live in a world of change. And not only is the world changing, even change is changing, because, as Alvin Toffler has reminded us in *Future Shock,* change is happening at a faster and faster pace as the years speed on. In the midst of a rapidly changing world it is a comfort to know that God himself is unchanging. He is today what he was for our fathers and mothers—and what he was for Paul and Mary and Joseph and David, indeed for all the patriarchs of the faith back to and including our first parents. Moreover, he can be counted on to remain as he has been. Spurgeon said, "As our fathers found him faithful, so will our sons and their seed forever."[3]

Has God been good in the past? Of course! Then he will always be good. You need never worry that he might cease to be good or change his good ways.

Has God been loving? Of course. Then he will always be loving. His very nature is love. You need never worry that he will cease to love you.

Has he seen you through difficult times? Very few Christians have avoided such difficult times altogether. Yet those who have gone through them testify that God has kept them securely. Well, then, he will do it for you also, whatever may come. Has anyone ever had greater reasons to thank God than we who are his redeemed people, who know him not only as our Creator but also as our loving shepherd and Lord? Then let us shout with gladness:

> Enter his gates with thanksgiving
>   and his courts with praise;
>   give thanks to him and praise his name.
> For the LORD is good and his love endures forever;
>   his faithfulness continues through all generations.

Psalm 101

Pattern for an Upright Administration

I will sing of your love and justice;
   to you, O LORD, I will sing praise.
I will be careful to lead a blameless life—
   when will you come to me?

I will walk in my house
   with blameless heart.
I will set before my eyes
   no vile thing.

The deeds of faithless men I hate;
   they will not cling to me.
Men of perverse heart shall be far from me;
   I will have nothing to do with evil.

Whoever slanders his neighbor in secret,
   him will I put to silence;
whoever has haughty eyes and a proud heart,
   him will I not endure.

My eyes will be on the faithful in the land,
   that they may dwell with me;
he whose walk is blameless
   will minister to me.

No one who practices deceit
will dwell in my house;
no one who speaks falsely
will stand in my presence.

Every morning I will put to silence
all the wicked in the land;
I will cut off every evildoer
from the city of the LORD.
                              verses 1–8

It has been some time since we have come across a psalm attributed to David. The last one was Psalm 86, and this is the first in book four of the Psalter, though there is also one yet to come (Psalm 103).

Many scholars reject the ascription of the psalm to David. Nevertheless, it reads like a psalm of David, and it is an appropriate psalm for David as an anointed king of Israel to have written. In this psalm David extols the standards by which he intends to run his kingdom, and he commits himself to those standards. We know that he did not live up to these high standards completely. We are all sinners and therefore fail to live up to whatever moral standards we acknowledge. Nevertheless, David did pretty well, and the standards themselves are of abiding value. They are valuable for anyone in a place of authority in government, business, the church, or the home.

Charles Haddon Spurgeon wrote rightly,

> This is just such a psalm as the man after God's own heart would compose when he was about to become king in Israel. It is David all over, straightforward, resolute, devout; there is no trace of policy or vacillation—the Lord has appointed him to be king, and he knows it; therefore he purposes in all things to behave as becomes a monarch whom the Lord himself has chosen. If we call this the Psalm of Pious Resolutions, we shall perhaps remember it all the more readily.[1]

"How Can the Lord Come to Me?"

Any early period of David's rule would form an appropriate setting for this psalm, but there may be a clue in verse 2 that will help us narrow it down further. In the middle of that verse, in a phrase that seems to break the flow of thought and even be a bit inappropriate at that point, David suddenly asks the question: "When will you come to me?" When we read words like that we think of the coming of the Holy Spirit or of some special times in our lives when God seems to make himself unusually close to us. But that is a New Testament way of thinking and not something that we find very much in the Old Testament. In the Old Testament, particularly in the psalms, the saints speak of going up to God, by which they mean going to worship God at the temple in Jerusalem. But they do not speak of God coming to them.

What does this question refer to, then? Well, in 2 Samuel 6:1–11 we are told of an attempt to bring the ark of the covenant to Jerusalem. It had been at Kiriath Jearim. But David had it brought up from the house of a man named Abinadab, placing it on a new cart drawn by oxen. David was accompanying the ark along with thirty thousand of the men of Israel, all of whom were singing songs and making loud music with harps, lyres, tambourines, and cymbals, when suddenly something terrible happened. The oxen stumbled, shaking the ark, and a man named Uzzah, one of the sons of Abinadab, reached out his hand to touch the ark to steady it. It was an apparently innocent and well-meaning act. But we are told, "The LORD's anger burned against Uzzah because of his irreverent act; therefore God struck him down and he died there beside the ark of God" (v. 7).

Needless to say, the singing and instrumental music stopped. The party was over. The king was angry and embarrassed, and the ark was not moved forward any farther. For a long time it was left in the house of Obed-Edom.

But here is the important thing. David said in his distress, "How can the ark of the LORD ever come to me?" (v. 9). For David the presence of the ark and the presence of the Lord were very nearly the same thing. That is why he wanted the ark in Jerusalem, where he lived. Here God had shown himself to be an unbendingly holy God. David had mismanaged the attempt to move the ark. God had said that the ark was to be carried by priests in a certain way and was never to be touched, even by the priests. When Uzzah reached out his hand to steady the ark, however well intentioned he may have been, he violated God's law and contaminated what must never be contaminated and was therefore struck down. It seemed a little thing. But God took it seriously, as he does all sin. If God took that seriously, so seriously that he punished Uzzah with death, how could David ever hope to have a life and rule so blameless that God, in the presence of the ark, could dwell with him?

I suggest that it is this incident that lies behind the question, "When will you come to me?" in Psalm 101:2 and that it is why David is so eager to lay out the pattern for an upright administration in these verses.

Love and Justice

I do not often take issue with the translation provided by the New International Version, but I do so here by pointing out that the word *your* in the first line of this psalm ("I will sing of *your* love and justice") is not in the Hebrew manuscripts. The psalm actually begins: "I will sing of love and justice." In other words, the psalm is about love (or mercy) and justice, and the way David introduces these two ideas is much like the style of older writers who would compose essays with such titles as "On Friendship," "On Civil Government," and so on.

The New International Version translators obviously thought that it was God's love and justice that David had in mind. That is why they added the word *your,* meaning God's. But I think this is a mistake. It is true that love and justice are frequently noted as characteristics of God's rule, rather than man's, since human beings are usually neither just nor loving. But the words are used of good human rule in Isaiah 16:5, and this is what David writes about in the psalm. I think this is very important. For when we relate characteristics such as these to God, however appropriate that might be, we tend to avoid applying these same standards to ourselves, and this is harmful because it is precisely these characteristics that are needed for any upright administration.

Besides, we need both if we are to manage other people well, whether in government, business, the church, the home, or whatever. Mercy and justice operate as checks on one another. Justice checks love that might otherwise be wrongly indulgent and therefore harmful. Love checks judgment that might otherwise be unduly harsh and therefore also harmful. David wanted his rule to be marked by both of these. Hence, they are the theme of the song. What follows is essentially exposition.

When I was looking through what had been written on Psalm 101 by other writers in preparation for this study, I was startled to find that Martin Luther had done an exposition of the psalm that ran to *eighty* pages. The reason, I discovered, is that he was deeply concerned about civil government and wanted to expound the psalm as a listing of qualities toward which every Christian prince or magistrate should strive.

Luther saw love and justice as referring to desirable human qualities also, as I have, not primarily to divine qualities, at least in this psalm. He wrote:

> What the psalm calls "mercy and justice" is said not of the mercy and justice of God but of the mercy and justice which a prince practices toward his servants and his subjects. . . . A prince and lord must use both of these. If there is only mercy and the prince lets everyone milk him and kick him in the teeth and does not punish or become angry, then not only the court but the land, too, will be filled with wicked rascals; all discipline and honor will come to an end. On the other hand, if there is only anger and punishment or too much of it, then tyranny will result, and the pious will be breathless in their daily fear and anxiety.[2]

We are talking about government here, proper standards for an upright administration. But these words apply to our personal lives as well—that is, to how we relate to others. We must insist on upright conduct, modeling it ourselves. But we also need to be merciful, knowing that people are weak as well as sinful. We must remember that even God, who has a perfect standard of justice, does not deal with us strictly as we deserve, but is merciful. We should note that just two psalms after this we find David writing,

> He [the Lord] does not treat us as our sins deserve
>   or repay us according to our iniquities.
> For as high as the heavens are above the earth,
>   so great is his love for those who fear him (Ps. 103:10–11).

Blameless Heart and Blameless Life

The next characteristic we find David talking about in this psalm is personal moral character, which he refers to as leading a "blameless life" and having a "blameless heart" (v. 2). These are divided by the stanza breaks in the New International Version, but they belong together since the only way to lead a blameless life is to have a blameless heart. As Jesus said, "Out of the overflow of the heart the mouth speaks" (Matt. 12:34)—and acts as well.

What strikes me as significant about David's description of blameless moral conduct at this point is how he assumes its existence naturally, apart from any puzzle as to what leading a blameless life is. This is entirely different from how people approach ethics in our relativistic times.

Not long ago my attention was drawn to a column by Meg Greenfield, a columnist who writes regularly for *Newsweek* magazine. It was titled "Right and Wrong in Washington" and was a penetrating exposure of what is wrong in government when we require ethics officers, committees, or specialists to tell us what proper moral behavior should be. People should know what is right and wrong, she argued. But today they say, "'I asked the ethics office and they said it didn't fall within the category of impermissible activity.' Or, more frequently, when there is a flap about something that has already occurred, they say, 'We have directed the ethics office to look into it and report back to us in 60 days.' Good old '60 days'—for something that your ordinary, morally sentient person wouldn't need 60 seconds to figure out."[3]

There is none of that moral escapism with David. There is no excusing himself for not knowing what the right way is. He did not always walk in that right way, but if he did not, he acknowledged that it was he who had deviated, not that the standards were unclear. His goal was to walk "with blameless heart" and to set "no vile thing" before his eyes.

War against Evil

That last phrase ("no vile thing") takes us a step further in studying the standards David is unfolding, for they bring in the negative side of the virtues with which the psalm began. Love (mercy), justice, and a blameless life! These are his themes. But now, having affirmed the positive virtues, David also rejects the negatives, writing,

> The deeds of faithless men I hate;
>> they will not cling to me.
> Men of perverse heart shall be far from me;
>> I will have nothing to do with evil.
>
> Whoever slanders his neighbor in secret,
>> him will I put to silence;
> whoever has haughty eyes and a proud heart,
>> him will I not endure (vv. 3–5).

A number of vices are suggested by these stanzas.

1. *"Faithless men"* (v. 3). Faithless behavior means failing to keep faith—that is, breaking agreements. In regard to human agreements it means being dishonest or untrustworthy. In regard to God it has to do with being an apostate, one who has renounced the faith he once held. It is the exact opposite of the "covenant love" *(hesed)* idea introduced in verse 1.

2. *"Men of perverse heart"* (v. 4). Perverse means wicked, but with the added idea of having turned aside from what is known to be good, true, or morally right. It also has the idea of willfully diverting someone or some proposed course of action from those ends.

3. *"Slander"* (v. 5). Slander has to do with words, not actions, and is a reminder of how often in the psalms David in particular is concerned with the harmful, even deadly effects of words maliciously spoken. There must have been a great deal of this in David's court in spite of his desire for high standards. It is true of all government circles.

4. *"Haughty eyes and a proud heart"* (v. 5). This is what we call arrogance. Arrogance is supposing that we are able to handle everything in life by ourselves without the help either of God or other people, that we are entirely self-sufficient. People today actually think highly of this characteristic. But it is a terrible vice, for it was the sin of Satan, who thought he could take over the rule of the universe. In his study of Psalm 101, Martin Luther spends almost the entire first quarter of his study reminding government figures that nothing is accomplished apart from God and that no one should be arrogant about his or her own accomplishments or abilities. "Everything is a vain sham and deception if God is not in it!" wrote Luther.[4]

The vices listed in these verses are also mentioned in the psalm's second half, where David seems to be writing about evil "in the land" and not just "in my house," meaning in the central government (see vv. 7–8).

David is saying in both sections that he will neither encourage nor deal with such persons. On the contrary, he will "put to silence all the wicked in the land" and dismiss "every evildoer from the city of the LORD." Why? Because he knew that standing for the right means nothing if the opposing evil is not opposed and rejected at the same time. He knew, as H. C. Leupold says, that "disavowal of evil men is as important as are the acceptance and acknowledgment of those who are true and upright."[5]

Promoting the Faithful in the Land

This brings us back to the positive again. We have been introduced to three administrative virtues: love, justice, and upright behavior. They have been followed by four harmful vices: faithlessness, perversity, slander, and arrogance. David says that it is his intention to drive those who practice such things from his government and from any position of power or influence. Yet that is not all. In place of those who are to be repudiated for their faithlessness, David writes that he also intends to seek out the faithful in the land.

> My eyes will be on the faithful in the land,
>   that they may dwell with me;
> he whose walk is blameless
>   will minister to me (v. 6).

David wanted to surround himself with good people, people he could trust and whose walk was blameless. Sometimes, when people are in positions of power or responsibility, they turn to those who can "get the job done" and do not ask questions about how they do it. It is worldly wisdom to say, No one can rule effectively who cannot close his eyes and ears to some of the things that are going on around him. But a good government is one in which the high places are filled with upright and not unscrupulous people. Luther said, "If God wants to be good to a prince or a country, he gives him a fine Joseph or a Naaman to be near him, through whom all things fare well and prosper."[6]

May God give us many such for our own government today! And in the companies for which we work! And in the church! We need people who can get the job done, but we need "the faithful of the land" to do it. It is a wise leader who seeks out such people and then puts authority into their hands.

"Come, Lord Jesus"

But now I need to end on both a sad and happy note. The sad part is to say that although David possessed these high and wonderful ideals, he did not live up to them. He started well and was a mostly moral man. But the last years of his reign were marked by his own personal sin and by growing violence within his own family and government. It was not that he was not a good king or that he had inadequate moral standards, only that he was a man and thus also a sinner, as we all are. No human being, however noble his or her intentions may be, ever lives up to a perfect standard of righteousness. That is why otherwise good political administrations tend toward corruption in their later years. It is why old leaders often fail.

The good news is that there is one who does not fail. In fact, he can never fail, for he is Jesus, God's Son. God has placed the governing of the entire universe in his hands. Revelation says,

> The kingdom of the world has become the kingdom
> of our Lord and of his Christ,
> and he will reign for ever and ever (Rev. 11:15).

Meanwhile, is it not true that Jesus, like David, has his eyes alert for the faithful in the land, for those who will serve now and also dwell with him in glory at the end of time? Will you be one of them? The way to do it is by keeping close to him, serving him always and the best you can.

Psalm 102

Frailty Anchored in Eternity

Hear my prayer, O LORD;
let my cry for help come to you.
Do not hide your face from me
when I am in distress.
Turn your ear to me;
when I call, answer me quickly.

For my days vanish like smoke;
my bones burn like glowing embers.
My heart is blighted and withered like grass;
I forget to eat my food.
Because of my loud groaning
I am reduced to skin and bones.
I am like a desert owl,
like an owl among the ruins.
I lie awake; I have become
like a bird alone on a roof.
All day long my enemies taunt me;
those who rail against me use my name as a curse.
For I eat ashes as my food
and mingle my drink with tears
because of your great wrath,
for you have taken me up and thrown me aside.
My days are like the evening shadow;
I wither away like grass.

But you, O LORD, sit enthroned forever;
your renown endures through all generations.
                                        verses 1–12

One of the splendid delusions of the young is that they think they are immortal. No matter how recklessly they drive, no matter how many drugs they take or physical dangers they expose themselves to, they do not believe that anything bad can happen to them.

But that changes as we grow older. There come times in our lives when it dawns on us that our existence is filled with dangers and life is not unending. Physical ailments begin to trouble us, and we worry about still other fatal diseases that may come. Family members die. We realize that the time is coming when we will die too. As we move into retirement and later years, that realization grows even stronger. For now, not only do we know that we are not immortal, we realize, quite to the contrary, that life is extremely short and we are at best frail specks of existence hanging on at the very precipice of eternity. At any point in life, whether young or old, we can be made aware of these realities by serious illness.

This is what the author of Psalm 102 experienced. Sickness forced him to a sharp realization of his frailty. But in his weakness he turned to God, who is not weak, and found a refuge.

A Messianic Psalm

In the liturgy of the church Psalm 102 is considered one of the seven penitential psalms, no doubt because of the mention of God's "great wrath" in verse 10. But it is actually messianic, though not in the detailed sense suggested by Arno C. Gaebelein or William J. Pettingill. Gaebelein sees the psalm as a prophecy of Christ's earthly humiliation and redemptive work. Pettingill views it as a dialogue between God the Father and God the Son.[1] The psalm is messianic because of verses 25–27, which are used in Hebrews 1:10–12, as the Father's address to Jesus Christ. But this anticipation of the future work of Christ grows out of the psalmist's painful awareness of his own frailty, which means that the messianic focus of the psalm comes in only at the end.

Looked at another way, Psalm 102 is a patriotic psalm, which is how Charles Spurgeon saw it.[2] This is because the writer, although he is sick even to death, does not look to God only for his own restoration but links his personal survival to the restoration of Zion. Jerusalem and its environs are in ruins. Her toppled "stones" and even the "very dust" move God's servants to pity. But God is still her God and will therefore restore her in "the appointed time" (v. 13). It is the anticipation of this future time that leads the writer into those verses that look forward to Jesus.

There are echoes of other portions of the Old Testament in this psalm: some earlier psalms, Job, Isaiah, and Lamentations. I will not explore them here, except to say that they are natural in view of Jerusalem's ruin.

The Prologue: "Hear My Prayer"

The first eleven verses are a lament in which the writer describes his weakened condition. But the first two of these verses (vv. 1–2) are really a prologue to the whole in which, with much repetition and great passion, the suffering man appeals to God to hear him.

The single most noticeable feature of Hebrew poetry is repetition, especially what is called parallelism. This means that an idea stated in one line is followed by a second line in which that idea is repeated, though in slightly different words. Sometimes the repetition is synonymous. At other times it is antithetical. At still other times the second sentence adds a thought to the first as if to amplify its meaning. In these two verses repetition is carried to the extreme, for there are five requests in these six lines and they are virtually identical: "Hear my prayer," "Let my cry for help come to you," "Do not hide your face," "Turn your ear to me," and "Answer me quickly."

The impression intended is that this is no passive or halfhearted petition, no mere formal "saying of prayers." Quite the contrary. It is an impassioned prayer because the situation out of which it grows is desperate. Desperate conditions make for strong petitions.

An Afflicted Man's Lament

The psalmist is sick, but that is not all that is bothering him. He is concerned for Jerusalem too, and he is being taunted by his enemies. These conditions enter into his lament. Nevertheless, it is chiefly his sickness, frailty, and the brevity of life that trouble him and give force to his complaint. He describes his condition like this:

1. *My life is like smoke.* When Job was bemoaning his sad condition, that great sufferer said,

> Hardship does not spring from the soil,
> > nor does trouble sprout from the ground.
> Yet man is born to trouble
> > as surely as sparks fly upward (Job 5:6–7).

Since there are other indications in Psalm 103 that its author may have known and drawn upon Job, it may be that he got the ideas of life dispersing like smoke from Job's writing (v. 3). Job is saying that each generation of human beings is born to suffer, that they are merely logs thrown upon the blazing fire of life to be consumed and fly upward as sparks and be blown into oblivion. So is the psalmist. He feels that he has been thrown upon the fire and that his life is vanishing like smoke. Or to change the image, he is withering away like summer grass (v. 4).

2. *I am sick.* As in other psalms written by sick men, there is not very much in these verses to indicate the psalmist's particular affliction. But whatever it

was, it affected his appearance. It had taken away his appetite. As a result of this sickness and not eating he was "reduced to skin and bones" (v. 5).

3. *I am lonely and isolated.* This seems to be the meaning of the references to various birds in verses 6–7. The older versions referred to a pelican and an owl, but this was only because the translators did not know the birds the Hebrew words referred to. The New International Version is not certain either, which is why it translates: "a desert owl" (whatever that is) and an "owl" and a "bird alone on a roof."

4. *My enemies are mocking.* Suffering is a difficult enough burden to bear all by itself. But when enemies also mock you for it, it is virtually intolerable. Yet they do! These cowards would have been afraid to mock a strong man when he was on his feet fighting, but they attacked the author of the psalm when he was down and unable to fight back.

5. *My sufferings are unexplained.* In verse 10 the psalmist speaks of God having taken him up and thrown him aside "because of your great wrath." This shows awareness of sin on his part, but it is significant that nowhere in the psalm does the psalmist mention his sin specifically or confess it. This suggests that although he is aware that nothing that has happened to him is undeserved (we all sin and deserve God's fiercest wrath), still he is not at all sure what he has done to deserve that wrath or why God is afflicting him in this particular way. In other words, his experience was identical to Job's. Job was not sinless, far from it. But Job could not understand why he was being singled out for such particularly intense suffering. All the psalmist can say is that, in the final analysis, it is God who is responsible. He leaves it at that.

The Turning Point of the Psalm

Verse 12 is the important turning point of the psalm, so much so that Martin Luther said, "Everything that has gone before looks to this verse."[3] Everything that follows builds on it also. In the previous verses the psalmist has described his frail and wasting condition. He is like smoke that vanishes. Ah, but he has a God who is not at all like that! His is the eternal, immutable God, and it is God whom he is trusting.

> But you, O LORD, sit enthroned forever;
> your renown endures through all generations.

These words could have been said bitterly, of course. They could mean, "Look at you. You are sitting in eternal, unshakable splendor while I, whom you should be caring for and could help, if you wanted to, am wasting away and will soon die miserably and be gone forever. Why are you treating me like this?" They could be demanding. They could mean, "You are powerful. You are able to heal me. It is my right to be healed. I claim healing in Jesus' name." They are none of these things. They are simply a turning to God when everything else has given way.

This is a lesson that Christians today need to learn. Claiming a right to health or anything else may seem spiritual. It may be described as a proof of strong faith by faith healers. But it is not spiritual at all. It is actually a proof of worldliness or secular thinking in the church. Roy Clements, a Baptist pastor in Cambridge, England, has written a book on the psalms in which he has a helpful treatment of Psalm 102, emphasizing the contrast between the way people today think about health and the attitude of the psalmist. We are preoccupied with health issues because we are preoccupied with ourselves, Clements says. Nearly every article that appears in the *New England Journal of Medicine* becomes immediate front-page news. Every dietary quirk gets attention. Exercise routines proliferate. We think we have a right to live forever. So when the church gets into demands for healing, as many churches have, what is this but the invasion of Christianity by the world's way of thinking?[4]

Do not misunderstand. God is the source of all good, including good health. God can heal—and does, though not as frequently as the faith healers claim and certainly not on demand. When we are sick we can ask God to heal us. We should. But perfect health is not a right, and ill health is often as much a gift from God as wholeness.

Do you see how different it was with the author of this psalm? He is praying. He is laying his wasted condition before God. But his words are spiritual, because they are focused on God and express full confidence in the Almighty. In other words, the psalmist has reminded himself that God is sovereign. Therefore, what happens in his life is no accident. It has been given to him by God; so, regardless of what happens to him, he will anchor himself in God's eternity and go on from there. G. Campbell Morgan had it right when he said wisely, "There is nothing more calculated to strengthen the heart in suffering, or inspire the spirit with courage in days of danger and difficulty, than the sense of the eternity of God."[5]

A Transformed Outlook

But that is not all we can observe at this important turning point in the psalm. For it is not just a case of the writer turning his reflections from himself to God, anchoring himself in God's eternity. Having done that, and thus having broken the damaging preoccupation with self that so often strangles our spiritual lives, the psalmist now finds himself thinking about other situations and other people and praying confidently for them. In them he knows that the work of God will go on.

There are four separate things he prays for.

1. *The rebuilding of Jerusalem.* This is the only clue to the dating of the psalm, but the question of dating is only of academic interest. What matters is that the writer is concerned for his city. God's servants are moved to pity by its sad state (v. 14). Therefore, he reasons, God will surely show compassion too:

> You will arise and have compassion on Zion,
>> for it is time to show favor to her;
>> the appointed time has come (v. 13).

The psalmist sees a parallel between his condition and that of Jerusalem; but having turned his thoughts to God, he is concerned now for the greater of the two disasters. Moreover, his concern for the city embraces his concern for the people in it. They are the "destitute" of verse 17. Yet they are also praying, as he is.

May I suggest that this is what we need today. When the people of God cease thinking about themselves so much and begin thinking about the state of things around them, particularly our cities and those who are suffering in them, then God may indeed hear our prayers and send a revival.

2. *The conversion of the Gentile nations.* Not only does the psalmist pray for his own people—for Zion and its impoverished inhabitants—his concern reaches beyond Jerusalem to all the world's nations, whom he sees coming to worship God at some future day.

> The nations will fear the name of the LORD,
> all the kings of the earth will revere your glory. . . .
>
> So the name of the LORD will be declared in Zion
>> and his praise in Jerusalem
> when the peoples and the kingdoms
>> assemble to worship the LORD (vv. 15, 21–22).

This is nothing less than a worldwide missionary outlook, a view that has always marked the church in its best periods. We need it today. We need to do all we can to see that not only our own immediate neighborhoods and cities but the entire world hears the gospel of salvation through the work of Jesus Christ, and that people of all tongues and backgrounds come to him.

3. *The church of the future.* One of the most fascinating things about the transformed, global outlook of the psalmist is that it extends not only outward geographically but also forward into time. Indeed, he sees his own time relating to future time, for he is sure that what God is about to do to save and deliver his people will be recorded in writing to be a source of blessing for the future church.

> Let this be written for a future generation,
>> that a people not yet created may praise the LORD (v. 18).

Do we think about the future? Do we think that what we do now and what God will do for us and through us will be a blessing to future generations?

4. *The deliverance of the prisoners.* The final condition the writer anticipates is deliverance for prisoners, the "release" of "those condemned to death"

(v. 20). It is hard to know what he is thinking of, writing this way, perhaps the release of Jews who were retained in Babylon and who were thus unable to return to Zion to participate in the rebuilding of the city. It is hard for us not to think of Jesus, who announced his mission as the proclamation of spiritual freedom for prisoners when he spoke in the synagogue in Nazareth.

> The Spirit of the Lord is on me,
>> because he has anointed me
>> to preach good news to the poor.
> He has sent me to proclaim freedom for the prisoners
>> and recovery of sight for the blind,
> to release the oppressed,
>> to proclaim the year of the Lord's favor (Luke 4:18–19).

"Thou Who Changest Not"

It is good that we have come to this point too, because this is how the psalm itself ends, according to the messianic interpretation given to it by the author of Hebrews. In some ways these last verses (vv. 23–28) are a reprise in which the psalmist repeats his complaint and also once again turns to anchor himself in God. What is new about them is the force with which the psalmist affirms God's eternity. He talks about God being present from the beginning to lay "the foundations of the earth" and "heavens" (v. 25) and of being present still at the end even though the created order will pass away like a worn-out garment (v. 26). We perish,

> But you remain the same,
>> and your years will never end (v. 27).

When the psalmist wrote these words he was thinking of God the Father, as he has been throughout the psalm. There is very little intimation of the Trinity or the person of the Son of God in the Old Testament. Still, the author of Hebrews is right when he views these words as spoken by the Father to Jesus Christ. For he too is God, "the same yesterday and today and forever" (Heb. 13:8).[6] Jesus is also the one through whom Zion is restored, the Gentile nations converted, future generations of the church raised up and preserved, and those who have been enslaved by sin delivered from their spiritual bondage. Anchored in eternity means anchored in Jesus Christ.

> Change and decay in all around I see;
> O thou who changest not, abide with me.

Psalm 103

"Praise the LORD, O My Soul"

Praise the LORD, O my soul;
*   all my inmost being, praise his holy name.*
Praise the LORD, O my soul,
*   and forget not all his benefits—*
who forgives all your sins
*   and heals all your diseases;*
who redeems your life from the pit
*   and crowns you with love and compassion,*
who satisfies your desires with good things,
*   so that your youth is renewed like the eagle's. . . .*

Praise the LORD, you his angels,
*   you mighty ones who do his bidding,*
*   who obey his word.*
Praise the LORD, all his heavenly hosts,
*   you his servants who do his will.*
Praise the LORD, all his works
*   everywhere in his dominion.*

Praise the LORD, O my soul.

verses 1–5, 20–22

Some psalms are addressed to God, some are spoken to other people—the righteous, sinners, Israel, the Gentile nations, other groups. But in Psalm 103 the psalmist is speaking to himself.

We only have to read as far as verse 2 to learn why—to remind himself of God's blessings so he will continue to be grateful for all that God has done for him. Roy Clements, the pastor of Eden Baptist Church in Cambridge, England, explains: "He is cataloguing the goodness of God; enumerating his blessings, lest in a moment of depression or backsliding, he should forget the source of his prosperity and take God's grace for granted."[1] Do you take God's grace for granted? Others may murmur against God and complain about him. They did in David's day. Many still do today. David wanted his words to be praise. John Stott wrote of this psalm, "We have here the authentic utterance of a redeemed child of God, who piles up words to express his gratitude to the God of grace."[2]

Count Your Blessings

Several good hymns are based on this psalm. From the Psalter of 1912:

> O come, my soul, bless thou the Lord thy Maker,
> And all within me bless his holy name;
> Bless thou the Lord, forget not all his mercies,
> His pardoning grace and saving love proclaim.

Others are Joachim Neander's hymn of 1680 translated by Catherine Winkworth (1863), "Praise to the Lord, the Almighty, the King of Creation," and Henry Lyte's hymn of 1834:

> Praise, my soul, the King of heaven,
> To his feet your tribute bring:
> Ransomed, healed, restored, forgiven,
> Who, like me, his praise should sing?
> Praise him, praise him, praise him, praise him,
> Praise the everlasting King.

Another hymn that was popular some years ago and still is with many people is not based on Psalm 103 but perfectly captures what the psalmist is doing. It goes: "Count your blessings; name them one by one, and it will surprise you what the Lord has done."

Psalms 103 and 104 form a pair of praise psalms. Derek Kidner says, "In the galaxy of the Psalter these are twin stars of the first magnitude."[3] In the fourth book of the Psalter this is the last psalm (and only one of two) that is attributed to David. There are fifteen more in book five.

How Should a Person Praise God?

I want to address a number of questions to this psalm, arranging them in such a way that the successive verses of the psalm give the answers. First, How should a person praise God? The answer of this psalm is in verses 1–2. It is with "all my inmost being" or with all my soul.

> Praise the LORD, O my soul;
> > all my inmost being, praise his holy name.
> Praise the LORD, O my soul,
> > and forget not all his benefits.

In these verses David is rousing himself to remember God's benefits, and he does not want to do it superficially. He wants to do it with all his heart, with all his soul, and with all his strength (cf. Deut. 6:5). This is the place to begin noticing the "alls" in this psalm: "*all* my inmost being" (v. 1) and for "*all* his benefits" (v. 2), which include forgiveness for "*all* your sins" and the healing of "*all* your diseases" (v. 3). Later David will call on "*all* [God's] heavenly hosts" and "*all* his works" to join him in his praise (vv. 21–22).

What a rebuke to much of what passes for praise in our assemblies. We come to church, but we leave our minds at home. We hear of God's grace, but our hearts have been hardened by a critical and carping spirit. Jonathan Edwards believed that there is no true worship that does not touch the "affections." We often are strangely unaffected, honoring God "with our lips" while our hearts are "far from him" (cf. Matt. 15:8; Isa. 29:13).

Why Should a Person Praise God?

What is the problem? Obviously it is that we have forgotten God's many benefits or blessings. It is human to forget. But let us remember this at least: It is a terrible thing to forget God's "benefits." It is said of Hezekiah that his "heart was proud and he did not respond to the kindness shown him; therefore the LORD's wrath was on him and on Judah and Jerusalem" (2 Chron. 32:25). Similarly, God warned the Israelites,

> When you have eaten and are satisfied, praise the LORD your God for the good land he has given you. Be careful that you do not forget the LORD your God, failing to observe his commands, his laws and his decrees that I am giving you this day. Otherwise, when you eat and are satisfied, when you build fine houses and settle down, and when your herds and flocks grow large and your silver and gold increase and all you have is multiplied, then your heart will become proud and you will forget the LORD your God, who brought you out of Egypt, out of the land of slavery. He led you through the vast and dreadful desert, that thirsty and waterless land, with its venomous snakes and scorpions. He brought you water out of hard rock. He gave you manna to eat in the desert, something your fathers had never known, to humble and to test you so that in the end it might go well with you. You may say to yourself, "My power and the strength of my hands have produced this wealth for me." But remember the LORD your God, for it is he who gives you the ability to produce wealth, and so confirms his covenant, which he swore to your forefathers, as it is today (Deut. 8:10–14).

Here then is my second question: Why should a person praise God? The answer should be obvious by now: Because of "all his benefits." David gives this answer in verse 2 and then lists what he means by God's benefits in verses 3–5.

1. *Forgiveness of sins* (v. 3). The first thing David is thankful for is the forgiveness of his sins. Rightly so! For this is the greatest of all gifts that we can receive from God, and the first we need to have. It is true that we need to remember to thank God for our homes and jobs and wealth and all our material possessions, the very things the Israelites were reminded to thank God for in Deuteronomy 8:10–14. But where would we be if we were to acquire all these things and lose our souls? The forgiveness of our sins is the greatest benefit any of us can ever receive from God, and we can receive it only because God gave his Son over to death on the cross to procure it for us.

Some of the statements that occur in the first part of the psalm appear later too, including this matter of the forgiveness of sins. Verse 3 says, "He forgives all your sins." That has to do with the number of sins that are forgiven; it is *all* of them. But then in verse 12 the psalmist elaborates on that by bringing in the scope of the deliverance. To what extent does God forgive sins? He answers, "As far as the east is from the west, so far has he removed our transgressions from us." Since east and west are directions and not points on the compass there is an infinite, unmeasurable distance between them. This may be what David is thinking.

Or it may be, as Roy Clements suggests, that the psalmist is trying to point out that, "however many miles you think lie between west and east, you cannot look two ways at once." You have to turn your back on one in order to look in the direction of the other. "When God forgives us, he puts our sin and us on two different horizons. So when he looks at our sin, he is no longer looking at us, and when he looks at us, he is no longer looking at our sin. To use the vocabulary of Paul, he has justified us."[4]

2. *Healing* (v. 3). The second thing the writer is thankful for is healing, indeed healing of "all" his diseases. This verse has played an important but unwarranted role in some systems of theology that stress what is called "healing in the atonement," meaning that if we have been saved from sin by Christ, we have been healed or have a right to be healed of any physical affliction too. This is bad theology, because it is simply not true that those who have been forgiven for sin are spared or have a right to be spared all diseases. Believers do get sick, and many passages teach that God has his purposes in the sicknesses.

What does the sentence mean then? Some suggest that David is speaking about spiritual illness, such as the burdens of sin. But that is not it. I think he really is speaking of diseases. He is saying that when we are healed, as we often are, it is God who has done it. He is the healer of the body as well as of the soul. Therefore, such health as we have been given is a sure gift from God. God should be praised for it.

3. *Redemption from the pit* (v. 4). The interpretation I have given of verse 3 is reinforced by verse 4. For when David says that God redeems our lives from the pit, he is saying that God brings us back from the very brink of death. The "pit" is Sheol, where the dead go when they die. As far as he himself is concerned, he does not mean that God has rescued him from Sheol by taking him to heaven, for he is not in heaven yet. He means that God has redeemed him by sparing him from death, presumably by healing his diseases.

4. *Satisfaction with good things* (v. 5). And it is not a matter of a mere rescue either, as if our lives are spared but so far as anything else is concerned our lives are miserable. No. God satisfies us with good things "so that [our] youth is renewed like the eagle's." Hasn't that been your experience? Can't you praise God for an abundance of good things that he has graciously brought into your life?

What Is God Like That We Should Praise Him?

Verses 1–5 of Psalm 103 are so personal that most writers view them as the first stanza of the psalm, noting that from this point on (vv. 6–18) the writer seems to be talking about God's grace to other people, particularly to Israel. Yet what David is actually doing is talking about God himself, reminding himself and us of what God is like. He is answering the next question I want to ask of this psalm: What is God like that we should praise him?

Here a number of assertions come in: (1) God works "righteousness and justice" for the oppressed (v. 6); (2) God is "compassionate and gracious, slow to anger, abounding in love" (v. 8); (3) he does "not always accuse, nor will he harbor his anger forever" (v. 9); (4) "he does not treat us as our sins deserve or repay us according to our iniquities" (v. 10); indeed, (5) his love is "from everlasting to everlasting . . . with those who fear him, and his righteousness with their children's children" (v. 17). Basically these statements are variations of a single truth about God—he is gracious or merciful.

David has in mind the revelation God gave to Moses on Mount Sinai when Moses asked God if he could see his face. God told Moses that he could not, because no person can see the face of God and live. He did, however, place Moses in a place on the mountain, cover him with his hand, and then pass by. The text reads, "Then the LORD came down in the cloud and stood there with him and proclaimed his name, the LORD. And he passed by in front of Moses, proclaiming, 'The LORD, the LORD, the compassionate and gracious God, slow to anger, abounding in love and faithfulness, maintaining love to thousands, and forgiving wickedness, rebellion and sin'" (Exod. 34:5–7).

This is the incident David is referring to in verse 7, when he says,

> He made known his ways to Moses,
>> his deeds to the people of Israel.

and in verse 8, where he actually cites Exodus 34:6,

> The LORD is compassionate and gracious,
> slow to anger and abounding in love.

That verse is cited many times in the Old Testament, so much that it almost becomes a credal statement answering the question "What is God?" It is referred to in Nehemiah 9:17; Psalms 86:15; 103:8; 145:8; Joel 2:13; and Jonah 4:2. Our equivalent of this text is from the Westminster Shorter Catechism, where one question asks, "What is God?" and the answer is given: "God is a spirit, infinite, eternal and unchangeable in his being, wisdom, power, holiness, justice, goodness and truth." To the same question the Jewish believer might have responded, "God is compassionate and gracious, slow to anger and abounding in love." It is because of this characteristic that God forgives our sins and satisfies us with all good things.

There is one more thing to be said about God's mercy. It is like that of a father for his children, for God is the Father of those who have been redeemed by Jesus Christ.

> As a father has compassion on his children,
> so the LORD has compassion on those
> who fear him (v. 13).

We remember that it was Jesus who taught us to call God Father (Matt. 6:9).

Who Should Praise God?

The final question I want to ask of this psalm is this: Who should praise God? We might expect the answer to be "those whom God has forgiven, those whom he has rescued from the pit." Certainly these persons should. But as we come to the last stanza of the psalm (vv. 19–22) we find that the writer is not satisfied with the thought that only the redeemed should praise God. God is so great that nothing but the praise of all creation will do. So he cries out: (1) "Praise the LORD, *you his angels*" (v. 20); (2) "Praise the LORD, *all his heavenly hosts*" (v. 21); (3) "Praise the LORD, *all his works*" (v. 22); and (4) "Praise the LORD, *O my soul*" (v. 22).

These final praises echo the praises of the opening lines, which is a fitting way of bringing the psalm to a close. But although they expand the scope of the praise, progressing from the *my* of verses 1–5 ("Praise the LORD, O *my* soul") and the *our* of verses 10–18 ("*our* sins" and "*our* iniquities") to the *all* of creation in verses 19–22, they nevertheless end with the psalmist's personal note of praise, just as he began: "Praise the LORD, O *my* soul" (v. 22). There is no missing the point that David wants to praise God himself more than anything.

Do You Have a Share in These Blessings?

As we come to the end of the psalm, we need to ask ourselves if there is any real praise in our hearts to God and if we have any real share in these blessings.

1. *Is there any real praise in your heart to God?* This question is for Christians. Roy Clements asks it directly:

> We need to ask ourselves whether or not there is any real praise in our hearts. It is so easy to come to church out of habit. It is so easy to repeat "Amen" without ever really speaking to God. It is so easy to hear sermons without ever really listening to God. Spiritual lukewarmness is a common disease in a land like ours where being a Christian is respectable. If that is our condition, then we, like David, need to talk to ourselves. We need to stir our hearts up to a more appropriate emotional response to the truth about the God we know. If you find your heart cold, then do what David did and count your blessings.[5]

If you are a Christian, the most important result of this study may be that you become more aware of your blessings and begin to praise God for them.

2. *Do you have any real share in these blessings?* At first glance it might seem that David is speaking of blessings from God that are enjoyed by everybody, since he is calling on the entire creation to praise God. But that is not so. Actually the blessings he is speaking of are for "those who fear him" (v. 17) and for "those who keep his covenant and remember to obey his precepts" (v. 18). He wants us to ask: Have I experienced forgiveness of sins? Has God redeemed my life from the pit? Has God satisfied me with good things? Have I discovered for myself and do I truly know that "the LORD is compassionate and gracious, slow to anger, abounding in love"?

If you do not know that, let me suggest that the only place where you will ever discover it to be true is at the cross of Jesus Christ. The Bible says, "For God so loved the world that he gave his one and only Son, that whoever believes in him shall not perish but have eternal life" (John 3:16). God cannot be more merciful to you than that. Nor can he show his mercy to you in a more graphic fashion. What you need to do now is surrender to the claims of Jesus Christ and so join the great company of those who have been saved by him and bless his name.

Psalm 104

God and God's Creation

Praise the LORD, O my soul.

O LORD my God, you are very great;
*   you are clothed with splendor and majesty.*
He wraps himself in light as with a garment;
*   he stretches out the heavens like a tent*
*   and lays the beams of his upper chambers on their waters.*
He makes the clouds his chariot
*   and rises on the wings of the wind.*
He makes winds his messengers,
*   flames of fire his servants. . . .*

How many are your works, O LORD!
*   In wisdom you made them all;*
*   the earth is full of your creatures. . . .*

May the glory of the LORD endure forever;
*   may the LORD rejoice in all his works.*

verses 1–4, 24, 31

Psalm 104 is a splendid praise psalm, one of the finest in the Psalter. The first part (vv. 1–30) follows the account of creation in Genesis 1 in a general way and shows how the entire cosmos rejoices in its good God. The second, surprising part (vv. 31–35) shows God rejoicing in his creation.

Do you ever think of God taking pleasure in his creation? We do not have trouble as Christians thinking how the creation rejoices in God, or should. But for many of us the thought that God likes what he has made and takes pleasure in it will be a new idea. It was for John Piper, the Minneapolis Baptist pastor and author who wrote *The Pleasures of God.*[1] Before he wrote the sermons that eventually appeared as *The Pleasures of God,* Piper had already published a book titled *Desiring God,* which argued that God is most glorified in us when we are most satisfied in him. The theme of that book was the answer to the question "What is the chief end of man?" from the Westminster Shorter Catechism. (Answer: "Man's chief end is to glorify God *and to enjoy him forever.*") In his second book, *The Pleasures of God,* Piper added the truth that he had discovered in the meantime, namely, that "we will be most satisfied in God when we know why God himself is most satisfied in God."[2]

Piper says—and so did Jonathan Edwards in one of his most masterful treatises—that God delights in creation because creation displays his glory and the glory of God is God's chief end in all his works. Edwards called attention to this on the basis of Psalm 104, which says, "May the glory of the LORD endure forever; may the LORD rejoice in all his works."[3]

Psalms 103 and 104 go together. John Stott says, "Psalms 103 and 104 form a perfect pair and illustrate the balance of the Bible. Both begin and end with the words *Praise the LORD, O my soul.* Psalm 103 goes on to tell of the goodness of God in salvation, Psalm 104 of the greatness of God in creation (v. 1). Psalm 103 depicts God as the father with his children, Psalm 104 as the Creator with his creatures. Psalm 103 catalogues his benefits (v. 2), Psalm 104 his works (vv. 13, 24, 31)."[4] One writer calls Psalm 104 "the most perfect hymn the world has ever produced,"[5] a glowing but not unreasonable tribute to have made.

God and God's Creation: Two Accounts

I mentioned that the first section of this psalm (vv. 1–30) follows the account of creation in Genesis 1, though only in a general way. Derek Kidner sees the pattern like this:

Day 1 (Gen. 1:3–5): Light (Ps. 104:2a)

Day 2 (Gen. 1:6–8): The "firmament" divides the waters (Ps. 104:2b–4)

Day 3 (Gen. 1:9–10): Land and water distinct (Ps. 104:5–9; plus 10–13?);
　　　　(Gen. 1:11–13): Vegetation and trees (Ps. 104:14–17; plus 18?)

Day 4 (Gen. 1:14–19): Luminaries as timekeepers (Ps. 104:19–23; plus 24)

Day 5 (Gen. 1:20–23): Creatures of sea and air (Ps. 104:25–26; sea only)

Day 6 (Gen. 1:24–28): Animals and man (anticipated in Ps. 104:21–24);
(Gen. 1:29–31): Food appointed for all creatures (Ps. 104:27–28;
plus 29–30)

There are some problems with this, since the psalm makes distinct and different points from the Genesis account as it moves through creation's various parts. This is why I have not followed the "days pattern," as some other commentators do. Nevertheless, the patterns are close enough to show that the psalmist had Genesis in mind as he worked on his composition. We will not be far wrong if we think of Psalm 104 as a poetic reflection on the more factual account in Genesis.[6]

God's Creation Glorifying God

I begin with verses 1–4, the first stanza in the New International Version translation. It parallels the account of creation on the first two days of Genesis 1: the creation of light on day one and the separation of the heavens above from the matter beneath on day two. However, in these verses the psalmist's interest is not so much in the sequence of God's acts as in God himself and the way these first elements of creation reveal his greatness and disclose his "splendor and majesty" (v. 1).

John Stott warns against taking this passage literally, a warning that should hardly be necessary. God is not literally wrapped in light, nor does he live in something like a great celestial tent resting on the oceans. These are images. However, Stott says, "What this passage does teach us is that God is the creator of the universe, and that he has revealed himself in it. In his essential being he is invisible, but he makes himself known in the visible order which he has made." It is in this sense that "the light is his garment, the heavens are his tent, the sky his chambers, and the clouds his chariot, while he makes the winds his messengers and fire and flame his servants."[7]

There is a very important difference here between the revealed religion of ancient Israel and the religions of virtually all the other ancient world cultures. Most of the ancient religions were pantheistic, which meant that they identified nature with various nature gods. Thus in order to worship God they worshiped nature. This was a degraded and debasing outlook, since in most cases it resulted in the worship of mere sex or procreation.

The ancient Jews separated God and nature, which God had taught them to do, and this meant that in their case nature could become a vehicle of God's self-revelation. "It is surely just because the natural objects are no longer taken to be themselves Divine that they can now be magnificent symbols of Divinity," wrote C. S. Lewis. "By emptying Nature of divinity—or, let us say, of divinities—you may fill her with Deity, for she is now the bearer of messages."[8]

Jonathan Edwards said that God's chief design in creation is to make himself known, to manifest his glory. For God to be glorified means for God to be known as he is. This means that creation is designed to show forth his might, wisdom, goodness, and, adds Edwards, "his happiness"[9]—as well as all his other attributes. This is exactly what the psalm shows, of course. The first verses display God's greatness in the creation of the heavens and earth. Verse 24 speaks of his wisdom in creating all things: "How many are your works, O LORD! In wisdom you made them all." Verses 27–30 emphasize God's perfect provision for his creatures. Verse 31, the key to the psalm, speaks of God's happiness:

> May the glory of the LORD endure forever;
> may the LORD rejoice in all his works.

This is not a wish for something that possibly might not happen, but rather a confident assertion that this is precisely what will happen. The lines are parallel. Because the glory of the Lord will endure forever, so will God's rejoicing in creation. This is why the older versions translated the line: "the LORD *shall* rejoice in his works."

No wonder this psalm has given us such happy hymns as: "God, All Nature Sings Thy Glory" by David Clowney (1960; sung to Beethoven's "Ode to Joy"); "O Worship the King" by Robert Grant (1833; sung to the tune *Lyons*); and "My Soul, Bless the Lord" (from the Psalter of 1912; sung to *Houghton*).

The Perfection of God's Creation

The next three stanzas of the psalm (vv. 5–23) cover days three and four of creation: day three, the separation of land and water (Gen. 1:9–10) and the creation of trees and vegetation (Gen. 1:11–13); and day four, the creation of the moon and sun as timekeepers (Gen. 1:14–19). But again, as in stanza one, the emphasis is not on creation itself or even on the sequence of God's creative acts, but on creation as it displays God's glory.

1. *The separation of land and water* (vv. 5–9). What makes this stanza interesting are the overtones of danger that to the Hebrew mind were always associated with water. The Jews were not seagoing people. They lived on land and loved the land. To their way of thinking the oceans were always dangerous, and in the rainy season even floods might sweep away either possessions or people. It was important to them, then, that God had "set the earth on its foundations" (v. 5) and that at his "rebuke the waters fled" (v. 7). In the last verse of this stanza there is a clear reference to the Flood of Noah's day and to God's promise that "never again will [the waters] cover the earth" (v. 9).

In this verse we begin to see something that emerges more clearly in the next stanza—that God continues to provide for his creation and that he does not turn his back on it. He is an ever-present Creator and an ever-sustaining God.

2. *Water and food for God's creatures* (vv. 10–18). In *Favorite Psalms* John Stott points out that although the verbs in the psalm have been mostly in the past tense up to now, "In this part of the psalm [through verse 23] the verbs are mostly in the present tense, and remind us that Christians are not deists."[10] What he means is that God has not merely created the cosmos as some skilled clock maker might have made a clock, winding it up and then placing it on a shelf to run by itself, showing no further interest in it. No Jews ever thought like that. To them God was always actively involved with creation, constantly sustaining it, since without his care it could not exist for a second, and graciously providing for each and every one of the creatures he has made.

As far as the wild animals are concerned, God provides water, without which they cannot live (vv. 10–13), and homes for them in the trees and mountains (vv. 12, 17–18). As for domesticated animals, such as cattle, he provides grass for food (v. 14). With human beings he is lavish. He gives

> wine that gladdens the heart of man,
>   oil to make his face shine,
>   and bread that sustains his heart (v. 15).

These were the three life staples of people living in the ancient Near East. Wine was important where water was usually unsafe. Oil was applied to the skin in a climate where the sun dried it out in short order. Bread was the food that kept most people alive.

The poet is describing what we call ecology, "God's marvelous adaptation of the earth's resources to the needs of living creatures, and vice versa."[11] Modern man attributes this to blind chance or mysterious "nature." The poet and all other knowledgeable believers attribute it to God.

3. *The beneficial regulation of time* (vv. 19–23). The fourth stanza of this psalm corresponds to the fourth day of creation, in which "God made two great lights—the greater light to govern the day and the lesser light to govern the night" (Gen. 1:16). In Genesis this has to do only with the separation of day and night and the marking of seasons and years. In Psalm 104 the night is established as the time for the animals of the night to seek their food, and the day is established as the time for man to go "out to his work, to labor until the evening" (v. 23). The alternating sequence of day and night is a reminder that there is a time to work but also a time to rest and recuperate from work. Work is good, but to do nothing but work is against God's wise and benevolent will.

God's Creation Rejoicing in God

Like the middle section of the psalm, the next two stanzas (stanzas five and six) speak of the dependence of creation on God and of God's provision for his creatures' every need. But the special note here is the joy of the creation in God's care. This is a beautiful section, holding out, first, the vast number and variety of God's creatures (vv. 24–26) and, second, their utter, childlike dependence on God (vv. 27–30).

> The earth is full of your creatures.
> There is the sea, vast and spacious,
>> teeming with creatures beyond number—
>> living things both large and small. . . .
>
> These all look to you
>> to give them their food at the proper time.
> When you give it to them,
>> they gather it up;
> when you open your hand,
>> they are satisfied with good things (vv. 24–25, 27–28).

H. C. Leupold wrote rightly, "This is a picture that is drawn on so vast a scale that one scarcely knows whether one should be more amazed at the prolific imagination of the writer or at the abounding gifts of God."[12]

Special attention should be drawn to verses 29–30. They state in a negative way the same creaturely dependence affirmed positively in verses 27–28. The author has just said that the creatures wait with open mouths for God to feed them, and that he does. Now he asserts that if God withholds their breath for even a moment, they die and return to dust. What is interesting here is that the word *breath* in verse 29 and the word translated "Spirit" in verse 30 are the same word, which reminds us that everything about us is dependent upon the Spirit or life-giving breath of God. This carries us back, on the one hand, to Genesis 2, where it is said that "God formed the man from the dust of the ground and breathed into his nostrils the breath of life, and the man became a living being" (Gen. 2:7), and forward into the New Testament, on the other hand, where we find Jesus teaching that no one can enter the kingdom of God unless he is "born of water and the Spirit" (John 3:5). In other words, both in regard to our physical lives and our spiritual lives, we are utterly dependent upon God. Without God we perish.

God Rejoicing in Creation

At the very end of the psalm we come to what I referred to earlier as its "surprising" second part. Here God is said to rejoice in his creation, just as the creation has already been said to rejoice in God.

John Piper calls attention to Job 38:4–7, where God asks Job where he was when God created the universe "and all the angels shouted for joy." Piper argues that since the angels are spirit beings, as God is, up to this point there must have been no matter or anything like matter in the universe. No angel had ever seen a star, a cloud, a sunset, or anything else that has form, weight, motion, texture, or color. Piper imagines God to have said, "Watch this!" Then he spoke the galaxies into existence. Piper adds,

> Imagine the awe and wonder that exploded among the angels. They had never seen or even imagined matter. They are all "ministering *spirits*" (Heb. 1:14) and have no material bodies as we do. When God brought material stuff into existence with all its incredible variety and utterly unheard of qualities of sight and sound and smell and touch and taste, this was totally unknown to the angels. God had made it all up. It was not like the unveiling of a new painting made of all the colors and paints we are all familiar with. It was absolutely, totally, unimaginably new! And the response of the sons of God was to shout for joy.[13]

It is true that Job 38 does not exactly say that *God* also shouted for joy, but can we doubt that he did? Especially when Psalm 104 says that he still rejoices in creation? And what did the angels do? They thrilled with what they saw, but they did not worship creation. Instead, they turned back to God alone and gave him the glory.

And this is how the psalmist ends too, vowing to sing to the Lord all his life and praise him as long as he lives. As far as he was concerned, an entire lifetime of praise would be insufficient to honor God properly.

There is only one jarring note, the writer's wish that "sinners [might] vanish from the earth and the wicked be no more" (v. 35). To us this desire seems harsh, self-righteous, and unnecessary. But it was not perceived that way by the biblical writers. They looked for a harmonious universe, and the only thing that was marring it for them was rebellious man. It is helpful to note that in Hebrew the psalm ends with the word *hallelujah,* meaning "Praise the LORD." This is the first occurrence of *hallelujah* in the Psalter, and it is significant that it is joined to a prayer for the destruction of the wicked, just as it is in Revelation 19. Sinners will perish. To God be the glory!

Psalm 105

God Remembered by Abraham's Descendants

Give thanks to the LORD, call on his name;
    make known among the nations what he has done.
Sing to him, sing praise to him;
    tell of all his wonderful acts.
Glory in his holy name;
    let the hearts of those who seek the LORD rejoice.
Look to the LORD and his strength;
    seek his face always.
Remember the wonders he has done,
    his miracles, and the judgments he pronounced,
O descendants of Abraham his servant,
    O sons of Jacob, his chosen ones. . . .

                           verses 1–6

We are coming to the end of the fourth book of the Psalter (Psalms 90–106), where we find two psalms that form a striking pair: Psalms 105 and 106. The first deals with the faithfulness of God to Israel from the time of his initial covenant with them through Abraham to their entering into the Promised Land. The second deals with their unfaithfulness to him during the same time period.

That they belong together is indicated in an interesting way. In the Septuagint the "hallelujah" (translated "Praise the LORD") that ends Psalm

104 is placed at the beginning of Psalm 105. If that is the way the psalms should be divided, then each of the last four psalms of book four ends as it began. "Praise the LORD, O my soul" both begins and ends Psalms 103 and 104. "Hallelujah" ("Praise the LORD") does the same for Psalms 105 and 106. So we actually have two sets of paired psalms. Psalms 103 and 104 form a pair; the first praises God as Savior, the second as Creator. The last two form a pair. These praise God for his faithfulness over against the continuing sin of his people.

The first fifteen verses of Psalm 105, the last two verses of 106, and, in between, the greater part of Psalm 96, appear in 1 Chronicles 16:8–36 as a hymn David committed to Asaph and his associates on the day the ark of the covenant was brought from the house of Obed-Edom to Jerusalem. This may be the original setting for Psalm 105 or part of it, but as it stands Psalm 105 would be a psalm of thanksgiving for Israel on any occasion—and for ourselves as well. Part of John Newton's hymn "Glorious Things of Thee Are Spoken" (1779) is based on verses 39–41.

Praise to Abraham's God

The first stanza (vv. 1–6) begins with a verse that tells us: (1) to give God thanks, (2) to call on his name, and (3) proclaim him to others. It is a wonderful way to begin the psalm:

> Give thanks to the LORD, call on his name;
>   make known among the nations what he has done.

Richard Baxter was one of the greatest of the nonconformist preachers of the seventeenth century. He lived from 1615 to 1692 and pastored at Kidderminster, where he died. His preaching ministry and his method of house-to-house catechizing of his flock were so successful that he was able to report toward the end of his pastorate, "On the Lord's Day there was no disorder to be seen in the streets; but you might hear a hundred families singing psalms and repeating sermons as you passed through them." There were probably many reasons for Baxter's amazing success in the ministry, but one clue can be found in the words of this verse inscribed on the pulpit from which he preached those many years in Kidderminster: "Give thanks unto the LORD, call upon his name; make known his deeds among the people" (KJV).[1]

Wouldn't it be wonderful if every minister or Bible teacher would make it his or her goal to do exactly that? Shouldn't this be the heart's desire and goal of every Christian?

There is even more to this opening stanza. Verse 1 gives us three great imperatives: "give thanks," "call on his name," and "make [his deeds] known." But the next verses continue this litany of appropriate response to God's goodness. Verse 2 tells us to "sing," "sing praise," and "tell of all his wonderful acts." Verse 3 advises, "glory in his holy name" and "rejoice." Verse 4 says, "Look to the LORD" and "seek his face always." Verse 5 says, "Remember." We need to remember what God has done on our behalf. This is precisely why the psalm was written, of course. It was written to remind Israel what God had done for them. We would be far more thankful people and more godly than we are if we would merely take time to remember God's many mercies to us, and not forget them.

God's Covenant

Important as the opening stanza may be for identifying Psalm 105 as a thanksgiving psalm, it is really not until stanza two (vv. 7–11) that we find out what the theme of the psalm is to be. It is God's covenant with his people, particularly his covenant with Abraham, which he confirmed with his son Isaac and his grandson Jacob. It is hard to miss this point since the word *covenant* occurs three times (in vv. 8, 9, and 10).

A covenant is a promise, in this case a promise made by God to Abraham and his descendants. For most of us *promise* is a better word than *covenant,* for *covenant* suggests a bargain, and God's covenants are established apart from any assets we might have to bargain with. On the other hand, we treat promises lightly, and God does not treat his promises lightly. So maybe we should use the word *oath* or talk about a *solemn commitment.* In any case, the commitment in view here is God's promise to give Abraham's descendants a land of their own.

The details are in Genesis 15. God caused Abraham to fall into a deep sleep and then appeared to him as a smoking fire pot and a blazing torch that passed between the divided carcasses of animals Abraham had previously slaughtered and laid out in the traditional manner for a covenant ceremony. God told him, "Know for certain that your descendants will be strangers in a country not their own, and they will be enslaved and mistreated four hundred years. But I will punish the nation they serve as slaves, and afterward they will come out with great possessions. . . . In the fourth generation your descendants will come back here, for the sin of the Amorites has not yet reached its full measure" (vv. 13–14, 16). This promise was repeated to Isaac a generation later (Gen. 26:24) and after that to Jacob (Gen. 28:10–15; 35:9–12; 46:1–4).

The covenant God made with Abraham and his descendants is called a unilateral covenant, meaning that God alone sets the terms and that he promises fulfillment apart from the faithfulness or lack of faithfulness of his people. Yet we are not to suppose that the people were absolved from any response at all. They had to own God as their God and promise him their allegiance, just as we do when we come to Jesus Christ as Savior. The psalm indicates this by having the people say in verse 7, "He is the LORD our God." This is their response, as well as a reference to the declaration of God himself at the start of the Ten Commandments: "I am the LORD your God, who brought you out of Egypt, out of the land of slavery" (Exod. 20:2).

The Early Stages

The middle section of the psalm (vv. 12–44) is a selective review of Israel's history, much as we have already seen in Psalm 78 and will see again in Psalm 106. But the emphasis here, unlike either Psalms 78 or 106, is on God's utter sovereignty in choosing and preserving Israel.

The third stanza (vv. 12–15) seems to be saying that God's choice was entirely apart from Israel's impressive numbers, for they were actually "few in number" (v. 12), and from their personal moral integrity, for even Abraham lied about his wife to Abimelech. The psalmist does not mention this directly; but it is the background for the word of God quoted in verse 15: "Do not touch my anointed ones; do my prophets no harm." The patriarch had deceived Abimelech by saying that Sarah was his sister rather than his wife, and Abimelech had almost taken her before God intervened to warn him that she was married to Abraham. It was then that God referred to Abraham as "a prophet" (Gen. 20:7). Yet a "lying" prophet! Obviously the emphasis here is upon God's faithfulness, not man's.

Israel in Egypt: Joseph

The most interesting part of the historical section of Psalm 105 is the fourth stanza (vv. 16–36), for it tells us about Israel's time in Egypt and her exodus from it. In telling about Joseph it introduces details not found in Genesis. Genesis emphasizes Joseph's character and spirit of service. In Psalm 105 the stress is on his cruel treatment.

Of particular interest is verse 18: "They bruised his feet with shackles, his neck was put in irons." This verse has a fascinating history. It tells us that when Joseph was first put into Potiphar's prison he was chained by his feet and neck, something we are not told in Genesis. But for some reason, when the Hebrew Old Testament was translated into Greek (the Septuagint version) the word for "neck" was rendered by the word *psyche*, which means "soul." That was the first mistake. Then, when Jerome came to do his Latin translation, he inverted the subject and object of the sentence and instead of saying, "His soul was laid in iron," he wrote, "Iron entered into his soul." That expression then passed into the English Prayer Book by Miles Coverdale's translation of the psalms (1534) and became a proverb.

Well, it was a complete error. But if there was ever a fortuitous mistranslation, this was it. For the phrase describes how a cruel fetter placed upon the body can in time seem to be placed on the soul, and after that to have entered the soul. You begin by trusting God in some affliction. But after a while, the monotony of the struggle wears you down and you begin to take on some of the rust of the manacle. This is what must have happened to

Joseph during the two long years Genesis records he was forgotten in the prison. He must have begun his imprisonment supposing that it would be for just a short time. After all, God had promised to make him a ruler over princes. But after a while he would have felt forgotten.

Yet he was not forgotten. The psalm tells us that this was only "till what he [that is, God] foretold came to pass" (v. 19). What is more, at the end Joseph looked back and understood it too; for he told his brothers, "You intended to harm me, but God intended it for good to accomplish what is now being done, the saving of many lives" (Gen. 50:20). His last words were: "I am about to die. But God will surely come to your aid and take you up out of this land to the land he promised on oath to Abraham, Isaac and Jacob" (Gen. 50:24). Thus Joseph too died trusting God and in his covenant with Abraham's descendants.

Israel out of Egypt: The Exodus

One striking characteristic of this psalm is its repeated use of the pronoun *he* to refer to God. It began in the second stanza: "*He* is the LORD our God" (v. 7), "*He* remembers" (v. 8), and "*He* confirmed" (v. 10). It occurred once more in stanza three: "*He* allowed no one to oppress them" (v. 14). However, in the fourth stanza it is dominant. First, in the story of Joseph: "*He* called down famine" (v. 16) and "*he* sent a man before them" (v. 17). Then in the story of the exodus: "*He* made them too numerous" (v. 24), "*He* sent Moses" (v. 26), "*He* sent darkness" (v. 28), "*He* turned their waters into blood" (v. 29), "*He* spoke, and there came swarms of flies" (v. 31), "*He* turned their rain into hail" (v. 32), "*He* struck down their vines" (v. 33), "*He* spoke, and the locusts came" (v. 34), and "*He* struck down all the firstborn in their land" (v. 35). It is hard to imagine a clearer way of teaching the sovereignty of God in human affairs, in this case over Israel and even over their enemies and their plans.

For some reason—we do not know why—Psalm 105 changes the order of the plagues somewhat and omits two. This listing begins with the ninth plague (the great darkness). Then it reverts to the original sequence, except that it inverts the order of the third and fourth plagues (gnats and flies, here flies and gnats) and omits the fifth and sixth plagues entirely (the death of the livestock and the boils).

In order to understand these plagues we need to understand that they were directed against the gods and goddesses of Egypt and were intended to show the superiority of the God of Israel to the Egyptian gods. There were about eighty major deities in Egypt, all clustered about the three great natural forces of Egyptian life: the Nile river, the land, and the sky. It does not surprise us, therefore, that the plagues God sent against Egypt in this historic battle follow this three-force pattern. The first two plagues were against the gods of the Nile. The next four were against the land gods. The final four plagues were against the gods of the sky, culminating in the death of the firstborn children of Egypt, including the firstborn of Pharaoh, who was to be the next "god."

1. *The great darkness* (v. 28; Exod. 10:21–29). The first plague mentioned in Psalm 105 is actually the ninth in Exodus, the terrible darkness that covered the land for three days. Ra, the sun god, was the most important god in the Egyptian pantheon, but he was suddenly banished from his place in the heavens. The importance of this plague in showing the superiority of Jehovah over Ra may be why this ninth plague is handled first in Psalm 105.

2. *The Nile turned to blood* (v. 29; Exod. 7:14–24). The second judgment, actually the first in Exodus, was against the waters of Egypt, primarily the Nile. Osiris was one of the chief Egyptian gods, and he was god of the Nile. The Egyptians believed that the Nile was his bloodstream. Khnum was considered the guardian of the Nile sources. Hapi was "the spirit of the Nile" and its "dynamic essence." In Upper Egypt Hapimon and Tauret were also Nile gods. Prayers had been addressed and offerings had been made to these gods for thousands of years, but they were revealed to be nothing by this judgment.

3. *The land overrun with frogs* (v. 30; Exod. 8:1–15). We know that the Egyptians worshiped frogs because archaeologists have found amulets carved in the form of frogs. Also, one of the most ubiquitous goddesses of Egypt was Hekt, and she was pictured with the head and often with the body of a frog. Since Hekt was embodied in the frog, frogs were sacred, as were many other animals. They could not be killed, just as cows, which are sacred to Hindus, cannot be killed in India. Because they could not be killed there was no way for the Egyptians to fight against this horrible and ironic proliferation of their goddess. They were forced to loathe the slimy symbol of their depraved worship, and when the frogs died their corpses must have turned the land into a stinking horror.

4. *The plague of flies* (v. 31; Exod. 8:20–32). Insects have always been a problem in Egypt. They are today. But in this fourth judgment they multiplied to a frightening and an intolerable extent. Many insects were identified with goddesses and gods and were worshiped, including flies. For example, the ichneuman fly was viewed as the god Uatchit.

5. *Dust turned to gnats* (v. 31; Exod. 8:16–19). The soil of Egypt is one of the most fertile in the world, thanks to the tons of rich earth carried downriver from the highlands of central Africa and deposited in Egypt by the river's annual inundation. Out of this soil came wonderfully nourishing grain, fruit, and vegetables. As part of God's judgment upon the god of the earth, known as Geb, the land produced even more insects to plague the people and defile their bodies.

6. *Thunder, hail, and lightning* (vv. 32–33; Exod. 9:13–35). This was the first of four plagues directed against the gods and goddesses of the sky. It does not hail in Egypt, and there is almost no rain. The city of Cairo has only two inches of rainfall annually, and there are years in the southern parts of

Egypt when no rain falls at all. Now the skies filled with clouds. The Bible says, "So the LORD rained hail on the land of Egypt; hail fell and lightning flashed back and forth. It was the worst storm in all the land of Egypt since it had become a nation. Throughout Egypt hail struck everything in the fields—both men and animals; it beat down everything growing in the fields and stripped every tree. The only place it did not hail was the land of Goshen, where the Israelites were" (Exod. 9:23–26). Shu, the god of the atmosphere; Horus and Month, the bird gods; and Nut, the sky goddess, were ineffective.

7. *The plague of locusts* (vv. 34–35; Exod. 10:1–20). The locusts devoured all that had been left in the fields or had regrown after the destruction by hail. Where was Nepri, the goddess of grain? Anubis, the guardian of the fields? Min, the deity of harvests?

8. *The death of the firstborn* (v. 36; Exod. 11:1–12:30). The last plague, both here and in Exodus, was the worst of all. The king was told that at midnight God would pass through the land to kill the firstborn son of every household, from the family of Pharaoh to that of the humblest slave girl and that even the firstborn of the cattle would die. It was a terrible judgment but a fitting one in view of Pharaoh's earlier slaughter of Israel's male children and the many long years of Jewish slavery. After this judgment, it was no surprise that "Egypt was glad when they left" (v. 38) and that the people were even sent away with gifts of gold and silver by the Egyptians (v. 37).

Never was God's word to man more plain, pointed, personal, or powerful, yet it took ten plagues to win Israel's freedom, and even then Pharaoh was unconverted. Do not be discouraged if people reject your witness. It will accomplish what God intends, for the word of God is never spoken without accomplishing its intended effect.

Through the Wilderness to Canaan

The last stanza of this psalm (vv. 37–45) follows Israel through the years of her desert wandering until God actually brought the people into Canaan, thereby fulfilling the promise made to Abraham. We can hardly miss this as the psalmist's major concern. For after mentioning the three great miracles of God's provision for the people during the desert years—the cloud that protected them from the fierce desert sun, the quail and manna given to them as food, and the provision of water from the rock—the writer mentions Abraham again, as he did earlier, saying that God

> remembered his holy promise
> given to his servant Abraham (v. 42).

The point is that nothing was lacking of all that God had promised. So his people, Abraham's descendants, should "give thanks," "call on his name," and "make known among the nations what he has done" (v. 1).

Shouldn't we, who have received even greater blessings than they, do the same?

And there is one more thought—a very important one. It occurs at the very end of the psalm, where it is said that God gave Israel the lands of the nations "that they might keep his precepts and observe his laws" (v. 45).

Derek Kidner has a wonderfully sharp comment on this closing verse in which he relates it to exactly the same point in the New Testament. He writes, "The final verse shows why grace abounded; not that sin might also abound, but (to quote a New Testament equivalent of verse 45), 'that the righteousness of the law might be fulfilled in us, who walk not after the flesh, but after the Spirit' (Rom. 8:4, AV)."[2] This is the ultimate point of God's covenant with us after all, not that those upon whom God sets his covenant love might be merely a select or unusual people, but that they might be holy, as he is.

Peter understood it. He wrote, "Just as he who called you is holy, so be holy in all you do; for it is written: 'Be holy, because I am holy'" (1 Peter 1:15–16). Are you? Are any of us?

Psalm 106

Let All God's People Say, "Amen!"

Praise the LORD.

Give thanks to the LORD, for he is good;
    his love endures forever.
Who can proclaim the mighty acts of the LORD
    or fully declare his praise?
Blessed are they who maintain justice,
    who constantly do what is right.
Remember me, O LORD, when you show favor to your people,
    come to my aid when you save them,
that I may enjoy the prosperity of your chosen ones,
    that I may share in the joy of your nation
    and join your inheritance in giving praise. . . .

Praise be to the LORD, the God of Israel,
    from everlasting to everlasting.
Let all the people say, "Amen!"

Praise the LORD.

verses 1–5, 48

W hen I end a sermon I like to end on a strong note, with a bang rather than a whimper, and generally I like to end a book or a lecture or anything else in the same way. I would expect this as we come to the end of the fourth book of the Psalter, but it is not what we find. True, the psalm is not exactly a whimper. But it is hardly a bang either. For the most part it is a long litany of the sins of Israel for which God chastised them again and again. In fact, if verse 47 is an accurate clue to when the psalm was written—

> Save us, O LORD our God,
>   and gather us from the nations—

the people seem to be in exile, and the final "Amen" ("Let all the people say, 'Amen!'" v. 48) is a recognition, in part at least, that God was right in having judged them as he did.

Psalm 106 is one of two psalms that go together. This means that although it is a somber note on which to end this section of the Psalter, it is nevertheless a realistic one. I pointed out in the last study that Psalms 105 and 106 represent two very different ways of telling the same story. Psalm 105 tells Israel's story from the point of view of God's faithfulness because of his covenant to Abraham and his descendants. Psalm 106 reviews the story from the point of view of Israel's unfaithfulness to that same covenant and over the same period of history. Derek Kidner calls the psalm "the dark counterpart of its predecessor, a shadow cast by human self-will in the long struggle against the light." Yet he also adds rightly, "For all its exposure of man's ingratitude, this is a song of praise, for it is God's extraordinary long-suffering that emerges as the real theme. This is the basis of the final prayer (v. 47), and this gives reality to the doxology that closes not only the psalm but the fourth book of the Psalter."[1]

We cannot miss the fact that Psalm 106 begins and ends with *Hallelujah* ("Praise the LORD"). Others that do the same are Psalms 113, 117, 135, 146–150, and probably 105.

Israel's Long-Suffering God

If Israel's history is one long litany of sin followed by God's just chastisement, as it is, why should Israel or anyone else "praise the LORD"? The answer is given immediately. It is because God "is good," because "his love endures forever" (v. 1). The people had sinned repeatedly, and God had disciplined them repeatedly. But he did not cast them off, as they deserved. Instead "he remembered his covenant" (v. 45) and restored them. Thus Israel's history is as much the story of God's mercy, faithfulness, and long-suffering as it is the story of Israel's faithlessness and unbelief. In fact, it is against the background of their sin that God's patience is most fully illuminated.

Isn't that your story too? And isn't that the chief content of your testimony when you praise God for his many mercies? We do not praise God because he is wonderful and we are wonderful too. We praise him because he is kind to us even when we sin and merciful to us when we don't deserve his mercy: "Give thanks to the LORD, for he is good; his love endures forever" (v. 1).

It is interesting that at the very start of this psalm of national confession of sin the writer addresses God on his own behalf, asking God to remember him and save him when he comes to the nation's aid (vv. 4–5).[2] He is certain God will deliver the people from their captivity because he has delivered them in the past, but the psalmist wants to be included in that blessing. You want to be included in times of God's future blessing on his people, don't you? Then do what the psalmist does: Confess your sin, recall God's past goodness to you, and look to him in faith for all present and future blessings.

Israel's Sin in Egypt

If verse 1 strikes the keynote of the psalm so far as God is concerned, crying, "Give thanks to the LORD, for he is good; his love endures forever," verse 6 strikes the keynote as far as the people are concerned. It has to do with Israel's sin and is a confession of it:

> We have sinned, even as our fathers did;
> we have done wrong and acted wickedly.

What follows from this point is a litany of Israel's transgressions (vv. 6–39). This section can be handled in a number of different ways, but it is probably most helpful to note that there are eight distinguishable sins spread out over three periods of the nation's history: the time of leaving Egypt, the years in the desert, and the occupation of the Promised Land.

The chief sin of the people when leaving Egypt was their *rebellion* against God, mentioned in verse 7:

> they did not remember your many kindnesses,
> and they rebelled by the sea, the Red Sea.

These "many kindnesses" would have been God's faithfulness in remembering his promises to Abraham to visit them and deliver them from their Egyptian captivity and his grace in sending Moses and Aaron as the agents of his deliverance. His "miracles" (v. 7) would be the plagues visited upon the Egyptians. These should have drawn the people to God in faith and grateful obedience. Yet as early as the border of the Red Sea, when they were not yet even completely out of Egypt, they rebelled against God and Moses, complaining, "Was it because there were no graves in Egypt that you brought us to the desert to die? What have you done to us by bringing us out of Egypt? Didn't we say to you in Egypt, 'Leave us alone; let us serve the Egyptians'? It would have been better for us to serve the Egyptians than to die in the desert!" (Exod. 14:11–12).

The psalm says that in spite of this rebellion God "saved them for his name's sake, to make his mighty power known" (v. 8). Indeed he did. He parted the waters of the Red Sea to bring them across on dry land. Then he caused the waters to return to drown the pursuing Egyptians so that "not one of them survived" (v. 11).

The psalm says,

> Then they believed his promises
> and sang his praise (v. 12).

It was not much credit to them to have done it then. "This is mentioned, not to their credit, but to their shame," wrote Spurgeon, since "those who do not believe the Lord's word till they see it performed are not believers at all. . . . Their song was very excellent, . . . but sweet as it was, it was quite short, and when it was ended they fell to murmuring."[3]

Is it that way with you? You see God's miracles, but at the first sign of any new opposition you forget what God has done and are soon rebelling against what you suppose to be your hard and painful life? Then, when God saves you again, you sing his praises but soon forget even that deliverance? That is exactly what you and I are like. Should we not say, as the psalmist, "We have sinned, even as our fathers did; we have done wrong and acted wickedly" (v. 6).

Israel's Sins in the Desert

Rebellion, the sin identified with the people's exodus from Egypt, is a root sin that lies at the heart of the other sins of Israel. Still, each sin is worth remembering separately, which is what the psalmist does at this point. He remembers six sins associated with Israel's years of wandering in the wilderness, then follows them with one more from the years in Canaan.

1. *The sin of discontent* (vv. 13–15). The first paragraph describing the sins of the wilderness seems to combine incidents recorded in Exodus 16 and Numbers 11. In Exodus 16 the people "grumbled against Moses and Aaron" because, they said, in Egypt "we sat around pots of meat and ate all the food we wanted, but you have brought us out into this desert to starve this entire assembly to death" (vv. 2–3). God answered by giving them the manna that they gathered each morning. In Numbers 11 they had grown tired of the manna and complained that they had no meat: "If only we had meat to eat! We remember the fish we ate in Egypt at no cost—also the cucumbers, melons, leeks, onions and garlic. But now we have lost our appetite; we never see anything but this manna!" (vv. 4–6). God answered this complaint by sending quail into the camp, so they had plenty of meat. But God was angry because of their discontent and "struck them with a severe plague" (v. 33).

How about us? We have been given much and have been preserved from much by God. Yet are we not also frequently sinfully discontented with our lives? Matthew Arnold, the English poet and essayist (1822–88), wrote that "one thing only has been lent to youth and age in common—discontent."[4]

2. *The sin of jealousy* (vv. 16–18). The next stanza of the psalm describes the time when Korah and 250 of his accomplices rebelled against Moses and Aaron because of jealousy, as recounted in Numbers 16. They said, "The whole community is holy, every one of them, and the LORD is with them. Why then do you set yourselves above the LORD's assembly?" (v. 3). God judged these men by having the earth open up and swallow their entire households, while fire came out from the tabernacle and consumed the 250. Even then the people were rebellious. God sent a plague that killed over 14,000 people before Aaron intervened to make atonement for their sin.

3. *The sin of idolatry* (vv. 19–23). The next incident is the best known, the sin of making the idol of the golden calf. It is told in Exodus 32. Moses had been on Mount Sinai receiving the law of God. But while he was on the mountain the people, who had grown impatient and restless, approached Aaron to ask for a "god" to lead them out of the desert to a better land. Aaron should have resisted, but he was weak, as so many leaders are. He asked for their gold earrings and other jewelry, melted them down, and fashioned them into a calf, which the people then began to worship. Since the calf reminded them of Apis, the bull god of Egypt, and since the worship of Apis had been orgiastic, the result was a sexual romp in which the people "ran wild" (see Exod. 32:25). On this occasion God told Moses that he would destroy the people and begin a new nation starting with Moses. But Moses interceded for them, offering himself in their place, and God spared them once again.

It is interesting that Paul quotes the first half of verse 20 in his indictment of the entire human race in Romans. The psalm says,

> They exchanged their Glory
>   for an image of a bull, which eats grass.

This refers to Israel's sin at Sinai. However, in Romans Paul broadens the verse to embrace the sin of mankind in general, writing, "Although they claimed to be wise, they became fools and exchanged the glory of the immortal God for images made to look like mortal man and birds and animals and reptiles" (Rom. 1:22–23). In other words, it is not Israel alone that has been guilty of the sin of idolatry. This is humanity's sin in general. We too are idolaters when we put anything but God in God's place.[5]

4. *The sin of unbelief* (vv. 24–27). The next of the eight serious sins highlighted by this psalm (six from the wilderness period) is the sin of unbelief connected with the refusal of the people to enter the Promised Land. The story is in Numbers 13–14. The psalm says,

> Then they despised the pleasant land;
>   they did not believe his promise.
> They grumbled in their tents
>   and did not obey the LORD (vv. 24–25).

Someone asked a Bible teacher, "What does the Lord want from me?" The teacher answered, "What God wants most of all is to be believed." Unbelief is the root of all sins, and the opposite of unbelief is faith, which is the way of salvation. The people of Israel disbelieved and refused to press forward into the Promised Land. Often we also miss the good God has for us, simply because we will not believe his promises and act upon them.

5. *The sin of apostasy* (vv. 28–31). Numbers 25 recounts the time when the men of Israel "began to indulge in sexual immorality with Moabite women, who invited them to the sacrifices to their gods" (vv. 1–2). The Baal gods (in this case the Baal of Peor) were fertility gods who were served by cultic immorality. In this story Phinehas, the grandson of Aaron the priest, killed two of the most blatant offenders and was rewarded by God giving him "a lasting priesthood" for his family (v. 13).

6. *The sin of insurrection* (vv. 32–33). The final representative sin of the wilderness period referred to in Psalm 106 is the insurrection at Kadesh, where the people had no water. The story is in Numbers 20. This was the time when even Moses sinned in frustration, being overcome by the people's angry unbelief. God told him to speak to the rock and it would bring forth water. But Moses struck it instead and also took some of God's glory to himself and Aaron, saying, "Listen, you rebels, must *we* bring you water out of this rock?" (v. 10). For this sin, though it may seem minor to us, Moses was kept from entering the Promised Land.

Israel's Sin in the Promised Land

Even in the Promised Land the unfaithfulness of the people continued. Here it was *accommodation* to the ways of Canaan (vv. 34–39). They had been warned against the sins of the Canaanites as far back as Exodus 34:11–14, where were told utterly to destroy the inhabitants or "they will be a snare among you" (v. 12). They refused to do it. Instead, as Psalm 106 says, they "mingled with the nations and adopted their customs" (v. 35), even to the point of "worship[ing] their idols" (v. 36) and "sacrific[ing] their sons and daughters to the demons" (v. 37).

The sacrifice of one's children to demons is so terrible that we can hardly imagine it. It was a sin caused by accommodation to pagan religions of a most debased kind. But are we so sure that we never practice it ourselves? We do if we desire worldly success for our children to the point of thrusting them into a pagan environment today or by encouraging them to live like the world, accommodating its morality, just to get ahead. If you worship any of the gods of this world—whether wealth, fame, sex, or power—they will become a snare to you and your children.

God's Response to Israel's Sin

When we come to the last section of this psalm, after the historical review of Israel's unfaithfulness to God, we are told of God's response to the people's sin (vv. 40–46). It was twofold.

First, there was *judgment*. Judgment we expect. We are told that God was angry with his people and therefore "handed them over to the nations" so that "their foes ruled over them" and "their enemies oppressed them" (vv. 40–42). This was the actual history of the people once they entered the Promised Land. They sinned by compromising with the values of the nations around them, God allowed an alien people to conquer and oppress them, they repented and called on God for help, and he delivered them—usually by the hands of the judges. But then the cycle started all over again. At last the northern kingdom was overcome by the Assyrians (in 721 B.C.) and the southern kingdom by the Babylonians (in 586 B.C.). The psalm seems to have been written during the time of the Babylonian captivity (see v. 47).

Second, there was *compassion and deliverance*. Compassion is unexpected and unmerited; yet that is what Israel experienced at the hands of God. We are told in verse 45 that, although the people had sinned often and greatly, God "remembered his covenant and out of his great love he relented" (v. 45). What a great reality! The compassionate God!

This is the first time the covenant has been mentioned in this psalm, but its mention takes us back to Psalm 105, where it was the central theme. It is one more feature that ties Psalms 105 and 106 together. Psalm 105 taught that God is faithful to his covenant. We are reminded here that, although the people were unfaithful to him, God nevertheless was faithful to them, which is why a psalm dealing with the sins of God's people can end on a positive note.

The lesson is that of Romans 3:3–4, where Paul asks, "What if some did not have faith? Will their lack of faith nullify God's faithfulness?" He answers, "Not at all! Let God be true, and every man a liar." God is faithful in spite of our unfaithfulness, and we had better be glad he is since his faithfulness is our sole hope. Can you say, "Amen" to that? "Amen" marks our assent to God's Word, and what God has chiefly said in Psalm 106 is this. First, the psalmist says "we have sinned, even as our fathers did; we have done wrong and acted wickedly" (v. 6). We hear and sadly agree. "Amen," we murmur. Second, God says he remembers his covenant (see v. 45). When we hear that we look up joyfully and cry in a very different tone of voice, "Amen!"

The psalm says: "Let all the people say, 'Amen!'"

Can you say Amen? "Praise the Lord!"

Notes

Psalms 42–43: *An Upward Look by a Downcast Soul*

1. D. Martyn Lloyd-Jones, *Spiritual Depression: Its Causes and Cure* (Grand Rapids: Eerdmans, 1965).

2. This seems always to have been the case, which accounts for William Bridge's masterpiece of 1649, *A Lifting Up for the Downcast* (Carlisle, Pa.: The Banner of Truth Trust, 1979), a 287-page study of Psalm 42:11, as well as Sherwood Eliot Wirt's more recent study, *A Thirst for God: Reflections on the Forty-second and Forty-third Psalms* (Minneapolis: World Wide Publications, 1970).

3. The Hebrew preposition before the words "Sons of Korah" can mean "to" as well as "of" or "by," in which case the title would mean that the poem was dedicated to the Sons of Korah so they could perform it. But the same preposition occurs before "David" in the titles bearing his name. If it means "by David" there, the preposition should mean "by" in this case also.

4. Franz Delitzsch, *Biblical Commentary on the Psalms,* vol. 2, trans. Francis Bolton (Grand Rapids: Eerdmans, n.d.), 51.

5. P. C. Craigie, *Psalms 1–50,* vol. 19 of the *Word Biblical Commentary* (Waco: Word, 1983), 325.

6. C. S. Lewis, *Reflections on the Psalms* (New York: Harcourt, Brace & World, 1958), 51–52.

7. Alexander Maclaren, *Expositions of Holy Scripture,* vol. 3, *The Psalms, Isaiah 1–48* (Grand Rapids: Eerdmans, 1959), part 1, 304.

8. Lloyd-Jones, *Spiritual Depression,* 21.

9. J. J. Stewart Perowne, *Commentary on the Psalms,* 2 vols. in 1 (Grand Rapids: Kregel, 1989), 1:351. Original edition 1878–1879.

Psalm 44: *Sheep That Conquer*

1. Murdoch Campbell, *From Grace to Glory: Meditations on the Book of Psalms* (Carlisle, Pa.: The Banner of Truth Trust, 1979), 83.

2. J. J. Stewart Perowne, *Commentary on the Psalms,* 2 vols. in 1 (Grand Rapids: Kregel, 1989), 1:360. Original edition 1878–1879.

3. E. W. Hengstenberg, *Kommentar ueber die Psalmen,* 4 vols. (Berlin: Ludwig Oehmigke, 1849), cited by H. C. Leupold, *Exposition of the Psalms* (Grand Rapids: Baker, 1969), 345.

Psalm 45: *A Messianic Wedding Song*

1. For a discussion of these suggestions and their proponents see J. J. Stewart Perowne, *Commentary on the Psalms,* 2 vols. in 1 (Grand Rapids: Kregel, 1989), 1:366–67. Original edition 1878–1879.

2. Alexander Maclaren, *Expositions of Holy Scripture,* vol. 3, *The Psalms, Isaiah 1–48* (Grand Rapids: Eerdmans, 1959), part 1, 307.

3. Walter J. Chantry, *Praises for the King of Kings* (Carlisle, Pa.: The Banner of Truth Trust, 1991).

4. Cited by H. C. Leupold, *Exposition of the Psalms* (Grand Rapids: Baker, 1969), 354.

5. Perowne, *Commentary on the Psalms,* 1:351. For a fuller discussion of this point see P. C. Craigie, *Psalms 1–50,* vol. 19 in the *Word Biblical Commentary* (Waco: Word, 1983), 336–37; Derek Kidner, *Psalms 1–72: An Introduction and Commentary on Books I and II of the Psalms* (Downers Grove, Ill.: InterVarsity, 1973), 172; and Leupold, *Exposition of the Psalms,* 360–61.

6. Chantry, *Praises for the King of Kings,* 100–101.

7. Ibid., 104.

Psalm 46: *Martin Luther's Psalm*

1. The story and quotation are from C. H. Spurgeon, *The Treasury of David,* vol. 1b, *Psalms 27–57* (Grand Rapids: Zondervan, 1968), 344.

2. H. C. Leupold, *Exposition of the Psalms* (Grand Rapids: Baker, 1969), 363.

3. Elisabeth Elliot, *Facing the Death of Someone You Love* (Westchester, Ill.: Good News Publishers, 1980), 8. This material was first published as an article in *Christianity Today* in 1973.

4. Franz Delitzsch, *Biblical Commentary on the Psalms,* vol. 2, trans. Francis Bolton (Grand Rapids: Eerdmans, n.d.), 91–92.

5. G. Campbell Morgan, *Notes on the Psalms* (Westwood, N.J.: Revell, 1947), 88–89.

6. Alexander Maclaren, *Expositions of Holy Scripture,* vol. 3, *The Psalms, Isaiah 1–48* (Grand Rapids: Eerdmans, 1959), part 1, 345.

Psalm 47: *King of All the Earth*

1. Derek Kidner, *Psalms 1–72: An Introduction and Commentary on Books I and II of the Psalms* (Downers Grove, Ill.: InterVarsity, 1973), 177.

2. Either from the armies of Ammon, Moab, and Mount Seir in the days of Jehoshaphat (2 Chron. 20) or from the forces of Sennacherib in the days of Hezekiah (2 Kings 18–19). See discussion of these options above, in the study of Psalm 46.

3. Arnold J. Toynbee, *A Study of History,* 12 vols. (London: Oxford University Press, 1934–61).

4. Or "UPARSIN," meaning "AND PARSIN."

Psalm 48: *City of Our God*

1. Derek Kidner, *Psalms 1–72: An Introduction and Commentary on Books I and II of the Psalms* (Downers Grove, Ill.: InterVarsity, 1973), 179.

2. Tremper Longman III says, "An *inclusio* gives the reader of the psalm a sense of closure, a sense of having read a complete poem. It imparts to the psalm a sense of unity, and perhaps most important, it sets the mood for the whole psalm" (*How to Read the Psalms* [Downers Grove, Ill.: InterVarsity, 1988], 107).

3. P. C. Craigie, *Psalms 1–50,* vol. 19 in the *Word Biblical Commentary* (Waco: Word, 1983), 352.

4. H. C. Leupold, *Exposition of the Psalms* (Grand Rapids: Baker, 1969), 375.

5. The points are cited in C. H. Spurgeon, *The Treasury of David,* vol. 1b, *Psalms 27–57* (Grand Rapids: Zondervan, 1968), 366.

Psalm 49: *You Can't Take It with You*

1. John White, *The Golden Cow: Materialism in the Twentieth-Century Church* (Downers Grove, Ill.: InterVarsity, 1979).

2. J. J. Stewart Perowne, *Commentary on the Psalms*, 2 vols. in 1 (Grand Rapids: Kregel, 1989), 1:395. Original edition 1878–1879.

3. For a discussion of these proposals see Alexander Maclaren, *The Psalms*, vol. 2, *Psalms 39–89* (New York: A. C. Armstrong and Son, 1893), 105; Derek Kidner, *Psalms 1–72: An Introduction and Commentary on Books I and II of the Psalms* (Downers Grove, Ill.: InterVarsity, 1973), 183, footnote 1.

4. C. H. Spurgeon, *The Treasury of David*, vol. 1b, *Psalms 27–57* (Grand Rapids: Zondervan, 1968), 378.

5. Alexander Maclaren, *Expositions of Holy Scripture*, vol. 3, *The Psalms, Isaiah 1–48* (Grand Rapids: Eerdmans, 1959), part 1, 365–75.

6. P. C. Craigie, *Psalms 1–50*, vol. 19 in the *Word Biblical Commentary* (Waco: Word, 1983), 361.

7. H. C. Leupold, *Exposition of the Psalms* (Grand Rapids: Baker, 1969), 386.

8. "Take me" is used again in Psalm 73:24, which is similar in many ways to this one. The Enoch story alone must have been understood by many people as teaching an afterlife for Old Testament believers.

9. Murdoch Campbell, *From Grace to Glory: Meditations on the Book of Psalms* (Carlisle, Pa.: The Banner of Truth Trust, 1970), 93.

10. Spurgeon, *The Treasury of David*, 1b:379.

Psalm 50: *The Mighty God, the Lord*

1. Psalm 50 is the first psalm ascribed to Asaph. It is the only one in the second book of Psalms, but in the next book there is an entire collection under his name, Psalms 73–83 (eleven in all). Asaph was one of the chief leaders of music appointed by David to preside over the Levite choirs (cf. 1 Chron. 15:14–17, 19; 16:4–6, 37). By the time of Hezekiah, Asaph was ranked with David as one of the greatest composers of praise hymns (2 Chron. 29:30). For a careful discussion of Asaph and the Asaphic psalms see Franz Delitzsch, *Biblical Commentary on the Psalms*, vol. 2, trans. Francis Bolton (Grand Rapids: Eerdmans, n.d.), 122–24.

2. J. J. Stewart Perowne, *Commentary on the Psalms*, 2 vols. in 1 (Grand Rapids: Kregel, 1989), 1:405. Original edition 1878–1879.

3. Alexander Maclaren, *The Psalms*, vol. 2, *Psalms 39–89* (New York: A. C. Armstrong and Son, 1893), 117–18.

4. Derek Kidner, *Psalms 1–72: An Introduction and Commentary on Books I and II of the Psalms* (Downers Grove, Ill.: InterVarsity, 1973), 187.

5. Ibid.

6. Maclaren, *The Psalms*, 2:124.

Psalm 51: *Cleansed by the Blood: Part 1*

1. Derek Kidner, *Psalms 1–72: An Introduction and Commentary on Books I and II of the Psalms* (Downers Grove, Ill.: InterVarsity, 1973), 189. The others are Psalms 6, 32, 38, 102, 130, and 143.

2. C. H. Spurgeon, *The Treasury of David*, vol. 1b, *Psalms 27–57* (Grand Rapids: Zondervan, 1968), v.

3. Rowland E. Prothero, *The Psalms in Human Life* (New York: E. P. Dutton, 1904). The deaths of Sir Thomas More and Lady Jane Grey are recounted on pages 130 and 155, Henry V on page 82, and the use of the psalm by William Carey on page 339.

4. Murdoch Campbell, *From Grace to Glory: Meditations on the Book of Psalms* (Carlisle, Pa.: The Banner of Truth Trust, 1970), 95–96.

5. Alexander Maclaren: "The psalm begins by at once grasping the character of God as the sole ground of hope" (*The Psalms*, vol. 2, *Psalms 39–89* [New York: A. C. Armstrong and Son, 1893], 128). H. C. Leupold: "Pardon has its base, not in the merit or worthiness of man, but in the fact that God is so good" (*Exposition of the Psalms* [Grand Rapids: Baker, 1969], 401).

6. Alexander Maclaren, *Expositions of Holy Scripture*, vol. 3, *The Psalms, Isaiah 1–48* (Grand Rapids: Eerdmans, 1959), part 2, 5.

7. J. J. Stewart Perowne, *Commentary on the Psalms*, 2 vols. in 1 (Grand Rapids: Kregel, 1989), 1:315–16. Original edition 1878–1879.

8. F. W. Robertson, cited in Perowne, *Commentary on the Psalms*, 1:418.

Psalm 51: *Cleansed by the Blood: Part 2*

1. Derek Kidner, *Psalms 1–72: An Introduction and Commentary on Books I and II of the Psalms* (Downers Grove, Ill.: InterVarsity, 1973), 192.

2. Quoted by C. H. Spurgeon, *The Treasury of David*, vol. 1b, *Psalms 27–57* (Grand Rapids: Zondervan, 1968), 419.

3. Arno C. Gaebelein, *The Book of Psalms: A Devotional and Prophetic Commentary* (Neptune, N.J.: Loizeaux, 1965), 222.

4. J. J. Stewart Perowne, *Commentary on the Psalms*, 2 vols. in 1 (Grand Rapids: Kregel, 1989), 1:421. Original edition 1878–1879.

5. Alexander Maclaren, *The Psalms*, vol. 2, *Psalms 39–89* (New York: A. C. Armstrong and Son, 1893), 137.

6. H. C. Leupold, *Exposition of the Psalms* (Grand Rapids: Baker, 1969), 405–6.

7. Perowne, *Commentary on the Psalms*, 1:422.

8. Maclaren, *The Psalms*, 2:141.

9. Kidner, *Psalms 1–72*, 194; Perowne, *Commentary on the Psalms*, 1:423.

Psalm 52: *Righteous Judgment for a Wicked Man*

1. Derek Kidner, *Psalms 1–72: An Introduction and Commentary on Books I and II of the Psalms* (Downers Grove, Ill.: InterVarsity, 1973), 195.

2. C. H. Spurgeon, *The Treasury of David*, vol. 1b, *Psalms 27–57* (Grand Rapids: Zondervan, 1968), 428.

Psalm 53: *A Psalm That Is Repeated*

1. C. H. Spurgeon, *The Treasury of David*, vol. 1b, *Psalms 27–57* (Grand Rapids: Zondervan, 1968), 433.

2. Matthew Henry, *Job to Song of Solomon*, vol. 3 of *Commentary on the Whole Bible* (New York: Revell, n.d.), 439.

3. Ibid.

Psalm 54: *Betrayed*

1. Derek Kidner, *Psalms 1–72: An Introduction and Commentary on Books I and II of the Psalms* (Downers Grove, Ill.: InterVarsity, 1973), 197.

2. A. Weiser, *The Psalms: A Commentary*, trans. H. Hartwell (Philadelphia: Westminster Press, 1962), cited in Marvin E. Tate, *Psalms 51–100*, vol. 20 of the *Word Biblical Commentary* (Dallas: Word, 1990), 49.

3. C. H. Spurgeon, *The Treasury of David*, vol. 1b, *Psalms 27–57* (Grand Rapids: Zondervan, 1968), 442.

Psalm 55: *Betrayed by a Close Friend*

1. G. Campbell Morgan, *Notes on the Psalms* (Westwood, N.J.: Revell, 1947), 101–2. But see also J. J. Stewart Perowne, *Commentary on the Psalms*, 2 vols. in 1 (Grand Rapids: Kregel, 1989),

1:436. Original edition 1878–1879; H. C. Leupold, *Exposition of the Psalms* (Grand Rapids: Baker, 1969), 420–25; and Alexander Maclaren, *The Psalms,* vol. 2, *Psalms 39–89* (New York: A. C. Armstrong and Son, 1893), 159–70.

2. Marvin E. Tate, *Psalms 51–100,* vol. 20 of the *Word Biblical Commentary* (Dallas: Word, 1990), 56.

3. C. H. Spurgeon is the only major commentator who has an outline similar to this (Spurgeon, *The Treasury of David,* vol. 1b, *Psalms 27–57* [Grand Rapids: Zondervan, 1968], 445).

4. Spurgeon, *The Treasury of David,* 1b:448.

5. Perowne, *Commentary on the Psalms,* 1:439.

Psalm 56: *"What Can Man Do to Me?"*

1. Derek Kidner, *Psalms 1–72: An Introduction and Commentary on Books I and II of the Psalms* (Downers Grove, Ill.: InterVarsity, 1973), 202.

2. J. J. Stewart Perowne, *Commentary on the Psalms,* 2 vols. in 1 (Grand Rapids: Kregel, 1989), 1:444. Original edition 1878–1879. The psalm is one of two that flowered from this crisis. The other is Psalm 34.

3. Alexander Maclaren, *Expositions of Holy Scripture,* vol. 3, *The Psalms, Isaiah 1–48* (Grand Rapids: Eerdmans, 1959), part 2, 46.

Psalm 57: *Hiding in Thee*

1. There are two caves to which the heading of Psalm 57 could refer: (1) the cave of Adullam (1 Sam. 22:1–2) and (2) the cave at En-gedi (1 Sam. 24:1–22). It is probably the first because of the obvious connection of this with the preceding psalm.

2. H. C. Leupold, *Exposition of the Psalms* (Grand Rapids: Baker, 1969), 431. See also J. J. Stewart Perowne, *Commentary on the Psalms,* 2 vols. in 1 (Grand Rapids: Kregel, 1989), 1:450–51. Original edition 1878–1879. Psalms 56 and 59 also have a repeated refrain and can be outlined similarly.

3. For a good listing see Franz Delitzsch, *Biblical Commentary on the Psalms,* vol. 2, trans. Francis Bolton (Grand Rapids: Eerdmans, n.d.), 173.

4. Derek Kidner, *Psalms 1–72: An Introduction and Commentary on Books I and II of the Psalms* (Downers Grove, Ill.: InterVarsity, 1973), 206.

5. Alexander Maclaren, *Expositions of Holy Scripture,* vol. 3, *The Psalms, Isaiah 1–48* (Grand Rapids: Eerdmans, 1959), part 2, 48–49.

Psalm 58: *Low Deeds in High Places*

1. Charles W. Colson, "The Problem of Ethics," a speech delivered to students at the Harvard Business School and published by the Wilberforce Forum, a division of Prison Fellowship (Washington: The Wilberforce Forum, 1992), 5.

2. Ibid., 3–4.

3. J. J. Stewart Perowne, *Commentary on the Psalms,* 2 vols. in 1 (Grand Rapids: Kregel, 1989), 1:454. Original edition 1878–1879.

4. Ibid., 455.

5. Alexander Maclaren, *The Psalms,* vol. 2, *Psalms 39–89* (New York: A. C. Armstrong and Son, 1893), 194.

6. For a particularly complete discussion of these options and a balanced suggestion of a good translation see Perowne, *Commentary on the Psalms,* 1:459. Alexander Maclaren is also helpful (see *The Psalms,* 2:194–96).

7. Maclaren, *The Psalms,* 2:195.

8. Cited in C. H. Spurgeon, *The Treasury of David,* vol. 2a, *Psalms 58–87* (Grand Rapids: Zondervan, 1968), 4.

9. Colson, "The Problem of Ethics," 22–23.

Psalm 59: *God Is My Fortress*

1. Marvin E. Tate has an interesting list of word parallels between this psalm and 1 Samuel 19 and 24, which also suggests a connection between the psalm and the historical setting: *watch* (v. 9), *morning* (v. 16), *innocence* (vv. 3–4), *seeing* (vv. 4, 10), *dogs* (vv. 6–7, 14–15), *ambush* (v. 3), and *blood* (v. 2). See *Psalms 51–100*, vol. 20 of the *Word Biblical Commentary* (Dallas: Word, 1990), 95.

2. See Derek Kidner, *Psalms 1–72: An Introduction and Commentary on Books I and II of the Psalms* (Downers Grove, Ill.: InterVarsity, 1973), 211.

3. Tate, *Psalms 51–100*, 99.

4. H. C. Leupold, *Exposition of the Psalms* (Grand Rapids: Baker, 1969), 443.

5. Albert Smith, *A Month at Constantinople*, quoted in C. H. Spurgeon, *The Treasury of David*, vol. 2a, *Psalms 58–87* (Grand Rapids: Zondervan, 1968), 20.

6. Alexander Maclaren, *Expositions of Holy Scripture*, vol. 3, *The Psalms, Isaiah 1–48* (Grand Rapids: Eerdmans, 1959), part 2, 61.

Psalm 60: *If God Does Not Go with Us*

1. Marvin E. Tate says that Aram-Naharaim is a name for Mesopotamia and that Aram-Zobah "refers to a major Aramean state during the time of David, located on the eastern slopes of the Anti-Lebanon mountain range in the Biqa Valley" (*Psalms 51–100*, vol. 20 in the *Word Biblical Commentary* [Dallas: Word, 1990], 104–5).

2. Derek Kidner, *Psalms 1–72: An Introduction and Commentary on Books I and II of the Psalms* (Downers Grove, Ill.: InterVarsity, 1973), 215.

3. A parallel account appears in 1 Chronicles 18:1–13.

4. First Chronicles 18:12 credits the slaying of the eighteen thousand to Abishai, another of David's commanders. He could have been a commander under David during the follow-up campaign.

5. C. H. Spurgeon, *The Treasury of David*, vol. 2a, *Psalms 58–87* (Grand Rapids: Zondervan, 1968), 27.

6. The first part of Psalm 108 is adapted from Psalm 57:7–11.

7. For a helpful study of these place names and their significance see H. C. Leupold, *Exposition of the Psalms* (Grand Rapids: Baker, 1969), 450–51, and J. J. Stewart Perowne, *Commentary on the Psalms*, 2 vols. in 1 (Grand Rapids: Kregel, 1989), 1:472–73. Original edition 1878–1879.

8. Leupold, *Exposition of the Psalms*, 448.

9. Ibid., 452.

Psalm 61: *The Rock That Is Higher Than I*

1. See Franz Delitzsch, *Biblical Commentary on the Psalms*, vol. 2, trans. Francis Bolton (Grand Rapids: Eerdmans, n.d.), 202; J. J. Stewart Perowne, *Commentary on the Psalms*, 2 vols. in 1 (Grand Rapids: Kregel, 1989), 1:478. Original edition 1878–1879; Derek Kidner, *Psalms 1–72: An Introduction and Commentary on Books I and II of the Psalms* (Downers Grove, Ill.: InterVarsity, 1973), 218–20.

2. H. C. Leupold, *Exposition of the Psalms* (Grand Rapids: Baker, 1969), 458.

3. Alexander Maclaren, *The Psalms*, vol. 2, *Psalms, 39–89* (New York: A. C. Armstrong and Son, 1893), 217–18.

4. Marvin E. Tate, *Psalms 51–100*, vol. 20 in the *Word Biblical Commentary* (Dallas: Word, 1990), 116.

5. See Psalms 18:2, 31, 46; 19:14; 28:1; 31:2–3; 40:2; 61:2; 62:2, 6–7; 71:3; 78:35; 89:26; 92:15; 94:22; 95:1; 144:1.

6. C. H. Spurgeon, *The Treasury of David*, vol. 2a, *Psalms 58–87* (Grand Rapids: Zondervan, 1968), 40.

7. See also Psalms 15:1; 23:6; 43:3; 84:4. "During the time the tabernacle was still being

moved from place to place we hear no such mention of dwelling in God's tabernacle or house. It was David who coined this expression for loving fellowship with the God of revelation, simultaneously with his preparation of a settled dwelling-place for the sacred Ark" (Franz Delitzsch, *Biblical Commentary on the Psalms*, vol. 2, trans. Francis Bolton [Grand Rapids: Eerdmans, n.d.], 203).

8. Spurgeon, *The Treasury of David*, 2a:46.

Psalm 62: *Rest in God Alone*

1. H. C. Leupold, *Exposition of the Psalms* (Grand Rapids: Baker, 1969), 458.

2. J. J. Stewart Perowne, *Commentary on the Psalms*, 2 vols. in 1 (Grand Rapids: Kregel, 1989), 1:480. Original edition 1878–1879.

3. Marvin E. Tate, *Psalms 51–100*, vol. 20 in the *Word Biblical Commentary* (Dallas: Word, 1990), 117.

4. Alexander Maclaren, *Expositions of Holy Scripture*, vol. 3, *The Psalms, Isaiah 1–48* (Grand Rapids: Eerdmans, 1959), part 2, 67.

5. John MacArthur, Jr., *Our Sufficiency in Christ* (Dallas: Word, 1991).

6. John Trapp, quoted in C. H. Spurgeon, *The Treasury of David*, vol. 2a, *Psalms 58–87* (Grand Rapids: Zondervan, 1968), 55.

7. Maclaren, *Expositions of Holy Scripture*, 3:70.

8. Derek Kidner, *Psalms 1–72: An Introduction and Commentary on Books I and II of the Psalms* (Downers Grove, Ill.: InterVarsity, 1973), 223.

9. Perowne, *Commentary on the Psalms*, 1:484.

Psalm 63: *A Love Better Than Life*

1. Murdoch Campbell, *From Grace to Glory: Meditations on the Book of Psalms* (Carlisle, Pa.: The Banner of Truth Trust, 1970), 109.

2. Derek Kidner, *Psalms 1–72: An Introduction and Commentary on Books I and II of the Psalms* (Downers Grove, Ill.: InterVarsity, 1973), 224.

3. J. J. Stewart Perowne, *Commentary on the Psalms*, 2 vols. in 1 (Grand Rapids: Kregel, 1989), 1:486. Original edition 1878–1879.

4. C. S. Lewis, *Reflections on the Psalms* (New York: Harcourt, Brace & World, 1958), 50–51.

5. C. H. Spurgeon, *The Treasury of David*, vol. 2a, *Psalms 58–87* (Grand Rapids: Zondervan, 1968), 65.

6. Augustine, *The Confessions*, book I, paragraph 1, in *Basic Writings of Saint Augustine*, ed. Whitney J. Oates (New York: Random House, 1948), 1:3.

7. Spurgeon, *The Treasury of David*, 2a:73.

8. John Donne, *Sermon 66*, quoted in Perowne, *Commentary on the Psalms*, 1:489.

9. G. Campbell Morgan, *Notes on the Psalms* (Westwood, N.J.: Revell, 1947), 112.

Psalm 64: *Sudden Destruction for the Wicked*

1. Alexander Maclaren, *The Psalms*, vol. 2, *Psalms 39–89* (New York: A. C. Armstrong and Son, 1893), 242–43.

2. C. H. Spurgeon, *The Treasury of David*, vol. 2a, *Psalms 58–87* (Grand Rapids: Zondervan, 1968), 83.

3. Paul is quoting from Psalms 14:1–3; 53:1–3; Ecclesiastes 7:20; Psalms 5:9; 140:3; 10:7; Isaiah 59:7–8; and Psalm 36:1.

4. Derek Kidner, *Psalms 1–72: An Introduction and Commentary on Books I and II of the Psalms* (Downers Grove, Ill.: InterVarsity, 1973), 228–29.

Psalm 65: *All Good Gifts from Our Good God*

1. C. S. Lewis, *Reflections on the Psalms* (New York: Harcourt, Brace & World, 1958), 77.

2. Derek Kidner, *Psalms 1–72: An Introduction and Commentary on Books I and II of the Psalms* (Downers Grove, Ill.: InterVarsity, 1973), 229.

3. H. C. Leupold, *Exposition of the Psalms* (Grand Rapids: Baker, 1969), 447.

4. J. J. Stewart Perowne, *Commentary on the Psalms,* 2 vols. in 1 (Grand Rapids: Kregel, 1989), 1:498. Original edition 1878–1879.

5. Leupold, *Exposition of the Psalms,* 475.

Psalm 66: *A Praise Psalm of Thanksgiving*

1. Psalms 65:2, 5, 8; 66:1–4, 7–8; 67:2–5; 68:32.

2. Marvin E. Tate, *Psalms 51–100,* vol. 20 in the *Word Biblical Commentary* (Dallas: Word, 1990), 151–52.

3. A number of commentators have argued that the deliverance in verses 8–12 seems to be a present experience of the people and suggest that it is probably the deliverance from the Assyrians in the days of King Hezekiah (2 Kings 18–19; Isa. 36–37), but this is only a guess. It could be anything or, as I suggest, nearly everything—that is, many national and even personal deliverances.

4. Quoted by C. H. Spurgeon, *The Treasury of David,* vol. 2a, *Psalms 58–87* (Grand Rapids: Zondervan, 1968), 126.

Psalm 67: *The Shining Face of God*

1. Alexander Maclaren, *The Psalms,* vol. 3, *Psalms 39–89* (New York: A. C. Armstrong and Son, 1893), 268.

2. C. H. Spurgeon, *The Treasury of David,* vol. 2a, *Psalms 58–87* (Grand Rapids: Zondervan, 1968), 129.

3. John R. W. Stott, *Favorite Psalms* (Chicago: Moody, 1988), 68.

4. William Binnie, cited in Spurgeon, *The Treasury of David,* 2a:130–31.

Psalm 68: *God Who Saves: Part 1*

1. Derek Kidner, *Psalms 1–72: An Introduction and Commentary on Books I and II of the Psalms* (Downers Grove, Ill.: InterVarsity, 1973), 238.

2. J. J. Stewart Perowne, *Commentary on the Psalms,* 2 vols. in 1 (Grand Rapids: Kregel, 1989), 1:512–18. Original edition 1878–1879.

3. Derek Kidner, *Psalms 1–72,* 240–41. Perowne also has a helpful list of these possibilities. See his *Commentary on the Psalms,* 1:524–26.

4. Perowne, *Commentary on the Psalms,* 1:523.

5. C. H. Spurgeon, *The Treasury of David,* vol. 2a, *Psalms 58–87* (Grand Rapids: Zondervan, 1968), 155.

6. Ibid., 156.

7. Ibid., 140.

Psalm 68: *God Who Saves: Part 2*

1. William L. Pettingill, *Christ in the Psalms* (Findlay, Ohio: Fundamental Truth Publishers, 1937).

2. Psalms 2, 8, 16, 22, 31, 34, 40, 41, 45, 68, 69, 102, 110, and 118.

3. Derek Kidner, *Psalms 1–72: An Introduction and Commentary on Books I and II of the Psalms* (Downers Grove, Ill.: InterVarsity, 1973), 244.

Psalm 69: *Man of Sorrows: Part 1*

1. Arno C. Gaebelein, *The Book of Psalms: A Devotional and Prophetic Commentary* (Neptune, N.J.: Loizeaux, 1939), 275–76.

2. Saint Augustine had trouble interpreting this verse because his way of explaining the psalms is to apply everything to Christ. He resolved the problem by deciding that the words apply to the members of Christ's body, not to the body's head.

3. Donald Grey Barnhouse, *God's Glory: Exposition of Bible Doctrines Taking the Epistle to the Romans as a Point of Departure,* vol. 10, *Romans 14:13–16:27* (Grand Rapids: Eerdmans, 1964), 39.

4. Ibid., 39–40.

5. Ibid., 40.

6. Ibid.

7. Ibid.

8. This material is covered in a fuller form by Barnhouse in *God's Glory,* 41–43.

Psalm 69: *Man of Sorrows: Part 2*

1. Alexander Maclaren, *The Psalms,* vol. 2, *Psalms 39–89* (New York: A. C. Armstrong and Son, 1893), 303.

2. Some of this material, including the Pearl Harbor illustration, is from Donald Grey Barnhouse, *God's Covenants: Exposition of Bible Doctrines Taking the Epistle to the Romans as a Point of Departure,* vol. 8, *Romans 9:1–11:36* (Grand Rapids: Eerdmans, 1963), 119–20.

3. Psalm 22 is predominantly a psalm prophesying Christ's crucifixion. But it ends with Jesus praising God for that "great assembly" of believers whom God will have given to him and announcing that generations yet unborn will glorify God because of his atoning work for them.

Psalm 70: *"Let God Be Exalted"*

1. Martin Luther, *First Lectures on the Psalms: I, Psalms 1–75,* vol. 10 in *Luther's Works,* ed. Hilton C. Oswald (St. Louis: Concordia, 1974), 391.

2. G. Campbell Morgan, *Notes on the Psalms* (Westwood, N.J.: Revell, 1947), 126.

Psalm 71: *A Psalm for Old Age*

1. Marvin Tate notes "the pleas for haste to help on the part of God in 70:2, 5 and 71:12; the prayer for deliverance or rescue in 70:2, 5 and 71:2 (note v. 11 also); the prayer for help in 70:2, 5 and 71:12; and the prayers regarding putting enemies to shame in 70:3 and 71:13, 24" (Marvin E. Tate, *Psalms 51–100,* vol. 20 in the *Word Biblical Commentary* [Dallas: Word, 1990], 211).

2. C. H. Spurgeon, *The Treasury of David,* vol. 2a, *Psalms 58–87* (Grand Rapids: Zondervan, 1968), 206.

3. H. C. Leupold, *Exposition of the Psalms* (Grand Rapids: Baker, 1969), 511.

4. John Wesley, *Journal from September 13, 1773 to October 24, 1790 (End),* vol. 4 in *The Works of John Wesley* (Grand Rapids: Zondervan, n.d.), 464.

5. Tate, *Psalms 51–100,* 217–18.

6. Spurgeon, *The Treasury of David,* 2a:208.

7. "The Martyrdom of Holy Polycarp, Bishop of Smyrna" in *The Apostolic Fathers: An American Translation,* trans. Edgar J. Goodspeed (New York: Harper & Brothers, 1950), 250–51.

8. J. J. Stewart Perowne, *Commentary on the Psalms,* 2 vols. in 1 (Grand Rapids: Kregel, 1989), 1:559. Original edition 1878–1879.

Psalm 72: *A Song of Solomon*

1. Two psalms are titled "of Solomon," this one and Psalm 127.

2. Derek Kidner, *Psalms 1–72: An Introduction and Commentary on Books I and II of the Psalms* (Downers Grove, Ill.: InterVarsity, 1973), 254.

3. Charles Hodge, *Systematic Theology,* vol. 1 (London: James Clarke & Co., 1960), 491–92.

4. There is a critical question here about how to translate the tenses in verse 2 and following. The verbs are imperfects, but they can be translated as optatives ("May he judge your people in righteousness," "May he defend the afflicted," and so on) or as futures ("He will

judge . . ."). If the verbs are to be understood as optatives, the psalm will be seen as an extension of the prayer for God's blessing on Solomon expressed first in verse 1. Most commentators, including the translators of the New International Version, prefer the future sense, thereby strengthening the thought that the psalm as a whole looks forward to the coming of Jesus Christ.

5. C. H. Spurgeon, *The Treasury of David*, vol. 2a, *Psalms 58–87* (Grand Rapids: Zondervan, 1968), 228.

6. Sheba was located to the southeast of Israel, Seba (Ethiopia) to the southwest. The mention of Sheba inevitably recalls the visit of the Queen of Sheba to Solomon, recorded in 1 Kings 10:1–13. The land was named after Sheba, one of the sons of Joktan (Gen. 10:28). Seba was among the sons of Cush (Gen. 10:7).

7. G. Campbell Morgan, *Notes on the Psalms* (Westwood, N.J.: Revell, 1947), 129.

Psalm 73: *A Paradigm Shift for Asaph*

1. In the second book of the Psalter, Psalms 42 and 44–49 are also titled "Of the Sons of Korah."

2. For a good discussion of the answers to the problem of the apparent successes of the wicked in Psalms 37, 73, and Job, see J. J. Stewart Perowne, *Commentary on the Psalms,* 2 vols. in 1 (Grand Rapids: Kregel, 1989), 2:3–7. Original edition 1878–1879.

3. Marvin E. Tate, *Psalms 51–100,* vol. 20 in the *Word Biblical Commentary* (Dallas: Word, 1990), 234.

4. Perowne, *Commentary on the Psalms,* 2:8.

5. Roy Clements, *Songs of Experience: Midnight and Dawn through the Eyes of the Psalmists* (Fearn, Scotland: Christian Focus Publications, 1993), 80–81.

Psalm 74: *Prayer amid the Ruins of Jerusalem*

1. See Rowland E. Prothero, *The Psalms in Human Life* (New York: E. P. Dutton, 1904), 217–18.

2. For a fuller discussion of this problem see Alexander Maclaren, *The Psalms,* vol. 2, *Psalms 39–89* (New York: A. C. Armstrong and Son, 1893), 349–50; J. J. Stewart Perowne, *Commentary on the Psalms,* 2 vols. in 1 (Grand Rapids: Kregel, 1989), 2:22–23. Original edition 1878–1879; and Marvin E. Tate, *Psalms 51–100,* vol. 20 in the *Word Biblical Commentary* (Dallas: Word, 1990), 246–47.

3. C. H. Spurgeon, *The Treasury of David*, vol. 2a, *Psalms 58–87* (Grand Rapids: Zondervan, 1966), 275–76.

4. Perowne, *Commentary on the Psalms,* 2:28.

5. Maclaren, *The Psalms,* 2:353–54.

6. John Wesley, *The Works* (Grand Rapids: Zondervan, from the authorized edition of 1872), 5:3.

7. Spurgeon, *The Treasury of David*, 2a:273.

8. Ibid., 278.

Psalm 75: *Our God Reigns*

1. C. H. Spurgeon, *The Treasury of David*, vol. 2a, *Psalms 58–87* (Grand Rapids: Zondervan, 1966), 273.

2. Ibid., 295.

3. Murdoch Campbell, *From Grace to Glory: Meditations on the Book of Psalms* (Carlisle, Pa.: The Banner of Truth Trust, 1970), 123–24.

4. For example, Marvin E. Tate, *Psalms 51–100,* vol. 20 in the *Word Biblical Commentary* (Dallas: Word, 1990), 259.

5. See H. C. Leupold, *Exposition of the Psalms* (Grand Rapids: Baker, 1969), 547; J. J. Stewart Perowne, *Commentary on the Psalms,* 2 vols. in 1 (Grand Rapids: Kregel, 1989),

2:38. Original edition 1878–1879; Alexander Maclaren, *The Psalms,* vol. 2, *Pslams 39–89* (New York: A. C. Armstrong and Son, 1893), 365; and Spurgeon, *The Treasury of David,* 2a:295.

Psalm 76: *The Fear of the Lord Is the Beginning*

1. C. H. Spurgeon, *The Treasury of David,* vol. 2a, *Psalms 58–87* (Grand Rapids: Zondervan, 1966), 302.

2. For details of these various military and other uses of the psalm see Rowland E. Prothero, *The Psalms in Human Life* (New York: E. P. Dutton, 1904), 168, 193, 276, and Herbert Lockyer, Sr., *A Devotional Commentary: Psalms* (Grand Rapids: Kregel, 1993), 252, 254.

3. Lord Byron, "The Destruction of Sennacherib" in *The Harvard Classics, English Poetry,* vol. 2, *From Collins to Fitzgerald* (Norwalk, Conn.: The Easton Press, 1994), 805.

4. Derek Kidner, *Psalms 73–150: A Commentary on Books III–V of the Psalms* (Downers Grove, Ill.: InterVarsity, 1975), 275.

Psalm 77: *Remembering*

1. Walter C. Kaiser writes, "Before verse 10 the psalmist had been too subjective and had looked only within himself in attempting to determine the mystery of God's dealings. The psalmist was thinking solely in light of his own experiences. Accordingly he experienced deep despondency. But when the psalmist's meditation *(hagih)* focused on the works of God, then he remembered that great deliverance of God experienced in the Exodus, which was a pledge of every other deliverance experienced by individuals or nations. Thus the text of the psalm emphasizes that it is a matter of great concern how one meditates and on what he fixes his heart and mind. Some meditation can be harmful, but biblically approved meditations strengthen" (Walter C. Kaiser, Jr., "What Is Biblical Meditation?" in John D. Woodbridge, ed., *Renewing Your Mind in a Secular World* (Chicago: Moody, 1985), 42–43.

2. H. C. Leupold, *Exposition of the Psalms* (Grand Rapids: Baker, 1969), 554.

3. C. H. Spurgeon, *The Treasury of David,* vol. 2a, *Psalms 58–87* (Grand Rapids: Zondervan, 1966), 312–13.

4. Alexander Maclaren, *The Psalms,* vol. 2, *Psalms 39–89* (New York: A. C. Armstrong and Son, 1893), 376.

5. For helpful discussions of these variations see Leupold, *Exposition of the Psalms,* 560–61; J. J. Stewart Perowne, *Commentary on the Psalms,* 2 vols. in 1 (Grand Rapids: Kregel, 1989), 2:50. Original edition 1878–1879; Maclaren, *The Psalms,* 2:377; and Franz Delitzsch, *Biblical Commentary on the Psalms,* vol. 2, trans. Francis Bolton (Grand Rapids: Eerdmans, n.d.), 352–53. Leupold prefers "This is my grief, that the right hand of the Most High has changed" (555). Perowne is similar: "This is my sorrow, that the right hand of the Highest hath changed" (50). Maclaren reads, "It is my sickness; [but I will remember] the years of the right hand of the Most High" (371). Delitzsch translates, "My decree of affliction is this, The years of the right hand of the Most High" (348). Marvin E. Tate, who discusses the problem only briefly in the notes, has, "My sorrow is this: the changing of the right hand of the Most High" (Marvin E. Tate, *Psalms 51–100,* vol. 20 in the *Word Biblical Commentary* [Dallas: Word, 1990], 268).

6. It might also be said in answer to the objection that this is an abrupt ending that the psalm was intended as a prelude to the next one, which deals with Israel's history more fully and ends with God shepherding the people by the hand of David, just as he is described as shepherding the people through the hands of Moses and Aaron here.

7. Delitzsch, *Biblical Commentary on the Psalms,* 2:349.

Psalm 78: *A Sermon from Israel's History*

1. This is what Jesus' parables did, which is why Matthew quotes verse 2 in 13:35, saying that Jesus spoke in parables to fulfill "what was spoken through the prophet." This is only one of many verses from Psalm 78 that are either cited or reflected in the New Testament:

1 John 1:1–4 echoes verse 3; Ephesians 6:4 builds on verse 4; Acts 2:40 may be referring to verse 8; 1 Corinthians 10:4 may refer to verse 15; 1 Corinthians 10:9 cites verse 18; John 6:31 quotes and Revelation 2:17 echoes verse 24; 1 Corinthians 10:3 refers to verses 24–29; 1 Corinthians 10:5 echoes verse 31; Acts 8:21 is like verse 37; and Revelation 16:4 may be thinking of verse 44.

2. J. J. Stewart Perowne, *Commentary on the Psalms,* 2 vols. in 1 (Grand Rapids: Kregel, 1989), 2:66. Original edition 1878–1879.

3. See Perowne, *Commentary on the Psalms,* 2:58; and Marvin E. Tate, *Psalms 51–100,* vol. 20 in the *Word Biblical Commentary* (Dallas: Word, 1990), 287–88.

4. Derek Kidner, *Psalms 73–150: A Commentary on Books III–V of the Psalms* (Downers Grove, Ill.: InterVarsity, 1975), 284.

5. The tabernacle had been at Shiloh during the whole period of the judges (see Josh. 18:10; Judg. 18:31; 1 Sam. 4:3), but God rejected Shiloh when the ark was given into the hands of the Philistines (1 Sam. 4:1–22), and it was never brought back. Instead, it was taken to Kiriath Jearim, to the house of a man named Abinadab (1 Sam. 6:21–7:1). The tabernacle itself was removed first to Nob (1 Sam. 21) and afterwards probably to Gibeon (1 Kings 3:4). It was David who finally brought the ark to Jerusalem (2 Sam. 6:1–19).

6. There is a significant link here with Psalm 77. Psalm 77 ended on God pastoring his flock by the hands of Moses and Aaron. Psalm 78 ends with God pastoring his flock by the hand of David. So we have two pastoral psalms, though in the first the psalmist is not aware of this until near the end.

Psalm 79: *"Where Is Their God?"*

1. For a careful discussion of this evidence from the side of the later dating see J. J. Stewart Perowne, *Commentary on the Psalms,* 2 vols. in 1 (Grand Rapids: Kregel, 1989), 2:73–77. Original edition 1878–1879. Maclaren also holds to this dating (Alexander Maclaren, *The Psalms,* vol. 2, *Psalms 39–89* [New York: A. C. Armstrong and Son, 1893], 397–98). In support of the earlier dating—that is, from the time of Nebuchadnezzar—see Marvin E. Tate, *Psalms 51–100,* vol. 20 in the *Word Biblical Commentary* (Dallas: Word, 1990), 298–99.

2. Tate, *Psalms 51–100,* 303.

3. Ibid., 301. Tate says, "This psalm deals with one of the basic issues in religious thought: how do the people of God cope with disaster in the face of God's seeming absence? The answer is: by hanging on to hope in him."

4. Saint Augustine, *The Confessions of St. Augustine,* trans. Edward B. Pusey, *The Harvard Classics Millennium Edition* (Norwalk, Conn.: The Easton Press, 1993), 141–42.

5. G. Campbell Morgan, *Notes on the Psalms* (Westwood, N.J.: Revell, 1947), 149. The others are "the sense that all the calamity which has overtaken them is the result of their own sin" and an "underlying confidence in God."

6. Derek Kidner, *Psalms 73–150: A Commentary on Books III–V of the Psalms* (Downers Grove, Ill.: InterVarsity, 1975), 288.

Psalm 80: *God's Flock and God's Vine*

1. The chorus is identical in all three instances, except that in the second and third occurrences the name of God is lengthened. In the first (v. 3), the word is "God" *(Elohim).* In the second (v. 7), the words are "God Almighty" or "God of Hosts" *(Elohim Sabaoth).* In the third (v. 19), the full title is the "Lᴏʀᴅ God Almighty" *(Jehovah Elohim Sabaoth).*

2. Franz Delitzsch, *Biblical Commentary on the Psalms,* vol. 2, trans. Francis Bolton (Grand Rapids: Eerdmans, n.d.), 383. However, the plea for restoration and the reference to the walls of God's vineyard having been "broken down" (v. 12) lead some to believe that it may have been written just after the northern kingdom's fall.

3. Alexander Maclaren, *The Psalms,* vol. 2, *Psalms 39–89* (New York: A. C. Armstrong and Son, 1893), 409.

4. See also 2 Samuel 7:10; Jeremiah 12:10; Amos 9:15.

5. H. C. Leupold, *Exposition of the Psalms* (Grand Rapids: Baker, 1969), 584.

6. J. J. Stewart Perowne, *Commentary on the Psalms*, 2 vols. in 1 (Grand Rapids: Kregel, 1989), 2:89. Original edition 1878–1879.

7. C. H. Spurgeon, *The Treasury of David*, vol. 2a, *Psalms 58–87* (Grand Rapids: Zondervan, 1966), 391.

8. Ibid., 397.

9. C. H. Spurgeon, "Without Christ—Nothing," *Metropolitan Tabernacle Pulpit*, vol. 27 (Carlisle, Pa.: The Banner of Truth Trust, 1971), 601.

Psalm 81: *"If My People . . ."*

1. Franz Delitzsch, *Biblical Commentary on the Psalms*, vol. 2, trans. Francis Bolton (Grand Rapids: Eerdmans, n.d.), 393.

2. There has been a great deal of debate about what service or feast this psalm was intended to introduce, but it is undoubtedly one of the feasts of the seventh month of the Jewish calendar, probably the Feast of Tabernacles. Trumpets were blown to announce the beginning of this month, the time of the new moon, and the shofar, or ram's horn, was sounded on the fifteenth day, which would have been the time of the full moon (Lev. 23:23–44). The first day of the month was a solemn assembly. The Day of Atonement was observed on the tenth of the month, and the Feast of Tabernacles (or Booths) began on the fifteenth and lasted for seven days. The Feast of Tabernacles was associated with the wilderness wandering, after the people had come out of Egypt, and was intended to remind them of God's care and provision during those days. Hence the psalm deals with remembering and has many echoes of the deliverance from Egypt and the instructions given at Mount Sinai.

3. Derek Kidner, *Psalms 73–150: A Commentary on Books III–V of the Psalms* (Downers Grove, Ill.: InterVarsity, 1975), 294.

4. Robert L. Wilken, "No Other Gods," *First Things*, November 1993, 13.

5. Ibid., 14. The quotes are from T. S. Eliot, *Christianity and Culture* (New York: Harcourt, Brace & World, 1949).

6. Wilken, 14.

7. Ibid., 18.

8. Alexander Maclaren, *The Psalms*, vol. 2, *Psalms 39–89* (New York: A. C. Armstrong and Son, 1893), 422.

9. Michael Scott Horton, *Beyond Culture Wars* (Chicago: Moody, 1994), 60.

Psalm 82: *All "Gods" Judged by God*

1. There are variants of these two possibilities, however. Some extend "human judges" to include those of the Gentile nations, largely because of verse 8, which speaks of God judging the entire earth, while others extend "principalities and powers" to include Gentile gods or goddesses, or angels.

2. H. C. Leupold is strong on this position (see *Exposition of the Psalms* [Grand Rapids: Baker, 1969], 592–94), but so are J. J. Stewart Perowne (*Commentary on the Psalms*, 2 vols. in 1 [Grand Rapids: Kregel, 1989], 2:101–4. Original edition 1878–1879) and Alexander Maclaren (*The Psalms*, vol. 2, *Psalms 39–89* [New York: A. C. Armstrong and Son, 1893], 2:426–28).

3. In verses 8, 9, and 28. In the case of verse 28, the New International Version reads, "Do not blaspheme God or curse the ruler of your people." The footnote indicates that the first half of the sentence may be parallel to the second half and might be translated, "Do not revile the judges."

4. Perowne, *Commentary on the Psalms*, 2:102.

5. Derek Kidner, *Psalms 73–150: A Commentary on Books III–V of the Psalms* (Downers Grove, Ill.: InterVarsity, 1975), 296–97; Marvin E. Tate, *Psalms 51–100*, vol. 20 in the *Word Biblical Commentary* (Dallas: Word, 1990), 332–33, 340–41. However, Tate sees this as "a false alterna-

tive. Both are involved because God's judgment of the gods has its parallel in God's judgment of unjust human officials. . . . The judgment of the gods is at the same time a judgment of their human agents" (341).

6. Martin Luther, *Selected Psalms II*, vol. 13 in *Luther's Works*, ed. Jaroslav Pelikan (St. Louis: Concordia, 1956), 44–45.

7. Ibid., 51.

8. Ibid., 56.

9. Tate, *Psalms 51–100*, 334.

10. Arno C. Gaebelein, *The Book of Psalms: A Devotional and Prophetic Commentary* (Neptune, N.J.: Loizeaux, 1965), 318–19.

Psalm 83: *The Encircling Foe*

1. See Will Durant, *The Age of Faith: A History of Medieval Civilization—Christian, Islamic and Judaic—from Constantine to Dante: A.D. 325–1300*, vol. 4 of *The Story of Civilization* (Norwalk, Conn.: The Easton Press, 1992), 385–94.

2. Durant, *The Reformation: A History of European Civilization from Wyclif to Calvin: 1300–1564*, vol. 6 of *The Story of Civilization* (Norwalk, Conn.: The Easton Press, 1992), 727–37.

Psalm 84: *The Psalm of the Janitors*

1. C. H. Spurgeon, *The Treasury of David*, vol. 2a, *Psalms 58–87* (Grand Rapids: Zondervan, 1966), 432.

2. Donald Grey Barnhouse, "The Christian and the Old Testament," booklet 86 in the series of Broadcast Notes issued to supporters of the Bible Study Hour (Philadelphia: Bible Study Hour, 1959), 25. The entire story is on pp. 23–25.

3. H. C. Leupold, *Exposition of the Psalms* (Grand Rapids: Baker, 1969), 604–5.

4. Donald Grey Barnhouse, *God's Remedy: Exposition of Bible Doctrines, Taking the Epistle to the Romans as a Point of Departure*, vol. 3, *Romans 3:21–4:25* (Grand Rapids: Eerdmans, 1954), 239.

5. Alexander Maclaren, *Expositions of Holy Scripture*, vol. 3, *The Psalms, Isaiah 1–48* (Grand Rapids: Eerdmans, 1959), 124–25.

6. Augustine, *The Confessions*, book 1, paragraph 1, in *Basic Writings of Saint Augustine*, vol. 1, ed. Whitney J. Oates (New York: Random House, 1948), 3.

7. Maclaren, *Expositions of Holy Scripture*, 3:128.

Psalm 85: *When Righteousness and Peace Meet*

1. The strongest champions of this view are H. C. Leupold (*Exposition of the Psalms* [Grand Rapids: Baker, 1969], 609–10) and J. J. Stewart Perowne (*Commentary on the Psalms*, 2 vols. in 1 [Grand Rapids: Kregel, 1989], 2:123–24. Original edition 1878–1879). Perowne says, "The most probable way of explaining this conflict of opposing feelings is by referring the psalm to the circumstances mentioned by Nehemiah (chap. 1–3)."

2. Derek Kidner, *Psalms 73–150: A Commentary on Books III–V of the Psalms* (Downers Grove, Ill.: InterVarsity, 1975), 308.

3. Rowland E. Prothero, *The Psalms in Human Life* (New York: E. P. Dutton, 1904), 259.

Psalm 86: *An Appeal to the Compassionate God*

1. C. H. Spurgeon, *The Treasury of David*, vol. 2a, *Psalms 58–87* (Grand Rapids: Zondervan, 1966), 464.

2. In the English versions *Adonai* is distinguished from *Jehovah* by being rendered *Lord* (with a capital *L* followed by small letters) as opposed to *Lord* (with large *L* followed by small capitals). In Psalm 86 *Lord* (*Adonai*) occurs in verses 3–5, 8–9, 12, and 15. *Lord* (*Jehovah*) occurs in verses 1, 6, 11, and 17. God is also called "God" or "my God" in verses 2, 10, 12, 14, and 15. These many references to God and the variety of names for God are characteristic of this psalm.

Psalm 87: *Zion, City of Our God*

1. Saint Augustine, *The City of God*, book 14, chap. 28, in *A Select Library of the Nicene and Post-Nicene Fathers of the Christian Church*, vol. 2, ed. Philip Schaff (Grand Rapids: Eerdmans, 1977), 282–83.

2. C. H. Spurgeon, *The Treasury of David*, vol. 2a, *Psalms 58–87* (Grand Rapids: Zondervan, 1966), 478.

3. This is quoted from an old work called "Plain Commentary" in Spurgeon, *The Treasury of David*, 2a:483.

4. H. C. Leupold, *Exposition of the Psalms* (Grand Rapids: Baker, 1969), 624–25.

Psalm 88: *The Dark Night of the Soul*

1. Derek Kidner, *Psalms 73–150: A Commentary on Books III–V of the Psalms* (Downers Grove, Ill.: InterVarsity, 1975), 316.

2. H. C. Leupold, *Exposition of the Psalms* (Grand Rapids: Baker, 1969), 626–27.

3. J. J. Stewart Perowne, *Commentary on the Psalms*, 2 vols. in 1 (Grand Rapids: Kregel, 1989), 2:40. Original edition 1878–1879.

4. For other references to Heman, presumably but not necessarily the same individual, see 1 Chronicles 2:6; 6:33; 15:17–19; 16:41–42; and 25:1–6; 2 Chronicles 5:12; 29:14; and 35:15.

5. Marvin E. Tate, *Psalms 51–100*, vol. 20 in the *Word Biblical Commentary* (Dallas: Word, 1990), 405.

6. Martin Marty in *A Cry of Absence: Reflections for the Winter of the Heart* (San Francisco: Harper & Row, 1988), 68, cited in Tate, *Psalms 51–100*, 404.

7. Tate, *Psalms 51–100*, 403.

8. C. S. Lewis, *Reflections on the Psalms* (New York: Harcourt, Brace & World, 1958), 38.

9. See Franz Delitzsch, *Biblical Commentary on the Psalms*, vol. 3, trans. Francis Bolton (Grand Rapids: Eerdmans, n.d.), 23–24.

10. Kidner, *Psalms 73–150*, 318.

11. Ibid., 319.

Psalm 89: *Our Covenant-Keeping God: Part 1*

1. Derek Kidner, *Psalms 73–150: A Commentary on Books III–V of the Psalms* (Downers Grove, Ill.: InterVarsity, 1975), 321.

2. H. C. Leupold lists some of the parallels: "If one would in a more detailed fashion note how this whole section is built on 2 Sam. 7, the following passages may be compared. Regarding v. 22 see 2 Sam. 7:10b. Regarding v. 25, 2 Sam. 8:3 and 13 may be compared—the only reference outside chapter 7. Regarding v. 26, 2 Sam. 7:14a. Regarding v. 30 see 14b; and regarding v. 33, 15a and 16" (H. C. Leupold, *Exposition of the Psalms* [Grand Rapids: Baker, 1969], 638). There are also references to other Scriptures. For example, verse 25 seems to echo Exodus 23:31, and verses 26–27 pick up on Psalm 2:7–9.

3. H. A. Ironside, *Random Reminiscences from Fifty Years of Ministry* (Neptune, N.J.: Loizeaux, 1939), 73–85.

4. Arthur W. Pink, *Gleanings in the Godhead* (Chicago: Moody, 1975), 47.

Psalm 89: *Our Covenant-Keeping God: Part 2*

1. See, for instance, Franz Delitzsch, *Biblical Commentary on the Psalms*, vol. 3, trans. Francis Bolton (Grand Rapids: Eerdmans, n.d.), 33–34.

2. H. C. Leupold, *Exposition of the Psalms* (Grand Rapids: Baker, 1969), 632.

3. Marvin E. Tate, *Psalms 51–100*, vol. 20 of the *Word Biblical Commentary* (Dallas: Word, 1990), 427.

4. J. I. Packer, *Knowing God* (Downers Grove, Ill.: InterVarsity, 1973), 68–72.

5. Ibid., 70–71.

6. J. J. Stewart Perowne, *Commentary on the Psalms*, 2 vols. in 1 (Grand Rapids: Kregel, 1989), 2:155. Original edition 1878–1879.

Psalm 90: *A Somber "Song of Moses"*

1. Psalm 90 is the oldest psalm in the Psalter. It is also one of only three psalms in this fourth book of psalms assigned to specific authors (Psalm 90 to Moses, Psalms 101 and 103 to David). It is a characteristic of the fourth book that most of the psalms are anonymous.

2. H. C. Leupold, *Exposition of the Psalms* (Grand Rapids: Baker, 1969), 645.

3. For example, verse 3 contains an obvious allusion to Genesis 3:19, and "the work of our hands" occurs seven times in Deuteronomy.

4. Herbert Lockyer, Sr., *Psalms: A Devotional Commentary* (Grand Rapids: Kregel, 1993), 312.

5. Alexander Maclaren, *The Psalms*, vol. 3, *Psalms 90–150* (New York: A. C. Armstrong and Son, 1894), 12.

6. Saint Augustine, *Confessions*, trans. R. S. Pine-Coffin (Baltimore: Penguin Books, 1961), 21.

7. William M. Taylor, *Moses the Law-Giver* (Grand Rapids: Baker, 1961), 373.

Psalm 91: *Under the Shadow of God's Wings*

1. H. C. Leupold, *Exposition of the Psalms* (Grand Rapids: Baker, 1969), 650.

2. C. H. Spurgeon, *The Treasury of David*, vol. 2b, *Psalms 88–110* (Grand Rapids: Zondervan, 1966), 88.

3. Ibid.

4. Ibid., 98.

5. Ibid., 92.

6. Martin Luther, *First Lectures on the Psalms: Psalms 76–126*, vol. 2 of *Luther's Works*, ed. Hilton C. Oswald (Saint Louis: Concordia, 1976), 208.

7. John R. W. Stott, *Favorite Psalms* (Chicago: Moody, 1988), 82.

Psalm 92: *A Psalm for the Sabbath*

1. Derek Kidner, *Psalms 73–150: A Commentary on Books III–V of the Psalms* (Downers Grove, Ill.: InterVarsity, 1975), 334.

2. C. H. Spurgeon, *The Treasury of David*, vol. 2b, *Psalms 88–110* (Grand Rapids: Zondervan, 1966), 116.

3. John Piper, *Desiring God: Meditations of a Christian Hedonist* (Portland, Oreg.: Multnomah, 1986), 225–26.

4. See Spurgeon, *The Treasury of David*, 2a:123.

5. Kidner, *Psalms 73–150*, 335. The quote is from James Boswell, *The Life of Dr. Johnson*, Everyman edition, vol. 1:464.

6. J. J. Stewart Perowne, *Commentary on the Psalms*, 2 vols. in 1 (Grand Rapids: Kregel, 1989), 2:181. Original edition 1878–1879.

Psalm 93: *A Psalm to God as King*

1. Franz Delitzsch, *Biblical Commentary on the Psalms*, vol. 3, trans. Francis Bolton (Grand Rapids: Eerdmans, n.d.), 73.

2. Psalm 94 is sometimes said to be an exception, a break in the pattern. However, although it does not specifically refer to Jehovah as a king, it does refer to his being the judge of the whole earth, which is an aspect of God's kingly rule. It is the psalm's theme. In a theocracy the roles of king and judge are one.

3. H. C. Leupold, *Exposition of the Psalms* (Grand Rapids: Baker, 1969), 663.

4. Putting the best possible face on this approach, Marvin E. Tate says, "The expressions used were doubtless conventional in Israelite worship and perhaps should be treated as personifications of the primeval forces which threaten creation" (*Psalms 51–100*, vol. 20 of the *Word Biblical Commentary* [Dallas: Word, 1990], 479).

5. See also Isaiah 51:9–15.

6. Delitzsch, *Biblical Commentary on the Psalms*, 3:75.

7. Tate, *Psalms 51–100*, 479.

8. Also many other times throughout that psalm (see vv. 14, 22, 24, 31, 36, 46, 59, 79, 88, 95, 99, 111, 119, 125, 129, 138, 144, 146, 152, 157, 167, 168).

Psalm 94: *All Hearts Open, All Desires Known*

1. C. H. Spurgeon, *C. H. Spurgeon's Sermons on the Psalms*, ed. Charles T. Cook (London: Marshall, Morgan & Scott, 1960), 164.

2. Ibid.

3. Marvin E. Tate, *Psalms 51–100*, vol. 20 of the *Word Biblical Commentary* (Dallas: Word, 1990), 488.

4. Derek Kidner, *Psalms 73–150: A Commentary on Books III–V of the Psalms* (Downers Grove, Ill.: InterVarsity, 1975), 340.

5. Cited in C. H. Spurgeon, *The Treasury of David*, vol. 2b, *Psalms 88–110* (Grand Rapids: Zondervan, 1966), 148.

6. Alexander Maclaren, *The Psalms*, vol. 3, *Psalms 90–150* (New York: A. C. Armstrong and Son, 1894), 40–41.

7. H. C. Leupold, *Exposition of the Psalms* (Grand Rapids: Baker, 1969), 671.

8. J. M. Neale, cited in Spurgeon, *The Treasury of David*, 2b:153.

Psalm 95: *How to Worship God*

1. John R. W. Stott, *Christ the Controversialist: A Study in Some Essentials of Evangelical Religion* (London: Tyndale, 1970), 160.

2. A. W. Tozer, *The Pursuit of God* (Harrisburg, Pa.: Christian Publications, 1948), 9.

3. C. H. Spurgeon, *The Treasury of David*, vol. 2b, *Psalms 88–110* (Grand Rapids: Zondervan, 1966), 164.

4. C. S. Lewis, *Reflections on the Psalms* (New York: Harcourt, Brace & World, 1958), 51–52.

5. John R. W. Stott, *Favorite Psalms* (Chicago: Moody, 1988), 83.

6. Derek Kidner, *Psalms 73–150: A Commentary on Books III–V of the Psalms* (Downers Grove, Ill.: InterVarsity, 1975), 343.

Psalm 96: *Worship in the Splendor of God's Holiness*

1. H. C. Leupold lists a number of these. See *Exposition of the Psalms* (Grand Rapids: Baker, 1969), 682.

2. Ibid., 681.

3. G. Campbell Morgan, *Notes on the Psalms* (Westwood, N.J.: Revell, 1947), 181.

4. Marvin E. Tate, *Psalms 51–100*, vol. 20 of the *Word Biblical Commentary* (Dallas: Word, 1990), 512.

5. J. J. Stewart Perowne, *Commentary on the Psalms*, 2 vols. in 1 (Grand Rapids: Kregel, 1989), 2:197. Original edition 1878–1879.

6. Leupold, *Exposition of the Psalms*, 684.

7. This verse played an unusual role in early church history because of the way it appeared in the bilingual (Greek/Latin) Verona Psalter (sixth century). It read, "Say among the nations, 'The Lord reigns *from the tree*.'" That was seen as a prediction of the reign of Jesus Christ from the cross with the result that many early crucifixes portrayed Jesus with a robe and a crown. An old Latin hymn declared:

> Fulfilled is all that David told
> In this prophetic song of old.
> "Amid the nations God," said he,
> "Hath reigned and triumphed from the tree."

For this and further versified expressions of the idea see Herbert Lockyer, Sr., *Psalms: A Devotional Commentary* (Grand Rapids: Kregel, 1993), 349–50. Earlier writers accused the Jews of having removed the words "from the tree" from the Hebrew text because of the apparent reference to Christ, but the words were probably not in the psalm originally.

8. From his book *Revolution by Candlelight,* cited by Ann Clark in "The Fall of the Wall: The Untold Story" (*reNEWS,* a Journal of Presbyterians for Renewal, December 1994, 17).

9. See C. S. Lewis, *Reflections on the Psalms* (New York: Harcourt, Brace & World, 1958), 9–19.

Psalm 97: *The Awesome God*

1. Arthur W. Pink, *The Sovereignty of God* (Grand Rapids: Baker, 1969), 263.
2. The story is from G. S. Bowes, "Illustrative Gatherings" (1862), and is cited in C. H. Spurgeon, *The Treasury of David,* vol. 2b, *Psalms 88–110* (Grand Rapids: Zondervan, 1966), 201.
3. Spurgeon, *The Treasury of David,* 2b:200.
4. For a short summary of his study see Spurgeon, *The Treasury of David,* 2b:204–5.
5. Cited by Spurgeon in *The Treasury of David,* 2b:205.

Psalm 98: *An Exuberant Praise Song*

1. Compare what was said about "a new song" in the study of Psalm 96.
2. Spurgeon provides a suggestive list of these from the writing of Adam Clarke, but Clarke's list is based on the King James translation and I have used the New International Version. Clarke describes this as correspondence between "the voice" (David) and "the echo" (Mary). C. H. Spurgeon, *The Treasury of David,* vol. 2b, *Psalms 88–110* (Grand Rapids: Zondervan, 1966), 214–15.
3. Marvin E. Tate, *Psalms 51–100,* vol. 20 of the *Word Biblical Commentary* (Dallas: Word, 1990), 525.
4. Cited in Spurgeon, *The Treasury of David,* 2b:212.

Psalm 99: *Holy, Holy, Holy*

1. C. H. Spurgeon, *The Treasury of David,* vol. 2b, *Psalms 88–110* (Grand Rapids: Zondervan, 1966), 222.
2. J. J. Stewart Perowne, *Commentary on the Psalms,* 2 vols. in 1 (Grand Rapids: Kregel, 1989), 2:206. Original edition 1878–1879.
3. Spurgeon, *The Treasury of David,* 2b:222.

Psalm 100: *The Psalm for Giving Thanks*

1. C. H. Spurgeon, *The Treasury of David,* vol. 2b, *Psalms 88–110* (Grand Rapids: Zondervan, 1966), 233.
2. Ibid.
3. Ibid., 234–35.

Psalm 101: *Pattern for an Upright Administration*

1. C. H. Spurgeon, *The Treasury of David,* vol. 2b, *Psalms 88–110* (Grand Rapids: Zondervan, 1966), 239.
2. Martin Luther, *Selected Psalms II,* vol. 13 of *Luther's Works,* ed. Jaroslav Pelikan (St. Louis: Concordia, 1959), 152–53.
3. Meg Greenfield, "Right and Wrong in Washington: Why Do Our Officials Need Specialists to Tell the Difference?" *Newsweek,* February 13, 1995, 88.
4. Luther, *Selected Psalms II,* 148.
5. H. C. Leupold, *Exposition of the Psalms* (Grand Rapids: Baker, 1969), 704.
6. Luther, *Selected Psalms II,* 170.

Psalm 102: *Frailty Anchored in Eternity*

1. Arno C. Gaebelein, *The Book of Psalms: A Devotional and Prophetic Commentary* (Neptune, N.J.: Loizeaux, 1939), 372–78; William J. Pettingill, *Christ in the Psalms* (Findlay, Ohio: Fundamental Truth Publishers, 1937), 115–24.

2. C. H. Spurgeon, *The Treasury of David*, vol. 2b, *Psalms 88–110* (Grand Rapids: Zondervan, 1966), 250.

3. Martin Luther, *First Lectures on the Psalms II: Psalms 76–126*, vol. 11 of *Luther's Works*, ed. Hilton C. Oswald (St. Louis: Concordia, 1976), 313.

4. Roy Clements, *Songs of Experience: Midnight and Dawn through the Eyes of the Psalmists* (Fearn, Scotland: Christian Focus Publications, 1993), 92–96.

5. G. Campbell Morgan, *Notes on the Psalms* (Westwood, N.J.: Revell, 1947), 189.

6. The author of Hebrews draws these words from the Septuagint text, where slight variations encourage their application to the Son rather than the Father. For a good discussion of the textual differences between the Hebrew Masoretic text and the LXX see Derek Kidner, *Psalms 73–150: A Commentary on Books III–V of the Psalms* (Downers Grove, Ill.: InterVarsity, 1975), 362–63.

Psalm 103: *"Praise the LORD, O My Soul"*

1. Roy Clements, *Songs of Experience: Midnight and Dawn through the Eyes of the Psalmists* (Fearn, Scotland: Christian Focus Publications, 1993), 135.

2. John R. W. Stott, *Favorite Psalms* (Chicago: Moody, 1988), 95.

3. Derek Kidner, *Psalms 73–150: A Commentary on Books III–V of the Psalms* (Downers Grove, Ill.: InterVarsity, 1975), 364.

4. Clements, *Songs of Experience*, 143.

5. Ibid., 147.

Psalm 104: *God and God's Creation*

1. John Piper, *The Pleasures of God* (Portland, Oreg.: Multnomah Press, 1991).

2. Ibid., 9.

3. Jonathan Edwards, "A Dissertation Concerning the End for Which God Created the World" in *The Works of Jonathan Edwards*, vol. 1 (Carlisle, Pa.: The Banner of Truth Trust, 1974), 94–121. The reference to Psalm 104 is on page 111.

4. John R. W. Stott, *Favorite Psalms* (Chicago: Moody, 1988), 98.

5. Ellicott, *Commentary*. See Herbert Lockyer, Sr., *Psalms: A Devotional Commentary* (Grand Rapids: Kregel, 1993), 402.

6. There are also similarities between Psalm 104 and the Egyptian "Hymn to Aten," though they have often been exaggerated by scholars. The hymn was written in the fourteenth century B.C. by that remarkable pharaoh, Amenhetep IV, who called himself Akhenaten. He tried to impose a form of religious monotheism on Egypt, and his hymn was praise to the singular sun god Aten. The hymn is similar to Psalm 104 in that it calls on creation to praise God. But it is remarkably different in that the sun is itself regarded as God. In Psalm 104 the sun, even light itself, is only a manifestation of the true and invisible God's greatness. For a helpful listing of the similarities and differences see Leslie C. Allen, *Psalms 101–150*, vol. 21 of the *Word Biblical Commentary* (Waco: Word, 1983), 29–30. C. S. Lewis also has an interesting but surprisingly uncritical discussion of this hymn in *Reflections on the Psalms* (New York: Harcourt, Brace & World, 1958), 85–89. The "Hymn to Aten" can be found in James B. Pritchard, *Ancient Near Eastern Texts Relating to the Old Testament* (Princeton, N.J.: Princeton University Press, 1955), 369–71.

7. Stott, *Favorite Psalms*, 98–99.

8. Lewis, *Reflections on the Psalms*, 81–83.

9. Edwards, "A Dissertation Concerning the End for Which God Created the World," 101.

10. Stott, *Favorite Psalms*, 99.

11. Ibid., 100.

12. H. C. Leupold, *Exposition of the Psalms* (Grand Rapids: Baker, 1969), 730.

13. Piper, *Pleasures of God,* 85.

Psalm 105: *God Remembered by Abraham's Descendants*

1. Psalm 105:1 also occurs almost word for word in Isaiah 12:4.

2. Derek Kidner, *Psalms 73–150: A Commentary on Books III–V of the Psalms* (Downers Grove, Ill.: InterVarsity, 1975), 377.

Psalm 106: *Let All God's People Say, "Amen!"*

1. Derek Kidner, *Psalms 73–150: A Commentary on Books III–V of the Psalms* (Downers Grove, Ill.: InterVarsity, 1975), 377–78.

2. Similar prayers of national confession are found in Deuteronomy 26, 1 Kings 8, Nehemiah 9, and Daniel 9.

3. C. H. Spurgeon, *The Treasury of David,* vol. 2b, *Psalms 88–110* (Grand Rapids: Zondervan, 1966), 366–67.

4. From "Youth's Agitations," cited in Angela Partington, ed., *The Oxford Dictionary of Quotations* (Norwalk, Conn.: The Easton Press, 1992), 29.

5. Leslie Allen points out how much Paul was dependent on this psalm. "Paul not only quoted v. 20 in Rom. 1:23 but echoed v. 14 at 1:24, v. 39 in 1:26, 27, and v. 48 in 1:26 (cf. vv. 23, 32, 40 with 1:18). Moreover, he used v. 41 as the basis for a threefold refrain in 1:24, 26, 28." See Leslie C. Allen, *Psalms 101–150,* vol. 21 in the *Word Biblical Commentary* (Waco: Word, 1983), 53.

Subject Index

627; unexpected, 778, 779

Washington Post, 481

Watts, Isaac, 456, 601, 740, 754, 796, 810

Weakness of old age, 594

Weapons, world's, 526

Wedding, king's, 383, 384

Wedding customs, 381, 382

Wedding song, messianic, 380–386

Wesley, Charles, 615

Wesley, John, 393, 594, 695, 800

Wesleyan Revivals, 374

Westminster Shorter Catechism, 756, 836, 839

White, John, 409

Whitefield, George, 698

Whitelock, Bulstrode, 790

Wicked, described, 482–484, 612; destiny of, 614; destruction of, 462, 463; prayer against, 484, 485; prosperity of, 611, 612;

sudden destruction of, 522–528

Wilken, Robert L., 670

Wilson, Woodrow, 709

Wine, 842

Wings of God, 476, 477

Wisdom, 414, 489, 744; path of, 409, 410

Word of God, 383, 511, 526, 792; building on, 725; famine for, 619, 620; power of, 547; see Bible

Word studies, atonement, 532; *elohim*, 792; glory, 785, 786; holiness, 805, 806; iniquity, 426; Jehovah ("I am"), 454, 455; *miktam*, 486; redeem, 414; *selah*, 417; sin, 426; transgressions, 426; vengeance and revenge, 769

Words, in worship, 777; king's, 383; weapon, 440, 441, 525

Wordsworth, William, 467

Work, established by God, 745

World, changeable, 764, 765

Worship, 531, 613, 808; call to, 782–784; formal, 812; how to, 774–780; in holiness, 781–787; joy of, 775–777; role of music in, 538–540; urgent, 779, 780; why we should, 777, 778

Wrath, 805, 827

Xerxes, 528

Yahweh, 490; see Jehovah

Zebulun, 564

Zedekiah, 732

Zion, 401, 450, 557–559, 561, 692, 708–714, 783, 792, 825; blessing for, 436; Mount, 367, 371, 416; praise of, 403–405

Scripture Index